Achim Truger, Eckhard Hein,
Michael Heine, Frank Hoffer (Hg. | eds.)

Monetäre Makroökonomie, Arbeitsmärkte und Entwicklung

Monetary Macroeconomics, Labour Markets and Development

Festschrift für | for Hansjörg Herr

Metropolis-Verlag
Marburg 2016

Bibliografische Information der Deutschen Bibliothek
Die Deutsche Bibliothek verzeichnet diese Publikation in der Deutschen Nationalbibliografie; detaillierte bibliografische Daten sind im Internet über <http://dnb.ddb.de> abrufbar.

Metropolis-Verlag für Ökonomie, Gesellschaft und Politik GmbH
http://www.metropolis-verlag.de
Copyright: Metropolis-Verlag, Marburg 2016
Alle Rechte vorbehalten
ISBN 978-3-7316-1229-2

Achim Truger, Eckhard Hein, Michael Heine, Frank Hoffer
(Hg. | eds.)
Monetäre Makroökonomie, Arbeitsmärkte und Entwicklung
Monetary Macroeconomics, Labour Markets and Development

Series of the Research Network Macroeconomics and Macroeconomic Policies

edited by Eckhard Hein, Torsten Niechoj and Engelbert Stockhammer

Volume 17

1   **Renaissance der Makroökonomik**, edited by Arne Heise, 1998, ISBN 3-89518-190-0

2   **Makropolitik zwischen Nationalstaat und Europäischer Union**, edited by Arne Heise, 1999, ISBN 3-89518-246-X

3   **Neue Weltwährungsarchitektur**, edited by Arne Heise, 2001, ISBN 3-89518-296-6

4   **USA – Modellfall der New Economy?**, edited by Arne Heise, 2001, ISBN 3-89518-353-9

5   **Neues Geld – alte Geldpolitik? Die EZB im makroökonomischen Interaktionsraum**, edited by Arne Heise, 2002, ISBN 3-89518-381-4

6   **Neu-Keynesianismus – der neue wirtschaftspolitische Mainstream?**, edited by Eckhard Hein, Arne Heise and Achim Truger, 2003, second edition 2005, ISBN 3-89518-422-5

7   **Finanzpolitik in der Kontroverse**, edited by Eckhard Hein, Arne Heise and Achim Truger, 2004, ISBN 3-89518-481-0

8   **Löhne, Beschäftigung, Verteilung und Wachstum. Makroökonomische Analysen**, edited by Eckhard Hein, Arne Heise and Achim Truger, 2005, ISBN 3-89518-512-4

9   **European Economic Policies. Alternatives to Orthodox Analysis and Policy Concepts**, edited by Eckhard Hein, Arne Heise and Achim Truger, 2006, ISBN 3-89518-560-4

10 **European Integration in Crisis**, edited by Eckhard Hein, Jan Priewe and Achim Truger, 2007, ISBN 978-3-89518-610-3

11 **Finance-led Capitalism? Macroeconomic Effects of Changes in the Financial Sector**, edited by Eckhard Hein, Torsten Niechoj, Peter Spahn and Achim Truger, 2008, second edition 2009, ISBN 978-3-89518-764-3

12 **Macroeconomic Policies on Shaky Foundations – Whither Mainstream Economics?**, edited by Eckhard Hein, Torsten Niechoj and Engelbert Stockhammer, 2009, ISBN 978-3-89518-757-6

13 **The World Economy in Crisis – the Return of Keynesianism?**, edited by Sebastian Dullien, Eckhard Hein, Achim Truger and Till van Treeck, 2010, ISBN 978-3-89518-806-0

14 **Stabilising an unequal economy? Public debt, financial regulation, and income distribution**, edited by Torsten Niechoj, Özlem Onaran, Engelbert Stockhammer, Achim Truger and Till van Treeck, 2011, ISBN 978-3-89518-878-7

15 **From crisis to growth? The challenge of debt and imbalances**, edited by Hansjörg Herr, Torsten Niechoj, Claus Thomasberger, Achim Truger and Till van Treeck, 2012, ISBN 978-3-89518-942-5

16 **Makroökonomik, Entwicklung und Wirtschaftspolitik | Macroeconomics, Development and Economic Policies**, edited by Sebastian Dullien, Eckhard Hein and Achim Truger, 2014, ISBN 978-3-7316-1099-1

Quelle: Institut für Weiterbildung Berlin / Berlin Professional School

Vorwort

Hansjörg Herr feiert in diesem Jahr seinen 65. Geburtstag, und nach dem Sommersemester 2016 gibt er damit seine Position als Professor an der Hochschule für Wirtschaft und Recht Berlin auf, die er seit 1994 ausgeübt hat. In der vorliegenden Festschrift sind Beiträge von Kolleginnen und Kollegen, akademischen Weggefährtinnen und Weggefährten und von ehemaligen Studierenden versammelt. Mit dieser Festschrift sollen Hansjörgs Jubiläum und seine Tätigkeit gewürdigt werden. Wir ehren einen hervorragenden Volkswirt und internationalen Makroökonomen, einen politisch engagierten Wissenschaftler – und einen Freund.

Zahlreichen Kolleginnen und Kollegen war es ein sehr persönliches Anliegen, zum Gelingen der Festschrift beizutragen. Dies spiegelt zum einen die große Beliebtheit wider, derer sich Hansjörg Herr bei allen, die ihn kennen, erfreut. Zum anderen zeigt die thematische Breite der vorliegenden Schrift, dass Hansjörg Herr seine wissenschaftliche Arbeit nicht nur auf Themen der Supranationalen Wirtschaftsintegration beschränkt hat, für die er seinerzeit berufen wurde.

Hansjörg Herr wurde 1951 in Baden geboren, sodass ihm seine Freude an gutem Essen und Trinken gleichsam in die Wiege gelegt wurde. Bezeichnenderweise absolvierte er nach Abschluss seiner Schulzeit eine Ausbildung als Koch. Bald danach arbeitete er als Schiffskoch und bereiste in dieser Funktion zahlreiche Meere der Welt. Allerdings drängte sich ihm nach einer schweren Havarie, dem Untergang des Schiffes und der damit einhergehenden Rettung aus dem Meer die Erkenntnis auf, dass eine wissenschaftliche Karriere eine echte Alternative zum SOS-Funken sein könnte. Im Ergebnis holte Hansjörg Herr den Realschulabschluss und die Fachhochschulreife nach und studierte von 1973 bis 1975 Betriebswirtschaftslehre an der Fachhochschule für Wirtschaft Berlin – der Vorgängerhochschule der Hochschule für Wirtschaft und Recht – und anschließend von 1975 bis 1981 Volkswirtschaftslehre und Wirtschaftspädagogik an der Freien Universität Berlin.

Unmittelbar danach erhielt er eine Anstellung als wissenschaftlicher Mitarbeiter am Institut für Wirtschaftspolitik der Freien Universität Berlin. Hier hatte er die Möglichkeit, an den theoretischen Arbeiten der seinerzeit so genannten „Berliner Schule" des Monetärkeynesianismus teilzunehmen, die maßgeblich von Hajo Riese, seinem späteren „Doktor- und Habilitationsvater" geprägt wurde. Er beteiligte sich mit mehreren Beiträgen zur Geld- und Währungstheorie und machte den monetärkeynesianischen Ansatz der „Berliner Schule" unter anderem zur Grundlage seiner kritischen Analysen des europäischen Integrationsprozesses.

Im Anschluss an seine Tätigkeit an der Freien Universität Berlin arbeitete er von 1986 bis 1993 als wissenschaftlicher Mitarbeiter und später als Projektleiter am Wissenschaftszentrum Berlin für Sozialforschung (WZB). Vor allem hier erwarb er seine Kenntnisse bei der Akquise und erfolgreichen Durchführung von Drittmittelprojekten. So bearbeitete er beispielsweise von der Deutschen Forschungsgesellschaft oder der VW-Stiftung finanzierte Forschungsprojekte. Thematisch beschäftigte sich Hansjörg Herr in dieser Zeit neben der Geld- und Währungspolitik vor allem mit fiskalpolitischen Themen und den Konstitutionsbedingungen einer erfolgreichen Transformation von vormaligen Planwirtschaften in geldgesteuerte Marktwirtschaften.

Im Jahr 1994 wurde Hansjörg Herr zum Professor für Supranationale Wirtschaftsintegration an die heutige Hochschule für Wirtschaft und Recht Berlin berufen. Als neuer Schwerpunkt seiner wissenschaftlichen Arbeit trat die Analyse der Entwicklungsrestriktionen und -bedingungen von ökonomisch „unterentwickelten" Ländern und Schwellenländern hinzu. Freilich beschränkte sich seine Arbeit nicht auf die Analyse, sondern Hansjörg Herr hat auch Zentralbanker, Politiker und Gewerkschafter vieler Länder sehr konkret beraten, Gutachten verfasst und Schulungen angeboten. Häufig hat er in diesem Kontext die Zusammenarbeit mit der Stiftung Internationale Weiterbildung und Entwicklung (ehemals Deutsche Stiftung für Internationale Entwicklung) gesucht. Schwerpunkte der Vortrags- und Beratungstätigkeit waren der zentralasiatische Raum und China. Darüber hinaus war er als Gutachter für die Gesellschaft für Technische Zusammenarbeit und die Hans-Böckler-Stiftung tätig.

Sein wissenschaftliches Engagement zeigt sich unter anderem in mehr als 200 Publikationen, die Hansjörg Herr im Laufe der Jahre verfasst hat. Darunter befinden sich Standardwerke wie beispielsweise seine mittlerweile in vierter Auflage erschienene Paradigmenorientierte Einführung in die Mikro- und Makroökonomie (zusammen mit Michael Heine). Hinzu kommen zahlreiche Drittmittelprojekte, die er erfolgreich durchgeführt hat. Aber sein Engagement zeigt sich auch in den vielfältigen Kontakten, die er seit Jahren mit nationalen und internationalen Persönlichkeiten und wissenschaftlichen Einrichtungen unterhält. So pflegt er intensive Kontakte mit chinesischen, vietnamesischen, russischen und US-amerikanischen Universitäten, mit Zentralbanken mehrerer Länder und mit Forschungseinrichtungen im In- und Ausland. Zuweilen interessieren sich besonders forschungsaktive Professorinnen und Professoren nicht sonderlich für die Lehre. Das gilt für Hansjörg Herr gewiss nicht. An seiner Hochschule war er am Aufbau und der Administration der Masterstudiengänge „Chinese-European Economics and Business Studies" und „Labour Policies and Globalisation" beteiligt. Darüber hinaus war ihm die Förderung besonders wissbegieriger Studierender geradezu eine Herzensangelegenheit. Und es gibt wenige Professorinnen und Professoren, die Lehre und Forschung so produktiv miteinander verbinden können, wie dies Hansjörg Herr gelungen ist.

Gerade diese Fähigkeit macht Hansjörg Herr auch zu einer der wesentlichen Stützen der Global Labour University (GLU), an deren Gründung und fortlaufenden Weiterentwicklung er seit den Anfängen im Jahre 2002 beteiligt ist. Die GLU ist eine weltweit einzigartige Kooperation von Universitäten, Gewerkschaften und der Internationalen Arbeitsorganisation, die sich in Lehre und Forschung mit den Themen globale Entwicklung, soziale Gerechtigkeit und grenzübergreifende Interessenvertretung befasst.

Hansjörg Herrs Vorschläge für einen „guten" Kapitalismus haben in diesem breitgefächerten Netzwerk kritischer Geister nicht immer Zustimmung gefunden, aber sie sind ein unschätzbarer Beitrag zu einer pluralen Diskussion, die Lösungen höher bewertet als ideologische Gewissheiten. Zahlreiche Studierende von Gewerkschaften und anderen sozialen Bewegungen haben im vergangenen Jahrzehnt im Rahmen des Master Programms „Labour Policies and Globalization" bei Hansjörg Herr erleben können, dass Makroökonomie nicht nur wichtig und komplex, sondern auch spannend und verständlich sein kann. Als Gastdozent an GLU-Partneruniversitäten in Indien, Brasilien und Südafrika wird er – auch nach seiner Pensionierung – weiter die internationale Debatte beeinflussen. Mit seiner vorurteilsfreien Weltoffenheit ist er ein herausragendes Beispiel gelingenden Engagements für internationale Debatte und internationales Verständnis.

Wer nun glaubt, diese jahrelange erfolgreiche Arbeit habe zu einer gewissen Arroganz und Hochnäsigkeit geführt, der kennt Hansjörg Herr nicht. Es gibt nur sehr wenige Menschen, die so gleichbleibend gut gelaunt und zu jedermann freundlich sind, wie er. Stets steht er mit Rat und Tat zur Seite, lässt alle, die es möchten, an seiner wissenschaftlichen Kompetenz und seinen Erfahrungen teilhaben und sagt bei Anfragen eigentlich zu selten Nein. Insofern ist es nicht überraschend, dass er überall nicht nur hoch anerkannt, sondern auch äußerst beliebt ist.

Wirklich überraschend ist eigentlich nur, dass Hansjörg Herr bei all dem Engagement noch Zeit findet, regelmäßig mit Freunden essen und trinken zu gehen oder sie zu bekochen. Bei diesen Gelegenheiten erweist er sich als geistreicher und witziger Zeitgenosse, der, als gelernter Koch, ein gutes Essen natürlich auch zu würdigen weiß. Kurzum: Wer Hansjörg Herr kennt, der muss ihn einfach mögen.

Diese Festschrift deckt bei weitem nicht das gesamte Spektrum von Hansjörg Herrs breit angelegten Forschungsinteressen und -arbeiten ab. Dennoch konnten wir insgesamt 29 Beiträge zu zahlreichen Themen aus Hansjörgs Forschungsspektrum zusammentragen. Wir haben sie grob vier Bereichen zugeordnet: Teil I widmet sich dem Themenfeld „Makroökonomie, makroökonomische Politik-Regime und ‚guter Kapitalismus'", Teil II dem Komplex „Finanzmärkte, Währungssysteme und Regulierung", Teil III dem Gebiet „Arbeitsmärkte und Lohnpolitik", während in Teil IV „Ökonomische Entwicklung und globale Wertschöpfungsketten" im Mittelpunkt stehen.

Abschließend möchten wir uns bei den Autorinnen und Autoren dieser Festschrift für die Kooperation und die Bereitschaft bedanken, an diesem Veröffentlichungsprojekt mitzuwirken. Bei Luisa Bunescu, Michael Nagel, und ganz besonders Isabell Kieser bedanken wir uns für die Unterstützung bei der Aufbereitung der Texte für den Druck, bei Hubert Hoffmann für die langjährige Veröffentlichung der Schriftenreihe des FMM in seinem Metropolis-Verlag und bei der Hans-Böckler-Stiftung für die großzügige finanzielle Förderung dieser Festschrift.

Berlin, im Juli 2016
Achim Truger, Eckhard Hein, Michael Heine, Frank Hoffer

Preface

This year Hansjörg Herr has celebrated his 65th birthday, and he has therefore retired from his position as a Professor at the Berlin School of Economics and Law, which he has held since 1994. For this Festschrift we have collected contributions by colleagues, academic companions and former students. With this volume we would like to honour Hansjörg and his work. We honour an eminent economist and international macroeconomist, a politically dedicated academic – and a dear friend.

Many colleagues had a strong personal wish to support this Festschrift with a contribution. This fact reflects, on the one hand, the high degree of esteem that Hansjörg enjoys with all those who have known him. On the other hand the topical breadth of this volume shows that Hansjörg's research has not at all been limited to matters of Supranational Economic Integration, the original denomination of his professorship.

Hansjörg Herr was born in 1951 in Baden/Germany which certainly explains his inclination to good food and beverages. Quite fittingly after leaving school he passed an apprenticeship as a professional cook. Soon after he worked as a ship's cook and travelled around the world's seas in this function. However, after having been saved from being shipwrecked it occurred to him that an academic career could offer a real alternative to sending out S.O.S. As a result Hansjörg acquired the advanced technical college entrance qualification and studied business administration at the Berlin School of Economics – which was later to become the Berlin School of Economics and Law – from 1973 to 1975. And then, from 1975 to 1981 he studied economics and economic pedagogy at the Free University Berlin.

Immediately after graduation he held a position as Junior Lecturer (Wissenschaftlicher Mitarbeiter) at the Insitute of Economic Policy of the Free University Berlin. This offered him the opportunity to participate in the development of the theoretical parts of the so-called "Berlin School" of Monetary Keynesianism which was founded by Hajo Riese, Hansjörg's academic teacher and the future supervisor of both his dotoral dissertation and his habilitation. Hansjörg contributed several works on monetary and currency theory and used the Monetary Keynesian approach of the "Berlin School" as a basis for his critical analyses of the process of European economic integration.

After having finished his doctorate Hansjörg worked as a Senior Researcher and project manager at the Berlin Social Science Center (WZB) from 1986 to 1993. It was here, above all, that Hansjörg acquired his experience in the acquisition and successful operation of research projects. For example he worked in projects financed by the Deutsche Forschungsgemeinschaft or the Volkswagen Foundation. At the time Hansjörg was precoccupied with monetary and curreny policies, but also with fiscal policy topics and the conditions of a successful transformation of formerly centrally planned to capitalist economies.

In 1994 Hansjörg Herr became Professor of Supranational Economic Integration at the Berlin School of Economics which added another new focus to his academic work: the analysis of the opportunities and obstacles to development in developing and emerging economies. His work, however, was not confined to academic analysis. Instead Hansjörg Herr also served as an advisor to central bankers, politicians und trade unionists in many countries. He wrote numerous studies and offered training courses. Often he cooperated with the Stiftung Internationale Weiterbildung und Entwicklung (formerly Deutsche Stiftung für Internationale Entwicklung). The central Asian region and China were the main foci of his advisorships. Furthermore, he served as a referee for the Gesellschaft für Technische Zusammenarbeit and the Hans Böckler Foundation.

Hansjörg's dedication to academia is reflected in more than 200 publications. Among the publications there is also a standard (German language) textbook (with Michael Heine), the paradigmatic introduction to microeconomics and macroeconomics which has already seen its fourth edition. On top of that Hansjörg has successfully conducted numerous research projects. His dedication is also witnessed by the numerous contacts with national and international persons and institutions that he built up. Among them are intensive contacts with Chines, Vietnamese, Russian and US universities, with several central banks as well as with research institutes at home and abroad.

Sometimes professors actively involved in resarch are not very much interested in academic teaching. Hansjörg is quite the opposite: At the Berlin School of Economics and Law he has been involved in the successful builtup and the administration of the master study programmes "Labour Policies and Globalisation" and "Chinese-European Economics and Business Studies". Furthermore, Hansjörg had a keen interest in promoting talented students.

There are few professors who are able to reconcile academic research and teaching as productively as Hansjörg has done for many years.

It is this ability that makes Hansjörg Herr also one of the essential pillars of the Global Labour University (GLU). Since the beginning in the year of 2002 he has been involved in the foundation and further developing of the GLU. It is a unique collaboration of universities, trade unions and the International Labour Organization addressing in teaching and research topics like global development, social justice and cross-border representation of interests. Hansjörg Herr's proposals for a "good" capitalism have not always found consent in this broad network of critical minds, but they are an invaluable contribution to a pluralistic debate that prefers discussing solutions instead of ideological certainties. Discussing with Hansjörg Herr many students from trade unions and other social movements did experience in the last decade as part of the Master program, Labour Policies and Globalization that macroeconomics can not only be important and complex, but also exciting and understandable. As a guest lecturer at GLU partner universities in India, Brazil and South Africa, he will – also after being a professor emeritus – continue to influence the international debate. With his unprejudiced cosmopolitanism he is an outstanding example of successfully contributing to international debate and understanding.

One might think that being that succssful for many years would breed a certain arrogance or vanity. Not so with Hansjörg. There are few people that manage to be steadily in a good mood and friendly towards everybody. He is always ready to help and shares his academic competence and experience with anybody who likes. He is rarely – maybe sometimes even too rarely – able to say 'no' if he is asked for something. Quite unsurprisingly, Hansjörg is not only respected by everybody, but indeed even liked very much.

It is, however, surprising that Hansjörg despite all his dedication to work still regularly finds the time to go out for dinner with friends or even to cook for them. At these occasions he proves to be a witty and funny person who – professional cook that he is – knows to appreciate a good meal. To put it shortly: If you know Hansjörg you will like him.

This Festschrift is far away from covering all of Hansjörg Herr's impressively broad range of research. Nevertheless, we were able to collect 29 contributions that are related to Hansjörg's numerous research topics. We have broadly structured them into four parts: Part I is dedicated to the subject area "Macroeconomics, Macroeconomic Policy Regimes and 'Decent Capitalism'", part II is preoccupied with the complex of "Financial Markets, Curreny Systems and Regulation", part III focusses on "Labour Markets and Wage Policy", whereas part IV is dedicated to "Economic Development and Global Values Chains".

Finally, we would like to thank the contributing authors of this Festschrift for their cooperation and their willingness to be part of this publication project. We also thank Luisa Bunescu, Michael Nagel, and in particular Isabell Kieser for their assistance in editing the papers and preparing them for the printing press, Hubert Hoffmann for the publication of the Series of the FMM in his publishing house Metropolis and the Hans-Böckler Foundation for the financial support of this Festschrift.

Berlin, July 2016
Achim Truger, Eckhard Hein, Michael Heine, Frank Hoffer

Inhalt | Contents

I. Makroökonomie, makroökonomische Politik-Regime und ‚guter Kapitalismus'
Macroeconomics, Macroeconomic Policy Regimes and 'Decent Capitalism'

‚Kritik der politischen Ökonomie' nach Keynes und Polanyi
Claus Thomasberger 21

Zwischen Gleichgewicht und Ungleichgewicht. Zur Kreislaufvorstellung bei Jean Baptiste Say
Siegbert Preuß 35

Was die Institutionenökonomie von der Ungleichheitsforschung lernen könnte. Eine kritische Auseinandersetzung mit dem Begriff „institutionelle Komplementaritäten"
Martin Kronauer 55

Das klassische Erbe der Makroökonomie – Anmerkungen zu einem vernachlässigten Thema
Hajo Riese 69

Macroeconomic policy regime: A heuristic approach to grasping national policy space within global asymmetries
Barbara Fritz 73

Three Post-Keynesian concepts within the periphery context
Zeynep M. Nettekoven 85

Finance-dominated capitalism and its crisis in Germany: Deep recession and quick recovery – Germany as a role model?
Daniel Detzer and Eckhard Hein 97

Saving 'decent capitalism': An emergency programme for fiscal policy in the Euro area
Achim Truger 113

Revitalising the Green New Deal. From a Keynesian stimulus to a sustainable growth strategy
Kajsa Borgnäs and Christian Kellermann 127

II. Finanzmärkte, Währungssysteme und Regulierung
Financial Markets, Currency Systems and Regulation

How to explain the exchange rate gyrations on the biggest foreign exchange market on the globe
Jan Priewe 141

The U.S. management of the financial crisis – a study of hegemony
Christoph Scherrer 157

Kommt nach der Krise der „gute Kapitalismus"? Bewertung der europäischen Finanzmarktreformen seit 2008
Sebastian Dullien 169

Realwirtschaft und Finanzwirtschaft in der neueren Krisendiskussion und in den Volkswirtschaftlichen Gesamtrechnungen
Klaus Voy 183

III. Arbeitsmärkte und Lohnpolitik
Labour Markets and Wage Policy

'There is power in a union': A strategic-relational perspective on power resources
Alexander Gallas 195

Issues concerning employment and minimum wages in India's urban informal economy
Sharit K. Bhowmik 211

Jobs and inequality in two Latin American countries blocs. Policy successes and diminishing returns for labor
Carlos Salas 223

Give that man a fishing rod: Reflections on job creation and cash transfers
Edward Webster and Khayaat Fakier 237

Decent wages for Decent Capitalism?
Patrick Belser 249

Price and non-price competitiveness – can it explain current account imbalances in the euro area?
Torsten Niechoj 263

Gender matters: Schnittmengen feministischer und (post-)keynesianischer Analyse
Friederike Maier 283

Herausforderungen und Grenzen der Lohnpolitik
Alexander Herzog-Stein und Gustav Horn 299

Verhindern nationale Lohnformeln Leistungsbilanzdefizite?
Die Rolle von Lohnstückkosten und Preisen in den Krisenländern des Euroraums
Heike Joebges und Camille Logeay 313

Hat das Bündnis für Arbeit zu Lohndumping geführt?
Michael Wendl 329

IV. Ökonomische Entwicklung und globale Wertschöpfungsketten
Economic Development and Global Value Chains

A comparison on trade dependence and industrial structure in China and India: A global value chain perspective
Yang Laike and Zheng Guojiao 347

The effect of FDI on industry value-added: Evidence from China
Behzad Azarhoushang and Jennifer Pédussel Wu 361

Global production networks: What has labour got to do with it?
Praveen Jha 383

Obstacles to development: Trade and labour market theory revisited
Bea Ruoff 395

The (im)possible developmental model of Albania:
A labour perspective
Edlira Xhafa 407

Nicaragua 37 years after the Sandinista Revolution
Trevor Evans 425

Lebenslauf Hansjörg Herr 437
Curriculum Vitae Hansjörg Herr 439
Publikationen von | Publications by Hansjörg Herr 441
Autor_innen und Herausgeber_innen | Authors and Editors 465

I.

Makroökonomie, makroökonomische Politik-Regime und ‚guter Kapitalismus'

Macroeconomics, Macroeconomic Policy Regimes and 'Decent Capitalism'

‚Kritik der politischen Ökonomie' nach Keynes und Polanyi

Claus Thomasberger

1. Einleitung

Es ist kein gutes Zeichen, dass die Kritik der politischen Ökonomie in den letzten Jahren an Bedeutung verloren hat, denn sie steht für eine realistische, die Auseinandersetzung mit der Wirklichkeit suchende Opposition gegenüber dem wirtschaftsliberalen Denken. Ihre Protagonisten sind sich der Tatsache bewusst, dass es unverzichtbar ist, die Grenzen der zielgerichteten Gestaltung der bestehenden Gesellschaft zu kennen, wenn die inhumanen, Mensch und Natur bedrohenden Auswirkungen der modernen technologischen Zivilisation überwunden werden sollen. Ohne das Bewusstsein der Ursachen der gesellschaftlichen Übel, so die Überzeugung, laufen alle Versuche der Umgestaltung der kapitalistischen Marktgesellschaft Gefahr, Resultate hervorzubringen, die entgegen den Absichten die konservativen Kräfte stärken.

Dass in der gegenwärtigen Phase voluntaristisch-utopische Ansätze an Boden gewinnen, die Werthaltungen und Modelle einer ‚guten Gesellschaft' für wichtiger halten als das Verstehen der Übel der gegenwärtigen Welt, schwächt die Möglichkeiten einer wirklichen Verbesserung der Verhältnisse. Umso bedeutender ist es, sich mit der Frage der ‚Kritik der politischen Ökonomie nach Keynes und Polanyi', den beiden wichtigsten Vertretern einer solchen Haltung im zwanzigsten Jahrhundert, auseinanderzusetzen. Marx' Werk ‚Das Kapital – Kritik der politischen Ökonomie', erschienen im Jahr 1867, markiert den ersten Höhepunkt der kritischen Auseinandersetzung mit den Grundlagen der kapitalistischen Marktwirtschaft. Marx stellt daher den unverzichtbaren Ausgangspunkt der folgenden Überlegungen dar.

2. Karl Marx

Das hervorstechende Merkmal der Zivilisation des neunzehnten Jahrhunderts bestand zweifellos in dem Nebeneinander von industriellem Fortschritt, wachsendem materiellem Reichtum auf der einen und Entwurzelung der Menschen, Kommodifizierung von Arbeit und Natur, Entfremdung sowie Verarmung der arbeitenden Bevölkerung auf der anderen Seite. Wie war es zu dieser gegensätzlichen Entwicklung gekommen? Was waren ihre Ursachen? Warum kamen die Vorteile der neugewonnenen produktiven Kräfte nicht allen Menschen zugute? Die klassische politische Ökonomie hatte auf diese Fragen durch den Verweis auf die ökonomischen Gesetze reagiert, die die gesellschaftliche Entwicklung bestimmen würden. Die Wirtschaft, so die Antwort, habe den Charakter eines selbstregulierenden Systems, das Gesetzen folge, die nicht der Kontrolle der Gesellschaft unterlagen, sondern denen die Gesellschaft ihrerseits untergeordnet war. Das Wertgesetz, das ‚eherne Lohngesetz' und die Gesetze der Akkumulation wurden von Malthus, Ricardo, Say und ihren Schülern als Naturgesetze der gesellschaftlichen Entwicklung präsentiert, die stärker waren als jede denkbare menschliche Einflussnahme. Nur durch die Anerkennung der Gesetze, so die Botschaft, wäre es möglich, die unvermeidlichen Übel so gering wie möglich zu halten.

Marx erfasst die Bedeutung der Entdeckung, dass die bürgerliche *Gesellschaft* von der *Wirtschaft* und von deren Gesetzen beherrscht wurde. Er stimmt Ricardo zu, dass die Arbeitswertlehre, die Verteilungsgesetze oder das ‚Gesetz der fallenden Profitrate' nicht einfach durch menschlichen Willen aufgehoben werden konnten. Marx' Kritik der politischen Ökonomie zielt auf einen anderen Punkt: den Naturalismus, d.h. die Interpretation der Gesetze quasi als Naturgesetze.

Marx' Einwand kennen wir: Die wirtschaftlichen Gesetze sind im Grunde Beziehungen von Menschen. Nicht die Natur, „die Menschen machen ihre eigene Geschichte", lautet die Gegenthese, allerdings „nicht aus freien Stücken, nicht unter selbstgewählten, sondern unter unmittelbar vorgefundenen, gegebenen und überlieferten Umständen" (Marx 1960: 115). Und auf letztere, die jeweiligen historischen Bedingungen, kommt es an. Die Gesetze der Wirtschaft sind historische Gesetze, die *Gesetze des Kapitals*.

Der historische Ausgangspunkt des Aufstiegs der bürgerlichen Gesellschaft, so Marx, war die industrielle Revolution. Die Einführung der Maschine in eine kommerzielle Gesellschaft bedeutete nicht nur die Ausweitung der Arbeitsteilung in einem in früheren Epochen unbekannten Ausmaß, sondern sie läutete auch eine grundlegende Umwälzung der gesellschaftlichen Verhältnisse ein, die auf der privaten Verfügung über die Produktionsmittel und dem ‚doppelt freien Lohnarbeiter' beruhte. Die Konsequenz war, dass die Menschen einander nicht länger als Menschen, sondern als Träger ökonomischer Funktionen oder Charaktermasken gegenübertraten. Die Herrschaft ökonomischer Gesetze und die Reduktion der Menschen auf bloße Funktionsträger waren zwei Seiten einer Medaille.

Das große Paradoxon der Marxschen Kritik der politischen Ökonomie besteht darin, den Gegensatz von Marktgesetzen und wahrhaft menschlichen Beziehungen, von Wirtschaft und Gesellschaft, zwar als konstitutiv für die Struktur der bürgerlichen Gesellschaft zu betrachten, den Motor der gesellschaftlichen Transformation aber nicht hier, sondern allein in der Wirtschaft zu verorten. Obwohl er die Kämpfe der Arbeiterklasse, ihre Forderungen und die Formen der Auseinandersetzung mit großer Akribie analysiert, obwohl er die proletarische Bewegung zum Adressaten seiner Theorie macht und obwohl er erwartet, dass sie in der Auseinandersetzung ihre partikularen Ziele überwindet und die Interessen der Gesellschaft in ihrer Gesamtheit vertritt, weist Marx die Rolle der die gesellschaftliche Transformation treibenden Kraft den ökonomischen Widersprüchen zu. Es ist erstaunlich. Aber angesichts des realen Kräfteverhältnisses im neunzehnten Jahrhundert scheint Marx das Vertrauen in den Opfermut, den Einsatz und die Fähigkeit der Arbeiterklasse, die bürgerliche Gesellschaft grundlegend zu verändern, zu fehlen. Daher der eigentümliche *ökonomische Determinismus*, der die Marxsche Kritik der politischen Ökonomie durchzieht.

Innerhalb der bürgerlichen Gesellschaft erscheint Marx der Gegensatz von Wirtschaft und Gesellschaft als unüberwindbar. Entsprechend gering schätzt er den Einfluss der Klassenauseinandersetzungen, der demokratischen Bestrebungen und der zivilgesellschaftlichen Kämpfe auf den Wandel der kapitalistischen Ordnung als solcher ein. Die Wirkung protektiver Maßnahmen wie Senkung der Arbeitszeit, Lohnerhöhungen und Verbesserungen der Arbeitsbedingungen betrachtet er als so beschränkt, dass er glaubt, sie theoretisch vernachlässigen zu können. Erst eine gesellschaftliche Revolution, durch die die Trennung der Wirtschaft von der Gesellschaft überwunden werde, so seine Vorstellung, schaffe die *Voraussetzungen* für eine zielgerichtete menschliche Einflussnahme. Ins andere Extrem verfallend, skizziert er die kommunistische Gesellschaft – den „Verein freier Menschen" (Marx 1972: 92) – als eine Form des menschlichen Zusammenlebens, in der die Einbettung der Wirtschaft in die Gesellschaft *vollkommen* hergestellt ist.

Zweifellos hat Marx, indem er die Verselbständigung der Wirtschaft gegenüber der Gesellschaft ins Zentrum der Betrachtung rückt, das entscheidende

Charakteristikum der Zivilisation des neunzehnten Jahrhunderts herausgearbeitet. Das ist der große Verdienst der Marxschen Kritik der politischen Ökonomie. Unter den Bedingungen dieser Epoche bewegte sich das kapitalistische Marktsystem tatsächlich weitgehend nach ‚seinen eigenen Gesetzen'. Aber Marx missinterpretiert die besonderen Bedingungen des neunzehnten Jahrhunderts als allgemeingültige Bestimmungsfaktoren der kapitalistischen Marktgesellschaft. Der ökonomistisch-deterministische Bias der Marxschen Kritik der politischen Ökonomie hatte die paradoxe Konsequenz, dass seine Anhänger kaum in der Lage waren, den faktischen Einfluss, den die protektiven Gegenbewegungen, die Demokratisierung und die ‚Politisierung der Politik' auf die Gesellschaft ausübten, in theoretisch-systematischer Weise zu reflektieren.

Tatsächlich aber spitzt sich gerade dieser Konflikt in der Periode zwischen den beiden Weltkriegen in fataler Weise zu. „Zwischen Wirtschaft und Politik ist eine Kluft aufgerissen. Das ist in dürren Worten die Diagnose der Zeit. Wirtschaft und Politik, diese beiden Lebensformen der Gesellschaft, haben sich selbständig gemacht und führen miteinander dauernd Krieg ... Eine Gesellschaft, deren politisches und wirtschaftliches System einander widerstritten, wäre unfehlbar dem Untergang – oder dem Umsturz geweiht", notiert Polanyi 1932. Die Weltkriege, die Weltwirtschaftskrise und der Aufstieg des Faschismus sind nicht zu verstehen, wenn dieser grundlegende Konflikt unbeachtet bleibt.

In der Folge der Ereignisse wurde die Überwindung des Gegensatzes von Wirtschaft und Gesellschaft zum wichtigsten Anliegen der Gesellschaft, die einer Lösung bedurfte, sollte der Fortbestand der westlichen Zivilisation nicht gefährdet werden. Nicht nur die Politik, auch die wirtschaftsliberalen Theorien wie ihre Kritiker hatten sich den daraus resultierenden Fragen zu stellen. Keynes' wie auch Polanyis Kritik der politischen Ökonomie, beide in der Zwischenkriegsperiode ausgearbeitet, reflektieren die veränderten Gegebenheiten. Für beide Autoren wurde die Frage, wie der Gegensatz von Wirtschaft und Gesellschaft überwunden werden kann, zur großen Herausforderung, auf die es eine Antwort zu finden galt.

3. *John M. Keynes*

Der ökonomische Liberalismus, mit dem Keynes in der Zwischenkriegsperiode konfrontiert war, hatte den Naturalismus des neunzehnten Jahrhunderts durch die Vorstellung ersetzt, die Gesellschaft könne als ‚Beziehung von Personen' verstanden werden. Das Nutzenoptimum rückte ins Zentrum der Gleichgewichtstheorie, weil es die kapitalistische Marktordnung als die logische Wahl der bestmöglichen gesellschaftlichen Ordnung erscheinen ließ. Die Ziel-Mittel-Logik, die in der Folge das wirtschaftsliberale Denken eroberte, schien die Herrschaft der Gesellschaft über die Wirtschaft zu bestätigen. Die Wahl der Ziele wurde als eine *ethische* Frage betrachtet, die von der Gesellschaft, nicht der Wirtschaft oder der ökonomischen Wissenschaft zu entscheiden sei. Wie Robbins in seinem berühmten Essay formulierte: „Society, acting as a body of political citizens, may formulate ends ... There are no economic ends. There are only economical and uneconomical ways of achieving given ends" (Robbins 1932: 128-129). Damit schien der Konflikt zwischen Wirtschaft und Gesellschaft der Vergangenheit anzugehören.

Keynes' Kritik der politischen Ökonomie (in Keynes' Jargon: der ‚klassischen Schule') bewegt sich in diesem Rahmen, bestreitet aber, dass der Konflikt sich quasi ‚von selbst' löst. Der Markt, so seine zentrale These, produziert, wenn sich selbst überlassen, nicht zwangsläufig ein gesellschaftliches Optimum. In ‚On Money' bestreitet er eine automatische Tendenz in Richtung Preisstabilität. In seinem zweiten Hauptwerk, der ‚Allgemeinen Theorie ...', versucht er nachzuweisen, dass ein ökonomisches Gleichgewicht nicht notwendigerweise die Vollbeschäftigung der Ressourcen beinhaltet. Das *wirtschaftliche* Ergebnis des Marktprozesses und das *gesellschaftliche* Ziel – ob Nutzenoptimum, Vollbeschäftigung oder Preisniveaustabilität – fallen auseinander.

Aber, so seine politische Message, der Konflikt zwischen ökonomischem Ergebnis und gesellschaftlichem Willen kann durch staatliche Intervention überwunden werden. Es genüge, wenn einige geld- und finanzpolitische Experten, mit dem richtigen Rüstzeug ausgestattet, die makroökonomischen Bedingungen kontrollierten. In der ‚Allgemeinen Theorie' fasst er zusammen: „If our central controls succeed in establishing an aggregate volume of output corresponding to full employment as nearly as is practicable, the classical theory comes into its own again from this point onwards" (Keynes 1936: 378). Mithilfe der staatlichen Eingriffe könne erreicht werden, was der ökonomische Liberalismus als Resultat des selbstregulierenden Marktsystems versprochen habe. Was bedeutet eine solche Position? Vier Aspekte scheinen entscheidend:

(1) Keynes' Kritik akzeptiert den Rahmen der Ziel-Mittel-Logik, aber schränkt diese in doppelter Weise ein: a) *die Ziele* auf solche wirtschaftlichen Zwecke, die vom ökonomischen Liberalismus geteilt werden: nicht Freiheit, Gleichheit, Brüderlichkeit oder die Überwindung der Ausbeutung, sondern

Preisniveaustabilität, Vollbeschäftigung der Ressourcen, außenwirtschaftliches Gleichgewicht; b) *die Mittel* auf marktkonforme Instrumente. Sein theoretischer Ansatz liefert die Grundlage, die den Zusammenhang von diesen Zielen und den wirtschaftspolitischen Instrumenten begründet.

(2) In der Konsequenz bedeutet dies, sowohl die Ziele wie auch die Mittel der marktwirtschaftlichen Logik *unterzuordnen*. Soweit die Ziele, die der ökonomische Liberalismus als Ergebnis des Marktprozesses annimmt, nicht automatisch erreicht werden, ist der Staat gefordert, eben genau dies herzustellen. Im Kern geht es Keynes um *marktkonforme Intervention* (auch wenn dieser Begriff üblicherweise in anderen Zusammenhängen verwendet wird). Ökonomische Experten stellen her, was der selbstregulierende Markt nach marktliberaler Interpretation zwar verspricht, aber nicht einzuhalten in der Lage ist.

(3) Die Charakterisierung der Keynesschen Position mit Hilfe des Begriffs ‚embedded liberalism' (Ruggie 1982) stellt den Zusammenhang auf den Kopf. Nicht die liberale Wirtschaft wird hier in die Gesellschaft eingebettet, sondern die Gesellschaft ordnet sich der Marktlogik unter. Der Marktmechanismus als zentrales, strukturbildendes System wird von Keynes mittelfristig in keiner Weise in Frage gestellt. Insofern bewegt sich sein Modell im Rahmen des wirtschaftsliberalen Denkens.

(4) Demokratischen Einrichtungen kommt in dem Keynesschen Modell keine entscheidende Rolle zu. Keynes mag darauf setzen, dass seine eigenen Politikvorschläge populärer sind als die seiner marktliberalen Widersacher, weil sie im Interesse der Mehrheit liegen. Letztendlich aber kommt es auf die ökonomischen Experten und die Umsetzung einer makroökonomisch orientierten Politik an. Nicht das Volk, ökonomisch ausgebildete Experten entscheiden.

Im Resultat läuft die Keynessche Kritik der politischen Ökonomie auf eine Ordnung hinaus, in der die Steuerung der Gesellschaft in den Händen von Experten der Geld- und Wirtschaftspolitik liegt, wodurch, so die Hoffnung, die Defizite des selbstregulierenden Marktsystems überwunden werden. Die dazu notwendige bewusste Unterordnung der Gesellschaft unter die ökonomische Logik des kapitalistischen Marktsystems ist das herausragende Merkmal des Keynesianischen technokratischen Systems.

Die Ziel-Mittel-Logik, einschließlich der Keynesschen Interpretation derselben, hatte nach dem Zweiten Weltkrieg – nicht zuletzt unter demokratisch-parlamentarischem Druck – in allen westlichen Industrieländern (sowie auf internationaler Ebene) einen merklichen Einfluss auf die politischen Entscheidungen gewonnen. Und es gelang zumindest zeitweise, die größten Übel der Zivilisation des neunzehnten Jahrhunderts durch protektive Gesetzgebung, geldpolitische Intervention und Nachfragesteuerung zu zähmen. Aber warum sollten weiterreichende Ziele, die der *Gesellschaft* als wünschenswert erschienen, negiert bzw. den Bedingungen der kapitalistischen *Marktwirtschaft* untergeordnet bleiben? Warum sollten die Grenzen marktkonformer Politik hingenommen werden? Seitens der Gesellschaft wurden in den sechziger/ siebziger Jahren Forderungen vorgebracht, die eine Stärkung der Demokratie (Fabrikräte, Mitbestimmung etc.), der ökologischen Protektion und der Persönlichkeit (Emanzipation des Einzelnen gegenüber seinem Dasein als bloßem Funktionsträger) bewirken sollten.

Man beachte: Eine Interpretation, die das Ende des ‚goldenen Zeitalters des Kapitalismus' zu Beginn des letzten Viertels des zwanzigsten Jahrhunderts primär wirtschaftlich zu erklären versucht, greift zu kurz. Das technokratische System der Nachkriegsperiode scheiterte nicht aus ökonomischen Gründen. Ähnlich wie das Marktsystem in der Zwischenkriegszeit zerbrach auch das technokratische System in den siebziger Jahren daran, dass der Einfluss der Gegenbewegung, als deren Vehikel nun in erster Linie die Studenten-, Frauen-, Ökologie- und Arbeiterbewegungen fungierten, mit den Funktionsbedingungen des internationalen Systems in Konflikt geriet.

Das Bretton-Woods-System setzte voraus, dass sich die Entwicklung der Löhne und Preise, der Geld- und Fiskalpolitik in den wichtigsten Ländern Europas und Asiens an jener der USA orientierte. Als der Vietnamkrieg und das parallel unter der Administration des demokratischen Präsidenten Johnson Mitte der sechziger Jahre aufgelegte „Great Society"-Programm die Hegemonie der USA und die internationale Position des Dollars schwächten, war diese Voraussetzung nicht länger erfüllt. Nachdem sich sowohl die finanzpolitischen Bedingungen wie auch die Handels- und Leistungsbilanz der USA verschlechtert hatten, konnte das System fester Wechselkurse gegen den Druck der Finanzmärkte nicht länger aufrechterhalten werden. Der Übergang zu flexiblen Kursen war das Signal, das das Ende der Keynesianischen Epoche einleitete. Auf nationaler Ebene bedingte der Konflikt das Ende des relativ stetigen Wachstumskurses. Steigende Inflationsraten und Boom-Bust-Zyklen wurden zum Merkmal der neuen Situation.

Damit stand die Alternative auf der Tagesordnung: entweder a) die Stärkung der Gesellschaft gegenüber der Wirtschaft oder b) eine noch konsequentere Unterordnung der Gesellschaft unter die Wirtschaft und die Aufgabe der Ziel-Mittel-Logik. Ersteres war die Forderung der Linken und der sozialen Bewegungen. Letzteres die Logik der konservativen Strömung innerhalb des ökonomischen Liberalismus. Ersteres hätte erfordert, den ökonomischen Herausforderungen mit einer neuen, kreativen Lösung zu begegnen, die eine ökonomische Alternative zu Markt und zentralwirtschaftlicher Planung beinhaltete. Die sozialen Bewegungen waren darauf nur ungenügend vorbereitet. Letzteres bedeutete, nicht den Keynesianismus, sondern die Logik des Ziel-Mittel-Denkens insgesamt durch eine deterministische Weltsicht zu ersetzen, in der das Marktsystem selbst als das *primäre* Ziel der gesellschaftlichen Planung anerkannt wurde.

4. Karl Polanyi

Polanyis Kritik der politischen Ökonomie (des ‚obsoleten marktwirtschaftlichen Denkens') entstand parallel zu den Arbeiten von Keynes. Polanyis Schwerpunkte lagen nicht auf theoretischem, sondern auf wirtschafts- und sozialhistorischem Gebiet. Polanyi würdigte Keynes als einen Vertreter des ‚englischen Neuliberalismus' (Polanyi 2002: 91). Was Keynes über Polanyis Arbeiten wusste oder dachte, ist nicht bekannt.

Das Verhältnis von Wirtschaft und Gesellschaft bildet den roten Faden von Polanyis bekanntestem Werk ‚The Great Transformation'. Erstens arbeitet er heraus, dass die Herauslösung der Wirtschaft aus der Gesellschaft (disembedding), die Marx zum Ausgangspunkt seiner Kritik an der klassischen Theorie gemacht hatte, ein Spezifikum der modernen kapitalistischen Marktgesellschaft, ein historisch beispielloses Phänomen ist, durch das sich die kapitalistische Marktgesellschaft von allen anderen Kulturen unterscheidet. In seinen späteren wirtschaftsanthropologischen Arbeiten vertieft er diesen Gedanken. Zweitens stützt er seine Interpretation des Aufstiegs, des Wandels und des schließlichen Niedergangs der Zivilisation des neunzehnten Jahrhunderts, die den Kern des Werkes ausmacht, auf die Untersuchung des Konflikts zwischen diesen beiden grundlegenden Seiten der menschlichen Existenz.

Polanyi stimmt nach der einen Seite mit Marx überein, dass das Marktsystem unter diesen besonderen historischen Bedingungen *tatsächlich* ein Eigenleben entwickelt, das auf die Bedürfnisse und Interessen der Gesellschaft keine Rücksicht nimmt. Gerade weil es von der Gesellschaft weitestgehend unabhängig ist und Letztere von sich selbst abhängig macht, könnte das selbstregulierende Marktsystem, wie er schreibt, „über längere Zeiträume nicht bestehen, ohne die menschliche und natürliche Substanz der Gesellschaft zu vernichten" (Polanyi 1978: 19-20). Letztendlich kann kein seelenloser Mechanismus die menschliche Kontrolle und Verantwortung für die zivilisatorische

Entwicklung ersetzen. Langfristig können die Widersprüche, die der modernen Gesellschaft inhärent sind, nur gelöst werden, so seine Folgerung, wenn dieser eigentümliche Zustand überwunden wird. Die Unterordnung der Wirtschaft unter eine demokratische Gesellschaft lautet seine Devise.

Polanyis Kritik der politischen Ökonomie unterscheidet sich andererseits von der Marxschen insofern, als er die Vorstellung, die gesellschaftliche Dynamik sei letztendlich durch ökonomische Gesetze determiniert, zurückweist. Es ist der Konflikt zwischen Wirtschaft und Gesellschaft selbst, so seine Gegenthese, der der Transformation der Zivilisation des neunzehnten Jahrhunderts zugrunde liegt.

Polanyi charakterisiert die daraus resultierende Dynamik als *Doppelbewegung*. Hier greift er eine Idee auf, die in der Marxschen Analyse zwar angelegt ist, aber – wie oben gezeigt – nicht entwickelt wird, dafür aber – mit umgekehrten Vorzeichen – von wirtschaftsliberalen Autoren wie Spencer, Mises oder Lippmann. Letztere hatten ihren Gegnern vorgeworfen, den gesellschaftlichen Fortschritt durch Interventionen der Gesellschaft, die durch kollektivistische Vorurteile und andere utopische Ideen fehlgeleitet waren, zu stören und zu destabilisieren. Polanyi legt eine entgegengesetzte Interpretation vor: Nicht die Gegenbewegung verfolgt utopische Ziele, sondern der ökonomische Liberalismus selbst, so sein Argument, ist das utopische Projekt, gegen das sich die Gesellschaft wehrt, um nicht ihrerseits von den Folgen bedroht zu werden.

Die Doppelbewegung setzte voraus, dass Klasseninteressen als das Vehikel der gesellschaftlichen Veränderung fungierten. In dem Maße, in dem es einzelnen Klassen gelang, sich nicht nur für ihre eigenen Interessen einzusetzen, sondern auch für die Belange, die für die Gesellschaft als Ganzes relevant waren, wurden sie zu Repräsentanten der Interessen der Gesellschaft (im frühen neunzehnten Jahrhundert fiel diese Aufgabe vornehmlich dem Landadel und der Bauernschaft, später der Arbeiterklasse zu). Diese Voraussetzungen zerbrachen in der Zwischenkriegsperiode. Als sich die Unternehmen, der Handel und die Gewerbetreibenden der Wirtschaft und die Arbeiterbewegung, gestützt auf ihren gewachsenen Einfluss innerhalb der demokratischen Einrichtungen, der politischen Sphäre bemächtigten, bedeutete dies das Ende der Doppelbewegung. Weltwirtschaftskrise und Faschismus, die die westliche Zivilisation in ihren Fundamenten bedrohten, waren das Ergebnis der daraus resultierenden Blockade.

An diesem Punkt trifft sich Polanyis Problemstellung mit der Keynesschen. In den dreißiger Jahren – und erneut nach dem Zweiten Weltkrieg – entsprach es dem Interesse der Gesellschaft in ihrer Gesamtheit, die Blockade, die durch den Gegensatz von Wirtschaft und Gesellschaft verursacht wurde, zu überwinden. Beide stimmen auch darin überein, dass weder selbstregulierende Märkte noch zentralwirtschaftliche Planung erfolgversprechende Antworten darstellten. Und dennoch schlagen beide entgegengesetzte Wege ein. Während Keynes für marktkonforme Lösungen plädiert, sucht Polanyi nach sozialistischen Alternativen, deren Kern in der Unterordnung der Wirtschaft unter eine demokratische Gesellschaft besteht. Schon frühzeitig wendet er sich explizit gegen die (nicht nur in den USA vorherrschende) Tendenz, „die Gesellschaft als Ganzes ... noch enger an das Wirtschaftssystem" anzupassen und dem Ideal einer Brave New World nachzueifern, „in der das Individuum darauf dressiert ist, eine Ordnung zu unterstützen, die von Klügeren für ihn entworfen worden ist" (Polanyi 1979: 147).

Aus dieser Perspektive betrachtet steht Polanyis Kritik der politischen Ökonomie der Marxschen näher als der Keynesschen: Der Gegensatz von Wirtschaft und Gesellschaft kann, wie er betont, letztendlich nur zugunsten der Gesellschaft gelöst werden. „Sozialismus", so der Kerngedanke, „ist dem Wesen nach die einer industriellen Zivilisation innewohnende Tendenz, über den selbstregulierenden Markt hinauszugehen, indem man ihn bewusst einer demokratischen Gesellschaft unterordnet" (Polanyi 1978: 311). Polanyis Kritik der politischen Ökonomie richtet sich nicht allein gegen die Verschwendung unausgelasteter Ressourcen, gegen die Ungerechtigkeiten und die ungleiche Verteilung von Einkommen und Lebenschancen. Er wendet sich primär gegen die Entfremdung, die Verdinglichung der menschlichen Beziehungen und die unmenschlichen Folgen, die aus der Herrschaft des ökonomischen Systems über die Gesellschaft resultieren.

Allerdings – und hier trennt sich sein eigener von Marx' Weg – sieht Polanyi das grundlegende Problem nicht allein im Privateigentum begründet, sondern in der sich dahinter verbergenden Komplexität und Unübersichtlichkeit einer technologischen Zivilisation. Daher erscheint ihm die Hoffnung, diese Übel durch den Fortschritt der Produktivkräfte und eine sich darauf stützende kommunistische Revolution vollständig überwinden zu können, als illusorisch und irreführend. Im Unterschied zu Marx betrachtet er die Ausweitung der Übersicht des Einzelnen, die Stärkung direkter Formen der Demokratie und die Vergrößerung der gesellschaftlichen Regulierungskapazitäten als eine unter den modernen Bedingungen *immerwährende* Aufgabe. Die umfassende Demokratisierung der Gesellschaft erscheint ihm als der einzig bekannte Weg, um die gesellschaftliche Kontrolle über die selbstregulierenden Mechanismen *auszudehnen*. Weder der Markt noch ein technokratisches System können den Menschen die Verantwortung für die Gestaltung ihrer

Gesellschaft abnehmen. Demokratie ist daher nicht nur eine Werthaltung, sondern eine unabdingbare Notwendigkeit, wenn die Herrschaft der Wirtschaft über die Gesellschaft zurückgedrängt werden soll.

Das bedeutet nicht, in die Logik des Ziel-Mittel-Denkens zurückzufallen. Polanyi macht keinen Hehl daraus, dass er sich am westlichen Ideal der individuellen Freiheit, die auf persönlicher Verantwortung basiert, orientiert. Aber *Polanyi bleibt Realist.* Nicht in erster Linie auf unterschiedliche Wertvorstellungen, sondern auf die Kenntnis der *gesellschaftlichen Gesetze* kommt es an. „Der Glaube an die Möglichkeit einer allein vom Wunsch und Willen des Menschen geformten Gesellschaft war eine Illusion" (Polanyi 1978: 341). Die Unterordnung der Gesellschaft unter die Wirtschaft kann nur überwunden werden, wenn wir *wissen*, was einer menschlicheren Gestaltung der Gesellschaft entgegensteht. Welches sind die *Hindernisse?* Wo liegen die *Grenzen* der menschlichen Kontrolle? Die Antworten auf diese Fragen verweisen zurück auf die Bedingungen einer technologischen Zivilisation. Polanyi folgt hier Adam Smith und Max Weber, Karl Marx und Ludwig Mises, die den grundlegenden Unterschied einer technologischen gegenüber einer vorindustriellen Gesellschaft betonten. Aber wie groß dieser Unterschied auch sein mag, es folgt daraus nicht, dass wir die Übel als selbstverständlich hinzunehmen haben.

Aus dieser Perspektive betrachtet, wird deutlich, was Unterordnung der Wirtschaft unter eine demokratische Gesellschaft bedeutet: die Verantwortung für die Gestaltung der gesellschaftlichen Verhältnisse im vollen Bewusstsein der Herausforderungen zu übernehmen, die mit dem technologischen Fortschritt verbunden sind. Das wirtschaftsliberale Denken führt uns in die Irre, wenn es den Eindruck erweckt, das Marktsystem befreie die Menschen von ihrer Verantwortung. „Der liberale Kapitalismus", so fasst Polanyi seine Kritik der politischen Ökonomie zusammen, „war im Effekt die erste Reaktion des Menschen auf die Industrielle Revolution. Um der Anwendung komplizierter und mächtiger Maschinen Raum zu geben, haben wir die Wirtschaft des Menschen in ein selbstregelndes System von Märkten umgewandelt und unsere Vorstellungen und Werte dieser einmaligen Innovation angeglichen. Heute ... stehen (wir) erneut vor der Frage, wie man das menschliche Leben in einer Maschinengesellschaft organisieren soll. Hinter dem verblassenden Gefüge des auf Wettbewerb beruhenden Kapitalismus erscheint das bedrohliche Bild einer Industriezivilisation mit ihrer lähmenden Arbeitsteilung, der Normierung des Lebens, der Vorherrschaft des Mechanismus über den Organismus, der Organisation über die Spontaneität. Die Wissenschaft selbst wird vom Wahnsinn heimgesucht. Dies ist unser vordringliches Besorgnis." (Polanyi 1979: 129)

5. Kritik der politischen Ökonomie heute

In den siebziger Jahren des zwanzigsten Jahrhunderts reagierte der konservative Liberalismus auf die Destabilisierung des internationalen Systems, die durch die Gegenbewegung ausgelöst worden war, in der Weise, dass er die Ansprüche Letzterer als utopisch zurückzuweisen versuchte. Nur jene politischen Entscheidungen, die auf einem wirklichen Verständnis der (vermeintlichen) ‚Gesetze der Wirtschaft' beruhten, so das zentrale Argument, erreichten ihre Absichten. Der Verweis auf die *nichtintendierten Folgen* menschlichen Handelns im Falle der Missachtung der ökonomischen Gesetze diente den marktliberalen Kräften dazu, eine ökonomistisch-deterministische Konzeption wiederzubeleben, ohne in die Logik des naiven Naturalismus zurückzufallen. Auch wenn dem menschlichen Wollen an sich keine Grenzen gesetzt seien, so könnten letztendlich nur jene Pläne verwirklicht werden, die die ökonomischen Gesetze anerkannten. Thatchers Motto fasste die marktliberale Logik des auslaufenden zwanzigsten Jahrhunderts in vier Worten zusammen: „There is no alternative!" Was auch immer die Gesellschaft anstrebe, letztendlich erreiche sie ihre Ziele nur dann, wenn sie sich den Gesetzen der Wirtschaft unterwerfe.

Die Gegenbewegungen, die sich der Unterordnung der Gesellschaft unter die Wirtschaft widersetzen, stehen heute vor der Alternative, entweder a) die Existenz gesellschaftlicher Gesetze grundsätzlich in Frage zu stellen oder b) sich auf eine Kritik der marktliberalen Interpretation einzulassen, um die irreführenden Annahmen und deren Widersprüche aufzudecken.

Die erste Variante schiebt die Forderung, die Politik auf Wissen, d.h. auf die Kenntnis der gesellschaftlichen Gesetze zu stützen, als obsoletes Vorurteil beiseite. In gewisser Weise wird die Existenz gesellschaftlicher Gesetze überhaupt geleugnet. Um der marktliberalen Utopie erfolgreich entgegentreten zu können, so die Hoffnung, komme es in erster Linie darauf an, Modelle einer ‚guten Gesellschaft' zu entwerfen und Beispiele ‚realer Utopien' zu propagieren. Die Schwächen einer solchen Strategie bestehen – abgesehen davon, dass die Überzeugungskraft eher gering ist – darin, dass sie die Fehler der Vergangenheit wiederholt, weil ihr das Verständnis der Versäumnisse früherer Bewegungen fehlt. Ohne klare Vorstellung darüber, wie sie den Problemen einer komplexen Gesellschaft, der globalen Arbeitsteilung, der Unübersichtlichkeit, den technologischen Herausforderungen etc. begegnen will, läuft sie Gefahr, den Konflikt zwischen Wirtschaft und Gesellschaft erneut auf die Spitze zu treiben. Gegenreaktionen marktliberaler, konservativer und anderer rückwärtsgerichteter Kräfte wären die notwendige Folge.

Die Alternative besteht darin, die marktliberale Interpretation der Gesetze der Gesellschaft einer kritischen Analyse zu unterziehen. Ihr Ziel ist es, zu einem *tieferen Verständnis* der gesellschaftlichen Gesetze vorzudringen, die die Möglichkeiten einer bewussten Gestaltung der Gesellschaft beschränken. Ihre Protagonisten stützen sich auf den Grundgedanken, dass die Kenntnis der gesellschaftlichen Gesetze die unabdingbare Voraussetzung jeder wirklichen Reform ist, die darauf zielt, die gesellschaftlichen Bedürfnisse gegenüber jenen der Wirtschaft zu stärken. Sie betrachten die inhaltliche Auseinandersetzung mit den herrschenden wirtschaftsliberalen Theorien und den diesen zugrunde liegenden Vorstellungen als unverzichtbar, weil nur die Kritik der herrschenden Vorurteile es erlaubt, ein *realistischeres* Bild der gesellschaftlichen Wirklichkeit zu zeichnen. Es ist dies der Weg, den Marx, Keynes und Polanyi eingeschlagen haben. Angesichts der Bedrohungen, die von der Destabilisierung der internationalen Beziehungen, der Krise der Demokratie, den wirtschaftlichen Unsicherheiten und den Gefahren des technischen Fortschritts für Mensch und Natur ausgehen, ist eine solche Orientierung heute wichtiger als je zuvor.

Literatur

Keynes, J.M. (1936): *The General Theory of Employment, Interest and Money*, London: Macmillan.

Marx, K. (1960): Der achtzehnte Brumaire des Louis Bonaparte, in: MEW 8, Berlin: Dietz Verlag, 111-207.

Marx, K. (1972): *Das Kapital* I, MEW 23, Berlin: Dietz Verlag.

Polanyi, K. (1978): *The Great Transformation*, Frankfurt a.M.: Suhrkamp.

Polanyi, K. (1979): Unser obsoletes marktwirtschaftliches Denken, in: ders., *Ökonomie und Gesellschaft*, Frankfurt a.M.: Suhrkamp, 161-180.

Polanyi, K. (2002): Liberale Wirtschaftsreformen in England, in: ders., *Chronik der großen Transformation. Artikel und Aufsätze (1920-1945). Bd. 1: Wirtschaftliche Transformation, Gegenbewegung und der Kampf um die Demokratie*, hg. und eingeleitet von M. Cangiani und C. Thomasberger, Marburg: Metropolis.

Robbins, L. (1932): *An Essay on the Nature and Significance of Economic Science*, London: Macmillan.

Ruggie, J.G. (1982): International Regimes, Transactions, and Change: Embedded Liberalism in the Postwar Economic Order, in: *International Organizations*, 36(2), 379-415.

Zwischen Gleichgewicht und Ungleichgewicht

Zur Kreislaufvorstellung bei Jean Baptiste Say

Siegbert Preuß

1. Einleitung

Für Ökonomen ist es selbstverständlich, das Modell der klassischen politischen Ökonomie auf das „Saysche Theorem" oder auch das „Saysche Gesetz" zu reduzieren. Insoweit hat diese Sprechweise die gleiche Dimension wie das Reden über die „invisible hand" oder der Hinweis „in the long run we are all dead". Oftmals jedoch verkommen solche Sätze führender Nationalökonomen zur Platitude und werden ihrer Intention nicht gerecht, denn die Verkürzung auf Schlagworte verkennt die ursprüngliche Absicht der Autoren, eine theoriegeleitete Aussage mit ökonomischen Folgen zu formulieren.

Das Erbe der klassischen politischen Ökonomie besteht in der optimistischen Variante darin, Gleichgewichtszustände auf allen Märkten feststellen zu können, weil eine inhärente Stabilität des marktwirtschaftlichen Systems unzweifelhaft vorhanden ist.[1] Prägnant findet sich diese Vorstellung in dem häufig zitierten Sayschen Theorem, dass sich jedes Angebot seine Nachfrage selber schafft, weil stets die angebotene Gütermenge abgesetzt werden kann. Diese Gleichgewichtsvorstellung muss auch eine Antwort auf die Frage nach der Einkommensverwendung finden, die sich immerhin durch Konsum oder

---

[1] Zu den Optimisten gehören in der Klassik Smith, Say sowie J. und J. St. Mill sowie später insbesondere die Vertreter der neoklassischen Theorie in der österreichischen Variante (Menger, Mises, Hayek) einschl. Vertretern der Chicagoer Schule (wie Friedman, Stigler, Becker) und in der deutschen Version des Ordo-Liberalismus (Eucken, Böhm, Röpke); demgegenüber sind Malthus, Ricardo und Sismondi skeptisch hinsichtlich der Entwicklung der kapitalistischen Gesellschaft.

Nichtkonsum (Sparen) auszeichnen und dadurch eine Gleichgewichtslösung verhindern kann, was zu einzel- bzw. gesamtwirtschaftlichen Veränderungen ggf. sogar zu Krisen führen kann. Positiv argumentierend, verweist Smith auf einen gesamtwirtschaftlichen Zusammenhang, bei dem zwar Investitionen, Sparen und Konsum zwischen den gesellschaftlichen Klassen auseinanderfallen, jedoch insgesamt alle makroökonomischen Größen im Wirtschaftskreislauf ausgeglichen sein müssen (Smith 1789: 278f.).

Allerdings wird im Denken der nachfolgenden Epochen auch deutlich, dass negative Folgen beim Fehlen einer effektiven Nachfrage entstehen können, die je nach theoretischem Standort zu neuen Theorieentwürfen führen. Heine und Herr zeigen Begründungsmängel und Folgen auf, die für eine mikro- bzw. makroökonomische Theorie entstehen, sofern sie eine Saysche Gesetzmäßigkeit unterstellen (Heine/Herr 2013: insbes. 211f., 340, 417, 643).[2]

Die nachstehenden Ausführungen befassen sich mit den theoretischen Erörterungen von Say, und zwar hinsichtlich einer frühen Diskussion zu Konjunkturzyklen (Abschnitt 2) und der sich anschließenden Debatte mit seinen Zeitgenossen (Abschnitte 3 und 4). Danach wird die moderne Interpretation vorgestellt und mit der wohl ursprünglich vertretenen Auffassung konfrontiert (Abschnitte 5 und 6). Abschnitt 7 schließlich zieht einige Schlussfolgerungen.

2. Der Konjunkturzyklus bei J. B. Say

In der ökonomischen Literatur wird Says Konjunkturerklärung unter dem Stichwort „Theorie der Absatzwege" behandelt. Roscher stellt diesen Aspekt als besondere Leistung heraus: „Zu den anerkanntesten und wirklich unzweifelhaftesten Fortschritten, welche die Wissenschaft Say verdankt, ist seine Theorie der Absatzwege zu rechnen, wobei er freilich die Möglichkeit einer allgemeinen Stockung zu sehr leugnet; ferner seine Betonung des Kapitals als eines besonderen Productionsfactors, während die Engländer meist so thaten, als wenn das gemeinsame Product eigentlich nur von der Arbeit herrührte" (Roscher 1874: 654).

Es handelt sich hierbei um Kapitel 15 des ersten Bandes, das den Titel „Von den Absatzwegen" trägt (Say 1803/1826 I: 189ff.; 1840 II: 10ff.). Hier wird der Frage nachgegangen, ob nur auf einzelnen Märkten oder auch gesamtwirtschaftlich Absatzkrisen entstehen können. Dies hat seinerzeit zu einer um-

---

[2] Siehe hierzu ausführlicher Gliederungspunkte 6. und 7. sowie Herr/Kazandziska (2011: 12); Dullien/Herr/Kellermann (2009: 86ff.).

fangreichen Diskussion zwischen Say, Malthus, Ricardo, Mill und Sismondi geführt, als deren vorläufiger Endpunkt Keynes' „Allgemeine Theorie" benannt werden kann.

Die allgemeine – Say zugeschriebene Aussage – lautet, dass sich jedes Güterangebot die eigene Nachfrage schafft und es demzufolge zu keinem Angebotsüberschuss kommen kann. Marktwirtschaftliche Systeme sind demzufolge inhärent stabil und führen stets zum Gleichgewicht. Mit einer Gleichgewichtsvorstellung, die sich durch flexible Preise auf Märkten einstellt, wird zugleich postuliert, dass neben der effizienten Allokation auch die Vollbeschäftigung gesichert werden kann. Damit ist ein Marktversagen auf Arbeitsmärkten grundsätzlich nicht möglich, denn konjunkturbedingte Nachfragemängel lassen sich grundsätzlich durch Preisflexibilität ausgleichen.

In Says Hauptwerkt trägt Kapitel XV die Überschrift „Von den Absatzwegen" und wird mit einem Untertitel eingeleitet, der bis heute die Gleichgewichtsvorstellung über Say bestimmt: „Producte kauft man nur mit Producten, und das zum Einkauf dienende Geld selber mußte erst mit irgend einem Producte eingetauscht werden" (Say 1803/1826 I: 189)[3], diese Chiffre für wirtschaftliches Gleichgewicht wird von ihm häufig verwendet (z.B. Say 1840 II: 12)[4]. Dieser Zusammenhang wird auch gegenüber Malthus vertreten: „Jeder, der seit Adam Smith sich mit der politischen Wirthschaftslehre beschäftigt hat, gibt zu, daß wir genau genommen, unsere Bedürfnismittel nicht mit dem Gelde, dem Umlaufswerkzeuge, wirklich kaufen, mit dem wir sie bezahlen. Wir müssen erst vorher dies Geld selbst durch den Verkauf unserer Erzeugnisse eingekauft haben" (Say 1820: 49).

Hintergrund dieser Argumentation ist die Vorstellung, dass sämtlichen Produktionsfaktoren (Say: Produktionselemente) bei der Herstellung von gesellschaftlich nachgefragten Gütern und Dienstleistungen ein Tauschwert – überwiegend als Marktpreis interpretiert – inhärent ist. Dieser Preis entspricht der Faktorentlohnung, die zu einem von Unternehmern vorgeschossenen Ein-

---

[3] „Man sollte nicht sagen, der Verkauf geht nicht, weil das Geld rar ist; sondern, weil die anderen Producte rar sind. Geld gibt es immer genug zum Behuf des Umlaufes und wechselseitigen Austausches der sonstigen Werthe, sobald diese Werthe wirklich existiren" (Say 1803/1826 I: 192).

[4] „Der Mann, dessen Industrie beflissen ist, den Dingen Werth zu geben, indem er ihnen irgend eine Brauchbarkeit beibringt, kann nur da hoffen, daß dieser Werth werde geschätzt und bezahlt werden, wo andere Menschen die Mittel zu seiner Anschaffung besitzen. Worin bestehen diese Mittel? In anderen Werthen, anderen Producten: – den Früchten von deren Industrie, Capitalen und Ländereien. Daraus geht hervor, [...] daß lediglich die Production den Producten ihre Absatzwege eröffnet" (Say 1803/1826 I: 190).

kommen führt,[5] das unmittelbar für Konsumzwecke verwendet wird. Es gilt also für jeden Unternehmer, diejenigen Güter herzustellen, die einem gesellschaftlichen Bedürfnis entsprechen, damit es zu einer Nachfrage kommt.[6] Insoweit kann das erfolgreiche Arbeitsangebot als Verkauf i.S. des Tausches von Arbeitszeit gegen Geld ebenso interpretiert werden wie der gelungene Verkauf von produzierten Gütern oder auch die durchgeführte Verpachtung eines Grundstücks, die beim jeweiligen Eigentümer der Produktionsfaktoren zu einer Einkommensgröße wird.

Nur durch die Entlohnung der verkauften Leistungen gegen Geld ist es möglich, andere Güter zu erwerben: „[...] Weil jeder von uns die Erzeugnisse der Anderen nur mit seinen eigenen kaufen kann, weil die Wertmenge, die wir einkaufen können, derjenigen gleich ist, die wir hervorzubringen vermögen, so werden auch die Menschen destomehr kaufen, jemehr sie hervorbringen werden" (Say 1820: 50). Bisher ist damit lediglich ein wechselseitiger Güter- und Leistungsaustausch charakterisiert worden, der auf einzelnen Märkten zu einer Überschussnachfrage führen kann, währenddessen Malthus auf einen gesamtwirtschaftlichen Nachfrageausfall abstellte.

Bislang ist bei dieser Argumentation noch kein Bezug zu einer Naturalwirtschaft ersichtlich. Wenn sich herausstellt, dass produzierte Güter nicht verkauft werden können, bedarf es einer Erklärung, die nämlich „[...] darin liegt, weil andere [Güter, S. P.] nicht hervorgebracht werden, und daß die Hervorbringung allein den Erzeugnissen Absatz eröffnet" (Say 1820: 50) und „[...] ob man außer Stande sey, das zu verzehren, was man im Stande ist hervorzubringen" (Say 1820: 63).

Mit dem skizzierten Wirtschaftskreislauf scheint auf den ersten Blick kein Problem zu entstehen. Dennoch geht es hier um die Frage nach den Ursachen und Folgen eines Nachfrageausfalls, der für Say auf einzelnen Märkten als ein Ergebnis von Konsumänderungen vorstellbar ist. Diese Situation wird jedoch – ähnlich wie bei Smith – durch andere Märkte ausgeglichen, auf denen

---

[5] Say unterscheidet erstmals in der ökonomischen Theorie zwischen dem Unternehmer, der Güter produzieren lässt, und dem Kapitalisten, der ggf. die Güterproduktion durch Kreditvergabe ermöglicht.

[6] „Eine Sache erzeugen, nach der kein Bedürfniß gefühlt wird, wäre soviel, als eine Sache ohne Wert hervorzubringen, als gar nicht hervorzubringen" (Say 1820: 101). Für Say existiert eine Rangreihenfolge der Bedürfnisse (1803/1826 I: 541ff.). Mit seiner Schrift „Entwicklung der Gesetze des menschlichen Verkehrs und der daraus fließenden Regeln für menschliches Handeln" wird 1854 Gossen die mikroökonomische Begründung liefern, die mit der individuellen Nutzenmaximierung begründet wird.

demzufolge eine Übernachfrage herrschen muss.[7] Bei steigendem Güterangebot kommt also zwangsläufig eine höhere Nachfrage zustande, weil dementsprechend die Summe der Einkommen gestiegen ist. Insoweit wird weiterhin ein „Geldschleier" unterstellt, der die realwirtschaftlichen Verhältnisse zusammenbringt.

Kreislauftheoretisch wird für den Güterkauf vorausgesetzt, dass vorher ein wertmäßig analoger Verkauf einer Ware oder Leistung erfolgreich durchgeführt werden konnte: „Sie müssen sich also durch den Tausch aller der Sachen, die sie verfertigen, entledigen, um die Sachen, deren sie bedürfen, zu erlangen. [...] In Folge des Tauschverkehrs kann Jeder die Fabrikation einer einzigen Art von Produkten so weit treiben, als es seine Mittel gestatten; und mit diesem Produkte erwirbt er Alles, was zum Unterhalte seiner Familie nothwendig ist. Das gemünzte Geld [...] dient beim Tauschverkehr nur als Werkzeug. Dasselbe ist nicht der Zweck des Austausches, sondern nur das Mittel" (Say 1845 II: 7).

Der Geldkreislauf bedingt den Verkauf von Gütern: „Wer kaufen will, muß zunächst verkaufen, und er kann nur das verkaufen, was er producirt hat, oder was man für ihn producirt hat" (Say 1845 II: 11). Diese Modellkonstruktion setzt voraus, dass nur die Summe von Gütern produziert wird, die auch konsumiert werden. Damit werden alle Mitglieder der Gesellschaft zu Produzenten und zugleich Konsumenten der hergestellten Produkte, die sie mit ihrem Einkommen erwerben, und zwar ohne Veränderung der Geldmenge. Dabei wird auch die Möglichkeit der Kreditaufnahme thematisiert. Sie erleichtert die Überbrückung von Ein- und Auszahlungen und führt zu Zinseinkommen bei Kapitalisten, die damit ihren Güterkonsum befriedigen (Say 1845 I: 174).

Say wird bei seiner Darstellung häufig unterstellt, er stelle eine Tauschwirtschaft mit unmittelbaren Austauschverhältnissen vor und behandle damit im Gegensatz zu einer monetären Ökonomie keine Geldfunktion als eigenständige Kategorie. Wir denken, dass Say durchaus eine monetäre Produktionsökonomie dargestellt hat. Allerdings sind Zweifel angebracht, ob Störungen des Gleichgewichts lediglich als Ursache einzelner Marktstörungen angemessen beschrieben werden können. Hinsichtlich eines gesamtwirtschaft-

---

[7] Deshalb die Schlussfolgerung: „Je lebhafter die Production, desto leichter der Absatz" (Say 1803/1826 I: 194).

lichen Erklärungsgehalts muss diese Interpretation scheitern.[8] Wir haben es hier mit einer frühen Darstellung zu tun, die keine monetäre Wirkungen kennt und dem Geld eine neutrale Rolle im Wirtschaftskreislauf unterstellt,[9] sodass Geldmengenänderungen lediglich zu Änderungen des Preisniveaus führen.

Wie muss eine monetäre Produktionsökonomie modelliert werden, damit ein Gleichgewichtszustand erreicht werden kann? Die vorgegebenen Handlungsbedingungen führen bei Say zu der gewünschten Gleichgewichtslösung. Diesem Aspekt, monetären Tauschwirtschaften immer einen unmittelbaren Güteraustausch zu unterstellen, ohne diese Situation methodisch zu untermauern, wird beispielsweise von Wicksell entgegengehalten: „[...] man hat sich ja daran gewöhnt, mit *J.B. Say* die Waren selber als gegenseitig die Nachfrage nacheinander konstituierend und begrenzend zu betrachten. Das sind sie auch in *letzter Hand*, aber hier handelt es sich umgekehrt gerade um das, was in *erster* Hand geschieht, nämlich um das Zwischenglied in dem definitiven Austausche einer Ware gegen eine andere, welche von der Nachfrage des Geldes nach Waren und dem Angebote der Waren gegen Geld gebildet wird. Jede Geldwerttheorie, die diesen Namen verdienen soll, muß daher imstande sein, nachzuweisen, wie und aus welchem Grunde die monetäre oder pekuniäre Nachfrage nach Waren unter gegebenen Umständen das Warenangebot übersteigen oder, umgekehrt, darunter bleiben wird" (Wicksell 1922 II: 181).

Andererseits lässt sich positiv herausstellen, dass Say durchaus einen Kreditmechanismus skizzieren wollte, der gerade nicht zu einer negativen Konjunktursituation führt, weil die gesparten Einkommen durch Unternehmer

---

[8] „[...] daß mit dem Eintritt des Geldes in die Wirtschaft ein neuer Bestimmungsgrund hinzutritt, der, weil das Geld nicht wie alle übrigen Gegenstände des wirtschaftlichen Handelns, selbst Bedürfnisse zu befriedigen, eine Nachfrage endgültig zu stillen vermag, die strenge Interdependenz und Geschlossenheit des Gleichgewichtssystemes aufhebt und Bewegungen der Wirtschaft ermöglicht, die innerhalb des Gleichgewichtssystemes unvorstellbar sind" (Hayek 1929: 14).

[9] „[...] das Geld ist nichts Anderes als der Transportwagen für den Wert der Producte. Sein ganzer Nutzen hat darin bestanden, den Werth jener Producte zu dir hinüberzuführen, welche dein Käufer verkauft hatte, um die deinigen einzukaufen; und ebenso wird es zu Dem, welchem du selber etwas abkaufen wirst, den Werth derjenigen Producte hinüberführen, die du an Andere verkauft haben wirst" (Say 1803/1826 I: 191).

akkumuliert werden.[10] Die weiteren Folgen der Kreditvergabe liegen nicht allein in der Produktionserweiterung, sondern führen zu Preisänderungen der nunmehr erzeugten Güter und – bei nicht gleichzeitiger Lohnsteigerung – ggf. zum Zwangssparen (Schumpeter, Hayek).

Kommt das Gleichgewicht immer zustande, wenn stets Güter mit Gütern ausgetauscht werden? Offensichtlich können Angebotsüberschüsse und Nachfrageschwankungen auftreten. Für einzelne Produkte kann das der Fall sein, während andere Knappheitspreise erzielen. Gesamtwirtschaftlich sind jedoch keine Nachfrageausfälle zu befürchten, weil das Gleichgewicht durch den Marktmechanismus hergestellt wird. Die am Markt gehandelten Güter haben einen Marktpreis, der den Opportunitätskosten des wechselseitigen Austauschvorteils entspricht (Say 1840 II: 16).

3. Optimistische Deutung: J. Mill, Ricardo und J. St. Mill

James Mill zeigt, dass die gesamtwirtschaftliche Nachfrage stets dem Güterangebot entsprechen muss, weil die entstandenen Einkommen konsumiert werden: „Every particle of the annual produce of a country falls as revenue to somebody. [...] It is either paid as wages to labourers, who immediately buy with it food and other necessaries, or it is employed in the purchase of raw materials. The whole annual produce of the country, therefore, is employed in making purchases" (J. Mill 1808: 83f.). Voraussetzung für jede Güterproduktion sind marktgängige Produkte: „Consumption in the necessary order of things is the effect of production, not production the effect of consumption" (J. Mill 1808: 79). Dabei stellt für den individuellen Konsum die freie Entscheidung der Leistungsabgabe die Budgetgrenze dar (J. Mill 1821: 323). Auch Sparen führt zu keinem Nachfrageausfall, weil in gleicher Höhe unmit-

---

[10] „Der Kreditmechanismus, auch wenn wir alle Kredite als Uebertragung von Ersparnissen auffassen, bedeutet also ein Moment der Elastizität im Produktions- und Zirkulationsprozeß. Werden *alle* irgendwie ersparten Summen sofort wieder als kreditierte Beträge dem Produktionsprozeß zugeführt, so bedeutet das in Tat, daß all in irgendeine Wirtschaft einströmenden Geldsummen auch wieder Waren kaufen. Insofern also Geldeingänge als Erlös von Produkten [...] gelten können, bedeutet dann restlose Zirkulation des Geldes, daß jede Produktion im gleichen Umfange Konsumtion auslöst [...]. So scheint der Kreditmechanismus ein weiteres Argument für die These Says zu bieten. [...] Indem der Kredit jedermann das Sparen wirtschaftlich sinnvoll erscheinen läßt, weil er (bei stabilem Geldwerte) über größere Gütermengen in der Zukunft als in der Gegenwart verfügen wird, kann er trotzdem eine Diskrepanz zwischen Produktion und Konsum im allgemeinen schaffen" (Lederer 1925: 379).

telbar Investitionen durchgeführt werden und damit eine zusätzliche Güter- und Einkommensentstehung erfolgt. Die Nachfrage wird wiederum durch Löhne und Profite gesichert: „Whatever be the additional quantity of goods therefore which is at any time created in any country, an additional power of purchasing, exactly equivalent, is at the same instant created; so that a nation can never be naturally overstocked either with capital or with commodities; as the very operation of capital makes a vent for its produce" (J. Mill 1808: 81f.).

Während das gesamtwirtschaftliche Gleichgewicht unzweifelhaft entstehen muss, kann selbstverständlich auf einzelnen Teilmärkten ein Angebotsüberschuss vorliegen (J. Mill 1808: 85), der jedoch durch Preisflexibilität wieder zu einem Marktgleichgewicht führen wird: „Wenn wir von irgend einer Nation sagen, daß zu einer bestimmten Zeit Angebot und Nachfrage bei ihr gleich seien; so meinen wir dieß nicht in Betreff einer oder einiger einzelnen Waaren, sondern, [...] daß der Betrag ihrer Nachfrage [...] dem Betrage ihres Angebots, in allen Artikeln zusammen genommen, gleich sei" (J. Mill 1821: 327).

Das gesamtwirtschaftliche Gleichgewicht wird zwar als Geldökonomie modelliert, denn im Mittelpunkt steht die deutlich hervorgehobene Quantitätstheorie und deren Wirkungen auf Güterpreise, sofern Geldmengenänderungen vorliegen. Eine weitere Wirkung wird dem Geld nicht unterstellt, weil alle ökonomischen Aktivitäten als Tausch modelliert werden, der immer eine gleichgewichtige Lösung hervorbringt: „Production ist die Ursache, und zwar einzige Ursache der Nachfrage. Sie erzeugt nie ein Angebot, ohne zugleich und in demselben Maaße eine Nachfrage zu erzeugen" (J. Mill 1821: 339).

John Stuart Mill stellt die Verbreitung des Sayschen Theorems insbesondere als ein Verdienst von Ricardo und J. Mill heraus. Für Ricardo ist evident, dass keine Absatzstockung vorkommen kann: „Say hat indessen in der befriedigendsten Weise gezeigt, daß es keinen Kapitalbetrag gibt, der in einem Lande nicht verwendet werden kann, weil der Nachfrage nur durch die Produktion Schranken gesetzt sind. Niemand produziert zu einem anderen Zweck als zu konsumieren oder zu verkaufen, und er verkauft nur in der Absicht, ein anderes Gut zu kaufen, das ihm unmittelbar nützlich sein oder das zu zukünftiger Produktion beitragen kann. Daher wird er durch Produzieren notwendigerweise entweder zum Konsumenten seiner eigenen Waren oder zum Käufer und Konsumenten der Waren anderer" (Ricardo 1821: 211f.) Damit wird auch die Geldfunktion beschrieben, die lediglich als Tauschmittel begriffen wird: „Produkte werden stets mit Produkten oder Diensten gekauft; Geld ist nur das Mittel, welches den Austausch bewirkt. Es kann zuviel von einem besonderen Gute erzeugt werden, von dem eine solche Fülle auf dem

Markte vorhanden sein kann, daß sich das dafür verausgabte Kapital nicht bezahlt macht. Jedoch kann das nicht bei allen Gütern der Fall sein" (Ricardo 1821: 213). Im Kapitel XXXI „Über Maschinenwesen" relativiert Ricardo seine Auffassung: „[...] daß sich mit jedweder Zunahme des Reineinkommens einer Gesellschaft auch ihr Roheinkommen vermehren würde; jetzt aber bin ich überzeugt, daß der eine Fonds, aus dem die Grundeigentümer und Kapitalisten ihr Einkommen beziehen, größer werden kann, während sich der andere, der, von welchem die arbeitende Klasse hauptsächlich abhängt, sich vermindern kann; und daraus folgt, [...] daß dieselbe Ursache, die das Reineinkommen des Landes vermehrt, gleichzeitig eine Übervölkerung herbeiführen und die Lage des Arbeiters verschlechtern kann" (Ricardo 1821: 287). Im Gegensatz zur optimistischen Einschätzung der Absatzmöglichkeiten steht die negative Wirkung des technischen Fortschritts, weil der immer stärkere Einsatz von Maschinen in der industriellen Produktion zu sinkenden Preisen gegenüber landwirtschaftlich erzeugten Gütern führen wird, was zu einem Rückgang der Marktpreise und dementsprechend auch der Profite führen muss. Als Folge wird laufend weniger investiert, was am Ende in einer stationären Wirtschaft mündet.

Wie bei seinem Vater steht auch für John Stuart Mill die Tauschfunktion des Geldes im Vordergrund. Geld wird als eine Ware modelliert, deren Einführung den Güteraustausch erleichtert, denn es werden die Schwierigkeiten vermieden, sich einen Tauschpartner suchen zu müssen. Das Medium Geld stellt die Brücke dar, ohne Zeitverlust den Tausch durchführen zu können. Damit entfällt die Notwendigkeit, das gewünschte Gut durch Tauschketten zu erwerben. In einer reinen Tauschwirtschaft führt der realisierte Gütertausch zu einem Gleichgewicht, weil Anbieter und Nachfrager ihre Vorstellungen realisieren konnten. Jeder ist nämlich sowohl Käufer als auch Verkäufer. Damit entsprechen die Einnahmen aus den Verkäufen den Ausgaben: Es herrscht ein Gleichgewicht zwischen Angebot und Nachfrage. Mit der Einführung von Geld ändert sich die Situation, weil der wechselseitige Tauschakt entfällt. Es besteht nunmehr die Möglichkeit, die Güternachfrage erst in einer späteren Periode vorzunehmen (J.St. Mill 1844: 90ff.).

Sofern zwischen Angebot und Nachfrage eine zeitliche Differenz besteht, erhält das Geld eine weitere Funktion, nämlich die Wertaufbewahrung. Damit ist allerdings nicht länger die Gleichgewichtslösung auf dem Gütermarkt sichergestellt (J.St. Mill 1844: 92ff.). Die Wirtschaftssubjekte können ihr Geld horten, während in der Zwischenzeit auf dem Gütermarkt Preissenkungen wegen des vorliegenden Überschussangebots auftreten. Die sinkenden Preise entsprechen den Preissteigerungen für die Ware Geld. Ein Gleichgewicht stellt sich ein, wenn der Geldwert in Relation zu den Güterpreisen so weit gestiegen ist, dass ein Tausch vom Geld- zum Gütermarkt einsetzt (J.St. Mill 1844: 93). Der Güterkauf erfolgt zu Herstellungskosten bzw. – entsprechend der Angebots-Nachfragesituation – zum jeweiligen Marktpreis. Sofern durch Sparen eine Kreditvergabe erfolgen kann, vergrößert sich die gesellschaftliche Güterproduktion. Dass damit ein allgemeines Überangebot auftreten kann, dem keine entsprechende Nachfrage gegenübersteht, wird bestritten. Lediglich Teilmärkte können sich im Ungleichgewicht befinden, allerdings nur kurzfristig, weil die Preisflexibilität auf dem Güter- und Geldmarkt zu einer Gleichgewichtslösung führen wird. Insoweit wird von J. St. Mill auf J. Mill und Say als hervorragende Vertreter der Nicht-Krisenvorstellung hingewiesen (J.St. Mill 1871: 117).

4. Pessimistische Antworten auf Say: Sismondi, Malthus

Im Gegensatz zur harmonischen Welt des ökonomischen Gleichgewichts wird mit der pessimistischen Auffassung die Grenze der kapitalistischen Produktion thematisiert. Theoriegeschichtlich beginnt die Auseinandersetzung mit Sismondi, wird von Malthus fortgesetzt und findet ihren Abschluss in der klassischen politischen Ökonomie bei Marx.

Sismondi hatte ursprünglich wie Say die Auffassung von Smith vertreten. Angesichts der sozialen Entwicklung als Folge von wirtschaftlichen Krisen in Frankreich, kann er seine ursprünglich positive Darstellung über den wirtschaftlichen Verlauf nicht länger aufrechterhalten und wechselt in der zweiten Auflage seines ökonomischen Hauptwerkes die Auffassung über die zukünftige kapitalistische Entwicklung. Er wird, wie Malthus, zu einem frühen Vertreter einer pessimistischen Auffassung, die von ihm auch ausführlich theoretisch begründet wird.

Die Güternachfrage ist das Ergebnis von Bedürfnissen und dem daraus erzielten Einkommen, wobei der Marktpreis sich durch die angebotene und nachgefragte Gütermenge einstellt, die dementsprechend nicht den Produktionskosten entsprechen muss. Ein zu geringes Einkommen führt zu einer sinkenden Nachfrage, „[...] sobald entweder das Bedürfnis oder die Kaufkraft der produzierten Menge nicht entspricht". Am Beispiel der damaligen Leipziger Buchmesse zeigt Sismondi den wechselseitigen Warentausch zwischen den Buchhändlern, ohne dass eine Nachfrageänderung eintritt, weil der Austausch dem Zweck dient, die Bücher des anderen Verlegers zu verkaufen.

Der tatsächliche Verkauf gegen Geld ist das Ergebnis zwischen den Buchhändlern und Lesern. Hier kann es selbstverständlich passieren, dass der Tauschakt zu keinem Verkauf beim lesenden Publikum führt (Sismondi 1820 II: 295ff.). Weiterhin ist zu berücksichtigen, dass die individuellen Entscheidungen das Arbeitsangebot und damit die kaufkräftige Nachfrage beeinflussen, ohne dass ein Zusammenhang zur hergestellten Gütermenge besteht: „Wenn in irgendeinem Zweig [...] die Anzahl der Maschinen und das Kapital erhöht werde, so wächst [...] die Produktion dieses Zweiges über den bisherigen Bedarf hinaus; und es wird erforderlich, daß entweder der Bedarf steigt oder aber daß diese vergrößerte Arbeitsleistung [...] irgendeiner anderen Produktion zugeführt werden". Damit wird gleichzeitig die Einkommensverteilung und deren Einfluss auf die gesamtwirtschaftliche Nachfrage thematisiert: „Wem fällt der Gewinn zu? Diese Frage ist wichtig: einmal in sittlicher Hinsicht [...] zum anderen aber in wirtschaftlicher Hinsicht, weil die Zahl der Konsumenten einen entscheidenden Einfluß auf den Umfang des Verbrauchs ausübt" (1820 II: 306). Hier wird die Produktivität problematisiert, die zwar ein Güterwachstum, jedoch nicht die erforderliche Nachfrage hervorbringt. Weiterhin sind bei der Produktion zukünftige Entwicklungen und Erwartungen zu berücksichtigen, die als unsicher hervorgehoben werden: „Jedes einzelne Produkt muss im richtigen Verhältnis zu den Wünschen, Bedürfnissen und der effektiven Kaufkraft einer bestimmen Klasse von Käufern stehen. Aber diese Wünsche und Bedürfnisse ändern sich unaufhörlich; und die Käufer, die von Produzenten obendrein nicht einmal überblickt werden können, sind über den ganzen Erdball verstreut. Kein Philosoph mit allen seinen Untersuchungen, keine Regierung mit ihrer ganzen Macht, hat jemals die Größe eines Marktes genau bestimmen können: wie sollten sie dann die Produzenten kennen?" (1820 II: 312).

Insoweit sind Absatzstockungen nicht nur auf einzelne Branchen beschränkt, sondern der Nachfrageausfall betrifft die gesamte Volkswirtschaft. In einer Wettbewerbsökonomie kann es den einzelnen Anbietern gelingen, einen Absatzvorteil zu Lasten der Konkurrenten zu erringen. Dabei ist jedoch die gesamtwirtschaftliche Nachfrage einkommensabhängig und damit nicht vom Güterangebot abhängig, sondern autonom. Sofern ein Teil des verfügbaren Einkommens gespart wird, führt das so lange nicht zu einem Nachfrageausfall, wie diese Summe wieder in den Produktionsprozess eingesetzt wird. „Jeder Verbrauch, der nicht gegen ein Einkommen ausgetauscht wird, stellt einen Verlust für den Staat dar [...]. Ein neues Einkommen entsteht für den Staat aus jedem fixen oder zirkulierenden Kapital, das zusätzlich aus Sparsamkeit hervorgegangen ist und angewendet wird, um eine neue Produktion und damit eine neue Nachfrage anzuregen. Ein neues Einkommen entsteht ferner aus jeder neuen Arbeit, die von einem Kapital im richtigen Verhältnis zur Nachfrage finanziert wird" (Sismondi 1827 I: 291). Darüber hinaus ist bei großen Einkommensunterschieden nicht sichergestellt, dass der Konsum im Inland vorgenommen wird und auch nicht auf Importgüter entfällt. In diesem Zusammenhang wird Ricardo zitiert, der offensichtlich eine Identität zwischen der gesamtwirtschaftlichen Nachfrage und der Güterproduktion unterstellt hat und damit keine Erklärung für Krisen erbringen konnte (vgl. Ricardo 1821: 211f.).

Die skeptischen malthusianischen Äußerungen zur Bevölkerungsentwicklung (Malthus 1798) finden ihre Entsprechung in den negativen Folgen der Kapitalakkumulation, denn einem steigenden Güterangebot steht nicht automatisch eine kaufkräftige Nachfrage gegenüber, sodass die Überproduktion mit der Unterkonsumtion konfrontiert wird. Gegen Malthus argumentiert Say in einem umfangreichen Briefwechsel. Bereits im ersten Brief macht er auf eine Fehlinterpretation seiner theoretischen Ausführungen aufmerksam: „[...] Ich habe nicht gesagt, daß die Waaren (Commodities) immer gegen Waaren vertauscht würden, sondern daß die *Erzeugnisse* (produits) *nur mit Erzeugnissen gekauft werden.* [...] Dieser Werth des Erzeugnisses, wofern er nur den Hervorbringkosten, d.i. dem Preise, welchen man für alle hervorbringenden Dienste verschließen mußte, gleich ist, reicht hin, die Gewinnste aller derer zu bezahlen, welche unmittelbar oder mittelbar zu dieser Hervorbringung mitgewirkt haben. [...] Mit der Landrente, den Zinsen, dem Arbeitslohne, welche die aus dieser Hervorbringung entspringenden Gewinnste bilden, kaufen die Erzeuger die Gegenstände ihrer Verzehrung" (Say 1820: 69ff.). Damit wird von Say hervorgehoben, dass er den Einkommenskreislauf beschrieben hat. Bevor Güter gekauft werden, muss eine kaufkräftige Nachfrage vorhanden sein, die den Verkauf eigener Leistungen erzwingt: „Um nun Ihre Beschuldigung wieder aufzunehmen, so sagen Sie, viele Güter müßten mit Arbeit gekauft werden. Ich gehe sogar noch weiter und behaupte dasselbe von allen Gütern, nämlich wenn man das Wort *Arbeit* auch auf den Dienst ausdehnt, welchen Erwerbsstämme und Ländereien leisten" (Say 1820: 73f.).

Leicht ironisierend wird gegen Say vorgebracht: „Einige sehr tüchtige Schriftsteller haben gemeint, es könne zwar eine leichte Überproduktion in einzelnen Waren eintreten, aber eine allgemeine Überproduktion sei unmöglich [...] Es ist keineswegs eine erwiesene Tatsache, daß Waren immer gegen Waren getauscht werden. Eine gewaltige Menge Waren wird unmittelbar gegen produktive Arbeit oder gegen persönliche Dienstleistungen getauscht; es ist ganz einleuchtend, daß diese Menge Waren im Vergleich zu der Arbeit, gegen die sie getauscht werden soll, infolge von Überproduktion so gut sinken kann, wie eine einzelne Ware infolge übergroßen Angebots im Werte sinkt, wenn man sie mit Arbeit oder Geld vergleicht" (Malthus 1820: 418f.). Sofern die Kapitalakkumulation als Folge des Sparens steigt, stellt sich die Frage, wer konsumiert diese Güter? Einerseits führt eine höhere Nachfrage zur Kompensation des Sparens, jedoch: „Ich will hiermit natürlich nicht geleugnet haben, daß Sparsamkeit oder sogar eine vorübergehende Einschränkung des Verbrauchs [...] durchaus notwendig für das Fortschreiten des Reichtums ist. [...] Ich will lediglich beweisen, daß ein Volk unmöglich nur durch eine Kapitalsanhäufung, die auf einer fortdauernden Abnahme des Verbrauchs beruht, reich werden kann" (Malthus 1820: 432).

5. Marx' Kritik an Say

Unter wachstumstheoretischen Aspekten zeigt Marx mithilfe der Reproduktionsschemata, dass die harmonische Welt der Klassik brüchig ist. Sofern für kapitalistische Gesellschaften eine dynamische Entwicklung unterstellt wird, führt deren Wachstumsrate zu Unterbeschäftigung und tendenziell sinkender Profitrate. Das steht offensichtlich im Widerspruch zu Smith und Ricardo. Denn die gesamtwirtschaftliche Nachfrage setzt sich aus der Konsumgüternachfrage der Arbeiter und Kapitalisten sowie der Investitionsnachfrage seitens der Kapitalisten zusammen. Unter dem Gesichtspunkt, dass die Klasse der Kapitalisten nur einen geringen Teil der Gewinne (Mehrwert) konsumiert und stattdessen Investitionen durchführt (Aufteilung des Mehrwertes in Konsum und Akkumulation), erfährt der Wirtschaftskreislauf negative Wirkungen: Arbeitskräfte werden aufgrund steigender Produktivität entlassen – es entsteht die industrielle Reservearmee –, während der permanente Investitionsaufbau zu Disproportionalitäten in der Produktion führt. Durch die industrielle Reservearmee ist gesichert, dass der Lohn nicht über das Reproduktionsniveau steigen kann.[11] Als Folge resultiert Unterkonsumtion aufgrund zu geringer Konsummöglichkeiten: „Denken wir uns eine Gesellschaft bloß aus individuellen Kapitalisten und Lohnarbeitern zusammengesetzt [...] Dann wäre eine Krise nur erklärlich aus dem Mißverhältnis der Produktion in verschiednen Zweigen, und aus einem Mißverhältnis, worin der Konsum der Kapitalisten selbst zu ihrer Akkumulation stände. [...] Der letzte Grund aller wirklichen Krisen bleibt immer die Armut und Konsumtionsbeschränkung

---

[11] Kurzfristig kann bei starker Nachfrage selbstverständlich auch der Lohn zu Lasten des Mehrwerts steigen (Marx 1894: 529).

der Massen gegenüber dem Trieb der kapitalistischen Produktion, die Produktivkräfte so zu entwickeln, als ob nur die absolute Konsumtionsfähigkeit der Gesellschaft ihre Grenze bilde" (Marx 1894: 500f.). Allerdings ist auch hier ein Gleichgewicht möglich, sofern die Kapitalisten ihre Konsumtion in einem bestimmten Verhältnis zur Akkumulation ausdehnen.

Marx übernimmt die ricardianische Vorstellung, dass die Arbeitskräfte zu Reproduktionskosten entlohnt werden, sie verkaufen ihre Arbeitskraft auf dem Arbeitsmarkt entsprechend den zu ihrer Reproduktion erforderlichen Güter. Der Kapitalist erhöht die notwendige Arbeitszeit durch oktroyierte, unbezahlte Mehrarbeit und erhält als Eigentümer der Produktionsmittel den Mehrwert. Mit dem Verkauf der Waren wird der Mehrwert als Profit realisiert. Die Ausgaben für die Produktion setzen sich aus dem vorgeschossenen Kapital, das aus zwei Teilmengen besteht, dem konstanten und dem variablen Kapital, zusammen.[12] Der konstante Teil beinhaltet Ausgaben für Rohstoffe, Anlagen und Arbeitsmittel, während der variable Teil der Entlohnung der Arbeitskraft entspricht.[13] Am Ende der Produktionsperiode hat sich der Produktionswert um den Mehrwert erhöht.[14]

Durch das Wachsen des Kapitalstocks – Akkumulation des Kapitals – verändert sich die organische Zusammensetzung zwischen dem eingesetzten konstanten und variablen Kapital (Marx 1867: 651ff.), und zwar zu Lasten des Arbeitseinsatzes. „Da die Nachfrage nach Arbeit nicht durch den Umfang des Gesamtkapitals, sondern durch den seines variablen Bestandteils bestimmt ist, fällt sie also progressiv mit dem Wachstum des Gesamtkapitals, statt, [...] verhältnismäßig mit ihm zu wachsen. [...] Die kapitalistische Akkumulation produziert vielmehr, und zwar im Verhältnis zu ihrer Energie und ihrem Umfang, beständig eine relative, d.h. für die mittleren Verwertungsbedürfnisse des Kapitals überschüssige, daher überflüssige oder ‚Zuschuß-Arbeiterbevölkerung'" (Marx 1867: 658).[15] Als Konsequenz resultiert eine stetig steigende Arbeitslosigkeit, die industrielle Reservearmee: „Rascheres Wachstum der Produktionsmittel und der Produktivität der Arbeit als der produktiven Bevölkerung drückt sich kapitalistisch also umgekehrt darin aus, daß die Arbeiter-

---

[12] Zum Kapitalbegriff siehe z.B. (Marx 1861-63: 22ff.).

[13] Für den Anfang der Produktion gilt für das gesamte eingesetzte Kapital C: $C = c + v$.

[14] Am Ende der Produktion steht die Wertschöpfung: $C' = c + v + m$. Die Veränderung der Zusammensetzung zwischen konstantem Kapital und Arbeitseinsatz entspricht der organischen Zusammensetzung des Kapitals: c/v.

[15] Im Gegensatz zu Malthus, der eine absolute Überbevölkerung behauptete, vgl. (Marx 1867: 660ff.).

bevölkerung stets rascher wächst als das Verwertungsbedürfnis des Kapitals" (Marx 1867: 674). Der Umfang der Arbeitslosigkeit führt zu Problemen bei der Einkommensbildung und damit zur Verelendung der Arbeiter: „Das Gesetz [...], welches die relative Überbevölkerung stets mit Umfang und Energie der Akkumulation in Gleichgewicht hält, [...] bedingt eine der Akkumulation von Kapital entsprechende Akkumulation von Elend. Die Akkumulation von Reichtum auf dem einen Pol ist also zugleich Akkumulation von Elend, Arbeitsqual, Sklaverei, Unwissenheit, Brutalisierung und moralischer Degradation auf dem Gegenpol, d.h. auf der Seite der Klasse, die ihr eignes Produkt als Kapital produziert" (Marx 1867: 675).

Der ständig sinkende Lohnfonds führt zu geringer Beschäftigung, der Herausbildung der industriellen Reservearmee, und stellt damit keine Grundlage für eine Gleichgewichtsituation dar. Die wachstumstheoretische Dimension wird mit den Reproduktionsschemata deutlich herausgestellt, ein Gleichgewicht setzt die Identität zwischen der Produktion und den Lohneinkommen der Arbeiter voraus, was nur zufällig eintreten kann. Says Gesetz hat in dieser Ökonomie keine Geltung.

6. Keynes: Geldfunktion und ökonomische Wirkungen

Die ökonomischen Theoretiker, die vor ihm publizierten, werden bekanntermaßen von Keynes als „Klassiker" bezeichnet, weil ihnen mit Ausnahme von Malthus die Akzeptanz des Sayschen Theorems unterstellt wird. „Seit den Zeiten von Say und Ricardo haben die klassischen Ökonomen gelehrt, daß das Angebot seine eigene Nachfrage schafft – womit sie in einem bedeutsamen, aber nicht klar definierten Sinn meinen, daß die gesamten Produktionskosten, unmittelbar oder mittelbar wieder ausgegeben werden müssen, um diese Erzeugnisse zu kaufen. [...] Die Doktrin wird heute nie in dieser rohen Form dargestellt. Sie bildet aber trotzdem noch die Grundlage der ganzen klassischen Theorie, ohne die sie zusammenfiele. Zeitgenössische Ökonomen [...] zögern nicht, Folgerungen anzunehmen, die Mills Doktrin als Voraussetzung fordern. Die Überzeugung, [...] daß das Geld keinen wirklichen Unterschied mache, es sei denn durch Friktionen, und daß die Theorie der Produktion und Beschäftigung [...] auf der Grundlage ‚realer' Tauschhandlungen ausgearbeitet werden könne, wobei das Geld im letzten Kapitel oberflächlich eingeführt wird, ist die moderne Fassung der klassischen Tradition" (Keynes 1936a: 16f.).

Diese Unterstellung erscheint zu pauschal angesichts von Äußerungen, die durchaus Hinweise von Kenntnissen über Konjunkturschwankungen als ein monetäres Problem erkennen lassen. Allerdings fehlt der klassischen politischen Ökonomie ein angemessenes Verständnis der Geldfunktion. Die Vorstellung eines Geldschleiers führt in Verbindung mit der Quantitätstheorie zu einer neutralen Sicht, denn mit Hilfe des Geldes wird lediglich der Güteraustausch ermöglicht. Erst eine Geldnachfrage, die zwischen Transaktions- und Spekulationskasse unterscheidet, kann Nachfrageausfälle interpretieren. Die unterstellte Identität von Spar- und Investitionsentscheidungen führt zwar im Modell zu einer Gleichgewichtssituation, muss aber an der Wirklichkeit scheitern. Das führt zu der Schlussfolgerung: „The division of Economics between the Theory of Value and Distribution on the one hand and the Theory of Money on the other hand is, I think, a false division. The right dichotomy is, I suggest, between the Theory of the Individual Industry or Firm and of the rewards and the distribution between different uses of a given quantity of resources on the one hand, and the Theory of Output and Employment as a whole on the other hand. So long as we limit ourselves to the study of the individual industry or firm on the assumption that the aggregate quantity of employed resources is constant, and, provisionally, that the conditions of other industries or firms are unchanged, it is true that we are not concerned with the significant characteristics of money. But as soon as we pass to the problem of what determines output and employment as a whole, we require the complete theory of a Monetary Economy" (Keynes 1936: 293).

Der klassisch-neoklassisch definierte Geldmarkt hat nur für den Gütermarkt Bedeutung, indem er das Tauschverhältnis zwischen Gütern abbildet, aber keine Beschäftigungswirkungen zulässt. Schon vor der „General Theory" hatte Keynes (1926; 1930) auf den Unterschied zwischen einer Tauschwirtschaft und einer Produktionsökonomie aufmerksam gemacht. Denn zu berücksichtigen ist, dass unternehmerische Entscheidungen nicht nur durch die Grenzleistungsfähigkeit des Kapitals bestimmt werden, sondern offensichtlich von den Entscheidungen der Vermögenseigentümer abhängig sind.[16] Entsprechend ihren Erwartungen auf dem Kapitalmarkt sorgen sie für eine Kreditvergabe und ermöglichen damit erst eine Investition (Riese 1986). Die Konsequenz besteht darin, eine monetäre Ökonomie zu begründen: „The theory which I desiderate would deal [...] with an economy in which money plays a part of its own and affects motives and decisions and is, in short, one of the operative factors in the situation, so that the course of events cannot be predicted, either in the long period or in the short, without a knowledge of the

---

[16] In diesem Zusammenhang stehen auch die Ausführungen zur Konzeption der Markthierarchie (Heine/Herr 2013: 345ff.).

behaviour of money between the first sat and the last. And this is which we ought to mean when we speak of a monetary economy" (Keynes 1933: 408f.).

Eine monetäre Theorie muss weiterhin die Möglichkeit von Unsicherheiten bei ökonomischen Entscheidungen berücksichtigen. Seinen Vorgängern – Keynes zitiert Marshall, Ricardo, Pigou – wirft er ein unangemessenes Gedankengebäude vor: „But these more recent writers like their predecessors were still dealing with a system in which the amount of the factors employed was given and the other relevant facts were known more or less for certain. [...] But at any given time facts and expectations were assumed to be given in a definite and calculable form; and risks, of which, though admitted, not much notice was taken, were supposed to be capable of an exact actuarial computation. The calculus of probability, though mention of it was kept in the background, was supposed to be capable of reducing uncertainty to the same calculable status as that of certainty itself; just as in the Benthamite calculus of pains and pleasures or of advantage and disadvantage, by which the Benthamite philosophy assumed men to be influenced in their general ethical behavior" (Keynes 1937: 112f.).

7. Schlussfolgerungen

Die klassische Gleichgewichtslösung ist das Resultat von wirtschaftenden Individuen, wobei als Handlungsnorm Interessen benannt werden, Bedürfnisse zu realisieren. Das gelingt, weil entweder Kenntnisse über die notwendigen Produkte vorliegen oder weil sich das Gleichgewicht durch die Identität von I und S einstellt. Gewinne, Löhne, Zinsen und Preise bestimmen das Verhalten der Wirtschaftsakteure, es fehlen jedoch Erwartungen über diese ökonomischen Größen und damit fehlt überwiegend auch die Vorstellung vom Scheitern. Erst mit der Einführung von Erwartungen gelingt es, ökonomisches Handeln angemessen zu charakterisieren.

Dass auf der anderen Seite die Problematik von Erwartungen schon früh bewusst war, zeigt Schumpeter am Beispiel von Thornton und J. St. Mill auf (Schumpeter 1954: 688ff.). Charakteristisch für das unternehmerische Alltagshandeln sind Erwartungen von Unternehmern über zukünftige Situationen: „Diese haben ja im allgemeinen nicht mit künftig steigenden Preisen zu rechnen, sondern alle Geschäftsunternehmungen gehen im Gegenteile, normalerweise von der Voraussetzung aus, daß die gegenwärtigen Preise auch in der Zukunft bestehen bleiben" (Wicksell 1922: 211).

Den vorläufigen Abschluss bildet Keynes. Unsicherheit und Ungewissheit sind nunmehr unmittelbar mit der ökonomischen Theorie verknüpft. Trotz vorherrschender Ungewissheit sind ökonomische Handlungen unumgänglich. Die Folge kann nur darin bestehen, weiterhin diesen Gesichtspunkt in die ökonomische Theorie zu integrieren, also Erwartungen über zukünftige Entwicklungen und deren vermutete Wirkungen anzustellen, anstatt sie bewusst auszublenden. Was im 21. Jahrhundert noch immer erstaunt, ist, dass den Erfahrungen mit historischen Wirtschaftskrisen weiterhin mit einer bewussten oder naiven Sichtweise begegnet wird, obwohl marktwirtschaftliche Systeme keineswegs inhärent stabil sein können. Auch die noch anhaltende Finanzmarktkrise hat bisher wenige Wirkungen in der ökonomischen Theorie hinterlassen. Offensichtlich erzwingt eine Geldwirtschaft zur Sicherung ihrer Stabilität weitergehende Haftungsregeln zwischen Gläubigern und Schuldnern und ggf. Verbote zur Durchsetzung von gesellschaftlich erwünschten Zielen. Mithilfe einer umfassenderen Theorie des Marktversagens, die nicht nur institutionelle, sondern auch verhaltenswissenschaftliche Elemente beinhalten müsste, kann eine derartige Stabilisierung modelliert werden.

Literatur

Dullien, S., Herr, H., Kellermann, C. (2009): *Der gute Kapitalismus. ... und was sich dafür nach der Krise ändern müsste*, Bielefeld: transcript.

Hayek, F.A. (1929): *Geldtheorie und Konjunkturtheorie*, 2. Aufl., Salzburg 1976: Wolfgang Neugebauer.

Heine, M., Herr, H. (2013): *Volkswirtschaftslehre. Eine paradigmenorientierte Einführung in die Mikro- und Makroökonomie*, 4. Aufl., München: Oldenbourg.

Herr, H., Kazandziska, M. (2011): *Macroeconomic Policy Regimes in Western Industrial Countries*, Abingdon: Routledge.

Keynes, J.M. (1926): *Das Ende des Laissez-Faire. Ideen zur Verbindung von Privat- und Gemeinwirtschaft*, München, Leipzig: Duncker & Humblot.

Keynes, J.M. (1930): *A Treatise on Money*, Volume I, II, deutsch, Vom Gelde, 3. Aufl., Berlin 1983: Duncker & Humblot.

Keynes, J.M. (1933): A Monetary Theory of Production, in: *Collected Writings*, Vol. XIII, 408f. London and Basingstoke 1973: Macmillan.

Keynes; J.M. (1936): *The General Theory of Employment, Interest and Money*. Reprint London and Basingstoke 1970: Macmillan.

Keynes, J.M. (1936a): *Allgemeine Theorie der Beschäftigung, des Zinses und des Geldes*, 10. Aufl., Berlin 2002: Duncker & Humblot.

Keynes, J.M. (1937): The General Theory of Employment, in: *The Quarterly Journal of Economics*, 51, 212-223, Reprint in: The Collected Writings of John Maynard Keynes, Vol. XIV, 109-123, London and Basingstoke 1973: Macmillan.

Lederer, E. (1925): Konjunktur und Krisen, in: *Grundriss der Sozialökonomik*, IV. Abteilung, Spezifische Elemente der modernen Kapitalistischen Welt, I. Teil, Tübingen: Mohr, 354-413.

Malthus, Th.R. (1798): *An Essay on the Principle of Population*, deutsch, Das Bevölkerungsgesetz, München 1977: dtv.

Malthus, Th.R. (1820): *Grundsätze der Politischen Ökonomie*, Berlin 1910: R.L. Prager.

Marx, K. (1861-1863): *Zur Kritik der politischen Ökonomie*, Marx-Engels-Werke, Band 43, Berlin 1990: Dietz.

Marx, K. (1867): *Das Kapital. Kritik der politischen Ökonomie*, 1. Band, in: Marx-Engels-Werke, Band 23, Berlin 1979: Dietz.

Marx, K. (1885): *Das Kapital. Kritik der politischen Ökonomie*, 2. Band, in: Marx-Engels-Werke, Band 24, Berlin 1986: Dietz.

Marx, K. (1894): *Das Kapital. Kritik der politischen Ökonomie*, 3. Band, in: Marx-Engels-Werke, Band 25, Berlin 1965: Dietz.

Mill, J. (1808): *Commerce Defended*, London: C. and R. Baldwin.

Mill, J. (1821): *Elements of Political Economy*, deutsch, Elemente der Nationalökonomie, Halle 1924: C. A. Kümmel.

Mill, J.St. (1844): *Essays on some Unsettled Questions of Political Economy*, London: John W. Parker, deutsch, Einige ungelöste Probleme der politische Ökonomie, hrsg. von H.G. Nutzinger, Frankfurt/Main 1976: Campus.

Mill, J.St. (1871): *Grundsätze der politischen Ökonomie*, 2. Band, Jena 1921: Gustav Fischer.

Ricardo, D. (1821): *Grundsätze der politischen Ökonomie und der Besteuerung*, hrsg. von Fritz Neumark, Frankfurt am Main 1972: Gustav Fischer.

Riese, H. (1986): Keynes, Schumpeter und die Krise, in: *Konjunkturpolitik*, 32(1/2), 1-26, Wiederabdruck in: Ders., Grundlegungen eines monetären Keynesianismus. Ausgewählte Schriften 1964-1999, Band 2, Angewandte Theorie der Geldwirtschaft, 867-893, Marburg 2001: Metropolis.

Roscher, W. (1874): *Geschichte der Nationalökonomik in Deutschland*, (Geschichte der Wissenschaften in Deutschland, 14), München 1874, Reprint Düsseldorf 1992: Wirtschaft und Finanzen.

Say, J.B. (1803/1826): *Traité d'économie politique*, deutsch, Johann Baptist Say's ausführliche Darstellung der Nationalökonomie oder der Staatswirthschaft, hrsg. von Carl Eduard Morstadt, Bd. I-III, 3. Aufl., Heidelberg 1830: Joseph Engelmann.

Say, J.B. (1820): *Lettres à M. Malthus, sur différens sujets d'économie politique, notamment sur les causes de la stagnation générale du commerce*; deutsch, Briefe an Malthus über verschiedene Gegenstände der politischen Ökonomie, insbesondere über die Ursachen der allgemeinen Stockung des Handels, in: Malthus und Say über die Ursachen der jetzigen Handelsstockung, übersetzt von Karl Heinrich Rau, Hamburg 1821: Perthes und Besser.

Say, J.B. (1840): *Cours complet d'économie politique practique*, deutsch, Ausführliches Lehrbuch der praktischen Politischen Ökonomie, hrsg. von Max Stirner (d.i. Johann Caspar Schmidt), Bd. I-IV, Leipzig 1845: Otto Wiegand.

Schumpeter, J.A. (1954): *History of Economic Analysis*, nach dem Manuskript herausgegeben von E. Boody Schumpeter, 4. Aufl., London 1961: George Allen & Unwin.

Sismondi, J.C.L. S. de (1820): Die Analyse einer Widerlegung der „Neuen Grundsätze der politischen Ökonomie" durch einen Schüler Ricardos in der „Edinburgh Review, in: Sismondi (1827): *Neue Grundsätze der Politischen Ökonomie oder vom Reichtum in seinen Beziehungen zur Bevölkerung*, hrsg. von A. Toepel, (Ökonomische Studientexte, 4), Band 1-2, Berlin 1971: Akademie, 290-315.

Smith, A. (1789): *Der Wohlstand der Nationen. Eine Untersuchung seiner Natur und seiner Ursachen*, München 1978: dtv.

Wicksell, K. (1922): *Vorlesungen über Nationalökonomie auf Grundlage des Marginalprinzipes*, Theoretischer Teil, Zweiter Band, Geld und Kredit, Jena 1922: Gustav Fischer.

Was die Institutionenökonomie von der Ungleichheitsforschung lernen könnte

Eine kritische Auseinandersetzung mit dem Begriff „institutionelle Komplementaritäten"

Martin Kronauer

Für Hansjörg Herr mit Dank für überaus angenehme Zusammenarbeit, für seine Denkanstöße und seine Offenheit für Einwände in den Diskussionen über den „guten Kapitalismus", die wir hoffentlich fortsetzen werden, und für seine Neugier darauf, was dabei herauskommt, wenn ein Soziologe den Kurs „International Institutional Economics" unterrichtet.

1. Die Ausgangsfrage

„Institutional complementarities" ist einer der zentralen Begriffe in der international vergleichenden Institutionenökonomie. Er spielt eine entscheidende Rolle bei der Unterscheidung zwischen „liberalen" und „koordinierten Marktökonomien" in Peter Halls und David Soskices (2001) „Varieties of Capitalism" und wird in der Debatte über typische Varianten kapitalistischer Gesellschaften immer wieder und mit wechselnden Interpretationen aufgegriffen. Im Folgenden will ich einen Blick auf den Begriff und die Debatte werfen, der insofern unüblich ist, als er von „außen" kommt, von einer Problemstellung her, die in der Institutionenökonomie zunächst keinen Platz zu haben scheint.

Dabei geht es um eine zentrale Frage der soziologischen Ungleichheitsforschung. Wie ist es möglich, dass sich soziale Ungleichheiten über unterschiedliche Dimensionen und „Funktionssysteme" des gesellschaftlichen Zusammenlebens hinweg ausbreiten und dabei verstärken können? Der Begriff der

„institutionellen Komplementaritäten" ist für eine Antwort auf diese Fragen insofern vielversprechend, als er in einem anderen Zusammenhang, dem der international vergleichenden Institutionenökonomie, ein vergleichbares Problem angeht: Unter welchen Bedingungen ergänzen sich die Institutionen verschiedener, für die strategischen Entscheidungen von Unternehmen wichtiger gesellschaftlicher „Sphären" (Hall/Soskice 2001: 6) in einer Weise, dass sie sich in ihren Wirkungen wechselseitig verstärken? In beiden Fällen geht es also um die Auswirkungen der „Verkoppelung" von unterschiedlichen gesellschaftlichen Handlungsebenen und deren Institutionen, mit ihren je eigenen Funktionsweisen. Im ersten Fall handelt es sich um einen negativen, im zweiten Fall um einen positiven Verstärkereffekt. Der Nachweis, wie „institutionelle Komplementaritäten" funktionieren, könnte deshalb dabei behilflich sein, auch das angesprochene soziologische Problem der Übertragung und Verstärkung sozialer Ungleichheit anzugehen. Um den Begriff auf diese Weise fruchtbar machen zu können, bedarf es allerdings einer Reihe kritischer Revisionen an seiner Verwendung bei Hall und Soskice.

Die soziologische Ungleichheitsforschung scheint also von der Institutionenökonomie etwas lernen zu können. Aber wie sieht es umgekehrt aus? Hat man erst einmal den „Umweg" über den Perspektivenwechsel der soziologischen Ungleichheitsforschung vorgenommen, dann geraten umso deutlicher einige Ungereimtheiten und Verkürzungen in den Blick, die sich in Halls und Soskices Rede von „institutionellen Komplementaritäten" finden. Sie haben Folgen für das ureigene Interesse dieser Autoren am institutionellen Wandel in Zeiten der Globalisierung. Vor allem aber wird deutlich, dass der institutionelle Umgang mit sozialer Ungleichheit auch für die „Varieties of Capitalism" von erheblicher Bedeutung ist. Ich werde also zu zeigen versuchen, dass die Institutionenökonomie ihrerseits etwas von der soziologischen Ungleichheitsforschung lernen kann. Der Beitrag stellt ein „work in progress" dar, wirft auf der Suche nach Antworten neue Fragen auf, in der Hoffnung, dass sie fruchtbares Weiterdenken in einer „Komplementarität von Disziplinen" ermöglichen.

2. „Institutional complementarities" bei Hall und Soskice

Institutionen verstehen Hall und Soskice ganz in der Tradition der griffigen Formel von Douglass North (1990: 3f.) als Spielregeln, die Organisationen (hier: Unternehmen) einen Rahmen bieten, in dem sie als Spieler ihre Ziele (hier: den Gewinn) verfolgen können. Die mit Sanktionen unterschiedlicher Intensität bewehrten, informellen und formellen Regeln erlegen den Akteuren

Beschränkungen auf, sie ermöglichen damit aber zugleich koordiniertes Handeln und Kooperation. Aus der Sicht der Institutionenökonomie reduzieren sie Unsicherheit und die aus ihr folgenden Transaktionskosten. Die Einschränkungen bilden aber auch immer wieder einen Ansporn für Unternehmen, sich für die Änderung von Regeln einzusetzen, institutionelle Grenzen zu verschieben und politische Allianzen zu schmieden, um dies zu bewerkstelligen.

Das Zusammenwirken *unterschiedlicher* Institutionen (zunächst im nationalen Rahmen) interessiert Hall und Soskice ausschließlich im Hinblick auf die strategischen Optionen von Unternehmen. Denn für diese bilden die institutionellen Arrangements einen begrenzten und begrenzenden Möglichkeitsraum. In fünffacher Hinsicht sind Unternehmen – wieder entsprechend den „Varieties of Capitalism" (Hall/Soskice 2001: 6f.) – auf die Leistungen von Institutionen angewiesen: für die Beschaffung von Kapital („corporate governance"), für die Beschaffung qualifizierter Arbeitskräfte („vocational training and education"), für das Aushandeln von Tarifverträgen und Arbeitsbedingungen mit den gewerkschaftlichen Interessenvertretungen („industrial relations"), für die Koordination der Beziehungen zu anderen Unternehmen („inter-firm relations") und für die Koordination der Arbeitsbeziehungen innerhalb des Unternehmens („firm-employee relations"; Hall/Gingerich 2009: 137).

Institutionelle *Komplementarität* sehen Hall und Soskice dann als gegeben, wenn die Existenz einer Institution den Ertrag der anderen bzw. deren „Effizienz" erhöht (Hall/Soskice 2001: 17). Komplementaritäten über die verschiedenen institutionellen Dimensionen hinweg lenken Unternehmen in die Richtung spezifischer Strategien. Diese unterscheiden sich typischerweise von den Strategien anderer Unternehmen, die entsprechend den Vorgaben anderer institutionalisierter Möglichkeiten und Zwänge agieren.

Hall und Soskice verweisen exemplarisch auf charakteristische Unterschiede zwischen „liberalen" und „koordinierten Marktökonomien". Erstere betonen Kooperation in hierarchisch geführten Unternehmensstrukturen und Koordination über den Markt (durch Konkurrenz), letztere Kooperation in institutionalisierten Aushandlungsprozessen und Koordination über die Konkurrenz abschwächende Abstimmungsverfahren („strategic coordination"; Hall/ Gingerich 2004: 8). Liberale und koordinierte Marktökonomien repräsentieren für die Autoren eigenständige Varianten des Kapitalismus. Sie zeichnen sich durch unterschiedliche institutionelle Komplementaritäten aus und unterstützen unterschiedliche Unternehmensstrategien, zum Beispiel im Hinblick auf Innovationen. Hall und Soskice folgern, dass technologischer Wandel (die Einführung und Ausbreitung neuer Informations- und Kommunikationstechnologien) und Globalisierung nicht notwendigerweise zu einer weltweiten

Angleichung von Institutionen (etwa in Richtung des marktliberalen Musters) führen müssten. Analog zu Ricardos komparativen Kostenvorteilen sprechen sie von „komparativen institutionellen Vorteilen" (Hall/Soskice 2001: 36). Unternehmen, die ihre Strategien in unterschiedlichen institutionellen Kontexten entwickeln, können unterschiedliche Stärken herausbilden, die es ihnen erlauben mögen, auf globalen Märkten zu koexistieren. So weit in aller Kürze der Ausgangspunkt.

3. Nachfragen an die „institutionellen Komplementaritäten" in den „Varieties of Capitalism"

Es geht im Folgenden nicht um eine umfassende Auseinandersetzung mit den theoretischen Voraussetzungen und empirischen Plausibilitäten des mittlerweile klassischen Einleitungskapitels zu „Varieties of Capitalism". Dazu ist inzwischen sehr viel und auch viel Kritisches geschrieben worden (vgl. Hancké 2009). Das Augenmerk gilt vielmehr allein der These von den „institutionellen Komplementaritäten" und dies unter dem eingangs formulierten Gesichtspunkt der möglichen Übertragbarkeit auf andere, soziologische Fragestellungen.

Die Annahme von „institutionellen Komplementaritäten" ist keineswegs selbstverständlich, und gerade das macht sie interessant. Das finanzielle System der Vergabe von Kapital an Unternehmen, das System der beruflichen Bildung, das Kapital-Arbeit-Verhältnis und das Verhältnis der Interaktion zwischen Unternehmen – sie alle folgen jeweils spezifischen Zweckbestimmungen, sind unterschiedlich geregelt und weisen somit in vielerlei Hinsicht unterschiedliche Institutionen auf. Wie können sie dann aber so aufeinander abgestimmt sein, dass sie sich in ihren Wirkungen ergänzen? Was macht ihre „Komplementarität" aus und wie kommt sie zustande? Warum sollten sie sich überhaupt ergänzen?

Die zuletzt aufgeworfene Frage scheint im Rahmen des „Varieties of Capitalism"-Ansatzes am leichtesten zu beantworten zu sein. Wenn die Erträge der Unternehmen von den (Vor-)Leistungen der Koordination und Kooperation in den angesprochenen unterschiedlichen gesellschaftlichen Dimensionen beeinflusst werden, dann hängen sie auch davon ab, ob sich deren Leistungen ergänzen oder einander zuwiderlaufen. Es kommt daher nicht allein auf die institutionellen Regelungen der Koordination und Kooperation *innerhalb* der jeweiligen „Sphären", sondern auch und vor allem auf deren institutionelle *Verknüpfungen* an.

Was zeichnet dann aber die besondere Verknüpfungsform der Komplementarität aus, und wie kommt es zu ihr? Bei Hall und Soskice finden sich dazu zwei Antworten. Die erste Antwort führt die Komplementarität von Institutionen auf die *Übertragung* des Koordinationsprinzips in einer „Sphäre" auf eine andere zurück. Komplementarität entsteht demnach durch eine *Analogie der Regelungsformen* („analogous forms of coordination"). Sie kann dadurch zustande kommen, dass die Akteure selbst jene Übertragung vornehmen. Als Beispiel führen die Autoren die Zusammenarbeit von Netzwerken bei der beruflichen Bildung an, die dann auf eine Kooperation bei der Etablierung kollektiver Standards ausgedehnt wird (Hall/Soskice 2001: 18). Die Kooperationsweise innerhalb eines institutionalisierten Handlungsfelds entscheidet demnach in einer Art institutionellen Lernens zugleich über die Koppelung mit anderen Handlungsfeldern.

Der zweiten Antwort zufolge bringen Unternehmen politische Akteure („governments") dazu, im Interesse der Effizienzsteigerung für eine Komplementarität von Institutionen zu sorgen (Hall/Soskice 2001: 18). In welcher Weise die Verknüpfung stattfindet, wird nicht eigens ausgeführt. Es liegt jedoch nahe, dass auch hier gemeint ist, dass Komplementarität über eine Analogie der Regelungsformen hergestellt wird. In einem späteren Text räumen Hall und Gingerich (2004: 21) allerdings ein: „... precisely why such congruence exists remains an open question".

Es gibt innerhalb der Institutionenökonomie eine Reihe von Einwänden gegen das Verständnis von „institutionellen Komplementaritäten", wie es in „Varieties of Capitalism" ausgeführt wird (vgl. Hancké 2009: 9). Für die hier zur Diskussion stehende Frage der Übertragbarkeit scheinen mir die von Bruno Amable (2003) vorgebrachten Argumente besonders einschlägig, weil sie am Gedanken der institutionellen Komplementarität festhalten, ihn aber in einer kritischen Auseinandersetzung mit Hall und Soskice auf seine Schwächen hin durchleuchten und zugleich erweitern.

Ein erster Einwand richtet sich gegen den Begriff der „Effizienz". Hall und Soskice hatten ihn als Steigerung des Ertrags einer Institution aufgrund der Wirkung einer anderen definiert, wobei Erträge als „total returns" gefasst werden (Hall/Soskice 2001: 17), etwa im Hinblick auf Qualität und sektorale Verteilung von Innovationen (Hall/Soskice 2001: 42f.) oder wirtschaftliches Wachstum (Hall/Gingerich 2009: 151). Was aber der Maßstab von Effizienz sein soll, quantitativ wie qualitativ, ist umstritten, wenn die Interessen unterschiedlicher Akteure in die Institutionenbildung eingehen. Sie können miteinander im Widerstreit liegen (Amable 2003: 10). Auch Hall und Soskice (2001: 15) gestehen zu, dass „considerations going well beyond efficiency" ins Spiel kommen, wenn Regierungen, politische Parteien und Organisationen der Arbeiterschaft bei der Formierung von Institutionen aufeinander und auf Unternehmensinteressen stoßen.

Infolgedessen lässt sich eine ökonomische Komplementarität von Institutionen auch nicht von vornherein sicherstellen – sollte diese von den involvierten Akteuren überhaupt angestrebt werden. Wenn Institutionenbildung, wie Amable (2003: 10, 12) argumentiert, das Ergebnis von Kompromissen ist, die aus Auseinandersetzungen zwischen Parteien mit unterschiedlichen Interessen erwachsen, die zudem mit ungleicher Macht ausgestattet sind, dann zeigt sich erst im Nachhinein, ob und inwieweit der gefundene Kompromiss auch dem ökonomischen Kriterium der Effizienzsteigerung durch Komplementarität genügt. Dieser spezifische Fall der Koppelung institutionalisierter Handlungsebenen wäre somit nur einer von mehreren möglichen Fällen. Und das Effizienzkriterium selbst kann je nach dem institutionalisierten Kompromiss variieren, etwa im Hinblick darauf, wie weit es neben wirtschaftlichem Wachstum Einkommensverteilung und Beschäftigung einbezieht oder gar nichtökonomische Gesichtspunkte wie soziale Rechte.

Fragwürdig wird schließlich auch das Prinzip der komplementären Koppelung durch eine Analogie der Regelungsformen. Auch hier gilt, dass ein solcher „structural isomorphism" (Amable 2003: 6) durchaus der Fall sein kann, aber nicht sein muss. Amable nennt als Beispiel für analoge Strukturen eine Ökonomie, in deren verschiedenen Bereichen Staatsintervention ein vorherrschendes Muster darstellt. Auch der von Hall und Soskice angeführte Fall der Netzwerkkooperation, die von einem Handlungsfeld in ein anderes übertragen wird oder die in beiden Handlungsfeldern existiert, weil sie auf gemeinsamen kulturellen Dispositionen beruht, gehört dazu.

Gleichwohl besteht kein eindeutiger Zusammenhang zwischen Analogie der Regelungsweisen und institutioneller Komplementarität: „Conformity to a single ‚logic' does not a priori guarantee the complementarity of institutions, which may itself exist without structural isomorphism" (Amable 2003: 6). Analoge Regelungsformen in den verschiedenen Handlungsebenen allein garantieren noch nicht eine Verknüpfung der Ebenen, die zu einer Komplementarität im Sinn der Effizienzsteigerung führen muss. Und umgekehrt sind komplementäre Verknüpfungen denkbar, die nicht auf einer Analogie der Koordinationsweisen in den unterschiedlichen „Sphären" beruhen. Komplementarität kann auch dadurch entstehen, dass die Leistungen einer Handlungsebene die möglichen negativen Wirkungen einer anderen dadurch kompensieren, dass sie gerade nicht einer gemeinsamen Handlungslogik folgen. Ein solcher Fall wird anschließend im Zusammenhang mit den möglichen institutionellen Verknüpfungen von Arbeitsmarkt und Sozialstaat näher zu betrachten sein.

Amable zeigt ein weiteres Problem bei der Komplementarität von Institutionen auf. Bei institutionellem Wandel in einer „Sphäre" kann institutionelle Komplementarität nicht intendierte Folgen in einer anderen nach sich ziehen (Amable 2003: 7). Streeck (2009: 107) schlägt deshalb vor, von positiven oder negativen Externalitäten statt von Komplementarität zu sprechen. Widersprüchliche Koppelung wäre die Folge. Darüber hinaus kann Effizienzsteigerung sogar in negative Verstärkereffekte umschlagen, wenn problematische Entwicklungen in einer „Sphäre" auf andere „Sphären" überspringen. Vor allem dieser Fall wird im Folgenden am Beispiel der Verknüpfungen von Arbeitsmarkt und Sozialstaat weiter zu verfolgen sein.

4. Eine folgenreiche Lücke in der Institutionenanalyse

Hall und Soskice weisen selbst darauf hin, dass der institutionelle Umgang mit sozialer Ungleichheit in einer international vergleichenden Institutionenökonomie durchaus seinen Platz hat. Gleich zu Beginn der Einleitung zu „Varieties of Capitalism" findet sich die folgende, bemerkenswerte Passage:

> „Political economists have always been interested in the differences in economic and political institutions that occur accross countries. Some regard these differences as deviations from ‚best practice'… Others see them as the distillation of more durable historical choices for a specific kind of society, since economic institutions condition levels of social protection, the distribution of income, and the availability of collective goods – features of the social solidarity of a nation" (Hall/Soskice 2001: 1).

Es gibt keinen Grund daran zu zweifeln, dass die Autoren eher der zweiten als der ersten Sichtweise zuneigen.

Umso überraschender – und inkonsequenter – ist es, dass „social protection", „distribution of income", „availability of collective goods", gar „social solidarity of a nation" in den anschließenden Ausführungen, ausgenommen das Arbeitsrecht, kaum mehr eine Rolle spielen. Erst in späteren Texten beziehen Hall und Gingerich auch eine Institution der Sozialversicherung, die Arbeitslosenversicherung, mit ein und erörtern sie im Hinblick auf ihre Komplementarität mit weiteren für die unternehmerischen Strategien wichtigen „Sphären" (Hall/Gingerich 2004: 19).

Zwar betonen Hall und Soskice (2001: 50f.) die Bedeutung von „social policy" für unterschiedliche unternehmerische Strategien im Kontext unterschiedlicher Ausprägungen des Kapitalismus und weisen in diesem Zusammenhang auch auf Esping-Andersens „The Three Worlds of Welfare Capitalism" hin, sie verstehen sich aber mehr als Anstoßgeber für weitere Forschung in dieser Richtung, als dass sie die Spur selbst weiter verfolgten. Es sind andere Autoren, die den Ähnlichkeiten zwischen der Unterscheidung von „liberalen" und „koordinierten Marktökonomien" bei Hall und Soskice und der Unterscheidung von Wohlfahrtsstaatsregimen bei Esping-Andersen nachgehen und beide miteinander zu verbinden suchen (z.b. Bosch et al. 2009: 10; McCann 2010: 134). Dabei beschränkt sich die Verbindung allerdings zumeist auf eine äußerliche Ergänzung und Kombination von typischen Merkmalen. Sie zielt weniger darauf ab, innerhalb der international vergleichenden Institutionenökonomie das Spektrum der zu berücksichtigenden institutionellen Ebenen auszuweiten und dabei die begriffliche Auseinandersetzung um die „Komplementarität von Institutionen" aufzugreifen.

Gerade dies wäre aber notwendig, um die analytische Lücke bei Hall und Soskice zu füllen. Ein solcher Schritt würde zugleich voraussetzen, den von ihnen abgesteckten Rahmen der Institutionenökonomie selbst zu erweitern. Wenn es zutrifft, wie Amable (2003: 10) argumentiert, dass in die Formierung von Institutionen, die für die strategischen Entscheidungen von Unternehmen relevant sind, auch die Interessen von politischen und gesellschaftlichen Akteuren eingehen, die nicht mit denen der Unternehmen identisch sind (oder sein müssen), dann kommt es analytisch darauf an, deren Interessen ebenfalls systematisch einzubeziehen; zu fragen, wie es mit der „Komplementarität von Institutionen" mit Blick auch auf diese Interessen bestellt ist und welche Widersprüche und Konflikte dabei entstehen können.

5. *„Institutionelle Komplementaritäten" und die Dynamiken sozialer Ungleichheit*

Die Interessen, die es zuallererst neben und zugleich mit denen der Unternehmen (des Kapitals) zu berücksichtigen gilt, wenn von Kapitalismus und seinen Varianten die Rede ist, sind selbstverständlich diejenigen der Lohnabhängigen. Mit den Hinweisen auf Institutionen der „social protection" und „social solidarity of a nation" deuten Hall und Soskice (2001: 1) Möglichkeiten eines institutionalisierten Interessenausgleichs (oder zumindest Interessenkompromisses) an, insbesondere in „koordinierten Marktökonomien". Allerdings interessieren sich die Autoren für diese Institutionen, soweit sie sie überhaupt in den Blick nehmen, nur in ihren Folgen für die Effizienzsteigerung von Unternehmen bzw. für makroökonomische Indikatoren wie wirtschaftliches Wachstum. Nur unter diesem Gesichtspunkt gehen sie auch in ihre Betrachtung „institutioneller Komplementaritäten" ein. Ausgeblendet bleiben die von Amable angesprochenen Ungleichheiten der Interessen und deren Auswirkungen bei der Institutionenbildung. Ausgeblendet bleibt ebenfalls, ob und in welcher Weise eine „Effizienzsteigerung" durch institutionelle Komplementarität auch bezüglich der Interessen der Lohnabhängigen stattfindet.

An dieser Stelle ist es angebracht, die soziologische Ungleichheitsforschung ins Spiel zu bringen. Denn gerade sie fragt nach den institutionellen Voraussetzungen für eine Abschwächung oder Verstärkung der durch Lohnarbeit geschaffenen sozialen Ungleichheiten über unterschiedliche gesellschaftliche „Sphären" hinweg. Hier besteht die Überschneidung mit der Thematik der „Komplementarität von Institutionen".

Über die Dynamiken der Verstärkung von sozialer Ungleichheit wird seit den späten 1980er Jahren insbesondere im Rahmen der sogenannten Exklusionsdebatte verhandelt (Kronauer 2010). Sie hatte ihren Ausgangspunkt in der Rückkehr und Verfestigung der Arbeitslosigkeit in Europa nach einer Phase relativer Vollbeschäftigung. Dabei wurden zugleich Schwächen in der sozialstaatlichen Absicherung gegen Arbeitsmarktrisiken und deren Folgen sichtbar. Es zeigte sich aber auch, dass für die von den Risiken am Arbeitsmarkt besonders betroffenen Lohnabhängigen die sozialen Netze jenseits der Erwerbsarbeit, die Hilfeleistungen in verschiedenen informellen Formen bereitstellen könnten, brüchig geworden waren. Die in der Exklusionsdebatte adressierte neue „soziale Frage" (Castel 2000) betrifft somit gleichermaßen sowohl den Arbeitsmarkt wie die „social protection". Was mit ihr in Frage steht, ist „social solidarity", um die von Hall und Soskice verwendeten Begriffe wieder aufzugreifen.

Einigkeit besteht trotz aller sonstigen theoretischen Differenzen in der soziologischen Literatur zur Exklusion darüber, dass sowohl Inklusion als auch Exklusion nur *mehrdimensional* zu begreifen sind. Auch darüber, welchen Dimensionen für gesellschaftliche Zugehörigkeit (bzw. deren Gegenstück, gesellschaftliche Ausgrenzung) eine besondere Bedeutung zukommt, besteht weitgehend Übereinstimmung. Der Erwerbsarbeit (und somit dem Arbeitsmarkt) fällt in Gesellschaften mit kapitalistischer Ökonomie direkt wie indirekt für Einkommen, gesellschaftliche Positionierung und Lebenschancen eine Schlüsselrolle zu. Daher wirken prekäre Beschäftigung und anhaltende Arbeitslosigkeit in der Tendenz ausgrenzend.

Die Lohnabhängigen (und ihre Angehörigen) sind aber nicht nur durch eine besondere Stellung in der (marktförmig organisierten) Arbeitsteilung gesellschaftlich eingebunden, sondern auch als Bürgerinnen und Bürger mit (noch immer abgestuften) persönlichen, politischen und sozialen Rechten. Dieser Status wurde ihnen erst nach langen und oft blutigen Kämpfen im Lauf des 19. und 20. Jahrhunderts zuerkannt (und Arbeitsmigranten wird er bis heute partiell oder völlig verweigert). Zu den sozialen Rechten gehören die im Begriff der „social protection" mit gemeinten Sozialversicherungen. Ausgrenzung bedeutet in dieser Dimension den formalen oder auch faktischen Ausschluss von der Wahrnehmung von Rechten. Sie findet aber bereits auch dann statt, wenn die über Rechte vermittelten Leistungen es nicht erlauben, am gesellschaftlichen Leben entsprechend den jeweils historisch-kulturell erreichten und erwarteten Mindeststandards teilzunehmen.

Und schließlich beruht gesellschaftliche Einbindung auf der Wechselseitigkeit sozialer Beziehungen in Haushalt, Verwandtschaft und Bekanntenkreisen, der Reichweite und Vielfalt sozialer Kontakte. Hier manifestiert sich Ausgrenzung in sozialer Isolation, sei es in Form einer zunehmenden Beschränkung von Kontakten auf Menschen in ähnlich marginalisierter sozialer Position, sei es in der noch krasseren Form der Vereinzelung.

Einigkeit besteht in der Debatte ebenfalls darüber, dass Exklusion als *Prozess* verstanden werden muss, der sich über die unterschiedlichen Dimensionen hinweg ausbreiten und dabei verstärken kann. Erst wenn dies der Fall ist, lässt sich von *sozialer* Ausgrenzung in einem strengen und umfassenden Sinn sprechen. Für solche Kumulationen von Ausgrenzungsrisiken und Verfestigungen von Ausgrenzungslagen gibt es empirische Belege. Wie lassen sie sich aber erklären?

Das Problem ergibt sich daraus, dass jede der angesprochenen Dimensionen mit ihren formellen und informellen Institutionen gesellschaftliche Zugehörigkeit auf unterschiedliche Weise vermittelt: Erwerbsarbeit durch die Einbindung in die wechselseitigen, objektivierten Abhängigkeitsverhältnisse der gesellschaftlichen Arbeitsteilung (*Interdependenz*); der Bürgerstatus über die Zuerkennung von (persönlichen, politischen, sozialen) Rechten (*Partizipation*); die sozialen Nahbeziehungen über informelle Verpflichtungen von Loyalität und *Reziprozität*. Es kommt hinzu, dass der Zugang zu den drei Vermittlungsinstanzen von gesellschaftlicher Zugehörigkeit auf jeweils unterschiedliche Weise ermöglicht wird: bei der Erwerbsarbeit über den Markt; beim Bürgerstatus durch die (rechtliche) Anerkennung als Mitglied eines Gemeinwesens; bei den sozialen Nahbeziehungen über Herkunft (Verwandtschaft) und soziale Wahl.

In welchem Verhältnis stehen dann die jeweiligen „Inklusionsfähigkeiten" dieser Dimensionen zueinander? Und wie ist es überhaupt möglich, dass Ausgrenzungen in einer Dimension auf andere Dimensionen übergreifen, wo sie doch je eigenen Zugangs- und Vermittlungslogiken folgen? Der Versuch einer Antwort verlangt, sich den institutionalisierten Verknüpfungen zwischen den Dimensionen zuzuwenden.

6. Die Zweischneidigkeit „institutioneller Komplementaritäten"

In der Einleitung zu „Varieties of Capitalism" verweisen Hall und Soskice (2001) auf Deutschland als typischen Fall einer „koordinierten Marktökonomie" im Unterschied zur „liberalen Marktökonomie" der USA. Es liegt deshalb nahe, sich zunächst den für die gesellschaftliche Einbindung der Lohnabhängigen durch „social protection" und „social solidarity" so wichtigen Verknüpfungen zwischen den Dimensionen Arbeitsmarkt, Bürgerstatus und Haushaltsformen bzw. soziale Nahbeziehungen in Deutschland zu widmen. Dabei zeigen sich institutionelle Komplementaritäten ganz besonderer Art. Denn sie entsprechen und widersprechen zugleich dem von Hall und Soskice dargelegten Muster in entscheidenden Aspekten.

Versteht man Effizienz in einem breiteren als nur ökonomischen Sinn als die jeweils spezifische Leistung, die von Institutionen erbracht wird, dann stellt das deutsche System der institutionellen Verkoppelung von Arbeitsmarkt, sozialen Sicherungssystemen (als einer Form der Institutionalisierung von sozialen Bürgerrechten) und Haushaltskonstellationen einen geradezu typischen Fall von institutioneller Komplementarität dar. Durch ihre Verbindung tragen sie zur Steigerung der „Effizienz" bei, und zwar sowohl im Hinblick auf den Ertrag von Unternehmen (worauf Hall und Soskice allein ihr Augenmerk richten) als auch auf die soziale Absicherung von in Erwerbsarbeit fest verankerten Lohnabhängigen.

Bekanntlich ist diese Verbindung in Deutschland in besonderer Weise „erwerbsarbeitszentriert". Die rechtliche Stellung im Arbeitsverhältnis und das Erwerbseinkommen entscheiden in hohem Maße über die Leistungen, die die Sozialversicherten und ihre Angehörigen im Fall von Arbeitslosigkeit, Krankheit und im Alter beziehen können. Die institutionalisierte Koppelung findet über die Finanzierung der Sicherungssysteme durch die Beiträge der Lohnabhängigen, abgestuft nach ihrem Einkommen, statt. Die Einbeziehung des engsten Kreises der Angehörigen im Haushalt wiederum erfolgt durch die institutionalisierte Koppelung der nicht-erwerbstätigen Haushaltsmitglieder (in der Regel Ehefrau und Kinder) an die Erwerbstätigkeit und die daraus abgeleiteten Versicherungsansprüche des Haushaltsvorstands in einem konservativen Familienmodell. Wer hier im Großen und Ganzen kontinuierlich vollerwerbstätig ist und zumindest tariflich entlohnt wird (damit dies geschehen kann, kommen weitere institutionelle Vorleistungen ins Spiel, vor allem die des Bildungs- und Ausbildungssystems und der industriellen Beziehungen), erfährt *zusätzlich* soziale Absicherung für sich und seine unmittelbaren Familienangehörigen. Darin besteht die „Effizienzsteigerung". Wer (entsprechend eingezahlt) hat, dem wird gegeben. Eine Variante des Matthäuseffekts also. Weniger offensichtlich, aber empirisch ebenfalls gut nachweisbar, sind die Verknüpfungen, die zwischen diesem Kernbereich von „social protection" und weiteren Dimensionen gesellschaftlicher Teilhabe bestehen, etwa der Reichweite und sozialen Zusammensetzung der Bekanntenkreise oder der politischen Partizipation.

Eine Effizienzsteigerung findet auf diesem Weg auch für die Unternehmen statt. Schließlich sind es die Lohnabhängigen selbst, die sich durch ihre eigenen Beiträge gegen soziale Risiken, die aus dem Kapitalismus erwachsen, absichern. Auch der Unternehmerbeitrag zu den Sozialversicherungen stellt, ökonomisch genau genommen, ja noch einen Lohnbestandteil dar. Darüber hinaus stärkt dies die Bindekraft von Belegschaften an die Unternehmerinteressen.

Die fatale Zweischneidigkeit dieser institutionellen Komplementarität besteht allerdings darin, dass gerade aus den engen institutionellen Koppelungen ein besonderes Risiko der sozialen Ausgrenzungen erwächst. Es betrifft diejenigen, die in den entscheidenden Phasen ihrer Biographie über längere Zeiten hinweg nicht oder allenfalls prekär erwerbstätig sind und auch keine indirekte Absicherung durch die Haushaltskonstellation, in der sie leben, erfahren. Diejenigen, die der sozialen Absicherung am meisten bedürften, stehen in der größten Gefahr, in eine Spirale der Ausgrenzung zu geraten. Die Kehrseite des Matthäuseffekts für die stabil in Erwerbsarbeit Eingebundenen ist der Teufelskreis, der für die am Arbeitsmarkt Marginalisierten in Gang kommt (Kronauer 2014). Dazu gehören auch diejenigen, die, weil sie in keinem konventionellen Familienhaushalt leben, auch am Arbeitsmarkt kaum Chancen haben (vor allem die von Armut besonders betroffenen alleinerziehenden Mütter). Es ist ein und dieselbe institutionelle Komplementarität, die für die entgegengesetzten Wirkungen sorgt.

In Deutschland werden die Erwerbsbiographien von immer mehr Menschen brüchig und damit auch deren soziale Absicherungen abgesenkt. Die Ausgrenzungsbedrohung wiederum wirkt auf die Konzessionsbereitschaft derer zurück, die im Erwerbssystem verankert bleiben. Damit verstärkt sich das Machtgefälle zwischen Kapital und Arbeit (das bereits der Prekarisierung von Erwerbsarbeit zugrunde liegt) und die soziale Ungleichheit nimmt zu. Der Charakter einer „koordinierten Marktökonomie" wird davon zunächst nicht berührt. Im Gegenteil, das Abkoppeln von Teilen der lohnabhängigen Bevölkerung mag die Effizienz der institutionellen Komplementaritäten für die Unternehmen noch steigern. Der Preis dafür ist jedoch, dass die „social solidarity of a nation" zurückgeht. Hall und Soskice blenden bereits die Möglichkeit einer solchen zwiespältigen Entwicklung aus, ebenso wie die ihr zugrunde liegende Zweischneidigkeit der institutionellen Komplementaritäten. Ob sie *auf Dauer* das Institutionengefüge der „koordinierten Marktökonomie" untergräbt, ist eine offene Frage.

Im Unterschied zu Deutschland haben die skandinavischen Länder bislang die „social solidarity of a nation" dadurch gestärkt, dass sie Erwerbsarbeit und individuelle soziale Absicherung stärker voneinander *entkoppelt* haben, durch einen größeren Anteil steuerfinanzierter Leistungen. Statt Komplementarität durch Effizienzsteigerung (mit ihren zweischneidigen Effekten) könnte man von Komplementarität durch *Kompensation* sprechen (Kronauer 2014: 94). Die grundlegende Abhängigkeit von kapitalistischer Akkumulation wird damit nicht beseitigt, ihre sozialen, Ungleichheit erzeugenden Wirkungen jedoch werden abgeschwächt. Wäre aber auch eine Art der institutionellen Verbindung denkbar, in der die Individuen gleichermaßen als arbeitende und tätige Subjekte, Bürgerinnen und Bürger und sozial gesellige Menschen gestärkt werden? In der die *Eigenständigkeit* der jeweiligen Dimensionen vor jeder zu engen Koppelung zu ihrem Recht kommt (Kronauer 2014: 95f.)? Denkbar schon, aber kaum als eine „Variety of Capitalism".

Literatur

Amable, B. (2003): *The Diversity of Modern Capitalism*, Oxford.

Bosch, G., Lehndorff, S., Rubery, J. (Hg.) (2009): *European Employment Models in Flux. A. Comparison of Institutional Change in Nine European Countries*, Basingstoke, New York.

Castel, R. (2000): *Die Metamorphosen der sozialen Frage. Eine Chronik der Lohnarbeit*, Konstanz.

Hall, P.A., Soskice, D. (2001): Introduction, in: Dies. (Hg.), *Varieties of Capitalism. The Institutional Foundations of Comparative Advantage*, Oxford, 1-68.

Hall, P.A., Gingerich, D.W. (2004): Varieties of Capitalism and Institutional Complementarities in the Macroeconomy. An Empirical Analysis, Köln, Max-Planck-Institut für Gesellschaftsforschung, Discussion Paper 04/5.

Hall, P.A., Gingerich, D.W. (2009): Varieties of Capitalism and Institutional Complementarities in the Political Economy: An Empirical Analysis, in: Hancké, B. (Hg.), *Debating Varieties of Capitalism. A Reader*, Oxford, 135-179.

Hancké, B. (Hg.) (2009): *Debating Varieties of Capitalism. A Reader*, Oxford.

Kronauer, M. (2010): *Exklusion. Die Gefährdung des Sozialen im hoch entwickelten Kapitalismus*, 2., akt. u. erw. Auflage, Frankfurt a.M., New York.

Kronauer, M. (2014): Matthäuseffekt und Teufelskreis. Inklusion und Exklusion in kapitalistischen Gesellschaften, in: *Mittelweg*, 36(2), 79-96.

McCann, D. (2010): *The Political Economy of the European Union*, Cambridge (UK), Malden (USA).

North, D. (1990): *Institutions, Institutional Change and Economic Performance*, Cambridge, New York.

Streeck, W. (2009): *Re-Forming Capitalism. Institutional Change in the German Political Economy*, Oxford.

Das klassische Erbe der Makroökonomie – Anmerkungen zu einem vernachlässigten Thema

Hajo Riese

Gibt man der Makroökonomie, wie es einer angemessenen theoriegeschichtlichen Perspektive entspricht, ein keynesianisches Fundament, so besteht ihre methodische Basis aus einer Werttheorie, die sich von der klassischen, tauschtheoretisch fundierten Version abgrenzt und an deren Stelle eine Theorie der Einkommensbildung und ihrer Komponenten, rückführbar auf die fabulöse (Einkommens-)Gleichung $Y = C + I$, setzt. Aus der Allokationstheorie ist eine Beschäftigungstheorie geworden. Bei der Einkommensbildung figurieren die Komponenten als Strömungsgrößen, werden also in Zeiteinheiten (1/t) gemessen; im einfachsten Fall lassen sie sich in Konsum (C) und Investition (I) gliedern. Dabei symbolisiert I ökonomische Dynamik im Sinne eines nicht konsumierten Einkommens, definiert als $Y - C$; sie schließt den Grenzfall einer Investion von Null und damit, in ökonomische Kategorien übersetzt, den Fall einer stationären Ökonomie ein.

Makroökonomie beinhaltet neben diesem theoretischen Fundament zugleich Makropolitik, indem sich die Einkommensbildung und ihre Komponenten als steuerbare Größen interpretieren lassen. Damit weist Makroökonomik ebenfalls ein teleologisches Fundament auf.

Zwar ist eine derartige Einsicht beim gegenwärtigen Stand der Wissenschaft trivial. Aber sie ist bis zum heutigen Tage, fast achtzig Jahre nach ihrer ersten Formulierung, eine Form ökonomischer Theoriebildung geblieben, die sich isoliert neben einer „eigentlichen", eben tauschtheoretisch fundierten ökonomischen Theorie herausbildete. Das macht ihren Charakter als Theorie der Einkommensbildung aus, begründet die Breite ihrer Anwendung und zugleich deren Beliebigkeit. Popularität wie Kritik der Makroökonomie haben hier ihre Wurzeln. Den Kontrapunkt (und zugleich eine Bestätigung der Beliebigkeit) stellt die in den siebziger Jahren einsetzende Renaissance der Mikroökonomie dar – ein theoriegeschichtliches Phänomen, aus dessen Umklammerung sich die Makroökonomie nur ganz allmählich zu lösen vermag und dabei immer den Geruch behält, doch nur angewandte Ökonomik zu repräsentieren. Dafür liefert Hansjörg Herr mit seinen Forschungen auf den unterschiedlichsten Gebieten der Ökonomie ein nachdrückliches Beispiel.

Nun kann es an dieser Stelle nicht darauf ankommen, die sich daraus ergebenden ungelösten Probleme ökonomischer Theoriebildung „end"gültig zu beantworten. Dennoch lassen sich Indizien für eine, wenn man so will, rigorose Interpretation der Ökonomie, die ihre Beliebigkeit überwindet, finden. Sie lassen sich angesichts einer sich nun bereits seit fast drei Jahrhunderten herausgebildeten Wissenschaftsentwicklung, die die Distinktion von Makro- und Mikroökonomik als selbstverständlich setzt, wie sich exemplarisch an der Lehrbuchliteratur zeigt, nur *ex negativo* deuten.

Dazu liefert wiederum der Blick auf die klassische Ökonomie, auf deren theoretisches Fundament, den Schlüssel. Denn die klassische Ökonomie vermochte eben nicht einen universellen gesamtwirtschaftlichen Zusammenhang zu begründen. Sie bleibt an ihre tauschtheoretischen Wurzeln gebunden, die ihr die Grenzen setzten und ihr bestenfalls, wie beispielsweise bei Ricardo und Walras angelegt, die Summation von Einzelentscheidungen erlauben. Das zeigt sich nicht zuletzt an der modernen Mikroökonomie, deren methodisches Fundament die Negierung einer gesamtwirtschaftlichen Orientierung und damit die Negierung einer Makroökonomie verlangt.

Die Akzeptanz dieser Kritik der Makroökonomik, allen voran ihr Nachweis einer unzulässigen methodischen Fundierung, ist unabweisbar. Denn ein mikroökonomisches Fundament lässt sich nicht makroökonomisch deuten. Die Wissenschaftsentwicklung bestätigt diese Einsicht, indem sie sich zunehmend mikroökonomisch orientiert. Aber dies kann für sich genommen lediglich bedeuten, dass sich die tradierten Wurzeln der Wissenschaftsentwicklung zwar einer makroökonomischen Bestimmung verschließen, dessen ungeachtet jedoch Makroökonomik ein Desiderat wirtschaftswissenschaftlicher Forschung bleibt.

Deshalb bedarf es eines Instruments, das *sui generis* Makroökonomik begründet, ihr theoretische Schlüssigkeit verleiht.

Dieses Instrument liefert die Einkommensbildung, eine Kategorie, die den doppelten Anspruch erfüllt, sowohl eine makroökonomische Kategorie zu sein, als auch ein eindeutiges (markt-)theoretisches Fundament aufzuweisen. Einkommen erweist sich dadurch als die entscheidende ökonomische Kategorie, die *sui generis* Makroökonomik begründet, die sie gleichsam überhaupt erst definiert.

Einkommen ist damit zugleich eine Kategorie, deren makroökonomischer Charakter sich der Beliebigkeit entzieht. Selbstverständlich ist Einkommen definitorisch stets ein Produkt aus (produzierter) Menge und (Güter-)Preis. Es ist jedoch dank seines genuin makroökonomischen Bezuges nicht auf „klassische" werttheoretische Wurzeln rückführbar. Vielmehr bedarf es zusätzlicher, sich aus einer speziellen Einkommens*bildung* ableitbarer Informationen, die hier nicht näher erläutert werden sollen. Entscheidend ist, dass deren Vielfalt ihre Mikrostruktur bestimmt und sich mikroökonomisch fundierte Werttheorie und makroökonomisch fundierte Einkommensbildung als unabhängig voneinander existierende Kategorien erweisen.

Es bleibt deshalb missverständlich, diesbezüglich lediglich von einem sogenannten Keynesianismus zu sprechen, wie es bei Hansjörg Herr und gelegentlich auch bei mir der Fall ist. Denn diese Kategorisierung verdeckt den universellen Charakter des Instruments der Einkommensbildung. Vielmehr entzieht sich diese, verstanden als Produkt aus (produzierter) Menge und (Güter-)Preis, der Beliebigkeit – und erhält jene theoretische Schlüssigkeit, die zugleich auch Makroökonomie begründet.

Mit der Kategorie der Einkommensbildung wird somit nicht nur die Dichotomie der Preis- und Mengenbildung der klassischen Schule – der klassischen wie der neoklassischen Ökonomie – überwunden, sondern zugleich der makroökonomischen Version ein genuines markttheoretisches Fundament gegeben, das sich der tradierten Trennung von Preis- und Mengenkomponente entzieht.

Macroeconomic policy regime: A heuristic approach to grasping national policy space within global asymmetries*

Barbara Fritz

1. Introduction: between the global and the domestic: Missing analytical links

It is trivial to state that economic globalization severely limits the nation state's capacity to pursue policies of its own. However, the search for concepts and analytical tools to describe and evaluate this limited yet not inexistent policy space at the national level is much less self-evident.

On the one hand, standard economic theory and policy advice, at least for a long time, have assumed that there exists a standard set of policies to be pursued if a country is in crisis (e.g. Williamson 1990). This highly voluntarist approach of an optimal economic policy assumes that problems on the way to a sustainable growth path should be explained by domestic policy failures. From a purely orthodox perspective, the usual suspects of this failure would be an inadequate monetary policy, insufficient fiscal adjustment, or structural reforms which fail to reach deep enough.

It is true that more recently, relevant work even within the economic mainstream has started considering external factors as a severe constraint for standard domestic policies. Especially high and volatile international capital flows have been a topic of analysis for their destabilizing effects on the exchange rate and the financial sector of countries receiving inflows. Following

---

* Special thanks go to my colleagues Daniela Prates and Luiz Fernando de Paula for what I learned in our collective work on the challenges and limits for domestic policies which are imposed by global economic asymmetries on emerging market countries.

earlier critical work from a Keynesian or heterodox perspective (e.g. Flassbeck 2001; Herr 2008; Ocampo 2001), a series of authors, based on empirical assessment, recognize the problems imposed especially by financial globalization which cannot be addressed by standard economic policies (Rey 2015) and would require unconventional measures such as capital account controls (e.g. Ostry et al. 2010). Yet, a look at current adjustment programs both in the Euro zone and in developing countries and emerging markets shows that supranational institutions such as the IMF still seem to be rather far away from taking into account these interdependencies between global economic features and policy design and outcome at the domestic level. For instance, Euro zone countries such as Spain, which came into deep trouble without having suffered from a fiscal slip before, but rather from a mixture of dysfunctional wage competition by other currency union members and the relaxation of financial regulation, are being left alone with a dysfunctional deflationist adjustment burden as well.

On the other hand, when looking to relevant non-orthodox approaches, we have a series of rather determinist concepts, especially in the case of countries denominated as developing, emerging or peripheral. Here, globalization of the capitalist system rather condemns countries to remain in a peripheral position, due to colonial and post-colonial global interdependencies (e.g. Wallerstein 1979, 2011; Korzeniewicz et al. 2009). In contrast to conventional approaches, here the focus lies exclusively on global conditions and limits which create powerful path dependencies, while domestic policies aimed toward changing this position do not receive systematic attention.

So, what we are missing is an approach capable of intermediating between both perspectives: the asymmetric nature of the global economy, on the one side, and the chances and limits of domestic policies on the other. Yet, there is little to be found in the literature.

2. The concept of the macroeconomic policy regime

The concept of the macroeconomic policy regime, as brought forward by Hansjörg Herr in various publications, may serve as an analytical tool to bring these two perspectives together. Even if he seems not to be considering this concept as key within his own research when presenting his "selected current work" on his homepage,[1] I argue here that this is indeed useful as an inter-

---

[1] See: http://www.hwr-berlin.de/fachbereich-wirtschaftswissenschaften/kontakt/personen/kontakt/hansjoerg-herr/

mediary concept between global structures and economic policies at the domestic level.

The term macroeconomic regime is understood as

> "the interaction between monetary policy, fiscal policy, wage policy and foreign economic policy within a framework of both: macroeconomic institutions which can be actively changed by policy-makers and become part of economic policy, and institutions which are beyond the control of policy-makers" (Herr/Kazandziska 2011: 2).

As this quote shows, one key characteristic of the concept of a macroeconomic regime[2] – or market constellation, as termed in an earlier publication (Herr 1995: 143ff.) – is that it encompasses a broad range of policy fields. Especially by including wage policies, it goes beyond standard analysis of the typical macroeconomic variables such as the fiscal budget, the monetary interest rate, and the exchange rate. This almost holistic perspective, similar to the French regulation school (e.g. Boyer 1990), also includes fields such as industrial policies and the form in which countries are integrated into the world market, the features of the financial sector, etc.

Second, the concept of the macroeconomic regime explicitly includes an institutional perspective, thus going beyond standard quantitative approaches which only focus on macro variables or quantifiable institutional features. Correspondingly, it is key that the concept analyzes policy options within their specific institutional context:

> "Institutions pave the way the policy instruments can be applied, and it is only when certain institutions are in place that certain types of policies become possible. Institutional changes can be induced by the decisions of the national governments, but they can also happen as a result of actions which are out of governments' reach" (Kazandziska 2013: 3, based on Heine/Herr/Kaiser 2006).

This focus on the interaction between policies and institutions allows for a specific insight: policy outcomes may differ from their intended aims for a variety of reasons, and failures in terms of policy implementation may be

---

[2] When using the concept of regime, Herr makes a cursory reference to its origins within social science, for example by hinting at its use within the field of International Relations (Krasner 1983). Yet, others using the concept of macroeconomic regimes within economics, such as Baele et al. (2011), also focus exclusively on the usage of the concept in terms of policy fields, simply defining it as the monetary policy with its implications on aggregate demand and supply.

only one among a series of reasons. With this perspective, (more or less) unsuccessful reform processes to foster sustainable growth can be assessed taking into account the specific conditions of a country which are not easy to be changed, at least in the short run. The way wage formation occurs according to country specific features represents one example. There might be strong labor unions which demonstrate a certain degree of politicization, pushing inflation with nominal wage increases which even counteract contractive monetary or fiscal policies. Or wage formation occurs in a highly decentralized manner, which makes the wage level pro-cyclical, thus fostering boom-bust cycles.

The encompassing perspective on the interaction of a broad set of policies and institutions is especially helpful in explaining why countries, despite significant policy efforts, may not experience a takeoff in terms of investment and growth. We see that macroeconomic policy regimes, or market constellations, show a high degree of inertia, or path dependency, due to the rigidity of institutions.

This gives us a powerful explanation of why economic actors may adjust to policy shifts only at the margin, but not fundamentally change their attitude. Instead, there is a high risk that investors remain in a sit-and-wait position, or procrastinate in their investment decisions, as long as they are not strongly convinced that the future will significantly differ from the past. Generally speaking, it is necessary to achieve strong structural breaks with a significant impact on expectations. At the same time, policies should be designed towards preventing negative feedback, and clearly embedded within he specific institutional setting.

Based on this broad definition, Herr applies the concept of the macroeconomic regime to all sorts of countries: advanced economies (e.g. Heine/Herr/Kaiser 2006; Herr/Kazandziska 2011); transformation countries (Herr 1995; Herr/Tober 1999); accession candidates to currency unions (Herr/Kazandziska 2007), and developing economies (e.g. Priewe/Herr 2005).

The aim is to classify, both in general and for specific cases or types or countries, regime types according to their effect on growth and stagnation. A regime deemed optimal would be comprised of some sort of a regulated financial system and labor market, together with active government policies aimed at reducing uncertainty and maintaining demand bringing about high investment, growth, employment, and low inequality. As this runs along the lines of the post-Keynesian literature, it will not be further described here.

A relevant part of the concept is the typology of regimes of growth or stagnation. When looking at developing and transformation economies specifically, as in Priewe/Herr (2005: 58ff.), growth regimes are classified as "growth without external debt", "growth with sustainable external debt", or "growth with unsustainable external debt", while stagnation regimes are characterized as "stagflation", "austerity", "structural non-competitiveness", or "social instability". This typology is rather flexible, offering somewhat different taxonomies in other publications, thus being adjustable to specific country case studies, and especially helpful for a comparative research design.

3. A methodologically open heuristic approach

I argue that from both an area studies and a methodological perspective, the macroeconomic policy regime approach is highly welcome as it highlights the relevance of deep and systematic knowledge of specific features of a certain economy, in contrast to purely econometric knowledge, the dominant requirement for economists at the moment.

This goes against standard economic wisdom, which is dominated by formalized models. Yet the implications of a purely formal and econometric approach are severe for several reasons. First, research inescapably has to be driven by data availability. Consequently, where data are missing, research is not possible. This is similar to searching for a lost key only where the light is shining and all the space outside the lamp's ray remains in the dark.

A second implication of the formalization of the economics discipline is that economic contexts, such as institutions and their complex interactions with policies, have to be translated into quantifiable variables, e.g. for describing institutional variety such as the form and degree of independence of a central bank. Instead of describing and analyzing this variety, which might include the multidimensional relationship between a central bank and fiscal institutions on primary and secondary markets for public bonds, or regulation of international capital flows, among other aspects, a formal model has to create proxy variables which translate this institutional richness into quantifiable indicators. In employing such a strategy, empirical content and context are downgraded to "anecdotal evidence", that is to say they are considered inferior in comparison to statistical evidence. For one institution or policy it still may be possible to elaborate on quantifiable variables, based on careful comparative analysis of institutional features, including their changes over time. Yet, this becomes impossible when trying to analyze the interdependency between a whole set of policies and institutions on the expectations of economic agents. Here, econometric models remain blunt, as the complexity of the interdependence of variables and related problems of endogeneity are left insolvable by formal models.

> "What is generally left of possible relevance in macroeconomics are cross-country regressions a la Barro which, in their more sophisticated manifestations, include relatively crude institutional and geographic variables which, at best, can be called the beginning but not the end of wisdom, i.e., something intermediate is needed beyond such regressions and old-fashioned country studies. (...) While there have been increasing challenges to the universalism of the machinery of neoclassical economics, emanating from an enhanced interest in institutions, behavioral and experimental economics, much of this remains something of a black box, reminiscent of Solow's technology 'residual' and requiring more convincing theoretical and empirical meat on the bones. It should, therefore, be no surprise that there has been increased questioning of the usefulness of economics in the public policy arena" (Ranis 2009: 3).

In this sense, the macroeconomic policy regime approach allows for methodological and disciplinary broadening.

> "While other social sciences have traditionally tried to imitate the methodology of economics, if with a substantial lag, non-economists, especially those in political science, are now ahead of economists in terms of their willingness to move into that no-man's-land between the disciplines and in recognizing that cross-area convergence is but a convenient illusion" (Ranis 2009: 4).

Political science offers important methodological tools for the combination of quantitative and qualitative methods (see e.g. Lieberman 2005). Some of the variables and their interdependence may be grasped by more or less sophisticated statistical instruments, for instance a monetary policy reaction function, which seeks to isolate the impact of monetary policy changes on specific variables such as the exchange rate, inflation and even short term output. Yet, the analytical quality of quantitative analysis will significantly improve if properly combined with a more comprehensive analysis of this interdependence with specific institutions and other policies.

4. Embedded in a Keynesian perspective

However, the macroeconomic regime approach certainly is no eclectic concept driven by nothing but the empirical assessment of institutions and policy outcomes. Here, three features are key. First, the concept departs from the Keynesian axiomatic assumption that uncertainty, and the attempt to reduce uncertainty, drive the behavior of economic actors and the results of their interaction.

This point is intrinsically linked to the Keynesian assumption that economic actors assume future development resembles the past, unless there are structural breaks.

"In practice we have tacitly agreed, as a rule, to fall back on what is, in truth, a convention. The essence of this convention – though it does not, of course, work out quite so simple – lies in assuming that the existing state of affairs will continue indefinitely, except in so far as we have specific reasons to expect a change" (Keynes 1936: 152).

Second, the approach explicitly covers the interaction of the real and the monetary sphere.

"The strength of the economy (say, in terms of real GDP per capita) depends to a large extend on a functioning monetary and financial system based in well-accepted local money" (Priewe/Herr 2005: 46).

Thus, the approach is especially capable of addressing problems as they emerged in the Great Financial Crisis, a situation which is not covered by most of standard economic models which focus on the real sphere.

Third, the concept of a macroeconomic policy regime assumes that the establishment of monetary stability is far from being sufficient to assure growth, as uncertainty undermines market coordination towards equilibrium with full employment. Thus, the state should take an active role in several kinds of economic policies. Specifically, monetary, exchange rate, fiscal, labor and sectoral policies should be coordinated to assure monetary and financial stability as well as sustainable growth and employment.

5. Relevance of highlighting interdependence of domestic and global regimes

As stated at the outset, I interpret the macroeconomic policy regime as (being) an analytical tool to intermediate between the global and the national perspective.

In most of the work related to this concept, Herr focuses on national policies. This may be explained by his engaged interest in policy advice for optimal policies. For this purpose, the scale for analysis unavoidably has to be the domestic sphere, as the nation state is the main actor being addressed.

Yet, it is possible to integrate the global perspective into this approach so as to elaborate on how global conditions concretely shape and delimit policy space and specific policy regimes at the national level. When looking at the above mentioned classification of growth and stagnation regimes for developing and transformation countries, avoiding unsustainable external debt, denominated in foreign currency, turns out to be the key variable for a growth regime. Behind this is the understanding of a hierarchical and asymmetric global monetary order where the competition between currencies results in a pattern where only a small number of countries are able to contract debt at the global level in their own money. The majority on the other hand, especially emerging market and developing economies, are forced to contract debt in other countries' currency. This hierarchical nature of the global monetary system and its changes over time have not only been analyzed by Herr (e.g. 1992). Eichengreen and Hausmann for instance, based on an empirical assessment of currency denomination of international financial contracts, have introduced into the economic mainstream the label of 'original sin' (Eichengreen/Hausmann 2005); in the field of International Political Economy, Cohen (1998, 2004) has established the concept of a 'currency pyramid'.

The fundamental implications of this global currency hierarchy on domestic policies, which depend on the position of a country's currency, have received some formalization by Riese (2004/1993). He offers a similar approach for developing a typology of growth and stagnation regimes against the backdrop of the hierarchical global monetary order, enriched by a simple yet convincing formalization of the equilibria condition for the foreign exchange market for the case of currencies at the lower stratum of this hierarchy. Departing from a difference in the liquidity premium among currencies, he deduces the necessity for a difference in terms of interest rates and profit rates. A similar approach, with links to the Latin American structuralist literature, is offered by Paula et al. (2015). Fritz et al. (2016), for their part, seek to organize concepts of developmentalist strategies combined with redistribution under the policy space constraints for emerging markets imposed by an international monetary asymmetry. In a similar vein, literature on the asymmetric patterns of global trade between center and periphery countries could be included in the analysis.

This perspective opens a promising research field. Bringing together in a more systematic manner the strands of literature on the hierarchical nature of the global monetary regime and related issues, and those on the interdependence between a broad set of policies and institutions at the domestic level, e.g. the macroeconomic policy regime, will certainly help to increase our understanding of the puzzle of stagnation and underdevelopment. And it can enhance our understanding of the limits and specific challenges for the design of adequate policies at the nation state level by concurrently taking into account the interdependence of global limitations and domestic policy space.

References

Baele, L., Bekaert, G., Cho, S., Koen, I., Moreno, A. (2011): Macroeconomic Regimes, NBER Working Paper, No. 170.

Boyer, R. (1990): *The regulation school: A critical introduction*, New York, NY: Columbia University Press.

Cohen, B.J. (1998): *The Geography of Money*, Ithaca: Cornell University Press.

Cohen, B.J. (2004): *The Future of Money*, Princeton, NJ: Princeton University Press.

Eichengreen, B., Hausmann, R. (eds.) (2005): *Other People's Money – Debt Denomination and Financial Instability in Emerging Market Economies*. Chicago: University of Chicago Press.

Flassbeck, H. (2001): The exchange rate – market price or economic policy tool, UNCTAD, Discussion Paper, No. 149.

Fritz, B., Paula, L.F., Prates, D. (2016): Developmentalism at the Periphery: Can productive change and income distribution be compatible with global financial asymmetries? Manuscript.

Heine, M., Herr, H., Kaiser, C. (2006): *Wirtschaftspolitische Regime westlicher Industrienationen*, Baden-Baden: Nomos.

Herr, H. (1992): *Geld, Währungswettbewerb und Währungssysteme*, Frankfurt a.M., New York: Campus.

Herr, H. (1995): Marktkonstellationen, Wirtschaftspolitik und Entwicklung – das Beispiel der Transformationsökonomien, in: Betz, K., Riese, H. (eds.), *Wirtschaftspolitik in einer Geldwirtschaft*, Marburg: Metropolis, 143-174.

Herr, H. (2008): Capital controls and economic development in China, in: Arestis, P., Paula, L.F. de (eds.), *Financial liberalization and economic performance in emerging countries*, Basingstoke, New York, NY: Palgrave.

Herr, H., Kazandziska, M. (2007): Wages and Regional Coherence in the European Monetary Union, in: Hein, E., Priewe, J., Truger, A. (eds.), *European Integration in Crisis*, Marburg: Metropolis

Herr, H., Kazandziska, M. (2011): *Macroeconomic policy regimes in western industrial countries*, London: Routledge.

Herr, H., Tober, S. (1999): Unterschiedliche Marktkonstellationen. Was unterscheidet die Entwicklung in der VR China von den Ländern der ehemaligen Sowjetunion und den Visegrádstaaten?, in: Herr, H., Hübner, K. (eds.), *Der "lange Marsch" in die Marktwirtschaft. Entwicklungen und Erfahrungen in der VR China und Osteuropa*, Berlin: Fachhochschule für Wirtschaft Berlin, Edition Sigma.

Kazandziska, M. (2013): Macroeconomic policy regimes in emerging market candidates for a currency union: the case of Latvia, Institute for International Political Economy, WP No. 21/2013.

Keynes, J.M. (1936): *The General Theory of Employment, Interest and Money*. London: Palgrave MacMillan.

Korzeniewicz, R.P., Moran, T.P. (2009): *Unveiling inequality: A world-historical perspective*, New York: Russell Sage Foundation.

Lieberman, E. (2005): Nested Analysis as a Mixed-Method Strategy for Comparative Research, in: *The American Political Science Review*, 99(3), 435-452.

Ocampo, J.A. (2001): International asymmetries and the design of the international financial system, CEPAL, Serie Temas de Coyuntura, No. 15.

Ostry, J., Ghosh, A., Habermeier, K., Chamon, M., Qureshi, M., Reinhardt, D. (2010): Capital inflows. The role of controls, IMF, Staff Position Note, 10/04.

Paula, L.F., Prates, D., Fritz, B. (2015): Centre and Periphery in International Monetary Relations. Implications for Macroeconomic Policies in Emerging Economies. desiguALdades.net, Working Paper 80, June.

Priewe, J., Herr, H. (2005): *The macroeconomics of development and poverty reduction. Strategies beyond the Washington Consensus*, Wiesbaden: Nomos.

Ranis, G. (2009): Economics, Area Studies and Human Development. Yale Economic Growth Center, Research Paper Series, Discussion Paper 975.

Rey, H. (2015): Dilemma not trilemma: The global financial cycle and monetary policy independence, National Bureau of Economic Research, NBER Working paper Series, No. w21162.

Riese, H. (1997): Stabilität und Entwicklung – Anmerkungen zur Integration der Dritten Welt in die Weltwirtschaft, in: Braig, M., Ferdinand, U., Zapata, M. (eds.), *Begegnungen und Einmischungen: Festschrift für Renate Rott zum 60. Geburtstag*, Stuttgart: Akademischer Verlag.

Riese, H. (2004): Building blocks of a macro-theory of transformation, in: Hölscher, J., Thomann, H. (eds.), *Money, development and economic transformation.* Selected essays by Hajo Riese, Basingstoke, New York, NY: Palgrave. [translated version of: Riese, H. (1993): Bausteine einer Makrotheorie der Transformation, in: Herr, H., Westphal, A. (eds.), Transformation in Mittel- und Osteuropa. Makroökonomische Konzepte und Fallstudien, Frankfurt a.M., New York, NY: Campus.]

Wallerstein, I. (1979): *The capitalist world-economy*, Cambridge: Cambridge University Press.

Wallerstein, I. (2011): *The modern world-system IV – Centrist Liberalism Triumphant, 1789-1914*, Berkeley, CA: University of California Press.

Williamson, J. (1990): What Washington means by policy reform, in: Williamson, J. (ed.), *Latin American adjustment, how much has happened?*, Washington, DC: Institute for International Economics, 7-20.

Three Post-Keynesian concepts within the periphery context*

Zeynep M. Nettekoven

1. Introduction

The schools of thought in economics carrying the name "Keynesian" do not necessarily have similar approaches to the original Keynesian thinking as exposed by Keynes (1936: 49). Among these schools, the Post-Keynesian (PK) one is considered to much more closely follow the original Keynesian thinking, albeit this school is divergent within itself concerning some areas. Despite the PK school's heterogeneity, it sets a realistic ground for understanding the modern economies and provides a solid ground to discuss the role of money.

The PK school has an extensive focus on the core economies. For instance, PK monetary policy proposals usually consider developed free market economies (Sawyer 2012). A certain degree of "normality" is assumed in a sense that the country should be free from fragilities such as an internal or external political conflict, large banking system vulnerabilities, the possibility of cross-border capital flow volatility, large exchange rate fluctuations or high inflationary environment, etc. (Sicsú 2001). This "normal" context also implies that the central bank can concentrate on the goals of the domestic economy by autonomously managing the interest rate. However, the peripheral economies lack most of the above-noted prevailing normality conditions. Nonetheless, the PK theory can be associated with a body of heterodox literature focusing on the periphery condition in the international monetary and financial system.

---

* I would like to thank Eckhard Hein for his valuable comments on this chapter and Luisa Bunescu for proofreading.

This chapter aims to contemplate the PK concepts of uncertainty, liquidity premium and endogenous money within a peripheral economy context. This will be achieved by reviewing the PK literature on these concepts together with some literature about the peripheral conditions in the international monetary and financial system. Before elaborating on the PK concepts in the second section considering the periphery context, this context will be described in the first section. Subsequently, the final section will conclude.

2. Periphery context

The peripheral economy context is understood in two dimensions in this paper. The first dimension is the currency hierarchy discussed by a heterodox body of literature[1]. After the breakdown of the Bretton Woods System (BWS), the leading position of the United States (US) in the world economic and financial system was sustained and correspondingly the US dollar has remained as the hegemonic currency (Fields/Vernengo 2013). Certainly, hierarchy is not simply between the US dollar and the rest of the world currencies; rather, it is also observed among the rest of the world currencies as well. The US dollar has a supreme "prestige", while a small number of currencies have a mediocre status in the international monetary system, such as the euro, Japanese yen, British pound and Swiss franc, as well as a few other currencies (Andrade/Prates 2013; Cohen 2009). The rest of the world currencies – particularly those of the peripheral countries – do not have this prestige in the international monetary transactions, as well as often in many short- and long-term domestic monetary transactions. This implies a "monetary asymmetry" within

---

[1] See Andrade/Prates (2013), Camara-Neto/Vernengo (2009), Cohen (2000), Cohen (2009), Fields/Vernengo (2013), Fritz/Prates/de Paula (2015), Hausmann (1999), Hausmann/Panizza (2011), Hausmann/Panizza/Stein (2002), Herr (2008), Herr/Hübner (2005), Herr/Priewe (2006), Herr (1992), Kindleberger (1967), Kindleberger (1970), Riese (2004), Vernengo (2006). For instance, Cohen (2009) categorizes the highest three levels in the currency hierarchy as follows considering the roles that an internationally acceptable currency can play based upon the usual three functions of money, namely medium of exchange, unit of account and store of wealth: top currency or currencies fulfilling all possible roles (foreign exchange reserves, exchange rate anchor, trade contracts, payments, financial assets, etc.). US dollar is considered as the only top currency with all these roles currently. At a lower level, there are the high-class currencies with many of these roles but not all. Euro and Japanese yen are considered in this category. Below there are some selected currencies with only some of these roles, for instance the British pound, Swiss franc, the Canadian and Australian dollars.

the international monetary system (Andrade/Prates 2013: 409), whereby the currencies of the periphery have lower premiums and thus interest rates tend to be higher than those of the core countries; moreover, the foreign debt of peripheral countries is denominated in the leading currencies such as the US dollar or the euro. Hausmann (1999: 66) describes these countries' inability to borrow from the international financial markets in domestic currency and even from domestic financial markets in the long term, being correspondingly bounded to accumulate foreign debt known as "the original sin".[2]

This monetary asymmetry is one of the key defining characteristics of the core-periphery division in the contemporary world. Vernengo (2006: 563) argues that "[t]echnological dependency (the ability to generate autonomous technological innovations) although important, is subsidiary, and financial dependency (the inability to borrow in its own currency) is central". The crucial ground behind this argument is that although the peripheral countries have industrialized to a certain extent in the 20th and 21st centuries, these countries' dependency on the core countries remains (Vernengo 2006). This implies that some dynamics other than the technological backwardness are working behind the sustained peripheral condition (Vernengo 2006). Indeed, a part of these dynamics is related to the financial sphere.

The second dimension is the "financial asymmetry" discussed by Andrade/ Prates (2013: 410), which concerns cross-border capital flows. First, cross-border capital flows are usually volatile and exogenous to the domestic economies, mainly because financial investment decisions depend on several factors, whereby they do not have definitive anchors (Andrade/Prates 2013; Kaltenbrunner 2011). Second, peripheral economies usually attract a relatively low extent of capital inflows compared to the core countries; however, due to their small and underdeveloped domestic financial systems, they are more vulnerable to the sudden shifts of these flows compared to the core countries (see the literature on this argument in Andrade/Prates 2013). These two factors describe the financial asymmetry in the international financial system, whereby the periphery is more fragile against the unanchored cross-border capital flows compared with the core countries.

These two dimensions of the periphery condition will be considered while discussing the three aforementioned PK concepts in the following section.

---

[2] See also Eichengreen/Hausmann/Panizza (2002) and Hausmann/Panizza (2011). Camara-Neto/Vernengo (2009) argue that the degree of "original sin" is strongly related to the development of the domestic bond market of a country.

3. Three PK concepts within the periphery context

The essential feature of the Keynesian theory is its emphasis on the functioning of an economy in which money exists, called a monetary economy.[3] Keynes (1963: 7) explains this as follows:

> "The theory which I desiderate would deal [...] with an Economy in which Money plays a part of its own and affects motives and decisions and is, in short, one of the operative factors in the situation, so that the course of events cannot be predicted, either in the long-period or in the short, without a knowledge of the behavior of money between the first state and the last and it is this which we ought to mean when we speak of a *Monetary Economy*" [emphasis in the original].

The sub-sections below will discuss this fundamental role of money in PK theory based upon three concepts – namely uncertainty, liquidity premium and endogenous money – and relate them to a peripheral economy context.

3.1 Uncertainty and financial asymmetry

The notion of uncertainty is key to Keynesian thinking, namely "there is no scientific basis on which to form any calculable probability whatever. We simply do not know" (Keynes 1937: 214). According to this view, the chance of the occurrence of future events cannot be predicted by probabilistic distributions based upon past information (Davidson 2011; Glickman 2003). The uncertainty notion occupies a central role in thinking about an economy that uses money, which, being liquid gives confidence to economic agents against the uncertainties of the future.

Due to this uncertainty notion, the expectations of the economic agents cannot be endogenized; rather, they are exogenous. Keynes argued that "conventional judgment" – meaning "anticipating what average opinion expects the average opinion to be" (Keynes 1936: 156) – leads the decision-making process in an uncertain world, whereby economic agents usually show a herd behavior. Conventional judgment is unstable because a "new conventional basis of valuation" (Keynes 1937: 215) might be imposed.

---

[3] Unlike Keynesian theory, Neoclassical theory divides the economy into a real versus monetary sphere, whereby money is irrelevant for understanding the real economy's dynamics: "According to this view the most important economic processes occur in the real sphere, and this can be seen and understood most clearly by constructing an analytical model in which money is first left out of the picture" (Evans/Heine/Herr 2007: 49).

The PK school argues that the foreign exchange market is volatile as it tends not to be based on economic fundamentals but rather shaped by a herd behaviour (Dow 1986; Herr/Priewe 2006; Kaltenbrunner 2011); as well as interest rate differentials between the core and periphery, the expectations of the financial investors about the nominal exchange rate movements and the risk premium of the domestic country (Herr/Priewe 2006). Capital flows are usually pro-cyclical in a Minskian fashion (see Minsky 1977), generating the boom-bust cycles as described by Kindleberger (1996).

The PK notion of uncertainty serves as solid basis for understanding the boom-bust cycles of the periphery and the dependency of their monetary policies on the fluctuations of the cross-border capital flows. As suggested by the herd behaviour in the international financial system, capital flows are highly exogenous to peripheral economies. Asset and real estate bubbles can burst when a domestic or external event triggers the financial investors' expectations about the future, whereby they would subsequently shift their asset portfolios across the borders. Based upon the financial asymmetry view, the periphery is more exposed to the herd behaviour or the consequences of uncertainty in the international financial system compared with the core.

3.2 Liquidity premium and monetary asymmetry

The notion of liquidity premium is explained as the rate of return that gives an individual a positive feeling of keeping money, which is determined by the individual's subjective estimations about the future (Herr 2008). Fluctuations in the degree of confidence among economic agents cause changes in the "propensity to hoard" or the "state of liquidity preference" (Keynes 1937: 216). Keynes (1937: 217) defines the interest rate as the "factor which adjusts at the margin the demand for hoards to the supply of hoards". Changes in the propensity to hoard affect the money market interest rates. The interest rate is the premium offered to the economic agents for not hoarding money.

For money to properly serve for the safety function against the uncertainties of the future, its purchasing power should not be very unstable (Carvalho 1997). Since the peripheral countries often face large fluctuations in the value of their currencies against the hard currencies – causing higher inflation rates and lower real incomes in these countries – their money is not as functional as that of the core countries in terms of safety against the uncertain future.

The Keynesian notion of money in a monetary economy thus facilitates understanding the functions of national currencies in the international monetary system (see Fritz et al. 2015; Herr 2008; Herr/Hübner 2005). Keynesian thinking depicts a negative relation between the amount of monetary wealth and its marginal liquidity premium, meaning the higher the amount of liquidity held by an individual agent, the lower the additional premium obtained from the last unit of the monetary wealth (Keynes 1936). The concept of liquidity premium is applied to different national currencies (see Andrade/Prates 2013; Fritz et al. 2015; Herr 2008). For this, the term "currency premium" is used, namely the credibility of a country's currency internationally and nationally, which – as argued by Herr (2008: 29) – primarily depends upon "the present and even more the expected internal and external stability" of that currency, as well as aspects such as "the size of the currency area, the size, liquidity and sophistication of the financial market in the currency or economic policies in favor of wealth owners" and factors beyond the economic dimension such as "political stability and the international role and economic and military power of the country issuing the currency" (see also Evans 2009). Just like a marginal liquidity premium curve describing the negative relation between the amount of monetary wealth and the marginal premium from the last unit of it, a "marginal currency premium" curve depicts the same relation, albeit particular to monetary wealth denominated in each currency (see Herr 2008: 130-131). Accordingly, the most prestigious currencies – such as the US dollar and the euro – are those with the highest position of the marginal currency premium curves in comparison to the rest of the world currencies. This implies a "monetary asymmetry" within the international monetary system (Andrade/Prates 2013: 409), whereby a hierarchy exists between the currencies. Thus, the PK notion of liquidity premium lays the ground for explaining the hierarchy in the international monetary system.

A lack of trust in the stability of the domestic currency is an obstacle for the monetary policy of the peripheral economies, thus hindering economic development. Due to the lower position of the marginal currency premium curve of the periphery compared to the core countries, the interest rate on domestic currency denominated assets pays higher returns than the core country currency denominated assets. For example, when the currency of a country has a low reputation or when there is a capital flight from domestic currency denominated assets, the domestic central bank tends to increase the interest rate to keep the domestic assets profitable. Therefore, benchmark interest rates in the international financial system or the international liquidity conditions can direct the periphery interest rate moves. This brings us to the endogenous money and "original sin" concepts discussed below.

3.3 Endogenous money and the "original sin"

As one of the early PK scholars, Kaldor (1985) argued that in modern economies where banknotes or credit money exists, a central bank can only directly affect the interest rates in the money market, whereas it cannot directly the money supply. Accordingly, this implies that the exogenous money supply assumption of Monetarism was incorrect because money supply can only be considered exogenous when money is in terms of a commodity such as precious metals (Kaldor 1985).

PK theory argues that money supply in an economy is mainly determined by the demand for loans by the public and the corresponding supply of loans extended by the banking system to creditworthy borrowers at a certain interest rate, which is determined by the central bank policy interest rate plus a certain margin added by the banking system to the policy interest rate; therefore, money supply is endogenous (Fontana 2004; Kaldor 1985; Lavoie 2003; Moore 1989, 2003). In other words, money creation depends on the banks' willingness to lend, as well as the willingness of firms, households and other sectors to borrow from the banks (Herr 2009). Borrowers demand loans from the banking system and loans granted by the banking system create deposits and money.

The endogenous money notion is highly relevant to understand the boom phases facilitated by the capital inflows in the periphery. Due to the currency hierarchy, peripheral countries cannot borrow from the international financial markets in terms of their domestic currencies, given that foreign capital inflows increase the debt in foreign currency in the balance sheets. Due to this "original sin", the balance sheets of the economic agents in the periphery become exposed to depreciation risk, which means a challenge for monetary policy. Capital inflows also appreciate the domestic currency in the peripheral economy and increase the asset prices, which in turn improves the balance sheet structures of the economic agents. Economic agents subsequently become more creditworthy and demand more credit. Accordingly, credit expansion in the economy speeds up, high indebtedness (in both domestic and foreign currency) is generated and asset and real estate price bubbles occur. To put it simply, the "original sin" of the periphery triggers the fast domestic credit expansion and thus asset and real estate price bubbles, which can burst abruptly.

A body of empirical studies supports the view that increased foreign credit inflows to non-banks in a domestic economy cause a more rapid domestic credit expansion (see for instance Avdjiev/McCauley/McGuire 2012; Brzoza-Brzezina/Chmielewski/Niedźwiedzińska 2010; Hilbers/Otker-Robe/Pazarbaşıoğlu 2006). This creates a dilemma for the monetary policy of the peripheral economies. For instance, an empirical analysis by Brzoza-Brzezina et al. (2010) shows that the central banks increased their interest rates to contain the domestic credit expansion, while increasing the domestic interest rate stimulated more foreign borrowing in some Central European countries. In a similar vein, considering the rapid credit growth in some Central and East European countries, an IMF publication (Hilbers et al. 2006: par. 11) notes: "[o]pen capital accounts limit the ability of some countries [...] to use monetary policy effectively, because increasing the interest rate tends to attract capital inflows that can further boost money and credit". Indeed, one of the policy responses to rapid credit expansion in these countries was increasing their benchmark interest rates.

The asset and real estate price bubbles burst when the international financial flows shift away from the domestic economy. The periphery is subsequently more exposed to exchange rate instability and balance sheet insolvency and hence the risk of a financial and economic crisis compared with the core and with the countries at the mediocre levels of the currency hierarchy. Accordingly, the "original sin" notion and the PK notion of endogenous money complement each other in terms of understanding the periphery's boom-bust cycles.

4. Conclusion

While the PK school offers a realistic ground to approach the dynamics of the modern economies, it usually bases its theories and policy proposals upon the assumption of "normality" as defined in this chapter. In other words, its focus is on the core economies. This raises the question of concepts and policy proposals designed for the peripheral economies by the PK school. This chapter has shown that understanding the core-periphery division in the international monetary and financial system and thus the differences between the periphery and the core country contexts requires further heterodox concepts. The sound analytical basis of the PK school enables understanding the peripheral economies' dynamics, if it is applied to these countries.

References

Andrade, R.P., Prates, D.M. (2013): Exchange rate dynamics in a peripheral monetary economy, in: *Journal of Post Keynesian Economics*, 35(3), 399-416.

Avdjiev, S., McCauley, R.N., McGuire, P.M. (2012): Rapid credit growth and international credit: challenges for Asia, BIS Working Papers No. 377.

Brzoza-Brzezina, M., Chmielewski, T., Niedźwiedzińska, J. (2010): Substitution between domestic and foreign currency loans in Central Europe. Do central banks matter?, ECB, Working Paper Series No. 1187.

Camara-Neto, A.F., Vernengo, M. (2009): Beyond the original sin: a new regional financial architecture in South America, in: *Journal of Post Keynesian Economics*, 32(2), 199-212.

Carvalho, F.J.C.D. (1997): Economic policies for monetary economies. Keynes' economic policy proposals for an unemployment-free economy, in: *Revista de Economia Política*, 17(4/68), 31-51.

Cohen, B.J. (2000): *The Geography of Money*, Ithaca, NY: Cornell University Press.

Cohen, B.J. (2009): Currency and state power. Paper presented at the conference to honor to Stephen D. Krasner, Stanford University.

Davidson, P. (2011): *Post-Keynesian Macroeconomic Theory, Second Edition. A Foundation for Successful Economic Policies for the Twenty-First Century*, UK: Edward Elgar.

Dow, S. (1986): Post-Keynesian monetary theory for an open economy, in: *Journal of Post Keynesian Economics*, 9(2), 237-252.

Eichengreen, B., Hausmann, R., Panizza, U. (2002): Original sin: the pain, the mystery, and the road to redemption. Paper presented at the Currency and Maturity Matchmaking: Redeeming Debt from Original Sin, Inter-American Development Bank, Washington, D.C.

Evans, T. (2009): International finance, in: Grahl, J. (ed.), *Global Finance and Social Europe*, Cheltenham: Edward Elgar, 29-52.

Evans, T., Heine, M., Herr, H. (2007): Elements of a monetary theory of production, in: Hein, E., Truger, A. (eds.), *Money, Distribution and Economic Policy. Alternatives to Orthodox Macroeconomics*, Cheltenham: Edward Elgar.

Fields, D., Vernengo, M. (2013): Hegemonic currencies during the crisis: the dollar versus the euro in a cartalist perspective, in: *Review of International Political Economy*, 20(4), 740-759.

Fontana, G. (2004): Rethinking endogenous money: a constructive interpretation of the debate between horizontalists and structuralists, in: *Metroeconomica*, 55(4), 367-385.

Fritz, B., Prates, D.M., de Paula, L.F. (2015): Center and periphery in international monetary relations. Implications for macroeconomic policies in emerging economies, desiguALdades.net, Working Paper Series No. 80.

Glickman, M. (2003): Uncertainty, in: King, J.E. (ed.), *The Elgar Copanion to Post Keynesian Economics*, Cheltenham, UK: Edward Elgar, 366-370.

Hausmann, R. (1999): Should there be five currencies or one hundred and five?, in: *Foreign Policy,* Fall (116), 65-79.

Hausmann, R., Panizza, U. (2011): Redemption or abstinence? Original sin, currency mismatches and counter cyclical policies in the new millennium, in: *Journal of Globalization and Development,* 2(1), 1-33.

Hausmann, R., Panizza, U., Stein, E. (2002): Original sin, passthrough and fear of floating, in: Blejer, M.I., Škreb, M. (eds.), *Financial Policies in Emerging Markets,* Cambridge, Massachusetts: MIT press.

Herr, H. (1992): *Geld, Währungswettbewerb und Währungssysteme: Theoretische und Historische Analyse der Internationalen Geldwirtschaft* (Vol. 20), Frankfurt a.M.: Campus-Verlag.

Herr, H. (2008): Financial systems in developing countries and economic development, in: Hein, E., Niechoj, T., Spahn, S., Truger, A. (eds.), *Finance-Led Capitalism?: Macroeconomic Effects of Changes in The Financial Sector,* Marburg: Metropolis-Verlag.

Herr, H. (2009): The labour market in a Keynesian economic regime: theoretical debate and empirical findings, in: *Cambridge Journal of Economics,* 33(5), 949-965.

Herr, H., Hübner, K. (2005): *Währung und Unsicherheit in Der Globalen Ökonomie. Eine Geldwirtschaftliche Theorie Der Globalisierung,* Düsseldorf: Hans-Böckler-Stiftung.

Herr, H., Priewe, J. (2006): Capital account regimes and monetary policy in developing countries. Liberalisation with regulation. mimeo.

Hilbers, P., Otker-Robe, I., Pazarbaşıoğlu, C. (2006): Going too fast? Managing rapid credit growth in Central and Eastern Europe, in: *Finance & Development. A Quarterly Magazine of the IMF,* 43(1). http://www.imf.org/external/pubs/ft/fandd/2006/03/hilbers.htm

Kaldor, N. (1985): How Monetarism failed, in: *Challenge,* 28(2), 4-13.

Kaltenbrunner, A. (2011): *Currency Internationalization and Exchange Rate Dynamics in Emerging Markets: A Post-Keynesian analysis of Brazil,* (PhD Thesis), University of London, UK.

Keynes, J.M. (1936): *The General Theory of Employment, Interest and Money,* Cambridge University Press: Cambridge.

Keynes, J.M. (1937): The general theory of employment, in: *The Quarterly Journal of Economics,* 51(2), 209-223.

Keynes, J.M. (1963): On the theory of a monetary economy, in: *Nebraska Journal of Economics and Business,* 2(2), 7-9.

Kindleberger, C.P. (1967): The politics of international money and world language, Princeton University, Essays in International Finance, No. 61.

Kindleberger, C.P. (1970): *Power and Money / The Economics of International Politics and the Politics of International Economics*, London: Macmillan

Kindleberger, C.P. (1996): *Manias, Panics, and Crashes. A History of Financial Crises* (3rd ed.), Basingstoke, Hampshire; London: Macmillan.

Lavoie, M. (2003): A primer on endogenous credit-money, in: Rochon, L.-P., Rossi, S. (eds.), *Modern Theories of Money: The Nature and Role of Money in Capitalist Economies*, Cheltenham, UK: Edward Elgar.

Minsky, H.P. (1977): The financial instability hypothesis: an interpretation of Keynes and an alternative to "standard" theory, in: *Nebraska Journal of Economics and Business*, 16(1), 5-16.

Moore, B.J. (1989): The endogeneity of credit money, in: *Review of Political Economy*, 1(1), 65-93.

Moore, B.J. (2003): Endogenous money, in: King, J.E. (ed.), *The Elgar Companion to Post-Keynesian Economics*, Cheltenham, UK: Edward Elgar, 117-121.

Riese, H. (2004): Building blocks of a macro-theory of transformation, in: Holscher, J., Tomann, H. (eds.), *Money, Development and Economic Transformation: Selected Essays by Hajo Riese*, New York: Palgrave Macmillan.

Sawyer, M. (2012): Economic policy, in: King, J.E. (ed.), *The Elgar Copanion to Post Keynesian Economics* (Second ed.), Cheltenham, UK: Edward Elgar, 101ff.

Sicsú, J. (2001): Credible monetary policy: a Post Keynesian approach, in: *Journal of Post Keynesian Economics*, 23(4), 669-687.

Vernengo, M. (2006): Technology, finance, and dependency: Latin American radical political economy in retrospect, in: *Review of Radical Political Economics*, 38(4), 551-568.

Finance-dominated capitalism and its crisis in Germany: Deep recession and quick recovery – Germany as a role model?[*]

Daniel Detzer and Eckhard Hein

Introduction

In the early 2000s Germany was widely perceived as the 'sick man of Europe'. However, this image had changed already before the financial and economic crisis. Based on strong net exports in 2006 and 2007, growth in Germany had resumed and, even though the financial and economic crisis hit Germany quite heavily in 2008/09, the economy recovered remarkably fast. This fast recovery, coupled with the enduring current account surpluses turned Germany into Europe's 'economic superstar' in public opinion. It is often argued that the wage moderation starting in the mid-1990s and the labour market reforms in the early 2000s were responsible for this favourable development and that the crisis countries of the Euro area periphery should now follow the German model.[1]

In this chapter we will challenge this view taking a broader perspective and interpreting the German development against the background of 'financialisation' or 'finance-dominated capitalism', a tendency which has become

---

[*] This chapter is part of the results of the project Financialisation, Economy, Society and Sustainable Development (FESSUD). It has received funding from the European Union Seventh Framework Programme (FP7/2007-2013) under grant agreement no. 266800 (Website: www.fessud.eu). The chapter draws on Detzer/Hein (2014) and has benefitted from the discussions with Hansjörg Herr in the context of the FESSUD project. We are grateful to Luisa Bunescu for editorial assistance. Remaining errors are ours, of course.

[1] See for example Dustmann et al. (2014).

increasingly relevant for Germany since the 1990s. Whereas other countries, like the US or the UK, under the conditions of financialisation generated a 'debt-led consumption boom' type of development, Germany followed the 'export-led mercantilist' type.[2] We will show that the rise in net exports and current account surpluses starting in the early 2000s was not primarily the reward for the wage moderation and labour market reforms, but were largely due to subdued domestic demand and a resumption of external demand for specific German products. Germany's vulnerability to the worldwide financial and economic crisis can also be explained by this specific growth model. With the collapse of world trade and decreased international investment activity, export markets for German goods collapsed and dragged down the German economy in 2008/09. At the same time, global financial integration and high capital exports associated with the current account surpluses made the German financial system conducive to contagion via financial markets. The fast recovery from the crisis can be attributed to a range of domestic factors, such as the stabilising effects of fiscal policy packages, the successful containment of financial stress within a few large institutions, with the rest of the credit system still functioning well, and stable consumption demand, due to specific labour market institutions, which all coincided to keep unemployment low during the crisis. In particular, however, the quick recovery was caused by external stimulus, when emerging market economies started to resume their investment activities and ordered German capital goods on a large scale. Finally, we will argue that the German type 'export-led mercantilist' regime cannot serve as a role model for other countries for two reasons. First, the underlying structural conditions (high quality, rather price inelastic export industries) cannot easily be replicated. Second, the world is a closed economy; neo-mercantilist strategies in one country necessarily imply current account deficits in other parts of the world and hence global imbalances.

2. The pre-crisis export-led mercantilist regime in Germany

As analysed in detail in Detzer et al. (2013) and Detzer (2014a), the most important changes related to the German financial sector which then contributed to an increasing dominance of finance took place in the course of the 1990s: in 1991 the abolition of the stock exchange tax, in 1998 the legalisa-

---

[2] See, for example, Hein (2012) for the macroeconomics of finance-dominated capitalism and for a typology of related demand and growth regimes.

tion of share buybacks, in 2002 the abolition of capital gains taxes for corporations, and in 2004 the legalisation of hedge funds, among others. At the same time, many of the big banks shifted their activities from traditional commercial banking towards investment banking and the German company network was increasingly dissolved. With those changes, a much more active market for corporate control emerged, along with the establishment of new financial actors, such as hedge funds and private equity funds. The rising dominance of finance was accompanied by a considerable redistribution of income at the expense of the wage share, and of low-income households in particular, as well as by weakened investment in the capital stock (Detzer/ Hein 2014). Against this background, significant changes in real GDP growth and its composition, as well as in the trends of the financial balances of the main macroeconomic sectors could be observed.

Comparing the development of the two trade cycles from the early 1990s until the Great Recession (1993-2002 and 2003-2008) with the trade cycles before 1993, we find that average real GDP growth over the cycle slowed down considerably with the increasing dominance of finance (Table 1). Furthermore, the relevance of the growth contributions of the main demand aggregates changed significantly. Real GDP growth in the cycles of the 1960s, 1970s and 1980s was mainly driven by domestic demand, while the balance of goods and services only contributed up to 0.25 percentages points to real GDP growth, which amounted to just 10 per cent of total GDP growth. In the trade cycles of the 1990s and early 2000s, however, the growth contributions of net exports went up to 0.47 and 0.64 percentage points, respectively, which meant 33 and 40 per cent of real GDP growth.

The increasing reliance on net exports as the driver of growth since the early/mid 1990s finds its expression in the development of the financial balances of the main macroeconomic sectors (Figure 1). The financial balance of the external sector (RoW), which had turned positive in the 1990s after German re-unification, became negative in the early 2000s and decreased to -7.5 percent of nominal GDP in 2007. The current account surplus – the mirror image of the deficits of the external sector – reached thus a historically unprecedented extent.

Table 1: Real GDP growth in Germany (in per cent) and growth contributions of the main demand aggregates (in percentage points), 1961-2013, cyclical averages

	1961-1966	1967-1974	1975-1981	1982-1992	1993-2002	2003-2008	2009-2013
Real GDP growth (per cent)	4.49	3.82	2.40	2.77	1.40	1.59	0.66
Growth contribution of (percentage points)							
domestic demand including stocks	4.49	3.59	2.36	2.52	0.93	0.94	0.58
private consumption	2.47	2.25	1.55	1.42	0.72	0.28	0.60
public consumption	1.03	0.84	0.70	0.21	0.28	0.17	0.26
gross fixed capital formation	1.28	0.47	0.38	0.69	0.04	0.40	-0.10
change in inventories and net acquisition of valuables	-0.29	0.03	-0.28	0.20	-0.11	0.10	-0.19
the balance of goods and services	-0.01	0.23	0.04	0.25	0.47	0.64	0.08

Notes: The beginning of a trade cycle is given by a local minimum of annual real GDP growth, 1961-1966 and 2009-2013 are incomplete cycles.

Source: European Commission (2014), our calculations

Figure 1: Financial balances, Germany, 1980-2013 (per cent of nominal GDP)

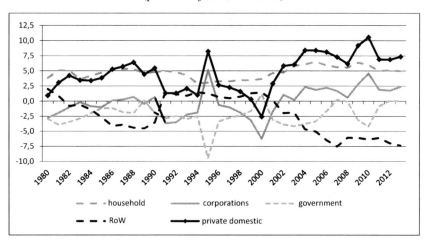

Notes: In 1995 the deficit of the 'Treuhandanstalt' was shifted from the corporate sector to the government sector. In 2000 the payments for UMTS licences from the corporate sector to the government sector are included. RoW is 'Rest of the World'.

Source: European Commission (2014), our calculations

The financial balances of the German private households have had a long tradition of being in surplus, but these surpluses increased even further in the early 2000s. Weak consumption demand and growing household saving were accompanied by weak investment in the capital stock and positive and rising financial balances of the corporate sector in this period. This meant large and increasing financial surpluses of the private sector as a whole, which were only temporarily and partly compensated by government sector deficits; the public sector was balanced in 2007, just before the Great Recession.

As can be seen from Figure 2, the main contribution to the high German current account surpluses in the early 2000s came from net exports. However, net primary incomes based on an improving net international investment position generated by rising net exports of capital contributed significantly, too.

Figure 2: Current account, Germany, 1960-2014 (per cent of GDP)

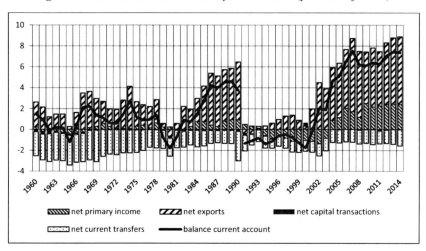

Notes: until 1990 W-Germany, from 1991 Germany; 2014 estimates
Source: European Commission (2014)

From international trade theory in general, and Thirlwall's (1979) concept of a balance of payments constrained growth rate (BPCGR) in particular, three important factors can be identified to explain the development of Germany's trade and current account balances: the price competitiveness of German producers in international markets, the development of external demand for German export goods, and the actual growth rate of domestic demand in Germany. The latter has already been touched upon above.

Considering the development of price competitiveness of the German economy with respect to different country groups (Figure 3), it is important to notice that the two periods with rapid increases in German net exports, the 1980s and the 2000s (Figure 2), were not associated with improved price competitiveness against the main trading partners. In the 1980s, price competitiveness deteriorated. And in the early 2000s it remained constant, because the improvement with respect to the other Euro area member countries was more or less compensated by a deterioration of German price competitiveness with respect to the non-Euro trading partners due to the euro appreciation.

Figure 3: Indicator of the German economy's price competitiveness against selected countries, based on the deflators of total sales, 1972-2013 (Index, March 1999 = 100)

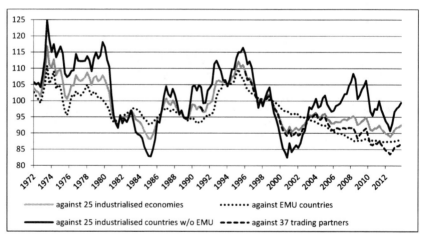

Notes: Decrease of the indicator is an increase in competitiveness, West Germany until 1990.
Source: Deutsche Bundesbank (2014)

Considering Germany's non-price competitiveness and the demand for its goods in the rest of the world, it is important to notice that Germany, unlike other developed countries, maintained a relatively high share of manufacturing in net value added before the crisis (24 per cent in 2007, France 12 per cent, UK 12 per cent, US 13 per cent (OECD 2014)). Large industrial firms, together with a vibrant sector of small and medium sized companies, have focused on the production of high quality, R&D intensive products. Additionally, in international comparison production has been heavily geared towards capital goods.[3] According to Jannsen/Kooths (2012) this focus on top quality segments of R&D intensive products has provided German exporters with high non-price competitiveness, an argument which is supported by the analyses by Botta (2014) and Simonazzi et al. (2013) on the production structure of the German economy in comparison to other Euro area countries. Storm/Naastepad (2015) relate this high quality production to the resilience of the German corporatist model, which they claim still exists, despite political attempts to alter its structure during the 1990s and the early 2000s (Agenda 2010, Hartz Laws). And due to its focus on capital goods, Germany can particularly benefit from growth in countries that are 'catching up', with high rates of investment in capital goods.

Figure 4 shows the development of gross fixed capital formation in different regions of the world from 1980 until 2014. As can easily be seen, comparing Figure 2 and Figure 4, the accelerations of German net exports in the 1980s and the 2000s highly correlate with an acceleration of worldwide investment expenditures: After a relatively stagnant phase in the beginning of the 1980s,

Figure 4: Gross fixed capital formation for different country groups (Billion US-Dollar (lhs), in per cent (rhs))

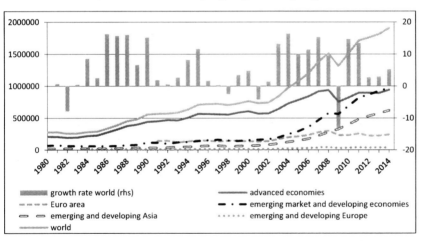

Source: International Monetary Fund (2014), own calculations

---

[3] The share of investment goods production in total value added in 2007 for Germany was about 15 per cent, Japan was at only 12 per cent, Spain 6 per cent, US 5 per cent, UK 5 per cent (Grömling 2014). See also European Commission (2010a).

worldwide investment picked up in 1984, which allowed Germany to strongly increase net exports. A similar pattern can be observed when worldwide gross capital formation picked up rapidly in 2002.

Our simple data inspection suggests that it is the non-price competitiveness of German exports and the dynamics in the trading partner countries – relative to modest domestic demand growth in Germany – which explain the pattern of German net exports much better than the development of German price competitiveness. This finding is in line with recent econometric results by Schröder (2011) and Storm/Naastepad (2015) who only find insignificant or very small effects of price competitiveness on German exports and hence on the trade balance in their estimations, in particular if relative unit labour cost growth is taken as an indicator for price competitiveness. According to these results, the development of the German trade balance is almost completely explained by foreign demand driving export, and domestic demand determining imports.[4] These findings contradict the exclusive focus of some heterodox authors, like Flassbeck/Lapavitsas (2013), on relative unit labour cost dynamics when it comes to the explanation of German export surpluses and intra-Euro area current account imbalances.

Summing up, under the conditions of increasing dominance of finance since the mid-1990s, weak investment in the capital stock, redistribution of income at the expense of labour and low income households, structural reform policies raising the degree of uncertainty and further dampening private consumption and investment, and overall restrictive macroeconomic policies,[5] the German economy suffered from weak domestic demand growth in the period before the financial crisis. Under these conditions, rising net exports became the main driver of demand and growth. Contrary to public and political opinion before the financial and economic crises, this German 'export-led mercantilist' model was as fragile as the 'debt-led consumption boom' type of development in the US, the UK and other countries. The moderate growth rates experienced in Germany were highly dependent on the dynamic growth of export markets, and hence on an expansion of the world economy. A collapse of the latter would therefore have major effects on

---

[4] See also the overview table in Storm/Naastepad (2015: 15) on further studies supporting the very low relative unit labour cost elasticities of German exports. See also Arghyrou/Chortareas (2008), European Commission (2010b), Gabrisch/Staehr (2014) and Schröder (2015) with similar results for current account imbalances in the EU or the Euro area.

[5] See Bibow (2005), Herr/Kazandziska (2011) and Hein/Truger (2007, 2009) for extensive analyses of the macroeconomic policy stance in Germany during the 1990s and the early 2000s.

German growth, in particular. At the same time, increasing capital exports to more dynamic economies carried the risk of contagion in the case of a financial crisis in these markets.

3. Deep recession – quick recovery

The 2008/09 recession in Germany proved to be particularly strong (Figure 5). This was mainly due to the fact that the export-led mercantilist German economy was particularly hard-hit by the global slowdown and the dramatic decline in export demand. Despite the deep recession, the loss in employment and the corresponding increase in the unemployment rate were much smaller (Figure 5). This can be partially explained by a dramatic rise in short-time work, heavily subsidised by the government, and the extensive use of so-called working-time accounts, allowing firms to flexibly adjust their labour volume without sacking workers (OECD 2010; SVR 2009b; Will 2011). After the large drop in GDP in 2009, growth picked up strongly in 2010 and 2011 and the unemployment rate fell to levels recently experienced only during the reunification boom.

Figure 5: Real GDP growth, growth contributions and unemployment rate, Germany, 2007-2014 (in percentage points (lhs), in per cent (rhs))

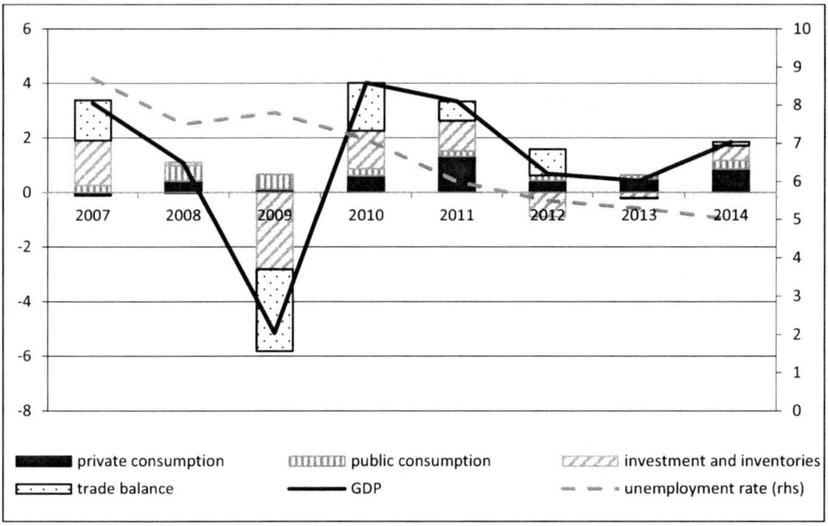

Source: European Commission (2014)

In line with our analysis so far, the German Council of Economic Experts has identified two main channels through which the crisis was transmitted into the German economy (SVR 2009a): the foreign trade channel and the financial market channel. The foreign trade channel became particularly effective because of the rapid increase in German dependence on exports and the specialisation in more volatile sectors and products (investment goods and cars in particular).

Of course, the financial transmission channel of the crisis into Germany was closely related to the rapidly increasing German current account surpluses in the course of the early 2000s. Net foreign financial assets held by German wealth owners rapidly increased up to 700 billion euro in 2007 (SVR 2009a: 91). Most of these foreign assets were held by German banks such that the ratio of foreign assets to equity of the German banking sector increased tremendously. While the entire foreign exposure stood at about 2.7 times banks' equity in 1995, it had increased to 7.6 times at the end of 2007. Correspondingly, German banks had to bear heavy losses when problems occurred internationally. The write-offs of large German financial institutions (banks and insurance companies) directly related to the financial crisis amounted to 102 billion euros in the period from 2007 to August 2009 (SVR 2009a).

Germany's quick recovery from the crisis depended on three main favourable factors: the successful containment of the crisis in the financial sector, macroeconomic policies supporting recovery and rising exports once again stimulating aggregate demand.

The losses in the financial sector rather swiftly translated into problems at large major banking institutions in Germany. First, public or partly public, then also increasingly private institutions were threatened with insolvency. However, the German government intervened on a massive scale to contain the problems in the financial sector, providing guarantees of up to €168 billion euros. It also recapitalised banks with almost €30 billion euros and allowed them to transfer their toxic assets to government-owned 'bad banks'. These interventions contributed to the stabilisation of the German financial sector and the avoidance of a widespread banking crisis in Germany. Furthermore, the diverse structure of the German banking sector in which public, cooperative and private banks as well as regionally, nationally and internationally active banks coexist helped to prevent a banking crisis and no widespread credit crunch undermined the recovery (Detzer 2014b).

Macroeconomic policies, and here in particular fiscal policies, also helped to stabilise the German economy. Regarding monetary policy, the ECB took over its role as a lender of last resort. Consistently low interest rates since

2011 have favoured Euro area member countries, and in particular countries like Germany, where economic expansion had already resumed.

Wage policies did not actively help to stabilise the German economy during the crisis. The compensation per employee only increased by 0.1 per cent in the crisis year 2009. However, a normalisation of compensation growth in the years 2010 (2.4 per cent), 2011 (3 per cent), 2012 (2.6 per cent), 2013 (2 per cent), compared to the years before the crisis, helped stabilising private consumption demand (OECD 2014).

It was therefore fiscal policy which mainly contributed to the quick recovery, reacting in a remarkably counter-cyclical way. After some hesitation and some merely 'cosmetic' measures, in the first months of 2009 a substantial stimulus package for 2009 and 2010 was enacted. Overall, the measures included substantial increases in public investment, as well as tax relief for business and households. The cumulative stimulus for 2009 and 2010 amounted to 3.1 per cent of 2008 GDP, which was certainly above the Euro area average level (OECD 2009; Hein/Truger 2010).

Despite these stabilisation measures, looking at quarterly data, the recovery in 2010 only set in after a resumption of export demand (Statistisches Bundesamt 2014). Demand and growth in Germany after the crisis, in particular between 2010 and 2012, were then again largely driven by net exports (Figure 5), stimulated by the recovery of the world economy (Figure 4).

However, this German type of recovery suffers from two major drawbacks. First, to the extent that it was driven by net exports, it relied on the neomercantilist type of development that had considerably contributed to world and regional imbalances and to the severity of the crisis in Germany in the first place. It therefore contains the seeds for further imbalances, fragilities and future vulnerabilities of the German economy, and it contributes significantly to the still persistent euro crisis (Cesaratto/Stirati 2010; Hein 2013/14). Second, as a political precondition for the German fiscal stimulus packages, the so-called 'debt brake' was introduced into the German constitution and has been imposed on the other Euro area member countries as well. This will severely limit the room for manoeuvre for German fiscal policy in the future, prevent current account rebalancing and constrain aggregate demand management in the Euro area as a whole (Hein/Truger 2014).

4. Conclusion: Germany should not be seen as a role model!

On the surface, it seems that Germany has transformed from Europe's 'sick man' to Europe's 'economic superstar'. This view is based on the strong export performance and Germany's quick recovery from the Great Recession. Many have related these successes to the wage moderation and the labour market reforms in the 1990s and early 2000s.

We have challenged this view and have examined the German development against the background of worldwide tendencies towards financialisation, which has become increasingly apparent in Germany since the mid-1990s. In this process, Germany has become one of the major 'export-led mercantilist' economies at the global scale.

The German economy has benefitted in particular from high non-price competitiveness, which provides a favourable position when world demand is strong. Therefore, when global investment demand picked up in the early 2000s, wage moderation policies, restrictive macroeconomic policies, and hence low private and public consumption, as well as weak public investment, together with the dampening effects of finance dominance on private investment in the capital stock, contributed to depress domestic economic activity and demand for imports, while growing activity in the rest of the world stimulated export growth, explaining the widely praised export performance of Germany. However, actual growth performance remained well behind several other developed countries.

This specific integration of Germany into the world economy explains to a large extent the transmission of the international financial and economic crisis to Germany, which was more severely affected than other countries, in particular through the international trade channel. But the specific German mercantilist export-led type of development, relying on high-quality exports, also provided the necessary conditions for a speedy recovery, as soon as world demand accelerated again. Rapid stabilisation of the financial sector and, in particular, active counter-cyclical fiscal policies contributed to this quick recovery, which was reinforced by the expansionary monetary policies of the ECB.

This German type of recovery suffers from two major drawbacks. First, it continues to rely on the neo-mercantilist type of development that has considerably contributed to world and regional imbalances, to the severity of the crisis in Germany itself, and also to the ongoing euro crisis. Second, as a political price for the active fiscal policies in the course of the crisis, Germany – and, under the pressure of Germany, the Euro area member countries – have either agreed to or have already implemented 'debt brakes' into their constitutions. This will mean highly constrained rooms for manoeuvre in future crises.

We can finally conclude that, on the one hand, Germany's extraordinary export performance and quick recovery from the crisis should not be attributed to the supposed benefits of the wage moderation and labour market flexibilisation of the 1990s and the 2000s. Instead, the performance seems to be based on high non-price competitiveness of German exports, and the industrial and institutional structure on which this has relied, in particular the specific corporatist German model, which seems to have survived in the export industries. It is based on long-term employment for core workers, which allows gaining firm-specific human capital, relatively decent wages for those core workers, participation of labour in decision making processes at the firm level, and still strong unions and employer organisations in this area. However, even if the German export model survives further liberalisation and financialisation pressures, it remains highly vulnerable. Another phase of stagnating worldwide investment activity will constrain the demand for German exports, and severely curtail prospects for growth.

Finally, this German type 'export-led mercantilist' regime cannot serve as a role model for other countries for two reasons. First, the underlying structural conditions (high quality, rather price inelastic export industries) cannot easily be replicated. Second, the world is a closed economy; neo-mercantilist strategies in one country necessarily imply current account deficits in other parts of the world and hence global imbalances.

References

Arghyrou, M.G., Chortareas, G. (2008): Current account imbalances and real exchange rates in the Euro area, in: *Review of International Economics*, 16, 747-765.

Bibow, J. (2005): Germany in crisis: The unification challenge, macroeconomic policy shocks and traditions, and EMU, in: *International Review of Applied Economics*, 19, 29-50.

Botta, A. (2014): Structural asymmetries at the roots of the Eurozone crisis: What's new for industrial policy in the EU?, in: *PSL Quarterly Review*, 67, 169-216.

Cesaratto, S., Stirati, A. (2010): Germany and the European and global crises, in: *International Journal of Political Economy*, 39(4), 56-86.

Detzer, D. (2014a): Inequality and the financial system – the case of Germany, Global Labour University Working Paper 23, The Global Labour University.

Detzer, D. (2014b): The German financial system and the financial crisis, in: *Intereconomics*, 49(2), 56-64.

Detzer, D., Dodig, N., Evans, T., Hein, E., Herr, H. (2013): The German financial system, FESSUD Studies in Financial Systems 3, University of Leeds.

Detzer, D., Hein, E. (2014): Financialisation and the financial and economic crises: The case of Germany, FESSUD Studies in Financial Systems 18, University of Leeds.

Deutsche Bundesbank (2014): Time Series Data Base, available at: http://www.bundes bank.de/Navigation/EN/Statistics/Time_series_databases/time_series_databases. html

Dustmann, C., Fitzenberger, B., Schönberg, U., Spitz-Oener, A. (2014): From sick man of Europe to economic superstar: Germany's resurgent economy, in: *Journal of Economic Perspectives*, 28, 167-188.

European Commission (2010a): Surveillance of intra-Euro-area competitiveness and imbalances, in: *European Economy*, 1/2010, Brussels: European Commission, Directorate-General for Economic and Financial Affairs.

European Commission (2010b): The impact of the global crisis on competitiveness and current account divergences in the euro area, Quarterly Report on the Euro Area, 9(1).

European Commission (2014): AMECO Database, Spring, available at: http://ec.euro pa.eu/economy_finance/db_indicators/ameco/index_en.htm.

Flassbeck, H., Lapavitsas, C. (2013): *The Systemic Crisis of the Euro – True Causes and Effective Therapies*, Berlin: Rosa Luxemburg Foundation.

Gabrisch, H., Staehr, K. (2014): The Euro Plus Pact: Cost competitiveness and external capital flows in the EU countries, Working Paper Series No. 1650, Frankfurt: European Central Bank.

Grömling, M. (2014): A supply-side explanation for current account imbalances, in: *Intereconomics*, 49, 30-35.

Hein, E. (2012): *The Macroeconomics of Finance-dominated Capitalism – and its Crisis*, Cheltenham: Edward Elgar.

Hein, E. (2013/14): The crisis of finance-dominated capitalism in the euro area, deficiencies in the economic policy architecture, and deflationary stagnation policies, in: *Journal of Post Keynesian Economics*, 36, 325-354.

Hein, E., Truger, A. (2007): Germany's post-2000 stagnation in the European context – a lesson in macroeconomic mismanagement, in: Arestis, P., Hein, E., Le Heron, E. (eds.), *Aspects of Modern Monetary and Macroeconomic Policies*, Basingstoke: Palgrave Macmillan.

Hein, E., Truger, A. (2009): How to fight (or not to fight) a slowdown, in: *Challenge: The Magazine of Economic Affairs*, 52(3), 52-75.

Hein, E., Truger, A. (2010): Financial crisis, global recession and macroeconomic policy reactions – the case of Germany, in: Dullien, S., Hein, E., Truger, A., van Treeck, T. (eds.), *The World Economy in Crisis – The Return of Keynesianism?*, Marburg: Metropolis.

Hein, E., Truger, A. (2014): Fiscal policy and rebalancing in the euro area: A critique of the German debt brake from a post-Keynesian perspective, in: *Panoeconomicus*, 61, 21-38.

Herr, H., Kazandziska, M. (2011): *Macroeconomic Policy Regimes in Western Industrial Countries*, Abingdon: Routledge.

International Monetary Fund (2014): World Economic Outlook Database, April, available at: http://www.imf.org/external/pubs/ft/weo/2014/01/weodata/index.aspx.

Jannsen, N., Kooths, S. (2012): German trade performance in times of slumping euro area markets, in: *Intereconomics*, 47, 368-372.

OECD (2009): *Economic Outlook, Interim Report*, Paris: OECD Publishing.

OECD (2010): *OECD Employment Outlook: Moving beyond the Job Crisis*, Paris: OECD Publishing.

OECD (2014): OECD.StatExtracts, available at: http,//stats.oecd.org/Index.aspx.

Schröder, E. (2011): Trade balances in Germany and the United States: Demand dominates price, Paper presented at the 15th conference of the Research Network Macroeconomics and Macroeconomic Policies (FMM), From crisis to growth? The challenge of imbalances, debt, and limited resources, October 27-29.

Schröder, E. (2015): Eurozone imbalances: Measuring the contribution of expenditure growth and expenditure switching, Working Paper 08/2015, Department of Economics, The New School for Social Research, New York.

Simonazzi, A., Ginzburg, A., Nocella, G. (2013): Economic relations between Germany and southern Europe, in: *Cambridge Journal of Economics*, 37, 653-675.

Statistisches Bundesamt (2014): Genesis-Online Data Base, Mai, available at: https://www-genesis.destatis.de/genesis/online.

Storm, S., Naastepad, C.W.M. (2015): Crisis and recovery in the German economy: The real lessons, in: *Structural Change and Economic Dynamics*, 32, 11-24.

SVR (2009a): *Deutschland im Internationalen Konjunkturzusammenhang. Expertise im Auftrag der Bundesregierung*, Wiesbaden: Statistisches Bundesamt.

SVR (2009b): *Die Zukunft nicht aufs Spiel setzen, Jahresgutachten 2009/10*, Wiesbaden: Statistisches Bundesamt.

Thirlwall, A.P. (1979): The balance of payments constraint as an explanation of international growth differences, in: *Banca Nazionale del Lavoro Quarterly Review*, 32, 45-53.

Will, H. (2011): Germany's short time compensation program: Macroeconom(etr)ic insight, IMK Working Paper 1/2011, Macroeconomic Policy Institute (IMK) at Hans Boeckler Foundation.

Saving 'decent capitalism': An emergency programme for fiscal policy in the Euro area[*]

Achim Truger

1. Introduction

In an important strand of his comprehensive research Hansjörg Herr – together with different co-authors – has spelled out the institutional features and the main economic policy conditions that define functional macroeconomic policy regimes from a Keynesian perspective (Heine/Herr/Kaiser 2006; Herr/Kazandziska 2011). More recently he has become preoccupied with the concept of a 'decent capitalism' as a blueprint for reforming economies in both an economically and socially beneficial manner (Dullien/Herr/Kellermann 2011). Most certainly, macroeconomic policy – and above all fiscal policy – in most Euro area countries have been characterised by almost the exact opposite of a functional macroeconomic policy regime: Since 2010 fiscal policy has been dominated by strict austerity measures implemented under the 'reformed' Stability and Growth Pact (SGP) and the 'fiscal compact' (FC). From a Keynesian perspective the outcome in terms of devastating economic, social and political consequences was predictable (Truger 2013).

Since summer 2014 the calls for a more expansionary fiscal policy in the euro area have become louder: In his Jackson Hole speech, Mario Draghi called for a more expansionary fiscal stance for the Euro area as a whole and a public investment programme insisting, however, that the existing rules of the SGP be respected. The European Council in June 2014 also saw the need to enhance growth, respecting, however, the current institutional framework.

---

[*] This contribution is partly based on Truger (2015a) and uses numerical results from Truger and Nagel (2016).

Against this background the central question is whether the existing institutional framework – that has even severely been tightened by the reforms of the SGP and the Fiscal Compact (European Commission 2013: 13-42) – still allows for a fiscal expansion strong enough to spark off a recovery in the stagnating Euro area economy. Without such a recovery, the Euro area economy and with it Hansjörg's project of a 'decent capitalism' is doomed. The current contribution, however, argues that there is substantial leeway for expansionary fiscal policies provided that the European Commission is willing to make use of the technical and interpretational leeway that is inherent in the central ambiguous concepts of the current framework.

In order to show this, section 2 briefly shows the incredible degree of austerity in the Euro area and how it is related to the concept of cyclical adjustment of public finances that is used by the European Commission. Section 3 argues that the European Commission recent strategy is insufficient before section 4 sketches a more ambitious re-interpretation of the SGP drawing on section 2. Section 5 briefly concludes.

2. Cyclical adjustment of public finances and austerity

The cyclical adjustment of public finances plays a major role in the European Commission's concept of budgetary surveillance within the framework of the SGP (Larch/Turrini 2010). With the exception of the excessive deficit threshold, all target values for the government budget balance are expressed in terms of structural, i.e. cyclically adjusted, values, and the cyclical condition of the economy plays a major role in assessing the necessary consolidation effort and potential exceptions. The most important concept in this respect is the structural budget balance, i.e. the cyclically adjusted government budget balance corrected for one-off measures in terms of which the consolidation requirements under the SGP and the FC are expressed.

The main problem is that the method employed by the EU Commission has proven to be highly sensitive to an endogeneity bias, i.e. the problem that potential output is highly sensitive to variations in actual output (see e.g. Klär 2013; Truger/Will 2013). During economic contractions – especially during large and durable contractions such as those observed in the Euro crisis – the estimates of potential output are revised substantially downwards.

Table 1: *Output gap in % of potential GDP, EMU-12 countries 2007-2015 with potential GDP growth of EU Commission's fall 2015 forecast compared to EU Commission's spring 2010 forecast*

	Output gap with potential GDP from EU Commission fall 2015							
	2007	2008	2009	2010	2011	2012	2013	2014	2015
Austria	2.0	2.0	-2.7	-1.7	0.4	0.4	-0.3	-0.8	-0.9
Belgium	3.3	2.6	-1.3	0.0	0.2	-0.6	-1.1	-1.0	-1.2
Euro area (12 countries)	2.5	1.6	-3.4	-2.0	-1.1	-2.2	-3.0	-2.7	-2.0
Finland	4.6	3.7	-5.1	-2.5	-0.2	-1.6	-2.8	-2.8	-2.4
France	3.1	1.8	-2.1	-1.2	-0.2	-0.8	-1.4	-2.0	-1.8
Germany	1.6	1.6	-4.7	-1.6	0.8	0.0	-1.1	-0.9	-0.7
Greece	5.2	4.2	0.5	-3.0	-8.8	-11.6	-11.9	-8.6	-5.6
Ireland	6.0	1.7	-4.6	-4.8	-2.7	-4.0	-5.5	-3.7	-3.7
Italy	2.2	1.0	-4.2	-2.2	-1.6	-3.3	-4.2	-3.9	-3.1
Luxembourg	3.9	1.2	-6.0	-2.7	-2.4	-4.9	-5.0	-4.8	-4.0
Netherlands	1.5	1.8	-2.5	-2.0	-1.1	-3.0	-3.9	-3.6	-2.9
Portugal	1.0	0.5	-2.5	-0.7	-2.1	-4.9	-5.6	-4.4	-2.9
Spain	3.1	1.3	-3.3	-4.3	-5.3	-6.8	-7.2	-5.5	-2.9
	Output gap with potential GDP from EU Commission spring 2010							
	2007	2008	2009	2010	2011	2012	2013	2014	2015
Austria	3.9	3.3	-2.2	-1.3	0.3	-0.5	-2.1	-3.7	-4.7
Belgium	3.1	2.5	-1.4	-0.1	0.4	-0.6	-1.5	-1.6	-1.7
Euro area (12 countries)	2.4	1.4	-3.9	-2.7	-2.2	-4.2	-6.1	-6.8	-6.9
Finland	7.2	5.2	-5.2	-3.0	-1.8	-4.5	-7.1	-8.6	-9.7
France	1.0	-0.5	-4.2	-3.9	-3.0	-3.8	-4.8	-5.8	-6.1
Germany	2.8	2.9	-3.7	-0.6	1.7	0.4	-1.1	-1.1	-0.9
Greece	3.0	1.1	-3.7	-8.9	-17.5	-23.3	-26.7	-26.7	-26.8
Ireland	2.2	-2.1	-7.9	-8.0	-5.7	-7.7	-10.2	-9.1	-9.0
Italy	2.1	0.5	-4.9	-3.5	-3.5	-6.9	-9.5	-11.0	-11.7
Luxembourg	7.5	-0.3	-8.7	-4.8	-4.6	-7.6	-9.0	-9.5	-9.6
Netherlands	3.3	3.0	-2.3	-2.0	-1.6	-4.5	-6.9	-8.0	-8.4
Portugal	3.9	3.0	-0.2	1.4	-0.9	-6.0	-8.8	-9.6	-9.6
Spain	1.3	0.6	-4.2	-4.9	-5.9	-8.8	-11.3	-11.7	-10.9

Source: Truger/Nagel (2016: 240-241) based on European Commission (2010, 2014a, 2014b, 2015a, 2015b)

In this contribution the spring 2010 forecast is used as a baseline, because at the time potential GDP estimates had already been revised downwards very substantially.[1] At the same time, most Euro area economies were recovering, before in the summer of 2010, a switch to austerity in the Euro area was decided (Blyth 2013). Table 1 shows the Commission's autumn 2015 estimates of the EMU-12 states' output gaps and contrasts them with the output gaps that would have been estimated had the spring 2010 potential GDP forecasts remained unchanged. Obviously, from 2013 to 2015, for almost all countries, with the exception of Germany, the output gap would have been substantially higher had it not been for the crisis induced downward revision of potential GDP since spring 2010.

Figure 1a: General government structural primary budget balance* in the Euro area, the European Periphery and selected countries in per cent of GDP, 2007-2015

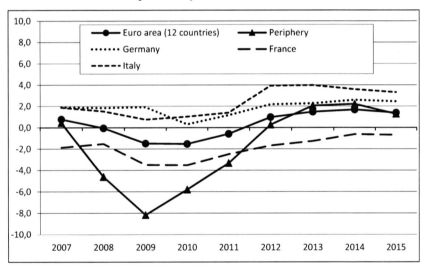

* Due to the revision of the national accounts to ESA 2010 the EU Commission no longer publishes structural balances for years before 2010 since the autumn 2010 economic forecast as the one-off measures have not yet been revised. In the calculations we use the unrevised values for the one-off measures to calculate the structural balances.

Source: Truger/Nagel (2016: 242) based on European Commission (2010, 2014a, 2014b, 2015a, 2015b)

---

[1] For the exact methodology of the calculations see Truger and Nagel (2016: 238-241).

Figure 1b: General government structural primary budget balance*
(with potential output as of EU Commission 2010 forecast)
for the Euro area, the European Periphery and selected countries in
per cent of GDP, 2007-2015

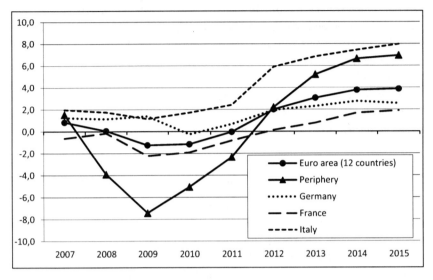

* Due to the revision of the national accounts to ESA 2010 the EU Commission no longer publishes structural balances for years before 2010 since the autumn 2010 economic forecast as the one-off measures have not yet been revised. In the calculatioplease find enclosed anns we use the unrevised values for the one-off measures to calculate the structural balances.

Source: Truger/Nagel (2016: 243) based on European Commission (2010, 2014a, 2014b, 2015a, 2015b)

Such dramatic downward revisions of potential GDP have substantial consequences for the calculation of structural budget balances and the assessment of consolidation efforts. These efforts will usually be underestimated because a substantial part of the fiscal effort is wiped out, as a larger part of the actual deficit is registered as structural although in fact it may well just be cyclical, i.e. caused by a temporary contraction. Figures 1a and 1b illustrate the point: Based on the official commission estimates (Figure 1a) the cumulative fiscal effort as measured by the change in the structural primary budget balance in the EMU-12 from 2009 to 2015 was about 3 per cent of GDP. For the countries in the periphery (Greece, Ireland, Portugal and Spain) the respective number was about 9 per cent of GDP. This is already an extreme degree of austerity. However, correcting for the potential output revision the estimate for the fiscal effort increases to 5.5 per cent and almost 15 per cent of GDP for the EMU-12 and the periphery, respectively (Figure 1b).

The European Commission already had to admit that the estimates of the fiscal effort based on the change in the structural (primary) budget balance tend to underestimate the true discretionary consolidation efforts and has developed complementary indicators to assess fiscal effort (European Commission 2013: 101-132 as well as Carnot/de Castro 2015). Using the results by Carnot and de Castro (2015: 10) the traditional estimate of fiscal effort underestimates discretionary fiscal effort for Portugal by 20 per cent, for Ireland by 45 per cent, for Spain by almost 75 per cent and for Greece by almost 90 per cent (see similarly Darvas et al. 2014: 10-15). It is obvious that such radical austerity necessarily has devastating economic and social consequences.

3. The EU Commission's insufficient strategy for fiscal stimulus

The European Commission led by president Jean-Claude Juncker has launched two initiatives to boost the economy. First, an Investment Plan for Europe, the 'Juncker-Plan' and second a re-interpretation of the SGP with the aim of providing more fiscal leeway for member states under adverse economic conditions and/or implementing structural reforms (European Commission 2014c and 2015c).

The Juncker-Plan aims at a European-wide total investment impact of 315 bn. Euros from 2015 to 2017. This is supposed to be reached by the creation of a European Fund for Strategic Investments (EFSI) which is guaranteed by 21 bn. Euros from the EU budget (16 bn. through reallocation from existing resources) and EIB reserves (5 bn.). The fund is to mobilise finance for investments in key areas such as infrastructure, education, research and innovation. Whether the Plan will really deliver is quite doubtful. The most important doubts relate to the question whether it will be possible to mobilise sufficient additional investment: If it is to stimulate private investment, particularly in the crisis countries it will be difficult to find investors almost irrespective of the terms of the programme due to pessimistic expectations. If investors are found, the danger of windfall gains will be large. If the fund offers private investors attractive returns then these returns will have to be paid for, either directly by the public contributor involved or indirectly through charges to the private sector that might otherwise have been avoided. If the fund is to stimulate public investment, one may wonder why this could not be realized by national governments' regular investment. All in all, therefore, the risk is high that the Investment Plan for Europe will deliver disappointingly little too late.

The clarifications and formalisations of the interpretation of the SGP contain several measures. All in all, they constitute some progress. They may contribute to relieve the pressure from public budgets and slow down the pace of consolidation somewhat, but obviously they are designed to permit only a slightly less restrictive fiscal stance but not to provide a truly positive fiscal stimulus.

4. Towards a more ambitious re-interpretation of the SGP

Of course, the current institutional framework with the SGP and the FC does not generally provide a favourable climate for a more expansionary fiscal policy. As in the short run major institutional reforms do not seem likely, alternative means will have to be found within the existing framework. If the Commission used the interpretational leeway that the current institutions afford, it would create substantial additional room for manoeuvre for national governments to switch to a truly expansionary fiscal policy. Indeed, the (too timid, see section 3) clarification by the Commission in relation to making optimal use of the flexibility can be seen as hinting at the direction that would need to be followed. It would at some points simply need a few further interpretational steps to enable a substantial fiscal boost. At least the following eight measures that are generally complementary to each other could be considered (see table 2).

Table 2: Eight ways to strengthen investment and facilitate an expansionary overall fiscal policy stance in Europe

(1) more active use of the 'investment clause'
(2) allow for temporary investment programmes (analogous to EFSI)
(3) interpret temporary investment programmes as structural reforms
(4) incorporate realistic investment multiplier in budgetary analysis ex ante
(5) use leeway in economically bad times
(6) use exception for severe downturn in EU or Euro area
(7) temporarily higher spending with a view to Europe 2020 goals
(8) implement better methods of cyclical adjustment

Source: author's compilation

There are at least four possibilities to explicitly strengthen public investment within the current fiscal framework (measures 1 to 4). Strengthening public investment should be of the highest priority: It is particularly conducive to growth both in the short and the long run (see Truger 2015b: chapter 3) and has suffered from austerity policies in a disproportionally strong manner (Barbiero/Darvas 2014).

First, the so-called 'investment clause' should at least be opened to unconditionally include all investment that is supported by European funds as was called for by the European Parliament (measure 1). Furthermore, additional net investment could be justified if it came in the form of a temporary investment programme, analogous to the way the Commission interprets contributions to the EFSI (measure 2). Additionally or alternatively, it may also be possible to treat a sufficiently comprehensive investment programme as a structural reform that temporarily allows for deviations from MTO or the adjustment path towards it (measure 3). All of this could further be supported if realistic multiplier values were used when assessing the budgetary impact of additional investment, which may not be significantly negative or even positive. This would mean that such additional investment could be irrelevant at least under the excessive deficit procedure as it would (almost) not increase the deficit: If the Commission adopted a realistic attitude to fiscal multipliers that was in line with the recent literature (see Gechert 2015), any increase in public (investment) spending would lead to a much smaller increase in the deficit due to its positive macroeconomic effects. Spending multipliers – especially for public investment – can be assumed to be well above one which means that such spending increases will be self-financing to a substantial extent (e.g. 50-75%).

In addition to the four measures specifically addressing public investment there are at least four more that could justify a more expansionary fiscal policy stance, be it to (further) promote public investment or other preferred stimulus measures (measures 5-8). For example, reference to adverse cyclical conditions may help to increase fiscal leeway even further (measure 5), although this could create the danger of a stop-and-go policy, if cyclical conditions improve as can be expected under a stimulus programme. Probably the most convincing way to avoid this would be to use the provision concerning a severe downturn in the Euro area or the EU to justify a temporary deviation from the consolidation path, thus allowing for a substantial European stimulus programme (measure 6). The Commission has explicitly made a comparison with the 2008 European Economic Recovery Plan (European Commission 2008) to give an example of the potential use of this provision (European Commission 2015c: 17). One option for the direction of the programme would be to use it in order to start phasing in traditional public investment. Alternatively or additionally, it could also be used to allow for spending needs beyond the narrow national accounts definition of public investment (measure 7). This could be investment in education, including child care, but it could more generally focus on spending with a view to achieving the currently neglected Europe 2020 goals that have strongly suffered from austerity over the last years (Aiginger 2014).

Last, but not least, a reconsideration of the European Commission's method of cyclical adjustment (measure 8) would help tremendously as it would increase the cyclical part of the budget deficit thus reducing the structural deficit. This could lead to a much more adequate indicator of the fiscal effort that has already been undertaken by the member states which in turn would make it easier to justify exceptional circumstances under both the preventive and the corrective arm. The upward revision of (negative) output gaps (table 1) would underline the extremely bad cyclical condition in which many member states are trapped. It not justified to assume (as the Commission does) that the Greek output gap in 2015 was only be -5.6% when the Greek economy has lost about a quarter of its pre-crisis output. Finally, the estimates of the structural budget balance would then be revised upwards lifting a number of member states above their MTOs so that they would enjoy additional leeway. For example, as table 3 shows, in addition to Germany, Italy, the Netherlands, Austria and Finland would already have reached their MTOs in 2015 if the structural balance had been calculated with the potential growth estimates of the pre-austerity-era in spring 2010. And for almost all other countries the distance to their MTOs would have been reduced substantially. For some countries still subject to an excessive deficit procedure like Spain, Portugal and France the justification for such a procedure would be weakened as they would have reached their MTOs. How can they fulfil the MTO criterion while at the same time having excessive deficits?

Table 3: output gap, structural budget balance (EU Commission fall 2015 estimate and modification) 2015 and medium term objective for 12 Euro area countries in % of GDP

	Output gap 2015 (Commission)	Output gap 2015 (modification)	Structural balance 2015 (Commission)	Structural balance 2015 (modification)	Medium term objective (MTO)
Austria	-0.9	-4.7	-0.6	1.7	-0.45
Belgium	-1.2	-1.7	-2.5	-2.1	0.75
Euro area (12 countr.)	**-2.0**	**-6.9**	**-1.1**	**1.4**	**-0.3**[1]
Finland	-2.4	-9.7	-1.7	2.4	0
France	-1.8	-6.1	-2.7	-0.2	-0.4
Germany	-0.7	-0.9	0.9	1.0	-0.5
Greece	-5.6	-26.8	-1.1	9.3	0
Ireland	-3.7	-9.0	-3.0	-0.2	0
Italy	-3.1	-11.7	-1.0	3.7	0
Luxembourg	-4.0	-9.6	0.7	3.2	0.5
Netherlands	-2.9	-8.4	-1.1	2.6	-0.5
Portugal	-2.9	-9.6	-1.8	1.6	-0.5
Spain	-2.9	-10.9	-2.5	2.4	–
[1] weighted average of available values.					

Source: Truger/Nagel (2016: 250) based on European Commission (2010a, 2014a, 2014b, 2015a, 2015b, 2015d)

Taking all of the proposals for a more expansionary interpretation of the existing institutional framework together, a Euro area-wide expansionary fiscal stance of two to three per cent of GDP would be quite realistic. This would not solve all of the Euro area's economic problems and would have to be accompanied by measures addressing the current account imbalances, but it would be a major step forward shifting the focus to the pressing macroeconomic questions and away from the useless debate about 'structural reforms'.

5. Conclusion

Most parts of the Euro area have seen seven years of deep economic crisis. Austerity policies have played a major role in this economic, social and political tragedy which is also totally against the spirit of Hansjörg Herr's 'decent capitalism'. The EU must address these problems. The previous strategy of tightening the fiscal constraints of the SGP was wrong as it has almost completely disempowered national fiscal policy as a macroeconomic policy instrument. In the current situation, with still depressed aggregate demand, tendencies of deflationary stagnation and monetary policy at the lower bound, fiscal policy is the only instrument that could bring about a sustained recovery.

In the medium to long run the Euro area and the EU will probably need a far-reaching reform of its institutional framework to foster growth and employment and to protect and strengthen the welfare state along the lines spelled out by Hansjörg Herr and colleagues. Nevertheless, even in the short run, the current institutional framework offers substantial interpretational leeway to allow for a substantial fiscal expansion that could boost the European economy at least for the next two or three years. If the European Commission used the opportunity in a way similar to the one sketched, the prospects for a strong recovery in the Euro area would not be too bad. All it would need is the will to be a bit more consequential in using the leeway provided by the current framework.

References

Aiginger, K. (2014): The Europe 2020 strategy at midterm: Disappointing assessment calls for an urgent change driven by long run priorities. Response of the Austrian Institute of Economic Research (WIFO) to the public consultation on the Europe 2020 strategy: European Commission IP/14/50405/05/2014, Wien.

Barbiero, F., Darvas, Z. (2014): "In Sickness and in Health: Protecting and Supporting Public Investment in Europe", Bruegel Policy Contribution 02/2014.

Blyth, Mark (2013): *Austerity. The history of a dangerous idea.* New York: Oxford University Press.

Carnot, N., de Castro, F. (2015): The Discretionary Fiscal Effort: an Assessment of Fiscal Policy and its Output Effect, European Commission, Economic Papers no. 543, Brussels.

Darvas, Z., Huettl, P., de Sousa, C., Terzi, A., Tschekassin, O. (2014): Austerity and Poverty in the European Union, Study for the Committee on Employment and Social Affairs of the European Parliament, Brussels.

Dullien, S., Herr, H., Kellermann, C. (2011): *Decent Capitalism. A Blueprint for Reforming Our Economies*, London: PlutoPress.

European Commission (2008): Communication from the Commission from to the European Council: A European Economic Recovery Plan, Brussels, 26.11.2008 COM(2008) 800 final.

European Commission (2010): Annual macro-economic database (Ameco), May 2010.

European Commission (2013): Report on Public Finances in the EMU, European Economy No. 4, Brussels: European Commission, Directorate-General for Economic and Financial Affairs.

European Commission (2014a): Annual macro-economic database (Ameco), Spring 2014.

European Commission (2014b): Annual macro-economic database (Ameco), Autumn 2014.

European Commission (2014c): Communication from the Commission to the European Parliament, the Council, the European Central Bank, the Economic and Social Committee, the Committee of the Regions and the European Investment Bank;, An Investment Plan for Europe, Brussels, 26.11.2014, COM(2014) 903 final.

European Commission (2015a): Annual macro-economic database (Ameco), autumn 2015.

European Commission (2015b): Circa database on output gaps, autumn 2015.

European Commission (2015c): Communication from the Commission to the European Parliament, the Council, the European Central Bank, the Economic and Social Committee, the Committee of the Regions and the European Investment Bank; Making the best use of the flexibility within the existing rules of the Stability and Growth Pact, Strasbourg, 13.1.2015 COM(2015) 12 final.

European Commission (2015d): The 2015 Stability and Convergence Programmes: An Overview, European Economy, Institutional Paper No. 002, July, Brussels: European Commission, Directorate-General for Economic and Financial Affairs.

Gechert, S. (2015): What fiscal policy is most effective? A meta-regression analysis, in: *Oxford Economic Papers*, 67(3), 553-580.

Heine, M., Herr, H., Kaiser, C. (2006): *Wirtschaftspolitische Regime westlicher Industrienationen*, Baden Baden: Nomos.

Herr, H., Kazandziska, M. (2011): *Macroeconomic Policy Regimes in Western Industrial Countries*, Abingdon: Routledge.

Klär, E. (2013): Potential Economic Variables and Actual Economic Policies in Europe, in: *Intereconomics*, 48(1-2), 33-40.

Larch, M., Turrini, A. (2010): The Cyclically Adjusted Budget Balance in EU Fiscal Policymaking, in: *Intereconomics*, 45(1-2), 48-60.

Truger, A. (2013): Austerity in the euro area: the sad state of economic policy in Germany and the EU, in: *European Journal of Economics and Economic Policies, Intervention*, 2/2013, 158-174.

Truger, A. (2015a): Austerity, cyclical adjustment and the remaining leeway for expansionary fiscal policies within the current European fiscal framework, in: *Journal for a Progressive Economy*, 6(July), 32-37.

Truger, A. (2015b): Implementing the Golden Rule for Public Investment in Europe. Safe-guarding Public Investment and Supporting the Recovery, Materialien zu Wirtschaft und Gesellschaft, Working Paper Reihe der AK Wien No. 138, Abteilung Wirtschaftswissenschaft und Statistik der Kammer für Arbeiter und Angestellte für Wien.

Truger, A., Nagel, M. (2016): Austerity, Cyclical Adjustment and How to Use the Remaining Leeway for Expansionary Fiscal Policies within the Current EU Fiscal Framework, in: *Turkish Economic Review*, 3(2), 235-255.

Truger, A., Will, H. (2013): The German 'debt brake': A shining example for European fiscal policy?, in: *Revue de l'OFCE / Debates and Policies*, The Euro Area in Crisis, 127, 155-188.

Revitalising the Green New Deal

From a Keynesian stimulus to a sustainable growth strategy

Kajsa Borgnäs and Christian Kellermann

1. Introduction

For most of the past decade it has seemed as if the world – and especially Europe – has been caught up in a perpetual state of crisis. Or rather than speaking of a single crisis, it is probably more accurate to speak of multiple crises. The financial crisis starting in 2008 was followed by the Euro-crisis in 2011, which was subdued only to be revived in 2014. Highly volatile oil prices accompanied the financial crisis and plummeted to around US$30 per barrel a few years later. Meanwhile, climate change has been the object of growing concern, which culminated in the Paris agreement in December 2015 where the target mark of aiming for no more than 1.5 degree Celsius warming by the end of the century was established. In addition, there are creeping crises relating to growing income and wealth inequalities, continued high levels of unemployment in many countries and most recently dramatic migration and refugee movements. Looming global economic slowdown currently unsettles policy-makers across the globe in fear of being caught up in a long-term 'secular stagnation'. One would assume that public investment strategies based on, or at least inspired by, Keynesian textbook advice would be quick at hand. However, they are not, even though there are good concepts available.

The concept of a Green New Deal (GND) gained momentum in the immediate aftermath of the financial crisis as a way to handle interrelated economic and ecological challenges. Several multilateral and non-governmental organizations, such as the United Nations Environment and Development

Programmes (UNEP and UNDP), the International Labor Organization and the New Economics Foundation (NEF), published proposals to combine green investments and job creation. The United Nations in 2009 called for a Global Green New Deal, and drew attention to the Millennium Goals of eradicating extreme poverty as well as the need for developed countries to step up their efforts to support (sustainable) development trajectories in developing countries as well. Although the GND-strategies had partly different focuses, they all put emphasis on the necessary replacement of fossil-fuel based energy infrastructure and consumption patterns with those based on renewable energies. This was to be achieved through broad programmes for public and private investments into green sectors and technologies.

The rationale for a GND was straight-forward, and several governments launched GND programmes during 2008-2009. However, a number of early reviews revealed that there were legitimate questions on how "green" these programmes actually were. Since 2011, and with the world economy recovering slowly, the concept of the Green New Deal lost much of its political momentum.

Not only have there been concerns related to practical implementation, but questions concerning the fundamental (theoretical) *essence* of green investments have been raised. The conundrum of whether economic growth can be reconciled with the need to drastically reduce greenhouse gas emissions as well as improving on issues such as biodiversity loss, acidification and water usage, is still unsolved. The concept of 'green growth', although popular among many politicians, has proven rather elastic. The general technological optimism underlying the 'Ecological Modernization' school of thought has been challenged. It has become increasingly clear that technological improvements alone seldom suffice to change the growth path of an economy in a truly sustainable direction. The 'rebound-effect', i.e. the correlation of efficiency gains and more – not less – usage (of electricity for example), is difficult to bypass. As a result, although some 'greening' of economic growth may certainly be achieved, it remains a central question of our time how economic growth can actually be made sustainable.

Against the background of high political ambitions on the one hand and persistent difficulties in achieving a sustainable economic development on the other hand, it is easy to stick to the well-known. However, the necessity for a sustainable transformation of our growth models is real and eminent.

In our contribution, we develop the argument for a revived Green New Deal as a functional political strategy to deal with the ongoing crises. In section 2 we analyse selected countries' records in what they had announced and then actually implemented concerning the GND in the aftermath of the year 2008. In section 3 we then briefly discuss some fundamental principles for a future, more effective sustainability strategy. Finally, we propose a strategy which could serve as a stepping-stone for a more long-term politico-economic transformation. Section 4 serves as a short summary and conclusion.

2. The "balance sheet" of the Green New Deal

2.1 What were the promises?

In this section, we briefly recap what major international actors proposed as an economic-ecological remedy in the course of the 2008/9 crisis.

G20

On 15 November 2008, the G20 met in Washington D.C. to decide on common strategies to boost economic growth. Among the measures discussed were fiscal stimuli through increased public spending, investments and lowering taxes to create jobs and hasten economic recovery. In total, the subsequent national proposals amounted to extra spending of over US$2 trillion, or about 3 percent of global GDP at the time. The sum consisted (among others) of a Chinese package amounting to about US $ 586 billion (over 8 percent of its GDP), a US package of US $ 827 billion and a European Union Package of US $ 259 billion (or just under 2 percent of its GDP) (UNEP 2009b). Although it was not the main aim to focus on green growth, it was broadly acknowledged that a large proportion should go into 'green' sectors. Reviews, however, showed that countries targeted green sectors to a very varying degree (Zenghelis 2012).

United States

As part of its general stimulus program, the US government launched green investments of about US $ 100 billion over the years 2009 to 2011 (about 0,7 percent of GDP). The green stimulus was to be invested primarily in four sectors: retrofitting buildings to improve energy efficiency; expanding mass transit and freight trail; constructing a 'smart' electrical grid transmission system, and developing renewable energy sources. It was claimed that the programme would create at least 2 million jobs, or that every US$1 billion in government spending would lead to about 30.000 new jobs per year (which would mean that such a job creation scheme would be 20 percent more efficient than more traditional fiscal stimulus measures, UNEP 2009b). Another target was, of course, to reduce GHG emissions. Early evaluations in 2009 concluded that about 11.5 percent of total US stimulus spending went into green sectors (Robins et al. 2009a).

The European Union

In November 2008 the EU adopted the European Economic Recovery Plan (EERP) outlining national and EU-level stimulus measures amounting to 200 billion euro (1.5 percent of GDP). In terms of green investments, about 60 percent of the stimulus spending of the EU could be termed green (Schepelmann 2009). Two thirds of the total green stimulus spending targeted energy efficiency (buildings, grids, rails and low-carbon vehicles). Tax incentives aimed at promoting greater fuel efficiency in vehicles or the use of electric vehicles. The European Investment Bank raised annual investments for energy and climate change-related infrastructure to EUR 6 billion per year.

Germany, Italy and France

Among EU member states Germany's stimulus plan represented the largest one, amounting to about 20 percent of the overall EU stimulus (ILO 2009). About 13 percent of total German stimulus could be termed green, focusing on climate protection and energy efficiency (in particular in buildings), rails and vehicles. Italy had among the largest stimulus packages of EU countries but with the lowest share of green investments (only about 1.3 percent). France had a rather limited stimulus package (US$34 billion) but with a clear green focus (21 percent) (Robins et al. 2009b).

In sum, there seems to have been widespread consensus among governments that (Keynesian) investment and spending was needed to restore growth and jobs, and that those investments at least partly would have to go into a 'greener' economy rather than the business-as-usual 'brown' economic activities. In terms of the nature of stimulus, most spending went into general wage and labour market spending, tax cuts and infrastructure (including R&D) investments. The 'greening' aspect of the stimulus programmes primarily focused on increases in energy efficiency and investment in renewable energies, grids, transport and buildings. The growth aspect was primarily founded on expected returns from investments in infrastructure, new technologies, productivity increases and the creation of new jobs. It was generally assumed that rather than reproducing the current crises by reinvigorating the same sectors and activities that had brought the crises around in the first place, societies would better prepare themselves for the future by reducing (economic and environmental) vulnerabilities and mitigating the imbalances and unsustainable economic patterns.

From the outset it was disputed whether the spending quantity and quality were enough to set the major OECD economies on a more sustainable path. Although job creation of stimulus spending is difficult to quantify, early reviews showed that it actually had a sizeable effect (ILO 2009; Aldy 2012). In terms of the environmental scale and scope of GND programmes, they were in line with what most studies at the time proposed as a reasonable level for providing the critical mass of green infrastructure needed for considerable greening of the global economy. Both the Stern report as well as other studies (e.g. UNEP 2009a) had suggested that green investments of about one percent of global GDP annually would be necessary to achieve this goal. Focusing on the EU, Barclays Capital and Accenture (2011) estimated that the transition to a low-carbon economy would take 2 percent of GDP in annual investment, added to accumulated investment levels at around 19 percent of GDP. This amounts to about 360 billion Euros annually. Another report foresaw that the investment levels would have to increase to about 22 percent, if the more ambitious GHG reduction targets by the EU were to be achieved (Jaeger et al. 2011). Most reviews of the share of green investments in EU countries' national stimulus spending concluded that between 1.3 (Italy) and 21 (France) percent of total monetary commitment had been on 'green investments'. A study in 2011 found that about US$3 trillion had been proposed as fiscal stimulus for GND globally up until 2011. This well exceeded the one percent of global GDP (roughly US $ 750 billion) target (UNEP 2009b). In sum, the world was – on the aggregate – rather on a positive track to take on the challenge of 'greening' unsustainable economies.

In the years following the initial phase of the financial crisis, government strategies concerning GND spending differed even more. Whereas programmes of some countries focused on the longer term (including the US program which was to be implemented over 10 years), a number of countries, in particular in Europe, adopted smaller and more short-term packages. An IMF report in 2011 concluded that global renewable green investments in 2009 and 2010 were largely on par with those in 2008 (Eyraud et al. 2011). However, whereas green investments spending in Asia increased, US spending dropped in 2009 only to pick up in 2010, whereas EU spending seemed to show a falling trend (ibid.: 15). In the course of the Euro crisis, the EU adopted a reinforced "Stability and Growth Pact", which emphasised fiscal responsibility and structural reforms rather than investments. However, in 2014, EU Commission president Jean Claude Juncker introduced a "European Fund for Strategic Investment", showing that there was a renewed will of EU leaders to emphasise investment (Jaeger et al. 2015).

2.2 What were the effects?

There are a number of selective evaluations of the effects of global and national GND-measures on jobs and sustainability. Whereas most scrutinised the early implementation of proposed GND plans (e.g. Barbier 2010; Pollitt 2011), others have examined the development of the GND debate more broadly (Asici/Bünül 2012). However, there are only few comprehensive evaluations of GND programmes (plans *and* implementation) spanning the whole post-crisis period until today (see e.g. Mundaca/Richter 2015).

We are not attempting such an evaluation of global GNDs in this contribution. Instead, we ask how some key indicators have developed between 2005 and 2014 as an indication of whether the world is set on a more sustainable path-way. This is the time-span where GND plans could be expected to have taken some effect. Although country developments differ widely, we focus on the EU-28 as a whole. We do not argue that this is a perfect way of establishing the effects of GND plans on sustainable growth. However, it might give a hint on whether the post-financial crisis investment strategies have contributed to pushing the economic development in a more or less sustainable direction.

In order to trace the possible impact of GND plans on 'sustainabilising' growth, we take a look at the following six indicators between 2005 and 2014 (Figure 1):

1. The share of GDP going into environmental protection
2. Government investment as a share of GDP
3. Total investment as a share of GDP
4. Unemployment rate
5. Share of renewable energy in gross final energy consumption
6. GHG emissions

The data was transformed so as to show relative developments over time (base-year 2005=100).

Figure 1: Six sustainable growth indicators in the EU-28 (2005=100) from 2005 to 2014

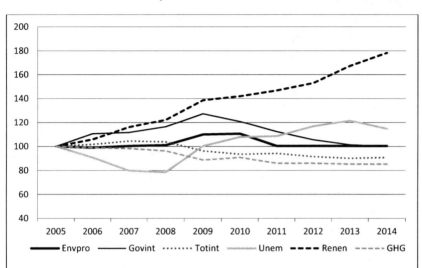

Source: Eurostat

We see that – although public investment (*Govint*) in the EU-28 increased during the acute phase of the crisis, this was reverted after 2009. As total investment (*Totint*) remained low after 2008, we conclude that private investment has failed to fill the gap. Instead it has dropped considerably throughout the period. The unemployment rate has mostly been high and rising since the crisis, and the share of GDP going to environmental protection (*Envpro*) grew somewhat in 2009-2010, only to revert to pre-crisis levels after 2011. GHG emissions have slowly decreased. The biggest (permanent) change is in renewable energy as a percentage of final energy consumption (*Renen*). However, the positive development seems mostly unaffected by the crisis.

Interpreting this picture we observe that national GND spending seems to have served primarily as short-term injection for stabilising EU-economies in the acute phase of the financial crisis. Once the most urgent phase was over, there is little evidence that EU economies have been continuing on a path towards more sustainable growth.

3. Reviving Green New Deal principles

Recent research into the processes of innovation and growth (with renewed strength) suggested that the neoliberal claim of efficient market allocation is more propaganda than serious economics (e.g. Mazzucato/Perez 2015). Major technological transformations of the past have been possible thanks to a dominant role of the state as both a facilitator and guide of innovation and investment. In her groundbreaking analysis of the history of investment and innovation regarding the ICT developments (especially internet and software), Mariana Mazzucato revealed that public capital had played a crucial role in bearing risks during most of the formative decades, long before private (risk) capital came to the table (Mazzucato 2013). Mazzucato draws the conclusion that private capital is efficient at commercialising products on existing 'technological platforms'. However, it is not very efficient (or willing to bear the risk) when it comes to innovating and shaping these platforms in early (and riskier) stages of development. Instead, the role of the state is to provide both *direction* and *capital* for early innovation phases. Mazzucato (amongst others) has suggested that the green transformation is similarly not a matter of commercialising niche-innovations (for which market mechanisms would suffice), but a matter of transforming basic platforms and therefore a genuine task of the state. Taking Keynes as a starting point, she argues that the specification of the direction for innovation is crucial of any state investment policy.

Following up on this we argue that the 'green' transition is not primarily a matter of specific technologies, but of transforming broader unsustainable socio-technological platforms. Naturally, such broader regimes take time to transform, which is why we suggest effective GND strategies should have much longer time-horizons than most plans had post-2008. Innovation and infrastructure is required in particular in relation with four main socio-technological regimes: electricity generation, mobility, materials use and building. The target is to reduce usage of carbon down to very low or even zero levels while at the same time securing jobs, wealth and welfare. Rather than proposing policies for each and one of the sectors however, we suggest that such a long-term GND strategy should aim for a three-faced development: some sectors and activities have to grow; some sectors and activities have to become more efficient; and some sectors and activities have to shrink or vanish entirely. In all these cases, government direction, investment and public spending are required.

In practical terms, what is needed is a mix of public investments and consumption on the one hand and new financial rules and economic incentives for private investments and consumption on the other.

Growing sustainable activities and sectors
Sustainability requires an appropriate infrastructure. National investment targets in 'green' infrastructure should therefore be increased to about 2 percent of GDP. Increased public investment should go primarily into the enhancement of energy efficiency of buildings and construction. It should encourage the use of low-carbon vehicles and build railways, renewable energy, electrical stations and more efficient electricity grids. Moreover, low-carbon energy sectors should be further developed. A practical example of a relatively sustainable sector with high economic potential is the biomass sector, which is under-developed in many countries (i.e. the Nordic countries). Developing this could provide the basis for a more sustainable production and export regime. Moreover, one of the most important tasks of the state is to help reduce production costs for sustainable technologies. One positive example is the German policies on solar and wind power. From a global perspective, the dramatic price reductions achieved through these policies benefit all. In general, a much stronger integration of environmental policy and economic policy is needed. To stabilize employment effects, this should be combined with educational investments.

Efficiency increases
Efficiency increases is one of the core pillars of green investments. All countries need to become more energy efficient, but in particular Eastern European countries still have problems with high energy intensity. An EU-wide strategy should focus efficiency investments towards these countries. Moreover, the green transformation requires new and better technologies as well as knowledge about how to apply them in any given socio-economic context. Any efficiency gain is a potential environmental gain. R&D needs more public money.

Phasing out unsustainable activities and sectors
There are activities and sectors that will never be able to adjust to a low or zero carbon economy. In particular some basic materials sectors (including steel production and mining) will be difficult to 'green' throughout. In part, these activities and sectors can be made to specialize more specifically on

those products that are necessary also in a future more sustainable economy. But there is also a possibility that economies and businesses relying heavily on intrinsically unsustainable activities will have to find new ways to produce, export and consume. Policy makers will have to intensify the efforts to identify those activities and sectors that cannot be expected to be part of a zero carbon society, and plan for their gradual phase-out. The German *Energiewende* has targeted nuclear power as an unsustainable sector. Europe should launch a joint *Energiewende* focused on the rapid phase-out of coal and oil.

A two percent increase in annual investment plus costs for helping people and businesses to transform will have to be paid for by a combination of higher taxes, new credit and private capital.

- Among the bundle of taxes that will have to be used to pay for the transition, an internationally stringent and strict carbon pricing is important. This includes setting a long-term carbon tax trajectory (rising with time).

- The removal of fossil fuel subsidies (direct and indirect) is necessary. It has been calculated that governments globally subsidise fossil fuel usage by $493 billion per year (IEA, 2016). Removing these could reduce GHG emissions considerably.

- The dogma of no new borrowing does not hold, if GND should be any long-term or ambitious strategy. Governments should ditch the fear of new credit, borrow money and start to invest in the economic structure underpinning a greener future.

- Similar to what the UK has achieved, private capital should be activated to contribute to co-financing of projects (via a "Green Investment Bank") or through various forms of "green financial rules".

4. Summing up

Although there is nothing intrinsically positive with a crisis, crises can be handled in more or less constructive ways. Outcomes are respectively more or less 'positive'. The current assemblage of crises provide such an opportunity to strike a new and better balance between economic development and the need to sustain the environment and climate for future generations. This opportunity stems primarily from three conditions. First, there is a growing acceptance – and indeed expectation – that our business-as-usual model of economic development does not work anymore and that it must be replaced by something better. Second, most of the crises of the past decade relate to the misallocation of capital rather than to insufficient technological knowhow, pointing towards the political aspects of handling the crises. Third, the crises all highlight the central role of the state in ensuring a sustainable development pathway and therefore provide an opportunity to break with the market-dogma of past decades.

We have argued that rather than seeing the Green New Deal as a one-off injection into the global economy, it should be conceptualised as a long-term strategy for transforming our economies in a more sustainable direction – indeed a long-term 'Sustainable New Deal'. The GND plans of most countries following the financial crisis were short-term plans, aiming primarily at increasing growth and create job opportunities at a time when the global economy was recovering from financial collapse. As a result, the GND spending largely ebbed when the global economy improved (in particular in the EU). There are countries (as well as local level governments) that have continued their GND efforts even after immediate economic recovery. However, for the world and the EU as a whole, stuck in the bottle-neck of low growth, low investment, high unemployment and severe environmental destruction, much more will have to be done in order for a 'green growth' to be achieved.

The investments needed for a sustainability transition (2 percent of GDP annually) are not outrageously large or expensive. The technological knowhow is there to exploit. The theoretical case for such a transformation is convincing. What is still lacking is political clout.

References

Aldy, J. (2012): A Preliminary Review of the American Recovery and Clean Energy Package. Washington D.C. Resources for the Future.

Asici, A., Bünül, Z. (2012): Green New Deal: A Green Way out of the Crisis, in: *Environmental Policy and Governance*, 22, 295-306.

Barbier, E. (2010): How is the Global Green New Deal going?, in: *Nature Opinion*, 464, 832-33.

Barclays Capital and Accenture (2011): *Carbon Capital, Financing the Low Carbon Economy*, London, UK.

Edenhofer, O., Stern, N. (2009): Towards a Global Green Recovery, https://www.pik-potsdam.de/members/edenh/publications-1/global-green-recovery_pik_lse

Eyraud, L., Wane, A., Zhang, C., Clements, B. (2011): Who's Going Green and Why? Trends and Determinants of Green Investment, IMF Working Paper WP/11/296.

IEA (2016): World Energy Outlook 2015 Special Report, http://www.worldenergyoutlook.org/energyclimate/

ILO (2009): Green Stimulus Measures, EC-IILS Joint Discussion Paper Series, No. 15.

Jaeger, C.C., Paroussos, L., Mangalagiu, D., Kupers, R., Mandel, A., Tabara, J.D. (2011): A New Growth Path for Europe, Synthesis Report European Climate Forum.

Jaeger et al. (2015): Investment-Oriented Climate Policy: An Opportunity for Europe, Global Climate Forum, Berlin.

Mazzucato, M. (2013): *Das Kapital des Staates. Eine andere Geschichte von Innovation und Wachstum*, München: Kunstmann.

Mazzucato, M., Perez, C. (2015): Innovation as Growth Policy: The Challenge for Europe, in: Fagerberg, J., Laestadius, S., Martin, B. (eds.), *The Triple Challenge for Europe*, Oxford University Press, UK.

Mundaca, L., Richter, J. (2015): Assessing 'green energy economy' stimulus packages: Evidence from the U.S. programs targeting renewable energy, in: *Renewable and Sustainable Energy Reviews*, 42, 1174-1186.

Pollitt, H. (2011): Assessing the Implementation and Impact of Green Elements of Member States' National Recovery Plans, Final Report for the European Commission, DG Environment.

Robins, N., Clover, R., Singh, C. (2009a): A Global Green Recovery? Yes, but in 2010, HSBC Global Research, London.

Robins, N., Clover, R., Singh, C. (2009b): Building a Green Recovery, HSBC Global Research, London.

Schepelmann, P. (2009): 'A Green New Deal for Europe. Towards green modernization in the face of crisis', Presentation at Resource Efficiency Allinace Committee of the Regions, Wuppertal Institute.

UNEP (2009a): Rethinking the Economic Recovery: A Global Green New Deal, Edwards B. Barbier, UNEP-DTIE.

UNEP (2009b) Global Green New Deal. Policy Brief, http://www.unep.org/pdf/A_Global_Green_New_Deal_Policy_Brief.pdf

Zenghelis, D (2012): A Strategy for Restoring Confidence and Economic Growth through Green Investment and Innovation. Policy Brief April 2012, Grantham Research Institute.

II.

Finanzmärkte, Währungssysteme und Regulierung

Financial Markets, Currency Systems and Regulation

How to explain the exchange rate gyrations on the biggest foreign exchange market on the globe

Jan Priewe

The dollar-Euro foreign exchange (FX) market – comprising spot and forward markets, swaps, options and others – has a market share in global currency markets of 24%, outpacing the second biggest FX market, the dollar-Yen market with 18% (2013, BIS 2013), The annual turnover of the dollar-Euro market was 34 times the Euro area GDP (2013). Since this market is absolutely unregulated, let alone a few rare central bank interventions, it might be a model of a FX market in a perfectly flexible exchange rate regime. Even though many authors have analysed this market, neither the exchange rates themselves nor the volatility and the dynamics could be explained with econometric methods. Despite many differences, mainstream theories are united in arguing that the short and perhaps even the medium term performance cannot be explained, whereas "fundamentals" reign the long-run (see standard textbooks). There is no explanation of the long short-run chaos, nothing about the alleged eventual switch to fundamentals, and the short long-run which quickly gyrates into new non-fundamental short-runs. This set of theories is in big crisis (Priewe 2016).

Hansjörg Herr has published intensively on exchange rate theory but did not delve into empirical analyses. He follows a theoretical approach in the track of Hajo Riese (Berlin) which considers FX markets as a special asset market in which financial investors seek portfolio equilibrium (Herr 2014; Heine/Herr 2013: 679ff.). The equilibrium is based in this approach on the interest-rate-parity theory complemented by differential currency premiums; exogenous expectations of wealth owners are added. I doubt the extended interest-rate-parity theory, which is an equilibrium approach, but follow the asset-speculation-approach. Yet I hold that "fundamentals", a term encompassing quite different variables, do have an impact. My approach is similar to exchange rate theories based on behavioural economics, which is in many aspects akin to Keynes, Kindleberger and Minsky. Keynes himself had not delivered an exchange rate theory except his consent to the purchasing-power-parity theory for the long run, limited to tradable goods (Keynes 1923; cp. Priewe 2015).

I will show, firstly, the cyclical performance of the dollar-DM and dollar-Euro markets since 1970, with a focus on the latter. Secondly, I use the behavioural approach with heterogeneous agents for a general interpretation of the empirical riddle. Thirdly I analyse empirically the role of standard fundamental variables with attention to the turning points in the exchange rate cycle and, fourthly, develop narratives to explain the exchange rate performance 1999-2015. Admittedly, my explanations are very limited, but I explain why this limitation is the core of the problems. In the conclusion I show that the dollar-Euro exchange rate has far reaching impacts, going beyond the transatlantic trade.

1. Performance of the dollar-DM-Euro exchange rate since 1970

Graph 1 shows the daily dollar-DM-Euro exchange rate (DM converted in Euro for the period 1970 to 1998). The DM started to appreciate even before the demise of the Bretton-Woods-system in 1973 and continued so until 1980, by around 114%, collapsed until 1985, rose again steeply over four peaks until reaching its climax 1995, after the collapse of the European Exchange Mechanism (ERM). The rise 1985-1995 lifted the DM 155%, then the rates turned into a steep fall, especially after the introduction of the Euro on January 1, 1999. The somewhat enigmatic weakness of the Euro was averted 2002, giving rise to an appreciation by around 90% until mid-2008, shortly before the Lehman-crisis. Over three steep zig-zag-cycles the Euro fell below 1.10 in early 2016.

Graph 1: US-dollar per DM/Euro (DM converted in €)
1970-2016 (daily rates)

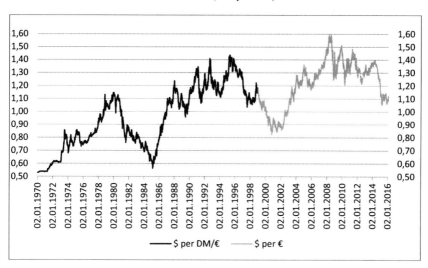

Source: ECB, Deutsche Bundesbank, own calculations

What needs to be explained (i) are the long spells of strong rise and fall, with many short and very short ups and downs but clear trends, (ii) and the upward and downward turning points, the main ones being 1980, 1985, 1995, 1999, 2002, 2008 and 2014 apart from the three "teeth" before 1995 and in the phase 2008-2014. Volatility, spikes and troughs between the DM era and the Euro era seem very similar.

Controlling for the inflation differential between the US and Germany or Euro area, respectively, shows clearly less inflation in the DM-era in Germany, so that the real exchange rate (RER: dollar per DM, inflation adjusted) rose 1973-1980 "only" by 23%, fell from then until 1985 by 46% and rose again until 1995 by 107%. Since the advent of the Euro, the inflation differential between the Euro area and the US was somewhat smaller. Hence the Euro plummeted in real terms by 16% 1999-2001 and gained by ca 60% 2001-2008. The pattern of ups and downs of the inflation adjusted exchange rate is similar to the pattern of the nominal rate, but somewhat attenuated.

The swings of the real effective exchange rates (REER: trade-weighted inflation-adjusted exchange rates vis à vis the trading partners) of the DM, Euro and the dollar. are much less extreme than nominal or real ones (cp. graph 2). The REER for the US is less volatile since many countries peg their currency tightly or softly to the dollar, and within the Euro area nominal exchanges rates are abandoned so that only price and cost differences occur due to labour cost and price divergence. Germany's nominal appreciation against the dollar was strongly alleviated by lower prices and lower unit labour cost changes in the critical periods 1985-1995 and 2002-2008, also by switches in the regional structure of trade between extra Euro area trade and intra Euro area trade. Overall, real effective appreciations and depreciations between Europe and the US seem to match symmetrically.

Graph 2: DM and Euro/US-dollar exchange rate, real and real effective exchange rates RER and REER)

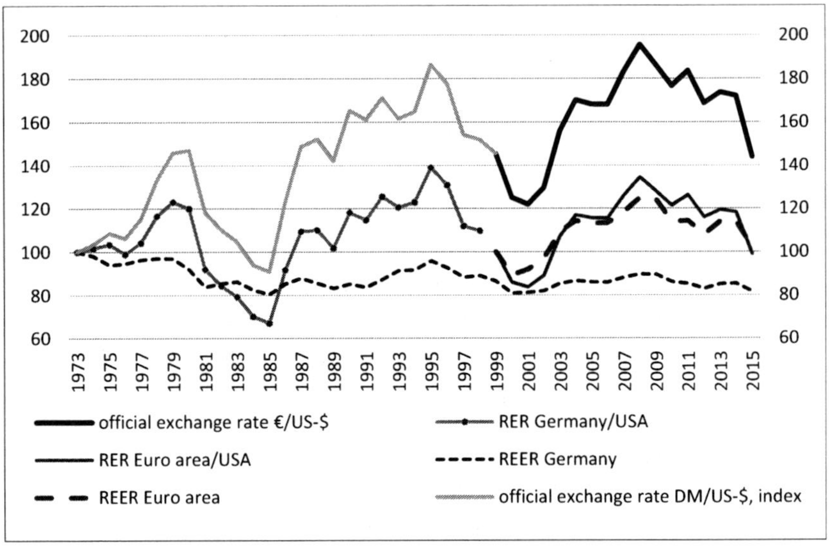

Source: BIS, OECD.Stat, AMECO; own calculations. REER against 26 trading partners (CPI based) for Germany from BIS and for 67 trading partner (ULC based) for Euro area from Bruegel

Graph 3 shows the purchasing-power-parity rate (PPP) for Germany since 1973 and the Euro area since 1999, compared to the actual exchange rate. OECD.Stat calculates PPP exchange rates, comprising tradeable and non-tradable goods and services. Prices of non-tradables are not subject to transnational arbitrage, assuming full competition; but price dynamics are similar to tradables, although the *level* of prices for non-tradables is likely to differ (often following the income level of a country). Therefore, the PPP rate can signal fairly correctly the *trend* in prices for tradables, not necessarily the level. The upward trend of the PPP rates is driven by a trend in lower inflation in Europe compared to the US, indicating a modest degree of appreciation of DM and Euro.

The actual market exchange rates deviate from PPP rates up to 30 percentage points at the peaks of over- and under-valuation. At first glance, PPP rates look like the trend line for market rates, with strong over- und undervaluations. Such a view is misleading. The result of long-standing overvaluation of a currency would be the crowding-out of considerable segments of output and employment. The baskets of production on both sides of the Atlantic would adjust adversely. Production would be forced to adjust to changing exchange rates, not the exchange rates to production – the opposite of the intention of PPP exchange rate theory.

Graph 3: US-dollar per DM/Euro: official exchange rate and PPP for Euro area (19 members) and Germany

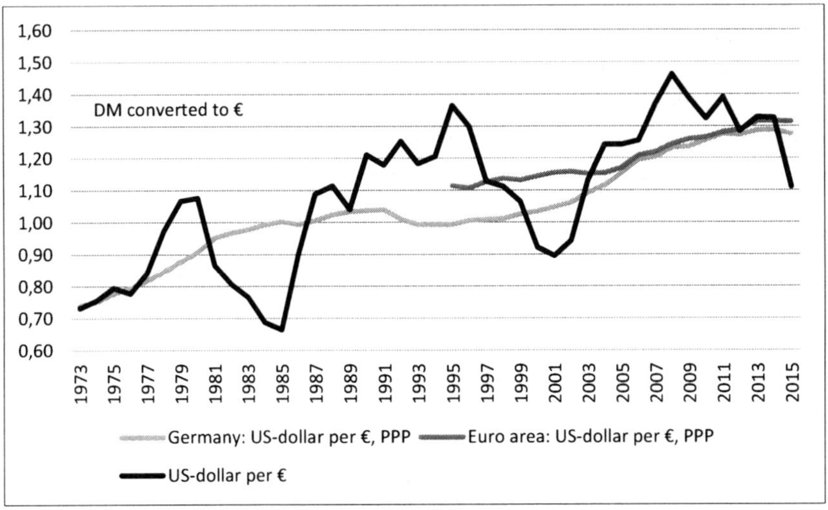

Source: OECD.Stat, own calculations

Can one see any "equilibrium" in the biggest FX market on the planet? Of course – there is always equilibrium since disequilibrium is by definition impossible. The definition is, as always, that demand equals supply on the FX market. The other side of the coin is that all equilibria are ultra-short and thus ephemeral – no *stable* equilibrium, not even for a second. Market agents seem permanently discontent with market outcomes. If one defines equilibria in fundamental terms, the answer would differ, see below.

After this rough overview on the extreme exchange rate gyrations – strongly in contrast to the expectations of the early proponents of flexible exchange rates, such as Milton Friedman in the 1950s – I will attempt to decipher the mix of volatility and long phases of misalignment in three steps.

2. The behavioural finance approach to exchange rates

Despite many analyses of the prime FX market on the globe, mostly econometric ones, the only consensus is that in the short and medium run the exchange rate cannot be explained better than random walk, endorsing an early paper of Meese/Rogoff (1983). The addition that in the long run fundamentals are the key determinant, is neither proven nor explained which fundamentals are identified. Not so the approach mentioned, based in behavioural finance and Keynesian economics (De Grauwe/Grimaldi 2006; Schulmeister 2009; Kindleberger 2000). The main proposition is that heterogeneous agents on FX markets, the dealers, are separated in two camps, the technical analysts following trending with mostly adaptive expectations, and the minority of the fundamentalists. The first camp behaves rationally in the sense of following past experience for short steps in an environment of great uncertainty. They go beyond arbitrage, speculate or they follow blindly the speculators like a herd – and make more profits than losses in doing so. They seem to be aware of neglecting fundamental determinants, but as long as the second camp cannot convince or predominate them, they continue heading unidirectionally. The sequence of many short steps, perhaps at times interrupted by short setbacks or stalemates, can lead to long trending phases. If nobody stops the music they continue dancing.

Through this lens, foreign exchange is a financial asset, perfectly suited – under a flexible exchange rate regime – for building up speculative bubbles. The dealers using their own capital as well as borrowed funds may have small profit margins, but dealing with a huge volume of transactions enables them to make sizable profits with little equity. They bet on rising (or falling) rates, and find counterparts who may do the same but may have a stronger or lower risk orientation, apart from counterparts who pay more attention to the fundamental criteria. Hence, heterogeneous expectations are exchanged on the various FX markets. Another group of agents is involved too, namely agents of banks and nonfinancial institutions which purchase and sell securities across different countries and currencies. Currency for trade of goods and services is negligible on FX markets. Capital flows, chiefly short-term, dwarf trade-related transactions. The two main camps on FX markets are not totally separated and antagonistic. The fundamentalists may prefer to behave opportunistically if they recognise that herding is more profitable than calling for a change in the direction.

There is seemingly much empirical evidence for this micro-setting of players at FX markets. To mention just one: Ehrmann/Fratzscher (2005) found that news perceived by FX dealers included to some extent fundamental data, but in most periods they received little attention. Unexpected news, i.e. "new news" were more important; bad new as well as news on the US rather than on Europe had a heavier weight. News from central banks were often not clear in their consequence, but subject to different interpretations. Under extreme time pressure news were sorted mainly by "good" or "bad" relative to economic growth. In episodes of great uncertainty, dealers tend to listen more to the fundamentalists.

If the microeconomic structure of FX agents is similar to this picture, fundamentalists indeed have a hard time. I add to the behavioural approach that fundamentals themselves are heterogeneous, see below. The most important group of fundamentalists, central banks and perhaps also ministries of finance, are largely absent – according to the rules in floating exchange rate regimes.

The outcome of this micro structure is that long phases of appreciation or depreciation of a currency can occur, as long as the voices of the fundamentalists are silent or absent. The dealer might attempt to forecast the behaviour of the potential key agents, the central bank, be it the ECB alone or the Fed alone or their collaboration, but the latter's main orientation is following the markets and avoiding interventions. However, exchange rates cannot appreciate/depreciate forever, as trees cannot grow into the sky. Hence, there is great certainty that a point of deviation exists where a return will be precipitated, in most cases after extreme peaks or troughs, often in the form of sudden turnarounds similar to other bursting bubbles on asset markets.

3. Fundamentals and the dollar-Euro exchange rate

Now I turn to the dollar-Euro market and the influence of suspected eight fundamental determinants of exchange rates (see also Rossi 2013; Menkhoff/ Taylor 2007; Beckmann/Belke/Kühl 2011). It is presumed, following the behavioural approach, much in line with Keynes's analysis of speculative asset markets (e.g. the beauty contest, the role of adaptive expectations and the role of uncertainty), that one or several fundamentals will gain predominance when it comes to turning points. I look at eight fundamentals for the dollar-Euro exchange rates in the period 1999-2015 with annual data[1], regarding the differential between the Euro area and the US: (1) GDP growth, (2) growth forecasts for the year ahead, (3) inflation, (4) the current account balance (% of GDP), (5 and 6) short- and long-term interest rates (the former close to the policy rates of Fed and ECB), (7) the real long- term interest rates and (8) the deviation of the actual exchange rate from the notional PPP-rate, as calculated by OECD.

The results convey a clear message. In all years, some of the eight fundamentals signal the need for appreciation, others for depreciation. There was never a year with an unequivocal sign of all fundamentals for one direction. Only in nine of the 17 years analysed the majority of the fundamentals shows in the direction of the actual annual change of the exchange rate – in the other eight years the majority of fundamentals would call for a change of the exchange rate in the opposite direction than the actual one. Let alone the strength of appreciation and depreciation, not even the direction, the sign, of fundamentals is in line with the actual changes of the exchange rate. There is not a single fundamental indicator out of the set of eight which is better than showing in 10 of 17 years in the direction of the actual exchange rate. A few fundamental indicators, in particular the current account balance, the spread of real long-term interest rates and the deviation from PPP, call for 10-12 years of the total of 17 years in the opposite direction to where the actual exchange rate was moving. Even in two of the five years of the crucial turning points of the exchange rate – 1999, 2002, 2008, 2012 and 2014 – the fundamental indicators signaled the wrong messages to the FX markets, namely 2008 and 2012. In the year 2008, the year of the grand financial crisis and the sudden fall of the Euro after July, ending a long phase of enormous Euro-appreciation, the fundamentals voted 7:1 for further appreciation. Even 2009, when the Euro continued to fall, the fundamentals signaled 5:3 need for

---

[1] Data from OECD.Stat, IMF, World Development Indicators, Eurostat, computations by the author.

appreciation. One may question the results due to using rough annual data rather than quarterly or monthly data, for not weighing fundamentals and for not controlling for time lags. A quick look at quarterly data for some fundamentals does not change the overall picture. Giving more weight to some indicators, say short-term interest rates, does not improve forecasts. Besides, most fundamentals do not change quickly. If there were strong time lags, one would have to ask why these were not anticipated and priced in early on. Long time lags, as e.g. for the deviation of the exchange rate from PPP, show that corrections from strong aberration – up to almost 29% as in the year 2001 – take several years to start rectification, and once the latter is reached it triggers a new wave of strong and lasting deviations in the other direction.

Misleading is the focus on policy interest rates, the Federal Funds Rate of the Fed and the Main Refinancing Rate of ECB. From the launching of the Euro until April 2001, the US-policy rate was up to 200 basis points above the European level – the Euro plunged heavily, seemingly in line with standard theory. However, from November 2004 until December 2007, the Fed raised the policy rate 200 basis points above the ECB's, but the Euro soared in value. After end-2007 until 2014 the ECB kept its policy rate above the Federal Funds rate, and the Euro fell, interrupted by short ups. What is also striking is the fact that the current account balance seems almost irrelevant for the exchange rate gyrations. It could be argued that the Euro area-US-trade can at best account for a bilateral small chunk in the overall trade or current account balance and that one should better look at the real effective exchange rate, but both currencies are tightly or softly pegged to a bunch of other currencies, not least the Renminbi to the dollar until 2005 (afterwards to a basket with a strong weight of the dollar). It is also striking that most fundamental indicators differ only slightly across the two sides of the Atlantic over long spells, with the exception of the current account and the deviation from PPP.

However, the conjecture that seemingly fundamentals play a minor or even negligible role in explaining the dollar-Euro-rate is premature. What is more important than the numerical values of the indicators is their peculiar interpretation, including a basket of some fundamentals and perhaps other indicators, which had formed expectations of agents. For instance, the initial weakness of the Euro 1999-2002 might have been influenced by higher interest rates in the US coupled with much higher growth 1999-2000. But we don't know what drove the expectations of bears and bulls at FX markets. Hansjörg Herr would respond that expectations are always exogenous. But this implies that exchange rates and their gyrations are totally exogenous as well. I contend that fundamentals and their varying interpretations feed into expectations, sometimes more, sometimes less. Further, when fundamentals convey in many phases unclear signals, then adaptive expectations might predominate, and they are endogenous. Keynes would probably agree.

Let us now try to interpret the main turning points of the dollar-Euro-rates by telling more or less plausible narratives, namely the weakness phase 1999-2002, the turn to appreciation in early 2002, the sudden drop starting in mid-2008 and the turn to strong depreciation of the Euro after 2012 until early 2016 when this analysis ends (see also the interpretations in Priewe 2015; cp. Mussa 2005/2012; Salvatore 2005; Rogoff 2002).

4. Narratives on the ups and downs

The Euro devalued 30% from 1.18 dollar per Euro, as the starting value 1999, until October 2000, reaching a low of 0.84 (data in this section are from ECB, Bundesbank, OECD.Stat, Eurostat). The reversal started not before February 2002. Both the Euro area and the US-economy were in a fairly strong growth phase until 2002 and 2001, respectively, stronger in the US than in Europe. During September-November 2000, ECB, Fed and Bank of Japan intervened jointly to weaken dollar and Yen. This may have helped to dampen the thrust of devaluation of the Euro somewhat. As mentioned before, US-short-term interest rates lay more than 200 basis points above the ones in the Euro area. Maybe the NATO-led Kosovo war in the year 1999 invoked uncertainty on Europe's economic prospects, and later the 9/11 attacks in the year 2001 and the ensuing bursting of the dot.com bubble contributed to the slow weakening of the dollar. Some hold that the initial change of DM reserves in Russia and Eastern Europe into dollars rather than Euro had supported the Euro's weakness. But why should all these events have devalued the Euro by 30% leading to an undervaluation of the Euro, relative to PPP, of almost 29%? It is very likely that the uncertainty, caused by the advent of a brand-new currency, and the neglect of guidance by the central banks opened the doors for speculative traders who profit from overshooting. Several commentators assume that this infant phase of the Euro cannot sufficiently be explained by fundamentals (De Grauwe 2000; Wollmershäuser 2003; SVR 2000, no. 350ff.).

The start of Euro appreciation 2002 was commenced by stronger reduction of interest rates in the US than in the Euro area. The interest rate differential changed the sign. The US authorities were interested in the weakening of the dollar, since the current account deficit was on the rise. The strengthening of the Euro was supported by the pressure of the undervalued Renminbi and other emerging countries' currencies on the dollar. Again, it remains somewhat enigmatic whether the change in the interest rate spread was enough to cause a turnaround of the exchange rate. In other phases the interest rate differential was irrelevant. It could likely be that traders started to bet on a weakening dollar, and authorities on both sides of the Atlantic were happy to see this. But again it led to overshooting Euro appreciation, after a temporary setback of -12% during the year 2005.

The appreciation of the Euro from end-2005 until July 2008 was in line with most fundamentals, but the strength of 35% – up to a peak of 1.60 – was made by the traders who pushed trending – despite a strong overvaluation of the Euro relative to PPP of some 15%. When the subprime crisis broke out in 2007, the Fed started to lower interest rates while the ECB continued to tighten. The US authorities had no reason to intervene to strengthen the dollar, since the US-current account deficit was still on a high level. The ensuing financial crisis and uncertainties regarding the financial stability of US-investment banks led to the reversal in July 2008. Wealth owners sold assets held abroad and returned to the US as the safe haven. This shock wave hit the emerging economies' currencies most, but also the Euro. Wealth owners reduced their risk proclivity and turned risk-averse, switching from low to high liquidity preference in times of uncertainty and emergency. The breakdown of the interbank markets reduced the supply of liquidity, until the Fed opened the faucets to flood the economy with liquidity. The turnaround of the year 2008 was not driven by fundamentals, let alone the current account and the violation of PPP. It was a clear consequence of the crisis, which demonstrated which currency is the prime money on the globe. The paradox that the currency of the country that was the epicenter of the crisis appreciated against the rest of the world reflects the hierarchy of currencies and the predominant trust in the US-authorities to cope with the mess better than other competing currencies.

Within four months – July to November 2008 – the Euro plunged 31%, a feast for FX traders. After a series of three strong ups and downs 2009-2014 the Euro fell further to a low of 1.06 end-2015. The ups-and-down phase reflects mainly the uncertainties of the diverging recoveries on both sides of the Atlantic and the outbreak of the Euro crisis 2010. The milestones were the announcement of ECB-president Mario Draghi 2012 to support the Euro "whatever it takes" and Quantitative Easing (OE) in the US in three forms. QE started in the US in November 2008, a second round came in November 2011 (QE2) and a third round in late 2012 (QE3 without a time limitation). By the end of 2013 tapering was announced and bond purchases came to a halt in February 2014. The Fed started to raise interest rates for the first time since almost a decade in December 2015, while the ECB had started to purchase assets in the framework of the "Expanded Asset Purchase Programme" (APP) as late as in March 2015. The QE strategy of monetary policies in the US, in Japan and especially by the ECB de facto triggered – be it intentional or as an unintended but tolerated side effect – depreciations of the currencies, especially against China and other emerging economies. This started a wave of "currency wars", initiated by the Fed, followed by Japan in 2010, later in the context of "Abenomics", while China responded with a return to depreciation against the dollar in late 2013 (by -8% until February 2016) and the ECB came in belated (see also SVR 2010, no. 59 regarding QE2; similarly Sosvilla-Rivero/Fernández-Fernández 2015).

Growth performance after the financial crisis was much better in the US than in Europe, thus strengthening the dollar, although policy interest rates remained higher in the Euro area until 2014. Although Mr Draghi announced to start the European QE in the form of OMT in 2012, it started three years later, as mentioned but in the form of the APP while the OMT was never applied. Hence the dollar appreciation after 2008, in particular after 2014, was pressured by central bank policies and the much better economic performance in the US, whereas the Euro area fell into recession 2013 and 2014 and crept into a very weak recovery 2015. The strength of the depreciation of the Euro may again be determined by the technical traders leading to an undervaluation of the Euro, relative to PPP, by almost 16% 2015.

Overall, a solely fundamentally determined equilibrium exchange rate, not disturbed and distorted by short-term speculation, as stipulated by the German Council of Economic Advisers (SVR 2000, no. 350ff.) has never existed – there is no uniform and unambiguous set of fundamentals, at least not in the reality of a floating exchange rate regime. They always contradict each other. Such a fundamental equilibrium exchange rate is a myth. Determining a fundamental exchange rate requires normative evaluations, gauging trade-offs, weighing advantages and downsides (Cline 2008)[2].

---

[2] Based on the work of John Williamson, Cline estimates bilateral exchange rates which are in line with fundamental real effective exchange rates that allow sustainable current account balances.

5. The impact of fickle exchange rates on trade, investment and finance

One might raise the question how important and relevant the dollar-Euro exchange rate really is in face of a small share of transatlantic trade for the European Union and the US in the past, excluding the period after 2008 when this trade rose markedly with a devalued Euro and stagnating growth in Europe. Intercontinental trade gains importance relative to regional trade, especially for Germany.

In general, misalignments of exchange rates are like heavy subsidies or taxes on exports and imports (cp. Salvatore 2005). They distort trade and world market prices (commodity prices are, for instance, strongly dependent on the strength of the US-dollar). This is in stark contrast to the idea of free trade on global markets as the dollar-Euro exchange rate is a key factor for all the other exchange rates (with 180 currencies on the globe, there are 32,220 exchange rates).

Heavy and long Euro appreciation against the US-dollar, like 2002-2008, lead to complex adjustments of corporations. The vast majority of intercontinental trade is intra-firm trade with pricing to markets strategies. This implies that profits of European exporters into the dollar bloc are squeezed. Firms strongly engaged in extra-EU-trade, many of them from more advanced Euro area countries, had sought to compensate this with pressure on unit labour costs and outsourcing of production, chiefly to low-wage Eastern European locations. This had contributed to diverging unit-labour costs and diverging current account balances in the Euro area. While market share expansion in the dollar-bloc is difficult under a strong Euro, competition within the Euro area will likely increase. The fragile peripheral countries in the Euro area are most likely the losers; they might respond, tentatively, to use a too strong dose of fiscal policy or tolerate inflationary wage increase with domestic-demand led growth, coupled in some countries with real estate booms and ensuing house price bubbles. Capital flows are attracted by bubbles and booms in places within the Euro area and of course also on the American side of the Atlantic, often originating from financial institutions with over-leveraging and from export-led countries that repress their domestic demand. All this had paved the complex ways into the Euro crisis and the US-subprime crisis as well.

Trade can, in principle, be protected against exchange rate risks by forward contracts and FX swaps, normally for maximum one-year duration. Yet investment in fixed asset for producing tradables, be it export goods or domestically used goods exposed to international competition, cannot be insured against exchange rate changes. Multinational companies as multi-currency-corporations have superior opportunities to cope with these imponderables, but countries with high shares of small and medium companies, mainly less advanced or developing countries, face severe investment risks in the production of tradables.

Exchange rates are *grosso modo* determined by capital flows, but the former boomerang on capital flows. The dollar-Euro exchange rate has strong and complex repercussions on capital flows. I see mainly two impacts. First, capital flows are tilting in their composition towards short-term flows, due to exchange rate risks. This does not necessarily preclude rising foreign direct investments in order to bypass exchange rate risks. Second, exchange rate gyrations distort asset prices. Since exchange rate changes can hardly be foreseen, as analysed above, and if they are key prices to value financial assets in other currency areas, asset pricing becomes fickler, nearly unforeseeable and infected by uncertainty rather than calculable risk. No question, this makes financial assets worldwide more volatile, affects balance sheets and increases the vulnerability of financial institutions. The functions of money as store of value, standard for credit contracts and standard of value are hollowed out if the external value of a currency is so unstable. What we have gained from more internal price stability (coined "great moderation" regarding inflation) in recent decades we have lost on external stability of our moneys. Speculation on currencies furthers speculation on financial assets. Hence, floating exchange rates in a speculation-prone regime for the prime and second prime currency on this globe are key ingredients of what has been coined financialisation, the increasing dependence of the real economy from the whims and follies of financial markets of which the global FX markets are the biggest. And the biggest among the latter is the dollar-Euro market. It is an epicentre of financialisation.

References

BIS – Bank for International Settlements (2013): *Triannual Central Bank Survey*. September. Basle.

Beckmann, J., Belke, A, Kühl, M. (2011): The dollar-Euro exchange rate and macroeconomic fundamentals: a time-varying coefficient approach, in: *Review of World Economics*, 147(1), 11-40.

Cline, W.R. (2008): Estimating Consistent Fundamental Equilibrium Exchange Rates. Working Paper 08-06. Peterson Institute for International Economics

De Grauwe, P. (2000): Exchange Rates in Search for Fundamentals: The Case of the Euro-Dollar-Rate, in: *International Finance*, 33, 329-356.

De Grauwe, P., Grimaldi, M. (2006): *The Exchange Rate in a Behavioral Finance Framework*. Princeton University Press, Princeton and Oxford.

Ehrmann, M., Fratzscher, M. (2005): Exchange Rates and Fundamentals: new evidence from real time data, in: *Journal of International Money and Finance*, 24, 317-341.

Heine, M., Herr, H. (2013): *Volkswirtschaftslehre. Paradigmenorientierte Einführung in die Mikro- und Makroökonomie*. München: Oldenbourg.

Herr, H. (2014): Der Wechselkurs in ökonomischen Paradigmen, in: Dullien, S., Hein, E., Truger, A. (eds.): *Makroökonomik, Entwicklung und Wirtschaftspolitik*. Marburg: Metropolis, 43-70.

Keynes, J.M. (1923): *A Tract on Monetary Reform*. Reprint 2000. Amherst, NY: Prometheus Books.

Kindleberger, Ch. (2000): *Manias, Panics, and Crashes. A History of Financial Crises*, 4th edition, New York: John Wiley.

Meese, R.A., Rogoff, K.S. (1983): Empirical Exchange Rate Models of the Seventies: Do They Fit out of Sample?, in: *Journal of International Economics*, 14 (February), 3-24.

Menkhoff, L., Taylor, M.P. (2007): The Obstinate Passion of Foreign Exchange Professionals: Technical Analysis, in: *Journal of Economic Literature*, 45(4), 936-972.

Mussa, M. (2005/2012): Reprint of: The euro and the dollar 6 years after creation, in: *Journal of Policy Modeling*, 34, 585-593.

Priewe, J. (2015): Rätsel Wechselkurs – Krise und Neuanfang der Wechselkurstheorie, in: Hagemann, H., Kromphardt, J. (eds.), *Für eine bessere gesamteuropäische Wirtschaftspolitik*. Marburg: Metropolis, 205-248.

Priewe, J. (2016): The enigmatic dollar-euro exchange rate and the world's biggest forex market – performance, causes, consequences, IMK Study 49, Düsseldorf, http://www.boeckler.de/imk_5023.htm?jahr=

Rogoff, K.S. (2002): Why Are G3 Exchange Rates so Fickle?, in: *Finance and Development*, June, 39:2. http://www.imf.org/external/pubs/ft/fandd/2002/06/rogoff.htm

Rossi, B. (2013): Exchange Rate Predictability, in: *Journal of Economic Perspectives*, 51(4), 1063-1119.

Salvatore, D. (2005): The euro–dollar exchange rate defies prediction, in: *Journal of Policy Modeling*, 27, 455-464.

Schulmeister, S. (2009): Technical Trading and Trends in the Dollar-Euro Exchange Rate. November. WIFO, Wien.

Sosvilla-Rivero, S., Fernández-Fernández, N. (2015): Unconventional monetary policy and the dollar-euro exchange rate: further evidence from event studies, in: *Applied Economics Letters*, 1466-4291.

SVR – Sachverständigenrat zur Begutachtung der gesamtwirtschaftlichen Entwicklung (2000): Jahresgutachten 2000/2001. Bonn, Bundestagsdrucksache 14/4792.

SVR – Sachverständigenrat zur Begutachtung der gesamtwirtschaftlichen Entwicklung (2010): Jahresgutachten 2010/2011. Bonn, Bundestagsdrucksache 17/3700.

Wollmershäuser, T. (2003): Sterilisierte Devisenmarktinterventionen – ein umstrittenes währungspolitisches Instrument, in: *ifo Schnelldienst*, 19, 34-44.

The U.S. management of the financial crisis – a study of hegemony

Christoph Scherrer

1. Introduction

Hansjörg Herr introduced me to the concept of currency hierarchies. Having just finished a PhD dissertation on the auto and steel industries, I became curious to learn more about currencies as their valuations have significant ramifications for the international competiveness of industries. Hansjörg's co-authored book on currency competition (Währungskonkurrenz und Deregulierung der Weltwirtschaft, 1989) provided an excellent starting point for delving into the topic and inspired me to a lengthy book review (Scherrer 1989). Very recently, I could also introduce some PhD students in Kassel to his work on currencies and he was even so kind as to come to us for a small but intensive workshop on dollarization. In other words, Hansjörg is an imcportant source of information on issues of currencies and finance for me who takes a political science perspective on these phenomena. Thus, I want to contribute to his Festschrift some thoughts on the management of the recent financial crisis with a focus on the country whose currency remained on the top of the global currency hierarchy despite being the epicenter of that crisis.

The ongoing financial crisis which originated in the United States of America (USA) in 2007 has not only rejuvenated interest in the financial system but has also opened up the academic discourses about it. The neo-classical theories on finance enjoy no longer a monopoly. While the bulk of the literature on the financial crisis is focused on problem solving, a fundamental critique of the money economy, be it inspired by Karl Marx or Silvio Gesell, is experiencing a renaissance. This classical critique can rightly feel justified by the current crisis. However, it has little to offer beyond a "millennialistic" solution which aspires to overcome the ambivalences of money completely. New approaches which are critical of the current financial system but are neither offering practical solutions nor are aiming at overcoming finance for good, have emerged with the objective of understanding finance's prominent position in society. They are inspired by the writings of Antonio Gramsci or by poststructuralism. They explore the genesis and the form of hegemony in the financial system. Given the brevity of this contribution, I want to focus on a Gramscian reading of the US management of the financial crisis. A concise introduction to the poststructuralist reading of the financial system has been written by Wullweber (2015).

The Gramscian analysis of finance capital has a bit longer tradition than the poststructuralist approaches (Gill 1990). It is mainly concerned with the question to what extent finance capital has become hegemonic. As it is well known, the Gramscian concept of hegemony includes the dimension of consent in addition to coercion. It thereby opens up space for discourse as an important part of any explanation of social power relations. This seems to be of special importance for a reading of the financial crisis of 2007-2009, since the controversies that followed in the wake of the crisis illustrate very pointedly that the causes, the ramifications – even the very existence – of a crisis are not self evident. A Gramscian perspective does not remain at the level of analyzing the frames used in the debate (cp. Boin et al. 2009); it also inquires into the other power sources of the actors in the field, such as their position in the accumulation process and in the institutional set-up of any given society.

A major difference between the above mentioned poststructuralist approaches and the Gramscian research agenda revolves around the question, who or what exerts hegemonic power. Gramsci belongs to the Marxist tradition of class analysis. The question, who or what exercises hegemonic power, would clearly be limited by Gramsci to that of "who" and would be answered with reference to a social class or fraction. Nonetheless he takes account of structures first through referring to class and secondly via the emphasis placed on the necessary correspondence between "progressive" forces of production and hegemony. In contrast, the research on hegemony following the work of Michel Foucault focuses rather on long-term transformations in world-view, power- and governance techniques, which cannot be ascribed to a specific societal group.

Together these inquiries into hegemonic conditions promise more fundamental insights into the genesis of financialization, the causes of the financial crisis and its management. Firstly, they point out the conflictual, contingent genesis of modern finance. Secondly, they highlight the societal character of money, i.e. the dependence of modern financial instruments on interpersonal trust within networks. Thirdly, they shed light on the power effect of specific understandings of economic relations. And fourthly, their concept of identity allows for a better understanding of the way actors in the financial system see their interests, roles, responsibilities and possibilities. All in all these studies of hegemony focus on the complex interactions of ideas, material reproduction and political strategies and thereby go in their critique beyond a mere scandalizing of the excesses in the markets.

A Gramscian perspective focuses more on the actors of finance capital. A ruling class is said to be hegemonic and not just dominant if it succeeds in winning approval for its authority among the members of other societal classes. The more this authority is not merely passively tolerated but actively supported, the more secure the hegemony is. The degree of approval generally rests on how far the ruling institutions address the respective interests of the other classes. One particularly effective form of hegemony by deception, Gramsci argued, is the co-option of the leadership of subordinate classes, so-called transformism. The ethical side of hegemony – leading other groups to the pinnacle of knowledge, technology, and culture – pertains only to allied classes, not to rival, 'ruled' classes (Gramsci 1991).

In the following I will apply these insights first to finance capital's pre-crisis hegemony and then to the management of the crisis itself. I will conclude with some thoughts on how the insights of Gramscianism and poststructuralism might complement each other.

2. Dimensions of pre-crisis hegemony

Financial capital's supremacy over other factions of capital in the last two decades is visible in its increasing share of gross domestic product (GDP) and its above-average rate of returns (Krippner 2005: 178-179). Finance capital's ability to mobilize large amounts of capital for mergers and acquisitions, has allowed it to commodify businesses, thereby creating a market for corporate control. This forces industrial groups to orient themselves in terms of expected rates of return on financial markets (Zorn et al. 2004).

After initial resistance, "productive" management has learned how to come to terms with financial market capital. Large industrial corporations actually spearheaded the trend towards "financialization" (Krippner 2005). Through stock option plans, the remuneration of management has become tied to developments in the stock market. In 1992 CEOs from U.S. corporations commanded over 2% of total equity capital; ten years later this figure had increased to over 12% (Sablowski 2003: 224).

The material basis of finance capital's hegemony rested in the "financial-market-driven" growth model (Boyer 2000) which substituted for out-of-fashion Keynesian demand policies. Increasing stock values (especially in the 1990s) and real estate prices (up until 2006) emboldened households to spend more on consumption. In a way, demand became financialized, fuelled by private households' ever expanding debt in the face of stagnating or declining income; a kind of "privatized Keynesianism" (Crouch 2008; Young 2009).

Does finance capital's hegemony go beyond management and reach the general populace? Here, the above discussed authors provide important insights. Financial speculation has lost some of its negative connotations, thanks to the rise of mathematical finance theory (MacKenzie 2006). These changes in sentiment towards speculation have coincided with some major institutional reforms which have tied the general populace more closely to the financial markets; especially the expansion of capital funded pension systems and the mortgage revolution. Debt has thus become "the American way of life" (Langley 2008). For these institutional reasons the interests of the population mostly run parallel to those of financial capital: rising share prices and low interest rates.

These trends translated into political power and were, at the same time, reinforced by the power gained in politics: financial deregulation, government bail outs, and the occupation of top positions within the state apparatus (the Treasury-Wall Street complex, Bhagwati 1998). The next section will show how valuable this political power proved to be for finance capital during the current crisis.

3. The management of the financial crisis

The crisis was preceded by a spectacular rise in housing prices, which was driven by, among other things, an expansion in the market for mortgage backed securities. Since the mortgages were taken out in the belief that real estate prices would continue to rise, a crisis should have been anticipated once prices started to stagnate, which occurred in May of 2006. It was not until the second largest mortgage bank in the U.S.A., New Century Financial Corporation, declared bankruptcy in April 2007 that the media started paying attention. This bankruptcy was dealt with however as if it was an isolated case that was the result of a particularly aggressive expansion strategy and ill-considered dealings with low-income households (Veiga 2008). Signs of crisis multiplied after that. In December 2007 the Fed started to allow banks to use the questionable mortgage bonds as collateral for loans. In this *first phase of the crisis*, misconduct on the part of finance capital was scarcely a topic of interest: the focus lay instead on the imprudent debtors and individual financial institutions. The strategies for coping with the crisis were, in the main, monetary policies; and the first victims of the crisis, heavily indebted homeowners, did not receive help. Finance capital's hegemony remained undiminished.

The *second phase of the crisis* began with the imminent collapse of the investment bank Bear Stearns in March 2008. It was bought up by the bank JPMorgan Chase with the help of government guarantees. After this rescue, everyone believed that the major financial institutions would be saved. In fact, the bail out of further financial institutions ensued and in September of 2008 the U.S. Treasury had to place the two giants of the mortgage industry, Freddie Mac and Fannie Mae, under state conservatorship. In this phase the systemic dimensions of the crisis became visible. At first the bank collapses were treated as single instances, which could be dealt with through state organized private takeovers. Even after Fed and taxpayer money had become massively involved, there remained the pretence that the state would hold bank capital responsible. However, the Fed and the Treasury thereby contributed to a further concentration of banks. The banks with the best political connections survived (Gapper 2008). While finance capital did loose its previous aura of success as the crisis unfolded, its place in the management of the crisis still remained undisputed. Homeowners and the ordinary employees of the collapsed banks received little or no help. The hegemony of finance capital persisted unbroken.

On September 14, 2008, only a few days after the Freddie Mac and Fannie Mae rescue, the fourth largest US investment bank, Lehman Brothers, applied for creditor protection. This time, the Treasury failed to broker a private rescue operation with state guarantees. The decision not to support Lehman Bros. with public money, plus the announcement on September 16 of guarantees in the amount of $85 billion for the world's largest insurance company, A.I.G., deeply unsettled the financial world and ushered in the *third phase* of the crisis. In order to stem an ensuing panic on the financial markets, the Fed responded with further loosening of the standards for the quality of assets pledged in exchange for its loans to financial institutions and the Treasury drafted a comprehensive rescue plan. Fed and Treasury now defined the crisis as a systemic one. Claiming great urgency, they demanded an open cheque for the amount of $700 billion from Congress. The Emergency Economic Stability Act of 2008 (EESA), signed into law by President Bush on October 3, 2008, did not stray far at its core from the original version (Sorkin 2009).

In this phase the systemic dimensions of the crisis became undeniable. However, the view that too little governmental oversight had caused the crisis was in competition with views that blamed the crisis on big government or the greed of all consumers. More important for the fate of finance capital was the fact that the immediacy of the crisis overshadowed any controversy about who to blame for the crisis. Finance capital could make use of its "panic power", causing the state to come to its rescue with few questions asked. The fear of another Great Depression forced even critics of finance capital to support the rescue. Thus, the acknowledgement of the systemic character of the crisis actually worked in favor of finance capital: its rescue meant the rescue of the whole system. Ironically, the strongest opposition originated in the camp of the stalwarts of free enterprise. The management of the crisis stayed in the hands of the friends of finance capital. The costs of the crisis were nearly fully shifted onto tax payers. Again homeowners took a back seat. Popular sentiment, however, turned against the major representatives of finance capital. Their rescue was not actively supported, only more or less passively accepted for lack of alternatives. Finance capital's hegemony was sliding towards dominance.

While promising quite sweeping changes in many policy areas, especially in health care, Barack Obama was remarkably restrained on the issue of the financial crisis in his campaign for the presidency. This cautious position may have reflected the weight of campaign donations from the financial sector (Phillips 2008: 174). Obama signaled right after his election victory, by the way he selected his economic team that he did not intend to rein Wall Street (Peschek 2011: 439). The Democrats in Congress were likewise not inclined to provoke finance capital. The financial centers of the USA have been a Democratic stronghold since 1992. Democrats have received three times as much campaign money as Republicans from hedge funds since 2006 (Phillips 2008: 170-174). Nevertheless, shortly after the presidential elections Democrats had to act in response to a popular outcry over high bonus payments to executives at some of the banks rescued with tax payers' money (Story 2009). The action remained mainly symbolic (see below).

In sum, in this *fourth phase of the crisis*, this time under President Obama, finance capital again proved able to manage the crisis and to pass on the costs to the U.S. tax payer. In addition, it successfully fought off the imposition of any strict limitations on its operations. It was less successful in defining the causes of the crisis, as many among the public blamed its leading managers. However, public wrath focused more on the level of their remuneration and less on their business model. Finance capital remained hegemonic in the policy arena, but suffered a loss of consent among the general public. This loss did not challenge their business model. In fact, the surviving large banks held even larger market shares and were again able to achieve high returns (Craig/Dash 2011).

In early 2010 President Obama surprised many with a call for a return to a modern version of the Glass-Steagall act. Named for its champion, Paul A. Volcker, the former Federal Reserve Chairman, the so-called Volcker Rule would prohibit banks that receive federally insured deposits from making trades that are for their own accounts, and not to the benefit of their customers. President Obama's push for banking regulation was widely seen as a reaction to an increasing resentment among the US population of his closeness to Wall Street (Chan/Dash 2010). On closer inspection, however, Obama's 2010 proposal sounds a lot more radical than it is in reality. The prohibition of proprietary trading does not limit speculation in general; it only restricts the financial dealings of one group – the banks. Private investors would still be able to use hedge funds for risky deals with derivatives.

A watered-down version of the Volcker rule eventually found its place as Sec. 619 in the Dodd-Frank Wall Street Reform and Consumer Protection Act (signed in July 2010). A telling example of the mainly symbolic character of the Act is its section on derivatives, the main instruments of speculation. The call for trading all derivatives within clearing and exchange systems suffered the same fate as the Volcker rule. This "radical" proposal would not have outlawed speculation; it would have just introduced more transparency and safety cushions (by requiring contracting parties to provide capital, so-called collateral) in the trading of derivatives, i.e. rules which are prevalent in stock markets around the world (Story 2010). This weakening of the already timid regulatory proposals of the Obama administration is the result of heavy lobbying by banks, the dependence of the Democrats on campaign donations from the financial sector, and the closed ranks of the Republicans (Johnson/ Kwak 2010). But it also mirrored the weakness of progressive forces in general (Dark 2011) and in particular in the field of finance (Scherrer 2010).

In this *fifth phase of the crisis*, finance capital seemingly suffered a defeat concerning its freedoms of operation. It failed to prevent quite comprehensive regulatory legislation. In the face of upcoming mid-term elections, the Democratic majority in Congress wanted to demonstrate its ability to reform the financial sector. It received intellectual support from academe and also from regulatory agencies. However, the business community, fearful of further regulation of their own lines of business, sided more or less with the financial industries. Thus, in the end the reform did not limit many of the freedoms finance capital had become accustomed to.

The mid-term elections in November 2010 ushered in the *most recent phase of the crisis*. An ideologically fairly united, right wing Republican Party gained sixty-three seats in the House of Representatives. They rally behind the slogan "market discipline": If banks will not be rescued in the future, they will behave more prudently now. This may sound strange for those remembering the Bush administration's grand bail-out of banks. However, the Republicans find financial rewards (the finance industry favored them in the midterm elections of 2010; Orol 2010) as well as popular support for their position. The "Tea Party Movement" turns its wrath against the federal government and Obama's slightly progressive policy proposals. They consider that Washington has been taken over by a finance-led cosmopolitan conspiracy (MacGillis 2014). The Republicans have acted in this belief. They have slowed down the implementation of the Dodd-Frank Act (Weisman/Lipton 2015).

4. The political – beyond system immanent reforms

The above presented approach to the study of finance capital highlights various dimensions of its hegemony in the past decades and in the current crisis. The Gramscian approach sheds light on the actor-centered dimensions of hegemony, i.e. the strategies of finance capital to universalize its particular interests. This approach tries also to identify the material foundations of these strategies. Although the Gramscian approach acknowledges power to ideas, the poststructuralist inspired approaches are the ones that explicitly try to trace the genesis of ideas, the conditions for their diffusion, and their embeddedness in societal practices (cp. de Goede 2005; MacKenzie 2006; Langley 2008). While de Goede and Langley would identify with the label poststructuralists, this label does not quite fit the sociologist of knowledge MacKenzie. Nevertheless, the parallels are obvious (a view shared by Langley 2010).

Common to both approaches is that they emphasize the political dimension of the genesis of the predominant position of finance capital in today's world. Finance capital's status does not follow from "natural" necessities but from struggles over meanings and practices. This denaturalization of the status quo opens space for envisaging change. This focus on the political origins of specific balances of power does not lead to voluntarism. It rather questions the belief in the efficacy of enlightenment strategies concerning ideological positions. It is not sufficient to denounce mainstream financial wisdom as ideology, as "false consciousness". The same holds true for a fixation with statist interventions. While the Gramscian analysis highlights finance capital's allies, its material and institutional resources, the poststructuralist approach traces the roots of financial markets to the knowledge practices of financial elites as well as to the every day practices of large segments of the population (de Goede 2005; MacKenzie 2006; Langley 2008).

Given that finance capital kept its central place in the financialized regime of accumulation, and that it received continued support from most other fractions of capital up to now, to talk of a loss of hegemony would be premature. What it mainly lost was the passive consensus of the American public. It therefore had to rely on its institutional power and its ability to raise financial resources for lobbying and election campaigns. The mixture of coercion and consensus underlying hegemony has shifted slightly more towards coercion in relation to the general public; but finance capital's main message concerning the right to keep one's money and to invest it according to one's preferences continues to resonate with a sizeable portion of the American electorate.

While finance capital had to accept some new restrictions on their business models, it continues to enjoy great liberties. In fact, as the poststructuralists warn us, more regulatory oversight may stabilize the power of finance capital. Regulation and market should not be seen as opposites, de Goede tells us. More rules can legitimize stock market operations and, thereby, fortify its social status (de Goede 2005: 148). Langley points to a similarly ambivalent impact of the call for a pay moratorium for "underwater" home owners (whose mortgage is higher than the current market price of their house). On the one hand, the deferral of repayments loosens the disciplinary norms for the debtors and opens space for a discussion of the co-responsibilities of the creditors for the debtor's plight. On the other hand, the debtors will be subjected to the legal, calculative, and self-disciplinary techniques of power (Langley 2009).

The poststructuralist authors' reflectivity is very receptive for ambivalences, however, they face the danger that their high level of reflexivity stands in the way of action. A surplus of illusion about the power of one's own action to overcome the status quo is a requirement for making change happen. For devising strategies one can learn more from Gramsci who shows how allies can be found and ones own interests can be furthered.

References

Bhagwati, J.N. (1998): The capital myth: the difference between trade in widgets and dollars. *Foreign Affairs* [online], May/June. Available from: http://www.foreignaffairs.com/articles/54010/jagdish-n-bhagwati/the-capital-myth-the-difference-between-trade-in-widgets-and-dol.

Boin, A., 't Hart, P., McConnell, A. (2009): Crisis exploitation: political and policy impacts of framing contests, in: *Journal of European Public Policy*, 16(1), 81-106.

Boyer, R. (2000): Is a finance-led growth regime a viable alternative to Fordism? A preliminary analysis, in: *Economy and society*, 29(1), 111-145.

Chan, S., Dash E. (2010): Obama moves to limit 'reckless risks' of big banks, in: *The New York Times* [online], 21 January. Available from: http://www.nytimes.com/2010/01/22/business/22banks.html

Craig, S., Dash, E. (2011): Study points to windfall for Goldman partners, in: *The New York Times* [online] 18 January. Available from: http://dealbook.nytimes.com/2011/01/18/study-points-towindfall-for-goldman-partners/

Crouch, C. (2008): What will follow the demise of privatised Keynesianism?, in: *The political quarterly*, 79(4), 476-486.

Dark, Taylor E., III (2011): The Economic Crisis and Organized Labor: resentment over Solidarity, in: *New Political Science*, 33(4), 525-539.

de Goede, M. (2005): *Virtue, Fortune, and Faith: A Genealogy of Finance*, Minneapolis: University of Minnesota Press.

Gapper, J. (2008): Whatever is good for Goldman ..., in: *The Financial Times* [online], Gapper Column, 24 September. Available from: http://blogs.ft.com/gapperblog/2008/09/whatever-isgood-for-goldman/.

Gill, S. (1990): *American hegemony and the Trilateral Commission*, New York: Cambridge University Press.

Gramsci, A. (1991ff.) *Gefängnishefte 1-15, 7 Bände*, eds. K. von Bochmann and W.F. Haug, Hamburg, Berlin: Das Argument Verlag.

Johnson, S., Kwak, J. (2010): *13 Bankers: the Wall Street takeover and the next financial meltdown*. New York: Pantheon.

Krippner, G.R. (2005): The financialization of the American economy. in: *Socio-economic review*, 3(2), 173-208.

Langley, P. (2008): *The Everyday Life of Global Finance: Saving and Borrowing in Anglo-America*, Oxford: Oxford University Press.

Langley, P. (2009): Debt, discipline, and government: foreclosure and forbearance in the subprime mortgage crisis, in: *Environment and Planning*, 41(6), 1404-1419.

Langley, P. (2010): On the materiality of markets, in: *Journal of Cultural Economy*, 3(3), 395-402.

MacGillis, A. (2014): Tea Party Populism Is Dead. The GOP Is Back in Bed With Wall Street, in: *New Republic*, 30. Oct.

MacKenzie, D. (2006): *An Engine, Not a Camera: How Financial Models Shape Markets*, Cambridge, Mass.: MIT Press

Orol, R.D. (2010): Wall St. banking on GOP to ease new rules. *Marketwatch* [online], 28 October. Available from: http://www.marketwatch.com/story/wall-st-banking-on-gop-to-ease-new-rules-2010-10-28

Peschek, J.G. (2011): The Obama Presidency and the Great Recession: Political Economy, Ideology, and Public Policy, in: *New Political Science*, 33(4) 429-444.

Phillips, K. (2008): *Bad money*, New York City: Viking.

Sablowski, T. (2003): Bilanz(en) des Wertpapierkapitalismus. Deregulierung, Shareholder Value, Bilanzskandale, in: *Prokla, Zeitschrift für kritische Sozialwissenschaft*, 33(2), 210-234.

Scherrer, C. (1989): Hinter den Sieben Siegeln. Weltwährungskonkurrenz und Weltwirtschaft, in: *Kommune*, 7(11) 54-56.

Scherrer, C. (2010): Finance capital will not fade away on its own, Global Labour Column Nr. 17, Aril, http://column.global-labour-university.org/

Sorkin, A.R. (2009): *Too Big to Fail. Inside the Battle to Save Wall Street*, London: Penguin.

Story, L. (2009): A rich education for summers (after Harvard), in: *The New York Times* [online], 5 April. Available from: http://www.nytimes.com/2009/04/06/business/06summers.html.

Story, L. (2010): A secretive banking elite rules trading in derivatives, in: *The New York Times* [online], 11 December. Available from: http://www.nytimes.com/2010/12/12/business/12advantage.html.

Veiga, A. (2008): Faulty accounting blamed for New Century's collapse, in: *Arizona Daily Star* [online], 27 March. Available from: http://azstarnet.com/real-estate/article_d285b336-eaf6-5014-ac80-a0dbcce05307.html

Weisman, J., Lipton, E. (2015): In New Congress, Wall St. Pushes to Undermine Dodd-Frank Reform, in: *New York Times*, 13. Jan.

Wullweber, J. (2015): Die Performativität des Finanzsystems und die Selektivität stratifizierter Finanzstrukturen, in: *Leviathan*, 43(2), 270-298.

Young, B. (2009): Vom staatlichen zum privatisierten Keynesianismus. Der globale makroökonomische Kontext der Finanzkrise und der Privatverschuldung, in: *Zeitschrift für Internationale Beziehungen*, 16(1), 141-159.

Zorn, D. et al. (2004): Managing investors: how financial markets reshaped the American firm, in: Knorr Cetina, K., Preda, A. (eds.), *The sociology of financial markets*, London: Oxford University Press, 269-289.

Kommt nach der Krise der „gute Kapitalismus"?

Bewertung der europäischen Finanzmarktreformen seit 2008

Sebastian Dullien

1. Einleitung

Seit 2008 befindet sich die Euro-Zone in einer wirtschaftlichen Dauerkrise. Zum Zeitpunkt der Erstellung dieses Beitrags (Anfang 2016) hatten die Länder des Währungsraums insgesamt bei ihrer Wirtschaftsleistung gerade wieder das Vorkrisenniveau erreicht (siehe Abb. 1). Wie viele Länder Lateinamerikas in den 1980ern hat damit Europa nun ein „verlorenes Jahrzehnt" erlebt, an dessen Ende der Lebensstandard vieler Menschen spürbar niedriger ist als zu Beginn des Jahrzehnts.

Für Europa begann die Krise im Sommer 2008 mit dem Überschwappen der Folgen der US-amerikanischen Subprime-Hypothekenkrise auf die europäische Wirtschaft und erreichte einen ersten Höhepunkt nach der Pleite der US-Investmentbank Lehman Brothers im September desselben Jahres. Nach einer kurzen Erholung schlug ab 2010 die Euro-Krise zu, die in eine zweite Rezession führte, deren Wendepunkt erst mit einem leichten neuen Zuwachs des BIP im zweiten Quartal 2013 erreicht wurde.

Da das Finanz- und Bankensystem für die Genese und den Verlauf der Krise(n) eine zentrale Rolle spielte, gab es von 2008 an Forderungen nach einer kräftigen Re-Regulierung des globalen Finanzsystems sowie der nationalen Finanzsysteme. So war ein wichtiger Konsens unmittelbar nach Ausbruch der Krise, dass übermäßig leichtsinniges Verhalten von Banken und anderen Finanzintermediären bei der Kreditvergabe und bei Investitionsentscheidungen eine der Hauptursachen der Krise gewesen seien. Auch im Verlauf der Euro-Krise wurden Strukturprobleme im Bankensystem wie übermäßig geringes Eigenkapital oder national konzentrierte Bankportfolios für die Länge und Tiefe der Krise verantwortlich gemacht, sodass auch in diesem Zusammenhang immer neue Forderungen zur Reform des Finanzsystems gestellt wurden.

Abbildung 1: Wirtschaftliche Entwicklung im Euro-Raum seit 2008

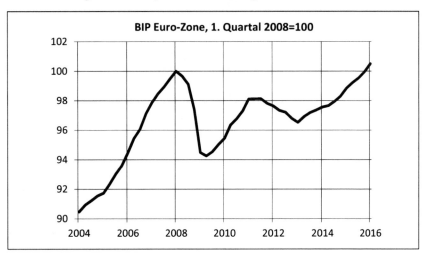

Quelle: Eigene (HTW based on Macrobond data)

Hansjörg Herr beteiligte sich an dieser Diskussion unter anderem mit dem von der Friedrich-Ebert-Stiftung geförderten Projekt des „guten Kapitalismus", das 2009 in der Veröffentlichung eines gleichnamigen Buches zusammen mit Christian Kellermann und dem Verfasser dieses Beitrags mündete (Dullien et al. 2009). Das Buch versucht sich einerseits an der Aufarbeitung der Krisenursachen, andererseits an einer Skizze eines regulierten Kapitalismus, der durch gezielte staatliche Eingriffe zum einen weniger krisenanfällig wäre als der derzeit in entwickelten Industrieländern anzutreffende real existierende Kapitalismus, zum anderen eindeutiger und besser zur Steigerung des Wohlstands der Menschen beitragen kann. Lange Passagen des Buches beschäftigen sich dabei mit notwendigen Reformen des Finanzsektors.[1]

---

[1] Eine überarbeitete und gekürzte Version erschien 2011 auf Englisch (Dullien et al. 2011), weitere Versionen in den Folgejahren auf Chinesisch, Koreanisch, Persisch und Indonesisch.

Dabei blieb es nach der Krise nicht bei theoretischen Debatten. Statt dessen startete die Politik schnell nach der Krise einen wahren Reformmarathon, was sowohl die Finanzmarktregulierung in Europa als auch die Strukturen der Europäischen Union angeht. Nach einer ersten Welle von Finanzmarktreformen unmittelbar nach der Krise entschieden sich die Staats- und Regierungschefs im Sommer 2012, eine „Bankenunion" für die Euro-Zone zu bilden und in dieser die Aufsicht und Regulierung aller Banken im Währungsraum zusammenzuziehen.

Bislang ist allerdings der Erfolg dieser Bemühungen immer noch nicht greifbar: Trotz der massiven Reformen dauern Anfang 2016 die Probleme im Bankensektor wichtiger Euro-Staaten wie Italien an. Es gibt weiter Streit zwischen der italienischen Regierung, der Europäischen Kommission und der deutschen Regierung über den richtigen und zulässigen Umgang mit den faulen Krediten im italienischen Bankensystem. In vielen Euro-Ländern ist die Kreditvergabe des Finanzsystems weiter verhalten, während an den Finanzmärkten Zweifel an der Stabilität wichtiger Banken, wie unter anderem sogar der Deutschen Bank, die Runde machen.

Vor dem Hintergrund dieser empirischen Erfahrungen und der Analyse des „guten Kapitalismus" soll der vorliegende Beitrag die Frage beantworten, was eigentlich bei den Reformen falsch gelaufen ist. Dafür wird zunächst in Abschnitt 2 herausgearbeitet, was genau die Reformblaupausen im „guten Kapitalismus" von anderen Reformkonzepten in der Krisenliteratur unterscheidet. Abschnitt 3 gibt einen kurzen Überblick über die tatsächlich erfolgten Finanzmarktreformen seit 2009 und Abschnitt 4 versucht zu ergründen, warum bislang wenig greifbare Erfolge dieser massiven Reformen zu erkennen sind.

2. Der gute Kapitalismus im Verhältnis zu anderen Reformvorschlägen nach der Krise 2008/9

Nach der Krise erschien eine Vielzahl von Büchern zur Reformnotwendigkeit des Finanzsystems, sowohl mit globaler als auch mit eher europäischer Ausrichtung. Als repräsentative Beispiele aus den Federn renommierter Ökonomen lässt sich der Bericht der sogenannten Stiglitz-Kommission (Stiglitz 2010), der Beitrag des damaligen Ifo-Präsidenten Hans-Werner Sinn (2009) oder des früheren Vorsitzenden des Vereins für Socialpolitik Martin Hellwig (Hellwig/Admati 2014) nennen. Radikalere Vorschläge gab es sowohl von eher linker Seite (Huber 2014) als auch von konservativer Seite durch den früheren Deutsche-Bank-Chefökonomen Thomas Mayer (2015).

Dabei wurde eine Reihe von mehr oder weniger weitreichenden Forderungen aufgestellt, wie man das Geld- und Finanzsystem reformieren müsse, um Krisen künftig zu vermeiden. Praktisch allen Werken ist gemein, dass eine Korrektur falscher Anreize im Finanzsystem gefordert wird. Schnell war etwa ausgemacht, dass eine Krisenursache gewesen war, dass Banken zu wenig Eigenkapital für ihre Aktivitäten vorgehalten hatten. Nach vorherrschender Argumentation hatte dies dazu geführt, dass die Aufnahme weiterer Risiken für die Banken im Konkursfall keine weiteren Verluste gebracht hätte (mehr als das Eigenkapital gibt es ja für Aktionäre nicht zu verlieren), die bei glücklichem Verlauf der Dinge resultierenden Gewinne aber die erwartete Rendite erhöht hätten.

In eine ähnliche Richtung gingen Forderungen, dass Banken bei Verbriefungen einen signifikanten Anteil der Risiken in der eigenen Bilanz behalten sollten, damit sie bei der Kreditvergabe ausreichend Sorgfalt walten lassen. Auch hier sollten die Banken durch eine höhere Beteiligung am Risiko zu vernünftigerem Verhalten bewegt werden.

Ebenfalls recht einmütig wurden Forderungen nach einer Reform von Vergütungsstrukturen vorgebracht, die zuvor bei Managern zu übermäßig großer Risikofreude geführt hatten. Aktienoptionen für Entscheidungsträger wurden hier oft als problematisches Beispiel genannt, weil sich bei diesen ein Aktienkursanstieg über einen recht kurzen Zeithorizont als zusätzliches Einkommen der Optionshalter materialisierte, mittelfristige und langfristige Risiken für die Bank allerdings kein symmetrisches Einkommensrisiko für die Manager bedeuteten.

Ebenso unumstritten war die Forderung, sowohl in den USA als auch in der EU die bestehenden Flickenteppiche von Aufsichts- und Regulierungsbehörden zu vereinheitlichen und Möglichkeiten zum Regulierungsarbitrage zu begrenzen.

Dagegen eher umstritten waren Außenseiterpositionen, die wie Huber (2014) und Mayer (2015) gleich eine Fundamentalreform des Geldsystems forderten, das den Banken die Giralgeldschöpfung untersagen sollte. Zwar gab es für solche radikalen Vorschläge Sympathisanten sogar bis in den Internationalen Währungsfonds (wo in einzelnen Papieren der sogenannte Chicago-Plan wiederentdeckt und analysiert wurde, der ebenfalls die Giralgeldschöpfung der Banken beendet hätte[2]), jedoch waren diese Vorschläge für die breitere politische Diskussion wohl doch zu esoterisch.

---

[2] Siehe etwa Benes/Kumhoff (2012).

Die Vision des „guten Kapitalismus" hebt sich von diesen Werken durch zweierlei Dinge ab. Erstens nimmt sie eine breite, gesamtwirtschaftliche Perspektive der Interaktion verschiedener Märkte ein, aus der Forderungen nicht nur nach Reformen des Finanzsektors und des Geldwesens folgen, sondern auch nach solchen für Arbeits- und Devisenmärkte und der öffentlichen Investitionstätigkeit. Zweitens kombiniert sie Mainstream-Argumentationen von mikroökonomischen Anreizproblemen im Finanzsektor mit einer Reihe von nicht-neoklassischen Argumenten wie Herdenverhalten und makroökonomischen Ungleichgewichten.

Paradigmatisch macht der „gute Kapitalismus" hier wichtige Anleihen an den Denktraditionen Joseph Schumpeters, John M. Keynes', Hyman Minskys und Karl Polanyis: Aus der schumpeterianischen (und zum Teil auch keynesianischen) Tradition stammt die Einsicht, dass Banken und die Kreditschöpfung eine wichtige Rolle im Investitions- und Innovationsprozess einer Volkswirtschaft spielen, die weit über die von der Neoklassik dem Finanzsektor zugesprochenen Allokationsfunktion hinausgeht. Nach diesem Verständnis kann das Finanzsystem Giralgeld „aus dem Nichts" schöpfen und dieses an Kreditnehmer verteilen. Unternehmer können sich mit der so geschaffenen Kaufkraft ohne vorherige Ersparnisse Produktionsmittel aneignen und damit einen Produktionsprozess in Gang setzen, der wiederum Einkommen und Beschäftigung in der Volkswirtschaft erhöht (Schumpeter 1912). Ebenfalls aus dieser Denktradition kommt die Idee, dass das Bankensystem helfen kann, Realkapital zu „monetisieren" (Tobin 1998), indem es auf der einen Seite Realkapitalakkumulation bei den Kreditnehmern ermöglicht, gleichzeitig aber den Sparern Geld in Form von liquiden Depositen zur Verfügung stellt. Das Ergebnis ist ein höheres Level und – bei Berücksichtigung der Erkenntnisse der endogenen Wachstumstheorie – eine höhere Wachstumsrate des Outputs einer Volkswirtschaft.

Eng verknüpft mit diesem Argument ist die (keynesianische) Erkenntnis, dass es enge Verbindungen zwischen dem Finanzsystem und der Wirtschaft als Ganzer gibt. Mit einem disfunktionalen Bankensystem, das keine Kredite vergibt, ist eine Rückkehr zu nachhaltigem Wachstum in einer Geldwirtschaft nach dieser Argumentation nicht möglich. Andererseits bedeutet aber auch ein deflationäres, makroökonomisches Stagnationsumfeld, dass das Eigenkapital von Banken durch Kreditausfälle zunehmend aufgezehrt wird und diese deshalb ihrer Funktion als Transmissionsmechanismus der Volkswirtschaft nicht mehr nachkommen können.

Gleichzeitig übernimmt der „gute Kapitalismus" aus dem Denken Minskys (1986) und auch Keynes' die Erkenntnis, dass sich Märkte nicht unbedingt selbst stabilisieren, sondern dass insbesondere Finanzmärkte zur inhärenten Instabilität neigen und dass so für eine reibungsfreie, stabile Wirtschaftsentwicklung im Kapitalismus permanente und umfangreiche Eingriffe des Staates in den Wirtschaftsprozess notwendig sind.

Zu guter Letzt erkennt der „gute Kapitalismus" die von Polanyi (1944) konstatierten Grenzen marktwirtschaftlicher Ordnung an, nach denen Natur, Arbeit und Geld keine normalen Güter sind und deshalb einer besonderen staatlichen Regulierung unterliegen müssen.

Aus dem Zusammenspiel dieser paradigmatischen Wurzeln ergeben sich Schlussfolgerungen, die den „guten Kapitalismus" deutlich von anderen Reformblaupausen nach der Krise abgrenzen. Zwar kommt der „gute Kapitalismus" wie viele andere Werke zu dem Schluss, Banken und Finanzinstitutionen wesentlich stärker zu regulieren und zu überwachen. Anders aber als Werke aus der neoklassischen Tradition, die vor allem auf mehr Haftung von Kapitalgebern und Managern setzen, werden dabei von Dullien et al. (2009) nicht nur höhere Eigenkapitalforderungen und Selbstbehalte bei Verbriefungen gefordert, sondern es wird ein Schwerpunkt auf die Reduktion der Komplexität des Finanzsektors gelegt. So fordern Dullien et al. (2009) eine Standardisierung von Finanzprodukten anhand eines „Finanz-TÜV" und einer Positivliste, wonach alle nicht explizit zugelassenen Finanzprodukte verboten wären.

Da der „gute Kapitalismus" auf der anderen Seite die positive Rolle der endogenen Geldschöpfung unterstreicht, wird in ihm radikalen Forderungen zum Umbau des Geldsystems, etwa durch ein Vollgeld-System (was ein Ende der Kreditschöpfung und der Fristentransformation durch das Bankensystem bedeuten würde), eine Absage erteilt.

Die Kombination mit der Einsicht in die zentrale Rolle des Bankensystems im Investitions- und Wachstumsprozess einer Volkswirtschaft rechtfertigt im „guten Kapitalismus" auch die gelegentliche Rettung von Banken durch Steuergelder: Da das Bankensystem durch den fördernden Einfluss der Monetisierung von Kapital auf das Wirtschaftswachstum positive externe Effekte mit sich bringt und aufgrund der inhärenten Instabilität der Finanzmärkte eine perfekte Stabilisierung des Bankensektors wegen seiner Fristentransformation ohnehin nicht möglich ist, ist es nach dieser Argumentation völlig angebracht, dass der Staat die Banken durch gelegentliche Bankenrettungen implizit subventioniert. Was den Autoren zufolge jedoch sichergestellt werden muss, ist, dass diese Subvention für gesamtwirtschaftlich nützliche Aktivitäten wie insbesondere die Kreditvergabe stattfindet, nicht aber für unnütze oder gar schädliche Aktivitäten wie die Spekulation. Aus diesem Grund fordern Dullien et al.

(2009), den Banken Eigenhandel ebenso zu verbieten wie Kreditvergabe an Nicht-Bank-Finanzinstitute. Ebenfalls klar aus diesen Prämissen folgt der Schluss, dass ein Sanieren des Bankensystems nicht im deflationären Umfeld gelingen kann und deshalb die Stabilisierung der gesamtwirtschaftlichen Nachfrage vorrangige Aufgabe aller Felder der Wirtschaftspolitik sein muss und für dieses Ziel auch die bestehenden Fiskalregeln der EU verändert bzw. zumindest zeitweise ignoriert werden müssten.

Die Kombination aus mikro- und makroökonomischer Analyse des „guten Kapitalismus" erlaubte dabei zum Zeitpunkt seiner Erstveröffentlichung eine Vorhersage des weiteren Krisenverlaufs, der anderen Werken aus der Zeit verwehrt blieb. So warnt das 2009 (deutlich vor dem Ausbruch der Euro-Krise, die mit den Finanzproblemen Griechenlands im Frühjahr 2010 begann) erschienene Buch vor den Ungleichgewichten im Euro-Raum. Es heißt da:

„Solange aber die Institutionen der europäischen Währungsunion nicht grundlegend angepasst werden, besteht weiter die Gefahr, dass sich [...] Ungleichgewichte aufbauen und krisenhaft [...] korrigiert werden – mit dramatischen Folgen sowohl für die deutsche Wirtschaft als auch für die anderen Volkswirtschaften des Euroraums. Ohne weitere Reformen wäre somit der Versuch der Europäer, sich mithilfe ihrer Währungsunion der Irrationalität der globalen Devisenmärkte zu entziehen, nur zum Preis neuer Probleme erkauft worden." (Dullien et al. 2009: 84)

Auch gelang es durch die Analyse der makroökonomischen Verbindung mit dem Finanzsystem, im „guten Kapitalismus" die Euro-Rettung vorherzusagen, die zum Erscheinungszeitpunkt im Jahr 2009 für die meisten Politiker und Experten noch völlig ausgeschlossen schien. So heißt es weiter:

„Der Bankrott eines einzelnen Eurostaates würde Schockwellen durch das Bankensystem der gesamten Währungsunion senden. [...] Da eine solche Bankenkrise am Ende extrem hohe Kosten [...] bedeutet, werden im Zweifel die europäischen Partner kein einzelnes Land in die Zahlungsunfähigkeit laufen lassen [...]. Die im Maastricht-Vertrag enthaltene sogenannte No-Bail-Out-Klausel, nach der die anderen Eurostaaten nicht für die Schulden eines einzelnen Mitglieds einstehen, dürfte somit im Ernstfall an der ökonomischen Realität der engen wirtschaftlichen Verflechtungen in Europa scheitern." (Dullien et al. 2009: 192f.)

Genauso kam es: Im Frühjahr 2010 wurde zunächst ein Hilfspaket für Griechenland aufgelegt, weil die europäischen Partner Angst vor einer Ansteckungsgefahr nach einem Zahlungsausfall Griechenlands hatten. Es folgten verschiedene Pakete für andere Länder und zu guter Letzt die Einrichtung des permanenten Rettungsschirms ESM – eine Maßnahme, die Anfang 2010 noch von vielen Politikern kategorisch ausgeschlossen worden war.

3. Tatsächlich umgesetzte Reformen

Auch den Politikern in den wichtigsten Industrieländern war nach Ausbruch der Krise schnell klar, dass es kein „Weiter so" im Finanzsektor geben könnte. Mit markigen Worten kündigten sie an, die Finanzmärkte so an die Kandare zu nehmen, dass eine Wiederholung der Krise 2008/9 nicht möglich sei. So heißt es im Abschlussdokument des G20-Treffens in Pittsburgh vom September 2009:

> „Where reckless behavior and a lack of responsibility led to crisis, we will not allow a return to banking as usual. [...] We committed to act together to raise capital standards, to implement strong international compensation standards aimed at ending practices that lead to excessive risk-taking, to improve the over-the-counter derivatives market and to create more powerful tools to hold large global firms to account for the risks they take. Standards for large global financial firms should be commensurate with the cost of their failure. For all these reforms, we have set for ourselves strict and precise timetables." (G20 2009: 2)

Diesen Worten folgten auch Taten: Auch wenn in der Öffentlichkeit heute gelegentlich der Eindruck vorherrscht, die Banken seien nach der Krise nicht weiter von Aufsehern und Gesetzgebern behelligt worden, entspricht dies nicht der Realität. Vielmehr sind sowohl in den USA als auch in Europa eine Vielzahl von neuen Regeln für den Finanzsektor erlassen worden. In den USA manifestiert sich die Re-Regulierung des Finanzsektors in erster Linie im „Dodd-Frank Wall Street Reform and Consumer Protection Act" von 2010, der auf fast 1000 Seiten neue Regeln für das Finanzsystem definiert, neue Aufsichtsbehörden schafft und auf den mehr als 10000 Seiten nachgelagerte Regulierungen von untergeordneten Behörden folgten.

Die Reformen der Finanzmärkte und des Bankensystems in der Europäischen Union vollzogen sich – anders als in den USA – in zwei Wellen. In einer ersten Welle wurden unmittelbar nach der Krise 2008 im Großen und Ganzen die G20-Versprechungen umgesetzt (Dullien 2012). So wurde(n) in einer Vielzahl von Richtlinien und Verordnungen

- Eigenkapitalanforderungen im Einklang mit dem unter Basel III vereinbarten Rahmen kräftig erhöht,

- größere (systemrelevante) Banken zu noch höheren Eigenkapitalquoten verpflichtet,

- Banken verpflichtet, bei Verbriefungen größere Anteile der zugrunde liegenden Kredite in der Bilanz zu behalten,

- ein „European Systemic Risk Board" eingeführt, das systemische Risiken im europäischen Bankensystem beobachten sollte,

- europäische Aufsichtsbehörden für Kapitalmärkte (ESMA), Versicherungen (EIOPA) und Banken (EBA) eingeführt, die die Tätigkeit der nationalen Aufsichtsbehörden besser koordinieren sollten,

- bestimmte Derivate standardisiert und organisiertem Handel unterworfen,

- Ratingagenturen einer Registrierungspflicht unterworfen,

- Hedgefonds stärkeren Regulierungen unterworfen,

- bestimmte Bonuspraktiken bei Banken verboten.

Die zweite Stufe der Finanzmarktreformen in Europa besteht aus den Regeln der Bankenunion, die nach 2012 auf den Weg gebracht wurden. Bei diesen Regeln handelt es sich zum einen um eine weitere Zentralisierung der Bankenaufsicht bei der Europäischen Zentralbank, die anders als die zuvor geschaffene europäische EBA Durchgriffsrechte für vormals national regulierte Banken erhielt, zum anderen um einheitliche europäische Regeln zur Abwicklung oder Rettung notleidender Banken.

Diese Regeln schreiben vor, dass EU-Staaten nicht mehr wie bisher Banken in Schieflage einfach mit öffentlichen Mitteln retten dürfen, sondern dass zuvor sowohl das Eigenkapital der Banken wie auch die Forderungen zumindest eines Teils der Bankgläubiger zur Deckung von Verlusten herangezogen werden müssen (das sogenannte „Bail-in"). Um für den Fall vorzusorgen, dass betroffene Banken danach noch immer Kapitalprobleme haben, die aus dem normalen Staatsbudget nicht zu leisten sind, müssen die EU-Staaten Abwicklungsfonds aus Beiträgen des Finanzsektors aufbauen, damit im Ernstfall systemwichtige Banken gerettet werden können, ohne auf das allgemeine Staatsbudget zurückgreifen zu müssen. Für die Euro-Zone wurde dabei (mit langen Übergangsfristen) ein gemeinsamer Bankenrettungsfonds geschaffen.

Weitere ursprünglich vorgeschlagene Elemente der Bankenunion befinden sich zum Zeitpunkt der Erstellung dieses Beitrags noch im politischen Limbo.

So wurde zwar im ursprünglichen Konzept der Europäischen Kommission (2012) eine gemeinsame Einlagenversicherung avisiert, diese ist bislang allerdings an deutschem Widerstand gescheitert. Ebenfalls ungewiss ist zum Zeitpunkt des Erstellen dieses Beitrags die Zukunft des Vorhabens der EU-Kommission, Aufsichtsbehörden bei zu großen systemrelevanten Banken ein Aufspalten der Banken zu erlauben, um das reguläre Bankengeschäft besser von gefährlichen spekulativen Aktivitäten zu trennen.

4. Umgesetzte Reformen und die Analyse des „guten Kapitalismus"

Wenn man diese Reformen betrachtet (Tab. 1), fällt auf, dass viele von den Veränderungen tatsächlich so oder ähnlich im „guten Kapitalismus" gefordert worden sind, wie ebenso von der Stiglitz-Kommission oder von Hellwig/ Admati (2014). Allerdings fällt ebenfalls auf, dass wichtige Forderungen sowohl der Stiglitz-Kommission als auch des „guten Kapitalismus" gerade nicht aufgegriffen wurden. So wurde die Idee eines Finanz-TÜV, der eine Positivliste für Finanzprodukte erstellt, ebenso verworfen wie das Verbot für Banken, Kredite an Finanzinstitute, die nicht zu den Banken zählen, zu vergeben.

Trennt man die Ursachenanalysen in solche, die auf neoklassischen Anreizargumenten beruhen, und solche, die sich entweder auf nicht-rationales Verhalten von Individuen oder auf makroökonomische Koordinationsprobleme beziehen, so fällt auf, dass die umgesetzten Reformen praktisch ausschließlich mikroökonomische Anreizeffekte angehen.

Ein Teil der nun umgesetzten Reformen läuft sogar den Grundideen des „guten Kapitalismus" völlig entgegen. Eine der Hauptforderungen des „guten Kapitalismus" ist, Politikspielraum zu erhöhen, um angesichts der inhärenten Instabilität der Finanzmärkte den Kapitalismus stabilisieren zu können. Das Verbot der Bankenrettung ohne vorheriges Bail-In von Gläubigern tut genau das Gegenteil: Es engt die staatliche Fähigkeit zur Stabilisierung von Erwartungen im Fall von Schwierigkeiten im Bankensektor ein. Begründet wurde dieses immer wieder mit der Hoffnung, dass rationale Kreditgeber so in Zukunft einen größeren Anreiz haben würden, Banken vor Kreditvergabe genauer zu überprüfen; allerdings basiert dieses Argument auf der Annahme kühl und immer rational agierender Investoren. Geht man von einer inhärenten Sprunghaftigkeit der Investoren aus, ist der Nutzen dieser Regeln alles andere als klar. Zwar mögen sie in dem ein oder anderen Fall die Banken zu vorsichtigerem Verhalten bewegen; dies geschieht aber auf Kosten massiv eingeschränkter Handlungsfähigkeit im Fall systemischer Krisen.

Tabelle 1: Krisenursachen, Reformempfehlungen des „guten Kapitalismus" und in der EU umgesetzte Reformen

	Theoretische Krisenursache	Empfehlung im „guten Kapitalismus"	In der EU umgesetzt
Traditionelle Anreiz- und Informationsprobleme (mit neoklassischen Instrumenten zu analysieren)	Moral Hazard bei Kreditverträgen	Erhöhte Eigenkapitalanforderungen	Erhöhte Eigenkapitalanforderungen (Basel III)
	Moral Hazard bei Kreditvergabe und Verbriefung	Reform der Verbriefungsregeln	Reform der Verbriefungsregeln
		Verstärkte Regulierung von Ratingagenturen	Registrierungspflicht von Ratingagenturen
	Too big to fail	Erhöhte Eigenkapitalanforderungen für große Banken	Erhöhte Eigenkapitalanford. für große Banken
			Beschränkung staatlicher Bail-outs
	Inkohärente Aufsichtsstrukturen	Einheitliche Aufsichtsstrukturen	Neue EU-Aufsichtsbehörden
			Bankenaufsicht durch EZB
	Interessenskonflikte	Europäisierung der Bankenaufsicht	Neue EU-Aufsichtsbehörden & Bankenaufsicht durch EZB
		Zurückdrängen von Ratings in Regulierungen	Ansätze zur Aufwertung von eigenen Bewertungen durch Banken
	Regulatorisches Arbitrage zwischen Banken und Schattenbanken	Verbot von Geschäften von Banken mit Schattenbanken	Höhere Eigenkapitalanforderungen für Geschäfte von Banken mit Schattenbanken
Probleme außerhalb des neoklassischen Analyserahmens	Instabilität durch Spekulationen von Banken	Trennbankensystem	–
	Exzessive Komplexität des Finanzsektors	Finanz-TÜV und Positivliste von Produkten	–
	Makroökonomische Ungleichgewichte (schwache gesamtwirtschaftliche Nachfrage; Einkommensungleichheit; Leistungsbilanzungleichgewichte)	Umfassendes makroökonomisches Management Kapitalverkehrskontrollen Begrenzung von Leistungsbilanzungleichgewichten durch internationale Vereinbarung	–[a]
	Inhärente Instabilität des Finanzsektors durch Herdenverhalten und irrationale Investoren	Zurückdrängen der Finanzmärkte bei gesamtwirtschaftlicher Allokation	–

[a] Mit dem sogenannten „Six Pack" ist zwar der Versuch unternommen worden, Leistungsbilanzungleichgewichte innerhalb der Euro-Zone zu begrenzen, allerdings sind die Regeln zum einen asymmetrisch ausgestaltet, zum anderen sind sie bislang in einer wenig bindenden Form angewendet worden.

Quelle: Eigene Zusammenstellung in Anlehnung an Dullien (2013)

Ebenfalls klar den Forderungen des „guten Kapitalismus" entgegen gelaufen ist in den vergangenen Jahren die Ausrichtung der Fiskalpolitik in der Euro-Zone. Seit dem Ausbruch der Euro-Krise 2010 haben sich die Mitgliedsstaaten mit verschiedenen neuen Regelwerken und Vereinbarungen einem raschen Abbau der strukturellen Budgetdefizite verschrieben. Das Ergebnis war eine jahrelange, spürbare Belastung der gesamtwirtschaftlichen Nachfrage und insbesondere ein Rückgang der staatlichen Investitionen, an deren Ende die staatlichen Nettoinvestitionen in der Euro-Zone sogar negativ geworden sind. Dies steht in brutalem Widerspruch nicht nur zu Forderungen einer antizyklischen Finanzpolitik, sondern auch zu Forderungen nach einer konstruktiven und wachstumsfördernden Investitionstätigkeit des Staates.

5. Warum gibt es weiter Probleme im Bankensektor?

Baut man auf die paradigmatischen Wurzeln des „guten Kapitalismus" auf, so sollte es wenig verwunderlich sein, dass trotz nun fast eines Jahrzehnts der Reformen am Bankensektor dieser immer noch eine akute Bedrohung für die gesamtwirtschaftliche Stabilität zu sein scheint. Zwar ist nach der Analyse des „guten Kapitalismus" eine kohärente Anreizstruktur der Akteure im Finanzsektor ebenso wie eine gute Aufsichtsstruktur wichtig, um Krisen zu verhindern. Eine solche Anreizstruktur ist bei Annahme inhärent irrationaler und instabiler Finanzmärkte allerdings nur eine notwendige, nicht aber eine hinreichende Bedingung für Finanzsystemstabilität.

Ebenfalls vernachlässigt wurde aus der Perspektive des „guten Kapitalismus" die Verbindung zwischen Makroökonomie und Mikroökonomie: Die Kombination von Bankenreformen, die höhere Eigenkapitalstandards von den Banken fordern, mit einer Politik fiskalischer Austerität bei ohnehin schwachen Nachfragetrends und niedrigen Inflationsraten muss in einem keynesianischen Paradigma scheitern. Zum einen wird es in einer Situation ohnehin schwacher gesamtwirtschaftlicher Nachfrage den Banken durch Erhöhung der Eigenkapitalstandards erschwert, ihre Kreditvergabe auszuweiten, zum anderen wird es durch die Nachfrageschwäche und den tendenziellen Preisverfall für Unternehmen schwieriger, ihre Kredite zu bedienen, was zu neuen Problemen im Bankensektor führt.

6. Schlussfolgerungen

Ein Sprichwort lautet: „In jeder Krise liegt eine Chance". Der britische Premier Winston Churchill wird oft mit den Worten zitiert: „Never let a good crisis go to waste".

Unmittelbar nach Ausbruch der Finanzkrise schien es einen Moment lang so, als gäbe es tatsächlich ein Zeitfenster für weitreichende Reformen der Wirtschaftsordnung in Europa und möglicherweise auch in anderen OECD-Ländern und ein grundsätzliches Zurückdrängen der Rolle volatiler Finanzmärkte in der Steuerung unserer modernen Volkswirtschaften. Die Öffentlichkeit, aber auch die herrschenden Politiker waren so entsetzt von den Folgen des ungebremsten Finanzkapitalismus für die Weltwirtschaft, die Arbeitsmärkte und ihre eigenen öffentlichen Budgets, dass es eine Bereitschaft zu geben schien, jahrzehntelang vorherrschende Paradigmen über die richtige Machtverteilung von Markt und Staat in Frage zu stellen. Ein echter Fortschritt hin zu einem „guten Kapitalismus" schien greifbar.

Acht Jahre später muss man konstatieren: Die Krise 2008/9 ist nicht in diesem Sinne genutzt worden. Zwar gibt es eine Reihe von neuen Regeln für Banken und andere Finanzinstitutionen. Da allerdings zumindest die europäische Re-Regulierung praktisch alle Erkenntnisse jenseits einer engen neoklassischen Anreizargumentation außer Acht gelassen hat, ist unser Wirtschaftssystem immer noch nicht stabilisiert. Insgesamt mögen die neuen Regeln zwar die eine oder andere zukünftige Krise unwahrscheinlicher gemacht haben, aufgrund der unterlassenen Veränderungen etwa bei öffentlichen Investitionen und eines übertriebenen Fokus auf den Abbau der Staatsdefizite und die Erhöhung der Haftung von Kapitalgebern im Bankensektor bleibt aber nicht nur das Risiko einer neuen Krise bestehen, sondern es ist überhaupt fraglich, ob man davon sprechen kann, dass die Euro-Zone bislang die Krise überhaupt schon hinter sich gelassen hat. Ein „guter Kapitalismus" ist leider heute kaum näher als 2008, unmittelbar vor der Krise.

Literatur

Benes, J., Kumhoff, M. (2012): The Chicago Plan Revisited, IMF Working Paper WP/12/202, Washington, D.C.

Dullien, S. (2012): Anspruch und Wirklichkeit der Finanzmarktreform: Welche G20-Versprechen wurden umgesetzt?, IMK Study 26, Düsseldorf.

Dullien, S. (2013): Finanzmarktreformen nach der Krise: Unzureichende Reformen durch einseitige Problemanalyse, in: *Wirtschaftsdienst*, 2012/7, 431-434.

Dullien, S., Herr, H., Kellermann, C. (2009): *Der gute Kapitalismus: ... und was sich dafür nach der Krise ändern müsste*, Bielefeld.

Dullien, S., Herr, H., Kellermann, C. (2011): *Decent capitalism: A blueprint for reforming our economies*, London.

Europäische Kommission (2012): Towards a Banking Union, MEMO/12/656, 10 September 2012, URL: http://europa.eu/rapid/press-release_MEMO-12-656_en.htm (zuletzt abgerufen am 23.02.2016).

G20 (2009): Leaders' Statement: The Pittsburgh Summit: September 24-25, 2009, https://www.treasury.gov/resource-center/international/g7-g20/Documents/pittsburgh_summit_leaders_statement_250909.pdf (zuletzt abgerufen am 19.02.2016).

Hellwig, M., Admati, A. (2014): *The Bankers' New Clothes: What's Wrong with Banking and What to Do about It*, Princeton, N.J.

Huber, J. (2014): *Monetäre Modernisierung: Zur Zukunft der Geldordnung: Vollgeld und Monetative*, 4. Auflage, Marburg.

Keynes, J.M. (1936): *The General Theory of Employment, Interest and Money*, London.

Mayer, T. (2015): *Die neue Ordnung des Geldes: Warum wir eine Geldreform brauchen*, 2. Auflage, München.

Minsky, H. (1986): *Stabilizing an Unstable Economy*, New Haven.

Polanyi, K. (1944): *The Great Transformation*, Boston.

Schumpeter, J. (1912): *Theorie der wirtschaftlichen Entwicklung*, Leipzig.

Sinn, H.-W. (2009): *Kasino-Kapitalismus: Wie es zur Finanzkrise kam, und was jetzt zu tun ist*, Berlin.

Stiglitz, J. (2010): *The Stiglitz report: Reforming the international monetary and financial systems in the wake of the global crisis*, New York.

Tobin, J. (1998): *Money, credit, and capital*, Boston, Mass.

Realwirtschaft und Finanzwirtschaft in der neueren Krisendiskussion und in den Volkswirtschaftlichen Gesamtrechnungen

Klaus Voy

Einleitend werden *politökonomische Paradigmen*, insbesondere das monetär-keynesianische mit der Betonung der Geld- und Kreditwirtschaft, und der Zusammenhang mit den Volkswirtschaftlichen Gesamtrechnungen (VGR) kurz skizziert. Die *Realwirtschaft als neues Modewort* im Gegensatz zur Finanzwirtschaft kennzeichnet die Aktualität des Themas seit der Finanzkrise. Die realen und finanziellen Dimensionen in den VGR werden in zwei Schritten beschrieben: zunächst als die Welt der *deflationierten Größen*, sodann die verschiedenen Möglichkeiten, *Real- und Finanzwirtschaft* in den VGR zu unterscheiden. Finanzwirtschaft wird einerseits dargestellt als Finanzsektor und andererseits als finanzielle Dimension aller Sektoren. Im Anhang *„Darstellungsebenen der Buchführung"* wird gezeigt, dass die Finanzbuchhaltung und die Gewinn- und Verlustrechnung die gleichen Unterscheidungen repräsentieren.

Der knappe Überblick verfolgt den Zweck, in der laufenden Diskussion zu begrifflichen Klärungen beizutragen.

1. Politökonomische Paradigmen

Für das monetär-keynesianische Paradigma (Heine/Herr 2013) ist bereits seit den achtziger Jahren die Sichtweise prägend, dass die nationalen Gesamtwirtschaften und die Weltwirtschaft nicht realwirtschaftlich bestimmt – und daher zu erklären – seien, wie die neoklassische Synthese annimmt, sondern umgekehrt ganz wesentlich finanzwirtschaftlich, also als Geldwirtschaften. In der neoklassischen Synthese steht die Realwirtschaft im Zentrum, am Ende ist der Ausgleich von Sparen und Investieren das große Thema, wobei die ganze Finanzsphäre gedacht wird als der Realwirtschaft dienend – wenn sie nur frei genug sei.

In ökonomischen Theorien werden diese Zusammenhänge in makroökonomischen ökonometrischen Modellen abgebildet. Die meisten makroökonomischen Modelle legen die Gleichungssysteme der VGR zugrunde, mehr oder minder weit ausdifferenziert und ergänzt um Verhaltensfunktionen für Bereiche und Sektoren. Die Orientierung an den VGR bzw. die Übernahme der VGR in der Volkswirtschaftslehre hat sich seit den fünfziger Jahren durchgesetzt, weil sie standardisierte praktische Konzepte boten, die international breiten Rückhalt hatten, in die Lehrbücher übernommen wurden und nicht zuletzt auch, weil sie Daten zur Verfügung stellten. Die VGR wurden so zur Grundlage der Makroökonomie, allerdings nur als quasi technisch gesehenes Begriffssystem und als Quelle für Daten, welche für die Illustration theoretischer Aussagen genutzt wurden. Diese konnten keynesianisch hergeleitet sein, aus der neoklassischen Synthese stammen oder auch rein neoklassischer Herkunft sein. Selbst „österreichische" Marktfundamentalisten verwenden die Daten der VGR.

In den vierziger bis sechziger Jahren wurde wie selbstverständlich auf die Kreislauftheorie verwiesen, ohne dass diese produktions-, preis- und verteilungstheoretisch über einzelne Ansätze hinaus systematisch ausgearbeitet worden wäre. Stattdessen kam es zur faktischen Durchsetzung des neoklassischen Marktdenkens (Hesse 2010) bis hin zur Umdeutung des Wertschöpfungskonzepts der VGR im Sinne der Produktionsfaktoren-Vorstellung (Hauf/ Voy 2009).

2. Realwirtschaft als neues Modewort

Die Finanzkrise 2008/9 bekam ihren Namen, weil die Journalisten, Analysten und kommentierenden Wissenschaftler/innen akzeptieren mussten, dass es sich zunächst und vor allem um eine Krise des Finanzsystems – Banken, Schattenbanken, Fonds aller Art auf den Finanzmärkten – handelte, die zu einer allgemeinen Vertrauenskrise und Blockade der Geldmärkte und großer Teile der Geschäftswelt führte, die als Rückwirkung der Finanz- auf die Realwirtschaft thematisiert wurde. Konservative entdeckten bald, dass es sich letztlich – wie für sie immer – um eine Krise des Wohlfahrts- bzw. Sozialstaats, wahlweise auch gewerkschaftliches Anspruchsdenken, handelte, in diesem

Fall um die berühmten staatlich geförderten Immobilienkredite in den USA. Angesichts der offensichtlichen Krisenphänomene und des zeitlichen Verlaufs verstummten bald die einzelnen Stimmen, welche die Thematisierung von Real- versus Finanzwirtschaft als „Antisemitismus" sehen wollten (grundsätzlich Heinrich 2005).

Die *Realwirtschaft* wurde rasch zu einem neuen Modewort, das gleichzeitig auch an den Kapitalismus der Nachkriegs-Prosperität erinnerte, während die finanzielle Dimension – als Finanzkapitalismus, Finanzialisierung etc. bezeichnet – ins Zentrum der Kritik geriet. Und damit auch die Geldwirtschaft und das Geld als solches.

Die Entgegensetzung von Real- und Finanzwirtschaft hat viele theoretische politökonomische Dimensionen, die hier nur in Teilen gestreift werden können. In den Diskussionen während und nach der Finanzkrise als tatsächlichem Ereignis (und nicht als Anlass für kulturpolitische, philosophische und psychologische Spekulationen oder weit ausholende historische Darstellungen von Geld und Kredit) spielte der Bezug auf empirische Daten und Konzepte eine große Rolle, und damit auch der Bezug auf die VGR, besonders auch auf das Teilsystem Finanzierungsrechnung (FR), weil – so eine verbreitete Schlussfolgerung – das Nichtvorhersehen der Finanzkrise auf die Vernachlässigung der Finanzierungsrechnung in ökonomischen Modellen und empirischen Untersuchungen zurückzuführen sei.

3. Real in den VGR (I): Das „reale" BIP

Die VGR sind nach einer langen Entstehungs- und Entwicklungsgeschichte (vgl. für die Nachkriegszeit Voy 2009) ein vielgestaltiges und komplexes System zur statistischen Darstellung nationaler Gesamtwirtschaften. In der öffentlichen Wahrnehmung, besonders bei kritischen Wissenschaftlern, sind sie oft beschränkt auf das Bruttoinlandsprodukt (BIP). Trotzdem zunächst einige Anmerkungen zu diesem bekanntesten Begriff der VGR, sowohl in positivem als auch negativem Sinn in der Diskussion um das Wirtschaftswachstum.

Das Wachstum des BIP, früher Bruttosozialprodukt (BSP), wird meist „real" dargestellt, erläutert als preisbereinigt oder deflationiert. Obwohl das „real" in diesem Sinn in der aktuellen Diskussion um die Realwirtschaft nicht direkt gemeint ist, soll es kurz erläutert werden, um das gesamte, zusammenhängende Begriffsfeld und die inhaltlichen Themen zu überblicken.

Die beiden BSP-Größen wurden früher „real" und „nominal" genannt, was die Vorstellung suggerierte, dass zunächst die Gesamtgröße real, quasi natural ermittelt wurde und dann mit Preisen bewertet sich die nominale Geldgröße ergab. Ganz entsprechend dem ‚Geldschleier' in den Denkwelten der neoklassischen Synthese. Tatsächlich sind alle diese gesamtwirtschaftlichen Größen Aggregate, die von vorneherein nur in Geld ausgedrückt existieren und nur als solche überhaupt buchhalterisch und statistisch erfasst werden können, also Geldgrößen wie Umsätze, Einnahmen, Ausgaben usw., zu welchen Preisen auch immer nachträglich umbewertet. Statistisch ermittelt werden die Gesamtgrößen in den gegebenen bzw. jeweiligen Preisen. Die Größen, die real, preisbereinigt, deflationiert, in konstanten Preisen, in Preisen eines Basisjahres genannt werden, sind von jenen abgeleitete Rechengrößen, wofür es unterschiedliche Konzepte gibt (Räth/Struck/Voy 2009). Da es nur um die zeitliche Entwicklung dieser Größen geht, werden die Aggregate in Indizes umgerechnet, deren Veränderung (Wachstum oder Schrumpfung) mittels Preisindizes in eine Preis- und eine Volumenkomponente aufgespalten wird. Diese schließt Menge und Qualität ein, ist also keine reine Mengengröße, wie oft angenommen wird, sondern eine Wertgröße, deren Entwicklung nach rechnerischer Ausschaltung der reinen Preisveränderungen dargestellt wird.

Das „reale" Wirtschaftswachstum ist also das Ergebnis der Anwendung mehr oder minder komplexer Algorithmen und damit zwar eine abstrakte quantitative Größe, die aber nicht nur Menge, sondern Volumen im eben genannten Sinn ausdrückt. Die Umrechnung in konstante Preise etc. ist natürlich nur sinnvoll und möglich für die Aggregate und Teilgrößen der VGR, welche Transaktionen in Waren und Dienstleistungen repräsentieren, deren Preisveränderungen gemessen werden können.

4. Real- versus Finanzwirtschaft in den VGR (II)

In der Literatur besteht keine Einigkeit darüber bzw. ist nicht wirklich klar, was jeweils mit Real- und Finanzwirtschaft gemeint ist. Meist werden zu dieser wohl die Banken und Finanzmärkte – was schon empirisch unscharf –, zu jener wohl jeweils die übrige Wirtschaft gezählt. Oft wird auch der Begriff Finanzsektor verwendet, der nicht ganz so unbestimmt ist, da er sich auf eine Gruppierung von Wirtschaftseinheiten bezieht – obwohl der Begriff Sektor selten klar definiert verwendet wird.

Im Kernbereich der VGR werden die – überwiegend geldwirtschaftlichen – Vorgänge zwischen den Wirtschaftseinheiten in aggregierter Form dargestellt, aggregiert in Bezug auf die Einheiten und die Transaktionen. Es ist ein vereinfachtes Kontenschema zugrunde zu legen, das vom Integrierten Kontensystem der internationalen VGR-Systeme abgeleitet ist (ESVG 2010 und SNA 2008). Die anderen Bestandteile oder Ebenen des Gesamtsystems werden im Weiteren mit einbezogen.

In diesem Schema wird für die jeweilige Gesamtwirtschaft (national, EU bzw. EURO-Gebiet, international) und für eine mehr oder minder tiefe Untergliederung nach Sektoren jeweils eine Abfolge von Konten dargestellt, welche die verschiedenen ökonomischen Tätigkeiten repräsentieren.

Übersicht: Integriertes Kontensystem in einem vereinfachten Schema

	Sektoren					
	Gesamte Volkswirtschaft	Nicht-finanzielle Kapitalgesellschaften	Finanzielle	Staat	Private Haushalte u. priv. Org. o.E.	Übrige Welt
Produktionskonten						
Einkommenskonten						
Entstehung						
Verteilung						
Umverteilung						
Verwendung						
Finanzierungskonten						

Der Kern der VGR ist das Integrierte (sektorale) Kontensystem. Dieses ist entstanden aus der systematischen Zusammenfassung der Finanzbuchhaltung von Unternehmen und der privaten und öffentlichen Haushaltsrechnungen zu einer nationalen Gesamtrechnung, die gegenüber der übrigen Welt bzw. dem Ausland abgegrenzt wird. Diese gesamtwirtschaftliche Darstellung spannt ein Tableau auf mit den beiden Dimensionen der institutionellen Wirtschaftseinheiten bzw. Sektoren einerseits und ihrer wirtschaftlichen Tätigkeiten andererseits, dargestellt mit Transaktionen in Kontenform. Für diese gesamtwirtschaftliche Darstellung werden rechtlich-finanzielle Institutionen zugrunde gelegt, weil nur für diese (und nicht z.B. für Betriebe) die ganze Breite und Vielfalt der wirtschaftlichen Transaktionen und Vorgänge in einer Volkswirtschaft dargestellt werden kann.

Für die Untergliederung einer Volkswirtschaft nach Sektoren und Teilsektoren sind verschiedene Kriterien anwendbar. In der Sektorenbildung werden jeweils Einheiten zusammengefasst, die gemeinsame Charakteristika aufweisen. Daraus hat sich die Bildung der Sektoren Kapitalgesellschaften einerseits und der privaten und öffentlichen Haushalte andererseits als grundlegender Rahmen ergeben.

Für die jeweilige sektorale Gliederung werden die wirtschaftlichen Transaktionen in einer einheitlichen Kontenfolge dargestellt, und zwar ausgehend von der Produktion über die Einkommensentstehung, Verteilung und Umverteilung bis zur Einkommensverwendung und Finanzierung. Deren Saldo ist dann – gewissermaßen spiegelbildlich – die Abschluss- bzw. Ausgangsgröße der Finanzierungskonten bzw. der gesamten Finanzierungsrechnung.

Das System der VGR beruht grundlegend auf einzelwirtschaftlichen Buchführungen und Haushaltsrechnungen in einer gesamtwirtschaftlich integrierten Form. Die verschiedenen Teile, Sphären oder Ebenen des VGR-Systems können besser verstanden werden, wenn von der Buchführung für Unternehmen ausgegangen wird, weil deren Sachlogik für die Ausgestaltung der gesamtwirtschaftlichen Darstellungen leitend war; die Rechnungen für private und öffentliche Haushalte wurden eingepasst.

In dem Versuch, die Unterscheidung von Real- und Finanzwirtschaft konkret in den Begriffen der VGR zu fixieren, ist von der finanziellen Dimension auszugehen. Mit *Finanzwirtschaft* kann im VGR-System gemeint sein entweder der *Sektor* (finanzielle Kapitalgesellschaften, Einschränkung auf Banken möglich) oder die *Finanzierungskonten* aller Sektoren. Wenn der Finanzsektor gemeint ist (siehe die graue Spalte in der Übersicht), dann sind alle anderen Sektoren Realwirtschaft. Wenn die Finanzen aller Sektoren gemeint sind (siehe die graue Zeile in der Übersicht), dann sind Realwirtschaft die Leistungskonten aller Sektoren. Die Finanzkonten aller Sektoren sind in der *Finanzierungsrechnung* zusammenfassend dargestellt.

In beiden Fällen hat das „real" im Begriff Realwirtschaft, und vergleichbar Realsektoren, jetzt eine andere, erweiterte Bedeutung gegenüber den oben beschriebenen deflationierten Größen. Es handelt sich immer um Geldwirtschaft. Realwirtschaft meint hier den Teil, der auch als Leistungswirtschaft bezeichnet wurde, also Produktion, Einkommensverteilung und -umverteilung in allen Formen, zuletzt Einkommensverwendung. Finanzwirtschaft meint dann die Ebene, auf der es zwar genauso um Geld geht, aber fast immer verbunden mit Kreditverhältnissen.

In einer Welt, wie sie bis in die achtziger Jahre des vergangenen Jahrhunderts existierte, in welcher die meisten Kreditbeziehungen über Kreditinstitute (Banken) und Versicherungen vermittelt sind und der Aktienbesitz einer eher stabilen Unternehmenskontrolle dient, ist die Macht der Finanzen – soweit in diesen wesentlich auch durch Regulationen geschaffenen Verhältnissen überhaupt wirksam – in den Banken konzentriert, weil sie Kredit und Geld schöpfen können. Es ist dann auch die Betrachtung zentral des *Bankensektors* sinnvoll.

In einer Welt hingegen, wie sie sich in den letzten drei Jahrzehnten herausgebildet hat, in welcher immer größere Teile der Kreditbeziehungen in Gestalt von frei handelbaren Wertpapieren und Verbriefungen gestaltet werden und diese Titel bzw. Produkte nicht nur im Finanzsektor, sondern auch von den anderen Sektoren (nichtfinanzielle Kapitalgesellschaften, private Haushalte) und international ausgegeben und gekauft werden, wird die finanzielle Dimension aller Sektoren immer wichtiger und damit die *Finanzierungsrechnung*.

Die mit dieser Entwicklung verbundene Herausbildung von Geld- und Kapitalmärkten kann zwar in der sektoralen Finanzierungsrechnung nicht direkt gezeigt werden, weil in dieser die finanziellen Beziehungen zwischen Institutionen aggregiert dargestellt werden und keine ganz anders abzugrenzenden Geld- und Kapitalmärkte. Es kommt erschwerend hinzu, dass diese Finanztransaktionen zu großen Teilen mittlerweile nicht auf freien öffentlichen transparenten Märkten stattfinden, sondern von Schattenbanken auf Schwarzmärkten abgewickelt werden, welche aufgrund der Deregulierungen seit den achtziger Jahren entstehen konnten.

Anhang: Darstellungsebenen der Buchführung

Das betriebliche Rechnungswesen – oder auch Rechnungswesen der Unternehmen – ist ein zusammenfassender Begriff für die Finanzbuchhaltung und die Betriebsbuchhaltung (= Kosten- und Leistungsrechnung).

Im betrieblichen Rechnungswesen werden vier Transaktionsebenen unterschieden (vgl. auch Reich/Braakmann 1995).

„Je nach abgebildeter Transaktionsebene unterscheidet man folgende Rechnungsgrößen:
Das Begriffspaar Ein- und Auszahlungen bezieht sich auf die Zahlungsebene des Unternehmens und erfasst die Bewegung von liquiden Mitteln (...).
(...)
Dagegen umfassen Ausgaben und Einnahmen nicht nur die liquiden Mittel, sondern das gesamte Geldvermögen, zu dem neben den liquiden Mitteln auch die kurzfristigen Forderungen abzüglich der kurzfristigen Verbindlichkeiten gehören. Eine Ausgabe und eine Auszahlung können also, wie bei einem Barkauf, identisch sein; eine Ausgabe liegt darüber hinaus aber auch vor, wenn keine Zahlung erfolgt, sondern eine Verbindlichkeit entsteht (analoges gilt für eine Einnahme durch die Entstehung einer Forderung). (...)

Will ein Unternehmen nun für eine Periode, etwa ein Geschäftsjahr, seinen Erfolg ermitteln, darf es nur die dieses Geschäftsjahr betreffenden Ausgaben den entsprechenden Einnahmen gegenüberstellen. (...) In diesem Sinne periodisierte (auf eine Abrechnungsperiode bezogene) Einnahmen/Ausgaben nennt man Erträge bzw. Aufwendungen, ihr Saldo ergibt als Jahresüberschuß bzw. Jahresfehlbetrag die Veränderung des Reinvermögens. (...)
Aufwendungen und Erträge sind pagatorische Größen, da sie die Veränderungen des Geldvermögens darstellen; sie beziehen sich auf die Kapitalebene des Unternehmens. Auf der Güter- und Leistungsebene interessieren dagegen nicht die pagatorischen Veränderungen des Reinvermögens, sondern nur die leistungsbezogenen Güterverbräuche bzw. Güterentstehungen. Als Kosten (Leistungen) definiert man somit den wertmäßigen, sachzielbezogenen Güterverbrauch (Güterentstehung). Der Saldo aus Kosten und Leistungen ergibt das Betriebsergebnis." (Förschle/Scheffels 1993: 4f.)

Die vier Ebenen sind also:

- Zahlungsebene,
- Geldvermögensebene,
- Reinvermögens- oder Kapitalebene,
- Güter- und Leistungsebene.

Diese vier Ebenen lassen sich auf die bisweilen schon angedeuteten zwei Ebenen reduzieren, die im obigen Zitat (Förschle/Scheffels 1993) bezeichnet werden als

- Kapitalebene des Unternehmens,
- Güter- und Leistungsebene (Betriebsergebnis).

In der Kapitalebene werden die ersten drei Ebenen zusammengeschlossen, weil es sich gleichermaßen um Transaktionen mit anderen Wirtschaftssubjekten handelt, die Geldvermögenspositionen verändern, deren Zusammensetzung oder insgesamt. Sie unterscheiden sich nur in der zeitlichen Zuordnung. Denn der Übergang von den Ein- und Auszahlungen zu den Ausgaben und Einnahmen bezieht Kreditbeziehungen mit ein, also das Auseinanderfallen von Entstehung von Forderung/Verbindlichkeit und Zahlungen in der Zeit. Der nächste Übergang zu den Erträgen und Aufwendungen ordnet die Transaktionen den Zeiträumen zu, die sie betreffen (Vorauszahlungen u.ä.), es handelt sich aber weiterhin um Transaktionen.
Auf der Güter- und Leistungsebene hingegen werden nicht mehr alle Transaktionen dargestellt; hier wird eine auf die Produktion bezogene Darstellung

der ‚realwirtschaftlichen' Prozesse geliefert, in die auch interne Vorgänge/ Transformationen (siehe Abschreibungen) mit einbezogen werden. Auf den beiden Ebenen werden auch unterschiedliche Darstellungseinheiten zugrunde gelegt. Während sich die Transaktionen notwendig auf rechtlich finanzielle Einheiten beziehen, auf Wirtschaftssubjekte, die hier Unternehmen genannt werden, beziehen sich die Leistungen und Kosten auf den Betrieb als Produktionseinheit.

Diese Ergebnisse der Betriebswirtschaftslehre, welche in der Bilanztheorie bzw. Theorie der Buchführung erarbeitet wurden (Kosiol 1976), konnten in den VGR nicht direkt zugrunde gelegt werden, da deren Entwicklung und die Entstehung der VGR in den vierziger bis sechziger Jahren parallel liefen, wobei es eine wechselseitige Beeinflussung gab. Auf die Buchführung der Unternehmen ist nur hinzuweisen, um deutlich zu machen, dass die Unterscheidung zwischen Finanzsphäre und Realwirtschaft keine Erfindung der VGR ist, sondern zur praktischen Grundstruktur der Geldwirtschaft und damit auch des Kapitalismus gehört.

Literatur

ESVG (2010): Europäisches System Volkswirtschaftlicher Gesamtrechnungen, Europäische Kommission (eurostat), Luxembourg 2014.
Förschle, G., Scheffels, R. (1993): *Buchführung. Grundzüge und Praxis*, Bonn.
Hauf, S., Voy, K. (2009): Produktions- und Einkommensbegriffe der Volkswirtschaftlichen Gesamtrechnungen, in: Voy (2009), 149-176.
Heine, M., Herr, H. (2013): *Volkswirtschaftslehre. Paradigmenorientierte Einführung in die Mikro- und Makroökonomie*, München.
Heinrich, M. (2005): *Kritik der Politischen Ökonomie. Eine Einführung*, Stuttgart.
Hesse, J.-O. (2010): *Wirtschaft als Wissenschaft. Die Volkswirtschaftslehre in der frühen Bundesrepublik*, Frankfurt, New York.
Kosiol, E. (1976): *Pagatorische Bilanz. Die Bewegungsbilanz als Grundlage einer integrativ verbundenen Erfolgs-, Bestands- und Finanzrechnung*, Berlin.
Räth, N., Struck, B., Voy, K. (2009): Zur Geschichte der Deflationierung in den Volkswirtschaftlichen Gesamtrechnungen, in: Voy (2009), 209-230.
Reich, U.-P., Braakmann, A. (1995): *Das Sozialprodukt einer Volkswirtschaft. Grundsätze, Berechnung, Bedeutung*, Stuttgart, Berlin, Köln.
SNA (2008): System of National Accounts 2008, Internetseite der Statistikabteilung der Vereinten Nationen (http://unstats.un.org/unsd/nationalaccount/sna2008.asp)
Voy, K. (Hg.) (2009): *Kategorien der Volkswirtschaftlichen Gesamtrechnungen. Band 4: Zur Geschichte der Volkswirtschaftlichen Gesamtrechnungen nach 1945*, Marburg.

III.

Arbeitsmärkte und Lohnpolitik

Labour Markets and Wage Policy

'There is power in a union':
A strategic-relational perspective on power resources

Alexander Gallas

1. Introduction

> There is power in the factory
> Power in the land
> Power in the hands of a worker
> But it all amounts to nothing if together we don't stand
> There is a power in a union

As singer-songwriter Billy Bragg suggests in the lyrics to his song *There Is Power in A Union* (1986), the labour question is a question of power. Numerous labour scholars follow this route when they analyse labour relations and the strategic choices of workers. They establish how workers make use of 'power resources' when they act collectively; for them, the composition of these power resources accounts for strategic choices.[1]

Arguably, the power resource approach (PRA) has become one of the most popular methodologies in the field of labour studies.[2] Its attractiveness lies in the fact that it offers a clearly defined conceptual framework providing parsimonious explanations for empirical observations in the field. In this article, I want to provide a critical appraisal of this methodology.

---

[1] See, for example, Korpi (1974, 1985); Korpi/Shalev (1979); Batstone (1988); Wright (2000); Silver (2003); Brinkmann et al. (2008); Dörre et al. (2009); Dörre/Schmalz (2013); AK Strategic Unionism (2013); McGuire (2014); Webster (2015) and Russell (2016).

[2] The PRA has also been used extensively for studying welfare states, but for the sake of clarity and rigour, I will focus in this article exclusively on contributions that examine labour relations.

In particular, I discuss a tension visible in the conceptual framework of the PRA: it assumes that the mobilisation of institutional power resources both represent an exercise of workers' power and a set of activities with potentially detrimental effects on that power. In my view, it is possible to alleviate this tension by reconceptualising power resources with reference to the insights of materialist class and state theory. I will briefly sketch how this can be done by drawing upon Bob Jessop's strategic-relational approach and Nicos Poulantzas's conjunctural Marxism.

2. The pyramid of workers' power: The Jena power resource approach

2.1 Mutations of workers' power

In this article, I will focus on a version of the PRA developed by a circle of labour scholars called Arbeitskreis Strategic Unionism. This circle is based at the University of Jena in Germany. In my view, the Jena PRA currently represents the most elaborate version of the PRA in the field of labour studies.

The explanatory strategy of the Jena PRA consists in accounting for workers' power by relating the "strategic choice" (Dörre/Schmalz 2013: 14; cf. Brinkmann et al. 2008: 23) of unions to the power resources they mobilise through their activities. [3] In order to capture differences in configurations of power resources, the Jena PRA distinguishes three fundamental or, in its language, 'primary' resources of worker's power: "structural power", "associational power" and "societal power". Structural power refers to the capacities of workers that result from their positions in the economic system. It highlights the fact that workers can disrupt the accumulation of capital – for example because they work in strategic industries where strikes have far-reaching consequences for the economy as a whole or because labour power is scarce. In contrast, associational power is associated with the capacity of workers to build organisations that facilitate collective action – both at the economic and the political level (AK Strategic Unionism 2013: 351). Furthermore, there is societal power, which relates to the capacity of workers' organisations to link up with other collective actors and become hegemonic, that is, to popularise a vision of society that is shared across different classes, segments and milieus of society (347ff.; cf. Brinkmann et al. 2008: 25; Dörre/Schmalz 2013: 16ff.).

---

[3] All quotes from German-language texts have been translated by the author of this chapter.

Importantly, the Jena circle adds a fourth power resource, institutional power, which reflects the institutional capacities of workers' organisations (356). This is presented in the Jena PRA as resulting from, and retroacting on the three other power resources. We end up with a pyramid-shaped model of power resources with two tiers (see figure 1). The Jena circle comments (363): "The fact that institutional power is located at the top of the pyramid is not meant to suggest that it is more important than the other power resources. Much rather, its position illustrates the fact that institutional power is the result of the mobilisation of the primary power resources, but that it also structures the relationships between the different power relations among themselves." This suggests that power resources are not strictly separated entities. Rather, they modify each other: "Power resources (...) are (...) mutually connected." (Brinkmann/Nachtwey 2013: 26)

Figure 1: The pyramid of workers' power

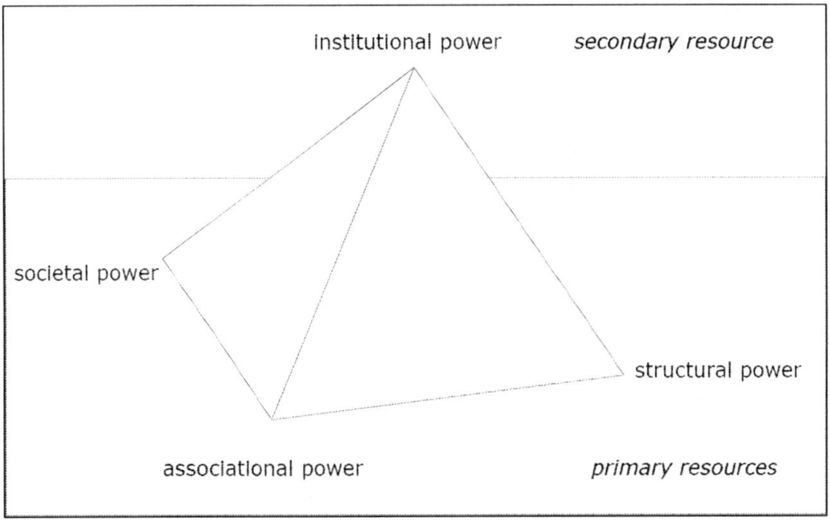

institutional power	*secondary resource*
societal power	
associational power	*primary resources*
	structural power

Source: AK Strategic Unionism (2013: 364), translated and amended

According to Klaus Dörre and Stefan Schmalz (2013: 19), the connection is visible in the historical development of the configurations of power resources: "For the sake of stylisation, it is possible to argue that in the countries undergoing early industrialisation there occurred, up until the 1880s, a shift from structural to organisational power, and, later, to institutional power."

This suggests that one type of power resource gets translated into another type over time: initially, workers went on strike spontaneously; once they started to form unions, they did not stop striking but the conditions of struggles changed due to the existence of organisations. Finally, labour relations became institutionalised through the emergence of regulations and trade union law, which provided labour with certain avenues for organisation and collective action but closed off others. Correspondingly, the Jena circle highlights that institutions should be seen as resulting from past mobilisations of power, which means that they reflect primary power resources (2013: 356). However, they work according to their own logic and with their own temporality so that they have effects on the primary power resources. These effects remain inexplicable with reference to the primary resources themselves.

This is visible in the diverging ways in which power resources change over time: a union may still dispose of institutional power resources even if union density has gone down significantly. This is due to institutional inertia, that is, the fact that institutional safeguards are often enshrined in law and thus cannot be removed easily. Over the medium term, however, the developments affecting primary resources will also start impacting on the secondary resource, which is why the Jena circles argues that the former can still have a significant effect on the latter. In their view, a union without an organisational base will eventually be stripped of its institutional capacities (358).

The result is a mutation model of workers' power: the character of the power resources at the disposal of labour is being changed considerably through struggles; in turn, these changes, which consist in organisation and institutionalisation, impact strongly on the modalities of struggles (cf. AK Strategic Unionism 2013: 352). The Jena circle exemplifies this scenario with reference to recent developments in the German system of labour relations. As Ulrich Brinkmann and Oliver Nachtwey argue (2013: 39ff.; cf. Dörre/ Schmalz 2013: 22ff.), the structural and the organisational power of German trade unions has been eroding for four decades thanks to rising unemployment, internationalisation, precarisation and the rise of the service sector. Nevertheless, unions managed to protect skilled workers for a long time – they were able to achieve substantial wage increases for this group through the existing institutions of collective bargaining up until the mid-1990s. In other words, the German unions pursued a corporatist strategy that heavily relied on the mobilisation of institutional power resources; they refrained from tackling the erosion of primary powers, which would have required a more confrontational approach. This was successful for a certain time, but in the end the Schröder government decided to curb the institutional capacities of unions. It did so by limiting entitlements to unemployment benefits, weakening the protection from unfair dismissal and rolling out temporary work. This "amounted to a reduction of industrial citizenship rights", to which the union leaderships, on the whole, did not respond with industrial action (41).

2.2 The 'double character' of institutional power

Inherent to the mutation model is a tension: On the one hand, all the different power resources are presented as facilitating the exercise of workers' power, which is visible in the fact that members of the Jena circle usually portray 'union power' as an instance of workers' power;[4] on the other hand, strategies of labour that are based on institutionalisation are said to change the modalities of the mobilisation of workers' power, which suggests that they can produce obstacles to its exercise. In fact, it may be the case that they weaken the position of labour vis-à-vis capital.

According to Brinkmann and Nachtwey, this is what happened in Germany during the global economic crisis: The unions operated on the grounds of a form of "crisis corporatism", which involved tripartite negotiations. They were able to secure short-time compensation and the institution of a car scrappage scheme, which protected jobs (2013: 43). However, this strategy came at a price: "Works councils' and trade unions' strategy during the crisis to accept concessions led to an undermining of their own power resources in the long-term through the extension of temp and other forms of precarious work. The underlying problem is related to the institutional basis: Institution stabilizing policy, although leading to short-term stability, in the long term, however, leads to further institutional destabilization." (44)

In a nutshell, institutional strategies seem to be a double-edged sword for unions. If institutional power resources are mobilised successfully by unions in order to safeguard achievements or even secure improvement for core work forces, this may weaken labour altogether over the medium term, not only 'peripheral', precarious workers. Against this backdrop, the Jena circle qualify the workings of institutional power somewhat: "Since institutional power results from antagonistic class relations, a 'double character' is inherent in it. It grants far-reaching rights to unions, but also restricts their agency. In this respect, the mutual concessions between capital and labour have an ordering function for the accumulation of capital – even if the representation of the in-

---

[4] See for example Dörre/Schmalz (2013: 16).

terests of wage dependent people is at the same time improved in this logic." (AK Strategic Unionism 2013: 356f.).

In my view, this observation has far-reaching theoretical implications for the mutation model of power, which are not clearly spelled out by the Jena circle. If institutionalisation may contribute to the accumulation of capital due to its 'ordering function', it does not necessarily work in favour of labour. By implication, the same can be said about the structural and associational capacities of unions that work with institutional strategies, for example, their ability to bargain collectively and to recruit new members. After all, they may focus on making concessions and on organising core workers. To put it bluntly, the activities of unions may enhance the power of capital under certain conditions.

All of this suggests that the capacities of unions should not simply be equated with workers' power. In fact, the above quote implies that the institutions framing labour relations have to distinguished from the level of the class relations of forces underpinning these institutions; the activities of unions are only instances of the exercise of working class power if they defend, consolidate or improve the position of the working class. This is consistent with the Josef Esser's conception of unions, who stresses that they are *"class organisations with the purpose of pursuing the economic interests of workers"* (1982: 228) plus "mass integrative apparatuses" that display "specific structures of organisation (...) and functional mechanisms [Funktionsbezüge]" transforming those interests in such a manner that they no longer pose a threat to capital (239). Notably, the Jena circle concedes that there is the case of the "'intermediary' or 'fortified' union", which is characterised by a "contradictory institutionalisation of workers' power" (AK Strategic Unionism 2013: 373).

3. Towards a strategic-relational model of class power

3.1 Class power and union capacities

I will try, in the remainder of the article, to alleviate the tension between describing institutional power as both as a form of workers' power and an ensemble of capacities with ambiguous effects on workers' power. I will first of all outline a re-conceptualisation of class power that is informed by Bob Jessop's strategic-relational approach (Jessop 2002; 2007) and Nicos Poulantzas's analyses of political conjunctures (1970; 1975; cf. Gallas 2015). In a second step, I will briefly explain how this re-conceptualisation can be used for a conjunctural analysis of labour relations. Needless to say, it is impossible in a short book chapter to provide a detailed picture; I will just provide a rough sketch.

Much like the Jena PRA, I aim to explain the strategic choices of workers acting collectively with reference to the power resources at their disposal. But in contrast to them, I refrain from equating workers' power with 'union power'. Instead, I propose distinguishing between

- the power resources that can potentially be mobilised by collective actors operating on behalf of the working class;
- working class power as it emerges when such actors make strategic choices that mobilise power resources; and
- the capacities of unions, which may or may not overlap with these power resources

The opening move of my re-conceptualisation of class power follows Poulantzas (1978: 14) insofar as my analysis starts from the capitalist relations of production (CRP). This approach is not entirely alien to the Jena PRA, which refers to Poulantzas approvingly at at least one point (AK Strategic Unionism 2013: 357). Correspondingly, the above quote on the 'double character' of institutional power suggests that the CRP are of fundamental importance for the structure and dynamics of capitalist societies. Consequently, my approach represents a creative engagement with the Jena PRA, not a complete rupture with it.

Following Marx (1867/72, 874), the CRP are antagonistic relations: They pit the owners of the means of production (capitalists) against people owning nothing but their labour power (workers). This makes class conflict unavoidable and unresolvable in capitalist societies. Against this backdrop, Marx argues that the conflict inherent in the CRP facilitates class formation, that is, the emergence of collective actors actively aiming to shift class relations of forces in the direction of either capital or labour (344; cf. Althusser 1973: 49). These actors, which can be labour movements, other social movements, business circles or political networks, act on behalf of a class if their activities can be seen as attempting to actively shift class relations.

This indicates that there is class agency in the Marxian framework. Marx famously observed in the *Eighteenth Brumaire* (1852) that "[m]en make their own history, but they do not make it as they please; they do not make it under self-selected circumstances, but under circumstances existing already, given and transmitted from the past". This suggests that class actors are capable of transforming the conditions under which they act – even if the conditions influence their choices in some way or another (cf. Marx 1852; Collier 1994: 144).[5] To use a concept coined by the Jena PRA (2013: 369), they can be said possess "strategic agency". This implies that the course and outcome of class conflict is not predetermined. However, the capitalist mode of production contains numerous selectivities (cf. Jessop 1985: 347; 1990: 9f.; 2002: 40f.) that favour strategies benefitting capital.

It follows that the constant confrontations between the two sides produce shifts in the relations of forces between capital and labour. Class power is *relational*: it is the effect of a relation of forces between two sides, which is characterised by the fact that advances of one side equal retreats of the other side. Furthermore, it is *strategic*: it is exercised through the strategic choices made by actors operating on behalf of one or the other side and in reaction to strategic choices made by the opponent. These strategic choices consist in activities that aim either reproducing (defensive and consolidating steps) or shifting (offensive steps) the class relations of forces (Gallas 2015: 57; cf. Poulantzas 1970).

Against this backdrop, it becomes possible, in principle, to determine

– whether the strategies of collective actors operating in a specific historical and spatial context such as labour movements amount to exercising class power at all;

– whether they constitute offensive, consolidating or defensive steps in the class struggle; and

– which power resources are mobilised in which way for this purpose.

Importantly, this suggests that workers do not simply possess working class power so that any of their collective activities can be assumed to reflect their power (cf. Poulantzas 1978: 146f.). Rather, they may or may not exercise working class power through their activities; it depends on their strategies. This also implies that the resources they mobilise when they act cannot be equated with being sources of working class power straight away. Furthermore, if agency is taken seriously, what constitutes or does not constitute a power resource also depends on the strategic environment and the strategy embarked on. In a certain context, a successful recruitment drive by a union may strengthen labour vis-à-vis capital because it is possible to bind workers to a collective approach to labour relations. But in another context, the reverse may hold true: Unions with a very broad membership may find it more

---

[5] For a more detailed account of class agency, see Gallas (2015: 52-56).

difficult to mobilise for industrial action than unions that have a small (and committed) base. In sum, what is needed is a *conjunctural* analysis of strategies and relations of forces. 'Conjuncture' here refers to a concrete constellation of strategies and relation of forces at a given time in a given space, for example Germany during the global financial and economic crisis or Brazil during the political and economic crisis that accompanied the final phase of the Dilma presidency (Althusser/Balibar 1968: 311; Poulantzas 1968: 93ff.; Jessop 2012; Gallas 2015; Gallas 2016).

3.2 Conjunctural analysis

The first step of a conjunctural analysis consists in determining the *strategic environment* workers find themselves in, that is, the existing class relations of forces and class strategies. Against this backdrop, it becomes possible, in a second step, to determine the *configuration of power resources* specific to the situation and the strategic options for workers that result from this configuration. This allows, in a third step, for explaining *strategic choices*.

Obviously, the assessment of a strategic environment starts with determining a social field in time and space that can be examined. If we assume that class relations of forces undergo constant shifts, it makes sense to limit the field to a demarcated period in the course of class conflict. Likewise, it is plausible to restrict the space of analysis because collective agency requires a connection of the individuals assumed to be acting together – for example, the fact that they are members of unions that belong to the same federation.

Against this backdrop, the key collective actors in the field need to be identified. Among them are the labour movements or unions plus the business circles or employers' associations that are of relevance in the field, but also the political networks (parties, governments) whose activities impact on class relations of forces. Likewise, it is necessary to pinpoint the institutions underpinning labour relations and, in a cursory fashion, the workings of the state apparatuses and of civil society.

Once this is done, it is possible to assess the status of the class relations of forces, which has two components. In line with what was said about the danger of conflating union power with class power, the first component consists in identifying strategies and their class effects. If the strategic choices of a union are consistently sectionalist in the sense that the emerging strategy only favours a specific group of workers, overrides the interests of other groups, cannot be expanded or transferred to other sectors and does not have a mobilising effect on workers, the union cannot be said to exercise working class power. In fact, its choices may weaken the working class and have, at the same time, an ordering function for capital accumulation, which is why there may be scenarios in which they can be called an exercise of capitalist class power. The activities of certain professional unions with an exclusive focus on highly skilled specialists in a particular field (technicians, medics, lawyers, pilots etc.) are cases in point. In countries with a tradition of corporatist arrangements, the class character of union strategies may be difficult to assess because they tend to contain both elements aimed at expanding workers' power and concessions that curb it. In these cases, the assessment of the class character of a certain strategy requires a careful weighing up of the different elements. If we follow Brinkmann and Nachtwey (2013: 41f.), the German unions, on the whole, were not prepared to underpin the political protests against Agenda 2010 – the defining political project of the Schröder government that amounted to a far-reaching retrenchment of the welfare state and a restructuring of labour relations in favour of capital – with industrial action. This suggests that they refrained from exercising working class power.

The second component is constituted by an assessment of the purpose of the class strategies embarked on. Are the activities chosen aimed at advancing (offensive step), containing an advance of the other side (defensive step) or at securing a shift in the relations of forces that has been achieved (consolidating step)? This is important for the evaluation of strategic choices because actors may misread conjunctures and opt for strategies that do not adequately respond to the activities of the other side, which can lead to crushing defeats. As Poulantzas points out in his seminal study *Fascism and Dictatorship* (1970: 159), the mainstream of communist movement misread the conjuncture of the interwar period in Continental Europe: it assumed that a revolution was imminent when in fact it should have embarked on a defensive strategy and built a united front to check the rise of fascism. This historical example shows that it is worth taking into consideration purposes of strategies when strategic options and choices are assessed.

After the first step, that is, the analysis of the strategic environment, has been completed, it becomes possible to assess power resources available in a conjuncture. The point here is that the class character and the availability of different power resources for workers is not set in stone; it shifts from one conjuncture to the next. Rather than identifying power resources in a schematic manner that is not sensitive to conjunctural conditions, what needs to be done, from a strategic-relational perspective, is to determine a configuration of constraints and opportunities that is specific to the conjuncture. This configuration can then be used in order to explain, in a third step, the strategic choices that collective actors have made.

In other words, a strategic-relational perspective calls for a reconceptualisation of power resources. In line with Poulantzas (1974: 22ff.), it makes sense to distinguish the capitalist mode of production from capitalist social formations and particular conjunctures of these social formations. The first concept refers to a "deep structure" (Collier 1994: 7, 11), that is, an ensemble of mechanisms with the CRP at its heart. It encompasses everything that makes capitalism capitalist, most importantly, the existence of wage labour and private property of the means of production. Moreover, it is fundamentally different from other modes of production like slavery in antiquity or feudalism, which are not based on wage labour. Capitalist social formations are societies in which the capitalist mode of production dominates, for example Britain during the age of empire or South Africa under the apartheid regime. They differ vastly over time and space in terms of the ways in which the fundamental mechanisms of the capitalist mode of production are institutionalised, which is visible, for example, in different regimes of labour relations. This implies that the fundamental mechanisms are the same everywhere, but they may produce diverging effects because their workings are modified by the institutions specific to the social formation. Finally, conjunctures are particular situations in the sense spelled out above. They are connected to a specific social formation and specific events that occur in the course of its reproduction. Again, events and development of a certain conjuncture impact in different ways both on the effects of the fundamental mechanisms and the effects of their institutionalisation.

Against this backdrop, it makes sense to see power resources as potentials that are located at the level of mode of production. A strategic-relational analysis of power resources identifies them at this level and then traces how they are converted both into conjunctural opportunities and constraints through (a) the existence of institutions specific to the social formation, and (b) conditions specific to the conjuncture.

This can be exemplified with what the Jena circle calls "market power" (2013: 349f.), which is a sub-form of 'structural power'. Market power refers to the capacities of workers arising out of shortages in the labour market. At the level of the mode of production, it is possible to argue that a key precondition for capital accumulation to succeed is the existence of a sufficient supply of labour power (Harvey 2010: 58). This implies that there is a potential opportunity for the exercise of working class power inherent in the existence of labour power, which can be activated in particular in situations when the labour supply is tight. However, this potential opportunity is also a potential constraint: whenever the "industrial reserve army" (Marx 1867/72, 784) of unemployed workers expands and the labour supply increases, capitalists find it much easier to put workers under pressure. We can say, at this very general level, that there is a potential for the existence of a power resource called 'market power', but that the activation of this potential depends on political-economic institutions affecting the labour market, sectoral conditions and the economic cycle.

If the level of the social formation is considered, it becomes clear that market power is a resource that is not always available for workers: During the times of the post-war settlement in Britain, when the unions traded industrial peace for full employment and a welfare state, the size of the industrial reserve army was limited. As a result, workers were in a comparably strong negotiating position. Once the Thatcher government did away with what was left of the settlement and put in its place a finance-driven accumulation strategy that drove up unemployment, things changed drastically. Workers were, on the whole, in a weak position; it was capital that used its 'market power' to crush the organised working class (Gallas 2015: 133).

However, these observations at the level of the social formation still need to be qualified with reference to conjunctural factors: first of all, there were vast differences in the labour market depending on where in Britain one looked (136), and, second, the economic cycle still made it possible for those who were employed to make wage gains once the recessions of the early 1980s had ended (161). In sum, a strategic-relational approach to power resources produces a nuanced account of opportunities and constraints than versions of the PRA that simply assume the existence of a resource called 'market power'.

Turning back to the case of Germany in the crisis, it appears that a strategic-relational take on power resources can introduce distinctions into the analysis that are useful for explaining the strategic choices of unions. Referring to the run-up to the crisis, Brinkmann and Nachtwey mention that the main unions joined political protests against Agenda 2010, but they refrained, on the whole, from underpinning these protests with strikes or other disruptive activities at the economic level (2013: 41). From a strategic-relational perspective, this can be interpreted as 'actionism', that is, activity for activity's sake with a limited impact on power relations (Gallas 2015: 58). Considering the significant weakening of organised labour through the expansion of temporary and precarious work that resulted from Agenda 2010, this can be seen as misinterpretation of the conjuncture with dire consequences. It appears that there was a considerable shift of power relations in favour of capital at the time.

In light of this, it turns out that workers were facing significant constraints once the crisis hit: the industrial reserve army increased; thanks to the economic situation, it was easy for capital to question the legitimacy of strikes by alleging that they had dangerous effects on businesses; and the expansion of temporary and precarious work in the run-up to the crisis made exposing oneself to the threat of the sack an even more risky endeavour. At the same time, union density had been falling for a long time, and Agenda 2010 had proven that governments were prepared to turn against tripartite negotiations when it came to restructuring labour relations. In this situation, it appears that there were two strategic options for the German unions: revive corporatism in order to come to a negotiated settlement or form an alliance with civil society actors against the neoliberal strategies of crisis management. In the light of the fact that protests against the political management of the crisis were very weak, it is no surprise that the unions opted for "crisis corporatism" (Brinkmann/Nachtwey 2013: 43). This was successful insofar as it lead to a regime of crisis management that protected core workforces through short-term work, a car scrappage scheme and other forms of public investment. In terms of the relations of forces, however, 'crisis corporatism' further weakened workers in Germany because it left precarious workers uncovered and deepened the divide between core workforces and other workers. On the whole, this may have been the least bad option in a difficult strategic environment. Importantly, however, some of the unions may have made a contribution to creating this environment by opting against launching a defensive against Agenda 2010 and choosing to 'muddle through' instead.

4. Conclusion

The PRA is an important methodology for labour studies because it allows for a systematic discussion not just of the shape of labour relations and prevalent patterns of class conflict, but also of strategic options and strategic choices. The Jena circle deserves praise for developing the PRA systematically. However, it produces conflicting statements on the nature of 'institutional power'. As I have argued, strategic-relational conceptions of power and strategy are well-suited to address this problem because they call for a dynamic understanding of power resources that takes on board potential opportunities and constraints at the level of the mode of production, and their activation through institutions at the level of the social formation and events and processes at the level of the conjuncture.

In a nutshell, union capacities should not be conflated with class power. Poulantzas (1978: 148) famously argued that the state is neither an instrument in the hands of the ruling class, nor a subject that is above class relations. Following him, it has no power on its own; rather, it can be seen as field and a facilitator of class strategies. It may be added that unions work in a similar way (and hence can be seen as being part of the state): if they opt for institutional strategies, their activities may to be conducive to the reproduction of capitalist class domination (cf. Althusser 1995: 133ff.). At the same time, however, they also facilitate the formation of working class strategies. In short, there is power in a union even though a union has no power.

References

AK Strategic Unionism (2013): Jenaer Machtresourcenansatz 2.0, in: Schmalz, S., Dörre, K. (eds.), *Comeback der Gewerkschaften? Machtresourcen, innovative Praktiken, internationale Perspektiven*, Frankfurt: Campus, 345-375.

Althusser, L. (1973): Reply to John Lewis, in: idem, *Essays in Self-Criticism*, London: NLB, 1976, 33-100.

Althusser, L. (1995): *Sur la Reproduction*, Paris: Presses Universitaires de France.

Althusser, L., Balibar, E. (1968): *Reading Capital*, London: NLB, 1970.

Batstone, E. (1988): The Frontier of Control, in: Gallie, D. (ed.), *Employment in Britain*, Oxford: Basil Blackwell, 218-250.

Brinkmann, U. et al. (2008): *Strategic Unionism: Aus der Krise zur Erneuerung? Umrisse eines Forschungsprogramms*, Wiesbaden: VS Verlag.

Brinkmann, U., Nachtwey, O. (2013): Industrial Relations, Trade Unions and Social Conflict in German Capitalism, in: *La nouvelle revue du travail*, 3/2013, available at: http://nrt.revues.org/1382

Collier, A. (1994): *Critical Realism: An Introduction to Roy Bhaskar's Philosophy*, London: Verso.

Dörre, K., Holst, H., Nachtwey, O. (2009): Organizing: A Strategic Option for Trade Union Renewal, in: *International Journal of Action Research*, 5(1), 33-67.

Dörre, K., Schmalz, S. (2013): Einleitung: Comeback der Gewerkschaften? Eine machtsoziologische Forschungsperspektive, in: Schmalz, S., Dörre, K. (eds.), *Comeback der Gewerkschaften? Machtresourcen, innovative Praktiken, internationale Perspektiven*, Frankfurt: Campus, 13-38.

Esser, J. (1982): *Gewerkschaften in der Krise*, Frankurt/M: Suhrkamp.

Gallas, A. (2015): *The Thatcherite Offensive: A Neo-Poulantzasian Analysis*, London: Brill.

Gallas, A. (2016): Konjunktureller Marxismus: Poulantzas und Althusser über den kapitalistischen Staat, in: Ekici, E., Nowak, J., Wolf, F.O. (eds.), *Althusser – Die Reproduktion des Materialismus*, Münster: Westfälisches Dampfboot, 140-168.

Harvey, D. (2010): *The Enigma of Capital and the Crises of Capitalism*, London: Profile.

Jessop, B. (1985): *Nicos Poulantzas: Marxist Theory and Political Strategy*, New York: St Martin's Press.

Jessop, B. (1990): *State Theory: Putting the Capitalist State in its Place*, Cambridge: Polity.

Jessop, B. (2002): *The Future of the Capitalist State*, Cambridge: Polity.

Jessop, B. (2007): *State Power: A Strategic-Relational Approach*, Cambridge: Polity.

Jessop, B. (2012): Left Strategy, in: *transform!*, 10/12, available at: http://www.transform-network.net/journal/issue-102012/news/detail/Journal/left-strategy.html

Korpi, W. (1974): Conflict, Power and Relative Deprivation, in: *The American Political Science Review*, 68(4), 1569-1578.

Korpi, W. (1985): Power Resources Approach vs. Action and Conflict: On Causal and Intentional Explanations in the Study of Power, in: *Sociological Theory*, 3(2), 31-45.

Korpi, W., Shalev, M. (1979): Strikes, Industrial Relations and Class Conflict in Capitalist Societies, in: *British Journal of Sociology*, 30(2), 164-187.

McGuire, D. (2014): Analysing Union Power, Opportunity and Strategic Capability: Global and Local Union Struggles Against the General Agreement on Trade in Services (GATS), in: *Global Labour Journal*, 5(1), 45-67.

Marx, K. (1852): The Eighteenth Brumaire of Louis Bonaparte, available at: https://www.marxists.org/archive/marx/works/download/pdf/18th-Brumaire.pdf

Marx, K. (1867/72): *Capital: A Critique of Politcal Economy*, vol. 1, Harmondsworth: Penguin, 1976.

Poulantzas, N. (1968): *Political Power and Social Classes*, London: NLB, 1970.

Poulantzas, N. (1970). *Fascism and Dictatorship*, London: NLB.

Poulantzas, N. (1974): *Classes in Contemporary Capitalism*, London: NLB, 1975.

Poulantzas, N. (1975): *The Crisis of the Dictatorships*, London NLB, 1976.

Poulantzas, N. (1978): *State Power Socialism*, London: NLB.

Russell, H. (2016): London 2012 Olympics and the Power of the British Trade Unions: A Golden Opportunity?, in: *Global Labour Journal*, 7(1), 35-49.

Silver, B. (2003): *Forces of Labor: Workers' Movements and Globalisation since 1870*, Cambridge: University Press.

Webster, E. (2015): Labour after Globalisation: Old and New Sources of Power, Institute of Social and Economic Research, Working Paper 1/2015, available at: https://www.ru.ac.za/media/rhodesuniversity/content/iser/documents/Labour%20after%20Globalisation%20-%20Edward%20Webster%20%282015.1%29.pdf

Wright, E.O. (2000): Working-Class Power, Capitalist-Class Interests, and Class Compromise, in: *American Journal of Sociology*, 105(4), 957-1002.

Issues concerning employment and minimum wages in India's urban informal economy

Sharit K. Bhowmik

This paper attempts to look critically at the position of the expanding informal economy in India. This section which comprises 93% of the labour force has minimum social protection and other benefits that lead to decent work. The first part deals with the dimensions of informal employment and later it discusses the issue of minimum wages which would provide a minimum economic protection to the workforce.

The labour force: An introduction

With a total population of 1.2 billion India is the second largest country in the world next to China. The population of India is 1.2 billion in 2011 census and the decennial growth rate is 17% which is lower than the previous decade but much higher than China's decennial rate of around 5%. India should be overtaking China in population by 2030.

The literacy rate is an important variable in determining the nature of the labour force. A high level of literacy could mean a high level of skill. According to the Census of India any person aged 7 or above who can read and write in any language is a literate. It mentions that a person who can read but not write is not literate. In 2011 census there were 1.05 billion over 7 years of age and 75% of them were literate. This could be considered a leap as in the 2001 census 65% of the population were literate. Nonetheless, India has the highest number of illiterates in the world. This leads to the growth of unskilled and vulnerable labour.

Formal and informal employment

The labour force all over the world is divided into two types of employment, namely, formal and informal. In the case of India this division is very sharp. Around 93% of the work force is in informal employment (including self-employment) and only 7% is in formal employment. The distinction between the formal and informal sectors is crucial for understanding employment relationship. Workers in the formal sector are engaged in factories, commercial and service establishments and are under the purview of legal regulation. Around 69% of the workers in this sector are employed in government, quasi-government and public sector enterprises. The private sector provides employment to only 31% of the labour in the formal sector (GoI 2005: 230). Wages of formal sector workers are substantially higher than those engaged in the urban informal sector. One study shows that the average wage of a formal sector worker is four or five times higher than wages in the informal sector (CMIE 1989: Table 10.1). Moreover, a range of labour laws, guaranteeing permanency of employment, health facilities and provision for retirement benefits, protect their jobs.

Though in principle, labour laws in India are expected to apply to all sections of industrial labour, there are in-built provisions in these laws which exclude large sections of the labour force. The most important law regulating work in industries is the Factories Act of 1948. All other laws such as Employees State Insurance Act, Workmen's Compensation Act, Provident Fund and Family Pension Act, Payment of Gratuity Act, apply only to establishments covered by the Factories Act. This Act is applicable only to manufacturing units that employ a minimum of 10 workers and which use power in manufacturing and a minimum of 20 workers if the unit does not use power. Hence a large section of industrial workers employed in small industries do not have legal protection in their work. We can thus see that the composition of the labour force in India shows wide contrasts. The new government (elected to power in May 2014) has sought to bring about greater changes by introducing amendments to the Factories Act that seeks to increase the minimum numbers to 20 and 40 respectively. Such changes in the factory laws have been made in Maharashtra, the most industrialised state in the country. As a result 14,300 of the factories in the state are not covered by the Factories Act (HT 2015: 08).

Composition of the labour force

According to the 68th round of the National Sample Survey (2011-2012), the worker population ratio (WPR) in the country is around 40% (GoI 2013). This indicates a high rate of dependency as 60% of the population is dependent on 40% who constitute the work force. The workforce in 2011-2012 was 459 million of which 336.4 million were in rural areas while 136.5 million were in the urban areas. If we subtract the 28 million engaged in the formal employment the total number in urban informal employment would be over 100 million. Informal employment in rural areas is also very high.

The 68th round of the NSS reports that the informal workers were mainly engaged in manufacturing, construction, wholesale and retail trade and transportation and storage. These four sectors provide employment to 73% of the non-agricultural rural informal employment and 75% of urban informal employment (GoI 2013: iii).

These statistics provide only a part of the picture. There are a lot of hidden people who work in informal employment. For example, the Commissioner of Small Scale Industries organises surveys on small and micro-enterprises, including the self-employed. These surveys record only those who have fixed places of work. This means that street vendors who have no fixed places of work are not included in the surveys (Kundu 1999: 12 footnote). There are millions of street vendors in the country and they are not included as informal workers. The National Policy for Urban Street Vendors (2009) estimates that 2% of the urban population is engaged in street vending. This would mean that they number around 6 to 7 million.

Besides street vendors, there are other sections of the working population that are not included as workers. These are home-based workers and a large section of domestic workers both of whom are mainly women. My own research on informal employment in Mumbai showed that domestic workers believed that because the work they did in their own homes (cleaning, cooking washing clothes etc.) was extended to other people's houses it did not constitute work. They believe that they were getting extra money for doing house work. The female home-based workers too have the same misgiving. They were engaged in semi-cooked food, making trinkets, embellishments on cloth or garments, stitching buttons on shirts etc. which are out-sourced by local contractors. Since they worked from their homes they did not consider it as work. Many of them thought of their work as a form of "time-pass" at home. This belief was further reinforced by the fact that they were in most cases not the main earner. Their husbands were regarded as the main earners and they were supplementing the main wage earner. Hence when the census or the surveys take place they would never give their returns as worker. They are thus excluded from the category of worker. Hence there is every possibility that the actual number of workers in informal employment may be much more than those provided in the official statistics.

Changes in policies and their effects

The radical changes in India's economy came after the policies of liberalisation and structural adjustment were introduced. On 24 July 1991 the then finance minister, Dr. Manmohan Singh placed before parliament the Statement on Industrial Policy. This was passed by parliament soon after. This policy was in many ways different from the past policies. Though the policy statement started with Jawaharlal Nehru's vision of modern India, the subsequent sections did not reflect any of this vision. There can be no denying that employment increased after the policies of liberalisation were introduced. Improvement in technology, especially in telecommunications, has given rise to the IT based employment, in call centres, back office activities, medical transcriptions and in IT enables services (ITES). This has provided employment to a section of the educated youth.

At the same time lower end jobs not requiring high levels of skills or no skills too increased. These were in the services sector such as cable TV, courier services, security services and others. In manufacturing there was no increase in formal sector jobs but those in informal employment increased. The annual *Economic Survey* of the Government of India for 2004-05 noted that labour in small scale industries recorded an increase of over 4% per annum. The report mentioned that this sector was able to absorb the excess labour.

The formal sector, on the other hand, did not increase its employment scope. The data from the Census of India 1991 shows that the total labour force was 345 million of which 28 million was in formal employment. Though the total labour force has increased as the earlier data from the NSS 2009-10 shows, there was no change in employment in the formal sector. In fact the formal sector itself was employing informal labour. There has been steady growth in the employment of casual and contract labour.

Increase in informal employment after liberalisation

As mentioned above, the trends towards informalisation had started much before liberalisation was introduced. The difference was that the pace was considerably increased. The percentage of workers in formal employment was 8.5% in 1991, before the new policies were introduced. By 2001 this decreased to 7% (GoI 2005). A decrease in 1.5% may seem minimal but if the increase in the total workforce is taken into account a drop of 1.5% is quite substantial. The trends show that the proportion of informal employment is expected to increase.

Over the past two decades or so there has been an increase in insecure employment. This basically means that the new workers do not have security of employment as they can be fired from their jobs at the will of the employer. Other facilities enjoyed by those in formal employment too are not provided. These include health benefits, leave and, most important pension benefits. The government and also the employers' associations believe that allowing informalisation to increase would also mean creation of new jobs which are of utmost importance in this era of growing unemployment.

In the above sections we have attempted to show the insecurity of working in informal employment. Under these circumstances getting a fair reward for work becomes all the more necessary. This brings us to the issue of minimum wage for workers in informal employment. We will discuss this in the following section.

What is a minimum wage?

In most cases the state governments declare the minimum wages for different categories of workers. These differ between different industries engaged in manufacturing and in the services sector. These include engineering, printing, chemicals among others in manufacturing and in different activities in the services sector. Beside there are pay commissions and wage boards for the different types of employment in the formal sector. The government appoints pay commissions for government employees, college and university teachers, public enterprises and the armed forces every decade. These commissions fix the salaries and other facilities for the respective employees. In addition there are periodic increases in salaries that take into account the rise in cost of living. These commissions cover the entire employees in the country and, as in the case of college and university teachers and government employees, the respective state governments who are the employers have to abide by the decision of the respective pay commission. In the case of minimum wages for labour, the state governments have to declare the minimum wages.

There are two pieces of legislation governing wages in India, namely the Payment of Wages Act of 1936 and the Minimum Wages Act of 1948. The former deals with the dates for paying wages; if workers are paid by the month, they must be paid by the 7th of each month; if the wage is paid weekly it should be paid on the last working day of the week; and by the end of the working day in the case of a daily wage. The Minimum Wages Act states that if the state or central government declares a minimum wage, it must be paid by the employers in the sectors concerned.

The Minimum Wages Act does not specify how the minimum wage should be calculated or what inputs should be considered for its constitution. State governments usually declare the minimum wage every three years for each industry and for agricultural labour. Therefore the minimum wage for engineering units, for example, will be different from the minimum wage of workers in textiles. Generally, states also declare minimum wages in agriculture that are lower than those of urban or industrial workers.

The declared minimum wage is primarily for workers in informal employment, namely industries that are not under the purview of the Factories Act, workers in the services sector and shops, and agricultural workers. Neither act covers self-employed workers nor domestic workers, home-based workers and so on, who constitute one-third of the informally employed.

The issue of minimum wages does not arise for workers in the formal sector because it is settled through collective bargaining for private sector and by pay commissions in the public sector. These wages are significantly higher than the declared minimum wage. Hence wages of workers in small scale engineering units will be lower than those of industrial workers in the formal sector. Since only 7% or 8% of the work force is in the formal sector, the vast majority of workers are entitled to the minimum wages declared by government.

How is the minimum wage calculated?

Right after the country was independent of colonial rule in 1947 the issue of minimum wage has been cropping up but there were no concrete guidelines on what should constitute a minimum wage. Finally in the 15th Session of the Indian Labour Conference (a tripartite body) held in 1957 decided that there should be a need based minimum. In other words the notified minimum wage should cover the basic needs that were necessary for reproducing one's labour.

The ILC unanimously decided that the minimum wage should cover the minimum needs in terms of food, clothing and shelter of three units of consumption, in other words a family of two adults and two children. The food consumption of each unit would amount to 2,700 calories. This would include carbohydrates (cereals), proteins (egg, meat, fish, milk), oils and fat. The clothing requirements for three units were fixed at 72 yards per annum. There should also be a component for house rent which should be around 15% of the wage. These would account for 80% of the minimum wage. The remaining 20% was for fuel, lighting and miscellaneous expenditure.

Soon after the resolution was passed, the central government announced formation of Minimum Wages Boards for 22 industries. This was the first time that such a massive exercise was undertaken for fixing minimum wages in almost all industries. The commissions for each industry comprised representatives of trade unions and employers while a senior official of the Ministry of Labour was appointed as chairperson. Each commission was to decide on the mode of fixing the minimum wage in their respective industry. Within a few months of setting up of the commissions the government announced that minimum wages would be implemented only if there was unanimity among the board members. This in fact went against the interests of labour as in most cases the employers representatives would differ from the decision of the labour or even the chair. A deadlock would mean that the declaration of the minimum wage for that industry would be delayed or, if the employers refused to budge, it could be delayed indefinitely. Hence in most cases labour had to make compromises in order to reach unanimity. In other words government ensured that labour could not get the real minimum wage as it had to be lower as the employers would descent. Hence the government managed to play up to the interests of the employers even after promising a fair deal to labour.

Supreme Court's ruling

In 1991 the Supreme Court ruled that the minimum wage should also include children's education, provision for old age and sudden expenses (births, deaths, marriage). These should constitute 25% of the minimum wage. Hence the total minimum comprises 55% for food, clothing and housing, 20% for fuel, lighting and miscellaneous and 25% for education, sudden expenditure and old age. The calculation of the minimum wage was mainly based on the costs of food, clothing and rent amounting to 55% and the remaining 45% was added on.

When a state government declares a minimum wage it is expected to be compulsory for all employers. The paying capacity of the employer is not a factor as there should be no negotiation for reducing this wage as it is the minimum need for reproducing the labour of the worker. However the states frequently try various means of reducing the wage. This is mainly done by reducing the weightage of each component that constitutes the wages. Prices for each component for the 55% that constitutes food and cloth are reduced so that the total wage is reduced. In most states the mechanism to enforce the minimum wage is weak. In fact after liberalisation the labour inspection machinery in the states have been considerably weakened.

Recent developments

The government has proposed a law that merges and modifies earlier laws, known as Labour Code on Wages Bill 2015. This Code merges four important legislations, namely, Payment of Wages Act, 1936, Minimum Wages Act, 1948, Payment of Bonus Act, 1965 and Equal Remuneration Act, 1976. The most crucial aspect of this Code is minimum wages but it merely repeats what has been said in the two acts of 1936 and 1948. The Code does not specify how the minimum wage should be calculated. One can understand that the Minimum Wages Act did not specify this because the idea of a need-based minimum wage had not been discussed then. As a result the states will be left to decide what they want to fix as daily minimum wage that it is happening at present. In most states the minimum wage for unskilled labour varies from Rs. 140 to Rs 400 per day (Rs 65= US$ 1). There is no way a need based minimum wage could vary to this extent if the basic criteria for fixing it are applied.

Another feature of the new system is that inspections by the relevant government department will be reduced or removed. While laying down the new plan for labour in November 2014, the prime minister stressed that employers should be trusted to invest in their employees (Pais 2014). He believed that since employers were concerned with the welfare of industry they would ensure that labour gets a fair deal so that they work hard and industry prospers. He therefore proposed a scheme of self-certification by the employers through which they would certify that all measures for labour welfare have been implemented (ibid).

The chief minister of Maharashtra too took a similar position of less intervention by government inspectors though he was not specific about employers' responsibilities towards employees. The new amendments to the Factories Act will ensure that factory inspectors will not be allowed to file cases against factories on their own. They would have to take the permission of the Chief Inspector of Factories before initiating any action. The chief minister was hopeful that the number of cases would decrease (ToI 2015: 07).

An effective trade union movement can ensure that minimum wages are enforced as it has happened in some states. In fact unless the trade union movement starts a broad-based movement for a need based minimum wage the government is least likely to consider it.

The attempts by trade unions have so far been not very successful. The trade unions at the national level have formed a joint co-ordination committee to tackle issues related to labour. Though till around a decade ago trade unions (with the exception of Self-Employed Women's Association, SEWA) were based mainly in the informal sector, however during the past decade the national unions have turned their interests towards the informal workers. In February 2013 when the trade unions decided to hold a joint two-day strike against the anti-labour policies of the government, six of the ten common demands related to issues concerning informal workers. One of the demands was of fixing a national floor level wage of Rs 10,000. There was no explanation of how this amount was agreed upon. However after the strike the unions did not make any further attempts at raising the issue of a minimum wage.[1]

More recently, on September 2, 2015, the national trade unions called for a strike against the policies of the present government[2] (discussed in the earlier sections). Two of the major demands related to informal workers namely, regularisation of casual workers and fixing a minimum wage of Rs 15,000. The trade union that is closely associated with the government initially supported the united trade movement. The government refused to negotiate with the unions on any of the issues till just two days before the strike. It proposed that it could guarantee a floor wage of Rs 7,000 and the other issues would be discussed later. On this 'assurance' the union backing the government (Bharatiya Mazdur Sangh, Indian Workers' Union) promptly withdrew from of the strike. The strike turned out to be fairly successful in most urban areas and in the public sector. However till March 2016, neither the government nor the trade unions have raised the issue of minimum wages.

There are cases where the minimum wages are enforced. SEWA has been very active in ensuring that their members get the minimum wage. The union

---

[1] For more details see *Global Labour Column* no. 125.
[2] For more details see *Global Labour Column* no. 221.

has appealed to the labour courts when violations occur. These unfortunately are long drawn struggles and even if the workers get a favourable verdict the employer can shut down the enterprise and move elsewhere. This is especially the case with small industries that operate on low capital.

At the same time there are positive cases of a section of informal workers in Mumbai who ensure that they are paid the minimum wage. These people are known as '*naka*' workers. *Naka* means street corner and these independent workers, male and female, who assemble daily at particular spots (*naka*) in the city to offer their labour power. The employers could be labour contractors or others who require labour for specific tasks. There are also *nakas* where other types of workers who specialise in specific tasks assemble. These include painting work, varnishing or wood polishing etc. These scenes are similar to what Keith Hart had noted in his study of labour markets in Accra, Ghana (Hart 1973). The other interesting feature about these workers is that they decide on the minimum wage that they would be paid which in most case is the minimum wage declared by the state government. They have an understanding among themselves that they will not accept any wage below the minimum wage, even if they do not get employment on that day. Hence it is impossible for a prospective employer to try to offer lower wages even when the concerned worker has no work for the day. In fact this is one of those rare cases where the minimum wage is actually paid and it is done because the workers are united in their decision. In fact this shows a high level of class consciousness as there is the underlying belief that if any worker breaks the rule s/he would be betraying the other workers.

References

CMIE – Centre for Monitoring Indian Economy (1989): *Wages and Income*, Bombay.

CRD – Centre for Research and Development (1995): *Socio-Economic Review of Greater Bombay (1994-1995)*, Mimeograph.

Davala, S. (ed.) (1993): *Unionisation and Employment in Indian Industry*, New Delhi: Friedrich Ebert Stiftung.

GoI – Government of India (2013): *National Sample Survey 68th Round*, New Delhi: National Sample Survey Organisation.

GoI (2009): *National Policy for Urban Street Vendors*, New Delhi: Ministry of Housing and Urban Poverty Alleviation.

GoI (2005): *Economic Survey, 2004-05*, Ministry of Finance.

Hart, K. (1973): Informal income opportunities and urban employment in Ghana, in: *Journal of Modern African Studies*, 11(1), 61-89.

HT – Hindustan Times (2015): "Assembly Clears Amendments to Factories Act", July 07, Mumbai.
HT (2015a): "Night Shift at factories open to women, state tweaks law", May 21, Mumbai.
MMRDA – Mumbai Metropolitan Regional Development Authority (1996): *Draft Regional Plan: 1994-2010*, Mumbai.
Kundu, A. (1999): *Urban Informal Sector in India: Macro Trends and Policy Perspectives*, Geneva: Development Policies Department, International Labour Organisation.
NCEUS – National Commission on Enterprises in the Unorganised Sector (2007): *Report on conditions of work and promotion of livelihoods n the unorganised sector*, New Delhi: Academic Press.
Pais, J. (2014): Limits to self-certification, in: *The Hindu*, 6 November.
ToI – Times of India (2015): Factory inspectors set to be reined in, 21 May, Mumbai.

Jobs and inequality in two Latin American countries blocs

Policy successes and diminishing returns for labor

Carlos Salas

Introduction

During the 1980 and 1990s, many Latin American countries were dominated by conservative governments with orthodox neoliberal policies that came alongside with stagnation and economic crisis, rising poverty and low-income jobs (Bulmer-Thomas 2003). By the end of the 1990s, the economic and political panorama of Latin America went through generalized transformations as the area gained a diversity of new governments and changes in the economic landscape (Panizza 2005) with renewed growth and rising exports (Rosnick/Weisbrot 2014). Among the achievements were general gains in GDP per capita and diminishing poverty rates, along with a reduction in income inequality throughout the Continent (Cornia 2012). Despite of similar trends, a careful look at the region exhibits important differences in worker's bargaining power. HansJörg Herr has emphasized in his recent work on elements that help to diminish inequality, the importance of such bargaining power for a sustained wage growth along with job creation (Herr/Ruoff 2014) and for policies to rise minimum wages (Herr/Kazandziska 2011).

For that purpose we will use a two-bloc division of countries. The first includes Pacific facing countries: Mexico, Colombia, Peru and Chile and the other one includes Atlantic facing ones: Argentina, Brazil, Venezuela, and Uruguay. Those countries in the first bloc have in common a pro-market orientation and right of center governments (save for the recent government in Chile, who has a more progressive orientation), while the other group is made up by countries that stress government activism in economic and social issues. Members of the first group embraced exports as means for growth (in strict accordance with trickle-down theories), while the other group pursued a combination of exports and internal market growth policies and strong social policies.

It is clear that these groups are not (and could not be) static, and several important developments occurred in 2015 that change this clear-cut divide. First, internal struggles spearheaded by extreme right-wing groups and the global slowdown led to political and economic crises in Argentina, Brazil, and Venezuela. As a neoliberal hawk was elected in late 2015 as Argentina's President, the Atlantic Bloc was exposed to a political rift. Also, in October 2015, a major trade agreement, the Trans-Pacific Partnership (TPP) was signed by eleven countries: Australia, Brunei, Canada, Chile, Japan, Malaysia México, New Zealand, Peru, Singapore, the United States and Vietnam. TTP is another free trade agreement that will increase pressures, both from inside and outside Latin America, to embrace free trade, neoliberal economic policies and to leave behind active social policies.

Here we will show that most countries in these blocs had a process of job creation, growth of average labor income evolution, and a better income distribution, the specific impacts of these variables on the workers' welfare are completely different among blocs. We present evidence that the economic success histories of the Pacific bloc countries are based on low wages and weak labor institutions, which run against the well-being of their workers. Thus our results support the policy prescription that is found in Herr's recent work on inequality.

To achieve these goals, in the first section, we will briefly examine the recent economic history of both blocs, paying attention to GDP and GDP per capita growth, and to the impact of GDP different components in the overall macroeconomic behavior of these blocs. In the second section, we discuss the evolution of occupations, income and income distribution, as well as union membership and the share of wages in GDP. In particular, we take into task the generalized explanation of raising incomes as based in "more and better human capital" that is the hallmark of many Orthodox arguments in this regard. We are able to show that in spite of similarities in macroeconomic performance, workers were benefited more from the pro-growth policies of the Atlantic bloc. Finally, conclude that the overall performance of the Pacific bloc is based on weak labor protection schemes. In the third section, we conclude with an examination of the possible labor developments of both blocs.

1. A little bit of recent economic history.

During the 1980 and 1990s, most Latin American economies went through major economic crises that led to substantial political and policy changes. Through vote or by the force of arms, countries gained conservative or extreme right wing regimes. From being inward looking, closed economies, with large sections of the economy controlled or owned by government enterprises, and with strongly regulated labor markets, at some time during those two decades, those characteristics and policies were profoundly transformed[1] in almost all Latin American countries. During those years there were slower rates of GDP and GDP per capita growth, greater trade opening, a diminished worker's bargaining power and increases in poverty rates (Weisbrot/Baker/ Rosnick 2006).

After 2003 there was a marked recovery in the growth rate, save for the case of Chile. Data from ECLAC shows that the main driver of GDP growth in the two blocs was domestic consumption, followed by investment, while exports and imports rates of growth played a more or less relevant role, depending on the specific economy (ECLAC 2015).

Credit for consumption, government investments, job creation and active minimum wage policies were among the national policies that helped to stimulate growth in Argentina, Brasil, Uruguay and Venezuela (Salas/Santos 2011; Weisbrot 2015). Those policies are in sharp contrast with the more market oriented path followed by Chile, Colombia, México and Peru. There is no space here to discuss the specific set of policies for each country, but an example of the contrasting policies and their impact on workers, can be found in a comparative analysis between Brazil and Mexico, that examines those diverging policies and their impact on growth and worker's wellbeing (Salas/Santos 2011).

As advanced capitalist countries regained growth after the 2000 Dotcom recession in the US and the demand pull coming from China started to accelerate (Erten/Ocampo 2013; Kaplinsky 2006), there was a visible impact on the region's exports. The average share of exports plus imports in Latin America GDP went from 28,5 in 1991 to 43,2 in 2002, as a result of the neoliberal trade opening thrust, led by the IMF and World Bank (Green 2003; Weisbrot 2015). But exports alone don't push the economies to a growth path – as the case of Mexico since 1994 shows clearly (Scott/Salas/Campbell 2006). Indeed, growth rebounded partially in response to the global scenario and

---

[1] Chile had already made those transformations, under the brutal dictatorship of A. Pinochet (Bértola/Ocampo 2010).

links with the world economy, but within a context of different national political regimes. Exports do not spur growth If they are concentrated in a few products, and if the exporting economy is not very diversified or if the export sector is not linked to the rest of the national economy. Because of the expansion of exports (both in terms of volume and in terms of prices), Inflows of foreign currency into the local economies had two important additional impacts (Weisbrot 2015), as they helped to confront balance of payments conflicts, that used to break off expansion cycles in the major Latin American countries (Bulmer-Thomas 2003) and second, as we shall see later, in some countries FDI flows came together with growing imports, and those flows also helped to stimulate final consumption.

In general terms, the positive evolution of the Latin American economies during the past 12 years was accompanied by a constant or slight rise in the share of gross fixed capital formation (for an exhaustive description and analysis of the FDI patterns in Latin America see (CEPAL 2015)

Both blocs show a growing concentration on exports based on primary commodities and minerals, that after 2005 includes even Brazil. The only exception to this trend is Mexico, because of its participation in NAFTA. In the case of Chile and Peru, metals such as copper, are an important source of foreign exchange. The United States has been traditionally a market partner of most of these countries (save for the case of Venezuela, since the late 1990s). But due to its growing demand for commodities (Jenkins/Peters/Moreira 2008), the whole area has seen the rise of China as a major trading partner, and in some cases as an active investor. Nevertheless, there is evidence that in general trade has not been diversified, either in terms of a number of products or number of trading countries (Dingemans/Ross 2012).

2. Labor, incomes and labor institutions

2.1 Job creation

Employment creation in both blocs followed GDP's growth trajectory of each country. Although several national specific trends have to highlighted: For oil exporting counties like Venezuela, whose government income comes mainly from oil revenues, greater income was used to support social programs like house construction for the poor, stimulating the construction industry and Colombia, where employment growth came as a result of the money inflow from exports.

Other commodities trading countries like Chile and Peru had employment growth linked to a growing external demand for the metals they produce. The case of Peru stands out, as exports needed infrastructure building in order to expand, bringing impulse to the construction sector. Mexico's performance was linked to the evolution of the US economy, and employment creation was severely affected by the 2007 crisis. In sharp contrast, Brazil the less trade open country of both blocs, had a job creation performance related to consumption growth, fueled by the availability of credits, public investment and other income related policies that we will discuss later on, while Argentina benefitted from domestic market growth policies after 2003 and (Weisbrot 2015; Salas/Santos 2011). In the case of Uruguay, after the 2004 election of a left oriented government in Uruguay, a set of economic and social policies were put in place (Pribble/Huber 2011), allowing for a sustained growth of the economy and employment. Policies like formalization of un-registered workers, a new labor status for paid domestic labor, monetary transfers for poor people, along with coordinated wage increases, allowed for a surge in consumption and investments, that followed 2004 (MIDES 2012); (UNDESA División de Desarrollo Social 2013).

The export demand pull on job creation was also affected by the size of the self-employment sector in each country. This is visible in the case of countries like Colombia, Peru and Mexico, where the self-employed workers are a high proportion of workers. This sector along with workers in very small scale units (which are usually referred as "informal sector activities") represent a major limit to poverty reduction, good quality job creation and to better bargaining conditions for wage workers (see chapters 4 and 5 of Jansen/ Peters/Salazar 2011). We don't have space to discuss unemployment figures in this paper, but it should be pointed out the economic significance of unemployment itself depends on the development levels of national labor markets, which are also linked to the general levels of economic development (Salas 2003). Thus countries with a dualistic economic structure, as Colombia, Mexico and Peru and to a lesser degree Chile, have levels of unemployment that do not reflect the lack or abundance of job opportunities. National comparisons for different moments of time might show a relation with the business cycle of each country, but comparisons among countries are difficult. As discussed in (Salas/Santos 2011) a typical example is given by Brazilian and Mexican unemployment levels. In the latter case, unemployment figures are low because of the existence of a large sector of self-employment and very small economic units, that absorb the surplus population that needs monetary income and cannot afford the luxury of long active job seeking process. In the Brazilian case, the existence of unemployment insurance and a more developed labor market, means that levels of unemployment reflect more closely the general conditions of the economy, than in the case of Mexico.

2.2 Wages and minimum wages

During the 2000s a minimum wage policy of constant growth was implemented in most of the countries considered in this paper, the exception being Mexico. As a result of the combination of growth and minimum wage policies, average wages rose expressively in these countries (Table 1) Mexico and Colombia had the lowest rates of growth of all the countries considered here, while Argentina and Uruguay had the highest rates. Those policy decisions had impact also on the incomes of the non-wage workers, because of the so called "lighthouse effect" on the lowest labor incomes. Wage growth had an important role in the reduction in inequality that we will examine next. In the case of Brazil, raising minimum wage had additional multiplier effects as some social payments are tied to the value of minimum wage.

Table 1: Average wages annual data, 2010=100

Country	2002	2008	2009	2011	2012	2013	2014
Argentina[*]	46.6	79.3	88.5	116.4	134.1	151.6	165.8
Brazil	98.7	96.3	98.5	101.4	104.9	107.1	108.8
Chile	85.3	93.4	97.9	102.5	105.8	109.9	111.9
Colombia	91.6	96.1	97.3	100.3	101.3	104.0	104.5
México	93.4	101.9	100.9	100.8	101.0	100.9	101.3
Peru[**]	97.7	100.0	103.1	108.4	111.0	114.7	117.9
Uruguay	87.1	90.2	96.8	104.0	108.4	111.7	115.4
Venezuela	130.2	112.1	105.6	103.0	109.1	104.3	...

[*] Data from 2010 to 2014 might be overvalued because of problems with CPI estimates
[**] Data for Peru includes only urban workers in Lima

Source: [A] CEPAL: Comisión Económica para América Latina y el Caribe – División de Desarrollo Económico. – http://www.cepal.org/es/areas-de-trabajo/desarrollo-economico

2.3 Income distribution

One of the most visible economic results in the last decade is the drop in inequality as measured by the Gini coefficient (Table 2). This fall results from a combination of factors that include a smaller household size, more jobs and better wages, anti-poverty programs (cash transfer programs). An enormous amount of papers has been written to explain this feat, mostly from a conservative point of view. These papers often dismisses the impact of specific social and economic policies (for a brief discussion see (Montecino 2012)) and include a growing educational levels as one of the explanatory variables of Gini's evolution. But there are other studies others that shown the relevance of social and economic policies in inequality reduction. For example (Montecino 2012) proves that the more progressive governments in the area (belonging to the Mercosur bloc) were more successful in diminishing inequality. Also, by means of a technique developed by (Shaikh/Ragab 2008), to measure the income of vast majority (average income of 70% percent of the population), that uses the Gini index and National Income data, (Gerstenfeld/Vega/Abeles 2011), show that the Atlantic bloc countries had a better redistribution performance, that is reflected in poverty reduction data (see next section)

Table 2: Gini index and changes

Country	2001	2002	2003	2006	2012	2013	Changes between first and last available data
Argentina	53.3	53.8	53.5	48.3	42.5	42.3	11.1
Brazil	59.3	58.6	58.0	55.9	52.7	52.9	6.5
Chile	..	..	54.7	51.8	..	50.5	4.3
Colombia	57.8	58.3	54.4	60.1	53.5	53.5	4.3
Mexico	..	49.5	..	48.0	48.1	..	1.5
Peru[*]	51.8	54.0	53.7	51.7	45.1	44.7	7.1
Uruguay	46.2	46.7	46.2	47.2	41.3	41.9	4.3
Venezuela	48.2	50.6	50.4	46.9	41.1	41.1	7.2

[*] Peruvian figures before 2004 are not strictly comparable to later data.

Source: World Development Indicators, For Venezuela 2012-2013 adjusted estimates based on CEPAL data

2.4 Poverty reduction

Falls in inequality were accompanied by a sensible drop in poverty levels, in particular, the extreme poverty levels. Although poverty numbers depend on the poverty line defined, one that varies from country to country, harmonized data show a similar tendency, albeit a smoothed one. This point along with critical examination of those numbers can be found in (Helwege/Birch 2007). With those caveats in mind, we find that poverty reduction was more intense in the Atlantic bloc countries. Once again, Mexico stands out with a lackluster performance.

Graph 1: Poor Population – percentage of total poulation

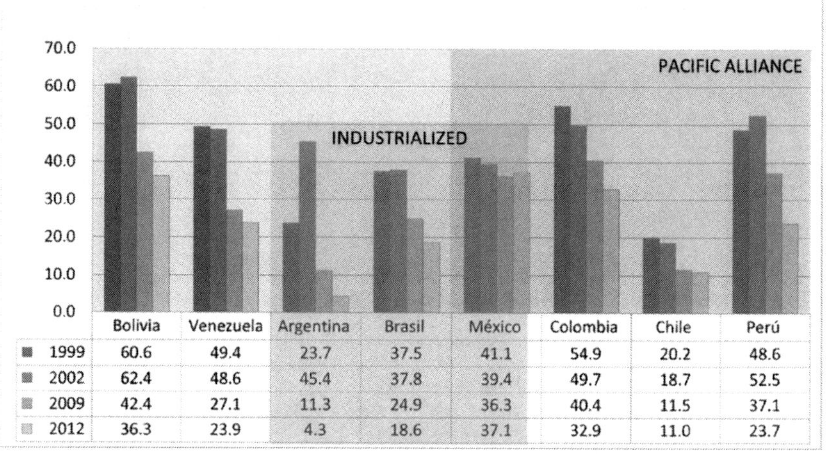

	Bolivia	Venezuela	Argentina	Brasil	México	Colombia	Chile	Perú
1999	60.6	49.4	23.7	37.5	41.1	54.9	20.2	48.6
2002	62.4	48.6	45.4	37.8	39.4	49.7	18.7	52.5
2009	42.4	27.1	11.3	24.9	36.3	40.4	11.5	37.1
2012	36.3	23.9	4.3	18.6	37.1	32.9	11.0	23.7

Source: Panorama Social de América Latina, CEPAL, several years

Poverty reduction results from of a combination of more jobs, better incomes and social safety nets. In both blocs the conditional cash transfer programs have been able to lower the extreme poverty rates, although if they are not accompanied by job creation programs, staying out of extreme poverty or poverty is very difficult. In fact several econometric exercises estimate a more important contribution of employment and income growth for a reduction of poverty levels (Inchauste et al. 2012; Zepeda et al. 2009).

Institutional labor developments

From an heterodox economic perspective, wages are not determined by some arcane entity named "marginal productivity of labor" as this entity cannot be measured and the neoclassical story behind wages being determined by marginal productivity, holds for a very restricted kind of perfectly competitive market that doesn't exists outside neoclassical theory (Kaufman 2007). Those arguments based on identifying better educational levels with higher skills as the reason why wages grow, assume the truth of marginal productivity argument for wage determination, and worse, assume that simply by rising skills, employers will open the adequate jobs for them. This kind of argument is a resurrection of Say's Law. In reality, wages are determined by productivity levels – a combination of skills, efforts and technology – and the bargaining power of workers, that is used to dispute for a larger share of the surplus available in the production of goods (Härring/Douglas 2012: chapter 5; Herr 2009).

A couple of variables that capture bargaining power are the share of labor (waged) in GDP and union density in a country. As can be seen in tables 3 and 4, both have, in general, greater values for countries in the Atlantic bloc. Even if instead of using the wage share, we use data for the labor income share in GDP to take into account self-employed workers, the comparisons between the two blocs will give similar results (Abeles/Amarante/Vega 2014).

Table 3 Share of wages in GDP, several years

Country	2005	2006	2007	2008	2009
Argentina	38.5	41.5	42.9		
Brazil	46.7	47.6	48.1	49.1	
Chile	37.5	34.8	35.2	39.4	40.6
Colombia	32.1	31.9	32.0	31.6	32.2
México	29.6	28.6	28.1	28.0	29.2
Peru	27.0				24.0
Uruguay					45.8
Venezuela	28.5	30.6	32.3		

Source: UNDP and Abeles et al. (2014)

In the case of union density, low values reflect either a less developed industrial structure, as in the case of Peru, or an explicit anti-labor bias, as is the case of Colombia and Mexico. The size and trends of both variables are influenced by government policies, which for the time lapse considered in this text, were pro-labor oriented in countries of the Atlantic bloc.

Table 4: Union density

Country	2003	2008	2009	2012	2013
Argentina		37.7			
Brazil	20.6	22.2	19.1	17.5	16.6
Chile	14.1	15.0	15.8	15.3	15.0
Colombia					6.5
México	16.9	15.7	15.3	13.6	13.6
Peru			4.4	4.2	
Uruguay			16.6		30.1

Source: IloStat

3. Conclusions

The social and economic impacts of the neoliberal reforms in the 1980-90s set up a popular reaction that in many countries led to social democratic and left wing governments into power, the first case being Venezuela in the late 1990s. Several other countries followed, Argentina, Bolivia Brazil, Chile, Ecuador and Uruguay. In other countries like Colombia and Mexico, the right retained power, and in the case of Chile they even regained government for a four year term. Our analysis of two blocs of countries, the Pacific Alliance formed by Colombia, Chile, Mexico and Peru, and the Mercosul bloc, Argentina, Brazil, Uruguay and Venezuela, show the results of two different sets of policies. It should be noted that we included Chile in the Pacific bloc because of its conservative trade policies.

From our review of the economic performance of each bloc, several important facts can be highlighted, the first one is it has been proved that neither growing prices of commodities (Adler/Magud 2015) nor better terms of trade (Rosnick/Weisbrot 2014)) by themselves pushed GDP growth in the region. For most of the Pacific bloc countries (and Venezuela) the key variable was their high degree of trade openness. Even though Argentina, Brazil and Uruguay did benefit from greater demand for their exports, for those countries the key for growth can be found in their economic and social policies that stimulated growth and demand. It goes without saying that the 2007 crisis showed the limits of export led growth policies and that there exists ample evidence that terms of trade deteriorate secularly (Erten/Ocampo 2013). The structure of trade in the Pacific bloc countries are examples of re-primarization processes with a strong private component. Being mostly primary commodities exporters, the consequences for workers are not very good as countries need to attract foreign investors to invest in extractive activities, frequently with weak links to the rest of the economy.

Although in most of the countries examined, poverty and income maldistribution was reduced and labor income increased, a closer look at the specific details in each bloc show important differences. The high numbers of self-employed and family workers in countries like Colombia, Mexico, Peru and to a lesser degree Chile, were not sharply reduced during the period considered. Those numbers are evidence of a lack of capitalist dynamism that could absorb that reserve army of labor, and they also show that the success of poverty reduction processes was based more by income transfers than on wage job creation.

The labor market institutional variables of union density and the share of wages in GDP show that workers from the Atlantic bloc countries have a greater degree of bargaining power than their counterparts in the Pacific bloc. Additionally, Mexico, Colombia and Peru have a long standing record of labor rights violations, as the annual Global Rights Index of ITUC shows (ITUC 2014).

Finally recent political developments in Latin America bring back the need to examine the economic policies of those countries that decided to confront poverty and low wages, along with job creation and general growth. Re primarization and sheer consumption growth cannot be the basis for a sustainable development process. Unless these societies stop and reverse the ongoing conservative offensive in Latin America, we could face more countries with backward policies based on low wages and weak labor protection schemes, to attract foreign investments. If those processes are not stopped, we might see the area's workers back to where they were in the final years of the past century: struggling to survive.

References

Abeles, M., Amarante, V., Vega, D. (2014): Participación del ingreso laboral en el ingreso total en América Latina, 1990-2010, in: *Revista CEPAL*, 114 (Diciembre), 31-52 (Retrieved from http://repositorio.cepal.org/bitstream/11362/37435/1/RVE114Amaranteetal_es.pdf).

Adler, G., Magud, N.E. (2015): Four decades of terms-of-trade booms: A metric of income windfall, in: *Journal of International Money and Finance*, 55, 162-192 (http://doi.org/10.1016/j.jimonfin.2015.02.007).

Bértola, L., Ocampo, J.A. (2010): *Desarrollo, vaivenes y desigualdad: Una historia económica de América Latina desde la independencia*, Madrid: SEGIB.

Bulmer-Thomas, V. (2003): *The Economic History of Latin America since Independence (Second)*, Cambridge: Cambridge University Press.

CEPAL – Comisión Económica para América Latina y el Caribe (2015): *La Inversión Extranjera Directa en America Latina y el Caribe*, Santiago de Chile: Naciones Unidas.

Cornia, G.A. (2010): Income Distribution under Latin America's New Left Regimes, in: *Journal of Human Development and Capabilities*, 11(1), 85-114 (http://doi.org/10.1080/19452820903481483).

Cornia, G.A. (2012): Inequality Trends and their Determinants: Latin America over 1990-2010 (No. 2012/09), Working Paper No. 2012/09 (Retrieved from http://hdl.handle.net/10419/81076\nhttp://www.wider.unu.edu/publications/working-papers/2012/en_GB/wp2012-009/).

Dingemans, A., Ross, C. (2012): Los acuerdos de libre comercio en América Latina desde 1990. Una evaluación de la diversificación de exportaciones, in: *Revista Cepal*, (108), 27-50 (Retrieved from http://www.cepal.org/publicaciones/xml/5/48615/RVE108DingemansRoss.pdf).

ECLAC (2015): *La Inversión Extranjera Directa en America Latina y el Caribe*, Santiago de Chile: Naciones Unidas.

Erten, B., Ocampo, J.A. (2013): Super Cycles of Commodity Prices Since the Mid-Nineteenth Century, in: *World Development*, 44, 14-30 (http://doi.org/10.1016/j.worlddev.2012.11.013).

Gerstenfeld, P., Vega, D., Abeles, M. (2011): *Crecimiento, distribución y desarrollo: Un enfoque integrado*, LC/W441. Documento de Proyecto 28, Santiago de Chile: Naciones Unidas.

Green, D. (2003): *Silent Revolution: The Rise and Crisis of Market Economics in Latin America*, New York: Monthly Review Press.

Härring, N., Douglas, N. (2012): *Economists and the Powerful: Convenient Theories, Distorted Facts, Ample Rewards* (Anthem Other Canon Economics), London: Anthem Press.

Helwege, A., Birch, M.B.L. (2007): Declining Poverty in Latin America? A Critical Analysis of New Estimates by International Institutions Declining Poverty in Latin America? A Critical Analysis of New Estimates by International Institutions (No. 07-02). GDAE Working Paper Series.

Herr, H. (2009): The labour market in a Keynesian economic regime: Theoretical debate and empirical findings, in: *Cambridge Journal of Economics*, 33(5), 949-965 (http://doi.org/10.1093/cje/ben044).

Herr, H., Kazandziska, M. (2011): Principles of Minimum Wage Policy – Economics, in: *Institutions and Recommendations. Policy*, 11, 1-28.

Herr, H., Ruoff, B. (2014): Wage Dispersion As Key Factor for Changing Personal Income Distribution, in: *Journal of Self-Governance and Management Economics*, 2(3), 28-71.

Inchauste, G., Olivieri, S., Saavedra, J., Winkler, H. (2012): What Is Behind the Decline in Poverty Since 2000? Evidence from Bangladesh, Peru and Thailand, World Bank Policy Research Working Paper No. 6199, Washington, DC.

ITUC – International Trade Union Confederation (2014): ITUC Global Rights Index 2014. The world's worst countries for workers.

Jansen, M., Peters, R., Salazar, J. (eds.) (2011): *Trade and Employment: From Myths to Facts*, Geneva: ILO (Retrieved from http://www.ilo.org/employment/areas/trade-and-employment/WCMS_162297/lang--en/index.htm).

Jenkins, R., Peters, E.D., Moreira, M.M. (2008): The Impact of China on Latin America and the Caribbean, in: *World Development*, 36(2), 235-253 (http://doi.org/10.1016/j.worlddev.2007.06.012).

Kaplinsky, R. (2006): Revisiting the revisited terms of trade: Will China make a difference?, in: *World Development*, 34(6), 981-995 (http://doi.org/10.1016/j.worlddev.2005.11.011).

Kaufman, B. E. (2007): The impossibility of a perfectly competitive labour market, in: *Cambridge Journal of Economics*, 31(5), 775-787 (http://doi.org/10.1093/cje/bem001).

MIDES – El Ministerio de Desarrollo Social (2012): *Vulnerabilidad y exclusión: Aportes para las políticas sociales*, Uruguay Social (Vol. 5), Montevideo.

Montecino, J.A. (2012): Decreasing Inequality under Latin America's "Social Democratic" and "Populist" Governments: Is the Difference Real?, in: *International Journal of Health Services*, 42(2), 257-275 (http://doi.org/10.2190/HS.42.2.g).

Panizza, F.E. (2005): The Social Democratisation of the Latin American Left, in: *Revista Europea de Estudios Latinoamericanos Y Del Caribe/European Review of Latin American and Caribbean Studies*, 79, 95-103 (http://doi.org/papers2://publication/uuid/94F28A32-463B-4365-AF5D-2A59EF82859E).

Pribble, J., Huber, E. (2011): Social Policy and Redistribution: Chile and Uruguay, in: Levitsky, S., Roberts, K.M. (eds.), *The Resurgence of the Latin American Left*, Baltimore: Johns Hopkins University Press, 117-138.

Rosnick, B.D., Weisbrot, M. (2014): *Latin American Growth in the 21st Century: The "Commodities Boom" That Wasn't*, Washington, D.C.: Center for Economic and Policy Research (http://www.cepr.net/documents/terms-of-trade-2014-05.pdf).

Salas, C. (2003): Trayectorias laborales entre el empleo,\r\nel desempleo y las microunidades\r\nen México, in: *Papeles de Población*, 9(38), 121-157 (Retrieved from http://www.redalyc.org/resumen.oa?id=11203804).

Salas, C., Anselmo, S. (2011): Diverging paths in development: Brazil and Mexico, in: *International Journal of Labour Research*, 3(1), 115-133.

Salas, C., Santos, A. (2011): Diverging paths in development: Brazil and Mexico, in: *International Journal of Labour Research*, 3(1), 115-133.

Scott, R., Salas, C., Campbell, B. (2006): *Revisiting NAFTA. Still not working for North America's workers*, Washington, D.C. (Retrieved from http://www.epi.org/publications/entry/bp173/).

Shaikh, A., Ragab, A. (2008): The Vast Majority Income (VMI): A New Measure of Global Inequality, Policy research brief, May/2008, no. 7, New York: SCEPA (Schwartz Centre for Economic Analysis).

UNDESA División de Desarrollo Social de la CEPAL (2013): Documento de país sobre kas políticas orientadas a las familias para la reducción de la pobreza y la conciliación de la vida laboral y familia: Uruguay.

Weisbrot, M. (2015) *Failed, What the "experts" got wrong about the global economy*, New York: Oxford University Press.

Weisbrot, M., Baker, D., Rosnick, D. (2006): The scorecard on development: 25 years of diminished progress, in: *International Journal of Health Services: Planning, Administration, Evaluation*, 36(31), 211-234 (http://doi.org/10.2190/AABL-CJ6J-G3P5-8G5U).

Zepeda, E., Alarcón, D., Soares, S., Osório, R. (2009): Changes in Earnings in Brazil, Chile, and Mexico: Disentangling the Forces Behind Pro-Poor Change in Labour Markets, Working Papers 51, International Policy Centre for Inclusive Growth.

Give that man a fishing rod: Reflections on job creation and cash transfers

Edward Webster and Khayaat Fakier

In August 2010 officials of the South African government began closing down clothing and textile factories in Newcastle, in the province of KwaZulu-Natal, in the face of angry protests from workers because the owners were paying less than the statutory minimum wage of R324 ($49) a week. Dudu Mabaso, who works in one of these factories, said that as much as she wants conditions to change at her company, closing down is not an option:

> People will revolt against closure. It's their source of survival, and working for these textile companies is the only way to survive. The wages are low at R250 ($36) per week but they are better than nothing (Oliphant 2010: 1).

The factory owners said they could not pay more and survive in the face of cheap Chinese textile imports. As Alex Liu, Chair of the Newcastle Chinese Chamber of Commerce, asserted:

> It is impossible for us to pay the minimum wage because we are competing with imports from China and the cut, make and trim (CMT) price from our customers will not sustain us if we paid the minimum wage of R324 ($49) a week (Khanyile 2010: 3).

This notion that "a bad job is better than no job" is rooted in popular discourse.[1] In the surveys of vulnerable workers in Gauteng, the only decent

---

[1] Our evidence is drawn from the results of research commissioned in 2009 by the Gauteng Department of Economic Development (GDED) (SWOP 2009). The studies were carried out in Westonaria (an urban area outside of Johannesburg) and Keiskammahoek (a rural area). We developed an instrument to monitor decent work (SWOP 2012).

work indicator for which there was *no* significant difference among the three sectors – hospitality, private security and agriculture – was Employment Opportunities (Webster et al. 2015: 58). As report on the Decent Work Indicators for South Africa states:

> The high rate of unemployment in South Africa emerges as a key issue in the area of Employment Opportunities ... If those who have given up looking for work are included, the expanded unemployment rate stood at 35.8% overall in 2010 – 31.5% for men and 40.7% for women (Department of Labour 2011: 3).

What is to be done overcome poverty – job creation or cash transfers? The answer, James Ferguson (2015) argues in his iconoclastic new book, lies in transferring cash unconditionally to the poor. Instead of "teaching a man to fish", as generations of development practitioners were taught, Ferguson believes it is more effective to simply "give a man a fish". This policy of cash transfers – what has become known as the Basic Income Grant (BIG) – entitles every person to a fixed regular income. It does not require much administration; all you have to do is "swipe your card at the ATM" (Ferguson 2015: 30).

Ferguson is convincing when he says that the South African government is doing the opposite of the standard neo-liberal model by "transferring 3.4% of the country's GDP directly to the poor via non-market cash payments to 30% of the population" (Ferguson 2015: 4).[2] These policies, he argues, are a direct challenge to the "productionist fundamentalism" of the traditional left. Ferguson draws on an alternative radical political tradition that goes back to the nineteenth century (Paine 1830; Kropotkin [1892]1995). It is an argument that states that everyone has the right to a share of the social product, and that "just distribution" is not based on the labour of individuals but on their share of the collective social product.[3]

---

[2] Even though modest, at 3.4 per cent of Gross Domestic Product (GDP) it is 'more than twice the median spending of 1.4 percent of GDP across developing and transition economies' (Woolard and Leibbrandt 2010: 1). Significantly, while expenditure on social security has shrunk across the globe, South Africa's expenditure has grown. Transfers also has to be seen as part of a larger package of social security which include the public provision of housing, health services and school feeding schemes for the poor.

[3] Currently expenditure on social assistance is +-R150 billion; estimates are that the BIG would cost +-R70 billion (for an income grant of R100 per month). If the two run concurrently, current expenditure rises by nearly 50%. This is clearly unaffordable. Even more so if the BIG is paid at a minimum wage rate of R1800 per month (the 2016 minimum wage rate for domestic workers in rural areas.

This is a utopian idea and is elegantly put by Ferguson. Our point of entry into this debate is through our research on the Community Work Programme (CWP). Ferguson dismisses these schemes as ineffective but, he says, the government continues to believe that job creation is "the solution to all problems" (Ferguson 2015: 60).[4] Ferguson turns this solution on its head; cash transfers, he proclaims, are the basis of a new welfare state and a "politics of distribution" (Ferguson 2015: 2-12).

While there has been a long-standing debate on whether South Africa should introduce a basic income grant, it is wrong to see the current system of social grants as a universal BIG. As Fouksman (2015: 290) points out in her recent review of Ferguson's book, social grants "are not universal but means tested, and they are far lower than the levels proposed by most BIG proponents...."

The origins of the debate on the BIG in South Africa goes back two decades to the report prepared for the Presidential Labour Market Commission by Guy Standing, a leading advocate of the BIG. (Standing et al. 1996). It was taken forward by the Congress of South African Trade Unions (COSATU), which proposed a BIG to the Presidential Jobs Summit in 1999 (Coleman 1999: 45). A statutory commission was set up in 2002 to investigate the feasibility of introducing a BIG, the so-called Taylor Commission, but its recommendations were largely ignored, both because of perceived fiscal constraints and a concern by government for what it called "dependency" (Bond 2014). Debates on the idea of a BIG have continued over the years, and a coalition to promote it was formed. But South Africa's social policy experts remain sceptical of the notion, either favouring embedding social policy in a "wider development strategy" (Adesina 2010: 1) or creating jobs through greater labour market flexibility (Seekings 2013: 34-35).

Our contribution to this Festschrift is an exploration of Hans-Jörg Herr's enduring interest in development policy and practice. In our research for the GDED on job creation, we first interviewed face-to-face over 3000 workers in the hospitality, private security and agricultural sectors in Gauteng (Webster et al. 2015). We then examined various labour-intensive job creation schemes, including the Community Work Programme.

In the first part of the article we present the results of our research on the CWP. Although participants felt that the scheme contributed to greater social cohesion in the community, the jobs were low-paid and part-time, and the project did not facilitate the creation of sustainable jobs. In the second part of

---

[4] See Franco Barchiesi (2011) for a fuller development of this argument.

the article we argue that the state has transferred its responsibility for care work to women in poor households.

We conclude that, while a "quiet revolution" is taking place in development policies in the Global South, cash transfers do little to tackle the structure of inequality (Fakier/Ehmke 2014: 245). Ferguson is right to identify spaces within neo-liberal capitalism where the poor are able to benefit from social grants; but to be sustainable "the politics of distribution" will need to link cash transfers to an alternative, job-creating developmental path.

1. The Community Work Programme

The CWP is "an experiment in key municipalities of an employment safety net providing a minimum level of regular and predictable work, usually two days a week, while wider policy processes to create sustainable employment take effect" (Philip 2010: 4). Although it does not meet many of the indicators identified in the International Labour Organisation's (ILO's) concept of "decent work", the CWP provides a work opportunity and a regular income with some degree of social protection. At the time that the research was undertaken in late 2010 and early 2011, the CWP had already created 100 000 work opportunities nationwide (SWOP 2011).

The CWP is based on a similar scheme in India, the Mahatma Gandhi National Rural Employment Guarantee Scheme (MGNREGS), which provides rural households with 100 days of "work opportunities" per year. It provides work for the unemployed "as they are", regardless of their skills, education or personal characteristics. It makes government the Employer of Last Resort. As a result of this approach, Employment Guarantee Schemes (EGSs) in India have become a key policy instrument in ameliorating endemic poverty and providing income relief through direct job creation. EGSs are suitable for job creation in developing countries, as they create "an infinitely elastic demand for labour at a floor or minimum wage that does not depend upon the long and short run profits of business" (Wray 2007). It provides a first step into the labour market, a staircase that contributes towards job creation.

The CWP provides access to a minimum level of regular work, two days a week (100 days per year) at a stipend rate of R63.18 ($9) per day. It is an area-based programme, and is intended to be ongoing. This allows it to target the poorest areas where market-based jobs are unlikely to come any time soon.

The CWP uses community participation to identify "useful work" and priorities. Work is decided in Ward Committees or local development forums; it is multi-sectoral and contributes to public/community goods and services. The start-up scale is 1 000 participants per site; the scheme has a 65% labour intensity – that is, 65% of total costs must be spent on wages.

The CWP programme provides a predictable and regular income of R480 ($69) per month to the participants. In addition, 93% of those interviewed in Westonaria and 92% of those interviewed in Keiskammahoek received R250 ($36) from the government child support grant.

However, the CWP had a limited impact on facilitating work searches; only 24% of the participants from Westonaria and 13% from Keiskammahoek had looked for work over the previous seven days. Of those who had looked for work, 65% (Westonaria) and 50% (Keiskammahoek) had used their CWP income to facilitate the search, to pay for transport or for mobile phone usage. Surprisingly, 21% of the participants in Westonaria and 25% in Keiskammahoek claimed to have been able to save some of their CWP money; 30% in Westonaria and 44% in Keiskammahoek saved on average over R100 ($14) per month.

In almost all of the sites (89% in Westonaria and 87% in Keiskammahoek), communal vegetable gardens had been established by participants; 50% of the respondents in (Westonaria) and 77% in Keiskammahoek had established vegetable gardens at their homes, and were able to provide their families with vegetables on a daily basis.

We concluded that the economic impact of the CWP was limited: its main contribution lay in facilitating greater social cohesion in these communities. Participants in the programme had made new friends (82% in Westonaria and 74% in Keiskammahoek) with whom they were able to share personal problems and gain social support.

The programme encouraged an ethic of care and support to the vulnerable in the community. Examples given by CWP participants included cooking and cleaning for the elderly and sick, collecting medicines for the bed-ridden, providing food parcels and clothing for child-headed households, and giving vegetables to crèches.

Many interviewees – 78% in Westonaria and 68% in Keiskammahoek – said that the CWP had improved community safety through community police forums. The community was taking greater care of their natural resources through clean-up campaigns, tree planting activities, clearing the environment of alien vegetation, repairing dams and water harvesting.

It could be argued that the CWP was a step towards a job. This seems to be the approach adopted by the former General Secretary of COSATU, Zwelinzima Vavi, when he gave qualified support for the programme:

We would like young people to get work experience knowing that it is not necessarily decent work on its own because CWP does not pay a living wage. These programmes are about providing those who are trapped in structural unemployment an opportunity to find their way out of that crisis (Vavi 2011).

But the opportunity of getting employment would be improved if participants in the CWP were provided with training. Participants do not have the option of, for example, working two days and spending the other three days in training for various skills in the Technical Vocational Education and Training (TVET) colleges. Currently the CWP is only about survival, and does not expand the capabilities of the participants through formal training.

2. Care work

The CWP is at the interface of social and economic policy (Philip 2010), and has both distributive (labour market) and redistributive (health, social welfare and education) ambitions (Seekings 2013).

Social welfare in South Africa is categorised into two systems. First is a system of public social assistance (or social grants) to the elderly, disabled persons, and some women and children. Second is the provision of direct welfare services to families, children, the disabled and the elderly. The Department of Social Development (DSD) spends "93% of the department's budget ... on social assistance, with just under 7% for other activities" (DSD 2007: 332). The income from state social grants is crucial for the survival of many poor and unemployed households (Fakier 2010; Mosoetsa 2011). But in prioritising social grants over direct care services, which institutions such as old age homes, crèches and facilities for the mentally and physically disabled could provide, care for the needy remains predominantly a private household concern and ultimately becomes the responsibility of women, who are not paid for this additional labour burden.

A combination of high unemployment with little provision to care for the very old, the young, the frail and the disabled has created a crisis of care. Our research on the CWP brought to light that many impoverished households prioritise care when they determine the "socially useful work" their communities require (SWOP 2011) A common menu of priorities emerged from the CWP communities and these have become the "anchor" programmes. These include:

- a strong focus on food security;
- home-based care, mainly for HIV- and TB-affected households and auxiliary care such as cooking and cleaning;
- care of orphans and vulnerable children, especially in child-headed households;
- social programmes to tackle alcohol abuse, violence and crime;
- development of recreation spaces and sporting facilities targeting youth;
- environmental rehabilitation and maintenance, informal settlement upgrading and road maintenance (Khanyile 2008; Luvhengo 2010).

The CWP also serves as a catalyst for crèches, old age homes, schools and voluntary associations to fulfil their development potential. The CWP does this by subsidising the cost of nutrition (by donating vegetables from food gardens to crèches, old age homes and vulnerable households). It also has the potential to facilitate training of community care providers, and provides the organisational infrastructure for care through its structures. In Keiskammahoek, for example, the non-governmental organisation (NGO) which runs the CWP has the physical structure and the organisational ability to bring together senior nurses and social workers to train CWP participants and volunteers to better deal with activities such as working with bed-ridden people and juvenile delinquents.

The CWP is not the only government programme that tries to make up for deficiencies in social welfare, health and education. The Home- and Community-Based Care (HCBC) programme was developed specifically to deal with the ravages of HIV and AIDS in the context of a struggling public health system, but has grown to include care services for other needy individuals as well. The programme is an attempt to provide care services to the frail, elderly and children in their homes by using "volunteers" in the consumer's immediate neighbourhood (Department of Health, not dated: 1).

In 2009, HCBC volunteers received a stipend of approximately R1 100 ($143) a month (more than twice the earnings of CWP workers) for their travel expenses. Many of them see this relatively high and stable income as an entry-point to a career, rather than a voluntary activity (Fakier 2010). However, despite greater resources devoted to the volunteers and the dependence of the HCBC programme on the organisational infrastructure of Community-Based Organisations (CBOs) and NGOs, the HCBC programme suffers from severe funding problems. At the base of the problem is the inadequacy of training and guidance for HCBCs to deal with the care needs of poor communities. Additional problems identified were their inability to deal with the physical and emotional needs and the effects of care, and the fact that [some of the] HCBCs themselves were plagued by illness and frailties due to old age (Fakier 2014: 133-146).

These problems with the HCBC means that very little assistance is provided by the state to people dependent on home-based care, other than what constitutes home "visits" (Hunter 2007). The state and desperate households revert to a dependence on woman family caregivers rather than state- or market-provided services. HCBC volunteers and CWP workers appear to be doing the work of the ministries of Health, Education and Social Development, in spite of the fact that these ministries are formally responsible for care work. As a result social development and welfare functions of the state are outsourced cheaply to "volunteers" who take it on with great empathy but little actual expertise and skill. The outcome is suboptimal social welfare delivered by the poor to the poor.

Across the globe, public sector employment has provided women an opportunity to enter formal wage employment and, as Crankshaw (1996) suggests, a vehicle for upward class mobility. However, in the case of some care workers, the state contradicts its reputation as a "good employer" and deliberately sidesteps its own labour regulations by "employing workers who are not even counted as part of the labour force" (Razavi/Staab 2010: 418). Razavi (2011) suggests that developing countries rely to a large extent on the "volunteer" or "community" work of women to care for and reproduce societies, relegating women to unpaid or underpaid positions. This is quite different from the Swedish case where care service expansion was financed and regulated by the state, and where care workers were public employees with all the rights and entitlements that this implied. An important outcome of the Swedish policy position was greater gender equality, in addition to high-quality care and decent work.

Those employed in the CWP and as HCBCs are overstretched and work for low pay. Clearly, the social sector has great potential of creating full-time jobs for the unemployed. These jobs could include child-care workers and teacher aides, as well as auxiliary work for school caretakers and school clerical workers. Antonopoulos and Kim (2008) go further and propose that the scaling up of these positions from public employment programmes to full-time work must include a permanent appointment for child-care, school nutrition, teacher aides and school caretakers, during which training is given and experienced gained. If the government is serious about this, it could lead to the creation of nearly 300000 jobs.

3. Conclusion: Building a basic social floor

The ILO has developed the concept of "a basic social floor of social security benefits", which could be introduced as a matter of priority in developing countries where there are wide coverage gaps (Cichon et al. 2011: 3). The crucial step in advancing this debate was the demonstration that a basic set of social security benefits, or at least parts thereof, is affordable in developing countries (ILO 2008). The realisation that, in the short term, it is possible to imagine building a global social floor – a basic pension, child benefits, access to health care, temporary employment guarantee schemes or income transfers for the long-term unemployed – broke the spell of the "non-affordability myth" (Cichon et al. 2011: 3).

But, as these authors emphasise, the argument for job creation and social security cannot be used "as a pretext for non-compliance" and that "resource scarcity does not relieve states of certain minimum obligations in respect of the implementation of the right to [social] security" (Cichon et al. 2011: 3). Social security systems, they argue, "have to grow in sync with economic and social development" (Cichon et al. 2011: 12). The metaphor that emerged is that of a social security "staircase", with the bottom step comprising a set of basic guarantees for all, and a second level and third level of ascending staircases where rights are strengthened (Cichon et al. 2011). Importantly, they argue:

> ...without investment in a social protection floor, many people will not reach a level of skills and productivity which would enable them to enter the formal economy but will remain trapped in informality and low productivity. Investing in a basic level of social protection that triggers a virtuous cycle of improved productivity and employability will ensure the sustainability of statutory schemes by enabling more and more people to move into contributory schemes (Cichon et al. 2011: 12).

This attempt at imagining an alternative development path is not some way-out revolutionary adventure, tilting at windmills as it were. Instead, it is swimming very much with the current by grounding political innovations in successful social policy initiatives in countries such as South Africa, Brazil and India (Chakraborty 2007; Cichon et al. 2011:15).

These emerging welfare regimes are different from the European welfare state that was constructed around the equal contribution of three pillars: permanent full-time employment, a strong professional public service and the nuclear family. Instead, the emerging welfare regimes of the South – what Gough (2004) calls informal security regimes – rely on informal work as well as a variety of livelihood strategies such as street trading, the extended family, and the villages and communities within which they are embedded.

The challenge is to link social policies to a new inclusive growth path.

Social assistance cannot be a substitute for decent employment, which needs a different macro-economic policy agenda and the strengthening of labour market regulations (e.g. on minimum wage) (Razavi 2011, cited in Fakier 2014: 144).

To achieve this goal, you cannot outsource the functions of the state to poor households where the poor have to carry the full costs of social reproduction. What is needed is a combination of cash transfers with a new job-creating developmental path. The answer to the developmental dilemma posed at the beginning is now clear: Giving a man a fish helps to alleviate poverty, but teaching him how to fish leads to sustainable development.

References

Adesina, J. (2010): *Rethinking the Social Protection Paradigm: Social Policy in Africa's Development*, Brussels, European Report on Development.

Antonopoulos, R., Kim, K. (2008): *The Impact of Employment Guarantee Strategies on Gender Equality and Pro-poor Economic Development in South Africa: Scaling up the Expanded Public Works Programme*, New York: Levy Economics Institute of Bard College and UNDP (Available online at www.levy.org/pubs/UNDP-Levy/EGS.html

Barchiesi, F. (2011): *Precarious Liberation: Workers, the State and Contested Social Citizenship in Post-apartheid South Africa*, Albany: State University of New York Press.

Bond, P. (2014): Tokenism in South African social policy, in: *Transformation*, 88, 48-77.

Chakraborty, P. (2007): Implementation of the National Rural Employment Guarantee Act in India: Spatial Dimensions and Fiscal Implications, Working Paper No. 505, New York: Levy Economics Institute of Bard College,

Cichon, M., Behrendt, C., Wodsak, V. (2011): The UN social protection floor initiative: Turning the tide, presented at the ILO Conference, Berlin Friedrich Ebert Stiftung.

Coleman, N. (1999): The basic income grant, in: *South African Labour Bulletin*, 23(2), 45.

Crankshaw, O. (1996): *Race, Class and the Changing Division of Labour under Apartheid*, London: Routledge.

Department of Health (Not dated): *National Guideline on Home-based Care/Community Based Care*, Pretoria: Dept of Health.

Department of Labour (2011): *Decent Work Indicators for South Africa*, Pretoria: Government Printers.

DSD – Department of Social Development (2007): *Estimates of National Expenditure 2007*, Pretoria: Government Printers.

Fakier, K. (2010): Class and social reproduction in migrant households in a South African community, in: *Transformation: Critical Perspectives on Southern Africa*, 72/73, 104-126.

Fakier, K. (2014): The Community Work Programme and care in South Africa, in: Fakier, K., Ehmke, E. (eds.), *Socio-economic Insecurity in Emerging Economies: Building New Spaces*, London, New York: Routledge, 133ff.

Fakier, K., Ehmke, E. (2014): Conclusion – building new spaces: Responses to insecurity in the Global South, in: Fakier, K., Ehmke, E., (eds.), *Socio-economic Insecurity in Emerging Economies: Building New Spaces*, London, New York: Routledge, 241ff.

Ferguson, J. (2015): *Give a Man a Fish: Reflections on the New Politics of Distribution*, Durham: Duke University Press.

Fouksman, E. (2015): What shall the fisherman become? Review of James Ferguson's Give a man a fish: Reflections on the new politics of distribution, in: *Basic Income Studies*, 10(2), 289-292.

Gough, J. (2004): Welfare regimes in developing contexts: A global and regional analysis, in: Gough, I., Wood, G. (eds.), *Insecurity and welfare regimes in Asia, Africa and Latin America: Social policy in development contexts*, Cambridge: Cambridge University Press.

Hunter, N. (2007): Crises in social reproduction and home-based care, in: *Africanus: Journal of Development Studies*, 37(2), 231-243.

ILO – International Labour Organisation (2008): Measurement of decent work, Discussion paper for the Tripartite Meeting of Experts on the measurement of decent work, Geneva.

Khanyile, M. (2010): Three pilots of the Community Work Programme: Munsieville, Bokfontein and Alfred Nzo, Addressing inequality and economic marginalisation, Presentation to Second Economy Strategy Workshop, 29 September.

Kropotkin, P. ([1892]1995): *The Conquest of Bread and Other Writings*, edited by Marshall Shatz, New York: Cambridge University Press.

Luvhengo, R. (2010): Consultative workshop to develop impact indicators for Community Work Programme, Johannesburg, 4-5 November.

Mosoetsa, S. (2011): *Eating from the Same Pot: The Dynamics of Survival in Poor South African Households*, Johannesburg: Wits University Press.

Oliphant, N. (2010): Labour trapped in the cracks, in: *Sunday Independent*, November 24.

Paine, T. (1830): *The Political Writings of Thomas Paine, Volume 2*, New York: Solomon Kings.

Philip, K. (2010): *Towards a Right to Work: The Rationale for an Employment Guarantee in South Africa*, Pretoria: Trade and Industrial Policy Strategies (TIPS).

Razavi, S. (2011): Challenges for making social security and protection gender equitable, in: *Development and Change*, 42(4), 34-42.

Razavi, S., Staab, S. (2010): Underpaid and overworked: A cross-national perspective on care workers, in: *International Labour Review*, 149(4), 407-422.

Seekings, J. (2013): Democracy, poverty and inclusive growth in South Africa since 1994, CSSR Working Paper No. 321, Centre for Social Science Research, University of Cape Town.

SWOP – Society, Work and Development Institute (2009): *A Policy Framework for the Progressive Realisation of the Goal of Decent Work in Gauteng, 2009*, Johannesburg: SWOP.

SWOP – Society, Work and Development Institute (2011): *The Socio-economic Impact of the Community Work Programme as a potential Employment Guarantee*, Johannesburg: SWOP.

SWOP – Society, Work and Development Institute (2012): *Decent Work and Development: The Decent Work Deficit Challenge in Gauteng*, Johannesburg: SWOP.

Standing, G, Sender, J., Weeks, J. (1996): *Restructuring the Labour Market: The South African Challenge*, Geneva: International Labour Organisation.

Vavi, Z. (2011): The idea of an employment guarantee in South Africa, Panel discussion at the University of Johannesburg, 7 June.

Webster, E., Budlender, D., Orkin, M. (2015): Developing a diagnostic tool and policy instrument for the realization of decent work, in: *International Labour Review*, 154(2), 123-145.

Woolard, I., Leibbrandt, M. (2010): The Evolution and Impact of Unconditional Cash Transfers in South Africa, Southern Africa Labour and Development Research Unit (SALDRU) Working Paper Number 51, Cape Town: SALDRU, University of Cape Town.

Wray, R. (2007): The Employer of Last Resort Programme: Could It Work for Developing Countries, Economic and Labour Market Papers, 2007/5. Geneva: ILO.

Decent wages for Decent Capitalism?*

Patrick Belser

Introduction

The title of this essay directly refers to an inspiring book called "Decent Capitalism" published in 2011 by Dullien, Herr and Kellerman. The book's objective is to convince readers around the world that there exists an alternative economic model to the one currently in place, which is be better suited to advance simultaneously the goals of prosperity, social justice and environmental sustainability. In essence, decent capitalism requires a move away from "naïve market radicalism" (p. 4) and a better balance between markets, the government and society.

As a first step, the book proposes to re-regulate finance so that it once again becomes a service provider for the rest of the economy, particularly enterprises which create jobs. While the role of finance is in principle to mobilise savings and allocate them to enterprises which generate employment, innovation and growth, the authors are not alone in observing that finance has recently become some sort of a "monster", interested mainly in its own profits (see for example Wolf 2014). Dullien, Herr and Kellerman emphasize that in the future a stronger regulatory framework should provide incentives for finance to support the transition towards "green" jobs – or else humanity will face a catastrophe.

But financial markets are only the tip of the iceberg.

"The rest of the economic framework must also be shaped in such a way that sufficient and sustainable aggregate demand growth can be generated without permanently rising indebtedness within countries and between countries" (p. 5).

---

* The responsibility of opinion expressed in this article rests solely with the author, and does not necessarily represent the view of the International Labour Office.

Active wage policies play a key role in this alternative model.

According to the book, "the key instrument for managing demand should be an active wage policy, which provides decent wages for all" (p. 6). This wage policy mostly consists of minimum wages and collective bargaining articulated and operated in such a manner as to ensure equity, price stability, and sustainable household consumption and aggregate demand.

"Decent capitalism" provides the "big picture" within which much of the work of Hansjöerg Herr and also the works of other scholars at the Berlin School of Economics on wage policies can be understood. In the following pages we briefly review and discuss three wage-related subjects. The first is the "wage norm", which according to Herr should guide policy makers and social partners in their wage setting and negotiations. The second section reviews works on inequality, and the role of minimum wages and collective bargaining in reducing inequality. The third section highlights the question of whether a strengthening of labour market institutions could reverse the downward trend in the share of labour compensation in GDP (hereafter the labour share).

The conclusion shows that these questions have found their way into discussions at global level, not only in the International Labour Organisation (ILO) but also at the level of the G-20, where recent declarations should give Herr and others some indication that there is hope for a future with "decent capitalism" for all.

1. The role of wage policies

1.1 The macro-economic perspective

In his different publications, Herr and his co-authors defend a macro-economic perspective of wage policies: labour market institutions should serve the objective of increasing average wages roughly at the rate of medium-term productivity plus the Central Bank's target rate of inflation (or some other low inflation rate if there is no explicit inflation target). This "wage norm" would guarantee price stability, ensuring that wage developments do not cause deflation or excessive inflation, leaving room for expansionary monetary policy, and providing a sound environment for growth and employment creation. The reference to medium-term productivity developments ensures that wage trends remain independent from the business cycle which statistically influences productivity.

Herr is aware of the difficulties in convincing governments and social partners to stick with this policy objective. Herr also recognizes that the "wage norm" works best in normal times. If there are substantial inflation pressures from other sources (say a currency depreciation or spikes in oil prices) realising the wage norm becomes more difficult, and may set off a wage-price spiral where higher nominal wages simply contribute to faster price inflation and fail to translate into higher real wages.

In normal times, however, bargained wages and minimum wages – once set at the right level – should be adjusted roughly in line with medium term productivity plus the target inflation rate. By following the wage norm, the minimum wage becomes an anchor against deflation in times of crisis or slow growth. Should the wage norm be cemented into an automatic adjustment formula? Herr views an automatic indexation as tempting, but ultimately social dialogue is better. "This allows for specific economic developments to be taken into account, supports political mobilisation and stimulates active trade union engagement" (Herr/Kazandziska 2011: 5).

1.2 Is the macro-economic view fighting back?

This macro-economic perspective is of course not new, but for some decades prior to the financial crisis it nearly vanished from mainstream policy debates, where – under the spell of neo-classical micro-economic textbooks – wage policies were mainly casted as a source of labour market "distortion" generating unemployment. The result has been a decoupling between real average wages and labour productivity.

Figure 1 from the ILO Global wage Report 2014/15 shows that for a sample of 36 developed economies wages have increased much less than labour productivity, including since 2010. There are differences across countries and the decoupling of wages and productivity does not apply everywhere, and in some countries it goes the opposite way. The ILO report shows that over the last 15 years, the decoupling was most obvious in Germany, Japan, Spain or the U.S.

Figure 1: Trends in growth in average wages and labour productivity in developed economies (index), 1999-2013

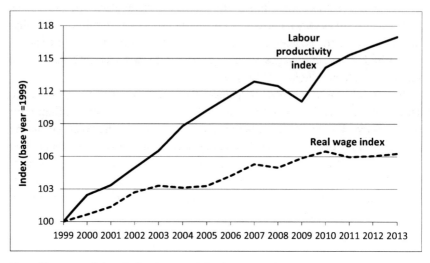

Note: Wage growth is calculated as a weighted average of year-on-year growth in average monthly real wages in 36 economies. Index is based to 1999 because of data availability.

Source: ILO Global Wage Report 2014/15 (ILO 2014)

In recent years, though, the macro view of wages has started an interesting comeback. A number of international organisations have pointed out that the broken link between wages and productivity has constrained household consumption and contributed to internal and global economic imbalances. Adding its voice to the debate, the 2012/13 ILO Global Wage Report on "wages and equitable growth" called for stronger institutions for wage determination, particularly minimum wages and more supporting and enabling environments for collective bargaining, as well as international coordination on wage policies to prevent a race to the bottom in wages and aggregate demand. The macro-view has also reappeared in some national policy debates. Within this context, it is unfortunate that policy coordination within the Eurozone still appears to be focused on the premise that the recipe for faster economic growth is lower wage growth.

2. Minimum wages, collective bargaining and wage inequality

2.1 Growing inequality as a source of concern

Inequality too has become a source of concern in recent years.[1] A large and growing literature has shown that inequality, measured in various ways, has been increasing in a majority of developed countries in recent decades. The OECD, for example, has documented in detail the rise in inequality in about two-thirds of developed economies between the early 1980s and the financial crisis of 2008-09. In some countries, including the United States and the United Kingdom, the rise in inequality has been particularly stark, although top income shares have increased in other countries too. Emerging and developing economies – where household income inequality is often greater than in developed economies – have also not been immune from this trend. Although inequality has diminished in several Latin American countries, inequality since the 1990s increased in a majority of developing countries for which household survey data are readily available (Ferreira/Ravallion 2009).

While some level of inequality is unavoidable in any market-based system, there is growing consensus (at least on paper) that current levels of inequality are problematic. High levels of income inequality undermine economic growth and make "equality of opportunity" and "social mobility" illusory. Recent work by the IMF recognizes that inequality reduces "the pace and durability of growth" (Ostry/Berg/Tsangarides 2014), and OECD research now also shows that greater social and economic inclusion is strongly associated with longer and stronger periods of sustained economic growth (OECD, 2014a). By depressing aggregate demand, inequality has also been highlighted as a factor increasing risk of crisis, and as a cause of the 2008 financial crisis in the United States (see for example Rajan 2010; Palley/Horn 2013; Sturn/Van Treeck 2013).

---

[1] The OECD has published a number of reports on the subject: see e.g. OECD 2008; OECD 2011; OECD 2014a. The IMF also recently studied the link between income inequality, economic growth and fiscal policy (see e.g. Berg/Ostry 2011; IMF 2014b). The ILO itself has issued various publications on inequality: see e.g. ILO/IILS 2008; ILO 2014b. These institutional reports have been published alongside a growing number of academic articles and books on inequality, including (to name just a few) Piketty 2013; Milanovic 2011 and Galbraith 2012. The growing academic research has also been summarized in large volumes such as Salverda/Nolan/Smeeding 2009.

2.2 Labour market institutions and wage inequality

Many factors have been advanced to explain the growth in inequality, with a dominant view attributing most of the problem to a side-effect of globalization and technological progress. Herr and is co-authors are amongst those challenging this conventional orthodoxy. According to Herr, the decline in the power of trade unions and the legal and institutional changes in the labour market are the main reason for inequality, not globalization and technological change – which is seen as "not very convincing" and as a way to pretend that inequality is due to reasons that "we cannot do anything about".

Herr defends the view that minimum wages and collective bargaining are key instruments to control wage dispersion and income inequality. In that he is widely supported by the recent literature, which documents the effect of labour market institutions on inequality. Recent studies have shown that minimum wages have contributed to reducing inequality in various European countries, as well as in Russia or different Latin American countries (see e.g. Belman/Wolfson 2014; Keifman/Maurizio 2012; Lukyanova 2011). On the other hand, in the U.S., it is clear that the decline in the real value of the minimum wage between 1979 and 2009 accounted for a large share of the increase in inequality in the lower half of the wage distribution (e.g. Autor/Manning/Smith 2010, cited in Belman/Wolfson 2014: 305).

This is hardly surprising given that in advanced economies wages represent the major source of income. The latest ILO Global Wage Report 2014/15 estimated that the share of wages in total household income for a sample of developed economies represents the largest proportion of total household income, between 50 to 80 per cent.

The evidence shows that countries where a larger proportion of workers are covered by collective agreements tend to have lower wage inequality (Visser/Checchi 2009). The extent to which collective bargaining can compress overall wage inequality depends on the position of unionized workers in the pay distribution, the outcome of bargaining for different types of workers, and the degree to which collective bargaining is centralized and coordinated (Bryson 2007). In particular, the extent to which unionization and collective bargaining affect the wage distribution depends on whether the collective bargaining system takes place at the company or workplace level, or if the system is more inclusive and encompassing – with collective bargaining taking place at the national, industry and/or branch level in multi-employer settings with coordination across levels (Visser/Checchi 2009; Hayter 2015). Governments can also take measures to extend the application of collective agreements to non-

signatories, thus reinforcing the equity-enhancing effects of collective bargaining.
As a matter of fact, where union movements are weak or do not cover all industries sufficiently, "statutory minimum wages are highly desirable and urgently needed to control wage dispersion" (Herr/Kazandziska 2011: 13).

Figure 2: Share of wages in household income, latest year: Selected developed economies and the European average

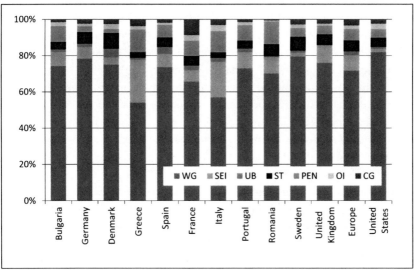

WG = wages; SEI = self-employment income; UB = unemployment benefits; ST = other social transfers; PEN = old-age pensions; OI = residual income; CG= capital gains.

The European average includes: Austria, Belgium, Bulgaria, Cyprus, Czech Republic, Denmark, Estonia, Finland, France, Germany, Greece, Hungary, Iceland, Ireland, Italy, Latvia, Lithuania, Luxembourg, the Netherlands, Norway, Poland, Portugal, Romania, Slovakia, Slovenia, Spain, Sweden and the United Kingdom.

Source: based on BILO Global Wage Report 2014/15 (ILO 2014: 36)

2.3 Minimum wages above the wage norm?

Where inequality is excessive, Herr are colleagues are prepared to advocate minimum wage increases in excess of the "wage norm". Indeed, if minimum wages are adjusted at the same rate as all other wages in the economy there will be no change in the wage structure. To compress the wage distribution minimum wages must increase more rapidly than average wages. If this means that wages increase more than the wage norm, this is acceptable as long as this will "moderately add to the inflation process".

In some cases average wages are structurally dependent on minimum wages. Wages of semi-skilled or skilled workers will be set at a multiple of minimum wages and thus automatically increased when minimum wages are raised. This means that if minimum wages are increased more than the wage norm, the wage structure will remain the same and inflation will be triggered. Minimum wages thus act as a substitute for coordinated wage bargaining. Herr recommends that in such cases "changing the wage structure must be negotiated separately" (p. 6).

According to Herr, in advanced economies minimum wages should remain simple and targeted at the 5% or 10% of workers at the lower end of the distribution. He considers however that there should be a possibility to set higher minimum wages rates in regions, counties of even cities where productivity is higher. "Only under this condition can minimum wages fulfil their function of compressing a market-driven wage structure from below and contribute to a relatively equal income distribution" (p. 10). Setting only one national minimum wage in large countries with large regional differences would imply that the minimum wage in many regions would be too low as the national minimum wage must take into account the situation of the least developed regions.

But minimum wages should not become too complex. He considers that the main purpose of minimum wages is to set a floor wages in the whole economy, and opposes occupational minimum wages, or wage floors by sectors, age or qualifications, because the greater the variety of minimum wages the more the characteristics of minimum wages as a lower boundary is lost. Differentiations of the wage structure according to occupations should for example be left to the wage bargaining process. He also warns against the risk that minimum wages crowd out independent and additional collective bargaining. Complex minimum wage systems are often a reflection of the fact that unions are unable to organise and bargain collectively at the industry level. But the right response is to develop collective bargaining, not to make minimum wage systems more complex.

2.4 Do labour market institutions distort the market and create unemployment?

Neoclassical economics indicates that labour market institutions create distortions in an otherwise perfectly efficient labour market, where supply and demand curves nicely intersect to create full-employment. Herr does not believe in the neoclassical model, which he thinks – like many others – has been undermined by the empirical literature of the "new minimum wage research" which did not show negative employment effects. Distinctively he also does not believe in the monopsony theory explanation, which he sees as a special case which neoclassical proponents have "exhumed" from the 1940s, and which can show higher employment and lower monopoly profits. He considers that all these explanations remain on the level of "partial analysis" applicable at the level of some industries, but not at the level of whole economies: "for a comprehensive judgement of the effects of minimum wages a mere partial analysis is not acceptable" (p. 6).

The best explanation for the "no employment" effect, in his view, is to be found in macro theory, based on Keynesian theory and going back to the original works of Keynes himself. In this framework, by changing the structure of wages and the relative labour costs of different types of employees, minimum wages result in a change in the relative structure of prices in the economy. This new structure of prices will change the structure of demand. In addition, households which receive minimum wages tend to have a higher propensity to consume then richer households. This enhanced level of consumption can have a positive impact on aggregate demand and employment, if the economy is wage-led (i.e. if the positive effects of higher wages on consumption exceed potential costs in terms of reduced exports or investment). There can be negative employment effects of these changes in some industries, but how overall employment is affected is theoretically open and extremely difficult to predict.

3. The puzzle of the labour share

What about the decline in the labour share? During much of the past century, a stable labour income share was accepted as a natural corollary or 'stylized fact' of economic growth. Yet it is now widely accepted that the labour share declined in a majority of developed economies in recent decades. The OECD has observed, for example, that over the period from 1990 to 2009 the share of labour compensation in national income declined in 26 out of 30 advanced countries for which data were available, and calculated that the median labour share of national income across these countries fell from 66.1 per cent to 61.7 per cent (OECD 2012b). The ILO Global Wage Report 2012/13 reported that the simple average of labour shares in 16 developed countries declined from about 75 per cent of national income in the mid-1970s to about 65 per cent in the years just before the global economic and financial crisis. It also showed a declining labour share in a group of developing economies, including China.

Figure 3: Labour income share in developed economies, Germany, the USA, and Japan, 1970-2010

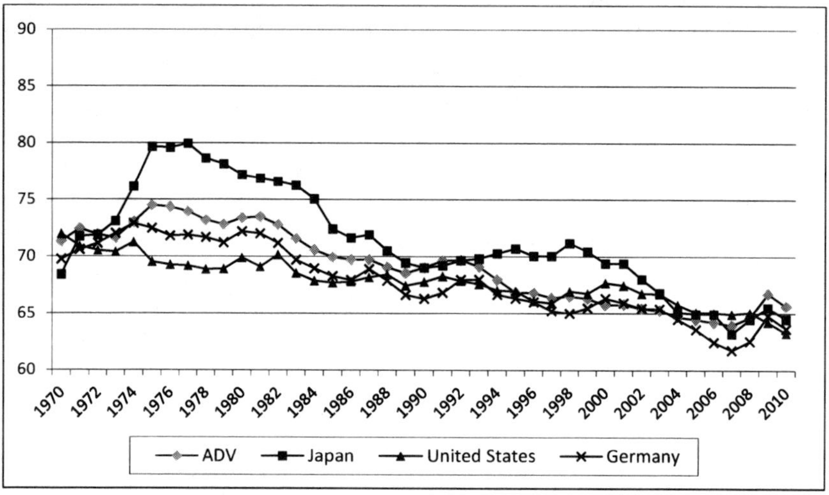

Source: ILO Global Wage Report 2012/13 (ILO 2012: 43)

The ILO report emphasized, consistently with Herr, that declining labour shares affect aggregate demand, reducing household consumption relative to other component (unless consumption is based on an unsustainable accumulation of debt, as was the case in the U.S. in the years before the financial crisis). The report also highlighted the problem of collective action at international level. While each individual country may in principle increase aggregate demand for its goods and services by exporting more, not all countries can do so at the same time. The world economy as a whole is a closed economy. If the labour share declines simultaneously in too many countries, the regressive effect of global wage cuts on consumption could lead to a worldwide depression of aggregate demand and employment.

What policies can reverse the downward trend in labour shares? Herr's publications reveal a deep scepticism about the ability of labour market institutions to influence the labour share. In his various publications, he sticks to the view that profits are always a "mark-up" above production costs, and so higher wages lead to higher prices instead of lower profit margins. This cannot be changed through collective bargaining or minimum wages. In Herr's view, the most important factor that explains changes of functional income distribution is the increased power of financial systems to push up firms' profit mark up. Naturally, then, to reverse the decline in labour income shares, what is needed is the re-regulation of the financial system and of corporate governance.

ILO publications come to a somewhat different conclusion, so perhaps more research is needed on this issue. Using research from a volume on wage-led growth (Lavoie/Stockhammer 2013) the ILO Global Wage Report 2012/13 adopted the view that the decline in the labour share in developed economies was indeed largely due to the growing weight of financial markets, but also found that falling union density and declining bargaining power of labour had contributed to the decline. It concluded that "internal rebalancing" requires both stronger institutions for wage determination as well as better regulation of the financial sector and restoring its function as channelling resources into productive and sustainable investments. It also called for a more detailed analysis of the role of taxation, as taxation scheme tends to be more generous to capital incomes relative to labour incomes, which increases pressure on both labour costs to employers and the take-home pay of workers.

Conclusion

Hansjoerg Herr's publications, and that of his colleagues at the Berlin School of Economics, did and continue to do much to promote the view that realistic alternative economic models exist. Some of this work has found a way into publications of international organisations, and also into global policy debates such those held at the G-20. The latest G20 Leaders' Communiqué[2] in particular committed to implementing the G20 Policy Priorities on Labour Income Shares and Inequality[3]. The latter notes that "Inequalities have increased over

[2] http://g20.org.tr/g20-leaders-commenced-the-antalya-summit/

[3] http://g20.org.tr/wp-content/uploads/2015/11/G20-Policy-Priorities-on-Labour-Income-Share-and-Inequalities.pdf

the last two decades in a majority of our countries and have become a source of growing concern. In some emerging countries, inequality has decreased significantly, but still remains at a high level. In most cases, increasing inequalities are associated with a sustained downward trend in the labour income share. Widening inequalities and declining labour income shares not only pose challenges for social and political cohesion, but also have significant economic costs in terms of both the level and sustainability of economic growth".

To reverse the rising inequalities and the falling labour shares, G-20 countries have among other measures agreed to: (a) strengthening labour market institutions (social dialogue, collective bargaining, wage setting mechanisms, labour legislation) based on respect for the Fundamental Principles and Rights at Work; (b) Reducing wage inequality, through policy tools such as minimum wages and the promotion and coverage of collective agreements, ensuring fair wage scales and that work pays; and (c) Improving employment outcomes for women, youth, older workers, persons with disabilities, migrants and other vulnerable groups in the labour market, by strengthening access to effective active labour market policies.

The G-20 Policy Priorities on Labour Income Shares and Inequality concludes like this: "We affirm the need for regular and effective monitoring of the evolution of the labour income share and inequalities, and their effect on the strength and sustainability of economic growth". While Hansjoerg Herr and his colleagues did not need to wait for such an encouragement from the G-20, the statement might hopefully motivate him and his colleagues to push on with their work towards a future with "decent capitalism".

References

Autor, D., Manning, A., Smith, C. (2010): The Contribution of the Minimum Wage to U.S. Wage Inequality over Three decades: A Reassessment, NBER Working Paper No.16533. Cambridge, MA.

Belman, D., Wolfson, P.J. (2014): *What does the minimum wage do?* Kalamazoo, MI: W.E. Upjohn Institute for Employment Research.

Berg, A., Ostry, J.D. (2011): Inequality and unsustainable growth: Two sides of the same coin?, Discussion Note SDN/11/08, Washington, DC: IMF.

Berg, A., Ostry, J.D., Zettelmeyer, J. (2012): What makes growth sustained?, in: *Journal of Development Economics*, 98(2), 149-66.

Bloomberg (2014): "Lagarde: US should increase the minimum wage", *Market Makers*, Bloomberg Television, 16 June, http://www.bloomberg.com/video/lagarde-u-s-should-increase-the-minimum-wage-kYnLLpMbQLGPxKD79_DYZQ.html [23 Sep. 2014].

Bryson, A. (2007): The effect of trade unions on wages, in : *Reflets et perspectives de la vie économique*, 46(2-3), 33-45.

Dullien, S., Herr, H., Kellerman, C. (2011): *Decent Capitalism: A Blueprint for reforming our economies*, London: PlutoPress.

Ferreira, F.H.G., Ravallion, M. (2009): Poverty and inequality: The global context, in: Salverda/Nolan/Smeeding (2009), 599-636.

Galbraith, J.K. (2012): *Inequality and instability: A study of the world economy just before the crisis*, Oxford: Oxford University Press.

Hayter, S. (2015): Unions and collective bargaining, in: Berg, J. (ed.), *Labour markets, institutions and inequality: Building just societies in the 21st century*, Geneva, Cheltenham, UK: ILO and Edward Elgar, 95-122.

Herr, H., Kazandziska, M. (2007): Wages and regional coherence in the European Monetary Union, in: Hein, E., Priewe, J., Truger, A. (eds.), *European Integration in Crisis*, Marburg: Metropolis, 131-162.

Herr, H., Kazandziska, M., Mahnkopf-Praprotnik, S. (2009): The Theoretical Debate about Minimum Wages, International Labour Office, Global Labour University, Working Paper No. 6.

Herr, H., Kazandziska, M. (2011): Principles of Minimum Wage Policy – Economics, Institutions and Recommendations, International Labour Office, Global Labour University, Working Paper No. 11.

Herr, H., Kazandziska, M. (2011b): *Macroeconomic Policy Regimes in Western Industrial Countries*, Routledge.

Herr, H., Horn, G. (2012): Wage Policy Today, Policy Brief, IMK Macroeconomic Policy institute.

ILO – International Labour Office (2012): *Global Wage Report 2012/13: Wages and equitable growth*, Geneva.

ILO – International Labour Office (2014): *Global Wage Report 2014/15: Wages and income inequality*, Geneva.

ILO – International Labour Office (2014b): *International Journal of Labour Research: The challenge of inequality*, Vol. 6, No. 1, Geneva.

ILO – International Labour Office, IILS – International Institute for Labour Studies (2008): *World of Work Report 2008: Income inequalities in the age of financial globalization*, Geneva.

IMF – International Monetary Fund (2014a): *United States: 2014 Article IV consultation*, IMF Country Report No. 14/221, July, Washington, DC.

IMF – International Monetary Fund (2014b): *Fiscal policy and income inequality*, Washington, DC.

Keifman, S.N., Maurizio, R. (2012): Changes in labour market conditions and policies: Their impact on wage inequality during the last decade, United Nations University World Institute for Development Economics Research (UNU-WIDER), Working Paper 2012/14, Helsinki.

Lavoie, M., Stockhammer, E. (eds.) (2013): *Wage-led growth: An equitable strategy for economic recovery*, Geneva, Basingstoke: ILO and Palgrave Macmillan.

Lukyanova, A. (2011): Effects of minimum wages on the Russian wage distribution, Working Paper WP BRP 09/EC/2011, National Research University Higher School of Economics, Moscow.

Milanovic, B. (2011): *The haves and the have-nots: A brief and idiosyncratic history of global inequality*, New York: Basic Books.

OECD – Organisation for Economic Co-operation and Development (2008): *Growing unequal? Income distribution and poverty in OECD Countries*, Paris.

OECD – Organisation for Economic Co-operation and Development (2011): *Divided we stand: Why inequality keeps rising*, Paris.

OECD – Organisation for Economic Co-operation and Development (2012b): *Economic Policy Reforms: Going for growth 2012*, Paris.

OECD – Organisation for Economic Co-operation and Development (2014a): *All on board: Making inclusive growth happen*, Paris.

OECD – Organisation for Economic Co-operation and Development (2014b): *Employment Outlook 2014*, Paris.

Ostry, J.D., Berg, A., Tsangarides, C.G. (2014): Redistribution, inequality, and growth, Discussion Note SDN/14/02, Washington, DC: IMF.

Palley, T.I., Horn, G.A. (eds.) (2013): *Restoring shared prosperity: A policy agenda from leading Keynesian economists*, CreateSpace Independent Publishing.

Piketty, T. (2013): *Le Capital au XXIe siècle*, Paris: Seuil.

Rajan, R. (2010): *Fault lines: How hidden fractures still threaten the world economy*, Princeton, NJ: Princeton University Press.

Salverda, W., Nolan, B., Smeeding, T. (eds.) (2009): *The Oxford handbook of economic inequality*, Oxford: Oxford University Press.

Sturn, S., Van Treeck, T. (2013): The role of income inequality as a cause of the Great Recession and global imbalances, in: Lavoie/Stockhammer (2013), 125-52.

USCEA – United States Council of Economic Advisers (2014): *The economic report of the President together with the annual report of the Council of Economic Advisers, 2014*, Washington, DC: US Government Printing Office.

Visser, J., Checchi, D. (2009): Inequality and the labor market: Unions, in: Salverda, W., Nolan, B., Smeeding, T. (eds.), *The Oxford handbook of economic inequality*, Oxford: Oxford University Press, 230-57.

Wolf, M. (2014): *The shifts and the shocks: What we've learned – and have still to learn – from the financial crisis*, London: Penguin.

Price and non-price competitiveness – can it explain current account imbalances in the euro area?

Torsten Niechoj

1. Introduction

The introduction of the European monetary union was accompanied by the so called Lisbon strategy, to make Europe the 'most competitive and the most dynamic knowledge-based economy in the world' (Lisbon European Council 2000). Sixteen years, a financial crisis and a Great Recession later, the results of both monetary union and Lisbon strategy (and its successors) are mixed. The common currency and the new regulatory framework amplified imbalances within the euro area as a result of two interwoven growth models, a domestic demand-led and an export-oriented growth model.

Both mainstream writers and heterodox authors like Flassbeck/Lapavitsas (2015) stress the role of price competitiveness, usually based on a comparison of unit labour cost developments or similar indicators. However, a sole focus on price competitiveness ignores two relevant aspects. Firstly, the effect of incomes on GDP growth and imports should not be underestimated. An increase in incomes leads to GDP growth but may worsen the trade balance due to higher imports (Thirlwall 1979; Schröder 2015). Secondly, and this is sometimes disregarded in the post-Keynesian camp, non-price competitiveness also impacts on the trade balance and thus the current account (Storm/Naastepaad 2015; Schulten 2015). Factors like institutions, infrastructure, culture, research & development and education determine the non-price competitiveness of firms and thus – at least partly – their market power and export volumes. Mainstream publications like the Global Competitiveness Report (2014) take this into account but their interpretation of the situation surely deviates from a heterodox point of view.

Therefore, this paper aims at presenting a more coherent picture of current account imbalances within the euro area by reviewing the available indicators and naming established proxies for non-price competitiveness like R&D expenditures or capital formation (CompNet 2015). This set of indicators is applied to four countries – Germany, Spain, Netherlands, and Greece – which represent combinations of the variables large vs. small and export oriented vs. domestic demand-led countries.

The paper is structured as follows. First current account imbalances within the euro area will be analysed. The subsequent sections will then examine indicators of both price and non-price competitiveness followed by a discussion that reviews the evidence and the limitations of the indicators and a conclusion.

2. Current account imbalances

Current accounts cover trade balance (exports minus imports), net income transfers and unilateral transfers. Usually the trade balance strongly dominates the current account. The current account balance indicates both the involvement of a country in international trade and its ability to finance its imports. If the current account is in deficit, the country as a whole has to borrow from other countries. If such a situation persists and if debt is denominated in foreign currency potential consequences include adjustment crises or even insolvency. In case of the euro area, most of the private and public debt is denominated in the own currency, the euro, but this currency is under control of a common monetary body, the European Central Bank (ECB). Moreover, public debt is subject to supranational regulations. Therefore, the ECB and the European Council may ask for austerity measures in exchange for the provision of fresh money and/or a debt restructuring. A surplus indicates either import restriction, be it due to low domestic demand or austerity measures or tariffs, or a situation favourable for export to other countries. This relates the current account to the competitiveness of a country. A country that sells goods or services at lower relative prices or products others cannot sell or cannot sell in this quality has a comparative advantage that leads to a surplus if there is sufficient foreign demand and if it is not overcompensated by rising imports. Current accounts signal the relative competitive position of countries, meaning the relative competitive position of firms of a country within a country- and/or union-specific framework of institutions. However, this signal needs to be interpreted carefully as the example of the US current account deficits shows. Due to its leading currency and relatively high GDP growth rates, a deficit is (at least currently) not a problem and does not indicate that US firms (as a whole) are not competitive. It signals that the lenders of the world have trust in the creditworthiness of the USA.

A depiction of current accounts within the euro area reveals three phases since its establishment (Fig. 1):

- In the *first three years* current account surpluses and deficits are relatively low. In 2001, the euro area as a whole shows a balanced current account with the rest of the world. Current accounts are roughly balanced between euro area members, too.

- In a *second phase*, current account imbalances accumulate in the years after 2001 which might demonstrate relative shifts in the competitive positions. Imbalances grow over the years and reach their peak before the Great Recession. Surpluses of the export-oriented member states roughly match the deficits of the other countries. Still the euro area as a whole has *cum grano salis* balanced current accounts with the rest of the world.

- Imbalances continue to exist in a different form in a *third phase*, starting in 2008. Firstly, due to the crisis there is a downward shift of current accounts in 2008. Then, imbalances decrease slightly and finally, since 2012, all countries depicted here, except Greece and France, reach current accounts in surplus.

In phases two and three a single country, Germany, dominates the picture and shows large surpluses vis-a-vis the euro area and countries outside this area. A few years after coping with the economic consequences of the German unification, the country takes up its old mercantilist pattern of export surpluses, which had been well established before the monetary union (Herr 1994).

*Figure 1: Current accounts in bill. euro of ten euro area members**

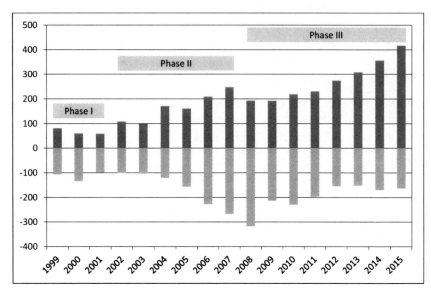

* Austria, Belgium, France, Germany, Greece, Ireland, Italy, Netherlands, Portugal and Spain.
Source: AMECO, own calculations

How can this development of emerging imbalances followed by a tendency towards surpluses for (nearly) all member states be explained? Two complementary growth models dominated the European scene after the monetary union had been established (Stockhammer 2011; Niechoj 2012; Hein 2013-14). Some countries massively gained from the introduction of the euro and low real interest rates and showed a good GDP performance for years which resulted in an increase of often debt-financed imports. The consequence for these countries was a deterioration of their current accounts. Export-led countries, however, improved their current accounts and were able to finance the debts of the other group of countries. Their export-orientation was fuelled by wage restraint which turned out to be favourable for exports but not for incomes, domestic demand and imports. Therefore, these two growth models were complementary and showed favourable results in the beginning. Both the increase in (mostly private) debt and the high dependence of some economies on exports aggravated, however, the impact of the financial crisis in 2007/8.

The crisis then not only led to a sharp fall in GDP in the euro area but also to a change in the pattern of current accounts. In order to shed light on this,

Figure 2 depicts the development of imports and exports for selected countries since 2007. The four countries represent the two growth models. Spain and Greece follow the model of debt-financed domestic demand and were both subject to massive austerity measures after the crisis. Spain represents a large and Greece a small country within this sub-sample. Germany is the largest and most prominent export-oriented country and is accompanied by the Netherlands as a second, but smaller export-led country.

As Figure 2 demonstrates, after the decline in 2008/9, German imports increase slightly in relation to exports but this does not severely dampen the positive trade balance. Similarly, the Netherlands keep their current account surplus. The increase in exports after the crisis is nearly identical to the increase in imports. Spain, however, shows a sharp decline in imports but also a significant increase in exports after 2009. The Greek plot indicates an even more pronounced drop in imports and no clear trend towards higher exports. If wages are depressed as in Greece, Spain and other countries, this can lead to export price reductions and thus to higher exports or a higher mark-up. However, it also leads to a reduction in incomes and thus to a lower domestic demand which limits imports (IMF 2014: 117-125, Niechoj 2014). For Spain and especially for Greece this import restriction has contributed massively to the improvement of the current account.

If economies recover, the euro area might return to a situation like in phase two, which was characterised by large imbalances, due to a rise of imports in the countries of the South. The mainstream idea of how to overcome such imbalances is to make use of a liberalisation of product and a deregulation of labour markets in order to increase competitiveness. If such a strategy is successful for all members of the euro area, it will lead to current account surpluses in all countries of the euro area with the rest of the world. This is exactly the strategy that is followed by the European Commission.[1] Such an approach, however, simply highlights the export-fostering price effects and ignores the negative side effects that structural reforms have on incomes and consumption. Moreover, the strategy to achieve a surplus with the rest of the world might not be compatible with the needs of the rest of the world and it ignores that developing an industry takes time and requires an adequate institutional setting and a sound infrastructure.

---

[1] Recently, the European Commission (2015) started a further initiative to increase the level of competitiveness in the European Union by promoting the idea of national competitiveness boards.

Figure 2: Exports (solid line) and imports (dotted line) at 2010 prices, 2007=100

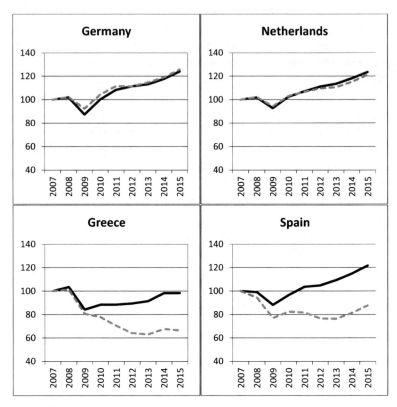

Source: AMECO, own calculations

3. Indicators of competitiveness

The concept of competitiveness is based on a rather microeconomic rationale but is nowadays applied to whole countries as well. The basic idea is that a firm or a nation can offer goods or services which are demanded by others due to certain comparative advantages. Traditionally, the focus is on relative prices. Indicators like (real) unit labour costs or export prices are used to cover such advantages in price competitiveness. Nevertheless, this is not the whole picture. As the New Trade theory has emphasised, price differentiation plays a crucial role (Krugman 1986). Goods and services might be demanded not due to relatively low prices but in spite of high prices when they offer a higher quality or are (relatively) unique. Moreover, among other authors, the debate about Varieties of Capitalism emphasised the role of other non-price factors like educational systems or innovations in the determination of GDP and exports (Hall/Soskice 2001). Finally, the impact of foreign and domestic demand on current accounts is not only relevant for the discussion of import restriction mentioned above but also for the emergence of current account deficits and surpluses. Demand determines investment and GDP growth which then impacts on imports and exports.

3.1 Indicators of price competitiveness

Usually, price indicators have to be corrected for changes in the exchange rate and differences in price levels. In a monetary union, as in the euro area, all prices are denominated in the same currency. Therefore, if the comparison is restricted to countries of the monetary union, such adjustments are not required. Against this background, the common indicator for competitiveness is unit labour cost in industry. Alternatively, unit labour costs of the whole economy are used.

Unit labour costs are an important part of the production costs of an exporting company but do not include other costs like capital or energy costs. Moreover, they focus on costs and thus cannot reflect changes in profit margins. As costs per produced unit, they cover differences and changes in productivity and hence should be preferred to simple labour costs. Both distinctions, industry vs. whole economy, have drawbacks. Part of the industry sector does not produce goods for export, it does not cover exports of services and it does not take into account that some services are sourced from other sectors which might have different unit labour cost developments. The whole economy covers all sectors, i.e. not only export relevant activities.

Unit labour costs have at least two advantages as a proxy for price competitiveness which is the reason why they are so widely used. Firstly, data is available, and secondly unit labour costs focus on wages, i.e. a field of interest for economic policy.

Figure 3a depicts the unit labour cost development starting in 2001[2] for industry, 3b for the whole economy. Both indicators show a similar picture.

---

[2] 2001 was chosen as the starting point for this and all following comparisons because the euro area as a whole then had a balanced current account with the rest of the world. Moreover, intra-euro area imbalances were low. Afterwards, imbalances started to develop. Having identified such a common starting point makes it obsolete to compare absolute

As can be seen, German unit labour costs decreased until 2007 and then increased due to labour hoarding in the crisis but were still below the euro average (Herzog-Stein et al. 2010). In recent years the German development resembles the development of the euro area. Hence, there is still a gap between the development of prices in the euro area and Germany. Greece and Spain have lost price competitiveness (according to the chosen indicator) in relation to Germany since the start of the monetary union but later converged again to the euro area average. The Dutch development was roughly in line with the development of the whole euro area.

Figure 3a: *Unit labour costs per hour, industry, in euro, 2001q1=100*

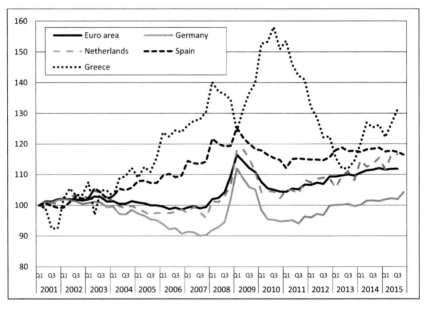

Source: Eurostat, own calculations

levels of competitiveness. This would have been problematic anyway since levels of competitiveness are hard to compare. The reason is that indicators are often subject to specific national contexts like taxation, educational systems or economic structure. Although harmonised, indicators might lead to inconclusive results due to these differences. Focusing on developments in relation to a common reference point, avoids this problem.

Figure 3b: Unit labour costs per hour, whole economy, in euro, 2001q1=100

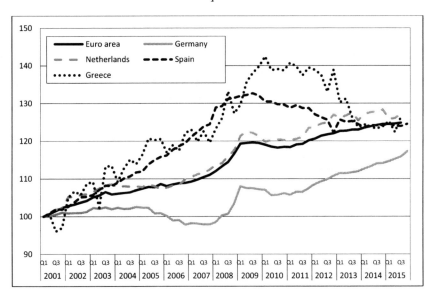

Source: Eurostat, own calculations

Other natural candidates for the measurement of price competitiveness are export prices (Fig. 4). They include not only production costs but also the profit margin and cover the products sold abroad. Unfortunately, this indicator has drawbacks, too. If the export composition changes, export prices change as well. In other words, qualitative differences lead to changes in prices. For example, an increase in prices can be caused by an increase in the quality of a product or a new product group. It signals a deterioration of price competetiveness but is indeed a sign of increasing competitiveness.

Figure 4: Export prices, 2001q1=100

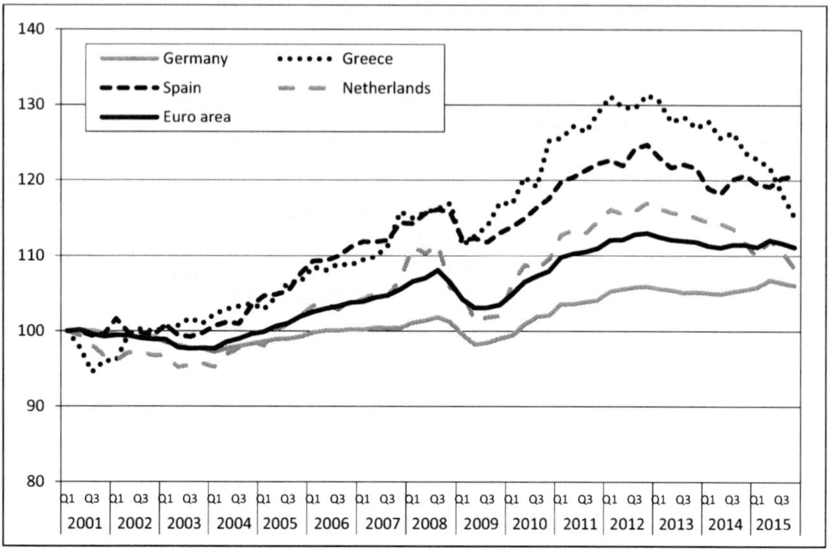

Source: Eurostat, own calculations

The development of export prices has resembled the development of the previous indicator (unit labour costs) for the four countries in question since the start of the monetary union. Differences can be explained by profit margins that have been squeezed or expanded due to differences in bargaining power between employers and employees and pricing-to-market behaviour of firms.

3.2 Indicators of non-price competitiveness and the role of macroeconomic aggregates

In order to shed light on non-price competitiveness, a variety of indicators is used. Basically, non-price competitiveness means to sell a product which customers perceive to have a higher quality or a distinguishing feature in comparison to similar products. Therefore, one can differentiate between vertical product differentiation, i.e. differences in quality, and horizontal product differentiation, i.e. variety of products (cf. Krugman 1989; Grossman/Helpman 1995). Both, higher quality and/or higher variety, can justify a premium, i.e. a higher price. There are several problems of measurement. In principle, a specification of physical characteristics in combination with an assessment of the value these characteristics have for consumers could be used. A single, omnipotent and direct indicator for quality and variety besides the price as a proxy for value is, however, not at hand and aggregated data does not offer the required information to differentiate between products.

Export prices can serve as an (insufficient) proxy to such an indicator because these prices partly not only measure prices but also non-price competetiveness if they are based on unit value indices, which measure the value of a unit of output. If so, part of the rise in export prices can be traced back to a change in the composition of exports towards products with higher quality (and unit value). Unfortunately, the indicator cannot separate the two effects, the price and the non-price effect.

Another way to measure non-price competitiveness would be to focus on unit values alone. If similar products differ in their unit values, it is reasonable to assume that a higher quality is ascribed to a higher-priced product. Then, different unit values are proxies for product differentiation. The development of exports and the market share has to be taken into account, too, in order to assess whether the products that are offered have also been demanded. However, the crucial difficulty is to compare similar products, not apples with oranges. Table 1 depicts unit values for cars. Against the background of a well-developed production of premium cars in Germany, the presented numbers make sense and reflect the higher quality of German cars in comparison to Spanish ones. However, some caveats apply. Not all countries produce a reasonable number of products; therefore, Greece is only listed here in order to complete the usual sample. Moreover, data is missing and extreme volatility in the number of units – cf. e.g. the data for the Netherlands from 2010-13 or the numbers for Greece – raises doubts about data consistency. Finally, due to fluctuations of the exchange rate between dollar and euro, one should not put too much emphasis on the development of absolute numbers but should focus on a comparison between the countries. Furthermore, for a lot of other products, unit values cannot be calculated due to missing data.

Table 1: Exported motor vehicles for transport of persons

	Germany			Netherlands			Spain			Greece		
	Units	Volume in mill. $	Unit value in $	Units	Volume in mill. $	Unit value in $	Units	Volume in mill. $	Unit value in $	Units	Volume in mill. $	Unit value in $
2001	5,221,109	67,408	*12,911*	368,329	3,470	*9,420*	2,194,021	16,943	*7,723*	3,604	38	*10,506*
2002	6,167,365	77,020	*12,488*	345,648	3,451	*9,985*	2,186,923	17,666	*8,078*	1,076	10	*8,880*
2003	6,692,795	91,510	*13,678*	255,489	2,875	*11,254*	2,325,389	22,744	*9,781*	3,021	37	*12,331*
2004	5,870,224	99,698	*16,984*	263,714	3,508	*13,301*	2,304,804	26,295	*11,409*	7,588	85	*11,163*
2005	6,436,649	108,685	*16,885*	208,548	2,754	*13,206*	2,027,430	24,088	*11,881*	9,051	64	*7,029*
2006	6,854,811	115,982	*16,920*	193,291	2,524	*13,058*	1,889,564	24,386	*12,906*	9,713	112	*11,533*
2007	7,579,370	138,803	*18,313*	136,469	1,824	*13,368*	2,130,964	29,815	*13,991*	17,898	320	*17,856*
2008	n.a.	140,158	n.a.	162,163	2,106	*12,986*	2,248,400	30,147	*13,408*	3,499	49	*14,120*
2009	n.a.	102,420	n.a.	2,588	n.a.		1,933,485	26,087	*13,492*	3,881	40	*10,355*
2010	6,804,435	128,671	*18,910*	185,171	2,356	*12,726*	1,961,162	26,011	*13,263*	9,289	49	*5,317*
2011	n.a.	154,290	n.a.	593,917	3,695	*6,221*	2,072,560	30,475	*14,704*	4,412	56	*12,730*
2012	7,301,342	146,851	*20,113*	661,574	3,829	*5,787*	n.a.	25,120	n.a.	10,367	96	*9,288*
2013	7,544,399	148,592	*19,696*	260,418	3,307	*12,698*	2,161,231	29,176	*13,500*	6,906	64	*9,318*
2014	8,372,972	160,306	*19,146*	279,618	4,511	*16,134*	1,975,420	31,932	*16,165*	3,540	57	*16,098*

Source: UN Comtrade, own calculations

A more indirect approach takes into account that non-price competitiveness is the result of an advantage in (applied) technology and thus innovative products and better production processes which allow a certain level of product differentiation and niches without much competition. Based on the assumption that horizontal and vertical differentiation is a result of previous investments in technology and education, non-price competitiveness can be derived tentatively from indicators describing the development of these investments or their outcome. Here, research & development (R&D) costs as an input factor, patent data or changes in productivity as a result of R&D, and education as a prerequisite for innovation can be used.

R&D expenditures are depicted in figure 5. Spain shows a huge increase until the crisis and is still above the euro area average. Germany as well as the Netherlands develop similar to the average but stay below it. The data for Greece and Spain point to an increase in competitiveness before the crisis, a sharp decline of R&D expenditures and thus competitiveness afterwards and no significant advantage to the euro area average for Greece in 2013.

Figure 5: Total Research & Development expenditures, in euro, 2001=100

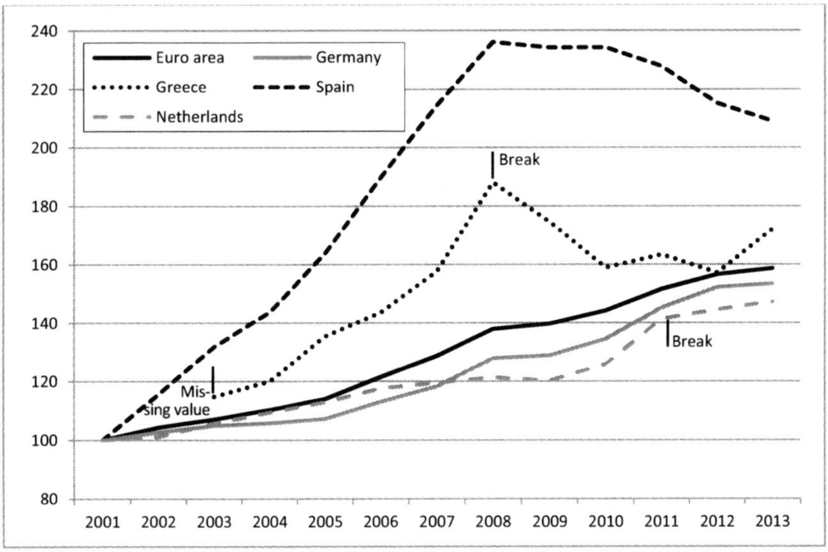

[Figure 5: Line chart showing R&D expenditures indexed to 2001=100 for Euro area, Germany, Greece, Spain, and Netherlands from 2001 to 2013. Notes indicate "Missing value" for Greece early in the series and "Break" markers in Dutch and Greek time series.]

Note: Data for Greece partly missing, breaks in Dutch and Greek times series
Source: Eurostat, own calculations

A further indicator to measure the outcome of innovations is the increase in capital stock. Figure 6 shows gross capital formation (without the construction sector).

The data of figure 6 shows a volatile development and a significant decline due to the crisis. In 2015, three of the countries have achieved a level well above the starting point. The evolution of the Greek capital formation, however, points to severe problems in the future due to disinvestment. The developments depicted here do not indicate a sustainable catch-up process of Spain and Greece. Furthermore, they do not resemble the development of current accounts since 2001.

Non-price competitiveness is related to the argument of effective demand – at least in the sense that exports are strong when foreign demand matches the dominant product groups or sectors in an economy. A comparison of export volumes and foreign demand helps to assess a change in competitiveness. If export volumes grow faster (slower) than foreign demand, this indicates an increase (decrease) in competitiveness, everything else constant.

Figure 6: Gross capital formation (without construction), constant prices, 2001q1=100

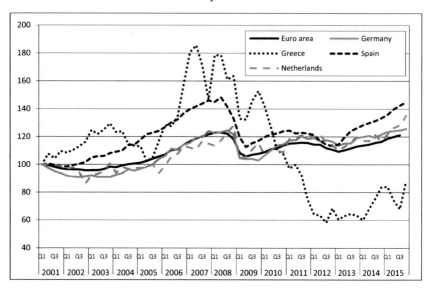

Source: AMECO, own calculations

Data is not easily available; therefore Figure 7 reports the development of total market shares. Although all countries in question lose market share to growing export economies like China, this is not fully reflected in the current accounts. Reasons can be that some countries of the rest of the world increase their current account deficits or that exports shrink but incomes due to foreign direct investments rise.

Figure 7: Total export market shares of euro area countries

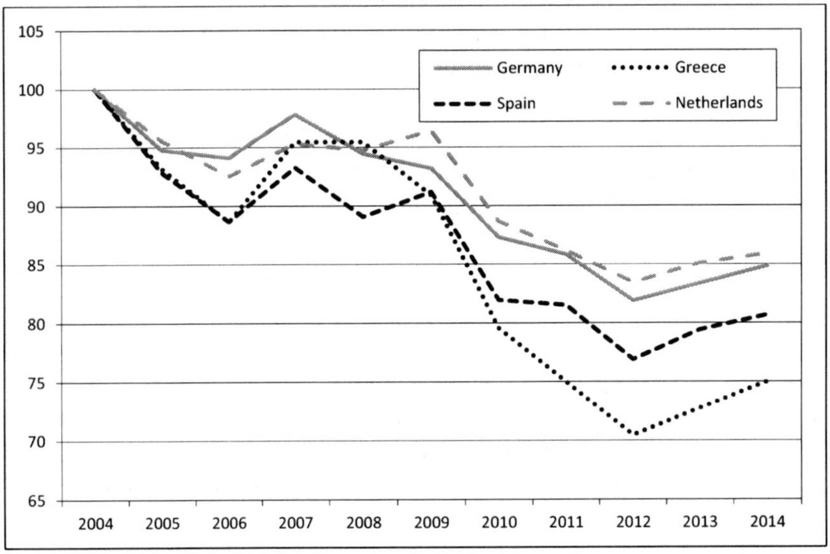

[Line chart showing export market share indices from 2004 to 2014 for Germany, Greece, Spain, and Netherlands, with values ranging approximately from 65 to 105.]

Source: Eurostat, own calculations

Ca'Zorzi and Schnatz (2007: 16) calculate a long-run elasticity of euro area export volumes in response to changes in foreign demand in the range of 0.80 to 0.93 for different indicators.

4. Discussion

The existing databases offer a variety of indicators for price and non-price competitiveness. All have advantages and disadvantages. Besides missing data, there are two important restrictions. Firstly, all indicators do not exactly match and measure what is happening in the export sector of a country. Secondly, none can directly and unambiguously measure competitiveness. Unit labour costs are only one component of production costs. Moreover, they do not include the profit margin and variations in the profit margin. Export prices directly measure the prices of exported goods. The drawback of this indicator is, however, that due to the calculation method, qualitative improvements that lead to price increases appear as a loss in competitiveness although an increase should be indicated. To measure non-price competitiveness is even harder. Data for quality and variety of products that allow firms to differentiate their product from others is only available in rudimentary form. A direct way to measure competitiveness would be to compare the prices of similar products and to assume that higher prices indicate higher quality. Unfortunately, unit values are not available in a sufficient amount and quality. Therefore, indirect indicators like R&D expenditures are used to measure this component of competitiveness. Again, these indicators are not only indirect but also insufficient indicators. Expenditures for research, for example, do not necessarily lead to improvements of competitiveness. In order to also cover the crucial effect of differences in demand, a further indicator was suggested: the market share indicating the development of exports in relation to foreign demand. But the role of demand is not limited to being an indicator for competitiveness. It directly serves as a crucial determinant of current accounts. For example, deficits of the current account can be caused by a growing economy as in the case of Spain. In contrast, an export oriented model leads to current account surpluses but restricts domestic demand. If such a situation is aggravated by a monetary union with an underdeveloped institutional framework, the whole union is at stake. And this is exactly the situation in the euro area which is characterised by a lack of fiscal transfers, a fragile financial system and a problematic construction of the monetary system (Terzi 2016; Bibow 2016).

With all the required caveats due to the insufficiencies of the indicators, the depicted findings show both consistency between the indicators and variety between the countries. All indicators of price competitiveness point at the same direction, and they are consistent with the current account developments of the countries. Deterioration in price competitiveness is reflected in a worsening of current accounts and vice versa. The indicators for non-price competitiveness describe a catch-up process of Greece and Spain and a decline in competitiveness for Greece after 2008 which is not surprising in view of the crisis and the austerity measures that caused disinvestment and unemployment. The improvement of the current accounts of Spain and Greece after the crisis should not be overestimated. Price developments play a role but more important is a decline in imports due to a fall in incomes.

The analysis supports the claim that each country has an individual story to tell. A simple and descriptive approach as suggested here might help to highlight such individual developments and to embed them into a macroeconomic story. This implies that fashionable rankings of competitiveness are not very helpful because they often do not adequately measure what they want to measure, they equate something which is not equal and ignore that countries cannot simply choose measures but always deal with a whole institutional and path-dependent setting.

5. Conclusions

A set of indicators was discussed in order to answer the question to what extent the recent current account imbalances in the euro area can be explained by price and non-price indicators of competitiveness. With all necessary caveats, the indicators support the existence of two growth models in the euro area. Germany has increased its price competitiveness and kept its level of non-price competitiveness. The country did not foster domestic demand in a way that would have been sufficient to increase GDP growth rates and to balance its current account. Other countries showed a catch-up process and high GDP growth rates in the past. At the same time, their current accounts deteriorated and they lost in price competitiveness. After the crisis, austerity policies forced these countries to reduce employment and wages. Even if this has increased their price competitiveness, evidence is rare that it has made up for the losses in non-price competitiveness caused by disinvestment and unemployment.

References

Bibow, J. (2016): Making the Euro Viable: the Euro Treasury Plan, in: *European Journal of Economics and Economic Policies: Intervention*, 13(1), 72-86.

Ca'Zorzi, M., Schnatz, B. (2007): Explaining and Forecasting Euro Area Exports. Which Competitiveness Indicator Performs Best?, ECB Working Paper Series, No. 833, European Central Bank.

European Commission (2015): Recommendation for a Council Recommendation on the establishment of National Competitiveness Boards within the Euro Area, 21.10.2015, COM(2015) 601 final, Brussels: European Commission, URL: http://ec.europa.eu/transparency/regdoc/rep/1/2015/EN/1-2015-601-EN-F1-1.PDF [accessed on March, 3rd, 2016].

Flassbeck, H., Lapavitsas, C. (2015): Confronting the failure of the European Monetary Union, in: Jäger, J., Springler, E. (eds.), *Asymmetric Crisis in Europe and Possible Futures. Critical Political Economy and Post-Keynesian Perspectives*, Abingdon, New York: Routledge.

Global Competitiveness Report (2014): The Global Competitiveness Report 2014-2105, ed. by Schwab, K., Sala-i-Martin, X., Geneva, World Economic Forum.

Grossman, G., Helpman, E. (1995): Technology and trade, in: Grossman, G., Rogoff, K. (eds.), *Handbook of International Economics*, vol. 3, Elsevier, Amsterdam, 121337.

Hall, P.A., Soskice, D. (2001): Introduction to Varieties of Capitalism, in: Hall, P.A., Soskice, D. (eds.), *Varieties of Capitalism. The Institutional Foundations of Comparative Advantage*, Oxford: Oxford University Press, 1-68.

Hein, E. (2013-14): The crisis of finance-dominated capitalism in the Euro area, deficiencies in the economic policy architecture and deflationary stagnation policies, in: *Journal of Post Keynesian Economics*, 36(2), 325-354.

Herr, H. (1994): Der Merkantilismus der Bundesrepublik in der Weltwirtschaft, in: Voy, K., Polster, W., Thomasberger, C. (eds.), *Marktwirtschaft und politische Regulierung*, Vol. 1, Marburg: Metropolis, 227-261.

Herzog-Stein, A., Lindner, F., Sturn, S., van Treeck, T. (2010): From a source of weakness to a tower of strength? The changing German labour market, IMK Report, No. 56e, URL: http://www.boeckler.de/pdf/p_imk_report_56e_2011.pdf [accessed on February, 11th, 2013].

IMF – International Monetary Fund (2014): World Economic Outlook. Legacies, clouds, uncertainties, October.

Krugman, P. (1986): Pricing to Market When the Exchange Rate Changes, NBER Working Paper, No. 1926, Cambridge, MA: National Bureau of Economic Research.

Krugman, P. (1989): Differences in income elasticities and trends in real exchange rates, in: *European Economic Review*, 33(5), 1031-1046.

Lisbon European Council (2000): Lisbon European Council 23 and 24 March 2000. Presidency Conclusions, URL: http://www.europarl.europa.eu/summits/lis1_en.htm [accessed on July, 14th, 2015].

Niechoj, T. (2012): Germany – best practice for the euro area? The Janus-faced character of current account surpluses, in: Herr, H., Niechoj, T., Thomasberger, C., Truger, A., van Treeck, T. (eds.), *From crisis to growth? The challenge of debt and imbalances*, Marburg: Metropolis, 389-419.

Niechoj, T. (2014): Kill or cure? Current accounts within the euro area after the austerity measures, in: Dullien, S., Hein, E., Truger, A. (eds.), *Makroökonomik, Entwicklung und Wirtschaftspolitik | Macroeconomics, Development and Economic Policies*, Marburg: Metropolis, 291-303.

Schröder, E. (2015): Eurozone Imbalances: Measuring the Contribution of Expenditure Switching and Expenditure Volumes 1990-2013, New School Working Paper, No. 8, New York: New School.

Schulten, T. (2015): Exportorientierung und ökonomische Ungleichgewichte in Europa, in: *Sozialismus*, 4/2015, 42-46.

Stockhammer, E. (2011): Peripheral Europe's debt and German wages: the role of wage policy in the Euro area, in: *International Journal of Public Policy*, 7(1/2/3), 83-96.

Storm, S., Naastepad, C.W.M. (2015): Crisis and recovery in the German economy: The real lessons, in: *Structural Change and Economic Dynamics*, 32, 11-24.

Terzi, A. (2016): A T-Shirt Model of Savings, Debt, and Private Spending: Lessons for the Euro Area, in: *European Journal of Economics and Economic Policies: Intervention*, 13(1), 39-56.

CompNet – The Competitiveness Network (2015): Compendium on the diagnostic toolkit for competitiveness, ECB Occasional Paper Series, No. 163, European Central Bank.

Thirlwall, A.P. (1979): The balance of payments constraint as an explanatioof international growth rate differences, in: *Banca Nazionale del Lavoro Quarterly Review*, 128, 45-53.

Gender matters: Schnittmengen feministischer und (post-)keynesianischer Analyse

Friederike Maier

1. Einleitung

An der HWR Berlin haben Ökonominnen und Ökonomen unterschiedlicher paradigmatischer Provenienz die Diskussion um die Frage, was eine gute volkswirtschaftliche Analyse in Lehre und Forschung ausmacht, in den vergangenen Jahren aktiv vorangetrieben. Hansjörg Herrs Arbeiten geben dazu ein hervorragendes Beispiel ab. So inspirierend seine Arbeiten, so anregend und angenehm die Diskussionen mit Hansjörg sind: Es bleiben doch auch blinde Flecken. Einer dieser blinden Flecken ist Gegenstand meines Beitrags: die Frage danach, ob und wenn ja wie die Geschlechterverhältnisse in volkswirtschaftlichen Analysen empirisch wie theoretisch systematisch einbezogen werden müssen. Auch wenn viele KollegInnen, wie auch Hansjörg, diese Frage im Prinzip bejahen, die Umsetzung dieses Anspruchs in der eigenen wissenschaftlichen Arbeit ist oft nicht geleistet worden. Im Folgenden soll daher gefragt werden, welche Schnittmengen zwischen feministischen und anderen Ansätzen erkennbar sind.

2. Die Relevanz der Geschlechterforschung für die Ökonomie

Die meisten ökonomischen Ansätze, neoklassisch oder heterodox, mikro- oder makroökonomisch fundiert, formulieren ihre Annahmen und Modelle ohne jeglichen Bezug auf Geschlecht. Das Geschlecht der „Wirtschaftssubjekte" wird weder als empirisches Phänomen noch als Analysekategorie zur Kenntnis genommen. Die Methode, ökonomische Phänomene ohne Bezug zu Geschlechterdimensionen analysieren zu können, führt bisweilen zu unerklärlichen Ergebnissen, wenn z.B. in der aktuellen Diskussion über die Arbeitsmarktentwicklung mit Verwunderung zur Kenntnis genommen wird, dass in manchen Ländern die Arbeitslosigkeit steigt, obwohl Beschäftigung und Wirtschaftswachstum ebenfalls steigen (vgl. European Commission 2011: 9). Wie kann dies der Fall sein, wo doch stabile Zusammenhänge herrschen sollen, die sich sogar Okun's law nennen, also mehr sein sollen als zufällige Ereignisse. Okun's law besagt, dass seit Beginn des letzten Jahrhunderts jeder Anstieg des Wirtschaftswachstums und der Beschäftigung zu einem Rückgang der Arbeitslosigkeit führte. Was ist jetzt anders, dass dieses Gesetz nicht mehr gelten soll? Die Lösung: „added workers", solche, die bisher nicht auf dem Arbeitsmarkt waren, treten auf und suchen (erfolgreich) Arbeit oder werden/bleiben arbeitslos. Und wer sind diese „added workers"? Frauen aller Altersgruppen! Aber nicht, dass nun angenommen wird, diese Frauen, die in den Arbeitsmarkt „drängen", täten dies, weil sie erwerbstätig sein wollten oder könnten – nein, die Welt der ÖkonomInnen bleibt im Rahmen des Ernährermodells intakt, denn es findet sich mehr als eine Studie, die zeigt, dass Frauen dies nur tun, weil das Einkommen der (Ehe-)Männer nicht mehr ausreichend hoch ist (European Commission 2011: 11).

Eine eigenständige Motivation der Frauen wird nicht angenommen, eine geschlechtsspezifisch differenzierende Analyse von Chancen und Risiken der ökonomischen Krisenfolgen auf dem Arbeitsmarkt ist nicht erforderlich, die Erwerbsbeteiligung der Frauen ist kein Phänomen, mit dem man sich weiter beschäftigen müsste: Primär die ökonomische Lage der Ehemänner erklärt die aktuellen Entwicklungen. Wissenschaftliche Analysen, die zeigen, dass sich das Erwerbsverhalten der Frauen in den letzten Dekaden radikal verändert hat, haben viele Volkswirtinnen und Volkswirte bisher nicht zur Kenntnis genommen (vgl. dazu den Überblick bei Jaumotte 2003).

Es lassen sich eine Reihe ökonomischer Felder aufzählen, in denen die Berücksichtigung von Geschlecht relevant wäre, wie die Arbeiten feministischer Ökonominnen zeigen, und in denen die Mainstream-Wissenschaft (aber auch die Politik) diese Erkenntnisse vollständig ignoriert oder als nicht relevant abtut. Es fallen einem Fragen ein wie Ursachen und Folgen von Krisen auf den Arbeits-, Kapital- und Gütermärkten, die Effekte von wirtschaftspolitischen Maßnahmen auf Wachstum, Preisstabilität und Staatsverschuldung und der Zusammenhang mit Geschlechterverhältnissen, die Entwicklung der Wirtschaftsstruktur und das Zusammenspiel von Markt, Staat und Privathaushalten bei der Produktion sowie bei Konsum und Verteilung von Gütern und Dienstleistungen.

Es gibt zu allen diesen Aspekten theoretisch wie empirisch fundierte feministische ökonomische Analysen, es gibt eine renommierte wissenschaftliche Zeitschrift „Feminist Economics" und auch eine internationale wissenschaftliche Vereinigung „International Association for Feminist Economics – IAFFE". Es finden sich vor allem im englischsprachigen Raum etablierte Lehrbücher (z.B. Blau et al. 2009; Jacobsen 2007), herausragende wissenschaftliche Grundlagenwerke (z.b. Ferber/Nelson 2003), lebhafte Kontroversen in Zeitschriften, disziplinäre und interdisziplinäre Konferenzen etc., kurzum eine lebendige wissenschaftliche community, die keinesfalls abgeschottet vom Mainstream, sondern in ständiger Auseinandersetzung damit agiert und – soweit das z.b. an den Mitgliederzahlen in der IAFFE ablesbar ist – kontinuierlich wächst.

Die Einbeziehung von Geschlecht als empirische Kategorie, geschweige denn die Beachtung der gesellschaftlichen Verhältnisse der Geschlechter, ist jedoch in der ökonomischen Wissenschaft nicht die Regel. ÖkonomInnen können logisch vollständig perfekt ableiten, dass eine höhere Frauenerwerbstätigkeit zu einer sinkenden Geburtenrate führen muss (vgl. Seyda 2003), dass die Spezialisierung der Frauen auf Hausarbeit (und der Männer auf Erwerbsarbeit) auch für Frauen ökonomisch vorteilhaft ist oder dass Frauen rational Berufe mit niedrigem Lohn wählen, weil sie höhere Abschreibungen ihres Humankapitals erwarten, wenn sie die Erwerbstätigkeit zur Kinderbetreuung unterbrechen (vgl. Weck-Hannemann 2003).

Es obliegt dann den feministischen Ökonominnen nachzuweisen, dass solche Aussagen nicht nur empirisch nicht fundiert sind, sondern oft das Gegenteil der Fall ist, und sie müssen darauf hinweisen, dass die als ceteris paribus gesetzten Rahmenbedingungen den Unterschied zwischen dem Modell und der Realität ausmachen. Hohe Frauenerwerbstätigkeit und hohe Geburtenraten gehen nämlich dann Hand in Hand, wenn es gesellschaftlich akzeptable Bedingungen zur Vereinbarung von Erwerbstätigkeit und Kindern gibt (Jaumotte 2003). Das neoklassische Spezialisierungsmodell der „New Home Economics" baut auf völlig inakzeptablen Annahmen über symmetrische Verhältnisse zwischen Mann und Frau im Kontext des privaten Haushalts auf und lässt nur deswegen die geschlechtsspezifische Spezialisierung als „freie" Wahl erscheinen (siehe Ott 1993 sowie Beblo/Soete 1999). Frauen, wie viele Männer auch, können zudem auf dem Arbeitsmarkt Berufe und Tätigkeiten keinesfalls entsprechend ihren Präferenzen und rationalen Kalkülen über Lebenserwerbseinkommen und Humankapitalabschreibungen wählen, sondern akzeptieren, was der „Markt" gerade bietet. Der „Markt" wiederum weist nach Geschlecht segregierte Arbeitsmärkte auf, auf denen – nicht nur wegen der unvollständigen Informationen – Geschlechterstereotype das AnbieterInnen- und NachfragerInnen-Verhalten prägen (Schmitt 2014). Aussagen zu ökonomischen und sozialen Problemstellungen, die auf der Basis rigider, aber geschlechtsfreier Modelle gewonnen werden, sind oft sehr suspekt – nicht nur Feministinnen, sondern auch vielen anderen Ökonominnen und Ökonomen erscheint dies problematisch. Auch sie erwarten von ihrer Wissenschaft keine gegen die Realität immunisierte Modellapologetik, sondern einen Beitrag zur Lösung gesellschaftlicher Probleme. Viele haben schon kritisiert, dass die Annahme rational handelnder Individuen, losgelöst von Zeit und Raum und Gesellschaft, ein fundamentaler Grundirrtum der meisten ökonomischen Modelle ist. Die Annahme von Gleichgewichtstendenzen auf Märkten stellt einen grundlegend falschen Ausgangspunkt der Analysen nicht nur in Gütermärkten und Arbeitsmärkten, sondern auch in Finanzmärkten dar. Der Staat ist für viele kritische ÖkonomInnen ein wichtiger Akteur, dessen Rolle bei der „Zähmung" des Profitstrebens gestärkt und nicht geschwächt werden sollte. Privatisierung, Liberalisierung von sozialpolitischen Rahmenbedingungen, Strukturanpassungen zugunsten der Unternehmen zulasten von Beschäftigten und der sozialen Kohärenz einer Gesellschaft, „mehr Markt – weniger Staat", all das sind Entwicklungen, die von ökonomisch argumentierenden think tanks und InteressenvertreterInnen mit vorangetrieben wurden. Die zum Teil verheerenden Folgen dieser Wirtschaftspolitik sind heute vielerorts sichtbar. Der „Autismus" der Wirtschaftswissenschaften, der beinhaltet, dass alles menschliche Verhalten mit Hilfe ökonomischer Modelle erklärt werden kann, ist schon von vielen Seiten kritisiert worden. Dieser Kritik stimmen die meisten feministischen Ökonominnen zu. Eine grundlegende Neuorientierung der Wirtschaftswissenschaften weg von der modellhaften mathematisierten „Zurichtung" der Realität, deren Ergebnisse dann auch noch in politischen Empfehlungen mit katastrophalen Folgen münden, hin zu einer echten Sozialwissenschaft in Kooperation und Austausch mit anderen sozialwissenschaftlichen Disziplinen, wäre ein notwendiger Schritt zur Reformierung der Disziplin.

Allerdings: Die Erklärungskraft und die Relevanz wirtschaftswissenschaftlicher Analysen könnte gesteigert werden, wenn Erkenntnisse der Geschlechterforschung Eingang fänden – gerade bei den heterodoxen Ansätzen, zu denen die Arbeiten von Hansjörg Herr ja zählen.

3. Unbezahlte Arbeit als blinder Fleck der Mainstream-Ökonomie

Im Folgenden wird auf einen zentralen blinden Fleck eingegangen: die Vernachlässigung der unbezahlten Arbeit. Gegenstandsbereiche der meisten ökonomischen Theorien sind Märkte: Gütermärkte, Geldmärkte und Faktormärkte, d.h. Märkte für Arbeit und Kapital (und Boden). Die kapitalistische Ökonomie wird als Marktwirtschaft verstanden, in der ökonomisch relevant ist, was über einen Markt gehandelt wird und einen Preis hat, der sich in Geld ausdrückt. Schon bei Adam Smith ist diese Definition des ökonomisch Relevanten angelegt, indem er darauf verweist, dass der Wohlstand der Nationen durch Arbeit entsteht. „Gemeint ist damit die Erwerbsarbeit. ...Was in der Erwerbsarbeit, in den Unternehmen, am Markt geschieht, ist Ökonomie – was in der Sorge-Arbeit, in der Familie, in den Haushalten geschieht, ist Nicht-Ökonomie" (Biesecker/Kesting 2003: 49). Smith war einer der Ersten, der den Arbeitsbegriff auf die Erwerbsarbeit reduzierte. Seine berühmten Beispiele zur Arbeitsteilung (Stichwort Stecknadel-Produktion) beziehen sich auf die Arbeitsteilung innerhalb einer Manufaktur und zwischen verschiedenen Manufakturen. Die Weiterentwicklung der ökonomischen Ansätze nach Adam Smith hat diese Dichotomisierung in Markt = ökonomisch relevant und Nicht-Markt = nicht relevant weiter vorangetrieben und führte letztlich zu einer Ausklammerung der unbezahlten Arbeit aus fast jeder ökonomischen Betrachtung. Insbesondere im zentralen Maß der ökonomischen Leistungsfähigkeit, dem Bruttoinlandsprodukt, taucht die unbezahlte Arbeit nicht auf. Als sich Ende des 19. Jahrhunderts die empirischen (und steuerrechtlichen) Definitionen der nationalen Rechnungslegungen herausbildeten, in denen die unbezahlte Hausarbeit nicht als Beitrag zur „national dividend" (zum Volkseinkommen) gezählt wurde, erschien es vielen zeitgenössischen Ökonomen doch als Paradox, dass die gleiche Tätigkeit als bezahlte Arbeit ökonomisch relevant sein soll, als unbezahlte Arbeit jedoch unberücksichtigt bleibt. Stellvertretend dafür sei Pigou zitiert: „The bought and the unbought kinds of services do not differ from one another in any fundamental respect and frequently an unbought is transformed into a bought one and vice versa. This leads to a number of violent paradoxes [...] the services rendered by women enter into the dividend when they are rendered in exchange for wages, whether in the factory or in the home, but do not enter into it when they are rendered by mothers and wives gratuitously for their own families. Thus, if a man marries his housekeeper or his cook, the national dividend is diminished. These things are paradoxes" (Pigou 1960: 32).

Während Pigou und andere Ökonomen dieser Zeit das Problem der Nicht-Erfassung der Hausarbeit immerhin noch als ein Paradox ansahen (was sie im Übrigen selbst geschaffen hatten, als sie sich auf das ökonomisch Relevante verständigt hatten!), gehen heutige VWLerInnen damit sehr viel unreflektierter um. In den meisten Lehrbüchern taucht das Pigou'sche Paradox allenfalls im Abschnitt über die Volkswirtschaftliche Gesamtrechnung auf, in dem die Definition und das Konzept des Bruttoinlandsprodukts erläutert werden. Es wird dabei dann darauf hingewiesen, dass unbezahlte Arbeit nicht erfasst wird, und zur Illustrierung folgt dann das Pigou'sche Beispiel (wobei der angesprochene Mann wahlweise als Junggeselle oder Manager bezeichnet wird, der seine Haushälterin heiratet). Weitere Beispiele sind dann die Schwarzarbeit und andere „Externalitäten" des Marktgeschehens (vgl. z.B. Bofinger 2003: 441; Heine/Herr 2003: 314[1])

Die lapidare Ausklammerung der unbezahlten Arbeit hat erhebliche Folgen: Da diese Arbeit den Frauen zugeordnet wird, verschwinden Frauen immer dann aus dem Blick der ÖkonomInnen, wenn sie nicht selbst erwerbstätig sind. Sie sind dann als vom Erwerbseinkommen eines Mannes oder der sozialen Wohlfahrt Abhängige keine eigenständigen, ökonomisch aktiven Akteurinnen – selbst als Konsumentinnen auf Gütermärkten sind sie demnach vom Geld anderer Akteure abhängig. Kein Wunder also, dass ihnen keine eigenständige Motivation zur Erwerbsarbeit zugesprochen wird, werden sie doch im Modell erst dann erwerbstätig, wenn der Reservationslohn den (indirekten) Wert der Hausarbeit übersteigt und der Zukauf von haushaltsnaher Arbeit weniger Kosten verursacht, als an Erwerbslohn erzielt werden kann (vgl. zur Kritik auch Ott 1993).

---

[1] Während Marktaktivitäten statistisch erfasst und dokumentiert sind, ist die Erfassung unbezahlter Hausarbeit lange Zeit ein ungeliebtes Thema der VolkswirtInnen und StatistikerInnen gewesen. In jüngster Zeit werden jedoch regelmäßig durch Zeitbudgeterhebungen Zeitwerte ermittelt, die die unbezahlte Hausarbeit abbilden. 2001 wurden danach in Deutschland 56 Mrd. Stunden Erwerbsarbeit und 96 Mrd. Stunden Hausarbeit im weitesten Sinn verrichtet. Multipliziert man diese unbezahlte Arbeit mit dem Nettostundenlohn einer Haushälterin (7 € pro Stunde), erhält man einen Wert der Haushaltsproduktion von 684 Mrd. Euro. Nach den Kriterien der Volkswirtschaftlichen Gesamtrechnung erfasst entspricht die unbezahlte Hausarbeit im Jahre 2001 40% des Bruttoinlandsprodukts Deutschlands (vgl. Statistisches Bundesamt 2003). Auch international vergleichende Daten liegen vor, die zeigen, dass die unbezahlte Hausarbeit wertmäßig zwischen 19% des BIP in Korea und bis zu 53% des BIP in Portugal ausmacht (Miranda 2011). Über die Erfassung und Bewertung herrscht dabei weitgehend Konsens, sodass die Einschätzung bei Heine und Herr (2003: 314), der Versuch einer Erfassung der Hausarbeit bereite immense methodische Probleme, doch inzwischen als überholt angesehen werden muss.

Die Ausklammerung der Arbeit zur „sozialen Reproduktion" (was nicht nur Kinderbetreuung meint) aus den gängigen ökonomischen Theorien folgt dabei zwei Argumentationssträngen (vgl. Humphries/Rubery 1984): Entweder wird die unbezahlte Arbeit als Teil der Gesellschaft angesehen, der unverbunden zur autonomen Marktökonomie steht – ein Zusammenhang zwischen Reproduktionsbereich und Entwicklungen auf Märkten, insbesondere dem Arbeitsmarkt, wird nicht systematisch angenommen. Oder aber der Reproduktionsbereich wird als integrierter und anpassungsfähiger Teil des Produktionssystems gesehen, in dem der Reproduktionsbereich entweder nach den gleichen Prinzipien funktioniert wie Märkte (und ökonomisch mit den gleichen Modellen analysiert werden kann) oder aber funktionalistisch den Arbeitsmarkt unterstützt (z.b. das Marx'sche Konzept der Reservearmee).

Indem man/frau annimmt, alle menschlichen Entscheidungen seien den gleichen Prinzipien unterworfen, können alle menschlichen Beziehungen als Märkte bezeichnet werden: der Heiratsmarkt, der Kindermarkt, der Markt für Diskriminierung, der Markt für Straftaten etc. Gary S. Becker war ein Vertreter dieser Theorierichtung. Er postuliert, dass der (orthodoxe) ökonomische Ansatz geeignet sei, jegliches menschliche Verhalten zu erklären: „Alles menschliche Verhalten kann vielmehr so betrachtet werden, als habe man es mit Akteuren zu tun, die ihren Nutzen, bezogen auf ein stabiles Präferenzsystem, maximieren und sich in verschiedenen Märkten eine optimale Ausstattung an Informationen und anderen Faktoren schaffen. Trifft dieses Argument zu, dann bietet der ökonomische Ansatz einen einheitlichen Bezugsrahmen für die Analyse menschlichen Handelns, wie ihn Bentham, Comte, Marx u.a. seit langem gesucht, aber verfehlt haben" (Becker 1993: 15).

4. Synergien zwischen Heterodoxie und feministischer Ökonomie

Das Konzept der autonomen Marktökonomie, das die soziale Lebenswelt und die natürliche Umwelt ignoriert, bzw. das Konzept, dass alles den gleichen ökonomischen Prinzipien unterworfen ist, ist von verschiedenen theoretischen Ansätzen her kritisiert worden. Es ist inzwischen hinreichend belegt, dass diese vermeintlich autonome Marktwirtschaft mit vermeintlich rationalem homo oeconomicus so mit der sozialen Lebenswelt und der natürlichen Umwelt verbunden ist, dass es unangebracht ist, weiterhin diese (Wechsel-)

Wirkungen als „externe Effekte" zu betrachten.² Diese Erkenntnis teilen auch viele heterodoxe VWLerInnen mit feministischen Kritiken.

Die Frauenbewegung und feministische Ökonominnen haben zudem die Marginalisierung der unbezahlten Arbeit, der sozialen Reproduktion bzw. der Versorgungsökonomie („care economy") zum wissenschaftlichen und politischen Thema gemacht. Insbesondere die Unsichtbarkeit der nicht marktvermittelten Arbeit in den meisten ökonomischen Kategorien und Modellen ist zentraler Gegenstand der Kritik, vor allem in einer Zeit, in der die Zurverfügungstellung öffentlicher und meritorischer Güter sowie sozialer Leistungen zum zentralen Kritikpunkt an der Mainstream-Ökonomie geworden ist.

Dabei können auch Mainstream-ÖkonomInnen nicht übersehen, dass sich das Verhältnis zwischen formeller und informeller Arbeit und der unbezahlten Arbeit im familiären Kontext in vielen Facetten aktuell neu formiert. Die Formen der Arbeitsmarktintegration verwischen, auch weil die Arbeitsmärkte dereguliert wurden und klare Grenzziehungen zwischen Normalarbeitsverhältnis (für Männer) und marginaler Erwerbsintegration (für Frauen) keinen Bestand mehr haben. Gleichzeitig sind Frauen heute keine Reservearmee mehr, sondern ihre Erwerbstätigkeit ist stabiler Teil der neuen Strukturen des Arbeitsmarkts. Dass Kinder- und Altenbetreuung keine Sphäre unbezahlter Arbeit mehr ist und viele Haushalte Dienstleistungen kaufen, ist in den entwickelten Volkswirtschaften Normalität und beeinflusst die Wirtschaftsstruktur, d.h. die Produktion von Gütern und Dienstleistungen. Die Arbeitsteilung zwischen Markt, Staat und Privatwirtschaft formiert sich z.B. in vielen Bereichen der personenbezogenen Dienstleistungen neu. Dabei ist unstrittig, dass diese Prozesse sehr unterschiedliche Auswirkungen auf Frauen und Männer haben, weil Frauen in der Regel in die unbezahlte Arbeit anders eingebunden

---

² Dass der homo oeconomicus nicht zufällig ein Mann ist, sondern in seiner Ausstattung mit bestimmten Merkmalen und Eigenschaften als Mann / männliches Wesen konzipiert wurde, hat u.a. Julie Nelson gezeigt (Nelson 1996). Insofern ist die orthodoxe Ökonomie nicht geschlechtsblind, sondern androzentrisch formuliert und konzipiert (vgl. dazu auch Maier 1994). Darüber hinaus ist der methodische Imperialismus der Ökonomen und ihres „homo oeconomicus"-Modells nicht nur von anderen SozialwissenschaftlerInnen kritisiert worden, sondern hat auch unter den ÖkonomInnen selbst eine nur noch begrenzte AnhängerInnenschaft: „Niemand im Vollbesitz seiner geistigen Kräfte möchte seine *Tochter* mit einem „homo oeconomicus" verheiratet sehen, mit jemandem, der sämtliche Kosten nachrechnet und stets nach dem Gegenwert fragt, der nie von verrückter Großzügigkeit oder nicht berechnender Liebe heimgesucht ist, der nie aus einem Gefühl innerer Identität handelt und der in der Tat keine innere Identität besitzt, auch wenn er gelegentlich von sorgfältig kalkulierten Erwägungen über Wohlwollen und Missgunst bewegt ist" (Boulding 1973: 12).

sind als Männer. Es ist aber für die zukünftige Entwicklung der Gesellschaften nicht „egal", wie Staat und Gesellschaft das Verhältnis zwischen öffentlichen und privatwirtschaftlich oder in den privaten Haushalten erbrachten Arbeiten organisieren und finanzieren (vgl. Karamessini/Rubery 2014).

Um Synergien zwischen heterodoxen Ansätzen und der feministischen Ökonomie zu schaffen, ist also eine Öffnung des Gegenstandsbereichs der ökonomischen Theorien gefragt: „Dieser weite Blick auf die Ökonomie hat nicht nur die Konsequenz, dass das ökonomische Geschehen in sozialen und natürlichen Grenzen analysiert wird, es hat auch zur Folge, dass der Ökonomiebegriff selbst sich verändert, dass sich der Gegenstandsbereich weitet – kommen doch neben der Marktwirtschaft oder Erwerbsökonomie die Hauswirtschaft oder Versorgungsökonomie in den Blick." (Biesecker/Kesting 2003: 13) Diese „eingebettete" Ökonomie unterscheidet sich dann u.a. in der Analyse der Frauenarbeit und der damit verbundenen Geschlechterverhältnisse erheblich von den vorherrschenden Orthodoxien, indem sie versucht, die Beziehungen zwischen Markt, sozialer Lebenswelt, natürlicher Umwelt und hierarchischem Geschlechterverhältnis systematisch zu analysieren.

Eine solche Analyse nimmt dann in den Blick, wie und unter welchen Rahmenbedingungen Arbeit zwischen privater Hausarbeit, öffentlicher oder privatwirtschaftlicher Erstellung aufgeteilt ist – zum Beispiel im Bereich der Kinder- und Altenbetreuung (Folbre 2001). Oder sie stellt die Frage, wie eine neue Arbeitsteilung zwischen Familie und Markt oder Staat zum Wachstum einer Volkswirtschaft beitragen kann, vielleicht sogar zum „qualitativen" Wachstum? Und dabei vielleicht Geschlechterverhältnisse hin zu mehr Geschlechtergerechtigkeit transformiert – zum Nutzen von Frauen und Männern (vgl. dazu Löfström 2009; Stotsky 2006; Maier 2011).

In den gesellschaftlich relevanten Fragen der Effekte von Wirtschaftspolitik auf die Gesellschaft, auf die Positionen und Entwicklungschancen sozialer Gruppen, darunter auch der Geschlechter, lassen sich viele gemeinsame Schnittmengen zwischen heterodoxen Ansätzen und den feministischen Anliegen finden. Es beschäftigt auch feministische Ökonominnen, wie staatliche Transfers und Dienstleistungen finanziert und organisiert sein können, denn viele der Transfers und Dienstleistungen beeinflussen z.B. die Einkommens- und Erwerbssituation von Frauen unmittelbar (Madörin 2010). Einschränkungen öffentlicher Dienste und Transfers können traditionelle Geschlechterarrangements wiederbeleben. Die „Re-Familiarisierung" von Aktivitäten und Tätigkeiten hat Auswirkungen auf Männer und Frauen – unter den aktuellen Bedingungen wirken sie auf eine „Re-Traditionalisierung" in den Privathaushalten hin.

Wirft man einen Blick auf die Integration von Geschlechteraspekten in wirtschaftswissenschaftlichen Analysen, so kommt man/frau zum Ergebnis, dass die moderne neoklassische Mikroökonomie durchaus in der Lage ist, Geschlecht als Variable in ihre Analysen einzubeziehen. Die moderne Mikroökonomik, die zum Beispiel Institutionen und ihre Wirkungen auf die Entscheidungen der Wirtschaftssubjekte untersucht, bezieht in ihre Analysen gesamtgesellschaftliche und gesamtwirtschaftliche Regelungen und Interdependenzen als Handlungsrestriktionen ein. Das bedeutet, dass diese Ansätze zwar dem Postulat des methodologischen Individualismus verpflichtet bleiben und davon ausgehen, dass ökonomische und soziale Sachverhalte aus Individualentscheidungen aggregiert werden können. Die in den institutionellen Regelungen sich niederschlagenden gesellschaftlichen Normen und Interessen werden jedoch nicht ignoriert, sondern in ihren Wirkungen auf den jeweiligen Märkten untersucht, indem sie als „constraints" in die Rahmenbedingungen der jeweiligen Maximierungsbestrebungen eingehen. Damit haben Studien neoklassischer FeministInnen erhebliches Wissen zu ökonomischen Fragestellungen produziert, basierend auf einem mikroökonomisch formulierten Paradigma. „Neo-classical economics is about marginal changes in prices and incomes, and it cannot give us a long-term vision. But using the tools of neo-classical economics with a gender awareness can give us arguments for reforms leading to a society which is at the same time more economically efficient and closer to the vision of a feminist" (Gustafsson 1997: 39).

Autorinnen wie Janet A. Seiz (1995), Frances R. Woolley (1993), Julie A. Nelson (1996), Michele Pujol (1995) und Jane Humphries (1995) weisen darauf hin, dass diese Ansätze zwar die Integration institutioneller Rahmenbedingungen erlauben und auch kulturelle Faktoren wie soziale Normen in die Kalküle der Individuen einfließen können. Dies kann als Fortschritt gegenüber den einfachen neoklassischen Modellen gewertet werden. Die Frage bleibt allerdings, ob der Ausgangspunkt der Analysen, die Annahme unabhängiger Individuen, die mit gleicher Verhandlungsmacht ausgestattet sind, nicht schon an sich falsch ist und zu falschen Schlussfolgerungen führt: „A bigger question for feminists is whether the way forward is to pursue analysis of power relations within the household using models of this kind, or to use structural models in which men as a socio-economic group oppress women." (Humphries 1995: 68).

Auch Ulla Knapp (1997) fragt, ob die neoklassischen Theorien als Methode nicht ohnehin auf die Erklärung eng begrenzter Aspekte des Angebots- und Nachfrageverhaltens am Gütermarkt eingeschränkt sind und für Arbeitsangebotsverhalten ungeeignet seien. Auch institutionalistische Neoklassikerinnen können dem Dilemma nicht entkommen, dass einer leeren Nutzenfunktion[3] ein prall gefüllter Datenkranz institutioneller Rahmenbedingungen gegenübersteht. „Diese Rahmenbedingungen sind irgendwann einmal von kollektiv handelnden Individuen, die sich aufgrund ihrer sozialen Lage miteinander auf gemeinsames politisches Handeln verständigt haben, geschaffen worden. Was das Geschlechterverhältnis angeht, so beeinflussen diese institutionellen Bedingungen – je nach Ausgestaltung – die den Haushalten übermittelten Preissignale und auch die Einstellungen (,Präferenzen') der Individuen ganz erheblich. Familienleitbilder, Frauenleitbilder, Vorstellungen darüber, ob und wie Kinder zu erziehen und wie ältere Menschen zu betreuen sind, sind Ergebnisse gesellschaftlicher Aushandlungsprozesse, in denen sich die (aus Interessen begründbaren) Ideale der Mächtigeren als herrschende durchsetzen und schließlich, geronnen in Traditionen und politischen Institutionen, individuelle Präferenzen und Preisstrukturen formen" (Knapp 1997: 13).

Die Nicht-Thematisierung dieser Aushandlungsprozesse selbst, die Ausklammerung der gesellschaftlichen und ökonomischen Dominanz der Männer als sozialer Gruppe begrenzt auch die analytische Reichweite der neueren neoklassischen Ansätze.

Die Ignoranz gerade (post-)keynesianisch orientierter ÖkonomInnen gegenüber den Geschlechterverhältnissen, der relativen Autonomie der Arbeitsangebotsentwicklung, der Verwobenheit der Haushalts- mit der Gütermarktproduktion und den Wirkungen der Geschlechterverhältnisse auf die gesamtwirtschaftliche Nachfrage ist besonders ausgeprägt. Sie stützt sich auf die tief verwurzelte Annahme, dass die Angebotsseite des Arbeitsmarktes im Wesentlichen einen Reflex der Nachfrageseite darstellt und insofern keiner eigenständigen Analyse bedarf (Humphries/Rubery 1984). Obwohl feministische Ökonomie und heterodoxe Ansätze gewisse Grundannahmen teilen (wie z.B. die Ablehnung des individualistischen Homo-oeconomicus-Konzepts, die zentrale Bedeutung von Institutionen, die wichtige Rolle des Staates für Produktion, Wachstum und Verteilung), bleiben die Welten doch getrennt. Als ein entscheidendes Hindernis betrachtet Dunby dabei Folgendes: „Perhaps because one strength of the school has been its theorization of a money-using economy, Post Keynesians are prone to sweep aside whatever does not entail the passing of money. Most Post Keynesian theorizing has no place for the work, like cooking, that goes on after consumer products are bought: once the

---

[3] Da die jeweilige Nutzenfunktion vom Individuum individuell auf Basis seiner Präferenzordnung bestimmt wird, ist sie inhaltlich nicht gefüllt und auch nicht bewertbar – sie ist das Ergebnis einer strikt individuellen Nutzenmaximierung.

earner's income has been turned into demand for produced goods, the story is over. (...) A comprehensive Post Keynesian doctrine uses the terms ‚household' and ‚consumer' interchangeably (in the way neoclassical orthodoxy does), something that feminist scholarship has critiqued for decades. In almost all Post Keynesian work, consumers/households are mere spenders of (monetary) incomes, and the unpaid labor that produces workers is invisible" (Danby 2004: 62).

Gesamtwirtschaftliche Kreislaufbetrachtungen z.B. die Wirkungen einer erhöhten Frauenerwerbstätigkeit auf Niveau und Struktur der Produktion von Waren und Dienstleistungen wurden bisher auch durch KeynesianerInnen kaum angestellt. Dies liegt sowohl an der Ausklammerung der Haushaltsproduktion als relevanter Größe der Gesamtwirtschaft, ein Ansatz, der auch von KeynesianerInnen geteilt wird, als auch an der fehlenden Verknüpfung von makroökonomischen Größen mit Strukturüberlegungen wie z.b. Geschlecht der Arbeitskräfte. Makroökonomische (post-)keynesianische Analysen sind – de facto – noch weniger „gender aware" als neoklassische Analysen.

Die makroökonomischen Poltitkansätze sind zur Zeit durch drei „biases" geprägt: den „male breadwinner bias", die beschäftigungs- und sozialpolitisch bedeutsame Annahme, dass Männer Familienernäher und Frauen lediglich „added workers" seien; den „commodification or privatization bias", der die Privatwirtschaft als prinzipiell effizienter bewertet als den öffentlichen Sektor und deshalb die „marketization" öffentlicher Leistungen als beste Sparpolitik betrachtet; und den „deflationary bias", der mit Hilfe einer restriktiven Geld- und Fiskalpolitik versucht, Preise zu stabilisieren und Preissteigerungen zu verhindern, dadurch aber auch Beschäftigungs- und Entwicklungsmöglichkeiten einschränkt (Elson 2010). Um diesen drei Fehlannahmen, die durchaus von heterodoxen Ansätzen geteilt werden, entgegenzuwirken, fordern feministische Ökonominnen von makroökonomischen Politiken und konjunkturpolitischen Maßnahmen, ex ante und explizit soziale und geschlechterbezogene Erwägungen orientiert am Ziel sozialer und geschlechterbezogener Gerechtigkeit einzubeziehen, statt sozialpolitische Maßnahmen ex post hinzuzufügen (vgl. Karamessini/Rubery 2014).

Die Analyse der geschlechtsspezifischen Entwicklung auf verschiedenen Märkten mit all ihren politischen Implikationen haben die (Post-)KeynesianerInnen nicht nur in Deutschland den NeoklassikerInnen und dem wirtschaftspolitischen Mainstream überlassen. Die OECD hat zum Beispiel zahlreiche Analysen zu den „Gender Gaps" und ihren Folgen für die ökonomische und gesellschaftliche Entwicklung erarbeiten lassen (OECD 2012), in denen sich neoklassische Ansätze und Geschlechteranalyse ergänzen und zu – nicht nur für feministische Ökonominnen relevanten – Anforderungen an eine geschlechtergerechte Wirtschaftspolitik führen. Es ist daher zu wünschen, dass die Schnittmengen zwischen den unterschiedlichen heterodoxen Ansätzen systematisch aufgriffen werden und das Nebeneinander von feministischer Ökonomik und allen anderen Heterodoxen langsam ein Ende findet.

„The possibility of full employment, price stability, and stabilization of effective demand is complementary to the possibility of socialization of unpaid care work and transformation of gender relations" (Todorova 2009: 20).

Literatur

Beblo, M., Soete, B. (1999): Zum Zusammenhang von Ökonomie und Geschlecht am Beispiel der Haushaltstheorie, in: Beblo, M. u.a. (Hg.), *Ökonomie und Geschlecht – Volks- und betriebswirtschaftliche Analysen mit der Kategorie Geschlecht*, München, Mering: Rainer Hampp Verlag, 11-33.

Becker, G. (1993): *Der ökonomische Ansatz zur Erklärung menschlichen Verhaltens*, 2. Auflage, Tübingen: Mohr.

Biesecker, A., Kesting, S. (2003): *Mikroökonomik – Eine Einführung aus sozialökologischer Perspektive*, München, Wien: R. Oldenbourg Verlag.

Blau, F., Ferber, M., Winkler, A. (2009): *The Economics of Women, Men and Work*, 6. Auflage, London u.a.: Prentice Hall.

Bofinger, P. (2003): *Grundzüge der Volkswirtschaftslehre – Eine Einführung in die Wissenschaft von Märkten*, München: Pearson Studium.

Boulding, K. (1973): Ökonomie als eine Moralwissenschaft, in: Vogt, H. (Hg.), *Seminar: Politische Ökonomie*, Frankfurt a.M.: Suhrkamp, 103-125 (zitiert nach Bofinger, P. (2003), 97.

Danby, C. (2004): Toward a Gendered Post Keynesianism: Subjectivity and Time in a Nonmodernist Framework, in: *Feminist Economics*, 10(3), 55-75.

Elson, D. (2010): Macroeconomic Policy and Employment generation: Gender Dimensions, in: Bauhardt, C., Caglar, G. (Hg.), *Gender and Economics*, Wiesbaden: VS Verlag, 221-232.

European Commission (2011): Labour Market Developments in Europe 2011, European Economy 2011.http://ec.europa.eu/economy_finance/publications/european_ economy-/2011/pdf/ee-2011-2_en.pdf/ (20.9.2015)

Ferber, M., Nelson, J. (Hg.) (2003): *Feminist Economics Today: Beyond Economic Men*, Chicago, London: Chicago University Press.

Folbre, N. (2001): *The invisible heart: Economics and Family Values*, New York: The New Press.

Gustafsson, S. (1997): Feminist Neo-Classical Economics: Some Examples, in: Dijkstra, A., Plantenga, J. (Hg.), *Gender and Economics – A European Perspective*, London, New York: Routledge, 36-53.

Heine, M., Herr, H. (2003): *Volkswirtschaftslehre*, 3. Auflage, München: Oldenbourg.

Humphries, J. (1995): Economics, Gender and Equal Opportunities, in: Dies., Rubery, J. (Hg.), *The Economics of Equal Opportunities, Equal Opportunity Commission*, Manchester, 55-86.

Humphries, J., Rubery, J. (1984): The Reconstitution of the Supply Side of the Labour Market: the Relative Autonomy of Social Reproduction, in: *Cambridge Journal of Economics*, 8(4), 331-346.

Jacobsen, J. (2007): *The Economics of Gender*, 3. Auflage, Malden/USA u.a.: Blackwell.

Jaumotte, F. (2003), Female Labour Force Participation: Past Trends and Main Determinants in OECD Countries. OECD Economics Department Working Papers, No. 376, OECD Publishing.http://dx.doi.org/10.1787/082872464507

Karamessini, M., Rubery, J. (2014): *Women and Austerity. The Economic Crisis and the Future for Gender Equality*, Oxon, New York: Routledge.

Knapp, U. (2002), Beschäftigung und Geschlechterverhältnis, in: Maier, F., Fiedler, A. (Hg.), *Gender Matters – Feministische Analysen zur Wirtschafts- und Sozialpolitik*, fhw- Forschung 42/2003, Berlin: edition sigma, 11-60.

Knapp, U. (1997): Wirtschaft für Frauen – eine ethische Frage? Eine kritische Auseinandersetzung mit einigen ökofeministischen Positionen, in: Evangelische Akademie Iserlohn, Tagungsprotokolle, Tagungsprotokoll 6/1997, 5-32.

Krug, B. (1997): Discrimination Against Women: A Neoinstitutionalist Perspective, in: Dijkstra, A., Plantenga, J. (Hg.), *Gender and Economics – A European Perspective*, London, New York: Routledge, 54-72.

Löfström, A. (2009): Gender Equality, Economic Growth and Employment, EUstudie _sidvis, http://ec.europa.eu/social/BlobServlet?docId=3988&langId=en

Madörin, M. (2010): Care Ökonomie – eine Herausforderung für die Wirtschaftswissenschaften, in: Bauhardt, C., Caglar, G. (Hg.), *Gender and Economics*, Wiesbaden: VS Verlag, 81-104.

Maier, F. (1994): Das Wirtschaftssubjekt hat (k)ein Geschlecht – Oder: Bemerkungen zum gesicherten Wissen der Ökonomen zur Geschlechterfrage, in: Regenhard, U., Maier, F., Carl, A.-H. (Hg.), *Ökonomische Theorien und Geschlechterverhältnis – Der männliche Blick der Wirtschaftswissenschaften*, fhw Forschung 23/24, Berlin: edition sigma, 15-39.

Maier, F. (2011): Macroeconomic regimes in OECD countries and the interrelation with gender orders, in: Young, B., Bakker, I., Elson, D. (Hg.), *Questioning financial governance from a feminist perspective*, Routledge IAFFE Advances in Feminist Economics, 11-37.

Manske, A., Young, B. (2002): Engendering der Makroökonomie: Eine Einleitung, in: *femina politica, Zeitschrift für feministische Politik-Wissenschaft*, 11(1), 9-12.

Miranda, V. (2011): Cooking, Caring and Volunteering: Unpaid Work Around the World, OECD Social, Employment and Migration Working Papers, No. 116, OECD Publishing. http://dx.doi.org/10.1787/5kghrjm8s142-en

Nelson, J. (1996): *Feminism, Objectivity and Economics*, London, New York: Routledge.

OECD (2012): *Closing the Gender Gap – Act now*, Paris: OECD publishing.

Ott, N. (1993): Die Rationalität innerfamilialer Entscheidungen als Beitrag zur Diskriminierung weiblicher Arbeit, in: Grözinger, G., Schubert, R., Backhaus, J. (Hg.), *Jenseits von Diskriminierung – Zu den Bedingungen weiblicher Arbeit in Beruf und Familie*, Marburg: Metropolis, 113-146.

Pigou, A.C. (1960): *The Economics of Welfare*, London: Macmillan, 2. Aufl. 1924, 4. Aufl. 1932 (zitiert nach: Pujol, M. (1992), *Feminism and Anti-Feminism in Early Economic Thought*, Aldershot: Edward Elgar).

Pujol, M. (1995): Into the Margin!, in: Kuiper, E., Sap, J. (Hg.), *Out of the Margin – Feminist Perspectives on Economics*, London, New York: Routledge, 17-34.

Schmitt, N. (2014): Gender Stereotypes and Individual Economic Decision Making, Inauguraldissertation Europa Universität Viadrina Frankfurt/Oder, Manuskript.

Seiz, J.A. (1995): Epistemology and the Tasks of Feminist Economics, in: *Feminist Economics*, 1(2), 110-118.

Seyda, S. (2003): Frauenerwerbstätigkeit und Geburtenverhalten, in: *IW-Trends*, 2(2003), 1-19.

Statistisches Bundesamt (2003): *Wo bleibt die Zeit? Die Zeitverwendung der Bevölkerung in Deutschland 2001/2002*, Bonn.

Stotsky, J. (2006): Gender and its relevance to macroeconomic policy: a survey, IMF working paper WP /06/233, Washington: International Monetary Fund.

Todorova, Z. (2009): Employer of Last Resort Policy and Feminist Economics: Social Provisioning and Socialization of Investment, Center for Full Employment and Price Stability, Working Paper # 56, http://econpapers.repec.org/paper/prampra pa/16240.htm

Weck-Hannemann, H. (2003): Frauen in der Ökonomie und Frauenökonomik: Zur Erklärung geschlechtsspezifischer Unterschiede in der Wirtschaft und in den Wirtschaftswissenschaften, in: *Perspektiven der Wirtschaftspolitik*, 1(2), 199-220.

Woolley, F.R. (1993): The Feminist Challenge to Neo-classical Economics, in: *Cambridge Journal of Economics*, 17(4), 485-500.

Herausforderungen und Grenzen der Lohnpolitik

Alexander Herzog-Stein und Gustav Horn

1. Lohnverhandlungen heute

Das Ritual der alljährlichen Lohnverhandlungen gerät immer wieder in die Kritik derjenigen, die glauben, dass ohnehin ein Ergebnis von vorneherein feststünde und der Rest ein Schaulaufen gegenüber der eigenen Mitgliedschaft sei. Ohne zu bestreiten, dass die Überzeugung der eigenen Mitgliedschaft ein wichtiger Teil von Tarifverhandlungen ist, wird diese Kritik dennoch der Komplexität der Anforderungen an ein „vernünftiges" Tarifergebnis nicht gerecht. Auch wenn Tarifverhandlungen auf Branchen oder gar nur Unternehmensebene stattfinden, steht doch die Frage nach den gesamtwirtschaftlichen Wirkungen eines Tarifabschlusses immer im Raum. Dies kann Zielkonflikte zur Folge haben, die gelöst werden müssen, sollen nicht letztlich alle Unternehmen mit ihren Beschäftigten leiden. Gleichzeitig sind Veränderungen im Wirtschaftsgeschehen wie der zunehmenden Heterogenität oder der Gefahr eines nachlassenden Produktivitätsfortschritts Rechnung zu tragen.

Diesen komplexen Problemen, mit denen sich Hansjörg Herr auch immer wieder beschäftigt hat, widmet sich der folgende Beitrag. Dem kommt vor dem Hintergrund einer immer noch schwelenden Krise des Euroraums eine besondere Bedeutung zu.

2. Was ist eine makroökonomisch orientierte Lohnpolitik?

Die Lohnpolitik ist neben der Geld- und der Fiskalpolitik das dritte zentrale makroökonomische Politikfeld. Sie unterscheidet sich jedoch aufgrund mehrerer Aspekte merklich von ihnen. So nimmt schon ihre entscheidende Stellgröße, der Arbeitslohn, im Hinblick auf seine grundsätzliche ökonomische

Bedeutung eine Sonderstellung ein, die sich aus der „Doppelfunktion des Lohnes als Kosten- und Nachfragefaktor" (Schulten 2004: 111) ergibt. Folglich ist die gesamtwirtschaftliche Lohnfindung keine einfache Setzung eines wichtigen ökonomischen Parameters, wie beispielsweise die Festsetzung der Höhe des Zinssatzes durch die Geldpolitik, sondern das Ergebnis eines komplexen Verhandlungsprozesses, der vielfältigen Einflussfaktoren ausgesetzt ist und insbesondere auch durch die makroökonomische Ausrichtung von Geld- und Fiskalpolitik beeinflusst wird, sodass die makroökonomische Lohnfindung zu einem hohen Grad als endogen angesehen werden muss. Insbesondere ergibt sich die Lohnsetzung aus dem Verhalten zweier antagonistischer Akteure, den Arbeitgeberverbänden und den Gewerkschaften, und jeder Lohnabschluss ist ein Kompromiss. Hinzu kommt, dass nicht über alle Löhne verhandelt wird, sondern nur über die, die im Geltungsbereich eines Tarifvertrags angesiedelt sind.

Je nach institutioneller Ausgestaltung des Arbeitsmarktes läuft der Lohnfindungsprozess sehr unterschiedlich ab. Erinnert werden soll hierbei insbesondere an den grundsätzlichen Unterschied zwischen einer kollektiven Lohnfindung und der arbeitsvertraglichen Festlegung des Arbeitslohns auf der Individualebene zwischen Arbeitnehmer und Arbeitgeber. Darüber hinaus gibt es im Unterschied zur Geld- und Fiskalpolitik mit ihren expliziten Akteuren, der Zentralbank und dem Staat, für die Lohnpolitik aus Sicht der ökonomischen Theorie nicht einen, sondern zwei Hauptakteure, Arbeitnehmer und Arbeitgeber bzw. ihre kollektiven Vertretungen (tarifliche Lohnpolitik), die sich die Zuständigkeit teilen müssen. Der dritte Akteur, der Staat als Gesetz- und Arbeitgeber, spielt je nach praktischer Ausgestaltung der Lohnfindung eine mehr oder minder große Rolle (staatliche Lohnpolitik).

Während die Lohnpolitik in der Neoklassik verstärkt auf der mikroökonomischen Ebene angesiedelt ist, hat die Idee einer gesamtwirtschaftlichen Lohnpolitik ihren Ursprung im Keynesianismus der Nachkriegszeit und ist in der keynesianischen Gedankenwelt seit Keynes selbst tief verwurzelt.[1] So ist die gesamtwirtschaftliche Bedeutung der Lohnbildung nach Herr und Horn (2012: 1ff.) erheblich, lassen sich doch nicht weniger als drei gewichtige Einflussbereiche der Lohnfindung ausmachen: Erstens beeinflusst die Lohnbildung über die Einkommenswirkung des Lohnes direkt und über ihre Verteilungswirkung aufgrund der unterschiedlichen Konsumneigungen verschiedener Einkommensgruppen indirekt die Binnennachfrage. Zweitens ist sie maßgeblicher Faktor für die Preisstabilität. Drittens schließlich hat die nationale

---

[1] Für eine ausführliche Darstellung siehe Schulten (2004), insbesondere Kapitel 4.2.

Lohnfindung mit der Schaffung der Europäischen Währungsunion eine weitere, europäische, Dimension erhalten:

„Mit der Abschaffung der Wechselkurse bei gleichzeitiger Aufrechterhaltung weitgehender nationaler Souveränitäten, die sich unter anderem in einem Verzicht auf europaweite Transfersysteme niederschlägt, stellt sich das Problem struktureller Leistungsbilanzungleichgewichte als Folge unterschiedlicher Wettbewerbsbedingungen in den Volkswirtschaften der einzelnen Mitgliedsstaaten. Die Löhne sind hierfür ein wesentlicher Faktor." (Herr/Horn 2012: 2)

Eine *makroökonomisch orientierte Lohnpolitik* (Herr/Horn 2012) sollte allen diesen gesamtwirtschaftlichen Aspekten der Lohnfindung Rechnung tragen und sie möglichst unter einen Hut bringen. Aus theoretischer Sicht gelingt der Lohnpolitik diese schwierige Aufgabe, wenn sich die Lohnentwicklung am gesamtwirtschaftlichen Verteilungsspielraum, der Summe aus dem Trend des gesamtwirtschaftlichen Produktivitätsfortschritts und der Zielinflationsrate der Zentralbank, orientiert (siehe Heine et al. 2005). Dabei sollte nicht nur die gesamtwirtschaftliche Lohnfindung makroökonomisch orientiert sein, sondern unabhängig davon, ob auf Branchen- oder auf Unternehmensebene über die Lohnentwicklung verhandelt wird, sollte generell der gesamtwirtschaftliche Verteilungsspielraum und damit der gesamtwirtschaftliche Produktivitätsfortschritt und das Inflationsziel der Zentralbank Richtschnur für die Lohnfindung sein. So wird gewährleistet, dass Branchen mit geringeren branchenspezifischen Produktivitätsfortschritten nicht systematisch von der Lohnentwicklung abgekoppelt werden. Durch den Fokus auf die trendmäßige Entwicklung der Produktivität anstelle des aktuellen Produktivitätsfortschritts und das Inflationsziel der Zentralbank anstelle der aktuellen Inflationsentwicklung wird zudem ein prozyklischer konjunktureller Impuls von Seiten der Lohnpolitik ausgeschlossen und eine makroökonomisch orientierte Lohnpolitik wirkt somit konjunkturell stabilisierend.

Nominale Lohnsteigerungen, die den Vorgaben einer makroökonomisch orientierten Lohnpolitik folgen, leisten somit einen wichtigen Beitrag zur Stabilisierung der gesamtwirtschaftlichen Entwicklung: Sie stabilisieren die effektive Nachfrage, leisten eine wichtige Voraussetzung für die Stabilität der Preisentwicklung, da von ihnen weder deflationäre noch inflationäre Impulse ausgehen, und im Rahmen eines gemeinsamen Währungsraums mit anderen Volkswirtschaften tragen sie mit dazu bei, dass makroökonomische Ungleichgewichte aufgrund von auseinanderlaufenden außenwirtschaftlichen Wettbewerbspositionen möglichst nicht entstehen. Gleichzeitig ergeben sich aus ihr aber Grenzen der tariflichen Lohnpolitik, die nicht immer einfach mit den einzelwirtschaftlichen Interessen der Unternehmen wie auch der Arbeitnehmer zu vereinbaren sind und deshalb zeitweise große Herausforderungen für die Tarifparteien darstellen, denen die wichtige Funktion zukommt, die berechtigten einzelwirtschaftlichen Interessen mit den Notwendigkeiten einer makroökonomisch sinnhaften Lohnpolitik in Einklang zu bringen. Denn aus solch einer makroökonomisch orientierten Lohnpolitik ergibt sich laut Herr und Horn (2012: 5), dass (*a*) Reallöhne langfristig nur über eine Erhöhung der Produktivität angehoben werden können, (*b*) eine solche Lohnpolitik ein ungeeignetes Instrument ist, um die funktionale Einkommensverteilung zu verändern, und (*c*) Preissteigerungen infolge eines exogenen Kostenschocks sinkende Reallöhne zur Folge haben, da sowohl die Geld- als auch die Lohnpolitik die Preiseffekte eines solchen exogenen Schocks akzeptieren und passiv hinnehmen sollten. Umgekehrt ergeben sich Reallohnsteigerungen, wenn exogene Kostensenkungen wie z.B. durch sinkende Energiepreise auftreten, was z.B. 2015 der Fall war.

3. Das deutsche System der Lohnfindung

Die Lohnfindung in Deutschland muss im Kontext des deutschen Systems der industriellen Beziehungen gesehen werden, welches in der Bundesrepublik traditionell durch ein duales System der Arbeitsbeziehungen geprägt ist.[2] Auf der überbetrieblichen Ebene handeln Gewerkschaften und Arbeitgeberverbände als Tarifparteien autonom – geschützt vor staatlichen Interventionen bei der Lohnfindung durch die verfassungsrechtlich geschützte Tarifautonomie – Tarifverträge vor allem in Form von branchenbezogenen Flächentarifverträgen in Hinblick auf Gehalt, vertragliche Arbeitszeit und Arbeitsbedingungen aus. Auf der betrieblichen Ebene kommt in Betrieben mit mehr als fünf Beschäftigten die betriebliche Vertretung von Arbeitnehmerinteressen durch Betriebsräte hinzu, die durch das Betriebsverfassungsgesetz eine Vielzahl von Mitbestimmungsrechten haben.

Das System der industriellen Beziehungen war im zeitlichen Verlauf erheblichen Veränderungen unterworfen. In der Lohnfindung fand in den letzten drei Jahrzehnten ein Prozess der Dezentralisierung statt (siehe Behrens, 2013a: 215f.), wobei zwischen einer „organisierten" oder „unorganisierten"

---

[2] Für einen Überblicksartikel siehe Behrens (2013a).

(Traxler 1995) beziehungsweise einer „kontrollierten" oder „wilden" Dezentralisierung (Bispinck/Schulten 1999) zu unterscheiden ist. Infolge der „unorganisierten" oder „wilden" Dezentralisierung kam es zu einer erheblichen Schwächung der kollektiven Lohnfindung und folglich der Möglichkeiten einer makroökonomisch orientierten Lohnpolitik. Zwischen 1998 und 2013 ging die Tarifbindung in Westdeutschland von 76% auf 60% aller Beschäftigten zurück, in Ostdeutschland von 63% auf 47% (Bispinck/ WSI-Tarifarchiv 2015). Die Gründe hierfür sieht Behrens (2013b: 475) vor allem auf der Arbeitgeberseite, da die Organisationsleistung der Arbeitgeber in erheblichem Maße für die hohen Tarifdeckungsraten in Deutschland verantwortlich ist. Nachdem in Folge der deutschen Vereinigung zuerst von einer „Verbandsflucht" unzufriedener Mitgliedsunternehmen die Rede war, hat sich im weiteren Verlauf gezeigt, dass es sich wohl eher um eine „Reproduktionskrise" handeln dürfte, da Mitgliederverluste unter aus dem Markt verschwundenen Altunternehmen nicht durch Mitgliedergewinne bei neuen jungen Unternehmen wettgemacht werden konnten. Teilweise als Antwort auf ihre Mitgliederkrise führten die Arbeitgeber, insbesondere nach der Jahrtausendwende, sogenannte Mitgliedschaften ohne Tarifbindung (OT-Mitgliedschaften) ein, wodurch das Problem der rückläufigen Tarifbindung verschärft und die kollektive Lohnfindung weiter geschwächt wurde.[3]

Darüber hinaus kam es innerhalb des kollektivvertraglichen Lohnfindungssystems seit gut 30 Jahren zu einem Prozess der „organisierten" oder „kontrollierten" Dezentralisierung, der zunächst mit einer Flexibilisierung tarifvertraglicher Regelungen einherging und letztlich zu der Vereinbarung einer Vielzahl von Öffnungsklauseln in Tarifverträgen führte. Die bekannteste Tarifvereinbarung ist das „Pforzheimer Abkommen" aus dem Jahr 2004 in der Metall- und Elektroindustrie (Bispinck et al. 2010: 6). Durch diese „organisierte" oder „kontrollierte" Dezentralisierung sollte „der verbreiteten Tendenz zur inoffiziellen Unterschreitung von Tarifnormen" ein Ende bereitet und ein tarifvertraglicher Rahmen für solche betrieblichen Bedürfnisse durch die Tarifparteien geschaffen werden (Kädtler 2014: 444). Im Zuge der „organisierten" Dezentralisierung werden betriebliche Interessen und Umstände ebenfalls stärker berücksichtigt, jedoch wurde gleichzeitig die Bedeutung des Flächentarifvertrags für die Zukunft gesichert und eine kollektive Alternative auf die „wilde" Dezentralisierung gefunden. Dadurch wurde sichergestellt, dass weiterhin die formale und praktische Möglichkeit besteht, durch die kollektive Vereinbarung von Flächentarifverträgen Vereinbarungen im Sinne

---

[3] Für Details zu diesen Punkten siehe Behrens (2013b).

einer makroökonomisch orientierten Lohnpolitik zu verfolgen. Ob der Erhalt des Flächentarifvertrags durch die „organisierte" Dezentralisierung in der Praxis dauerhaft gesichert ist, kann derzeit aus wissenschaftlicher Sicht noch nicht abschließend beurteilt werden (Kädtler 2014: 443ff.).

Von Seiten der Politik wurde in der ersten Hälfte der 2000er Jahre eine Lohnfindung im Sinne einer makroökonomisch orientierten Lohnpolitik erheblich erschwert. Durch die einseitige und enge Ausrichtung der Arbeitsmarktreformen und den auf die Absenkung des Reservationslohns gerichteten Fokus wurde einseitig die Verhandlungsposition der Arbeitnehmer geschwächt. In Verbindung mit der anhaltend hohen Arbeitslosigkeit erschwerte dies eine Lohnentwicklung im Sinne einer makroökonomisch orientierten Lohnpolitik erheblich. In den letzten Jahren, insbesondere während der Finanzmarktkrise und danach, ist in der Politik wieder ein stärkeres Bekenntnis zur tariflichen Lohnfindung festzustellen, und die Einsicht hat an Bedeutung gewonnen, dass auch die Politik ihren Beitrag leisten muss, um das kollektive Lohnfindungssystem zu stärken und seine Vorteile zu erhalten. Konkret führte dies dazu, dass die Große Koalition 2015 mit dem Gesetz zur Stärkung der Tarifautonomie (Tarifautonomiestärkungsgesetz) erstmalig einen allgemeinen gesetzlichen Mindestlohn in Deutschland einführte und dabei explizit den Tarifparteien durch ihre Rolle in der Mindestlohnkommission die zentrale Rolle bei der Festlegung der Höhe dieser allgemeinen Lohnuntergrenze zuwies. Zudem wurden die Möglichkeiten der Allgemeinverbindlichkeitserklärung von Tarifverträgen wieder etwas erleichtert.

4. Lohnpolitik, Produktivität und Lohnentwicklung in Deutschland

Die gesamtwirtschaftliche Lohnentwicklung kann im Zeitraum der Jahre 1992 bis 2015 in drei Phasen unterteilt werden (Abb. 1). In der ersten Phase bis Mitte der neunziger Jahre war die Lohnentwicklung zunächst vor allem von der deutschen Vereinigung und der Absicht geprägt, durch eine möglichst schnelle Anpassung der Löhne gleiche Arbeits- und Lebensbedingungen zwischen Ost- und Westdeutschland herzustellen.

Entsprechend hoch fielen die von den Tarifparteien vereinbarten Lohnabschlüsse aus. Auffällig ist in diesem Zeitraum aber auch die relativ stark negative Lohndrift, das heißt der relativ deutliche Abstand zwischen den jährlichen Tariflohnsteigerungen und den gesamtwirtschaftlichen Zuwächsen der effektiven Stundenlöhne, den Bruttolöhnen und -gehältern je geleisteter Arbeitsstunde. Diese Lohndrift ist nicht einfach zu interpretieren. Generell ist jedoch davon auszugehen, dass die negative Lohndrift in diesen Jahren zu einem erheblichen Grad auf den schwierigen wirtschaftlichen Vereinigungsprozess und den damit einhergehenden drastischen Arbeitsplatzabbau in Ostdeutschland zurückzuführen ist.

Abbildung 1: Entwicklung Tariflöhne und Effektivlöhne

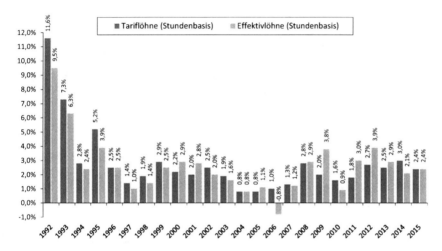

Quelle: Bundesbank (Tarifverdienste, Gesamtwirtschaft einschließlich aller Nebenvereinbarungen auf Stundenbasis), Statistisches Bundesamt: Fachserie 18, Reihe 1.2, Wiesbaden (Bruttolöhne und -gehälter je Arbeitnehmerstunde), eigene Berechnungen.

Ab 1996 kommt es zu einer langen Phase deutlich verhaltenerer Lohnsteigerungen; bis zum Krisenjahr 2009 sind die tariflichen ebenso wie die effektiven Lohnsteigerungen in jedem Jahr niedriger als drei Prozent. Insbesondere zwischen 2003 und 2007 liegt eine Phase ausgesprochen schwacher Lohnzuwächse. Im Jahr 2006 gingen die nominalen Effektivlöhne je Arbeitsstunde sogar zurück. Mit Ausnahme der Aufschwungjahre um die Jahrtausendwende ist die Lohndrift überwiegend negativ. Nach der Finanzmarktkrise lässt sich eine dritte Phase ausmachen. Im Vergleich zur vorherigen Phase nehmen die Löhne wieder etwas stärker zu. Die Zuwachsraten der Effektivlöhne betragen zeitweise drei Prozent und mehr.

Aus makroökonomischer Sicht ist ein bloßer Blick auf die Lohnentwicklung allein aber nicht aussagekräftig. Vielmehr muss sie in Relation zum gesamtwirtschaftlichen Verteilungsspielraum betrachtet werden (Abb. 2).

Abbildung 2: Entwicklung Verteilungsspielraum

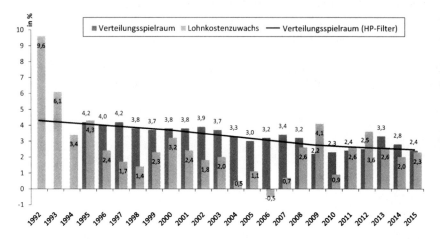

Quelle: Statistisches Bundesamt: Fachserie 18, Reihe 1.2, Wiesbaden, eigene Berechnungen. Berechnungen: Der Verteilungsspielraum ist die Summe der Veränderungsrate der Arbeitsproduktivität je Erwerbstätigenstunde und der Zielinflationsrate derEZB (1,9%). Bei der Veränderungsrate derArbeitsproduktivität je Erwerbstätigenstunde handelt es sich um die durchschnittliche Zunahme der letzten vier Jahre. Zusätzlich wird ein Verteilungsspielraum (HP-Filter) ausgewiesen, wo die Veränderungsrate mittels der Trendkomponente eines HP-Filters (Glättungsparameter = 100) ermittelt wurde. Der Lohnkostenzuwachs ist die jährliche Veränderungsrate derLohnkosten je Arbeitnehmerstunde.

Um den gesamten Beobachtungszeitraum seit Anfang der neunziger Jahre abbilden zu können, wurde der trendmäßige Produktivitätsfortschritt für die Ermittlung des gesamtwirtschaftlichen Verteilungsspielraums auf zwei verschiedene Arten berechnet. Neben der Verwendung eines gleitenden Durchschnitts der letzten vier Jahre (dunklere Balken), der bevorzugten Variante des Instituts für Makroökonomie und Konjunkturforschung (IMK), wird der Trend noch mittels des Hodrick-Prescott-Filters mit einem Glättungsparameter von 100 berechnet (durchgezogene Linie). Im Hinblick auf die Beurteilung der Lohnentwicklung in Deutschland seit der deutschen Wiedervereinigung ist die Wahl der Berechnungsmethode jedoch nicht relevant, insbesondere da der Fokus darauf gerichtet ist, ob die Lohnentwicklung über längere Zeiträume hinweg dem gesamtwirtschaftlichen Verteilungsspielraum entsprach. Ausreißer in einzelnen Jahren, nach oben oder unten, sind aufgrund von Sonderfaktoren immer möglich und letztlich für die Beurteilung nicht bedeutsam.

Insgesamt lässt sich feststellen, dass über den gesamten Zeitraum der Jahre 1992 bis 2015 die deutsche Lohnentwicklung die Vorgaben einer makroökonomisch orientierten Lohnpolitik nicht erfüllte. Über lange Zeiträume hinweg war genau das Gegenteil der Fall; die gesamtwirtschaftliche Lohnentwicklung war viel zu schwach. In der langen Phase zwischen 1996 und 2008 wurde der Verteilungsspielraum in keinem einzigen Jahr ausgeschöpft. Ganz im Gegenteil, in diesem Zeitraum lag der Lohnkostenanstieg teilweise erheblich unter dem, was im Sinne einer makroökonomisch orientieren Lohnpolitik für eine gesamtwirtschaftlich stabile Entwicklung notwendig gewesen wäre. In den letzten 24 Jahren war der Lohnkostenzuwachs lediglich in fünf Jahren höher als der ermittelte gesamtwirtschaftliche Verteilungsspielraum. Zwei dieser Jahre, 1992 und 1993, waren wie bereits weiter oben diskutiert, geprägt von der deutschen Vereinigung. Der merkliche Lohnkostenanstieg im Jahr 2009 war krisenbedingt und die Konsequenz der temporären Arbeitszeitverkürzung durch den Einsatz von Arbeitszeitkonten, Kurzarbeit und anderen Maßnahmen der intern-numerischen Flexibilität, die einen wichtigen Beitrag zur Beschäftigungssicherung während der Finanzmarktkrise leisteten. Die Stabilisierung der Monatslöhne und damit einhergehend der kurzfristige Anstieg der Stundenlöhne stabilisierten die effektive Nachfrage in der Wirtschafts- und Finanzkrise (Herzog-Stein et al. 2013). Das war ein wichtiger antizyklischer Impuls, der dazu beigetragen hat, dass Deutschland die Krise relativ rasch überwand. Gleichzeitig war der niedrige Lohnkostenzuwachs im darauffolgenden Jahr ebenfalls die, spiegelbildliche, Konsequenz dieser beschäftigungssichernden Krisenmaßnahmen.

Seit 2011 ist eine Rückkehr zu einer makroökonomisch orientierten Lohnpolitik auszumachen. So legten die Lohnkosten je Arbeitsstunde in den letzten fünf Jahren im Durchschnitt um 2,6% pro Jahr zu. Dies entspricht mehr oder weniger genau den Anforderungen einer makroökonomisch orientierten Lohnpolitik, der zufolge ein jährlicher Anstieg von rund 2,7% pro Jahr als stabilitätskonform anzusehen ist.

Besonders auffällig ist der deutliche Rückgang des stabilitätskonformen gesamtwirtschaftlichen Verteilungsspielraums. Lag er Anfang der 1990er Jahre noch bei über vier Prozent, so beläuft er sich aktuell lediglich auf rund zweieinhalb Prozent. Ursächlich hierfür ist die deutliche Reduktion des trendmäßigen Produktivitätsfortschritts, die kontinuierlich über den Beobachtungszeitraum auszumachen ist. Betrug der durchschnittliche jährliche Produktivitätsfortschritt je geleisteter Arbeitsstunde in den neunziger Jahren noch 2,0% und zwischen 2000 und 2007 noch durchschnittlich 1,7%, ist der Produktivitätsanstieg aktuell nun schon einige Jahre ausgesprochen schwach. Zwischen

2012 und 2015 belief sich der durchschnittliche jährliche Anstieg der Stundenproduktivität auf lediglich 0,5%. Dabei ist der aktuell zu beobachtende schwache Produktivitätsfortschritt kein (alleiniges) Dienstleistungsphänomen, denn auch in den industriellen Wirtschaftsbereichen ist der Produktivitätsanstieg am aktuellen Rand verhalten und im historischen Vergleich niedrig. Zwischen 2012 und 2015 nahm die Stundenproduktivität im Produzierenden Gewerbe durchschnittlich um 0,4% pro Jahr zu; im Verarbeitenden Gewerbe stagnierte sie faktisch in diesem Zeitraum.

Obwohl ab 1996 der gesamtwirtschaftliche Verteilungsspielraum nicht mehr ausgeschöpft wurde, trat der aus neoklassischer Sicht zu erwartende Effekt nicht ein. Vielmehr stieg die Arbeitslosigkeit bis 2005 deutlich an, und erst im Zuge des starken weltwirtschaftlichen Aufschwungs in der zweiten Hälfte der 2000er Jahre setzte danach der Rückgang der Arbeitslosigkeit ein. Genau umgekehrt scheint ein Schuh daraus zu werden. Die Verschlechterung der Arbeitsmarktsituation zwischen 1992 und 2005 schwächte die Verhandlungsposition der abhängig Beschäftigten, was sich dann ab Mitte der neunziger Jahre negativ auf die Lohnentwicklung auszuwirken begann. Die Arbeitsmarktreformen in der ersten Hälfte der 2000er Jahre schwächten die Verhandlungsposition der Arbeitnehmer weiter, die infolge der beschriebenen Veränderungen im deutschen System der industriellen Beziehungen ohnehin schon unter Druck stand. All dies wurde noch verstärkt durch eine falsche Ausrichtung der Fiskalpolitik in der ersten Hälfte der 2000er Jahre. Massive Steuersenkungen insbesondere für Unternehmen und Haushalte mit höheren Einkommen ab 2001 verursachten öffentliche Budgetdefizite, die die Regierung ab 2003 durch Ausgabensenkungen abzubauen versuchte. All dies belastete die Binnennachfrage in Deutschland anstatt sie zu stabilisieren, und infolgedessen entwickelte sich die Binnennachfrage in Deutschland über Jahre hinweg äußerst schwach (Herzog-Stein et al. 2013: 4ff.).

Die schwache Nachfrageentwicklung in Deutschland in Verbindung mit Nachfragebooms insbesondere in einigen südeuropäischen Staaten infolge der Einführung der gemeinsamen Währung hatte schwerwiegende Folgen für den gemeinsamen Währungsraum. Die zunehmenden Nachfragedifferentiale in den verschiedenen Mitgliedstaaten nach Einführung des Euros brachten Inflationsdifferentiale mit sich, die zu erheblichen Veränderungen der preislichen Wettbewerbsfähigkeit der Mitgliedstaaten und zum Aufbau von Leistungsbilanzungleichgewichten führten (Horn et al. 2009). Diese trugen zu einem gewichtigen Teil nach der Finanzmarktkrise mit zum Ausbruch der Eurokrise bei.

5. Herausforderungen für eine makroökonomisch orientierte Lohnpolitik

In einer immer komplexer werdenden Wirtschaftswelt, die sich zudem mit hoher Geschwindigkeit ändert, stellen sich hohe Herausforderungen für eine gesamtwirtschaftlich orientierte Lohnpolitik. Das gilt umso mehr, als es in Tarifverhandlungen häufig nicht nur um die Lohnfestsetzung geht, sondern auch um andere, häufig auch qualitative Ziele. Betriebliche Alterssicherung und Arbeitszeiten sind nur zwei weitere Dimensionen tarifvertraglichen Verhandelns.

Diese Mehrdimensionalität der Tarifverhandlungen erschwert eine gesamtwirtschaftliche Ausrichtung, da in solchen Verhandlungen Lohnprozente gegen andere Ziele getauscht werden. Daher ist es wichtig, diese in ihrer Kostenwirkung zu erfassen, um zumindest zu erkennen, ob gesamtwirtschaftliche Ziele erreicht oder verletzt werden. In den genannten Beispielen wäre dies zumindest leicht möglich. Diese Information ist insofern bedeutsam, als sie es erlaubt, adäquate flankierende Maßnahmen aus anderen Politikfeldern zu ergreifen.

Eine weitere Komplikation ergibt sich durch die zunehmende Heterogenität vor allem der Arbeitgeber- aber in einem gewissen Ausmaß auch der Arbeitnehmerseite. Auf der Arbeitgeberseite zeigen sich teilweise erhebliche Ertragsdivergenzen. Eine Orientierung am Durchschnitt würde daher auf der einen Seite zahlreiche Betriebe in Ertragsschwierigkeiten bringen, während andere hohe Gewinne ausweisen würden. In früheren Zeiten hätte man dies primär auf unterschiedliche Innovationsfähigkeit zurückgeführt. Würden sich die Tariflöhne am Durchschnitt der Unternehmen orientieren, hätte dies unter diesen Umständen den erwünschten Effekt, dass besonders innovative Unternehmen durch höhere Gewinne belohnt und weniger innovative durch niedrigere Erträge oder gar Verluste bestraft würden. Insgesamt entstünde dann ein Anreiz zu mehr Innovation, von dem letztlich die gesamte Volkswirtschaft profitieren würde. Auf der Arbeitnehmerseite wäre die Orientierung am Durchschnitt ein Beitrag zur Solidarität mächtigerer Berufsgruppen, die, wenn sie allein stünden, möglicherweise höhere Löhne durchsetzen würden, gegenüber weniger mächtigen, die auf diese Weise am gesamtwirtschaftlichen Wohlstandszuwachs stärker teilhaben, als wenn sie allein verhandeln würden. Aus gesamtwirtschaftlicher Sicht führt dies zu einer gleichmäßigeren Einkommensverteilung und begünstigt insbesondere innovative Unternehmen.

Diese im Grundsatz richtige Sichtweise ist in den vergangenen Jahren teilweise ins Wanken geraten. Das betrifft zum einen die Ursache der Heterogenität. Diese kann nicht mehr nur auf unterschiedliche Innovationsfähigkeit zurückgeführt werden. Vielmehr spiegeln sich in der Rentabilität vermehrt auch unterschiedlich starke Marktpositionen entlang der Wertschöpfungskette im globalen Wettbewerb wider. Große Endproduzenten vermögen häufig die Preise ihrer Zulieferer, die zudem teilweise Ausgründungen sind, massiv zu drücken, was deren Rentabilität beeinträchtigt. Gleiche Lohnsteigerungen würden daher Zulieferer nur deshalb in Schwierigkeiten bringen, weil sie eine schwache Marktposition gegenüber ihrem Endabnehmer haben. Durch die höheren Löhne wird ihre Position dann noch prekärer.

Vor allem aber wirkt die Drohung oder der Vollzug eines Austritts aus dem Arbeitgeberverband simplen Durchschnittszielen entgegen. Wenn Unternehmen der Meinung sind, die Tariflohnentwicklung sei für sie unter den gegebenen Bedingungen strukturell zu hoch, werden sie den Tarifbereich verlassen. Diese Drohung ist wirksam, weil unter den gegebenen Bestimmungen die Allgemeinverbindlichkeitserklärung von Tarifverträgen nur sehr restriktiv gehandhabt werden kann. Hemmend wirkt vor allem, dass die Verbände der Arbeitgeber zustimmen müssen. Mit der Einführung von OT-Mitgliedschaften in den Arbeitgeberverbänden ist dies aber nicht mehr in ihrem Interesse. Unter diesen Umständen haben die Arbeitgeberverbände somit ein hohes Drohpotenzial gegenüber an der Durchschnittsrendite orientierten Lohnabschlüssen, da sie die Gewerkschaften jederzeit mit einer geringeren Tarifabdeckung in Bedrängnis bringen können. Solange diese Praxis jedoch gilt, die die Unternehmensseite einseitig begünstigt, müssen die Gewerkschaften dies in ihrer Verhandlungsstrategie berücksichtigen.

Hinzu kommen (geringere) Heterogenitätsprobleme auf der Arbeitnehmerseite. Die Machtpositionen einzelner durch die Gewerkschaften vertretenen Berufsgruppen unterscheiden sich im Betrieb. Sehr deutlich ist dies im Fall einiger Unternehmen der öffentlichen Daseinsvorsorge. Es kann dann leicht die Tendenz entstehen, dass sich Berufsgruppen mit größerer Macht höhere Lohnzuwächse zuzubilligen wünschen als dem Rest der Belegschaft. Dass sich derartige Divergenzen aufschaukeln und letztendlich die Gewerkschaftsseite spalten können, haben die vergangenen Jahre gezeigt.

Wie können und sollen die Gewerkschaften mit den gesamtwirtschaftlichen Erfordernissen auf der einen Seite und der Heterogenität auf der anderen Seite unter den gegebenen Umständen umgehen? Durch den Prozess der „organisierten" oder „kontrollierten" Dezentralisierung wurden erhebliche Anstrengungen unternommen, um im Rahmen des Flächentarifvertrags den betrieblichen Flexibilitätsbedürfnissen und insbesondere dem Problem der heterogenen Ertragssituation auf Arbeitgeberseite Rechnung tragen zu können. Darüber hinaus muss es aber auch darum gehen, den Aspekt einer makroökonomisch orientierten Lohnpolitik im Auge zu behalten. Der gesamtwirtschaftliche Verteilungsspielraum aus gesamtwirtschaftlicher Trendproduktivität und Inflationsziel der Zentralbank stellt dabei einen Fixpunkt für die Lohnentwicklung dar. Wo tarifliche Öffnungsklauseln Spielräume für Betriebe in schwierigen wirtschaftlichen Situationen für (temporäre) Abweichungen nach unten bieten, sollten die Tarifparteien im Hinblick auf Tariflohnsteigerungen darüber nachdenken, als Zusatzelement und symmetrisch zu den Öffnungsklauseln vermehrt auch (Mindest-)Aufschläge auf das Tarifergebnis im Sinne von Abweichungen nach oben für Betriebe mit einer überdurchschnittlich guten Ertragslage zu vereinbaren. Welche Unternehmen in diesem Intervall einzuordnen sind, kann entweder bereits bei den zentralen Tarifverhandlungen festgelegt werden oder aber im Nachgang auf Unternehmensebene. Allerdings sollte dies dann von den Tarifparteien gebilligt werden müssen. Eine weitere Möglichkeit ist, mögliche Unterschreitungen des erstrebten Durchschnittswerts aufgrund von Öffnungsklauseln durch pauschale Aufschläge auf alle Löhne wieder auszugleichen, sodass der gesamtwirtschaftliche Verteilungsspielraum im Durchschnitt ausgeschöpft wird. So könnte am Ende ein flächentariflich vereinbarter Korridor vereinbart werden, der sicherstellt, dass im Durchschnitt eine makroökonomisch orientierte Lohnpolitik erreicht wird, die gleichzeitig verstärkten Heterogenitätsbedürfnissen Rechnung trägt.

Mit einer solchen Lohnbildung der gesamtwirtschaftlichen Flexibilität ließen sich die Konflikte in den Zielsetzungen überwinden. Sie würden sowohl den gesamtwirtschaftlichen Anforderungen gerecht als auch der zunehmenden Heterogenität des wirtschaftlichen Geschehens. Wichtige Voraussetzung hierfür wäre allerdings, dass die strukturelle Benachteiligung der Gewerkschaften durch die hohen Anforderungen an die Allgemeinverbindlichkeit in Kombination mit OT-Mitgliedschaften auf der Arbeitgeberseite beseitigt würde. Hier ist die Politik gefragt, denn sie hat es in der Hand. Durch eine Vereinfachung der Allgemeinverbindlichkeitserklärung würde die Attraktivität der OT-Mitgliedschaft im Arbeitgeberverband reduziert und das Tarifvertragssystem insgesamt gestärkt.

Literatur

Behrens, M. (2013a): Employment Relations in Germany, in: Frege, C.M., Kelly, J. (Hg.), *Comparative Employment Relations in the Global Economy*, London, New York: Routledge, 206-226.

Behrens, M. (2013b): Arbeitgeberverbände – auf dem Weg in den Dualismus?, in: *WSI-Mitteilungen*, 66(7), 473-481.

Bispinck, R., Schulten, T. (1999): Flächentarifvertrag und betriebliche Interessenvertretung, in: Müller-Jentsch, W. (Hg.), *Konfliktpartnerschaft, Akteure und Institutionen der industriellen Beziehungen*, München: Hampp, 185-212.

Bispinck, R., Dribbusch, H., Schulten, T. (2010): German Collective Bargaining in a European Perspective – Continuous Erosion or Re-Stabilisation of Multi-Employer Agreements?, WSI Discussion Paper No. 171, Düsseldorf.

Bispinck, R. und WSI-Tarifarchiv (2015): Statistisches Taschenbuch Tarifpolitik 2015, Düsseldorf.

Heine, M., Herr, H., Kaiser, C. (2005): Überforderte Lohnpolitik – Löhne im Spannungsfeld von Verteilung, Preisen und Beschäftigung, in: Hein, E., Heise, A., Truger, A. (Hg.), *Löhne, Beschäftigung, Verteilung und Wachstum – Makroökonomische Analysen*, Marburg: Metropolis Verlag, 93-118.

Herr, H., Horn, G.A. (2012): Lohnpolitik heute, IMK Policy Brief, Mai 2012.

Herzog-Stein, A., Lindner, F., Zwiener, R. (2013): Nur das Angebot zählt? Wie eine einseitige deutsche Wirtschaftspolitik Chancen vergeben hat und Europa schadet. IMK Report, Nr. 87.

Herzog-Stein, A., Horn, G.A., Stein, U. (2013): Macroeconomic Implications of the German Short-time Work Policy During the Great Recession, in: *Global Policy*, 4, Supplement 1, 30-40.

Horn, G., Joebges, H., Niechoj, T., Proano, C., Sturn, S., Tober, S., Truger, A., van Treeck, T. (2009): Von der Finanzkrise zur Weltwirtschaftskrise (I) – Wie die Krise entstand und wie sie überwunden werden kann, IMK-Report, Nr. 38.

Kädtler, J. (2014): Tarifpolitik und tarifpolitisches System, in: Schroeder, W. (Hg.), *Handbuch Gewerkschaften in Deutschland*, 2. Auflage, Wiesbaden: Springer VS, 425-464.

Schulten, T. (2004): *Solidarische Lohnpolitik in Europa. Zur Politischen Ökonomie der Gewerkschaften*, Hamburg: VSA-Verlag.

Traxler, F. (1995): Farewell to labour market associations? Organized versus disorganized decentralization as a map for industrial relations, in: Crouch, C., Traxler, F. (Hg.), *Organized Industrial Relations in Europe: What Future?*, Aldershot: Avebury, 3-19.

Verhindern nationale Lohnformeln Leistungsbilanzdefizite?

Die Rolle von Lohnstückkosten und Preisen in den Krisenländern des Euroraums

Heike Joebges und Camille Logeay

1. Einleitung

Hansjörg Herr hat allein und mit Koautoren zahlreiche Artikel zur Rolle der Lohnentwicklung nicht nur in Industrieländern sondern auch in Entwicklungsländern veröffentlicht. Statt Löhne in mikroökonomischer Tradition vor allem als Ergebnis von Angebot und Nachfrage auf dem Arbeitsmarkt zu betrachten, betont er zusammen mit Michael Heine deren makroökonomische Funktion: Durch die Auswirkungen auf Einkommen und Einkommensverteilung seien sie eine wichtige Bestimmungsgröße der Binnennachfrage (Heine et al. 2005). Im Euroraum komme durch den Wegfall unterschiedlicher Währungen hinzu, dass Löhne ein wichtiger Faktor für die Wettbewerbsfähigkeit einer Volkswirtschaft seien und damit auch zur Entwicklung struktureller Leistungsbilanzungleichgewichte beitragen. Daher sei ein gemeinsames lohnpolitisches Konzept für alle Mitgliedsländer des Euroraums nötig (Herr/Horn 2012). Die potentiell problematischen Auswirkungen unterschiedlicher Lohnentwicklungen im Euroraum wurden von Heine und Herr bereits zu Beginn der Einführung des Euros analysiert (Heine/Herr 1999) und mehrfach von Herr und Koautoren vor der Finanz- und Eurokrise aufgegriffen (z.B. Heine/Herr 2006; Herr/Kazandziska 2007).

Wichtig für das lohnpolitische Konzept ist, dass die Lohnentwicklung und vor allem die Lohndispersion nach Heine und Herr nicht vor allem technologischen Entwicklungen geschuldet sei, sondern durch Arbeitsmarktinstitutionen, Wirtschaftspolitik und internationale Entwicklungen beeinflusst werde.

Für das Niveau der Lohnentwicklung wird eine Orientierung am durchschnittlichen nationalen Produktivitätswachstum plus Zielinflationsrate der Zentralbank empfohlen (für Deutschland siehe Heine et al. 2005; Herr 2004). Müssten solche Lohnformeln von den Mitgliedsländern des Euroraums eingehalten werden, würden sie auch dazu beitragen, dass sich deren Inflationsraten nicht so stark auseinanderentwickeln, da Lohn- und Preisentwicklungen stark korrelieren. In einem gemeinsamen Währungsraum mit einheitlicher Geldpolitik führen persistente Inflationsdifferenzen aus nationaler Sicht zu einer prozyklischen Geldpolitik, die divergierende Konjunkturzyklen verstärkt. Daher waren solche Inflationsdivergenzen schon zu Beginn der Europäischen Währungsunion (EWU) eine Sorge der EZB, die in zahlreichen Publikationen geäußert wurde (z.B. ECB 2003).

Bis zur Eurokrise hatten sich einige makroökonomische Kenngrößen wie Lohnstückkosten, Inflationsraten und Leistungsbilanzsalden sehr unterschiedlich entwickelt. Divergenzen entstanden vor allem zwischen Deutschland und den „Krisenländern" des Euroraums, Griechenland, Spanien, Irland, Italien und Portugal.[1] Die Finanzkrise und deren Folgen setzten den in den Krisenländern kontinuierlich steigenden Leistungsbilanzdefiziten ein Ende (Abb. 1), ebenso wie der bis dahin überdurchschnittlichen Entwicklung von Preisen und Lohnstückkosten. Da die Entstehung der Leistungsbilanzdefizite vor allem auf die Verschlechterung der Wettbewerbsfähigkeit im Zuge von Lohnsteigerungen oberhalb des Produktivitätsanstieges zurückgeführt wurde, lag ein besonderer Fokus auf der Reduzierung der Lohnstückkosten zur Verbesserung der preislichen Wettbewerbsfähigkeit (siehe z.B. IMF 2013; European Commission 2013). Diese konnten zwar in allen Krisenländern reduziert werden, allerdings auf Kosten der binnenwirtschaftlichen Entwicklung. Feigl und Zuckerstätter kritisieren die Verengung auf wettbewerbsfähige Lohnstückkosten, die „… zu einer Überschätzung der Bedeutung der Warenexporte und deren Preise bei Unterschätzung von Gesamtnachfrage- und Vermögenseinkommensentwicklung führt" (Feigl/Zuckerstätter 2013: 1).

Angesichts der hohen Belastung des Faktors Arbeit durch Beschäftigungsabbau und schwache Lohnentwicklung widmet sich dieser Beitrag der Frage, inwieweit die Reduzierung der Lohnstückkosten vollständig in den Preisen weitergegeben wurde und damit auch wirksam werden konnte. Schon für den Zeitraum vor der Finanzkrise zeigen Feigl und Zuckerstätter (2013) auf Basis einer Zerlegung der Preisentwicklung für Deutschland, dass die Gewinnentwicklung problematischer für die Exportentwicklung war als die der Lohn-

---

[1] Kleinere Krisenländer wie z.B. Zypern werden hier nicht explizit behandelt.

stückkosten. Ziel dieses Beitrags ist zu klären, ob das auch für den Zeitraum nach der Finanzkrise der Fall ist. Die Antwort darauf soll auch dazu dienen, zu klären, ob das von Herr und Horn (2012) bzw. Herr und Kazandziska (2007) geforderte lohnpolitische Konzept ausreicht, um eine problematische Auseinanderentwicklung von Lohnstückkosten, Leistungsbilanzsalden und Inflationsentwicklungen im Euroraum zu verhindern.[2]

Der folgende Abschnitt widmet sich zunächst der Entwicklung der Leistungsbilanzsalden in den Krisenländern seit der Finanzkrise, um zu untersuchen, inwieweit die Reduzierung der zuvor gestiegenen Defizite auf gesteigerten Exporterfolgen oder reduzierten Importen beruht. Abschnitt 3 untersucht die wichtigsten makroökonomischen Faktoren für die Rückgänge: preisliche Wettbewerbsfähigkeit und die Entwicklung von Inlands- und Auslandsnachfrage. Abschnitt 4 analysiert den Zusammenhang zwischen Lohnstückkostenentwicklung und inländischer Inflationsrate. Der letzte Abschnitt fasst zusammen und beantwortet die Einleitungsfragen. Es soll deutlich werden, dass die Lohnstückkostenrückgänge weder in den Exportpreisen noch bei den inländischen Preisen vollständig weitergegeben wurden. Trotzdem trugen sie zum Abbau der Leistungsbilanzdefizite bei. Die von Feigl und Zuckerstätter (2013) konstatierte Bedeutung der Gewinnentwicklung scheint aber auch für den Zeitraum nach der Finanzkrise von Belang zu sein.

2. Abbau der Leistungsbilanzdefizite im Euroraum

Die bis zur Finanzkrise steigenden Leistungsbilanzdefizite hatten in den Krisenländern zu zunehmenden Auslandsverbindlichkeiten geführt. Die Krisenländer waren zu Nettoschuldnern gegenüber dem Ausland geworden. Die Nettoauslandspositionen lagen nach Daten des Internationalen Währungsfonds für Spanien, Portugal, Irland und Griechenland 2010 bei ungefähr 100% des BIP. Nur Italien wies mit ca. 25% des BIP eine deutlich geringere Nettoverschuldung gegenüber dem Ausland auf (siehe auch Joebges/Logeay 2012, für aktuellere Zahlen European Commission 2015: 17).

---

[2] Herr und Kazandziska fordern zusätzlich zur Vermeidung krisenhafter Prozesse im Euroraum aufgrund unterschiedlicher Lohnstückkostenentwicklungen ein gemeinsames Lohnverhandlungssystem, europaweite Mindestlöhne, wenn Löhne zu moderat steigen, aber auch EU-Besteuerungsregeln, wenn Löhne zu excessiv steigen (Herr/Kazandziska 2007).

2.1 Rückgang der Leistungsbilanzdefizite

Die Finanzkrise und deren Folgen setzten den bis dahin kontinuierlich steigenden Leistungsbilanzdefiziten ein Ende. Der Abbau der Defizite erfolgte in Spanien ab dem Jahr 2008, in den anderen Krisenländern ab 2009 (Abb. 1). Seitdem sind die Defizite in allen Krisenländern kontinuierlich zurückgegangen und in Irland bereits seit dem Jahr 2010 (mit Ausnahme des Jahres 2012) positiv, in den anderen Krisenländern seit 2013 (Abb. 1).

Da die Leistungsbilanzdefizite mit Ausnahme Irlands vor allem auf dem Außenhandel beruhen, wird im Folgenden die Entwicklung von Exporten und Importen von Gütern und Dienstleistungen und damit der Außenbeitrag genauer betrachtet. Es ist aber zu berücksichtigen, dass auch die Bilanz der Erwerbs- und Vermögenseinkommen zur Anpassung beigetragen hat, neben den weniger relevanten laufenden Übertragungen (vgl. z.B. IMF 2013).

Abbildung 1: Leistungsbilanzsalden der Krisenländer des Euroraums, in % des jeweiligen BIP

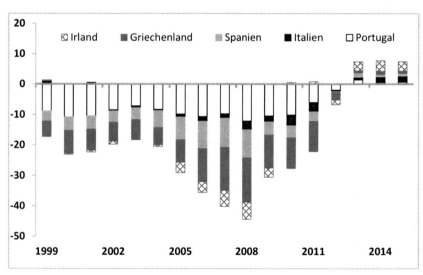

Quelle: IWF, WEO, Oktober 2015

2.2 Entwicklung von Exporten und Importen

Was hat vor allem zum Abbau der Leistungsbilanzdefizite in den Krisenländern geführt – ein Anstieg der Exporte oder der Rückgang der Importe? Beides war in den Krisenländern beobachtbar. Im Zuge der weltweiten Rezession im Jahr 2009 brachen die Exporte in allen betrachteten Ländern ein (Abb. 2). 2010 verzeichneten die Exporte der Krisenländer eine sehr schnelle und kräftige Erholung, die dazu führte, dass die Exporte in Irland, Spanien und Portugal annähernd wieder die Niveaus vor dem Rezessionsjahr erreichten. Für Italien war das erst ab 2013 der Fall. In Griechenland dagegen erholten sich die Exporte deutlich langsamer.

Abbildung 2: Entwicklung von Exporten und Importen in den Krisenländern, real, 1999=100

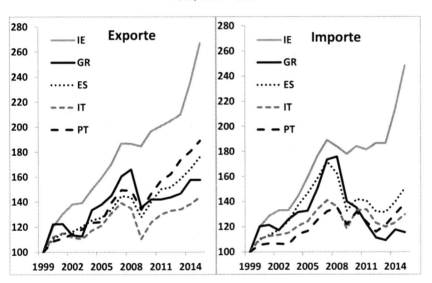

Anmerkungen: Preisbereinigte Werte; IE = Irland, GR = Griechenland, ES = Spanien, IT = Italien, PT = Portugal

Quellen: AMECO (OXGS, OMGS), Stand: Anfang März 2016

Betrachtet man die Importentwicklung, zeigt sich, wie relevant diese vor allem im Zeitraum von der Finanzkrise bis ungefähr 2013 für die Reduzierung der Leistungsbilanzsalden waren: Die Importe sind in den Krisenländern 2008/2009 eingebrochen. Nur in Irland haben sie sich in den letzten zwei

Jahren so stark erholt, dass das Vorkrisenniveau deutlich überschritten ist. In allen anderen Ländern ist dies nicht der Fall (Abb. 2). Zudem verdecken die Indexzahlen, dass die Importe mengenmäßig höher waren als die Exporte, sodass der Rückgang für die Leistungsbilanz via Außenbeitrag relevanter war. Seit 2013/2014 steigen die Importe in allen Krisenländern wieder und wirken damit nicht mehr entlastend auf die Leistungsbilanz.

2.3 Zwischenfazit

Der seit der Finanzkrise beobachtbare Rückgang der Leistungsbilanzdefizite der Krisenländer beruht sowohl auf schrumpfenden Importen als auch auf einem Anstieg der Exporte. Die Daten deuten darauf hin, dass zumindest im Zeitraum direkt nach der Finanzkrise der stärkste Rückgang der Leistungsbilanzsalden über den Einbruch der Importe erfolgte, die bereits ab 2008 reagierten.

Die Exporte stiegen dagegen erst ab 2010 an, nach dem durch die Finanzkrise bedingten Einbruch im Jahr 2009. Ihr Wachstum schwächte sich zwar vor allem für Griechenland und Italien vorübergehend ab dem Jahr 2012 ab, spätestens seit 2014 ist aber in allen Krisenländern ein hohes Exportwachstum zu beobachten, das zu den Leistungsbilanzüberschüssen beiträgt. Insgesamt scheint daher die stärkste Entlastung in der ersten Phase nach der globalen Finanzkrise von den Importen gekommen zu sein. Spätestens seit 2014 kann der Entlastungseffekt nur von den Exporten kommen, da die Importe seitdem in allen Krisenländern wieder steigen.

3. Faktoren für den Abbau der Leistungsbilanzdefizite

Für die ständige Zunahme der Leistungsbilanzdefizite seit Einführung des Euros wurde vielfach die stetige Verschlechterung der preislichen Wettbewerbsfähigkeit in den Krisenländern verantwortlich gemacht. Wird dieser Faktor als wesentlich angesehen, wird folgerichtig die Verbesserung der Leistungsbilanzsalden vor allem auf den Anstieg der preislichen Wettbewerbsfähigkeit zurückgeführt (siehe u.a. IMF 2013; European Commission 2013).

3.1 Entwicklung der preislichen Wettbewerbsfähigkeit

Preisliche Wettbewerbsfähigkeit eines Landes bezüglich seiner Exporte kann über unterschiedliche Indikatoren gemessen werden. Eine gebräuchliche Messung erfolgt über die nominalen Lohnstückkosten der gesamten Volkswirtschaft bzw. ausgewählter Sektoren. Die Lohnstückkosten messen nur die Arbeitskosten je Produktionseinheit, nicht aber die Herstellungskosten insgesamt, ebenso wenig wie Gewinnaufschläge durch die Unternehmen. Ein alternativer Indikator für preisliche Wettbewerbsfähigkeit ist daher der Exportpreisindex, der den durchschnittlichen (gewichteten) Preis misst, der für tatsächlich erfolgte Exporte gezahlt wurde. Beide Indikatoren zur Messung preislicher Wettbewerbsfähigkeit sind nicht unumstritten, haben sich aber in empirischen Untersuchungen als signifikante Erklärungsvariablen durchgesetzt, ohne dass es theoretisch noch empirisch eindeutige Argumente dafür gäbe, welcher Indikator vorzuziehen sei (Ca'Zorzi/Schnatz 2007: 8ff.; Chinn 2006; Herzog-Stein et al. 2013a).

Der Vergleich der Lohnstückkostenentwicklung mit der Entwicklung der Exportpreise (Abb. 3) zeigt zumindest für die ersten Krisenjahre eine Auseinanderentwicklung und deutet darauf hin, dass Veränderungen der Lohnstückkosten nicht in den Exportpreisen weitergegeben wurden.[3] Das war in vielen Krisenländern auch schon vor der Krise der Fall, ist aber direkt nach Kriseneinbruch bis 2012 augenfällig: Die Exportpreise nahmen trotz massiven Rückgangs der Lohnstückkosten (bis auf in Italien) zu, was eine Ausweitung von anderen Verteilungskomponenten wie Gewinn- und Kapitaleinkommen ermöglicht hat. Dass das auch der Fall war, wurde durch frühere Analysen von der Europäischen Kommission und dem Internationalen Währungsfonds gestützt (European Commission 2013; IMF 2013). Seit 2013 sinken jedoch auch die Exportpreise in allen Krisenländern. Im Jahr 2015 sind sie aber insbesondere in Irland wieder gestiegen, aber auch leicht in Spanien.

---

[3] Die bivariate Korrelation für 33 Länder (Europa und die Türkei) zwischen den Zuwächsen beider Variablen für die Zeiträume 2000-2007 bzw. 2008-2015 hat sich von 83% auf 57% reduziert.

Abbildung 3: Exportpreisindex und Lohnstückkosten in den Krisenländern, 1999=100

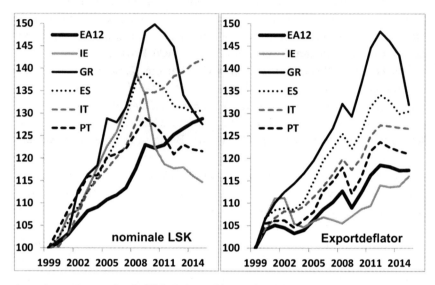

Anmerkung: Gesamtwirtschaftliche Lohnstückkosten, bereinigt
Quelle: AMECO (PLCD, PXGS), Stand: März 2016

3.2 Entwicklung der Nachfrage aus Inland und Ausland

Für Importe und Exporte spielen nicht nur die Unterschiede in den Preisen eine Rolle, sondern auch die Nachfrage danach. Dabei ist zu berücksichtigen, dass auch die Qualität der Güter und Dienstleistungen sowie deren Struktur über die Exporterfolge eines Landes entscheidet (vgl. z.B. Decramer et al. 2014 für Belgien). Es gibt aber kaum verlässliche Indikatoren für nicht-preisliche Wettbewerbsfähigkeit, sodass dieser Aspekt im Weiteren nicht verfolgt wird. Stattdessen wird auf die Entwicklung von inländischer versus ausländischer Nachfrage abgehoben: Während die Nachfrage nach Importen neben den relativen Importpreisen vor allem durch die Entwicklung der Binnenwirtschaft getrieben wird, ist für die Exporte neben der preislichen Wettbewerbsfähigkeit die Entwicklung der Nachfrage aus dem Ausland entscheidend.

Ein Großteil der divergenten Entwicklung des Außenbeitrags zwischen den Euroraumländern kann daher schon durch die unterschiedliche Dynamik der Binnennachfrage erklärt werden: Die Krisenländer verzeichneten im Vergleich zum Euroraumdurchschnitt bis zur Finanzkrise (in den Jahren 2000 bis 2007) mit Ausnahme Italiens und Portugals ein überdurchschnittliches BIP-Wachstum, das zu einer entsprechend überdurchschnittlichen Importentwicklung führte (siehe Abb. 2 und Tab. 1). Folgerichtig hat auch der wirtschaftliche Einbruch in den Krisenländern in Folge der globalen Finanzkrise und der wirtschaftlichen Rezession die Importentwicklung einbrechen lassen.

Tabelle 1: Wachstumsrate der Nachfrage aus dem Euroraum, vor und nach der Krise, in % p.a.

	2000-2015		2000-2007		2008-2015	
	Krisenland	EA12-ohne Krisenland	Krisenland	EA12-ohne Krisenland	Krisenland	EA12-ohne Krisenland
Irland	4,0%	1,3%	6,2%	2,5%	2,9%	0,4%
Griechenland	-0,2%	1,4%	4,4%	2,6%	-4,6%	0,6%
Spanien	1,6%	1,4%	4,3%	2,4%	-0,7%	0,6%
Italien	0,2%	1,6%	1,6%	2,8%	-1,0%	0,8%
Portugal	0,6%	1,4%	1,7%	2,6%	-0,5%	0,5%

Anmerkungen: Berechnung des durchschnittlichen jährlichen Anstiegs der preisbereinigten Endnachfrage im Krisenland und aus dem Euroraum (12 Länder) ohne das jeweilige Krisenland.

Quelle: AMECO (UUTT, OUTT), eigene Berechnungen; Stand: März 2016

Gleichzeitig war die Nachfrage nach Exporten der Krisenländer aus dem Rest der Welt, inklusive dem restlichen Euroraum (Tab. 1, 2000-2007), vor der Finanzkrise vor allem durch die stabile weltweite, aber auch europäische Konjunktur gestützt, auch wenn Deutschland bis 2005 stagnierte. Seit der Finanzkrise hat sich nicht nur das Wachstum weltweit abgeschwächt, sondern insbesondere die Nachfrage aus der EWU (Tab. 1, 2008-2015). Eine Analyse der Exporte nach Ziellländern in der EWU zeigt, dass die überdurchschnittliche deutsche Dynamik den dämpfenden Effekt einer ansonsten relativ schwachen europäischen Konjunktur nicht kompensieren kann. Da der Rest der Welt außerhalb des Euroraums vor und nach der Finanzkrise im Durchschnitt noch höhere Wachstumsraten verzeichnete, waren diejenigen Länder im Vorteil, deren Exporte vor allem auf stark wachsende Länder ausgerichtet waren. Deutschland profitierte zum Beispiel von starken Zunahmen der Exporte nach Asien, was für die Krisenländer weniger der Fall ist.

3.3 Zwischenfazit

Die Wettbewerbsfähigkeit der Krisenländer, die sich seit Beginn der EWU erheblich verschlechtert hatte, zeigt seit der Finanzkrise deutliche Verbesserungen, wenn sie auf Basis der Lohnstückkosten gemessen wird. Mit Ausnahme Italiens sind die seit 2000 kumulierten Divergenzen im Jahr 2015 komplett abgebaut worden. Der Rückgang der Lohnstückkosten wurde aber nur zeitverzögert in den Exportpreisen weitergegeben. Diese Verbesserung der preislichen Wettbewerbsfähigkeit dürfte die Exporte der Krisenländer auch künftig unterstützen. In der Phase direkt nach der Finanzkrise wurden die Leistungsbilanzdefizite aber vor allem über den Rückgang der Importe abgebaut, was der schwachen Binnennachfrage der Krisenländer geschuldet war. Fraglich ist, ob der steigende Außenbeitrag die schwache Binnennachfrage kompensieren kann (vgl. auch Feigl/Zuckerstätter 2013).

4. Wurden die geringeren Lohnstückkosten in den inländischen Preisen weitergegeben?

Wie bereits erwähnt, führen persistente Inflationsdivergenzen zu einer aus nationaler Sicht prozyklischen Geldpolitik und produzieren persistente und lang anhaltende divergierende Konjunkturzyklen in den einzelnen Ländern. Bis zum Krisenbeginn liefen die Inflationsraten innerhalb der EWU stark auseinander. Die Krisenländer verzeichneten deutlich höhere Zuwächse des harmonisierten Verbraucherpreisindexes (HVPI) als der Durchschnitt der EWU, deutlich über der EZB-Zielmarke von nahe, aber unter 2% jährlich. Nach der Finanzkrise kehrte sich diese Entwicklung um, denn die Inflationsraten in den Krisenländern liegen nun deutlich unter EWU-Durchschnitt (1,24% p.a.)[4] und unter EZB-Inflationsziel.

Die Lohnstückkostenentwicklung bleibt stark mit den Inflationsraten korreliert, auch wenn der Zusammenhang vor der Krise um einiges stärker ausgeprägt war.[5] Weitere Einflussfaktoren sind importierte Inflation und die Entwicklung der anderen inländischen Kostenfaktoren. Der folgende Abschnitt untersucht deren Entwicklung genauer.

---

[4] Eine Ausnahme bildet Italien mit 1,45% p.a.

[5] Die bivariate Korrelation für 32 Länder (Europa und die Türkei) zwischen den Zuwächsen beider Variablen für die Zeiträume 2000-2007 bzw. 2008-2015 hat sich von 88% auf 71% reduziert.

4.1 Importierte Inflation

Die Krisenländer sind, bis auf Irland, gemessen an der Importquote (Importe in % des BIP) nicht sehr offen, dafür aber relativ ölabhängig (gemessen an den Netto-Ölimporten in % des BIP). Der Ölpreis hat sich von 2000 bis 2007 in Euro mehr als verdreifacht und trug damit zu Inflationsdifferenzen bei. Seit der Krise verzeichnete er zwar bis 2011 zunächst einen vorübergehenden erneuten Anstieg. Seither bewegt sich der Ölpreis aber auf sehr niedrigem Niveau, was zusammen mit der seit 2000 gestiegenen Ölabhängigkeit der hier betrachteten EWU-Länder einen Teil der unterschiedlichen Inflationsentwicklung im Euroraum erklärt.

Hingegen wirkte die Abwertung des Euro, die sich in allen Krisenländern bis auf Griechenland für die Zeit nach der Krise in einem Rückgang des nominalen effektiven Wechselkurses[6] spiegelte, inflationär. Andere importierte Güter könnten in Euro nun teurer sein.

Eine genauere Berechnung der Beiträge zur inländischen Inflationsrate nach inländischen und ausländischen Kostenfaktoren ist mit dem HVPI nicht möglich. In der Systematik der volkswirtschaftlichen Gesamtrechnung können diese Kostenfaktoren aber für die Deflatoren der Endnachfrage bzw. des BIP berechnet werden.

Die Inflationsbeiträge zum Deflator der Endnachfrage[7] aus den Importen zeigen, dass sie in den acht Jahren nach der Krise im Vergleich zu den acht Jahren davor die Inflationsrate eher gedämpft haben. D.h., dass auch nach der Krise ein kleiner Teil der inländischen Preisentwicklung „importiert" wurde – aber in wesentlich geringerem Ausmaß als vorher. Die Haupttreiber der inländischen Inflation gemessen mit dem BIP-Deflator bleiben in dieser Abgrenzung nach wie vor die inländischen Kosten. Eine Ausnahme bildet Irland, bei dem Importpreisentwicklungen wichtiger sind als die inländische Kostenentwicklung, vermutlich aufgrund des hohen Offenheitsgrades.

4.2 Lohnstückkosten und BIP-Deflator

Da sich die Lohnstückkosten in allen Krisenländern (bis auf Italien) zurückgebildet haben (Abb. 3), hätte sich ein ausgeprägterer Rückgang der Inflationsrate[8]

---

[6] Quelle: AMECO (XUNNQ), Stand: März 2016. Griechenland verzeichnet einen leichten Anstieg.
[7] Quelle: AMECO (PUTT, YPUT0 und YPUT6), Stand: März 2016.
[8] Gemessen am BIP-Deflator, um die importierte Inflation herauszurechnen und etwaige auf Konstruktion des HVPI zurückgehende Diskrepanzen außen vor zu lassen.

als beobachtet einstellen müssen. Wie bereits in der Einleitung angesprochen, empfehlen Herr und Horn (2012) eine Formel für die nationale Lohnentwicklung, die sich am EZB-Ziel von nahe, aber unter 2% HVPI-Wachstum sowie der durchschnittlichen Produktivität der Vergangenheit orientiert. Ziel ist, eine auch im EWU-Kontext stabile Einkommens- und Verteilungsentwicklung zu gewährleisten, die für die Entwicklung der Binnennachfrage eine wesentliche Rolle spielt. Steigen die Löhne für die gesamte Wirtschaft nach dieser Formel und wird das Inflationsziel der EZB auch erreicht, bliebe die Verteilung des nominalen BIP auf Arbeit und Kapital mittelfristig konstant. Ergeben sich aber Abweichungen, kann man die Preisentwicklung ex post darauf untersuchen, welcher Faktor davon profitiert hat. Feigl und Zuckerstätter (2013) erweitern diesen Analyserahmen, indem die tatsächliche Preisentwicklung in drei Verteilungskomponenten unterteilt wird (Löhne, Gewinne, indirekte Steuern) und diese mit entsprechenden Zielmarken der Lohn-Formel verglichen werden. Damit kann sehr plastisch bewertet werden, ob die Preisentwicklung eines Landes seit Beginn der EWU stabilitätskonform verlaufen ist und wie die einzelnen Komponenten dazu beigetragen haben.

In den vorhergehenden Abschnitten wurde bereits angesprochen, dass sich die Lohnkomponente in den Krisenländern mit Ausnahme Italiens von einer inflationstreibenden zu einer inflationsdämpfenden Komponente mit z.T. deutlich negativen Beiträgen entwickelt hat. In Tabelle 2 ist zu sehen, dass die Löhne im Zeitraum vor der Finanzkrise (2000-2007) gesamtwirtschaftlich in allen Krisenländern stärker gestiegen sind („Ist") als nach der Lohnformel gerechtfertigt gewesen wäre („Soll"). Das gilt aber auch für Gewinne und indirekte Steuern, sodass die Lohnquote nicht unbedingt gestiegen ist. Da alle Komponenten um mehr als ihre verteilungsneutralen Werte gewachsen sind, lag die Inflationsrate in den Krisenländern über dem EZB-Ziel. Das hat sich im Zeitraum nach der Finanzkrise (2008-2015) deutlich verändert: Die Lohnzuwächse lagen nicht nur unter dem nach der Lohnformel („Soll") gerechtfertigten Wert, sondern gingen mit Ausnahme Italiens sogar zurück. Dass die Inflation nicht im gleichen Umfang gesunken ist, muss auf die anderen Verteilungskomponenten zurückgeführt werden. Tatsächlich hat die Gewinnkomponente in Irland und Portugal überhaupt nicht zu unterdurchschnittlicher Inflationsentwicklung beigetragen. In Griechenland und Spanien haben die Gewinne zur Inflationskorrektur geführt, aber nicht so stark wie die Löhne. Lediglich in Italien haben nur die Gewinne zur Inflationskorrektur geführt.

Verhindern nationale Lohnformeln Leistungsbilanzdefizite? 325

4.3 Zwischenfazit: Träger der Anpassungslast

Die Löhne haben nach der Krise stark dazu beigetragen, die Inflationsdivergenzen zu korrigieren, was die rückläufige Entwicklung der nominalen Lohnstückkosten auch zeigt. Die Gewinne haben mit Ausnahme Italiens wenig bis gar nicht dazu beigetragen. Vom BIP-Deflator zum HVPI sind aber noch einige externe Faktoren wirksam, wie Ölpreis und Wechselkurse. Diese sind zwar nicht zu vernachlässigen, spielen aber sowohl vor wie auch nach der Krise eine untergeordnete Rolle. Eine Ausnahme bildet Irland.

Tabelle 2: Inflationsbeiträge zum BIP-Deflator in Prozent(punkten)

		IE	GR	ES	IT	PT
		Insg. (%)				
2000-2007	IST	23,1%	22,5%	27,5%	18,3%	23,3%
	SOLL	14,0%	14,0%	14,0%	14,0%	14,0%
2008-2015	IST	-0,2%	-2,1%	1,4%	7,8%	5,9%
	SOLL	14,0%	14,0%	14,0%	14,0%	14,0%
2000-2015	IST	19,5%	24,7%	31,0%	28,6%	30,9%
	SOLL	30,0%	30,0%	30,0%	30,0%	30,0%
		Löhne (%-Punkte)				
2000-2007	IST	10,6%	10,4%	13,1%	8,3%	9,1%
	SOLL	5,3%	4,6%	6,7%	5,3%	6,7%
2008-2015	IST	-7,9%	-2,1%	-2,3%	4,0%	-0,7%
	SOLL	5,6%	4,8%	6,9%	5,6%	6,4%
2000-2015	IST	4,7%	10,3%	13,7%	14,1%	9,8%
	SOLL	11,8%	10,1%	14,5%	11,6%	14,0%
		Gewinne (%-Punkte)				
2000-2007	IST	9,3%	9,8%	11,3%	7,5%	10,1%
	SOLL	7,1%	7,9%	5,9%	7,0%	5,6%
2008-2015	IST	8,5%	-2,1%	1,5%	1,9%	5,5%
	SOLL	7,1%	7,6%	5,9%	6,7%	5,9%
2000-2015	IST	14,0%	9,4%	13,7%	10,6%	16,0%
	SOLL	15,1%	16,6%	12,6%	14,6%	12,3%
		Indirekte Steuern (%-Punkte)				
2000-2007	IST	3,2%	2,4%	3,1%	2,5%	4,1%
	SOLL	1,5%	1,5%	1,4%	1,7%	1,7%
2008-2015	IST	-0,8%	2,0%	2,2%	1,9%	1,2%
	SOLL	1,3%	1,6%	1,2%	1,8%	1,7%
2000-2015	IST	0,8%	5,0%	3,7%	3,9%	5,2%
	SOLL	3,0%	3,3%	2,8%	3,8%	3,7%

Quelle: AMECO (OVGD, UVGD, UWCD, UOGD, UTVN), eigene Berechnungen; Stand: Februar 2016

5. Fazit: Ist der Abbau der Leistungsbilanzdefizite nachhaltig?

Aus der Analyse der Leistungsbilanzen konnte die Erkenntnis gewonnen werden, dass die Lohnstückkostenreduzierung zwar zu deren Rückgang beigetragen hat, aber nur zeitverzögert. Wichtiger waren Verschiebungen zwischen inländischen und export-relevanten ausländischen Nachfrageentwicklungen. Ein wesentlicherer Faktor war der Einbruch der inländischen Nachfrage. Darauf deutet auch die Analyse der Preisentwicklung: Die Löhne haben sich in allen Krisenländern deutlich schlechter entwickelt, als es nach der Lohnformel gerechtfertigt gewesen wäre. Der daraus resultierende Effekt für das Wachstum ist aber problematisch: Wenn sich die Löhne und damit die Lohnstückkosten sowohl unter deren Soll als auch unterhalb des EWU-Durchschnitts entwickeln, können zwar gegenüber dem Nicht-Euroraum Exporterfolge erzielt werden, aber nur auf Kosten der Binnennachfrage. Für nicht ausreichend offene Volkswirtschaften kann der steigende Außenbeitrag die schwache binnenwirtschaftliche Entwicklung nicht kompensieren – eine Erfahrung, die Deutschland bis zur Finanzkrise machen musste.[9] Ähnliches zeichnet sich schon jetzt in den Krisenländern ab, die Wachstumseinbußen verzeichnen. Lediglich für Irland als sehr offener Volkswirtschaft ist der Nettoeffekt positiv. Für die anderen Krisenländer kann diese Konstellation zwar lange anhalten, führt aber nicht zu einer nachhaltigen, stabilen ökonomischen Entwicklung.

Wie gezeigt wurde, wurden die Lohnstückkostenrückgänge nicht vollständig in den Preisen weitergegeben. Stattdessen wurden mit Ausnahme Italiens die Gewinne erhöht. Eine solche Verteilungsänderung zwischen Arbeit und Kapital soll mit der von Herr und Horn (2012) vorgeschlagenen Lohnformel verhindert werden. Hätten sich in der Vergangenheit alle Länder des Euroraums bemüht, Lohnsteigerungen gemäß dieser Formel durchzusetzen, hätten sich weder die deutlichen Divergenzen bei den Lohnstückkosten und inländischen Preisen noch bei den Leistungsbilanzsalden ergeben.

Abweichungen von der Lohnformel sind daher gleichzeitig ein guter Indikator für Fehlentwicklungen, die sowohl Verstärker als auch Ursache von divergenten ökonomischen Entwicklungen in der EWU sind. Sie liefern wichtige Erkenntnisse, ob die Lohnentwicklung prozyklische makroökonomische Geld- und Fiskalpolitiken im Rahmen einer EWU verschärfen. Aber die Befolgung einer Lohnformel kann keine alleinige Lösung zur Eurokrise liefern: Denn wie gezeigt wurde, übersetzte sich eine dramatische Korrektur

---

[9] Herzog-Stein et al. (2013b), Joebges et al. (2009, 2010), Joebges/Logeay (2012).

der nominalen Lohnstückkostenentwicklung nicht komplett in der Preisentwicklung. Zudem spielen für die beobachteten Divergenzen weitere Faktoren eine Rolle, von denen hier nur auf die unterschiedliche Ölabhängigkeit sowie die unterschiedliche Zusammensetzung der Nachfrage aus dem Rest der Welt hingewiesen wurde.

Literatur

Ca'Zorzi, M., Schnatz, B. (2007): Explaining and forecasting euro area exports. Which competitiveness indicator performs best?, European Central Bank Working Paper no. 833, November.

Chinn, M. (2006): A Primer on Real Effective Exchange Rates Determinants, in: *Open Economies Review*, 17, 115-143.

Decramer, S., Fuss, C., Konings, J. (2014): How do exporters react to changes in cost competitiveness?; ECB Working Paper no. 1752, https://www.ecb.europa.eu/pub/pdf/scpwps/ecbwp1752.en.pdf

ECB – European Central Bank (2003): Euro area inflation differentials. Frankfurt: European Central Bank, September 2003. https://www.ecb.europa.eu/pub/pdf/other/inflationdifferentialreporten.pdf

European Commission (2013): Special topics on the euro area economy: Labour costs pass-through, profits, and rebalancing in vulnerable Member States, in: *Quarterly Report on the Euro Area*, 12(3), Ch. II, 19-25.

European Commission (2015): Macroeconomic Imbalances. Main Findings of the In-Depth Reviews 2015, European Economy, Occasional papers no. 228, http://ec.europa.eu/economy_finance/publications/occasional_paper/2015/op228_en.htm

Feigl, G., Zuckerstätter, J. (2013): „Wettbewerbs(des)orientierung", WWWforEurope Policy Paper, Nr. 2, April 2013, http://www.foreurope.eu/fileadmin/documents/pdf/PolicyPapers/WWWforEurope_Policy_Paper_002.pdf

Heine, M., Herr, H. (1999): Verdrängte Risiken der Euro-Einführung, in: *WSI-Mitteilungen: Zeitschrift des Wirtschafts- und Sozialwissenschaftlichen Instituts in der Hans-Böckler-Stiftung*, 52(8), 539-547.

Heine, M., Herr, H. (2006): Die europäische Währungsunion im Treibsand. Fehlende Lohnkoordination und fiskalische Schwächen gefährden das europäische Projekt, in: *Prokla: Zeitschrift für kritische Sozialwissenschaft*, 144(36/3), 361-379.

Heine, M., Herr, H., Kaiser, C. (2005): Überforderte Lohnpolitik – Löhne im Spannungsfeld von Verteilung, Preisen und Beschäftigung, in: Hein, E., Heise, A., Truger, A. (Hg.), *Löhne, Beschäftigung, Verteilung und Wachstum: makroökonomische Analysen*, Marburg: Metropolis, 93-118.

Herr, H. (2004): Der Arbeitsmarkt in Deutschland im Jahre 2003: Lage, theoretische Debatte und Reformvorstellungen, in: Zwengel, R. (Hg.), *Gesellschaftliche Perspektiven: Arbeitsmarkt, Ökologie und Reformpolitik, EU-Erweiterung*, Essen: Klartext Verlag, 29-54.

Herr, H., Horn, G.A. (2012): Lohnpolitik heute, IMK Policy Brief, Mai.

Herr, H., Kazandziska, M. (2007): Wages and regional coherence in the European Monetary Union, in: Hein, E., Priewe J., Truger, A. (Hg.), *European integration in crisis*, Marburg: Metropolis, 131-162.

Herzog-Stein, A., Joebges, H., Stein, U., Zwiener, R. (2013a): Arbeitskostenentwicklung und internationale Wettbewerbsfähigkeit in Europa. Arbeits- und Lohnstückkosten in 2012 und im 1. Halbjahr 2013. IMK Report Nr. 88.

Herzog-Stein, A., Lindner, F., Zwiener, R. (2013b): Nur das Angebot zählt? Wie eine einseitige deutsche Wirtschaftspolitik Chancen vergeben hat und Europa schadet. IMK Report Nr. 87.

IMF – International Monetary Fund (2013): Rebalancing the Euro Area: Where do we stand and where to go?, in: IMF Country Report No. 13/232, Euro Area Policies, 2013 Article IV Consultation, 21-44.

Joebges, H., Lindner, F., Niechoj, T. (2010): Mit dem Export aus der Krise? Deutschland im Euroraumvergleich, IMK Report, Nr. 53, August 2010.

Joebges, H., Logeay, C. (2012): Deutschlands Anteil an Stabilitätsproblemen im Euroraum, in: Sauer, T. (Hg.), *Die Zukunft der Europäischen Währungsunion: Kritische Analysen*, Marburg: Metropolis, 69-90.

Joebges, H., Schmalzbauer, A., Zwiener, R. (2009): Der Preis für den Exportweltmeister Deutschland: Reallohnrückgang und geringes Wirtschaftswachstum, IMK Studies Nr. 4/2009.

Hat das Bündnis für Arbeit zu Lohndumping geführt?

Michael Wendl

1. Die Kontroverse

Ende 2015 hatte sich die Debatte über die Lohnzurückhaltung der deutschen Tarifparteien in der Währungsunion wieder zugespitzt. Simon Wren-Lewis nahm einen Beitrag von Peter Bofinger, der die Lohnmoderation der deutschen Gewerkschaften ab 2000 durch eine Vereinbarung zwischen der Bundesvereinigung der deutschen Arbeitgeberverbände (BDA) und dem Deutschen Gewerkschaftsbund (DGB) zu erklären versuchte, zustimmend auf. Er vermutete dahinter eine beabsichtigte Lohnzurückhaltung und fragte: „Was German Wages Undercutting Deliberate" (Wren-Lewis 2015). Bofinger hatte nach einem Verweis auf das Bündnis für Arbeit, Ausbildung und Wettbewerbsfähigkeit geschrieben: „On 20 January 2000, trade unions and employers associates explicity declared that productivity increases should not be used in for increases in real wages but for agreements that increase employment. In essence, ‚wage moderation' is an explicit attempt to devalue the real exchange rate internally" (Bofinger 2015).

Diese Kritik hatte lange vorher mit einem Beitrag von Heiner Flassbeck in der „Frankfurter Rundschau" vom 31.10.1997 („Und die Spielregeln für die Lohnpolitik in einer Währungsunion?") begonnen. Hier schrieb Flassbeck, dass Deutschland wegen der zurückhaltenden Lohnpolitik seit 1987 mit einem Wettbewerbsvorteil von 8% in die Währungsunion starten werde. Flassbeck und Friederike Spiecker haben diese Kritik seit dieser Zeit kontinuierlich fortgesetzt (siehe Flassbeck/Spiecker 2000, 2005). Später hat Flassbeck diese Kritik ähnlich wie Bofinger begründet: „(Es) einigten sich 1999 die Gewerkschaftsführungen in einer dreiseitigen Vereinbarung (mit der BDA und der Bundesregierung, M.W.) darauf, die Formel aufzugeben, die bis dato zur Bestimmung des Lohnzuwachses benutzt worden war (gemeint ist die Lohnformel der produktivitätsorientierten Lohnpolitik, M.W.); stattdessen stimmten die Gewerkschaften zu, die Produktivität für die Beschäftigung zu reservieren" (Flassbeck/Lapavitsas 2015: 42). Die Terminierung überrascht, hatte doch Flassbeck diese Lohnzurückhaltung bereits 1997 moniert. Dessen ungeachtet werden diese Vereinbarung und ihre Wirkungen von Bofinger und Flassbeck überschätzt.

Es gibt solche Vereinbarungen, die erste zwischen DGB und BDA vom 6. Juli 1999 und eine zweite, im Inhalt gleichlautende, von der Sitzung im Bündnis für Arbeit vom 9. (!) Januar 2000. Darin heißt es, dass die Beteiligten für die Tarifrunde 2000 eine „beschäftigungsorientierte und längerfristige Tarifpolitik" empfehlen. „Dabei wird der sich am Produktivitätswachstum orientierende, zur Verfügung stehende Verteilungsspielraum vorrangig für beschäftigungswirksame Vereinbarungen genutzt" (Bündnis für Arbeit 2000). Unter „beschäftigungswirksam" verstanden die beteiligten Gewerkschaften überwiegend Modelle zur Frühverrentung, für die es keine gesetzliche Grundlage gab. Sie sollten tarifvertraglich ausgestaltet werden, was daran scheiterte, dass die Schröder-Regierung zu Gesetzesänderungen nicht bereit war. In den Gewerkschaften selbst wurde diese Vereinbarung überwiegend nicht als Lohnleitlinie interpretiert. Dass durch diese Lohnzurückhaltung ein Wettbewerbsvorteil zugunsten Deutschlands in der Eurozone gezielt initiiert werden sollte, ist unwahrscheinlich, weil die makroökonomischen Zusammenhänge von nationalen Arbeitskosten mit einer Währungsunion von den Tarifparteien auf beiden Seiten nicht verstanden wurden.

Auf den zweiten Blick sehen wir, dass die Theorie einer merkantilistisch wirkenden Lohnpolitik, die durch eine restriktive Geldpolitik der Bundesbank verstärkt wird, eine viel längere Vorgeschichte hat. Hansjörg Herr hatte bereits rund 10 Jahre vorher diese Rolle der Lohnpolitik, die zusammen mit der Geldpolitik der Bundesbank zu einer stabilitätspolitischen Unterbewertung der DM geführt hatte, im Rahmen des monetär-keynesianischen Paradigmas begründet. Er sprach von einem „stabilitätspolitischen Merkantilismus", der den einheimischen Finanzsektor stärkt und den relativ sicher Beschäftigten um den Preis von hoher Arbeitslosigkeit Wohlfahrtsgewinne gewährt (Herr 1992: 205). „Das generell kooperative Verhältnis zwischen Kapital und Arbeit drückt sich in moderaten Geldlohnerhöhungen bei hohen Produktivitätsraten aus – beides zusammen ergibt die Lohnstückkosten und bestimmt letztlich das Preisniveau" (Herr 1991: 237). Diese Unterbewertung wurde durch die Kombination von schwacher Nachfrage, die auf Lohnzurückhaltung basierte, und restriktiver Geldpolitik der Bundesbank, die mit diesem Lohnniveau eine niedrige Inflationsrate erreichen konnte, durchgesetzt. In den Gewerkschaften war diese makroökomische Sicht, die auch die Lohnpolitik der 1980er Jahre mit eingeschlossen hatte, kein Thema. Sie konnten das wegen ihres nur auf den Arbeitsmarkt konzentrierten Blicks nicht erkennen und versuchten, mit Arbeitszeitverkürzung, also einer Rationierung des Arbeitsangebots, die hohe Arbeitslosigkeit zu verringern. Aus dieser Kritik eines stabilitätspolitischen Merkantilismus wurde dann das normative Modell einer Lohnpolitik entwickelt, die sich an der Summe von trendmäßigem Produktivitätswachstum und Zielinflationsrate der Zentralbank orientieren sollte (Heine/ Herr 2004: 204).

2. Angebots- oder Nachfragetheorie?

In der Debatte um die produktivitätsorientierte Tarifpolitik haben wir es mit zwei konträren Sichtweisen zu tun, einmal mit der Interpretation der Rolle der Tarifpolitik als regulierende Instanz für eine möglichst gleichgewichtige Entwicklung von Angebot und Nachfrage in einem gesamtwirtschaftlichen Kreislauf, zum anderen mit einer angebotsorientierten Sicht, die Lohnkosten in ihrer neoklassisch interpretierten Rolle auf dem Arbeitsmarkt versteht und in einer Lohnkostenentwicklung unterhalb des Produktivitätsniveaus die entscheidende Voraussetzung für eine steigende Beschäftigung und zugleich für eine verbesserte relative Wettbewerbsposition sieht. Diese zweite Position wird vom Sachverständigenrat zur Begutachtung der gesamtwirtschaftlichen Entwicklung (SVR) mit seinen Vorschlägen zur Modellierung einer beschäftigungsorientierten Lohnpolitik vertreten.

Dieser Sicht schien sich die IG Metall mit ihrer Forderung nach einer kooperativen Lohnpolitik im Rahmen eines „Bündnis für Arbeit" anzuschließen. Klaus Zwickel zitierte in seiner Rede auf dem Kongress der IG Metall 1995 zunächst nahezu wörtlich aus dem DIW-Wochenbericht 38/95: „Es kann nicht Aufgabe der Gewerkschaften sein, auf Wechselkursschwankungen mit Lohnverzicht zu antworten. Das würde außerdem die Aufwertung nur beschleunigen" (Lindlar 1995). Unmittelbar daran anschließend wurde die Nichtausschöpfung des Verteilungsspielraums nach der produktivitätsorientierten Lohnpolitik angeboten und mit der Bedingung verknüpft, dass die Arbeitgeberseite verbindliche Beschäftigungszusagen macht. Diese Aussage bewegt sich im Rahmen der neoklassischen Arbeitsmarkttheorie, weil sie davon ausgeht, dass es bei der Lohnpolitik um eine Entscheidung zwischen Lohnwachstum oder Beschäftigung gehe. In den Gewerkschaften wird diese Alternative aber nicht neoklassisch interpretiert. Die Gewerkschaften verstehen Lohnverzicht, ähnlich wie Arbeitszeitverkürzung, als Voraussetzung für eine Umverteilung eines fixen Arbeits- und Lohnfonds auf mehr Beschäftigte. Diese Sicht basiert auf der folgenreichen Verwechselung von Arbeitskraft mit Arbeit (Marx 1972: 562).

Der Hintergrund für die innerhalb der IGM zunächst überraschende Offerte war der hohe Tarifabschluss der IGM in Frühjahr 1995 mit 6,3%, dem in Bayern ein 11-tägiger Streik vorangegangen war. Dieser Abschluss wurde damals von der Konjunkturabteilung des DIW unter der Federführung von Flassbeck als zu hoch kritisiert, weil am 1.10.1995 auch die letzte Stufe zur 35-Stundenwoche in Kraft getreten war. In der betreffenden Branche wurde damit der gesamtwirtschaftlich definierte Verteilungsspielraum überschritten. Die moderaten Tarifabschlüsse in anderen Branchen konnten das ausgleichen. Dieser Abschluss wurde in der Führung der IGM für die zunehmende Tarifflucht von Unternehmen verantwortlich gemacht. Das Angebot Zwickels war, so gesehen, eine tarifpolitische Friedensformel. Der Lohnverzicht sollte in erster Linie die Tarifbindung wieder stabilisieren. So sind auch die gleichzeitig beginnenden Versuche zu sehen, den Flächentarifvertrag durch betriebliche Öffnungsklauseln zu dezentralisieren, um seinen Bestand zu sichern. Innerhalb der IGM wurde diese Etablierung eines mehrstufigen Tarifvertragssystems gegen die innergewerkschaftliche Kritik als erfolgreiche Stabilisierung eines durch die Währungsunion und die Globalisierung gefährdeten Systems der kooperativen Arbeitsbeziehungen verteidigt (Schroeder 2003). Innerhalb der Gewerkschaften wurde das deutsche Modell der Lohnfindung aus Sicht der sozialwissenschaftlichen Beratung als „institutionelle Hochlohnökonomie" (Streeck 1999) (miss-)verstanden. In Verbindung mit den steigenden Sozialversicherungsbeiträgen in Folge der sozialpolitischen Integration der neuen Länder, kam es zu einer fast hysterischen Lohnnebenkostendebatte. Sie zeigte, dass die deutschen Arbeitskosten insgesamt für zu hoch gehalten wurden. Daran änderten auch die anders lautenden Studien aus dem DIW und dem Ifo-Institut (Ködderman 1996) nichts, weil sie weitgehend nicht wahrgenommen wurden.

Die vorherrschende Sicht war und ist aus mindestens zwei Gründen falsch: einmal wegen des dahinter stehenden „Tunnelblicks" auf den Arbeitsmarkt, auf dem eine nachlassende Nachfrage nach Arbeitskräften mit zu hohen Löhnen erklärt wird. Bei einer isolierten Betrachtung des Arbeitsmarktes werden Schwankungen der Beschäftigung als Resultate von Lohnkosten interpretiert. Beschäftigung entsteht aber nicht durch Bewegungen auf dem Arbeitsmarkt. Sie wird dort nur gemessen. Der zweite Fehler besteht darin, hinter der Größe der Arbeitsproduktivität sowohl die Grenzproduktivität des Faktors Kapital als auch die Grenzproduktivität des Faktors Arbeit zu sehen. Lohnzurückhaltung führt aus dieser Sicht zu einer steigenden Rate der Grenzproduktivität des Kapitals und damit zu steigenden Investitionen. Beides sind Denkweisen, deren einfache angebotstheoretische Sicht auf eine Gesamtwirtschaft, die durch eine Hierarchie der Märkte geprägt ist, in der der Arbeitsmarkt eine von der Entwicklung auf den Kapital- und Gütermärkten abgeleitete Größe ist, nicht angewandt werden kann. Durch die Verteilungsresultate einer produktivitätsorientierten Lohnpolitik findet eine pragmatische Zurechnung des Produktivitätszuwachses auf die beiden Seiten der Primärverteilung statt, eine eigene künstliche Berechnung der sog. Grenzproduktivität des Faktors Arbeit läuft durch die Konstruktion einer davon abgegrenzten Grenzproduktivität des Kapitals auf eine zusätzliche Erhöhung der Kapitaleinkommen heraus und widerspricht insofern dem Gedanken einer verteilungsneutralen Tarifpolitik.

Aus keynesianischer Sicht wird nicht angebotstheoretisch, sondern verteilungspolitisch und daraus folgend nachfragetheoretisch argumentiert. Niedrigere Löhne führen zu einer niedrigeren Inflation, diese wiederum führt in einem System fester Wechselkurse oder in einer Währungsunion zu einer realen Abwertung. Zugleich führen niedrige Löhne zu einer Änderung der Einkommensverteilung, die zunächst die konsumtive Nachfrage und darüber vermittelt auch die effektive, also aggregierte Nachfrage beschränkt. In einer Währungsunion, so die Argumentation, drückt sich Wettbewerbsfähigkeit nicht als physische Größe infolge technologischer Innovationen und einer entsprechend höheren Kapitalproduktivität aus oder in einer intensiveren Wertschöpfung, sondern als eine nominale „Wertproduktivität", die in einem durch Preise gekennzeichneten Output an Gütern und Dienstleistungen gesehen wird. Eine aus der Entwicklung der Nachfrage abgeleitete nominale Wertproduktivität setzt aber ein flexibles Angebot voraus, das entsprechend auf das durch die Entwicklung der gesamtwirtschaftlichen Lohnsumme bestimmte wachsende Nachfragevolumen reagiert. Diese Produktionselastizität ist aber in den Ländern der Eurozone nicht in gleichem Maß vorhanden. Empirisch orientierte Untersuchungen (Erber/Hagemann 2012) zeigen, dass in den Ländern in der Eurozone unterschiedliche Produktivitätsniveaus bereits vor der Einführung des Euro bestanden hatten. Diese „Produktivitätsschere" zwischen den exportorientierten und den importgetriebenen Ländern hat sich in der Währungsunion vergrößert. Dabei ist offen, was davon technologisch und was durch ein niedriges Lohnwachstum bestimmt war.

Die Entwicklung der gesamtwirtschaftlichen Lohnstückkosten kann daher zunächst nur die Nachfrage bestimmen, nicht aber das Angebot, weil dessen

Kosten von den Kapitalkosten und den Branchenlöhnen, also spezifischen Arbeitskosten, und nicht von den gesamtwirtschaftlichen Lohnkosten bestimmt werden. Für die Entwicklung der Nachfrage ist die gesamtwirtschaftliche Lohnsumme eine zentrale Größe. Die Kostenpreise der angebotenen Güter und Dienstleistungen bestehen aber nicht aus einem Aggregat von gesamtwirtschaftlichen Lohnstückkosten. Die Entwicklung der gesamtwirtschaftlichen Arbeitsproduktivität ist von mehreren Faktoren abhängig, dabei spielt die Entwicklung der Löhne als wichtige Größe der aggregierten Nachfrage und damit des Preisniveaus eine zentrale Rolle.

Dass eine zu zurückhaltende Lohnpolitik mit signifikant unterdurchschnittlichen Lohnstückkosten über eine niedrigere Inflationsrate zu realer Abwertung und damit zu einem Wettbewerbsvorteil führt, ist plausibel. Dieser Vorteil basiert aber nur auf einem „Quasi-Wechselkurseffekt", weil Deutschlands Exporte faktisch abgewertet haben. Es handelt sich um zwei Faktoren: einmal um die unterschiedlichen Produktivitätsniveaus in einzelnen Ländern und zusätzlich um den Wechselkurseffekt einer realen Abwertung. Nur der zweite Faktor ist direkt auf die Lohnmoderation zurückzuführen.

3. Was bestimmt die deutsche Tarifpolitik?

Diese Sichtweise, dass Lohnzurückhaltung auf eine Vereinbarung zwischen den Tarifparteien zurückzuführen ist, markiert ein simples und handlungstheoretisch überzogenes Verständnis der Entstehung und Durchsetzung tarifpolitischer Forderungen, das die Entwicklungen der ökonomischen Rahmenbedingungen zwischen 1990 und 2015 ausblendet. Wenn die Frage „Sprengt die deutsche Lohnpolitik die Währungsunion?" (Flassbeck/Spiecker 2005) in den Gewerkschaften gestellt wurde, hat das zu Erstaunen geführt. Zum einen war man verwundert, dass ausgerechnet den Gewerkschaften, trotz hoher Arbeitslosigkeit, so viel Macht zugetraut wird. Zum zweiten war man erstaunt, dass Lohnpolitik mit der Währungsunion direkt zusammenhängen soll. Die tarifpolitische Willensbildung von gewerkschaftlich organisierten Lohnabhängigen pendelt zwischen zwei Motiven: Lohnwachstum oder Beschäftigungssicherung. Die mögliche Auflösung dieser Frage, dass gerade Lohnwachstum Beschäftigung sichert und sogar ausweiten kann, ist im Alltagsbewusstsein nicht angelegt, weil dieses durch die einzelwirtschaftliche Sicht bestimmt ist.

Die Handlungsmöglichkeiten der Tarifpolitik werden weiter begrenzt durch die Höhe der Arbeitslosigkeit und durch die Stabilität des nationalen Tarif-

Hat das Bündnis für Arbeit zu Lohndumping geführt? 335

systems. Diese kann am Grad der Tarifbindung und am Verhältnis von Flächentarifverträgen und Firmentarifverträgen abgelesen werden. Die Tarifbindung war zwischen 1990 und 2009 dramatisch zurückgegangen und hatte zu einer deutlichen Erhöhung des Anteils der Firmentarifverträge bei gleichzeitiger Zunahme von Öffnungsklauseln in den Flächentarifverträgen geführt. Es kam zu einer starken Dezentralisierung und „Verbetrieblichung" des Tarifvertragssystems. In diese Zeit fällt auch der gescheiterte Streik für die Arbeitszeitverkürzung 2003 in der ostdeutschen Metallindustrie, in dem die IGM die Erfahrung machen musste, dass dieser Arbeitskampf in Westdeutschland nur unzureichend unterstützt wurde (Schmidt 2003).

Es ist voluntaristisch anzunehmen, dass die Resultate der Tarifpolitik einem aus Produktivitätswachstum und Preisentwicklung definierten Verteilungsspielraum folgen. Diese Norm basiert auf einem doppelten Missverständnis. Einmal sind die Parteien eines sogenannten Beschäftigungspakts auf der nationalen Ebene nicht identisch mit den Akteuren der Tarifverhandlungen. Zweitens regeln Tarifverhandlungen nicht ein nationales makroökonomisches Gesamtvolumen der Löhne. Es finden auf einer Vielzahl von Teilarbeitsmärkten voneinander getrennte und durch unterschiedlich regional und betrieblich geprägte Bedingungen Verhandlungen statt. Die Ergebnisse von Tarifverhandlungen hängen dabei nicht nur von den Kräfteverhältnissen der Tarifparteien auf diesen Arbeitsmärkten ab, sondern auch von der Interpretation dieser Situation durch die tarifpolitischen Akteure. Die normative Konzeption der produktivitätsorientierten Tarifpolitik ist zudem nicht klar genug, einmal, weil unterschiedliche Lohnformeln verwendet wurden, und zweitens, weil diese Konzeption, wenn sie überhaupt geläufig war, in den Gewerkschaften selbst umstritten ist. Manche der tarifpolitischen Akteure akzeptieren sie aus unterschiedlichen Gründen nicht. Das hängt damit zusammen, dass diese Lohnformel als Lohnleitline als zu theoretisch und praxisfremd abgelehnt wird. Dass die IGM und die DGB-Gewerkschaften sich 1998 innerhalb des Europäischen Metallarbeiterbundes (EMB) und mit den Gewerkschaften der Benelux-Länder (Abkommen von Doorn) auf das Konzept der produktivitätsorientierten Tarifpolitik verständigen konnten, ist auf die in Doorn handelnden Akteure und nicht auf einen bereits bestehenden Konsens in den Gewerkschaften des DGB zurückzuführen. Allerdings wurden die Abkommen danach in den Gewerkschaften diskutiert und nicht abgelehnt.

Das originäre Konzept der produktivitätsorientierten Lohnpolitik, welches 1965 vom neu gegründeten Sachverständigenrat entwickelt wurde, war in den Gewerkschaften nur noch wenig bekannt. Mit dem Modell wurde durch die Addition von Zuwachsrate der Arbeitsproduktivität und anzustrebender Inflationsrate versucht, eine preis- und verteilungsneutrale Lohnpolitik zu begründen. Praktische Bedeutung hatte es in der Zeit von 1965 bis 1981, war aber in diesem Zeitabschnitt als vermeintliche Lohnleitlinie umstritten. Dort, wo es als normatives Modell verwendet wurde, bestand die Formel aus dem Wachstum der Arbeitsproduktivität plus der Zuwachsrate der Verbraucherpreise. Gelegentlich wurde eine dritte Komponente, die auf eine Umverteilung zugunsten der Arbeitsentgelte zielte, hinzugerechnet.

Wenn wir die Lohnpolitik von 1951 bis 2008 bilanzieren, so wurde der aus dieser Sicht verteilungsneutrale Verteilungsspielraum nur in den Spätphasen der verschiedenen Konjunkturzyklen erreicht oder überschritten. In den 1950er und 1960er Jahren wurde er hingegen durchgängig unterschritten. Diese produktivitätsorientierte Tarifpolitik hat die Verteilungspolitik in Westdeutschland nicht gekennzeichnet. Überschritten wurde dieser Verteilungsspielraum nur Anfang der 1970er Jahre (bis 1974) und Anfang der 1990er Jahre, was aber ausschließlich auf die Lohnabschlüsse in den neuen Ländern zurückzuführen war. In Westdeutschland wurde er damals nicht ausgeschöpft. Generell gilt, dass es nur zu Tarifabschlüssen nach der Regel der produktivitätsorientierten Tarifpolitik gekommen ist, wenn die Nachfrage nach Arbeitskräften stark war. Umgekehrt wurde der Verteilungsspielraum nicht ausgeschöpft oder deutlich unterschritten, wenn die Arbeitslosigkeit hoch war. Für die Zeit nach 1982 kam es zu dieser stabilitätspolitisch motivierten Unterbewertung der DM, was von den Gewerkschaften nicht intendiert war. Auch die Mitte der 1980er Jahre beginnende Arbeitszeitverkürzung hatte daran nichts geändert, ihre Kosten blieben innerhalb dieses Verteilungsspielraums (Heilemann/Ulrich 2008).

Diese normative Lohnformel wurde nicht nur vom Sachverständigenrat wiederholt nach unten zu rechnen versucht, auch in den Gewerkschaften wurden unter den Experten unterschiedliche Modelle errechnet und diskutiert. Hartmut Görgens verwendete für sein Modell einer verteilungsneutralen Lohnpolitik nur die Größen Volkseinkommen und Löhne, um daraus eine Gleichverteilung von Arbeitseinkommen und Kapitaleinkommen zu berechnen. Er versuchte, so zwischen den Größen der Grenzproduktivität von Kapital und Arbeit zu unterscheiden (Görgens 2014). Damit wurden Abschreibungen und die Einnahmen aus der Mehrwertsteuer zu nicht verteilbaren Größen. Das ist eine Formel, die den kreislauftheoretischen Zusammenhang von Produktion, Investitionen und aggregierter Nachfrage nicht mehr berücksichtigt und insofern eine Umverteilung zu den Kapitaleinkommen akzeptiert. Wird diese Lohnformel zum Maßstab genommen, so wird der Verteilungsspielraum in den 1990er Jahren gering über- und in den 2000er Jahren etwas unterschritten. Von einer zu moderaten Lohnpolitik kann dann aus dieser Sicht nicht gesprochen werden.

Eine weitere Aktualisierung des Konzepts erfolgte durch Michael Heine und Hansjörg Herr und durch das 2005 neu gegründete Institut für Makroökonomie und Konjunkturforschung (IMK) in der Hans-Böckler-Stiftung. Beide kombinierten den trendmäßigen, also mittelfristigen Produktivitätsanstieg mit der Zielinflationsrate der EZB (Heine/Herr 2004; Horn et al. 2005; Herr/Horn 2012). Das Wirtschafts- und Sozialwissenschaftliche Institut (WSI) in der Hans-Böckler-Stiftung blieb dagegen bis heute bei der traditionellen Formel von Produktivität zuzüglich des Index der Verbraucherpreise. Das markierte auch die in den Gewerkschaften mehrheitlich übliche Formel, die aber eher zur Forderungsaufstellung und nicht als Abschlussnorm verwendet wurde. Das Konzept von Heine und Herr und des IMK ist schlüssiger, weil es nicht prozyklisch wirkt und durch die Beachtung der Zielinflationsrate gegen die deflationären Tendenzen einer restriktiven Fiskalpolitik wirken kann. Inzwischen hat die IG Metall diese Lohnformel übernommen. Daraus kann aber nicht geschlossen werden, dass diese Formel allgemein akzeptiert wird. Über solche Fragen diskutieren in den Gewerkschaften nur wenige.

Durch die Auffächerung und Dezentralisierung der Tariflandschaft spielen gesamtwirtschaftliche Größen in der Tarifpolitik zunehmend eine relativ geringe Rolle. Organisationspolitische Ziele, wie der Erhalt der tariflichen Bindung und die Gewinnung neuer Mitglieder durch den Kampf um Firmentarifverträge, rücken zunehmend in den Vordergrund. Die IGM und die IG BCE versuchten mit betrieblichen Öffnungsklauseln den „Wildwuchs" von rechtswidrigen betrieblichen Vereinbarungen, die ohne Öffnungsklauseln von den Normen der Branchentarifverträge nach unten abgewichen waren, wieder zu begrenzen. Das Pforzheimer Abkommen der IGM mit den Arbeitgebern der Metallindustrie 2005 zielte exakt auf dieses Problem und legalisierte damit Abweichungen nach unten, die jetzt von der IGM zu kontrollieren versucht wurden. Daneben wurden Notlagen- oder Sanierungstarifverträge, die direkt Nominallohnsenkungen zum Inhalt hatten, erheblich ausgeweitet. Damit wurde die Tarifpolitik organisationspolitischen Zwecken der Gewerkschaft untergeordnet.

Das galt besonders für den Bereich des öffentlichen Sektors, für den die Gewerkschaft ver.di und die Tarifunion des Beamtenbundes neue Tarifverträge für Bund, Länder und Gemeinden vereinbarten. Diese Vereinbarung sah vor, dass das Entgeltniveau für die neuen Beschäftigten, die nach den Stichtagen der Änderung (2005 bzw. 2006) eingestellt wurden, direkt abgesenkt wurde und für 2 Jahre eine Pause bei den Nominallöhnen eingelegt wurde, um die Tarifbindung für den öffentlichen Sektor im Großen und Ganzen zu erhalten und eine Angleichung der Ost-Entgelte an das West-Niveau zu vereinbaren. Angesichts der Größe dieses Beschäftigungssektors war der dadurch ausgelöste Druck auf die gesamtwirtschaftlichen Lohnstückkosten beträchtlich. Das wird in dieser Debatte über die Entwicklung gesamtwirtschaftlicher Lohnstückkosten kaum wahrgenommen, weil sich die Aufmerksamkeit auf die industriellen Löhne konzentriert. Deren Bedeutung für die Nachfrageseite ist geringer als die des öffentlichen Sektors. In diesem Bereich handelt es sich nicht um eine merkantilistische oder wettbewerbsorientierte Tarifpolitik, sondern um eine defensive Reaktion auf die finanzielle Lage der Gebietskörperschaften, die durch die Steuerpolitik der rot-grünen Bundesregierung erheblich unter Druck geraten waren.

Das wirft Schlaglichter auf einen Abschnitt der Geschichte der Tarifpolitik nach 1995, die zeigen, wie wenig die gewerkschaftliche Praxis von der Konzeption der produktivitätsorientierten Tarifpolitik bestimmt worden ist. Davon völlig abgewichen wurde 1990/91 im Prozess der Übertragung der Tarifverträge auf die neuen Länder. Hier wurde die Größe der Arbeitsproduktivität generell nicht berücksichtigt, nicht nur weil es dafür keine verwendbaren Daten, sondern nur grobe Schätzungen gab, sondern weil die Tarifverhandlungen in den neuen Ländern durch eine andere normative Formel bestimmt waren: gleicher Lohn für gleiche Arbeit. Das entsprach auch den Erwartungen der neuen Mitglieder. Faktisch wurden die Ergebnisse dieser Tarifpolitik nicht realisiert, da es sehr schnell zu einer flächendeckenden Arbeitslosigkeit gekommen war. Die Lohnentwicklung spielte angesichts des veralteten Kapitalstocks der früheren DDR-Wirtschaft dabei eine untergeordnete Rolle. Das Arbeitsmarktdesaster und die 1993 beginnende Konjunkturkrise waren dann die Basis einer weitreichenden tarifpolitischen Ernüchterung und Kehrtwende in den DGB-Gewerkschaften spätestens nach 1994.

4. Das Bündnis für Arbeit, Ausbildung und Wettbewerbsfähigkeit 1998 bis 2002

Nach der Regierungsbildung im Herbst 1998 stand ein neues Bündnis für Arbeit unmittelbar auf der Tagesordnung. Die Gewerkschaften hatten es nach dem ersten Scheitern dieser Versuche gefordert und die neue Bundesregierung war dieser Forderung bereitwillig nachgekommen. Von Anfang an hatten die sozialwissenschaftlichen Berater des Bundeskanzleramts für das Bündnis eine allgemeine Lohnzurückhaltung, eine stärkere Lohnspreizung nach unten und darüber hinaus eine steuerliche Subventionierung eines intendierten Niedriglohnsektors empfohlen (Streeck 1999). Diese Vorschläge waren seit dem Ende der 1980er Jahre in der Diskussion (Scharpf 1988, 1993). In den Gewerkschaften wurden diese Vorschläge kontrovers diskutiert, aber letztlich nicht akzeptiert, was kritische Kommentare aus dem Lager der sozialwissenschaftlichen Berater provozierte. Aus deren Sicht hatten die Gewerkschaften im Bündnis für Arbeit eine große Chance versäumt.

Ob die bereits erwähnte Vereinbarung vom 9. Januar 2000 als Lohnleitlinie für die anstehenden Tarifverhandlungen gewirkt hat, ist umstritten. Deutlich wird sie als Lohnleitlinie am Tarifabschluss für die chemische Industrie, als die IG BCE im März 2000 einen zweistufigen Abschluss von 2,2% für 12 Monate und danach 2,0% für weitere 9 Monate vereinbart hatte. Das konnte als Nachvollzug dieser Vereinbarung interpretiert werden, auch deshalb, weil die IG BCE ihre Bereitschaft erklärt hatte, im Bündnis auch über Tarifpolitik zu sprechen. Die IG BCE hatte den Kurswechsel zu einer „nachfrageorientierten" Tarifpolitik, der von Heiner Flassbeck und Oskar Lafontaine 1998 initiiert worden war, explizit abgelehnt. Der darauf folgende Abschluss der IGM in Nordrhein-Westfalen, dem Bezirk, der damals die tarifpolitische Pilotfunktion wahrnehmen wollte, konnte mit einem Volumen von 3,0% für 12 und 2,1% für die nächsten 10 Monate nebst Verbesserungen des Altersteilzeittarifvertrages auch als Nachvollzug dieser Vereinbarung gesehen werden. In der IGM selbst wurde dieser Abschluss heftig kritisiert (Urban 2000: 13f.), da das WSI für 2000 einen Verteilungsspielraum von 4,2 errechnet hatte (WSI 2014). In der ÖTV wurde für den Bereich des öffentlichen Dienstes ein Schlichterspruch von 1,8% für 12 und danach 2,2% für 9 Monate plus eines Stufenplans zur Angleichung der Ost-Entgelte bis 90%, entgegen dem Votum der Verhandlungsführung, in der zuständigen Tarifkommission abgelehnt. Es kam danach aber nicht zu einem Arbeitskampf. Die Urabstimmung hatte mit gerade 76% nur ein knappes Votum für einen Streik ergeben. Danach wurde ein geringfügig modifiziertes Ergebnis angenommen.

Damit war es in den wichtigen Tarifbereichen zu Abschlüssen gekommen, die der Lohnformel der Vereinbarung auf den ersten Blick gefolgt waren. Anders als die IG BCE haben die Verantwortlichen von IGM und ÖTV bestritten, dass diese Vereinbarung als eine Art Lohnleitlinie verstanden worden ist. Mit den nominalen Erhöhungen waren auch kostenwirksame Regelungen zur Altersteilzeit und zur Angleichung Ost vereinbart worden, die die Gesamtergebnisse etwas angehoben hatten. Entscheidend ist aber bei der Frage nach der Rolle dieser Vereinbarung, dass ihre Wirkung in den Gewerkschaften im Laufe des Jahres 2001 zunehmend in Frage gestellt wurde. In der ÖTV wurden die Resultate dieser Verständigung auf dem letzten Gewerkschaftstag vor der Gründung von ver.di in einem nahezu einstimmigen Beschluss heftig kritisiert: „Insofern war die zurückhaltende Tarifpolitik der Tarifabschlüsse des Jahres 2000 gerade nicht beschäftigungsfördernd (...). Eine am Verteilungsspielraum der Produktivitätsorientierung ausgerichtete Tarifpolitik hätte über die Stärkung des inländischen Konsums zu höheren positiven Beschäftigungseffekten geführt. Mit der zurückhaltenden Tarifpolitik der Jahre 2000/ 2001 wird auch die Doorner Initiative als Koordinierung der westeuropäischen Tarifpolitik unterlaufen. Damit inszeniert Deutschland einen Lohnsenkungswettlauf innerhalb des europäischen Binnenmarktes, der für die Beschäftigung im gesamten Binnenmarkt schädlich ist, auch wenn er kurzfristig einen nationalen Vorteil ermöglicht." (Bsirske et al. 2001)

Darin drückt sich eine deutliche Kritik am Bündnis für Arbeit, Ausbildung und Wettbewerbsfähigkeit aus, die dazu führte, dass es danach nur noch ergebnislos weitergeführt und im März 2003 beendet wurde. Bereits im Laufe des Jahres 2002 wurden um 5,5 bis 6,5% höhere Löhne gefordert. Faktisch war der Einfluss, der vom Bündnis 1999 und 2000 ausgegangen war, bereits 2002 beendet, obwohl sich die konjunkturelle Situation deutlich verschlechtert hatte und die Arbeitslosigkeit angestiegen war. Der SVR war entsprechend unzufrieden mit der Lohnpolitik des Jahres 2002: „Damit hat sich in der Lohnpolitik eine Abkehr von moderaten, unter dem Produktivitätsfortschritt liegenden Tariflohnsteigerungen vollzogen" (SVR 2002: Ziff. 198).

Diese Kritik motivierte die Mehrheit im Rat dann zu den 20 Programmpunkten für Wachstum und Beschäftigung, mit denen eine neoklassisch fundierte Konzeption für Lohnzurückhaltung und mehr Beschäftigung vorgeschlagen wurde, die dann als Richtschnur für die Agenda 2010 dienen sollte (SVR 2002: Ziff. 374ff.). Ein Jahr später stellte der Rat fest, „dass die Tariflohnpolitik ihrer Verantwortung für mehr Beschäftigung auch 2003 nicht nachgekommen ist. Die Tarifparteien nahmen keinen Abschlag vom erwarteten Verteilungsspielraum vor; lediglich durch Kürzungen der übertariflichen Leistungen, also durch eine negative Lohndrift, war es den Unternehmen möglich, eine vollständige Ausschöpfung des tatsächlich realisierten Verteilungsspielraums zu verhindern" (SVR 2003: Ziff. 63).

5. Viel Lärm um wenig?

Erst mit den aus der Agenda 2010 folgenden Entscheidungen zur Deregulierung des Arbeitsmarktes durch die sogenannten Hartz-Gesetze bei gleichzeitig hoher Arbeitslosigkeit wurde der längerfristige Lohndruck erzeugt, der für die ungleiche Entwicklung in den Ländern der Eurozone verantwortlich ist (Dustmann et al. 2014). Für den öffentlichen Dienst resultierte dieser Lohndruck aus der desolaten Haushaltslage der Gebietskörperschaften und dem dadurch verstärkten Trend zur Privatisierung öffentlicher Aufgaben. Das verleitete ver.di dazu, einen Niedriglohnbereich in den eigenen Tarifverträgen zu akzeptieren. Mit dem Rückgang der Arbeitslosigkeit 2006 und nach der schnellen Überwindung der Folgen der Finanzmarktkrise für die deutsche Exportindustrie 2009 konnte das deutsche Tarifvertragssystem wieder stabilisiert werden. Damit verbunden war ab 2011 in der Tendenz eine Rückkehr zur produktivitätsorientierten Lohnpolitik, die 2015 noch anhält. Dabei sehen wir eine divergierende Entwicklung: Die Industriegewerkschaften haben in den exportgetriebenen Branchen deutlich höhere nominale Steigerungen der Tarifentgelte durchsetzen können als die Gewerkschaften in den binnenmarktorientierten Dienstleistungssektoren. So stiegen nach Angaben des WSI die Tarifentgelte in der Metallindustrie indexiert von 2000 (= 100) bis 2015 auf 148,6, in der chemischen Industrie auf 148,1, während sie im öffentlichen Dienst nur auf 137,7 und im Einzelhandel auf 133,1 angestiegen waren. Der gleichzeitige Verbraucherpreisindex stieg auf 124,7. Dabei ist bezogen auf die absolute Höhe der Tarifentgelte die Spreizung zwischen den Industrie- und den Dienstleistungslöhnen beträchtlich (Horn et al. 2007).

Von dieser Entwicklung völlig abgekoppelt wurde der nicht tarifgebundene Beschäftigungssektor, der ab 2000 Reallohneinbußen hinnehmen musste, während die durchschnittlichen tariflichen Bruttolöhne real von 2000 bis 2014 um rund 10% gestiegen sind. Die Re-Stabilisierung des Tarifvertragssystems wird durch die Einführung des gesetzlichen Mindestlohns spürbar unterstützt, weil der Lohndruck aus den Bereichen der niedrigsten Löhne eingeschränkt werden kann. Wenn wir heute eine Bilanz dieses Bündnisses für Arbeit, Ausbildung und Wettbewerbsfähigkeit ziehen, so hat es ohne Zweifel für die Tarifbewegung 2000/2001 eine Rolle gespielt. Die Gewerkschaften hatten sich damals teils freiwillig, teils gezwungen auf diese „schiefe Bahn" der Lohnzurückhaltung führen lassen. Die zentrale tarifpolitische Fehlentscheidung geschah 1995 mit der Initiative von Klaus Zwickel. War diese Entscheidung mit Blick auf die Europäische Währungsunion „deliberate", also absichtlich, oder intentional? Dazu hätten die Akteure die Rolle der Löhne in einer Währungsunion verstehen müssen, was nicht der Fall war. Das gilt ebenso für den SVR und die seiner Sicht folgenden Ökonomen. Die SPD hatte sich zwischen 1999 und 2009 nach der Preisgabe ihrer früher moderat keynesianischen Position instinktiv dem neoklassischen Mainstream angeschlossen. Insofern akzeptiert sie nach wie vor diesen exportgetriebenen Merkantilismus. Das beeinflusste auch die gewerkschaftliche Willensbildung. Die Gewerkschaften hatten sich aber in erster Linie angestrengt, um ihre tarifpolitische Funktion zu verteidigen. Das ist ihnen, wenn auch mit Abstrichen, gelungen. Ob es ihnen gelingt, ihre Tarifpolitik zukünftig stärker nach makroökonomischen Gesichtspunkten auszurichten, bleibt eine offene Frage. Es mangelt hier nicht an der entsprechenden Beratung durch die beiden Forschungsinstitute der Hans-Böckler-Stiftung, sondern stärker an der Umsetzung der Erkenntnisse in die tarifpolitische Praxis.

Literatur

Bsirske F. et al.: Antrag C1 des a.o. Gewerkschaftstags der ÖTV 2001 (im Archiv des Verfassers).

Bofinger, P. (2015): German wage moderation and the EZ Crisis (http://www.voxeu.org/article/german-wage-moderation-and-ez-crisis).

Bündnis für Arbeit, Ausbildung und Wettbewerbsfähigkeit (2000): Gemeinsame Erklärung zu den Ergebnissen des Spitzengesprächs am 9. Januar 2000, in: Blätter für deutsche und internationale Politik, 2/2000, S. 250-252.

Dustmann, C., Fitzenberger, B., Schönberg, U., Spitz-Oener, A. (2014): From sick man of Europe to economic superstar: Germany's Resurgent Economy, in: *Journal of Economic Perspectives*, 28(1), 167-188.

Erber, G., Hagemann, H. (2012): Zur Produktivitätsentwicklung Deutschlands im internationalen Vergleich, WISO-Diskurs, Friedrich-Ebert-Stiftung.

Flassbeck, H. (1997): Und die Spielregeln für die Lohnpolitik in einer Währungsunion?, in: *Frankfurter Rundschau* v. 31.10.1997.

Flassbeck, H., Lapavitsas, C. (2015): *Nur Deutschland kann den Euro retten*, Frankfurt a.M.

Flassbeck, H., Spiecker, F. (2000): Reallohn und Arbeitslosigkeit. Es gibt keine Wahl – Die neoklassische Wahlthese erweist sich beim Vergleich der USA mit Europa als falsch, in: *WSI-Mitteilungen*, 53(11), 706-717.

Flassbeck, H., Spiecker, F. (2005): Die deutsche Lohnpolitik sprengt die Währungsunion, in: *WSI-Mitteilungen*, 58(12), 707-713.

Görgens, H. (2014): *Zur Ausschöpfung des Verteilungsspielraums*, Marburg.

Heilemann, U., Ulrich, J. (2008): Viel Lärm um wenig? Zur Empirie der Lohnformeln, Working Paper Nr. 68, Universität Leipzig.

Heine, M., Herr, H. (2004): *Die Europäische Zentralbank*, Marburg.

Herr, H. (1991): Der Merkantilismus der Bundesrepublik in der Weltwirtschaft, in: Voy, K., Polster, W., Thomasberger, C. (Hg.), *Marktwirtschaft und politische Regulierung*, Marburg.

Herr, H. (1992): *Geld, Währungswettbewerb und Währungssysteme*, Frankfurt a.M.

Herr, H., Horn, G.A. (2012): Lohnpolitik heute, IMK Policy Brief, Mai, Düsseldorf.

Horn, G.A., Logeay, C., Stephan, S., Zwiener, R. (2007): Preiswerte Arbeit in Deutschland, Auswertung der aktuellen Eurostat Arbeitskostenstatistik, IMK Report, Nr. 22, September.

Horn, G.A., Mülhaupt, B., Rietzler, K. (2005): Quo vadis Euroraum? Deutsche Lohnpolitik belastet Währungsunion, IMK Report, Nr. 1, August.

Köddermann, R. (1996): Sind Löhne und Steuern zu hoch? Bemerkungen zur Standortsicherung in Deutschland, in: *Ifo-Schnelldienst*, 20/96, 6-14.

Lindlar, L. (1995): Hat Westdeutschland ein Standortproblem?, in: *DIW-Wochenbericht*, 38/95, 653-661.

Marx, K. (1972): *Das Kapital*, Bd. 1, Marx-Engels-Werke, Bd. 23, Berlin.

Scharpf, F.W. (1988): Weltweite, europäische oder nationale Optionen der Vollbeschäftigungspolitik?, in: *Gewerkschaftliche Monatshefte*, 1, 14-25.

Scharpf, F.W. (1993): Von der Finanzierung der Arbeitslosigkeit zur Subventionierung niedriger Erwerbseinkommen, in: *Gewerkschaftliche Monatshefte*, 7, 433-443.

Schmidt, R. (2003): Der gescheiterte Streik in der ostdeutschen Metallindustrie, in: *Prokla*, 132, 493-509.

Schroeder, W. (2003): Die Transformation einer bundesdeutschen Basisinstitution, in: *Prokla*, 130, 147-158.

Streeck W. (1996): Anmerkungen zum Flächentarifvertrag und seiner Krise, in: *Gewerkschaftliche Monatshefte*, 2, 86-97.

Streeck, W. (1999): Der deutsche Kapitalismus: Gibt es ihn? Kann er überleben?, in: Ders., *Korporatismus in Deutschland: zwischen Nationalstaat und Europäischer Union*, Frankfurt a.M., New York, 13-40.

SVR – Sachverständigenrat zur Begutachtung der gesamtwirtschaftlichen Entwicklung (2002): Zwanzig Punkte für Beschäftigung und Wachstum. Jahresgutachten 2002/03, Wiesbaden.

SVR – Sachverständigenrat zur Begutachtung der gesamtwirtschaftlichen Entwicklung (2003): Staatsfinanzen konsolidieren – Steuersystem reformieren. Jahresgutachten 2003/04, Wiesbaden.

Urban, H.J. (Hg.) (2000): *Beschäftigungsbündnis oder Standortpakt?*, Hamburg.

Wren-Lewis, S. (2015): Was German Wage Undercutting Deliberate? (http://www.mainlymacro.blogspot.co.uk/2015/12/was-german-wages-undercutting-deliberate.html).

WSI (2014): *Statistisches Taschenbuch Tarifpolitik*, Düsseldorf:

IV.

Ökonomische Entwicklung und globale Wertschöpfungsketten

Economic Development and Global Value Chains

A comparison on trade dependence and industrial structure in China and India: A global value chain perspective[*]

Yang Laike and Zheng Guojiao

1. Introduction

China and India are the two largest developing countries with many common characteristics regarding economic development. As two members of BRICS countries, they are the typical representatives of emerging economies. In 2015, China's GDP reached $11 trillion and India's reached $2 trillion, making them the world's second and ninth largest economy respectively. With huge population and large-sized production, trade plays a significant role in both two countries' economic development. But since the economic system and industrial structure of the two countries are very different, China is much more depending on foreign trade than India according to the traditional trade statistics.

Thus, it is important and interesting to compare the trade dependence of the two countries and analyze the factors behind the differences. However, in recent years, due to the rapid integration in international production networks and the evolution of global value chains (GVC), international trade is increasingly dominated by the trade in parts and components. It then has been argued explicitly that standard trade statistics on final products do not give accurate information anymore about the actual value which a country adds in the global production process. Especially for countries which have to import a large amount of intermediate inputs to assemble their exports, such as China.

[*] The paper is supported by China National Social Science Fund (Key Project, Grant No. 16AGJ002) and Research Project from Ministry of Education in China (Grant No. 10YJA790221). However, viewpoints are of the authors and not of any of mentioned organizations. Any errors solely remain to the author.

In this paper we aim to estimate the effects of Chinese and Indian exports on their countries' economic development, namely, the ratio of trade dependence from the domestic value-added perspective, which contributes directly to their total gross domestic product. We then decompose the influential factors by structure decomposition analysis. Finally, we derive some policy recommendations for these countries.

The paper is organized as follows: Section 2 reviews the recent relevant literature in the field. Section 3 describes the methodology and data we use to measure the dependency ratio of trade and to analyze the factors of the trade dependence ratio. Section 4 shows the results of the factor decomposition analysis. Section 5 concludes and provides some policy implications.

2. Methodology and data

2.1 RDT calculation

There are two ways to calculate the RDT (dependence on foreign trade): the calculation by conventional trade data and calculation by trade in value added.

a. *Conventional RDT calculation.* This method was first developed by Grassman (1980) and quickly became the most commonly used formula for measuring the degree of a nation's openness. The formula is as follow:

$$RDT = \frac{\sum_{s=1}^{n} ex_s}{GDP} \qquad (1)$$

Where $\sum_{s=1}^{n} ex_s$ is the conventional total export, RDT is the conventional dependence on trade.

b. *Value added RDT calculation.* As previously mentioned, since the 2000s many scholars have criticized Grassman's method for its simplicity and for being imprecise. A modified calculation based on value-added trade has been developed based on the work of Johnson and Noguere (2012) and Koopman and Wei (2014). The formula is as follows:

$$RDT^{adv} = \frac{va_{ij}}{GDP} \qquad (2)$$

Where va_{ij} is the domestic value added in trade, RDT^{adv} is the dependence on trade base on the value added trade.

The key method to calculate domestic value added is Input-Output Analysis (IOA) which was first developed by Leontief in the 1950s. Earlier IOAs are all based on single region Input-output tables. Recently, it has been replaced by Multiregional Input-output tables when analyzing international trade. The most widely applied approach for calculating domestic value added is proposed by Johnson and Noguera (2012), based on the assumption that intermediate trade flows between regions are only determined by reproduction and final consumption.

In this paper, we assume there are S sectors and N countries. Each country produces a single differentiated tradable good within each sector, and we define the quantity of output produced in sector s of country i to be $y_i(s)$. This good is produced by combining local inputs with domestic and imported intermediate goods. It is then either used to satisfy final demand (equivalently, "consumed") or used as an intermediate input in production. The market clearing condition in value terms is:

$$y_i(s) = \sum_j \sum_t m_{ij}(s,t) + \sum_j c_{ij}(s) \tag{3}$$

In Eq. (3), i and j denote countries or regions. s and t denote the sectors. $y_i(s)$ denotes the output of country i in sector s. $m_{ij}(s,t)$ denotes country j's consumption of intermediate products from country i in sector s. $c_{ij}(s)$ denotes country j's consumption of final products from country i in sector s. Eq. (3) shows that output is divided into domestic final use, domestic intermediate use, and gross exports.

Assume there are N countries and S sectors, the world's total output can be shown in matrix form:

$$y = Ay + \sum_j c_j \tag{4}$$

where, y is the output block matrix, $y = \begin{pmatrix} y_1 \\ y_2 \\ \vdots \\ y_n \end{pmatrix}$,

A is the world's input-output matrix, $A = \begin{pmatrix} A_{11} & \cdots & A_{1n} \\ \vdots & \ddots & \vdots \\ A_{m1} & \cdots & A_{mn} \end{pmatrix}$,

c_j is country J's final consumption matrix, $c_j = \begin{pmatrix} c_{1j} \\ c_{2j} \\ \vdots \\ c_{Nj} \end{pmatrix}$

Using this framework, the world's output can be rewritten into Leotief's inverse matrix as:

$$y = \sum_j (I-A)^{-1} c_j \tag{5}$$

Eq. (5) thus decomposes output from each source country i into the amount of output from the source used to produce final goods absorbed in country j. To make this explicit, we define:

$$\begin{pmatrix} y_{1j} \\ y_{2j} \\ \vdots \\ y_{Nj} \end{pmatrix} = (I-A)^{-1} c_j \tag{6}$$

To calculate the value added associated with these implicit output transfers, define the ratio of value added to output for each sector within country i, as

$$r_i(t) = 1 - \sum_j \sum_s A_{ji}(s,t) \tag{7}$$

Thus, the total value added produced in sector s in source country i and absorbed in destination country j is

$$va_{ij}(s) = r_i(s) y_{ii}(s). \tag{8}$$

Total value added produced in i and absorbed in j is then

$$va_{ij} = \sum_s va_{ij}(s) \tag{9}$$

The sector-level bilateral value added to export ratio is given by $va_{ij}(s)/x_{ij}(s)$. $x_{ij}(s)$ represents the conventional gross export amount.

2.2 Structure decomposition analysis for RDT^{adv}

From above analysis, we can divide RDT^{adv} into two components as shown in equation 10, value added export ratio (VAX) and traditional RDT:

$$RDT^{adv} = \frac{va_{ij}}{\sum_{s=1}^{n} ex_s} \times \frac{\sum_{s=1}^{n} ex_s}{GDP} = Vax \times RDT \tag{10}$$

And the VAX ratio in one country can be decomposed as:

$$Vax = \frac{va_{ij}}{\sum_{s=1}^{n} ex_s} = \sum \left(\frac{va_{ij}(s)}{ex(s)} \times \frac{ex(s)}{\sum_{s=1}^{n} ex_s} \right) \tag{11}$$

Then, we can conclude that:

$$RDT^{adv} = Vax_{ij} \times xr_{ij} \times RDT$$

$$RDT^{adv} = Vax_{ij} \times xr_{ij} \times RDT \tag{12}$$

Further decompose the RDT^{adv}, we get:

$$\Delta RDT^{adv} = \underbrace{\Delta Vax \times xr_0 \times RDT_0}_{a} + \underbrace{Vax_1 \times \Delta xr \times RDT_0}_{b} + \underbrace{Vax_1 \times xr_1 \times \Delta RDT}_{c} \tag{13}$$

             VAX ratio effect   exports structure effect   demand expansion effect

2.3 Data sources

The data source for the structural decomposition analysis (SDA) in this paper is the World Input Output Database (WIOD) which provides time-series of inter-country input-output tables for 40 countries. Due to its clear description of inter-country and inter-sector flows along global production processes, the input-output method has been widely accepted to measure domestic-value-added of international trade (Koopman/Wei 2014). To highlight our analysis, we focus the measurement in 15 major economics, combine EU countries as integration and the rest of the world as ROW. Given that the service trade is limited in China and India, we combine the service industries into 2 catalogs, which are consumer services and producer services. The world input-output table contains 17 industries and 15 economics finally.

3. Literature review

The ratio of dependence on foreign trade (RDT) was originally conceived to illustrate the economic dependence among international markets (Grassman 1980). The traditional calculation method showed that China had seen a rising trend while India's trend was much flatter with minor fluctuations from 1995-2012. Since China joined the WTO in 2001, two important interrelated phenomena have attracted a great deal of interest by researchers. The first one is the slicing-up of the value chain, where the production processes are sliced into many stages in different locations, including different countries. The second one is, that – based on the gross trade statistics – China's RDT reached 67% of GDP while India's RDT was only 33.6%. High dependence on exports also pushes up China's trade surplus/GDP ratio from 2 % in 2000 to 7.6% in 2007, which makes China suffer from strong accusations of dumping by cheap products and currency manipulation.

However, many scholars argue that the traditional trade statistics exaggerated the RDT in China and call for a modification of the methods and new system of trade statistics (Shen Lisheng 2005; Huang Yan 2003). Therefore, how to precisely measure RDT is still one important question that needs to be answered. So far, most of the literature measuring the RDT has been focused on one country's export measured by nominal value. This can reflect the degree of dependence on foreign trade to some extent, however, some issues, such as the statistical standards, the exchange rate, the processing exports etc., have not been taken into consideration. For this reason, many scholars put forward a series of modifications for the calculation methods.

The first modification is using total economic activity (both domestic and foreign market activities) to substitute GDP. This modification can ensure the consistency of economic meaning between numerator (total foreign markets activity) and denominator (the total domestic market activity) in the equation of RDT. Using this modified equation, some scholars argue that China's

RDT is not as high as in the conventional calculation, and China's RDT is not so much higher than that of the US and Japan (Shen Lisheng 2005; Huang Yan 2003).

The second modification is to correct the conventional trade and GDP data. By calculating the ratio between trade in commodities and merchandise, some scholars confirmed that China's trade dependency ratio is not as high as when we use nominal GDP and traditional trade data (Zhang Xun/Zheng Guihuang 2006). But this correction is criticized because it fails to take into account the service trade. Other scholars trying to calculate the RDT using Purchasing Power Parity based GDP and trade data (Li Xin/Xu Tianqing 2013; Peng Jianping 2010). Their results also show that China's RDT is not as high as people believe.

Though the literature on RDT generally suggests that the conventional calculation method overestimated China's dependency ratio on foreign trade, most of them still mainly use the total trade database. There is very little literature providing both measurement on GDP and value added in international trade, based on the domestic value added database. In the context of the international division of labor and the deepening of the global production value chain, the value added trade statistics can settle the "double accounting" issues. The new trade statistics can truly reflect the contribution of a country's domestic production to the final consumption product. In 2013, the Trade in Value Added (TiVA) database has been developed by OECD and WTO. Since then, many more studies have been done based on the TiVA data. Li Xin and Xu Tianqing (2013) recalculated the RDT of China in 2007. Their study shows that China's RDT was actually only 31.6%. Yang Laike/ Zheng Guojiao (2015) using the new database analyzed Chinese-Japanese trade, also drew conclusions that were very different from those of previous studies.

This paper is to reanalyze the RDT of China and India using domestic value added as the indicator of economic benefits, which can give us a better understanding of the two countries' economic structure and the factors behind it.

4. Results and discussions

4.1 The trend of RTD in China and India

Based on the above mentioned method, we calculated the RTD of China and India from 1995-2009 from a domestic-value-added perspective. The results are as follows:

As displayed in Figure 1, China's RDT^{adv} generally is on an upward sloping trend. It rose from 19.2% to 28.8% during the period of 1995-2009; the average annual rate of growth is 2.9%. But according to traditional trade statistics China's RDT was much higher. Before joining the WTO, it remained around 18% with narrow fluctuations. Then after joining WTO, the export volumes increased rapidly which results in a fast increase in the export dependency ratio. The RTD reached the peak point of 34.5% in 2008. After that it decreased a bit, due to the global financial crisis.

Fig. 1: The dependence on international trade of China in1995-2009

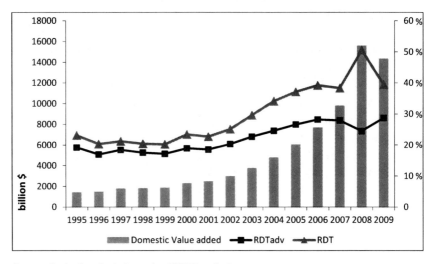

Source: Author's calculation using WIOD trade data

As shown in Figure 2, the situation in India was different. India's RDT^{adv} was increasing moderately till 2006, then descending ever since. The RDT^{adv} fluctuated around 10.5% from 1995-1999 and stayed at around 15% steadily after the liberalization policy implementation. Compared to RDT, it declines significantly. The gap between RDT and RDT^{adv} in India is much smaller.

This difference with respect to China can be explained by the fact that China is doing much more processing and assembly manufacture. The overestimation of RDT in China is accordingly much higher and therefore the need for adjustment is much higher. The results also tell us that China is involved in the international division of labor more deeply than India.

Fig. 2: *The dependence on international trade of India in1995-2009*

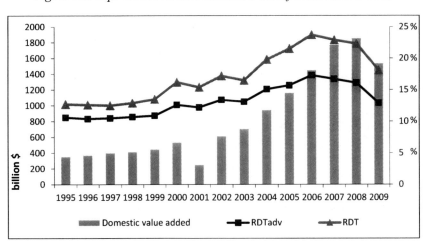

Source: Author's calculation using WIOD trade data

4.2 Overall RDT^{adv} decomposition

The decomposition of RDT^{adv} could offer insights into comprehension of dependence on trade and help us trace it by different industries. VAX ratio can measure a country's or region's integration in the global value chain (Johnson and Noguera, 2012). Figure 3 shows that both China and India see a decline in the VAX ratio. In China, it declines from 83.6% in 1995 to 75.5% in 2011. The peak point is 86.4% in 1998, the turning point of the VAX ratio is 2001 when China joins the WTO. Given that China has become the largest exporter taking active participation in global value chain. It contains much more domestic value, so its VAX ratio increased gradually since 2005. India's VAX ratio also showed a downward trend overall but in a slightly smoother way. Opposite to China, it did not stop declining in recent years which shows that India has enhanced its position in the outsourcing of manufacturing.

Fig. 3: The VAX ratio of China and India in 1995-2011

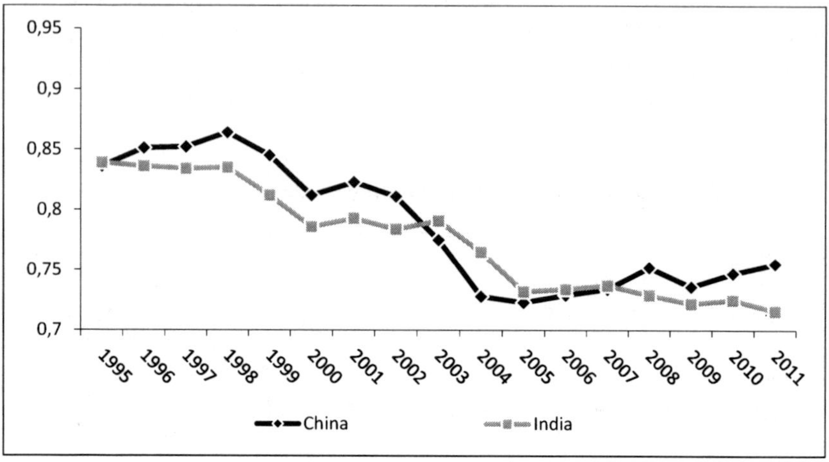

[Line chart showing VAX ratio for China and India from 1995 to 2011, with values ranging roughly from 0.7 to 0.9, both trending downward over the period.]

Source: Author's calculation using WIOD trade data

As shown in Table 1, in both countries, the demand expansion effect is positive and greater than the effect of the VAX ratio. The fact that China's demand-expansion-effect (0.1189) was significantly higher than India's (0.0375) while the VAX-ratio-effect was lower than India's indicating that China's export-oriented economic growth was more led by scale-expansion. China should increase local contents of its export products and lower the demand expansion effect on RDT.

Table 1: Overall decomposition of RDT^{adv} of China and India (1995/2009)

	Time	RDT	Total VAX Ratio	RDT^{adv}	VAX ratio effect (1995/2009)	Demand expansion effect (1995/2009)
China	1995	23.06%	0.836	19.15%	-0.0231	0.1189
	2009	39.34%	0.755	28.74%		
India	1995	12.73%	0.839	10.57%	-0.0140	0.0375
	2009	17.96%	0.716	12.93%		

Source: Author's calculation using WIOD trade data

From Table 1, we can see China's RDT^{adv} increased from 19.2% in 1995 to 28.7% in 2009, what are the factors behind this change? The decomposition analysis shows, among the three main factors determining the RDT^{adv}, the demand expansion effect is dominating followed by the exports structure effect. The VAX ratio effect is the weakest. The demand expansion effect is almost always positive which states the scales of China's exports expanded considerably. There are industrial differences in the structure effects. In labor-intensive industries its effect is negative while in capital and knowledge-intensive industries it is positive. This phenomenon reflects the optimization of China's export structure which means China's competitiveness in technology-intensive products has improved. As to the details, the structure effect of textiles and textile products is the most negative (-1.92%), the structure effect of transport and transport equipment is the most positive (0.4%). The result shows that in the last few decades, a considerable progress has been taken place in China's technology-intensive and capital-intensive industries, which played a leading role in China's international trade. But the service exports are still weak; its contribution in RDT^{adv} is limited.

There are many similarities between China and India. India's export structure has also been optimized to some extent, but the adjustment is smaller compared to China. For instance, the structure effect of recycling manufacture industries is the largest (0.39%). Consistent with China, the electronic industry's VAX ratio is the highest (0.77%). However, the consumer service's structure effect is negative (-0.36%). The producer service sector's competitiveness is stronger than China. Its pulling effect to India's economic development is significantly higher than in China.

From industrial perspective, the VAX ratio effect in most sectors is negative. As an indicator to measure the participation rate in the global value chain, the declinations in the VAX ratio tell us that although China has integrated in the world production network, China's share in the global value chain is decreasing.

Specifically speaking, the consumer service sectors and the mining sectors have a relatively higher domestic value added because their inputs are mostly from the domestic market. Oppositely, the producers' service sectors and most manufacturing industries have a lower value added, because they rely very much on components and intermediate products from the international market. Their VAX ratio is decreasing, too.

In India, The VAX ratio effect is almost negative in all industries. From 1995 to 2009, both the VAX ratio effect and the structure effect of textile products and the tobacco industry are all negative, which results in the RDT^{adv}

Table 2: Structure decomposition analysis (SDA) of RDT^{adv} of China and India

		1995/2009SDA (India)			1995/2009SDA (China)		
		VAX ratio effect	Export structure effect	Demand expansion effect	VAX ratio effect	Export structure effect	Demand expansion effect
Labor-intensive industries	Mining	0.0001	0.0016	0.0017	-0.0004	-0.0036	0.0006
	Food and tobacco	-0.0003	-0.0026	0.0015	-0.0005	-0.0006	0.0033
	Textiles and textile	-0.0029	-0.0119	0.0039	0.0005	-0.0214	0.0150
	Leather and footwear	-0.0001	-0.0036	0.0003	0.0003	-0.0064	0.0030
	Wood products	-0.0001	-0.0002	0.0004	-0.0001	-0.0023	0.0008
	Paper and printing	0.0000	-0.0021	0.0001	-0.0002	-0.0014	0.0005
	Plastics	-0.0002	-0.0009	0.0005	-0.0008	-0.0021	0.0034
	Other non-metallic mineral	-0.0002	-0.0074	0.0003	-0.0004	-0.0021	0.0015
	Total	-0.0018	-0.0290	0.0085	-0.0041	-0.0441	0.0291
Capital-intensive industries	Petroleum and nuclear fuel	-0.0001	0.0023	0.0011	-0.0003	-0.0002	0.0006
	Chemicals	-0.0007	-0.0019	0.0021	-0.0005	0.0041	0.0056
	Basic metals	-0.0003	0.0029	0.0024	-0.0025	-0.0041	0.0061
	Transport and equipment	-0.0002	0.0026	0.0020	-0.0004	0.0040	0.0047
	Other manufacturing	-0.0041	0.0039	0.0038	0.0000	0.0009	0.0044
	Total	-0.0031	0.0199	0.0071	-0.0040	0.0055	0.0218
Technol.-intensive industries	Machinery	-0.0001	0.0004	0.0013	-0.0008	0.0057	0.0076
	Electronic and optical	-0.0004	0.0077	0.0043	-0.0066	0.0192	0.0338
	Total	-0.0005	0.0080	0.0056	-0.0068	0.0221	0.0435
Services	Production services	-0.0002	0.0126	0.0094	-0.0009	0.0066	0.0144
	Consumption services	0.0003	-0.0036	0.0022	-0.0002	0.0069	0.0115

Source: Author's calculation using WIOD trade data

of labor-intensive industries declining a lot. The VAX ratio effect of leasing and business services is positive, indicating that it has a great deal of domestic value added in these industries and the competitiveness is relatively strong.

5. Conclusion

Based on the WIOD database and the RDT^{adv} calculation methods, the paper analyzes the RDT^{adv} and their decomposition factors determining the value-added trade in China and India during 1995-2009. The results show that China and India's RDT have significantly been overestimated using the conventional statistics methods of calculation. The differences between RDT and RDT^{adv} are about 10 percentage points in both two countries.

Both RDT and RDT^{adv} in China's hold an upward trend. While in India, both RDT and RDT^{adv} are more or less flat. This means that China's trade dependency ratio has been increasing consistently, whereas India's dependency ratio is not as high as in China and is not increasing. Precisely speaking, the RDT^{adv} was increasing before 2006 and then turn into a downward trend afterward.

The VAX ratio effect is negative in both countries, which results from reducing their share in obtained value added in exports of final products. The promotions of RDT^{adv} of both countries were mainly caused by export demand expansion in sample periods.

On the sector level, using the decomposition of RDT^{adv} methods, we found that the consumption expansion effect is the decisive factor, followed by the exports structure effect, and the VAX ratio effect is the weakest.

Under the value added export accounting, we can see that both China and India are shifting from labor-intensive industries to capital and technology-intensive industries gradually. The competitiveness of China's technology-intensive industries continues to improve, and India's services have shown a strong competitiveness.

As the 'world factory', China should focus on moving upward in the global value chain and improving her position in the international division of labor. China should shift from quantity expansion to quality improvement and increase the domestic value added in exports. The Chinese government should support the development of financial services and other knowledge-intensive services to optimize the export structure and maintain its pulling effects on economic growth.

References

Balassa, B. (1978): Exports and Economic Growth: Further Evidence, in: *Journal of Development Economics*, 5, 181-189.

Grassman, S. (1980): Long-term Trends in Openness of National Economics [J], in: *Oxford Economic Papers*, 32, 181-205.

Huang Yan (2003): A Study on China's Trade Openness [D]. Master Thesis of Jiangxi University of Finance and Economics.

Hummels, D. et al. (2001): The Nature and Growth of Vertical Specialization in World Trade, in: *Journal of International Economics*, 54, 75-96.

Johnson, R.C., Noguera, G. (2012): Accounting for Intermediates: Production Sharing and Trade in Value Added [J], in: *Journal of International Economics*, 86(2), 224-236.

Koopman, R. et al. (2012): Give Credit Where Credit Is Due: Tracing Value Added in Global Production Chains, NBER Working Paper No. 16426.

Koopman, R.Z, Wei, S.J. (2014): Tracing Value-added and Double Counting in Gross Exports, in: *American Economic Review*, 104(2), 459-494.

Li Xin, Xu Tianqing (2013): Reassessment of China's Trade Dependence-A Perspective of Value-added trade[J], in: *Chinese Social Science*, 1, 29-56.

Peng Jianping (2010): A comparison of China's Trade Dependency Based on Various Different Calculations [J], in: *Journal of Guangxi University of Finance and Economics*, 2, 101-106.

Lutz, E. (1980): Trade in non-factor Services: Past Trend and Current Issues, Staff Working Paper.

Shen Lisheng (2005): A Study on China's Trade Dependency [J], in: *Journal of Quantative and Technical Economics*, 7, 15-25.

Timmer, M.P. et al. (2012): New Measures of European Competitiveness: A Global Value Chain Perspective, WIOD Working Paper 9.

Wu, Y.R., Zhou, Z.Y. (2006): Changing Bilateral Trade Between China and India, in: *Journal of Asia Economics*, 17(3), 509-518.

Yang Laike, Zheng Guojiao (2015): A comparison on Trade in Service of China and India, in: *Journal of Economic Issues*, 8, 99-105.

Zhang Xun, Zheng Guihuan (2006): Current Situation and Issues of China's Trade Dependency [J], in: *Journal of Chinese Academy of Social Science*, 2, 113-119.

The effect of FDI on industry value-added: Evidence from China

Behzad Azarhoushang and Jennifer Pédussel Wu

1. Introduction

Since the 1990s, trade in intermediate goods and raw materials between Multi-National Companies (MNCs), their subsidiaries, and international subcontractors increased sharply and currently dominates world trade. In 2013, trade in the Global Value Chain (GVC) accounted for 80 percent of global trade (UNCTAD 2013). The revolution in Information and Communication Technology (ICT) due to innovative technology and decreasing trade costs encouraged MNCs to fragment production and outsource various stages to countries with lower factor costs (Baldwin 2013; Azarhoushang et al. 2016).

Opening subsidiaries in host countries via Foreign Direct Investment (FDI) is one method of outsourcing production stages and the amount of FDI has increased significantly in the past three decades, surpassing international trade in goods and services since the 1990s. According to UNCTAD (2013), the nominal stock of inward FDI tripled from 1980 to 2012. The patterns of international trade are clearly dependent on government interventions and FDI is no different. In addition, FDI has possible direct and indirect positive impacts on manufacturing value-added via technology spillovers and the creation of new employment opportunities. While various factors increase the positive effects of MNCs on the host country, the government policy of host countries is therefore one of the most important factors for directing FDI into constructive directions.

Currently among the top five FDI recipients in the world, four are developing economies (UNCTAD (2014) World Investment Report). Following economic reforms which began in 1978, China gradually became the top recipient of FDI among first, developing countries and in 2014, the world's largest recipient of inward FDI (World Bank 2012; UNCTAD 2014). During its gradual reform, China designed and implemented sound government policies to boost economic growth allowing a move from low value added to medium and high value-added industries (Naughton 2007; Azarhoushang 2013).

This paper observes the effects of FDI on China's manufacturing sector from 2003-2013. The value-added changes in manufacturing subsectors as well as Chinese government policies will be examined. Section 2 reviews different perspectives concerning the effects of GVC and FDI on the industrial development of developing countries. Section 3 evaluates Chinese government policy toward FDI, i.e., the national development plans and specific industrial policies. Section 4 analyzes and compares the performance of foreign and domestic firms in the textile, electronic machinery, and electronic equipment industries. The last section concludes with some future policy implications.

2. The global value chain and foreign direct investment

There are two types of FDI each linked closely to the two types of specialization in the GVCs: horizontal and vertical FDI, each of which has different effects on technology spillovers.

1. Horizontal FDI occurs when a company produces a product with the same production line and value chain in the host countries as in the home country. Therefore, horizontal FDI can improve horizontal specialization in host countries.

2. Vertical FDI takes place when a company wants to optimize its production cost by fragmenting each part of the value chain in countries with least costs. Since the 1990s, this type of FDI has become increasingly popular among MNCs to decrease their production cost and to keep their high profit mark up (Peng 2009).[1]

With horizontal FDI the probability of a positive technology spillover is higher than with vertical FDI as in the latter most production stages are outsourced to host countries including some R&D. Therefore, host countries benefit most from the attraction of higher value-added production stages such as design and R&D. Most horizontal FDI is within developed countries.

---

[1] Although it is difficult to statistically define the difference between Horizontal and Vertical FDI, Alfaro and Charlton (2009) by using firm-level database of 650,000 companies find that Vertical FDI is the dominant type of FDI among MNCs (more than 60 percent).

However, some developing countries also benefit from this type of FDI due to the increase in income levels and large domestic markets e.g., Volkswagen in China (Azarhoushang 2013). Zhu (2010) also found that FDI had positive spillovers for Chinese firms. Moreover, foreign companies practicing horizontal FDI in developing countries (including R&D) do not generally import the newest technologies; key competencies are kept in the country of the lead firm or in the developed 'North'. Alternatively, companies with market seeking motivations may establish research and development (R&D) centers in host countries in order to meet the special customers' demand in the host countries via product localization.

In order to accomplish market access goals, foreign companies normally work closely with domestic experts and local universities which allow the use of expertise concerning tastes and preferences of domestic customers. Local experts also benefit from working with new technologies and participation in R&D processes and the production of new goods. Their experiences can be used later in domestic companies (Damijan et al. 2003). Another factor which has effects on technology spillovers is the market structure. If host countries' markets have high entry barriers, for instance high tariffs or the existence of dominant domestic (or foreign firms in case of latecomers companies), foreign investors have to enter into host countries with a large amount of investment and relatively high technology in order to be competitive in the market.

Vertical FDI which dominates in developing countries, in contrast to horizontal FDI, does not show such positive technology and skills spillovers as it is typically focused on low tech specialized tasks in a small number of industries. Technologically very underdeveloped countries with very low skill levels can to a certain extent also benefit from vertical FDI. However, even after some upgrading of the technological skill level there is no incentive for headquarter firms to improve local technology and skills further.

If FDI mainly goes to developing countries for cost reduction motives, it can still lead to technology spillover and industrial upgrading through a variety of mechanisms. A common belief among mainstream economists is that being part of MNCs' GVC, developing countries do not need to build a wide and deep industrial base in order to be competitive in the world market, as they can be specialized in certain stages and industries. The latter may accelerate the industrialization process in these countries (OECD 2012). Foreign companies' investments in developing countries are generally in the lower value-added stages of production, a main feature of vertical specialization.

Access to managerial skills and advanced technologies are motives for host countries to attract FDI as foreign owned companies commonly have a higher technological standard, train local staff, or secure export channels. Local firms also benefit from the technologies and managerial skills of foreign firms through joint venture, reverse engineering, and hiring workers that are trained by working in foreign firms. Foreign owned firms also affect local companies through developing supply chains in the host countries and by forcing local firms via external control mechanisms to increase their quality and standards and/or help them to increase their managerial skills (Alfaro et al. 2010).

Benefiting from positive technology spillovers of FDI (either vertical or horizontal) depends on a number of different factors. Primarily, technology spillovers are highly reliant on the development level of the host country. If local companies do not have a relatively high technological and educational level, FDI cannot lead to positive technology spillovers and could lead to a crowding out of local companies due to their inability to compete with foreign firms (Singh 2011). Furthermore, if foreign companies invest in host countries only to export low value added goods and invest in labor intensive industries as well as in natural resources, it does not result in large positive technology spillover effects. Lin et al. (2009) examines Chinese domestic firms 1998-2005 and find that positive spillovers existed in terms of productivity resulting from both horizontal and vertical FDI although there was an important difference in the type (Non-Overseas or Overseas Chinese) of companies investing.

Thus, the type of FDI investment (i.e., wholly owned, joint venture or merger and acquisition) is an important factor. For instance, if foreign firms invest through mergers and acquisitions the level of technology spillover will be very low as usually foreign companies keep employees and production lines unchanged and only alter management. However, in many instances, foreign firms only invest to reap the benefits associated with cheap labor costs (or possibly government incentives) via vertical FDI and do not bring any additional positive technology spillovers.

In this sense, developing countries that want to accelerate their industrial development may face various risks resulting in a lock-in to the low value-added stages of production. These risks are as follows:

1. If developing countries only participate in the fabrication process then the GDP contribution of GVC will be limited.

2. The main part of GVC value-added is generated by MNCs' subsidiaries in developing countries leading to low value income capturing due to profit repatriation.

3. If governments do not invest in education and improvement of local firms' absorption capacity, the technology spillover from MNCs would be unlikely to result in improvements in higher value-added creation in these countries.
4. The results are negative environmental impacts and social effects in the absence of an efficient regulatory framework.
5. The potential unaccountability of GVC activities may increase the vulnerability of local firms when facing external shocks (UNCTAD 2013).

Without clearly defined policy objectives, a middle income trap or a glass ceiling for market based development even with a high level of FDI results (Ohno 2008). This is clearly identified for Asian countries in Figure 1. Countries that decreased their wage gap with developed countries are not necessarily uncompetitive nor does increasing wages in these countries necessarily reduce economic growth. However the problem of the middle income trap should also be approached from a human capital perspective so that as wages increase in some developing countries parallel improvements in technology and education are pursued. The latter changes the previous vertical specialization driven by wage differentials into the realm of horizontal specialization which can lead to trade in similar goods if a certain level of specialization is attained. Furthermore, horizontal specialization leads to increases in trade values as production stages being outsourced to these countries have higher value-added (e.g., the East-Asian Tigers).

Figure 1: Stage of Industrial Upgrading

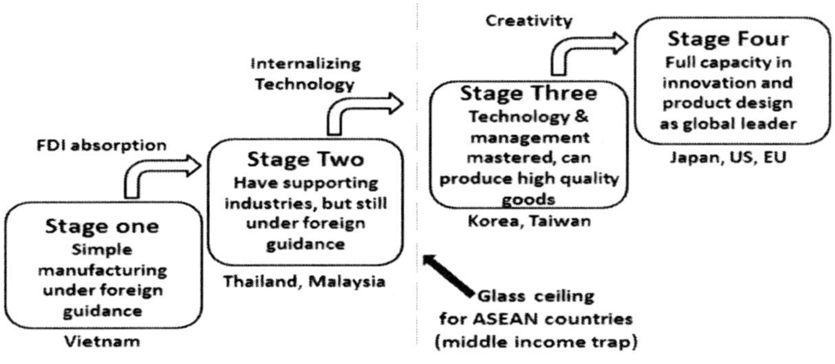

Source: Ohno (2008)

FDI can also lead to industrial upgrading for some developing countries under certain conditions, mentioned above, yet even in such an optimistic scenario self-market mechanisms will not lead to the same income level of developed countries. For this reason, to harness the positive spillovers resulting from FDI industrial policies are preferred. Furthermore, Baldwin (2011) argues that economists and government should rethink the role of the manufacturing sector in economic development, or at least reexamine the function of the fabrication stage in the modern era of globalization.

If FDI mainly goes to developing countries for cost reduction motives, how it leads to technology spillovers and industrial upgrading must be carefully managed. Moving toward higher value-added activities in developing countries depends on government policies. Designing and implementing sound industrial policies in line with national development plans has the main effect on the pace and direction of moving toward horizontal specialization (Mudambi 2008). China has in a comprehensive way dictated the conditions for FDI as concomitantly the level of economic development made China an attractive investment location (Azarhoushang 2013). Hale and Young (2011) found there existed systematic positive productivity spillovers in the case of China. We therefore continue this investigation using the example of Chinese government policy.

3. Chinese industrial policies, the National Development Plan and FDI

Industrial policy is a strategic plan for improving growth and development in the manufacturing sector. Government designs and implements a series of policies in order to increase productivity, competitiveness and the capacity of domestic firms. Supporters of strategic intervention argue that due to market failure, government has a responsibility to use industrial policies to support domestic industries. The successful experience of countries such as Japan, Taiwan, and South Korea showed that industrial policy could improve economic performance and employment (Chang 2003).

Policies and the regulation of FDI have therefore now become an important component of industrial policies. Most policy makers believe the positive effects of FDI (i.e., poverty reduction, technology spillovers, growth, etc.) outweigh the negative effects (i.e., inequality, weakening trade union, crowding out effects, etc.). A country's FDI strategy is determined based on all these positive effects, levels of factor endowment, and the ability of policy makers to choose the level of policy intervention (te Velde 2002). Consequently, the number of worldwide FDI related regulations rose by 25 percent in 2012 (Zhan 2013). Linden (2004) examined the design and implementation of Chinese industrial policy for high tech industries. He argued that China was more successful compared to other East Asian countries because of its large domestic markets, the support of national innovation and the pragmatic nature of policy. Furthermore, he argued although Chinese industrial policy is politicized, there is no additional economic cost to the economy while these political influences simultaneously force domestic companies to increase quality and productivity.

During the 1970s, China suffered from a lack of modern technologies, competitive advantages, and foreign exchange. After a long period of isolation, they needed to import machinery and equipment from more advanced countries yet protect the state-owned domestic industries (Naughton 2007: 378-380). After economic reforms in 1978, China attracted significant amounts of FDI stock, in 2011 becoming the primary recipient amongst developing countries and then second in the world after the USA (UNCTAD 2014). Sustained GDP growth, high rates of capital return and brisk economic development made China one of the leaders of manufacturing output in the world. The design of sound industrial policies according to the development plan in conjunction with absorbing huge amounts of FDI helped China increase its productivity, improve its competitive advantage ("Chinese miracle"), and generate millions of new jobs domestically (Azarhoushang 2013). After 1978, Deng Xiaoping opened the economy to foreign investment gradually and with a limited scope. In the first step, foreign export oriented companies were allowed to invest without access to local markets with additional regulation impeding them from exporting profit back to their own countries. However, with so many restrictions, China was unable to attract many foreign firms (Hou 2011).

Since 1979, China has passed a wide and relatively complete range of laws and regulations concerning FDI to encourage foreign firms' investment into China. These include the Law of the People's Republic of China for Wholly Owned Enterprises, the Sino Foreign Joint Venture Law, etc. Table 1 summarizes the main laws and regulation passed by the Chinese government regarding FDI promotion. The result has been constantly increasing levels of FDI accumulation (UNCTADstat 2015). Investing in infrastructure, changing regulations and laws in favor of foreign investors, opening Special Economic Zones (SEZs), keeping GDP growth high (10 percent) and moving toward a more liberalized market-based system, gave positive signals to investors.

In order to maintain economic growth and the trend of positive inward FDI, China decided to join the WTO in the early 1990s, completing its negotiations in 2001 (BBC 2001). As a result, foreign investors had more freedom to invest in different overall economic sectors and access to local markets. Institutional reforms and changes in regulations to meet WTO rules, a stable political and social environment, and optimistic perspectives about the economic situation encouraged increasing numbers of foreign firms to invest in China. Although following the most recent global financial crisis, China experienced a dramatic decline in its inward FDI, by preserving high GDP growth and increasing domestic investment, China showed that its economy was relatively unaffected and was still attractive to foreign investors.

Table 1: Chinese Regulation and Laws toward FDI

Year	Regulation	Main focus	Revision
1979	The Equity Joint Venture (JV) Law	CEO's of JV had to appointed by the Chinese partner; abolished in 1990	
1986	Wholly Foreign-Owned Enterprise Law	Foreign wholly owned firms in High-Tech could only exist in SEZs and Economic and Technological Development Zones (ETDZs)	2000 – to ease regulations for wholly owned Foreign Invested Enterprises(FIEs)
1988	The Contractual Joint Venture Law	Foreign firms are now allowed to do business as contractual joint ventures	2000 – to ease regulations for wholly owned FIEs 2001 – to ease Joint Venture laws for FIEs
1994	The Company Law	All foreign companies should be limited liability	2005 – for ease of registration
1995	Interim Provisions on Guiding Foreign Investment Catalogue for the Guidance of Foreign Investment Industries	Promotion of industries for FDI is based on industrial policy and national development plans Government consultation to aid investment in targeted strategic industries	2002 – Catalogue revised for simplified implementation 2004 – Catalogue revised for ease of implementation 2007 – Change of industrial categories from 2002; reclassification generally meant losing incentives. 2015 – Additional restrictions on service sectors lifted and more incentives offered to foreign companies investing in R&D in high tech industries.

2002	Provisions on Guiding the Orientation of Foreign Investment	These provisions divided FDI into four categories: encouraged, permitted, restricted and prohibited	
2003	Interim Provisions on Mergers and Acquisitions of Domestic Enterprises by Foreign Investors	3 year trial of M&A deregulation	2006 – provisions abolished restrictions on foreign firms M&A with Chinese firms 2009 – revised to ensure that all M&As conform to the *Anti-Monopoly Law*
2007	Anti-Monopoly Law	Government anti-monopoly regulations with special agreements for cost reduction to protect resources; technology development also exempted	
2007	The Enterprise Income Tax Law	Foreign companies should pay same taxes as domestic firms except for companies in high-tech and environmental industries and those in western regions	
2010	New Regulation on Foreign Investment by State Council	Incentives for high-tech companies, service sector, energy saving and environmental friendly projects	
2011	Notice for Public Consultation on the Catalogue for the Guidance of Foreign Investment Industries	The high-tech industries (e.g., aerospace, internet equipment, software and processors) encouraged via incentive packages; auto manufacturing exempted from encouraged category	

Source: Azarhoushang (2013) and Yao (2015)

The Chinese government uses a 5 year development plan to designate the direction of national goals and preferred approaches to their realization. The economic development goals and strategic sectors are designated by the government while governmental institutions and agencies determine their individual blueprints for policy implementation. Local government is also bound to implement the broad goals although they can also follow special policies for improving their specific regional sectors (Dorn/Cloutier 2013). Before the economic reforms of 1978, the national development plans mainly focused on the quantity of production. Following the 1978 reforms, the national development plans changed directions and began to include more market based incentive policies and openness to foreign trade. Additional incentives to encourage the direction of foreign firms' investment, especially in the manufacturing sector, came to the fore. The last national development plan (12th) running from 2011-2015 outlines its main objectives as sustainable growth, moving up the value chain, reducing disparity, scientific development, environmental protection, energy efficiency, and domestic consumption (KPMG 2011).

The Chinese government uses various tools for implementing their policies (some of which have been labeled as against WTO rules). The main tools are:

- Income tax breaks for companies with foreign investment, located in special development zones, or designated as having "high technology";
- Loans to "encouraged" industries from government-owned banks;
- Rebates of value added tax and import duties for equipment purchases;
- Low-priced land for SOEs and companies located in special development zones;
- The provision of goods and services at below-market prices by the government and SOEs;
- Cash payments to companies based on factors such as export performance.

The Chinese government provides a list with different criteria for foreign firms to fulfill to benefit from the above policies. These criteria include such items as a preference for foreign investment in "encouraged" activities; promoting R&D and the transfer of technology; developing integrated circuits; and encouraging companies to upgrade technology and equipment (Dorn/Cloutier 2013).

As the manufacturing sector is the main strategic sector for the economy, the Chinese government always designed industrial policies in line with national development for the same period of time. In the 12th national plan, nine industries including textile, machinery, and electronic appliances were chosen as strategic industries as an attempt to improve their quality, the industrial technology, as well as their brand images through 2015 (Dorn/Cloutier 2013). Before analyzing the performance of these industries, we first outline the industrial goals which were outlined in the national plan. Table 2 illustrates the main goals of industrial policies for these three industries.

Table 2: Chinese Industrial Policy Goals (2011-2015)

Industry	Goals
Textile	<ul><li>8 % increase in annual industry value-added.</li><li>Investment of at least 1% of total income on R&D.</li><li>Development of 5 to 10 reputable Chinese international brands as well as 50 to 100 famous domestic brands</li></ul>
Electronic Machinery	<ul><li>Replacement of all imported machineries by high quality domestic machines.</li></ul>
Electronic Appliances	<ul><li>Investment of at least 3% of sales revenue in R&D.</li><li>Establishment of 20 state supported technology centers.</li><li>Domestic products should aim to cover 30% of the world market.</li></ul>

Source: Dorn/Cloutier (2013)

Studying industrial policies and especially the policies for promoting the manufacturing industry aids in understanding the success of the Chinese government in the implementation of their policies. We evaluate the value-added resulting in FDI using textiles, electric equipment and machinery industries and electronic and telecommunication equipment as examples of low, medium and high value-added industries.

4. The economic performance of three industrial sectors in China

We choose to analyze the effects of government policies and FDI by concentrating on three industries: Textiles, Electronic Machinery and Communication equipment, Computers and Other Electronic Equipment. These are examples of low, medium and high value-added industries[2] and allows for the examina-

---

[2] The textile industry is among the low-tech sectors categorized in supplier dominated industries which include traditional sectors (e.g., food, textile, retail services) where innovative activities are less relevant, small firms are prevalent, and technological change is mainly introduced through the inputs and machinery provided by suppliers from other industries. Electronic machinery is classified as a high-tech industry categorized by specialized suppliers and their products are new processes for other industries. R&D is present but an important innovative input comes from tacit knowledge and design skills embodied in the labor force. Average firm size is small and innovation is carried out in close relation with customers. Communication equipment, Computers and Other Electronic Equipment is a high tech industry and is Science-Based. This category includes

tion of China's position in the GVC through analysis of the growth rate of value-added during 2003-2013. We consider the value-added tax payable[3] and total assets of foreign founded companies and compare them with stated-owned and private Chinese companies in each industry as well as their share of value-added in total manufacturing sector. This further enables the assessment of the role of FDI in the development of the Chinese position in the GVC.

The textile industry is generally considered a low value-added industry, especially in developing countries. Foreign companies which invest in developing countries mainly do so for vertical specialization motivations and look for low production costs. Due to the outsourcing of the fabrication stage to developing countries, foreign firms are assumed to not have significant effects on positive technology spillover to local firms. We examine the total assets as well as the value-added tax payables of foreign, state-owned (SOEs) and private Chinese companies to see the effects of foreign firm investment on domestic companies. Figure 2 confirms that private Chinese companies have the highest total assets in the textile industry and Chinese state-owned firms have the lowest. We confirm the same trend in their value-added tax payables in Figure 3. These two graphs show that the Chinese government did not choose to invest in the textile industry via SOEs. Furthermore, foreign founded companies did not have any meaningful technology spillovers to local firms.

---

sectors where innovation is based on advances in science and R&D, where research laboratories are important, leading to intense product innovation and a high propensity to patent (Bogliacino/Pianta 2011).

[3] This indicator was chosen as access to value-added data of these industries was limited. The only publicly available data for value-added was value-added tax payable, available for the chosen time period in the China Statistical Yearbook

Figure 2: Total Assets, Textile Industry

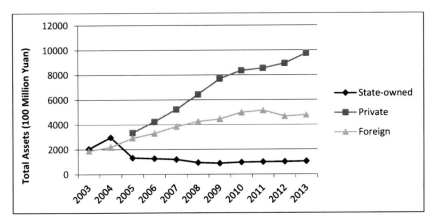

Source: China Statistical Yearbook (2004-2013)

Figure 3: Value-added tax payables, Textile Industry

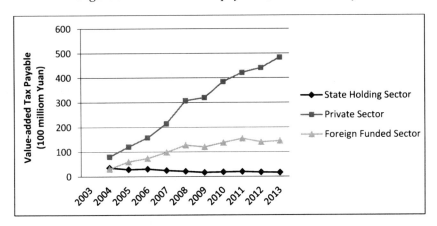

Source: China Statistical Yearbook (2004-2014)

In contrast to the Textile industry, the Electronic Machinery industry was considered a strategic industry as it is symbolic of a country's comprehensive strength. As seen in Figure 4, all companies had more or less same amount of total assets between 2003 and 2005. After 2005, foreign companies accumulated higher total assets compared to two other types of companies (with the exception of 2012). State-owned companies in this industry, as with those in the textile industry, have the lowest total assets. The small size of the companies in the electronic machinery industry is considered the main reason for the overall low investment of state-owned companies in this industry.

Figure 4: Total Assets, Electronic Machinery Industry

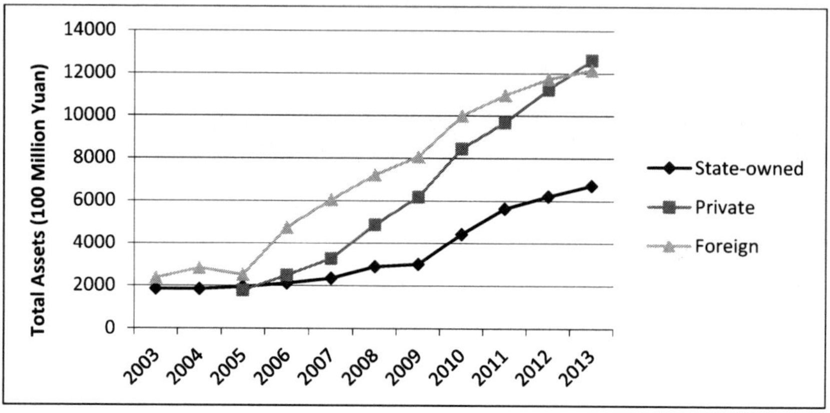

Source: China Statistical Yearbook (2004-2013)

As in the textile industry, SOEs in Electric Machinery have the weakest performance relative to their total assets. However, foreign companies had a similar performance compared to private companies until 2009. In 2009, private companies were able to catch up to the foreign firms perhaps due to the global financial crisis which led to a reduction in demand as well as the investment of foreign firms globally and resulting in the subsequent weak performance of foreign firms in China. Although the technology spillover in the machinery industry was higher than in the textile industry, these effects were not meaningful due to the similar performance of the private domestic and foreign companies. The presence of foreign firms encouraged private firms to increase their investment and improve their machinery which can be seen via the sharp rise in the total assets of private firms.

Figure 5: Value-added tax payable in Electronic Machinery

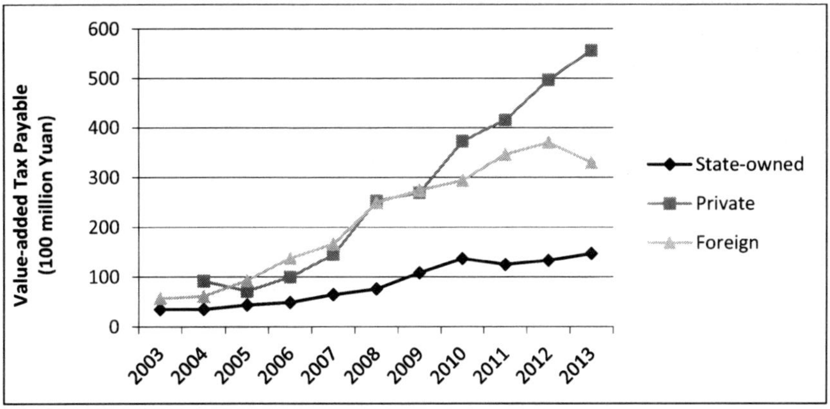

Source: China Statistical Yearbook (2004-2014)

The industry with the highest value-added is Communication equipment, Computers and Other Electronic Equipment where the Chinese government put a lot of emphasis on improving innovation and technology levels. Based on the definition of this industry and Figures 6 and 7 we ascertain that foreign companies have the highest total assets and the best performance. Unlike the other two industries, state-owned companies have higher assets and better performance compared to private companies which verifies our assumption that the Chinese government prefers to invest in high-tech industries due to their higher value-added and the additional benefits of technology transfer.

Moreover, the gap between foreign and local firms continuously increased during the chosen time period of 2003-2013, despite strong support of government for domestic firms. This elucidates the role of foreign firms as well as their better technology use and higher skilled workers in this industry. Furthermore, this widening gap indicates that the technology spillover is not significant in the electronic equipment industry.

Figure 6: Total Assets,
Communication equipment, Computers and Other Electronic Equipment

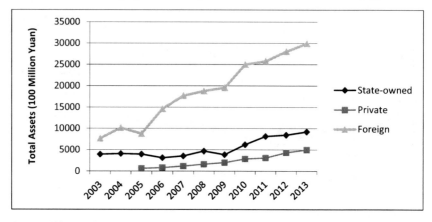

Source: China Statistical Yearbook (2004-2014)

Figure 7: Value-added tax payable,
Communication equipment, Computers and Other Electronic Equipment

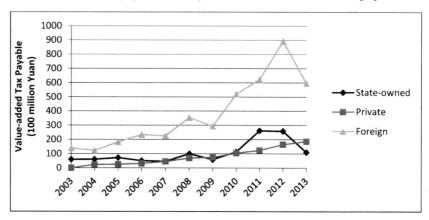

Source: China Statistical Yearbook (2004-2014)

By examining the share of value-added tax payable for these industries to total value-added of the manufacturing sector, it can be argued that despite value-added differences among the three industries, based on their value-added categories, the difference in China is not as high as expected. In order to ascertain why this might be the case, we report the difference in value-added, their growth rate and their share to total value-added in Table 3. For a more precise analysis, we also examine the ratio of total profit to total industrial costs to determine whether these small differences are related to the production level or simply reflect the value-added of these industries.

Table 3: Value-added, growth rate and share to total value-added

Year	Textile			Electronic Machinery			Electronic Equipment		
	Value-added	Growth rate %	Share of total value-added %	Value-added	Growth rate %	Share of total value-added %	Value-added	Growth rate %	Share of total value-added %
2004	217.62	n.a	3.40	238.12	n.a	3.72	216.18	n.a	3.38
2005	316.51	45.4	3.71	316.62	32.97	3.72	315.23	45.82	3.70
2006	381.77	20.6	3.57	426.09	34.57	3.98	410.52	30.23	3.83
2007	469.04	22.9	3.44	553.72	29.95	4.06	430.42	4.85	3.15
2008	606.07	29.2	3.43	618.95	11.78	3.50	846	96.55	4.78
2009	573.28	-5.4	3.28	914.16	47.70	5.23	577.8	-31.70	3.30
2010	720.78	25.7	3.21	1125.4	23.11	5.01	900.91	55.92	4.01
2011	814.14	13.0	3.10	1268.2	12.69	4.82	1326.1	47.20	5.04
2012	828.16	1.7	2.80	1462.2	15.30	4.95	1562.4	17.82	5.28
2013	892.34	7.7	2.96	1513.2	3.48	5.02	1163.2	-25.55	3.86

Source: China Statistical Yearbook (2004-2014); Growth rates and shares of total value-added calculated by author

The average share of total value-added tax payables (to the total) of textile, electronic machinery and electronic equipment for our time period are 3.29, 4.2 and 4.03 percent respectively illustrating the low levels of value-added in the electronic machinery and electronic equipment industries. Table 4 shows the ratio of total profit to total industrial costs for these three industries as well as the whole manufacturing sector. This indicator shows that the textile industry performed better than the electronic equipment industry. In addition, all three industries had a weaker performance in comparison with the total manufacturing sector.

Table 4: Ratio of Total Profit to Total Industrial Costs

Ratio of Total Profit to Total Industrial Costs (Percent)				
Year	Textile	Electronic Machinery	Electronic Equipment	Total
2004	3.09	5.1	3.99	6.52
2005	3.68	5.03	3.43	6.42
2006	3.95	5.03	3.58	6.74
2007	4.46	5.66	3.86	7.43
2008	4.74	6.59	3.71	6.61
2009	5.15	7.21	4.14	6.91
2010	6.45	7.94	5.47	8.31
2011	6.41	6.95	4.61	7.71
2012	6.24	6.62	4.71	7.11
2013	5.97	6.02	4.48	6.6
Average	5.01	6.22	4.20	7.04

Source: China Statistical Yearbook (2004-2014)

Given the above analysis, FDI inflows do not seem to have led to an automatic industrial upgrading in China. This is in contrast to the general argument that FDI inflow is desirable from a host country perspective because it should automatically lead to industrial technology transfer and thus an upgrade in the GVC. Furthermore although the Chinese government was quite successful in improving technology and value-added in the industrial sector, this success was rather lethargic.

5. Conclusion

International organizations and mainstream economists widely believe that being part of the global value chain and hosting foreign companies leads to industrial development especially in the case of developing countries. To this end, Washington Consensus Policies were recommended to developing countries as a best practice for economic development. However, there is little consensus among scholars and empirical studies about the existence of automatic industrial upgrading in the host countries.

This paper has examined the effect of FDI on the Chinese global value chain participation. In addition, the role of Chinese government policy (especially industrial policy), as a principal precondition for positive technology spillover to improve industrial value-added was examined in the context of the Textile, Electronic Machinery and Electronic Equipment industries.

Based on the analysis of industry data, it can be argued that FDI did not have a significant effect on the performance of Chinese companies. Ambitious goals were set by the Chinese government in its 12th development plan and the related industrial policy did not satisfy expectations. By closely examining the performance of these three industries, it is evident that China remains in a middle income trap as the overall improvement of technology level remains weak and Chinese companies have hitherto been unsuccessful in the creation of international brands. Increased investment into innovation development by the Chinese government seeks to remedy this situation. In the new national development plan (2016-2021; 13th) the Chinese government has accentuated domestic demand by increasing the cooperation between domestic companies and universities as well as improving financial and non-financial supports for new innovations and their development (Lou 2015). With continued emphasis on industrial policy, the Chinese government remains well positioned to continue its quest for improved industrial value-added and positive technology spillovers from foreign and domestic investment.

References

Alfaro, L., Chandra, A., Kalemi-Ozcan, S., Sayek, S. (2010): Does foreign direct investment promote growth? Exploring the role of financial markets on linkages, in: *Journal of Development Economics*, 91, 242-256.

Alfaro, L., Charlton, A. (2009): Intra-Industry Foreign Direct Investment, in: *American Economic Review*, 99, 2096-2119.

Azarhoushang, B. (2013): The effects of FDI on China's economic development; Case of Volkswagen, in China. Master Thesis, Berlin School of Economics and Law.

Azarhoushang, B., Bramucci, A., Herr, H., Ruoff, B. (2016): Global Value Chains, Under-Development and Unions Strategy, in: *International Journal of Labour Research*, Forthcoming.

Baldwin, R. (2011): Trade and Industrialization after Globalization's 2nd Unbundling: How Building and Joining a Supply Chain are Different and Why it Matters: NBER Working Paper 17716.

Baldwin, R. (2013): Global supply chains: why they emerged, why they matter, and where they are going, in: Elms, D.K., Low, P. (eds.), *Global value chains in a changing world*. Geneva: WTO Publications.

BBC (2001): China Joins the WTO – at Last. http://news.bbc.co.uk/2/hi/business/17 02241.stm (11 December 2001).

Bogliacino, F., Pianita, M. (2011): Innovation and Employment: a Reinvestigation using Revised Pavitt classes, in: *Research Policy*, 39, 799-809.

Chang, H.J. (2003): *Kicking Away the Ladder: Development Strategy in Historical Perspective*, London, New York: Anthem Press.

Chen, Z.H., Ying, G., Lai, H.W. (2011): Foreign Direct Investment and Wage Inequality: Evidence from China, in: *World Development*, 39(8), 1322-32.

China Daily (2010): China Unveils New Rules for Foreign Investment, in: China Daily 14 April 2010 (http://www.chinadaily.com.cn/china/2010-04/14/content_9725146.htm).

China Statistical Yearbook (2004-2014): China Statistical Yearbook, Beijing, China: China National Bureau of Statistics.

Damijan, J.P., Knell, M., Majcen, B., Rojec, M. (2003): The role of FDI, R&D accumulation and trade in transferring technology to transition countries: evidence from firm panel data for eight transition countries, in: *Economic Systems*, 27, 189-204.

Dorn, J.W., Cloutier, C. (2013): Report on Chinese Industrial Policies, King & Spalding.

Fujita, M., Krugman, P., Venables, A.J. (1999): *The Spatial Economy, Cities, Regions, and International Trade*, Cambridge, MA: The MIT Press.

Graham, O.L. (1992): *Losing Time; Industrial Policy Debate*, Cambridge/Mass.: Twentieth Century Fund, Inc.

Hale, G., Long, C. (2011): Did Foreign Direct Investment Put an Upward Pressure on Wages in China?, in: *IMF Economic Review*, 59(3), 404-430.

Hou, J.W. (2011): Economic Reform of China: Cause and Effects, in: *The Social Science Journal*, 48, 419-34.

KPMG (2011): China's 12th Five-Year Plan: Overview, http://www.kpmg.com/cn/en/issuesandinsights/articlespublications/documents/china-12th-five-year-plan-overview-201104.pdf

Krugman, P. (1991): *Geography and Trade*, Cambridge/Mass.: The MIT Press.

Lin, P., Liu, Z., Zhang, Y. (2009): Do Chinese Domestic firms Benefit from FDI Inflow? Evidence of Horizontal and Vertical Spillovers, in: *China Economic Review*, 20, 677-691.

Linden, G. (2004): China Standard Time: A Study in Strategic Industrial Policy, in: *Business and Politics*, 6(3).

Lou, J. (2015): 13th five-year plan focuses on economic development quality 2015, Xihuanet 02 November 2015 [Online]. Available at http://news.xinhuanet.com/english/china/2015-11/02/c_134776063.htm [Accessed 20th February 2016].

Mudambi, R. (2008): Location, control and innovation in knowledge intensive industries, in: *Journal of Economic Geography*, 8, 699-725.

Murray, J. (2011): Inward Investment and Market Structure in an Open Developing Economy: A Case of India's Manufacturing Sector, in: *Journal of Economics and Behavioral Studies*, 2, 286-297.

Naughton, B.J. (2007): *The Chinese Economy: Transitions and Growth*, Cambridge/Mass.: The MIT Press.

OECD (2007): *Moving Up the Value Chain: Staying Competitive in the Global Economy*, Paris: OECD.

OECD (2012): *Mapping Global Value Chains*, Paris: The OECD Conference Centre.

Ohno, K. (2008): *The Middle Income Trap. Implication for Industrialization Strategies in East Asia and Africa*, Tokyo: GRIPS Development Forum.

Peng, M.W. (2009): *Global Strategy*, Mason (USA): South-Western Cengage Learning.

Porter, M.E. (1985): *Competitive Advantage*, New York: Free Press.

Singh, J. (2011): Inward Investment and Market Structure in an Open Developing Economy: A Case of India's Manufacturing Sector, in: *Journal of Economics and Behavioral Studies*, 2, 286-297.

te Velde, D.W. (2002): Government Policies towards Inward Foreign Direct Investment in Developing Countries: Implications for Human Capital Formation and Income Inequality, Working Paper No. 193: OECD Development Centre.

UNCTAD (2010): Integrating Developing Countries' SMEs into Global Value Chains, New York, Geneva: United Nations.

UNCTAD (2013): Research on FDI and TNCs, available at: http://unctad.org/en/Pages/DIAE/Research%20on%20FDI%20and%20TNCs/Researchon-FDI-and-TNCs.aspx [Accessed 20th July 2015].

UNCTAD (2014): Foreign Direct Investment [Online]. New York, US: UNCTAD, available: http://unctad.org/en/Pages/DIAE/Foreign-Direct-Investment-(FDI).aspx [Accessed 25th February 2014].

UNCTADstat (2015): Available: http://unctadstat.unctad.org/wds/ReportFolders/reportFolders.aspx [Accessed 20th August 2015].

Williamson, J. (1990): What Washington Means by Policy Reform, in: Williamson, J. (ed.). (1990): *Latin American Adjustment: How Much Has Happened?*, Washington, DC.: Institute for International Economics, 7-20.

World Bank (2012): Stock of Inward FDI, http://databank.worldbank.org/data/reports.aspx?source=2&country=CHN&series=&period=

Yao, R. (2015): Update: Latest Guidance Catalogue for Foreign Investment Industries Released [Online]. China: China Briefing. Available at http://www.china-briefing.com/news/2015/03/20/breaking-news-updated-guidance-catalogue-foreign-investment-industries-released.html#sthash.O6DBBgpV.dpuf [Accessed 10th August 2015].

Zhan, J. (2013): Global Value Chains: Investment and Trade for Development, in: *World Investment Report 2013*, New York, Geneva: UNCTAD, 121-233.

Zhu, Y. (2010): An Analysis on Technology Spillover Effect of Foreign Direct Investment and Its Countermeasures, in: *International Journal of Business and Management*, 5(4), 178-182.

Global production networks: What has labour got to do with it?

Praveen Jha

I take great pleasure in contributing to a volume in honour of Professor Hansjörg Herr, an economist of great distinction and a wonderful human being. It has been a privilege to know Professor Herr and I am grateful to the editors of the volume for including me in this celebration. Professor Herr's research interests span a large canvas of themes and areas including monetary theories and policies, economics of developing and emerging economies, financial markets, regulation of shadow banks, currency regimes, labour markets, wage policies and income distribution. In a number of important contributions Professor Herr has recently engaged with the theme of the so called Global Value Chains (henceforth GVCs) or Global Production Networks (henceforth GPNs); this note attempts to connect with a couple of core issues that are central to Professor Herr's extremely insightful work in this important area.

1.

It is generally well-acknowledged that the global capitalist system has undergone a significant reconfiguration in its spatial organization of production in almost every sector, particularly in manufacturing and services, in the last few decades. Much talked about feature of this configuration is the "transnationalisation" of economic activities or the growing salience of the GPNs. The de-centring of production under neo-liberal capitalism is characterised by a shift of production from advanced capitalist countries to a handful of developing countries where metropolitan capital has strengthened its presence to take advantage of, *inter alia*, relatively inexpensive labour and raw materials as well as to tap the markets. Thus, in a whole range of activities, the value chains underlying a manufactured good (or service) for final consumption may well criss-cross different corners of the globe before it is assembled together (e.g., automobiles, electronic items, garments, shoes etc). With the powerful ascendency of the GPNs in the era of neo-liberal globalization, the "Fordist" production regime, that dominated manufacturing till about half a century ago, has now taken a back seat.

Apart from striking debates regarding the implications for labour due to the ascendancy of GPNs, a major, and again controversial, theme with respect to the GPNs has been about its conceptual location. On both these there is considerable contestation in the existing literature, analytically as well as empirically. To flag just one issue: some have argued that the post-Fordist regime is clearly a distinct advance, with features such as workplace participation, shop floor democracy, and re-skilling, over the 'despotic control and deskilling of workers' associated with the "Fordist-Taylorist" regime (a claim advanced by Harry Braverman in his iconic classic *Labour and Monopoly Capital* (Braverman 1974)); the counter argument is that post-Fordist GPNs have given a massive push to informalisation of workers and a further loss of control over the labour process by the working classes. In fact on almost every feature associated with this presumed transition from Fordist-Taylorist to the GPN regime there are major debates. It is not my objective to get into an adequate consideration of all the relevant issues. The purpose of this paper is limited specifically to two issues. First, in Section 2, it raises some concerns regarding the conceptual underpinnings of the GPN/GVC framework itself. Second, in Section 3, it tries to engage with a couple of arguments relating to the pathways with respect to the implications for labour. Section 4 concludes the paper.

2.

The basic aspects of the "Fordist" production regime of the so-called "Golden Age" (approximately three decades after the World War II) in advanced capitalist countries were marked by: standardized mass production driven by assembly-line techniques run by the semi-skilled workers, increasing productivity generated from the "economies of scale" together with rising levels of profits and real wages, and collective bargaining of unionized workers and management. By the end of 1960s the regime faced a a growing crisis of profitability and accumulation due to a host of economic, political and social factors. The so called 'oil shock' and 'stagflation' of the early 1970s only exacerbated the problem and contributed to a restructuring of production regime. The Keynesian demand management policy and the welfare State which had sought to embed the market into the society were presumed as failures; thus capitalism entered a neo-liberal phase with State regulation in economic affairs taking a back seat and trade union organizations facing severe attacks There was an aggressive push by capital to liberate itself from regulations, nationally and internationally, and ever-greater flexibilisation of economic activities to exploit economies of scale and scope (Jha/Chakraborty 2014). One of the inevitable consequences of this has been the acceleration of the internationalization of production, which has of course been dominated by multinational corporations, and *ipso facto*, has led to an increase in their 'extra territorial' powers.

To understand the phenomena and processes of accelerated trans-nationalisation of production and their myriad economic implications, analytical frameworks like Global Commodity Chains (GCC), Global Value Chains (GVC) or Global Production Networks (GPN) have been dominant in the recent literature, which are rich in insights and explanations. Though these frameworks have some broad similarities and are often used interchangeably, the GPN framework maybe analytically better as argued elsewhere (Jha/Chakraborty 2014). GPN approach is based on three conceptual categories – value, power and embeddedness (Mackinnon 2012: 229). The concept of value attempts to incorporate both Marxian notion of surplus value and the economic rent (Henderson et al. 2001). Power within the GPN is understood in terms of corporate power, institutional power (local, national state or supra-state institutions like EU, NAFTA, IMF, ILO, etc.) and collective power (which includes collective actors like employers' associations, trade unions or NGOs within given network) (ibid). Thus departing from GCC-GVC's narrow focus on the governance of inter-firm transaction, GPN attempts to incorporate the relevant actors and relationships (Coe et al. 2008) in a more comprehensive fashion and provides a multi-scalar approach and emphasizes that each stage of a production chain is embedded in much broader set of non-linear relationships. There are three kinds of embeddedness that have been highlighted in GPN literature – societal embeddedness, to emphasize broader regulatory and institutional framework; network embeddedness, to emphasize economic and social relationships of firms; and, territorial embeddedness, to "anchor" a GPN in different places (Mackinnon 2012).

It is important to emphasise, however, that the concerns and issues mapped by the GPN/GVC literature has a long theoretical ancestry and history. For reasons of space it is not possible here to get into a detailed discussion of the relevant issues and I would only focus on a couple of arguments which may be squarely located in the Marxist Political Economy paradigm. As is well known, amongst the various laws of motion of capitalism that Marx emphasized, those of a) the "combined and uneven development" and b) the "concentration and centralization of capital" help us understand a transition from a relatively dispersed and 'free' competitive capitalism to a oligopolistic/monopolistic stage in which giant corporations come to rule the roost in particular markets and industries. At certain junctures in their evolution, these large conglomerates start expanding the frontiers of their activities and the process continues till the global economy as a whole becomes their playing field. They do so, of course, to reap a whole range of monopolistic advantages by accessing cheaper sources of raw materials, relatively inexpensive labour, access to markets etc. It is some of these major issues which constitute the crux of the Marxist-Leninist theorizing about imperialism. In other words the ascendency of GPNs or trans-nationalisation of capital has been a central theme in Marxist theory to which Lenin (along with Luxemburg and others) made the most profound contributions (Lenin 2000; Bagchi et al. 1985). Scholars such as Paul Baran, Paul Sweezy and many others (many of whom are associated with the *Monthly Review*) made significant contributions to enriching our understanding (Baran/Sweezy 1966). Stephen Hymer, a major Marxist theorist of trans-national corporations, captured the essence of the thrust underlying Marxist thinking when he observed that: "multinational corporations are a substitute for the market as method of organizing international exchange" (Hymer 1979). In a similar vein Barnet and Muller in their justly famous book, *Global Reach* (1974) argued that: "The rise of global corporation represents the globalization of oligopoly capitalism". Thus, the mobility of capital from the global North to the global South ought to be located in the overall context of imperialism and ascendency of the international oligopolistic system.

In some of the recent literature ideas such as 'global labour arbitrage' (a phrase coined by Stephen Roach of Morgan Stanley) which suggests that powerful TNCs can reap major advantages by exploiting the wage hierarchy between the North and South, have become quite prominent (Roach 2004). Again, it is important to note that significant wage differences playing an important role in the globalization of oligopoly have been prominent in Marxist tradition almost since its inception. For instance, in the above noted work by Barnet and Muller (1974), the search for lowest unit of labour cost worldwide is central to the oligopolistic rivalry and it generates huge rents for the TNCs headquartered in the North. The point worth noting is that it is one among many advantages in the contemporary oligopolistic structure of the global economy. Of course there is considerable evidence to show, through the recent data, that indeed transnational corporations have enormously benefitted from wage hierarchies that exist in the world. For instance, as noted by Whalen, that (about a decade ago) hourly wages for a worker in a factory in the U.S. and China were $21 and 64 cents respectively. As per the US Bureau of Labour Statistics, the Chinese manufacturing workers received just about 4 percent of the compensation for American workers in comparable occupations. As per the World Development Indicators database of the World Bank (2016), if we compare set of countries approximately at two ends, namely, high income and low income, the ratio in 1990 was 57.1 which increased marginally to 58.9 by 2014. These data clearly show that the argument regarding the operation of the 'global labour arbitrage' has some merit in explaining why the transnational corporations are expanding their operations in developing and emerging economies. *However it needs to be located in the larger overall context of the structures of accumulation.*

Further, with respect to labour, the wage hierarchy argument needs to be connected, as is done in the Marxist Political Economy, with the inexorable tendency to perpetuate and exacerbate the Relative Surplus Population. As Marx explains in *Capital Volume I*, the General Law of Capitalist Accumulation results in, and requires, the maintenance of a relative surplus population which consists of a *floating*, the *latent* and the *stagnant* components. Relative surplus population is essential to maintain low wages and reproduce the high profits and concentration of wealth that characterises the capitalist system in general and the GPNs in particular. As Marx put it, pauperism "is the hospital of the active labour-army and the dead weight of the industrial reserve army. Its production is included in that of the relative surplus population. Its necessity is theirs; along with the surplus population, pauperism forms a condition of capitalist production and of the capitalist development of wealth. It enters into the *faux frais* of capitalist production; but capital knows how to throw these, from the most parts from its own shoulders on to those of the working class and the lower middle class." (Marx 1976: ch. 25, p. 797)

3.

The maintenance of low wages and a relative surplus population is one of the central features of the trans-nationalisation of capital under contemporary capitalism. The labour regimes that enable the reproduction of such conditions are characterised by persistent informality. Going by the ILO data the global labour force increased from approximately 2.26 to 3.09 billion between 1991 and 2010-2012. Over the same period the number of unemployed increased from approximately 150 to 195 million. The employed are distributed by the ILO into two main categories: wage and salaried workers (also known as employees) and self-employed workers (consisting of self-employed workers with employees, called employers; self-employed workers without employees or own-account workers and members of producers' cooperatives and contributing family workers, also known as unpaid family workers). Another distinction made by the ILO is between 'non-vulnerable' employment (consisting of employers as well as wage and salaried workers) and 'vulnerable' employment, consisting of all those who work but cannot be considered wage and salaried workers; basically it comprises of 'own-account workers' and 'contributing family workers'. The ILO data shows that the proportion of the wage and salaried workers, is well below 50 percent of the global labour force. Thus, the greater part of the world labour consists of 'vulnerably employed', as per the ILO classification, which along with unemployed, may be considered a proxy for the size of relative surplus population at any given juncture.

Recent literature on the GPNs and GVCs shows that the vulnerability of labour is maintained and reproduced through contracting and sub-contracting structures that reproduce informality and unfree labour relations. As several case studies show, a large part of the contract labour employed by the GVCs is migrant and casual who fail to get registered in national labour statistics (Barrientos 2011). The existence of migrant and contract labour indicates the presence of a labour reserve that structures the flexibility within global production systems. Several case studies and analysis of labour regimes highlight the multiple nature of flexible structures in GPNs. One such study by Barrientos (2007) characterises this flexibility in three ways: functional flexibility (or when specific jobs of workers can be varied and multiplied); pay flexibility (where variable piece rates can be used to have varied conditions of work and depressed wages); and numerical flexibility (where numbers employed can be varied at any point of time through either short term hiring or through the use of contractors). Examples of home based workers from India also point towards these flexible arrangements as signifiers of these new production regimes where more than 80 percent women workers in the non-agrarian sector work on piece rates and short term contracts (CITU 2013). Such flexibility is necessary to create and maintain a low wage labour force which is essential to maintain the 'global labour arbitrage'.

Given this situation, it is obvious that that informality and vulnerability of the labour conditions increase the order of difficulty in organising workers and increasing their collective bargaining power. Hence it is appropriate to ask: how can workers be organised and increase their bargaining power under GPNs? As Eric Olin Wright argues, the worker's power to influence capitalist accumulation may be twofold: structural power and associational power (Wright 2000). Structural power signifies the ability of the worker to disrupt the production process. In contrast, associational powers refers to the ability of the workers to come together, form workers organisations and protest. But this form of organisation is becoming more and more difficult especially in the case of vertical value chains which are integrated across regions and nations. Hence the problem of trade unionism is not only confined to local union organisation at the factory floor (as done under conventional trade unionism) but through the formation of Global Union Federations. The two forms of power described above are further elaborated by Silver (2003) where she reclassifies structural power in terms of 'marketplace bargaining power' and 'workplace bargaining power'. Marketplace bargaining power results from tight labour markets due to relatively high level of employment and the ability of labourers to leave the job and survive on some other sources of income; whereas workplace bargaining power arises from the 'strategic location of a particular group of workers within a key industrial sector'. The interrelation of these two powers vis-à-vis the strategies of capital determines the trajectories of working class movement and its capacity to sustain its agency in the dynamics of GPNs.

Within this broad framework, the labour control regimes and the worker's response to them have been classified in diverse ways. For example Anner (2015) identifies three types of labour regimes which structure collective action within GPNs. First, 'state controlled regimes' where 'officially' recognised unions do not call for strike actions, but workers on their own organise 'wild cat strikes' on the basis of their shop floor experiences. Second is the situation of 'despotic market control' where there are a few lead firms and many sellers who build national and international alliances to gain advantages. Third the 'oppressive employers labour control' where workers build cross-border solidarity to increase their support and bargaining power. These three forms of action are directly related to the way in which labour processes are structured within GPNs and show that the 'agency' of the working class may be diverse in nature because of the multiple forms of labour regimes that may exist within GPNs.

Structural and associational power of workers can be seen in multiple examples of labour unrest in the contemporary world. Here we explore two examples to explain how structural and associational power may work in different contexts to increase the bargaining power of workers. Perhaps the most significant example of the use of structural power or 'workplace bargaining power' in India is the continuing struggles of the Maruti and Honda workers. As described by Jha and Chakraborty (2014) these collective actions by contract workers are largely based on their experiences in the labour process. In case of Maruti Suzuki, the workers went for a sudden occupation of the factory on 4th June 2011 demanding recognition of their own union. But the actual genesis of this strike can be traced back to the worsening of working condition, increased managerial and supervisory control and intensification of work to meet the post-2008 increased demand.[1] The struggles used strategies that went beyond the traditional legal trade unionist framework of workers' struggle, and made capital vulnerable in new ways. At Maruti Suzuki, in the first and third phases of struggle, workers occupied the factory so that it would not be possible for management to continue production by training new workforce. Workers went for "go-slow" policy in production. Workers in factories like Suzuki Powertrain, Suzuki Castings, and Suzuki Motorcycle went on sustained solidarity strike, while those in seven other companies like Satyam Auto, Bajaj Motor, Endurance, Hi-lex, Lumax, etc., went on a one-day solidarity strike on 8 October 2011. All these were "illegal" – factory occupation, go-slow policy, and solidarity strike. The ongoing strike by Honda workers in multiple locations like Alwar and Gurgaon show the disruptive capacity of workers within the production process. But as Anner (2015) explains such 'wild cat' type of actions get incremental benefits and the display of structural power needs to be continuous and repeated in order to maintain and extend the benefits won through struggles.

The second example, the Asian Wage Floor Initiative, is a display of associational (or in Silver's classification marketplace bargaining) power where a concerted effort is made to break the stranglehold of the market. The Initiative is an alliance of Asian trade unions to improve the working conditions of vulnerable workers. The alliance makes demands on the basis of the paying capacity of global industry rather than the conditions within the national economies. The assumption is that there can be a common transparently worked out wage floor on the basis of labour costs and a living wage. However, this wage floor can only be implemented through an alliance of Asian

---

[1] It is worth noting that in spite of the global financial and economic crisis stating in 2007, the Indian economy continued to be in a buoyant state for the next 4 years; in fact the average growth rate increased marginally between 2008-09 and 10-11which started losing momentum only after 2011-12.

trade unions who have come together in an Asia Brand Bargaining Group. The group has four common demands i.e., the welfare of garment workers; living wage; freedom of association, abolition/regulation of contract labour and the end of gender based discrimination (Bhattacharjee/Roy, forthcoming). This example shows how associational power can be exercised across borders to increase the bargaining power of workers vis-a-vis lead firms. In this case even though buyers were few and many suppliers, the coming together of unions across countries seems to have made a difference by organising workers in a coordinated way across the vertical chain of the GPNs in the garment industry. This also highlights the importance of the role of global unions and alliances between workers' alliances whose outreach goes beyond the influence of Global Union Federations.

4.

This short essay was intended as a modest contribution to engage with the currently dominant frameworks for studying the trans-nationalisation of capital under contemporary capitalism. Reviewing the underpinnings of the contemporary GVC/GPN frameworks, the first part of the essay highlights the Marxist arguments regarding the internationalisation of oligopolistic capitalism, which itself, is best understood as powerful affirmation of the 'laws of uneven and combined development' and 'concentration and centralisation of capital'. In this sense the GPNs are embedded in a new form of oligopolistic and monopolistic capitalism. Such an understanding also entails that the rate of capitalist accumulation is maintained, and indeed also enhanced, through the maintenance of a relative surplus population perennially subjected to flexibility and informalisation.

In this context, the second issue flagged by this essay concerns the implications such an understanding has for the labour movement and the challenges facing it today. One of the major concerns here is to think in terms of alliances of workers across the globe. It is interesting to note that the issue was aptly stated by Karl Marx in his address to the First International in 1867 when he said: "A study of the struggle waged by the English working class reveals that in order to oppose their workers, the employers either bring workers from abroad or else transfer manufacture to countries where there is a cheap labour force. Given this state of affairs, if the working class wishes to continue its struggle with some chance of success, the national organisations must become international".

References

Anner, M. (2015): Labour control regimes and worker's resistance in global supply chains, in: *Labour History*, 56(3), 292-307.
Bagchi A.K, Ghosh, A., Misra, S. (1985): Industrial Policy and the Economy, in: *Social Scientist*, 13(9), 3-15.
Barnet, R., Muller, R. (1974): *Global Reach: The Power of Multinational Corporations*, New York: Simon and Schuster.
Baran, P.A., Sweezy, P.M. (1966): *Monopoly Capital*, New York: Monthly Review Press.
Barrientos, S. (2007): Global Production Networks and Decent Work, Ilo Working Paper Number 77, Geneva: International Labour Organisation.
Barrientos, S. (2011): "Labour Chains": Analysing the Role of Contractors in Global Production Networks, Brooks World Poverty Institute Working Paper 153, Manchester: University of Manchester.
Bhattacharjee, A., Roy., A. (Forthcoming): Bargaining in garment GVCs, in; Nathan, D., Tiwari, M., Sarkar, S. (eds.), *Labour in Global Value Chains in Asia*.
Braverman, H. (1974): *Labour and Monopoly Capital: The Degredation of Work in the Twentieth Century*, New York: Monthly Review Press.
Buroway, M. (1979): *Manufacturing Consent: Labour Process Under Monopoly Capitalism*, Chicago: University of Chicago Press.
CITU (2013). *A Survey on the Conditions of Homebased Workers in India*, Delhi: Centre for Indian Trade Unions.
Coe, N.M., Dicken, P., Hess. M. (2008): Global production networks: Realising the potential, in: *Journal of Economic Geography*, 8(3), 271-95.
Henderson J., Dicken, P., Hess, M., Coe, N.M., Yeung, H. (2001): Global production network and anaysis of economic development, in: *Review of International Political Economy*, 9(3), 436-464.
Hymer, S. (1979): *The Multinational Corporation*, Cambridge: Cambridge University Press.
ILO stats (2012): *Mean Monthly Income: Wages and Earnings* accessed on https://www.ilo.org/ilostat/ (accessed on 10 March 2016).
Jha, P., Chakraborty, A. (2014): Post Fordism, Global Production Networks and Implications for Labour: Case Studies from National Capital Region, India, ISID Working Paper 172, Delhi: Institute for Studies in Industrial Development.
Lenin, V.I. (2000, reprint): *Imperialism: The Highest Stage of Capitalism*, Delhi: Leftword Books.
Mackinnon, D. (2012): Beyond strategic coupling: Reassing firm region nexus in global production networks, in: *Journal of Economic Geography*, 12(1), 227-245.

Marx, K. (1976, reprint): *Capital Volume I: A Critique of Political Economy*, New York: Penguin Classics.

Nathan, D., Tiwari, M., Sarkar, S. (eds.) (Forthcoming): *Labour in Global Value Chains in Asia*, Cambridge: Cambridge University Press.

OECD stats (2013): *Global Value Chain Indicators*, accessed on 12 March 2016 at https://stats.oecd.org/Index.aspx?DataSetCode=GVC_INDICATORS

OECD stats (2014): *Dataset Outward Activity of Multinationals by Location*, http://stats.oecd.org/Index.aspx?DataSetCode=AMNE_OUT_PARTNER (accessed on 12 March 2016).

Roach, S. (2004): "How global labour arbitrage will shape the world economy", http://www.globalagendamagazine.com/2004/stephenroach.asp (accessed on 12 March, 2016).

Silver, B. (2003): *Forces of Labour: Working Class Movement and Globalisation Since 1870*, Cambridge: Cambridge University Press.

Whalen, C.J. (2005): Sending Jobs Offshore from the United States, in: *Intervention: European Journal of Economics and Economic Policies*, 2(2), 33-40.

Wright, E.O. (2000): Working class power, capitalist class interests and class compromise, in: *American Journal of Sociology*, 105(4), 957-1002.

Obstacles to development: Trade and labour market theory revisited*

Bea Ruoff

1. Introduction

The 'wealth of nations' – or more precisely: positive developments of labour markets and international convergence in terms of decreasing income inequality – is not necessarily a result of international free trade. Moreover, shortcomings of the underlying theories depict why trade liberalisation is such a controversial topic. However, usually when policies fail to increase a nation's wealth, it is not the theory being challenged but it is the lax implementation, which is blamed.

Empirically, neither macroeconomic development nor international convergence among developed and developing countries – and their workforces – can clearly be attested as positive effects of trade openness. Even though the empirical evidence is quite split on this issue,[1] there seems to be consensus among economists that international integration of (labour) markets leads to a situation, which is not necessarily socially just, but improves the wealth of all participating nations in terms of employment and consumption possibilities, as well as development. In fact, the promised positive effects of free trade and labour market flexibility are distributed unequally, and can as well be interpreted as being negative for certain groups, such as low-skilled workers. Nevertheless, free trade and labour market flexibility are policy recommenda-

---

* I would like to thank Eckhard Hein and Luisa Bunescu for their helpful comments.
[1] For a review of the extensive literature see for example Winters, McCulloch, and McKay (2004), Milanovic (2005). Globally, income per capita tends to converge; personal income distribution however diverges in many countries (Milanovic 2013).

tions where economists seem to be almost unified (Fuller/Geide-Stevenson 2003, 2014).[2]

There are several explanations for international divergence and income inequality – globalisation, technological progress, institutional changes etc. (Dabla-Norris et al. 2015). International trade – and generally conventional trade theories such as theory of comparative advantage and its advancements – implies a division of labour and builds on marginal productivity theory.

In order to discuss free trade and labour market flexibility, the theoretical background of trade openness with a focus on labour market effects will be scrutinized.

2. Ricardian trade model, its advancements and labour markets

David Ricardo (1814) formulated the basis of the free trade argument benefitting all nations. His basic idea was that England, producing cloth, and Portugal, producing wine, both can increase their welfare by specialising their production according to their comparative advantage. Exogenously given country specific differences determine the production levels – Portugal is more productive than England and needs less workers to produce cloth and wine. However, in comparison to England, the comparative advantage in producing wine is bigger than in producing cloth. Portugal thus should produce (and trade) wine, England cloth. International free trade and the division of labour increases even England's (and any less developed country's) income, because consumption and output increases.

Advancements of Ricardo's formulation by Heckscher (1919) and Ohlin (1933) stress different factor endowments, but same levels of technology, and a specialization in trade in production with the abundant factor. Here it is assumed that factor prices – wages and profits – even equalize due to free international trade.[3]

Trade between countries with similar factor endowments increased in the last decades. Such a trade pattern cannot be explained by comparative advantages. Economies of scale and diversified production explain gains from free trade according to new trade theories (Krugman 1979). The more realistic

---

[2] Or Kearl, Pope, Whiting and Wimmer (1979), Rickets and Shoesmith (1990), Frey and Eichenberger (1992), Alston, Kearl and Vaughan (1992).

[3] See the factor price equalisation theory by Samuelson (1948) and Lerner (1952). Another advancement – the Stolper-Samuelson theorem – states that trade increases the real return of the ample factor.

these trade theories became, they all lead to the same trade pattern – developed countries have capital and technology, developing countries have cheap labour (Priewe 2015) – and ground on marginal productivity theory. This is the starting point to show how international trade affects labour markets.

In a simple case, homogenous labour, perfect competition and full information was assumed. With these prerequisites this labour market model became mainstream thinking until today. The basis for explaining labour demand in the neoclassical paradigm is the so-called macroeconomic production function. Assuming the capital stock as given, the marginal productivity of labour is decreasing when labour input increases. Confronted with a given real wage (w_r) firms will employ workers as long as the marginal product a worker produces is higher than the real wage the company has to pay. The difference between the higher marginal product and the real wage is used to pay profits respectively interest. A firm fixes employment at the point when the marginal product of the last worker is equal to the real wage.[4] Given such a profit maximising constellation and reducing the real wage, a profit maximizing firm moves along the marginal productivity curve and will increase its demand for labour. To sum up, the demand curve of labour (LD^1 in Figure 1) is identical with the marginal productivity curve of labour. It has to be noted that a marginal product of labour can only be calculated when a fixed capital stock is assumed.

Usually a labour supply function is assumed, which shows an increase in labour supply when real wages increase (LS in Figure 1), as higher real wages lead to higher consumption opportunities and stimulate utility maximising households to sacrifice some leisure time to work and consume more.

Equilibrium is realised when the labour demand and the labour supply curve intersect. In such a constellation all workers willing to work for the equilibrium wage, find a job; and all firms, which want to hire workers for the equilibrium wage are able to do so. The precondition to realise the equilibrium are, of course, flexible real wages.

Labour has increasingly become internationally divided as production globalises (Azarhoushang et al. 2015). To integrate this development theoretically we will now assume that countries switch from autarchy to free trade. Figure 1 shows the effects of international trade on labour demand in two diagrams. On the left side the effects on (a) homogeneous labour demand in developing countries, (b) low-skilled labour demand in developing countries, and (c) high-

---

[4] A firm maximizes profits up to the point when marginal output (marginal revenue) is equal to real wages (marginal costs).

skilled labour demand in developed countries is shown. On the right side one can see the effects on (d) homogeneous labour demand in developed countries, (e) low-skilled labour demand in developed countries, and (f) high-skilled labour demand in developing countries.

According to the trade theories mentioned above countries rich in labour (developing countries) would exploit their cheap workforce and trade labour intensive goods, while countries rich in capital (technology) (developed countries) would specialise in a capital or skill intensive production. The demand for labour as well as wages would increase in developing countries (a). Labour demand as well as wages would shift downwards in developed countries (d). Convergence would be the consequence in a constellation of homogeneous labour.

Figure 1: Effects of free trade on demand of homogeneous/ heterogeneous labour

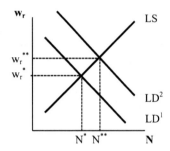

(a) homogenous labour demand in developing countries
(b) low-skilled labour demand in developing countries
(c) high-skilled labour demand in developing countries

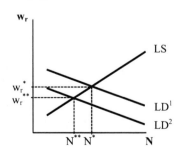

(d) homogenous labour demand in developed countries
(e) low-skilled labour demand in developed countries
(f) high-skilled labour demand in developed countries

This basic model only functions when the very specific assumptions named above hold true. Let us come to inequality and divergence in the case of heterogeneous labour.

Two types of labour are assumed, low-skilled and high-skilled labour. Both labour market segments have labour demand and labour supply functions similar to the case of homogenous labour. Undistorted markets and flexible wages lead to equilibrium in all labour market segments and full employment. Low-skilled workers are less productive than high-skilled workers; the level of the marginal productivity curve of low-skilled workers will be well below the one of high-skilled workers. This leads in almost all circumstances to lower real wages of low-skilled workers. 'Objective' factors based on technology together with labour supply based on utility determine the marginal productivity in equilibrium and income inequality. In the end any single worker has his/her own skills and work experience and is remunerated according to his/her marginal productivity.

We assume now international trade (or a technological revolution) which substitutes low-skilled labour by machines and increases the demand for high-skilled workers, who produce the machines. The result of such a change is a downward shift of the demand for low-skilled workers (e) and an upward shift of the demand of high-skilled workers in developed countries (c), specialised in skill-intense or capital-intense production. Low-skilled workers have to accept a wage cut from w_r^* to w_r^{**}. Wages for high-skilled workers would increase. In developing countries, specialising in labour-intensive production, wages for low-skilled workers would increase (b), while wages for high-skilled workers would decrease relatively (f).[5] Specialisation and international trade would benefit all trading countries in a Ricardian, Heckscher-Ohlin, or Stolper-Samuelson world.

Irrespective of the difficulty to prove these effects of convergence and increasing welfare of nations empirically,[6] there are still fundamental shortcomings of the conventional trade theory and neoclassical labour market theory.

---

[5] The consequences are the same as with skill-biased technological change. See e.g. Acemoglu (2002), Lemieux (2008), or Herr and Ruoff (2014).

[6] See e.g. Stone and Cavazos (2011) and Kierzenkowski and Koske (2012).

3. Shortcomings of conventional trade theories and labour market theory

The first deficiency of neoclassical labour market theory lies in the complexity of labour inputs. If one assumes perfectly substitutable inputs, then marginal productivity theory is an excellent tool. But this assumption neglects the diverse appreciation of labour (movie stars or nurses) and complementary inputs (craftsmen and their tools, teamwork, know-how, or skill level). It is difficult to measure marginal productivities if, for instance, specific tasks are appreciated more than others or output is produced as part of a teamwork (Stiglitz 2012).

Secondly, according to the labour market theory drafted above increasing real wages (or minimum wages) would result in decreasing labour demand due to rising labour costs for firms. However, rising real wages may also increase labour demand when the employer is price taking in the goods market but the only buyer of labour in the labour market (Herr/Ruoff 2014).

Thirdly, increasing labour demand even though real wages increase can also be explained by economies of scale, because output increases faster than input increases. The macroeconomic production function – itself being questionable because of the existence of many capital goods and capital intensities – assuming constant returns to scale is inappropriate for industries characterised by rising economies of scale (Herr/Ruoff 2014).

Last but not least, increasing wages can also be an incentive to work in a more productive and efficient way (Stiglitz 1987).

This basic idea can be combined with the theory of comparative advantage. Here gains from trade are only static. Technological progress and productivity growth however are an effect of international trade. These dynamic gains are missing in the theory (Milberg 2013; Schumacher 2013).

The assumption of full employment of labour and capital is also controversial. Un- and underemployment are phenomena that can be seen all over the world (Felipe/Vernengo 2002). If for example, one country increases output and consumption because its factors of production are not fully utilized, international trade could even lead to unemployment and decreasing output and consumption (Schumacher 2013).

Moreover, for the theory of comparative advantage to function an automatic adjustment via exchange rates, wages or the specie-flow mechanism (or quantity theory of money) (Hume 1793) has to be assumed to balance trade. However, there is no automatic mechanism of real exchange rates (Rose 1991) or wages balancing trade (Schumacher 2013).

Additionally, it is assumed that capital and labour cannot move freely from one country to the other, but domestically they can. International immobility of capital and labour stems from the insecurity one faces when migrating to a foreign country (Ricardo 1814: 161f.). However, there is no theoretical and empirical justification for this inclination because since the 1990s we are witnessing both increasing international labour mobility (UN 2013) and rising international capital mobility (Lund et al. 2013). Empirically one can see that labour is highly mobile and progress of now developed countries came differently than proposed by Ricardo. Britain, Germany, and the United States of America for example did not catch-up with the help of free trade. The opposite – protectionism of their infant industries via trade regulations – was the case (Chang 2002). Trade regulations to protect infant industries as well as industrial policy do not only support technological progress but labour markets as well. Less skilled workers get trained to meet the new requirements of diversified production processes. It seems that thriving developing countries did benefit if diversification and skill upgrading were part of their catch-up strategies. If developing countries rather relied on policy recommendations based on the theory of comparative advantage in the early stage of growth it was difficult to overcome an underdevelopment trap because a specialisation in low-tech but labour intensive production is less likely to foster diversification and skill upgrading (Imbs/Wacziarg 2003; Rodrik 2004; Azarhoushang et al. 2015). Singer (1949) and Prebisch (1950) conclude that the terms of trade of developing countries producing primary commodities and simple manufacturing goods tend to decrease, leaving developing countries in a trap if they only stress international trade and industrialisation. The latter should be diversified, protected via import substitution, and strengthened through skill upgrading (Singer 2003).

Shaikh (2007) and Singer (2003) state that developed countries benefit at the expense of developing countries (as importers of cheaper products and exporters of products achieving higher incomes), thus not equalisation but divergence is the result of free trade.[7]

---

[7] There are exceptions: China, India, South Korea, and Taiwan tend to converge to other "super-countries" (Singer 2003: 4).

4. Flexible to adjust when the facts are changing?

International integration happened anyways, disregarding the difficulty to explain its effects theoretically. It is argued, for instance, that development can be financed by large capital inflows filling a country's 'financing gap'. The amount of foreign direct investment (FDI) has increased significantly and even has surpassed the amount of international trade since the 1990s. According to UNCTAD (2016), the nominal stock of inward FDI increased from US $ 701 billion in 1980 to US $ 24,626 billion in 2014 worldwide and from US $ 294 billion to US $ 8,310 billion in developing countries in the same period. However, simply relying on the "ghost of the financing gap" (as Easterly (1990) terms the still used Harrod-Domar growth model by international financial institutions such as the World Bank or International Monetary Fund) to encourage development, makes no sense from a theoretical and empirical point of view. According to this growth model, saving translates into investment and growth one-to-one in the short-run. The so-called financing gap is the difference between savings of a country and the required investments to achieve a certain level of growth. If there is a gap, it has to be filled by aid paid by donors, so the story goes. However, testing 88 countries with cross-country data only China, Hong Kong, Tunisia, Morocco, Malta, and Sri Lanka show a positive significant relationship between foreign aid and investment. The assumed short-run linkage between lagged investment and growth in a test of 136 countries is only verified by Israel, Liberia, Réunion and Tunisia. Thus, the Harrod-Domar growth model only fits Tunisia (Easterly 1990, 1997). Azarhoushang et al. (2015) argue that it is rather the process of income creation via domestically financed investment than the injection of missing resources (savings and aid) what matters for development. An import oriented development strategy strongly relies on the willingness of other countries to cooperate (and foreign aid). Underdevelopment can even be cemented by longer periods of current account deficits and high foreign indebtedness.

However, policy recommendations of the 'Washington Consensus' to promote development partly neglect the questionable theoretical and empirical fundamentals. Openness to FDI is an essential recommendation of the agenda and is thought to overcome the problem that countries are pushed into an international distribution of labour, which does not necessarily lead to development. The name 'Washington Consensus' stands for a series of "prudent macroeconomic policies, outward orientation, and free-market capitalism" (Williamson 1990: 18) that firstly were imposed on Latin American countries in the 1980s and 90s by Washington based institutions such as the U.S. Congress, the International Monetary Fund, the US Treasury, or the World Bank, and now are used for developing countries in general. It has been augmented with policy reforms such as flexibilisation of of the labour markets (Herr/Priewe 2005; Rodrik 2006). Even though it does not directly praise trade openness, the neoliberal rationale of development coming alongside – or as an effect of – free markets is still very strong (Priewe 2015).

Stiglitz (2008: 44) argues that the Washington Consensus missed the point and rather post-Washington Consensus policies no more relying on one-size-fits-all solutions are needed to foster development, especially because there are countries (e.g. China, Korea, Taiwan) where the state played an important role for development by using industrial policies. What does this mean for conventional trade theory and labour market theory?

5. Conclusion

Real wages and employment are not directly related, therefore it is not a decreasing wage level or more flexible wages in general which should improve international competitiveness and development (Herr/Ruoff 2014). Unregulated (labour) markets seem to reproduce underdevelopment. Import substituting industrialisation together with social upgrading, industrial policy, strong governments and labour market institutions are of vital importance for development. Instead of testing comparative advantage and conventional labour market theory empirically again and again – coming to mixed results – it is worthwhile to reassess if these theories are appropriate to be used for policy advice in the first place.

It is inappropriate to state that free trade is inevitably beneficial for all nations given the deficiencies of comparative advantage theory and its advancements. Labour market flexibility as the preferred buffer to cope with increasing international trade is a questionable policy recommendation. Neither free trade nor flexible labour markets are adequate solutions. They rather seem to be obstacles to development, according to our review of the theoretical and empirical literature.

References

Acemoglu, D. (2002): Technical Change, Inequality, and the Labor Market, in: *Journal of Economic Literature*, Vol. 40 (1), 7-72.

Alston, R., Kearl, J., Vaughan, M. (1992): Is There a Consensus Among Economists in the 1990's?, in: *The American Economic Review*, 82(2), 203-209.

Azarhoushang, B., Bramucci, A., Herr, H., Ruoff, B. (2015): Value Chains, underdevelopment and union strategy, in: *International Journal of Labour Research*, 7(1-2), 153-175.

Chang, H. (2002): *Kicking Away the Ladder*, London: Anthem press.

Dabla-Norris, E., Kochhar, K., Suphaphiphat, N., Ricka, F., Tsounta, E. (2015): Causes and Consequences of Income Inequality: A Global Perspective, IMF Discussion Note, SDN/15/13.

Easterly, W. (1990): The Ghost of the Financing Gap: Testing the Growth Model Used in the International Financial Institutions, in: *Journal of Development Economics*, 60(2), 423-438.

Easterly, W. (1997): The Ghost of the Financing Gap: How the Harrod-Domar Growth Model Still Haunts Development Economics, The World Bank Development Research Group, Policy Research Working Paper 1807.

Felipe, J., Vernengo, M. (2002): Demystifying the Principles of Comparative Advantage: Implications for Developing Countries, in: *International Journal of Political Economy*, 32(4), 49-75.

Frey, B., Eichenberger, R. (1992): Economics and Economists: A European Perspective, in: *The American Economic Review*, 82(2), 216-220.

Fuller, D., Geide-Stevenson, D. (2003): Consensus among Economists: Revisited, in: *The Journal of Economic Education*, 34(4), 369-387.

Fuller, D., Geide-Stevenson, D. (2014): Consensus among Economists – An Update, in: *The Journal of Economic Education*, 45(2), 131-146.

Heckscher, E. (1919): The effect of foreign trade on the distribution of income, in: *EkonomiskTidskriff*, (21), 497-512. Translation in American Economic Association: Readings in the Theory of International Trade (Philadelphia, PA, Blakiston), 1949, 272-300.

Herr, H., Priewe, J. (2005): *The Macroeconomics of Development and Poverty Reduction: Strategies beyond the Washington Consensus*, Baden-Baden: Nomos Publication House.

Herr, H., Ruoff, B. (2014): Wage dispersion as key factor for changing personal income distribution, in: *Journal of Self-Governance and Management Economics*, 2(3), 28-71.

Hume, D. (1793 [1752]): Of the Balance of Trade, in: Ders., *Essays and Treatises on Several Subjects, Essays, Moral, Political and Literary*, Vol. 2, Basil: J.J. Tourneisen, 66-86.

Imbs, J., Wacziarg, R. (2003): Stages of Diversification, in: *American Economic Review*, 93(1), 63-86.

Kearl J., Pope, C., Whiting, G., Wimmer, L. (1979): A Confusion of Economists?, in: *The American Economic Review*, 69(2), 28-37.

Kierzenkowski, R., Koske, I. (2012): Less Income Inequality and More Growth – Are they Compatible? Part 8.The Drivers of Labour Income Inequality – A Literature Review.OECD Economic Department Working Papers, No. 931, OECD Publishing.

Krugman, P. (1979): Increasing returns, monopolistic competition, and international trade, in: *Journal of International Economics*, 9(4), 469-479.

Lemieux, T. (2008): The Changing Nature of Wage Inequality, in: *Journal of Population Economics*, (21), 21-48.

Lerner, A. (1952): Factor Prices and International Trade, in: *Economica*, 19(73), 1-15.

Lund, S., Daruvala, T., Dobbs, R., Härle, P., Kwek, J., Falcón, R. (2013): Financial globalization: Retreat of reset?, Global capital markets 2013, March.

Milanovic, B. (2005): Can we discern the effect of globalization on income distribution? Evidence from household budget surveys, in: *World Bank Economic Review*, (1), 21-44.

Milanovic, B. (2013): Global Income Inequality in Numbers: in History and Now, in: *Global Policy*, 4(2), 198-208.

Milberg, W., Winkler, D. (2013): *Outsourcing Economics: Global Value Chains in Capitalist Development*, New York: Cambridge University Press.

Ohlin, B. (1933): *Interregional and international trade*, Cambridge, MA: Harvard University Press, (RP 1966).

Prebisch, R. (1950): The economic development of Latin America and its principal problems, ECLAC Paper No. E/CN.12/89/Rev.1.

Priewe, J. (2015): Eight Strategies for Development in Comparison, Institute for International Political Economy Berlin Working Paper, No. 53/2015.

Ricardo, D. (1814): *On the Principles of Political Economy, and Taxation*, London: John Murray.

Ricketts, M., Shoesmith, E. (1990): *British Economic Opinion: A Survey of a Thousand Economists*, London: Institute of Economic Affairs.

Rodrik, D. (2004): Industrial Policy for the Twenty-First Century, Harvard University, John F. Kennedy School of Government, Faculty Research Working Papers Series No. RWP04-047.

Rodrik, D. (2006): Goodbye Washington Consensus, Hello Washington Confusion? A Review of the World Bank's Economic Growth in the 1990s: Learning from a Decade of Reform, in: *Journal of Economic Literature*, 44, 973-987.

Rose, A. (1991): The role of Exchange Rates in a Popular Model of International Trade: Does the 'Marshall-Lerner' Condition Hold?, in: *Journal of International Economics*, 30(3-4), 301-316.

Samuelson, P. (1948): International Trade and the Equalisation of Factor Prices, in: *The Economic Journal*, 58(230), 163-184.

Schumacher, R. (2013): Deconstructing the Theory of Comparative Advantage, in: *World Economic Review*, 2, 83-105.

Shaikh, A. (2007): *Globalization and the Myths of Free Trade: History, theory, and empirical evidence*, New York: Routledge.

Singer, H. (1949): Economic progress in under-developed countries, in: *Social Research*, 16(1), 236-266.

Singer, H. (2003): The terms of trade fifty years later: Convergence and divergence, in: South Letter, No. 30. Available at: http://www.southcentre.org/southletter/sl30/South%20Letter%2030trans-12.htm.

Stiglitz, J. (1987): The Causes and Consequences of The Dependence of Quality on Price, in: *Journal of Economic Literature*, 25(1), 1-48.

Stiglitz, J. (2008): Is there a Post-Washington Consensus Consensus?, in: Serra, N., Stiglitz, J. (eds.) (2008): *The Washington Consensus Reconsidered: Towards a New Global Governance*, Oxford: Oxford University Press, 41-56.

Stiglitz, J. (2012): *The Price of Inequality*, London: W.W. Norton.

Stone, S., Cavazos, R. (2011): Wage Implications of Trade Liberalisation: Evidence for Effective Policy Formation, OECD Trade Policy Working Paper, No. 122.

UN (2013): *International Migration Report 2013*, Department of Economic and Social Affairs, Population Division, New York: United Nations.

UNCTAD Statistics (2016): Available at http://unctadstat.unctad.org/wds/TableViewer/tableView.aspx?ReportId=96740

Williamson, J. (1990): What Washington Means by Policy Reform, in: Williamson, J. (ed.). (1990): *Latin American Adjustment: How Much Has Happened?*, Washington, DC.: Institute for International Economics, 7-20.

Winters, A., McCulloch, N., McKay, A. (2004): Trade liberalization and poverty: Evidence so far, in: *Journal of Economic Literature*, 42, 72-115.

The (im)possible developmental model of Albania: A labour perspective

Edlira Xhafa

More than two decades since the transition from a command economy to an open market economy, Albanians continue to take up any opportunity to leave their country in search of a better life. Indeed, in 2015, they were second only to Syrians among the asylum seekers in Germany (Ristic, 2016). Once considered the "star pupil" and the "success story" of the region by the IMF and World Bank officials (Abrahams 2015: 169), Albania remains one of the poorest countries in Europe (World Bank 2015a) with the highest rate of migration, relative to its population, in Central and Eastern Europe (IOM Albania, undated). This paper takes a labour perspective on the developmental model of Albania, and more specifically on the way Albania is integrated in the world economy. The model, which has relied heavily on low-wage jobs and flexible labour, has not met the promise of economic and social progress and has instead led to high levels of unemployment and underemployment, especially among the youth, and a shockingly high incidence of vulnerable employment. Breaking with this failed model, requires a model of development grounded on the principle that decent work is a cornerstone to achieving freedom from poverty, and economic and social progress.

1. Albanian labour market: A snapshot

High rates of migration and reports of stable economic growth have been unable to ease the pressure of unemployment in the country, which has only been exacerbated by the Eurozone crisis. The official unemployment rate in 2014 stood at 17.9 percent, with youth unemployment reaching 32.5 percent

(INSTAT 2015a). Having a job, however, offers limited protection against poverty particularly for the most vulnerable workers receiving the minimum wage, the lowest in the Balkans and in Europe both in absolute terms and in purchasing power (Monitor 2016). The incidence of poverty, for example, was 11 percent among the families with both heads of family employed (World Bank 2015b).

Data on the magnitude of low-wage and precarious jobs are rather scarce. Some estimates put the share of the informal employment at around half of the overall employment outside agriculture and almost three-fourths of employment in the construction sector (World Bank 2015b). While official data are lacking, anecdotal evidence suggests a significant presence of underemployment, especially among the university graduates and the self-employed who make up a quarter of all employment[1]. The share of vulnerable workers – lacking decent working conditions and voice, and access to social security – is over 58 percent (UNDP 2015). A 2013 survey of medium and large companies by the Albanian Institute of Statistics showed that Albanians work longer and receive a much lower pay than workers in neighbouring countries with the same level of development[2] (INSTAT 2015c). High job insecurity is another major issue as seen during the Eurozone crisis where 27 percent of Albanian households had at least one member who had lost a job versus a Europe and Central Asia average of 18 percent (World Bank 2015c). Research in MSE found out that almost all workers in the construction sector, whether unionised or not, were faced with job insecurity (Xhafa 2008).

The scant research on the nature and prevalence of precarious work reflects a lack of attention to the issue of job quality and decent employment as a cornerstone to a broader concept of development which goes beyond growth to consider development as freedom from poverty. But even in a paradigm of development as economic growth, the complete disregard of the link between quality jobs and productivity is rather confounding, although it may reflect a (not very uncommon) thinking that as the country climbs up the global value chain, the quality of jobs will eventually improve. So, after two decades of

---

[1] Only 41.6 percent of those employed are employees; 26 percent are self-employed (with or without employees) and 32.4 percent are contributing family workers with women being 1.7 time more likely to belong to the latter category (INSTAT 2015b).

[2] In 2012, the average annual hours of work in Albania was 2,102 as compared to 1,702 average of European countries (OECD 2012; INSTAT 2015c). Meanwhile, the average hourly labour cost was €2.2 euro as compared to €3.4 in Bulgaria, €3.5 in Macedonia, €4.1 in Romania, €5.1 in Serbia, €5.3 in BiH and €5.8 in Montenegro (INSTAT 2015c).

opening up to the market economy, to what extent has the Albanian model of integration in the global economy resulted in more and better jobs?

2. Albanian's integration in the global value chain: Climbing the ladder or caught in the middle-income trap[3]?

One of the political aims shared by all Albanian governments since the early years of transition has been to attract FDI and increase exports as a way of promoting economic growth, increasing employment, upgrading technology, and improving labour productivity. This was all the more important considering the very high levels of unemployment in the early 1990s due to massive privatisation programs, very low levels of productivity, and obsolete industrial capital stock and production technology that Albania inherited from the command economy (World Bank 2000).

The last two decades have seen FDI flows increase by around 18 times[4] (Open Data Albania Undated, UNCTAD 2014) and exports by around 20 times[5] (INSTAT 2015d). According to the Bank of Albania (2015), the composition of FDI stock in 2014 was dominated by transport and communication (27 percent); the industry sector, including extractive and manufacturing industry, (24 percent); and financial services (17 percent). The period 2012-2014 has seen the domination of Greek FDIs (mainly manufacturing), followed by Canadian (mainly oil extraction) and Italian FDI (mainly manufacturing) (Figure 1).

---

[3] ADB (Asian Development Bank) uses the term for countries "unable to compete with low-income, low-wage economies in manufactured exports and with advanced economies in high-skill innovations... such countries cannot make a timely transition from resource-driven growth, with low cost labour and capital, to productivity-driven growth" (Felipe 2012: 14).

[4] FDI flows went from $68 million in 1993 to over $1.2 billion in 2013 mainly as a result of privatisation of four hydro power plants and of acquisition of a 70 percent share of the main oil-refining company by an Azerbaijani corporation.

[5] Albanian exports grew from a low of 12,499 million ALL in 1993 to 243,183 million ALL in 2015.

Figure 1: Distrubution by country of origin of FDI annual stock (%), 2012-2014

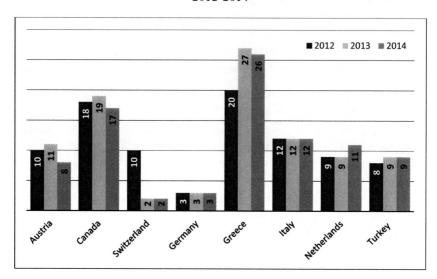

Source: Author's calculations based on data from Bank of Albania time series database

The top exporters, in 2013, were textile and footwear (37 percent); followed by minerals[6], fuels and electricity (27 percent); and construction materials and metals (15 percent) (Figure 2).

The overall data may seem impressive, yet the model of integration in the global economy is not unproblematic. Although FDIs flows have increased steadily, thanks also to a very liberal legal framework, the stock of FDI per capita and the weight of FDI flow to GDP remain the lowest in the region (UNDP/UNCTAD 2012; Demeti/Rebi 2014). The sharp drop in net FDI due to the repatriation of a significant amount of foreign capital (E & Y 2014) has disturbed the country's fragile economic stability. Also, despite significant growth in exports, the country, as of 2015, is a net importer as exports made up less than half (44.6 percent) of imports (INSTAT 2016). A deeper analysis of the industry sector – and more specifically apparel and footwear, and extractive industry of oil and minerals – which are among the top sectors both in terms of exports but also of attracting FDI flows, reveals even more fundamental problems with the Albanian model of integration in the global economy.

---

[6] Main metals exported are chromite, crude steel, copper and ferrochromium.

Figure 2: Sectoral share of exports (%), 1933-2015

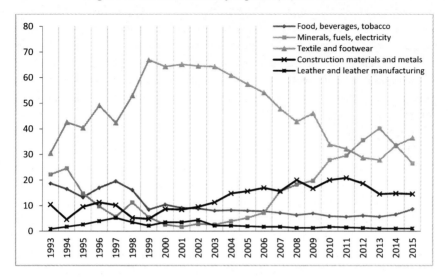

Source: Author's calculations based on data from INSTAT, 2016.

2.1 Apparel and footwear industry[7]

Apparel and footwear industry, which produced a wide range of products of the value chain (such as fiber and leather) as well as final products for domestic market, were two of the main industries in the country before the full privatisation in the early 1990s. As for many developing countries, the industry was considered the starting point for industrial development due to low wages and the simple management skills required (World Bank 2009). Apparel and footwear industry attracted foreign investors since the early 1990s[8] and has remained the country's top export, peaking 67 percent of total exports in 1999

---

[7] The World Bank's report (2009) shows that in 2007, the share of apparel exports was 97.7 percent of all textile and apparel products. Similarly, exports of footwear dominated footwear and leather products. Unless labelled differently in official statistics, this paper uses the terms apparel and footwear industry to include also textile, and leather and leather manufactured products. This is also in conformity with the INSTAT's Statistical Classification of Economic Activities (2014) which groups these activities together as "Textile, apparel, leather manufacturing and footwear". The paper provides disaggregated data whenever available.

[8] The stock of FDI in the apparel and footwear sector stood at 16-17 percent in 2004. (World Bank 2009).

(Figure 2). Meanwhile, around 11 percent of foreign capital or joint-stock companies operate in the apparel sector (E & Y 2014). The industry, which has operated mainly on the basis of Outward Processing Trade[9], known in Albania as *fason*, has concentrated on labour-intensive products rather than textiles that are relatively more capital-intensive (World Bank 2009). This has important implications for the sustainability of the export model followed by Albania. On the one hand, the model relies heavily on foreign buyers, most often intermediaries who are looking for the lowest price, preventing *fason* producers to reap higher margins by sourcing the inputs themselves and weakening the possibility of spill-overs from exports in the local economy in terms of backward linkages (ibid). On the other hand, the intermediaries have no incentive (and/or capacity) to transfer advanced technology and knowledge (ibid). Moreover, the concentration of exports on three notable destination markets[10], has made Albania highly dependent on foreign buyers for markets, inputs and design (ibid), but also susceptible on the fluctuations of the economic situation in those countries, particularly Italy which is the destination of the bulk of the country's exports. The high uncertainty has further discouraged investment in learning and upgrading (ibid).

While a number of companies, especially those operating in the footwear exports, have been able to grow and operate as independent exporters (Liperi, 2015), the majority of exporting companies remain micro and small[11] (INSTAT 2015d), and hence unable to invest in technological upgrading and to improve labour productivity. The small gap in labour productivity between foreign-owned and domestic companies operating in the manufacturing sec-

---

[9] Since 1992, Albania has been benefiting from the EU's General System of Preferences, with textile and footwear products specifically benefiting from this status, according to Regulation 39 17/1992 of 21 Dec. 1992. Further liberalization of textile and apparel trade was granted with the Autonomous Trade Preferences, based on Regulation No. 1763 o f 29 July 1999, while in 2000, with Regulation No. 2007, Asymmetric Regional Preferences were granted to Albania and other Balkan countries, which allowed for export with 0 percent customs duties on OPT, namely apparel exports that were produced using materials that originated only from the EU or the beneficiary country. (World Bank 2009).

[10] Three main export destinations are Italy, Greece and Germany, with Italy being the destination of 75 percent of exports, compared to 25 for Slovakia's exports and 36 for Romania's (World Bank 2009).

[11] Of all companies operating in the industry sector, 89 percent are micro (1-4 employees); 5.2 percent are small (5-9 employees); 4.2 percent are medium (10-49 employees); and 1.6 percent large (over 50 employees).

tor indicates a relatively low technological level of the former (Demeti/Rebi 2014). Regional comparisons indicated that Albania's capital intensity in the apparel and footwear sector and value added in apparel was amongst the lowest in the region (World Bank 2009). The expectation that integration of apparel and footwear industry in the global supply chain would have created conditions for industrial upgrading has not materialized, leaving Albania trapped in a manufacturing model of low value added, limited technological upgrading, and low productivity and skills. Not surprisingly, the importance of the industry has waned both in terms of its contribution to export and its ability to attract FDI (Figure 2 & 3).

Figure 3: Share of annual FDI stock for selected sectors (%), 2007-2013

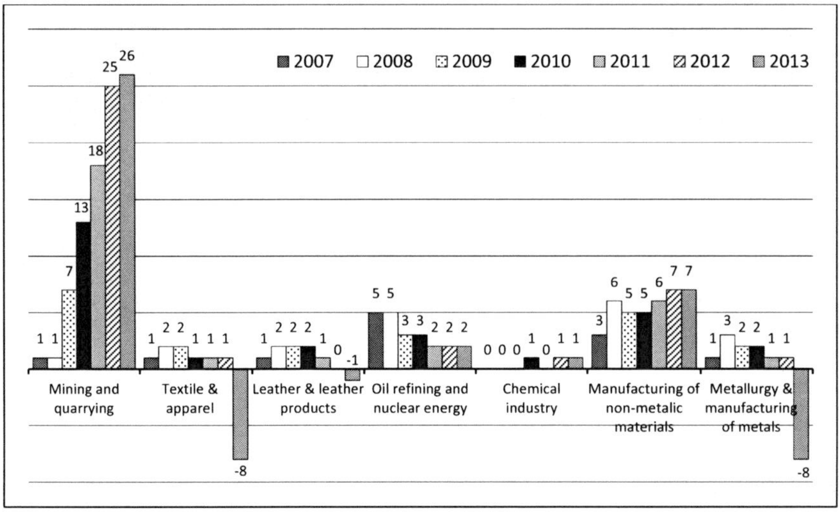

Source: Author's calculations based on data from Bank of Albania time series database

The industry's record of employment, too, is rather unimpressive, averaging at about 8 percent for the years there are available data (Figure 4). Research on working conditions in the sector is rather scant. World Bank findings on apparel and footwear sector show that low wages, high turnover rates and very limited investment on training for workers are prevalent in the sector (2009). Similarly, a micro survey of occupational health and safety issues in unionised garment factories in the region of Shkodra pointed to a number of health issues such as tiredness, headache, irritation and stress (Xhafa 2005).

A number of investigative reports in the media have also exposed the harsh working conditions in the sector, including informal employment and child labour[12].

Figure 4: Sectoral share of employment (%), 2011-2014

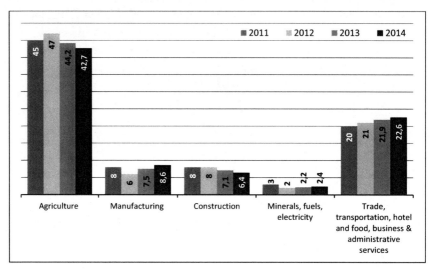

Source: Author's calculations with data from INSTAT's labour surveys 2011-2012 and 2013-2014

2.2 Extractive industry: Oil and minerals

FDI stock in the extractive industry of oil and minerals has expanded from 1 percent in 2007 to 26 percent in 2013 (Figure 3). The exports have also grown from a low of 2 percent in 2001 to 40 percent in 2013 (Figure 2). These signs of revival, and indeed the whole trajectory of the extractive industry, needs to be seen in the light of the importance of the sector during the period

---

[12] Translation of newspapers' titles by the author is offered to provide an idea on the content of the articles. DurresLajm. 2011. Fasonet fshehin shifrat e te punesuarve (*Fason factories hide the numbers of employees*); Agjensia e lajmeve SOT. 2013. Në Shqipëri mbi 50 mijë fëmijë të punësuar, qeveria vazhdon demagogjinë "mbrojtëse" të tyre (In Albania, more than 50 thousand children are working: the government continues with the demagogy of "protecting" the children; Shqip. 2014. Kur skllaveria quhet punesim (*When slavery is called employment*).

of the command economy and the dramatic decay after the 1990s. A detailed report of the World Bank sheds light on such developments in the mining sector. As the Bank puts: "After serving for more than fifty years as a foundation of industrial growth and economic linkages, the mineral industry of Albania has succumbed to underinvestment, cannibalization and decay" (World Bank 2009: 56). The industry went from "integrated mine/metallurgical operations ... feeding raw materials to downstream industrial activities that included steel, metals fabrication and value-added metallurgical products for exports" to "highly fragmented ... assets", so that the "remaining operations today realize only 10 percent of rated plant capacities" (ibid: 58). As the reinvestments ceased and a process of assets' stripping was set in motion, mineral production and exports dramatically fell from $140 million in 1989 (chrome, copper and nickel accounted for 80 percent of the exports' value) to $20 million in 1992, in a very short period of three years. In 1998, the Albanian government's response was the fragmentation of mining operations into dissociated units and license transfers. In addition, exploration and exploitation rights were reassigned to individuals who lacked any technical capacity or financial resources to recover the sector. Thus, what followed was "a decade of lax contractual enforcement [which] enabled these license holders to passively hold resources, and thus effectively sterilizing key assets and restricting access to qualified investors... Within two years, nearly all remaining productive capacity of the large, diversified, integrated mining sector had been stripped away" (ibid).

Oil extraction had a similar trajectory although a much less glorious past as the sector already faced difficulties back in 1980s. Problems related to obsolete technology, lack of exploration to replace produced reserves, lack of investment in extraction equipment and limited and aging transportation and refining infrastructure were only exacerbated with the breakdown of the command economy (Balkan Analysis 2012).

As for all other sectors, Albanian governments chose the path of privatisation for the extractive industries. The expansion of FDIs in the oil and mineral extraction in recent years reflects major privatisations and licensed drilling in the oil sector, and concessions for construction and operation in the mining industry. The number of mining permits reached 600 in November 2015, of which around 20 percent was for chromium extraction (Ministry of Energy and Industry 2016). In 2013-2014, there were 11 private companies operating in the oil producing and exploration, while the only state-owned company involved in oil and gas exploration and producing has delegated its rights to private companies (EITI 2014). However, the returns have been far from impressive. In 2014, the sector's share to GDP stood at 5 percent, while its contribution to employment was a negligible less than 1 percent to total employment (Ministry of Energy and Industry 2016). In fact, the transfer of oil wells to private companies has resulted in more jobs losses (ibid). Further, the Ministry of Energy and Industry reports that none of the private companies operating in Albania paid any tax on profits for years 2013 and 2015. Despite being a crude oil producer in Europe, the country's oil imports are still high as the refining capacities do not meet the domestic needs and even the part of oil refined domestically does not meet the EU environmental standards (Hoxha 2015). This suggests that FDIs in the extractive industries have failed to bring the expected technological upgrading and improve productivity.

Moreover, the 'success' of the extractive industry is overshadowed by its impact on working conditions, communities and environment. Sectoral studies and reports cited in this paper are silent on these issues. Indeed, the World Bank's praise of the mining industry before the 1990s, as cited earlier in this paper, and its current support for the mining and oil[13] extracting industry, ignores this devastating impact. In contrast to the apparel and footwear sector, however, the number of investigative media reports analysing the issues is much larger. These reports point to use of child labour in the industry[14], appalling working conditions, very serious violations of occupational health and safety regulations, very low wages, tax evasion, criminality and pervasive corruption[15]. Indeed, Albania makes no exception to other "natural resource rich countries [which] show a high level of corruption and a low level of democracy as the incentives for powerful groups in society to grab some of

---

[13] World Bank (2015a) reports that its financial arm (IFC) invested $75 million to a Canadian based oil and gas exploration and production company, exclusively focused on Albania.

[14] Toronto Sun. (2014): Albanian child labour takes shine off chrome industry. http://www.torontosun.com/2014/06/06/albanian-child-labour-takes-shine-off-chrome-industry

[15] Translation of newspapers' titles by the author is offered to provide some idea on the content of the articles. Lajme.gen.al. 2009. Viktimat ne miniera nga varferia dhe moszbatimi i teknikes (Mine victims due to lack of OSH). Tema. 2011. Ne Bulqize po perleshet uria masive me mafien e kromit. (In Bulqiza, the massive hunger is facing the mafia of chromium); Independent Balkan News Agency. 2014. Bankers Petroleum accused of $40 million tax evasion; MAPO. 2015. Mallkimi i naftes: Jeta midis ndotjes dhe vdekjes ne Patos-Marinze (The curse of oil: Life between pollution and death in Patos-Marinze); Focus News. 2015. Minierat, galerite e vdekjes (Mines, the death mineshafts); Reporter.al. 2016 Kromi i përgjakur: "Mafia" me mbështetje politike kontrollon nëntokën e Bulqizës (Blooded Chromium: The politically supported "mafia" controls the mines of Bulqiza).

the natural resource rents are high" (Humphreys et al. 2007, in Herr et al. forthcoming: 8).

There are no official data on the number of mine workers injured or killed while working in the 'death mineshafts', but some media have reported that in less than three years, 11 mineworkers have lost their lives and nine have been injured in the mines of the Bulqize e Martanesh area alone (Rusta 2014). The Albanian Helsinki Committee (2015) has raised serious concerns over the environmental degradation caused by the extraction activities in the oil fields of Patos-Marinze with severe health consequences for the lives of the community. Media investigations have reported on cases of cancer, serious respiratory, neurological, skin and kidney problems (MAPO 2015; Ekolevizja 2015). In March 2015, explosions from gas exploration by the Bankers Petroleum, the Canadian company which received financing also from IFC and EBRD for its operations in the area, resulted in further pollution and in many damaged houses (MAPO 2015; Panorama 2015).

The analysis of the apparel and footwear and extractive industries shows that the Albanian model of integration in the global economy, at least the industry sector, is rather precarious. Heavy reliance on the international markets has made the industry sector highly susceptible to external crisis. Low value added exports due to low technology has constrained the possibility for technological spillover and increased productivity levels. FDI flows in high technology production are very limited (Figure 3) and the country's productivity remains the lowest in the region (Demeti/Rebi 2014). Unable to transition from labour- and resource-intensive growth to productivity-driven growth, Albania has tried to maintain its competitive advantage of low costs by freezing its minimum wage[16]. Thus, the initial improvements in the welfare of consumers that came with the development of the industry have been halted. Indeed, "without a substantial increase in the level of productivity in developing countries, a conversion of living standards between developing and developed countries will not be possible" (Herr et al. forthcoming: 3). In fact, an Asian Development Bank paper has included Albania in the list of 37 countries considered to be experiencing the "middle-income trap" and "will likely be there for another 2-3 decades" (Felipe 2012: 22). A model of reliance on market solutions has clearly failed in delivering economic and social progress in Albania.

---

[16] The decision of the Socialist Government to freeze the minimum wage for four years, may be influenced by the package of demands from *fason* producers in 2013 (Monitor 2014).

3. As a way of conclusions: Policy considerations

"It is not just the creation of market economy that matters, but the improvement of living standards and the establishment of the foundation of sustainable, equitable and democratic development" (Stiglitz 1999: 3)

Increasing exports and attracting FDIs may help the development of a country, but it does not translate automatically into technological and productivity improvement and even less to decent work and development as freedom from poverty. In fact, the two industries discussed here prove that left to the market, the model not only fails to meet the promise of economic development, but in addition it can result in perverse outcomes, such as working for low wages and in inhumane working conditions, environmental degradation, increased corruption and further weakening of democracy and the state.

While a comprehensive elaboration of a policy package for the development of the industry sector is beyond the scope of this paper, a number of policy considerations can be suggested.

With regard to the apparel and footwear sector, the argument of keeping minimum wages low as a competitive strategy suffers from short-termism and short-sightedness for a number of reasons. First, meeting the challenge of skills upgrading requires not only quality and free vocational training (World Bank 2009; Monitor 2014), but also putting in place incentives, such as higher wages and improvement of working conditions, to attract and retain qualified workers. This, in turn, may also have a positive impact on productivity. The available literature suggests that higher job quality is positively associated with higher productivity, profitability and sustainability of growth and development of enterprises, including MSMEs (Fenwick et al. 2006; Eurofound 2012; Croucher et al. 2013; Eurofound 2014).

Second, low wages may be one of the reasons behind the persistent dominance of low-value added exports. Experiences from the sector in countries such as Hong Kong, Korea, Taiwan and Portugal, show that raising domestic labour costs makes low-value production uncompetitive and forces firms to invest in upgrading their technology and move up the value chain production (World Bank 2009). Third, shipping costs from Albania to Italy are substantially lower when compared to China, 1.43 percent of imports vs. 11.8 percent, and even lower than the other countries in Western Balkans (World Bank 2009). This provides significant room for raising wages which in combination with public investment in quality and free public services – education, health care[17], water, electricity and housing – can help lift the living standards of a substantial proportion of the working poor. Fourth, far from causing contraction of employment, as *fason* producers argue (Monitor 2014), raising minimum wages can increase the aggregate demand, which in turn may have a general positive effect on employment and economic growth (Herr et al. 2009). Finally, moving up the value chain necessitates a comprehensive and diversified industrial policy which, among others, supports the building of clusters with backward and forward linkages (for a comprehensive discussion on this, see Herr et al. forthcoming).

This paper has shown that the benefits from the oil and mineral extraction industry are outweighed by its limited potential for employment generation and economic growth. Already back in the 1950s, it was forcefully argued that "the concentration of countries on the production of natural resources including basic agricultural products will in the long-term lead to a deterioration of the terms of trade in developing countries" (Singer 1950; Prebisch 1950, in Herr et al. forthcoming: 7). Moreover, the serious impact of the sector on people's health and environment is a sufficiently compelling reason to look at sustainable sources of energy, such as solar energy[18], to meet the country's needs for energy and to export.

Although the analysis of this paper pertains only to the industry sector, the perspective of the analysis may be insightful also for the other sectors of the economy. For example, the relatively high FDIs and the domination of foreign-owned banks – 14 out of 16 commercial banks (E & Y 2015) – may not necessarily increase credit availability for the domestic economy. Foreign owners may prefer to channel deposits out of the country rather than finance small and medium enterprises (Herr et al. forthcoming), which was one key constraint faced both by small and large firms in the apparel and footwear sector (World Bank 2009). Similarly, the rise of call centers in Albania[19] needs to be seen in light of the newest wave of outsourcing, i.e. services that can outsource the low-value added activities. While this may alleviate pressing employment problems, especially for the youth, it may also represent another trap, locking such employment in 'pure voice' services rather than 'higher-end' jobs of the Business Process Outsourcing (BPO).

---

[17] As the country spends only 2.6 percent of GDP on health care, out-of-pocket expenditure at the point of services account for 60 percent of sectoral (World Bank 2015c).

[18] With an average of 240-260 sunny days per year, Albania has an enormous potential for developing solar energy.

[19] Over 400 companies employing around 9,500 employees (Liperi 2015, 2016).

Finally, a key policy consideration pertains to the critical role of the government. The legacy of a "failed state" (World Bank 2001: 22) which has marked the painful transition to market economy, cannot be addressed with more of the same. Privatisation of the remaining strategic public companies[20] will not resolve the fundamental problems of the model, most notably the missing elements of a developmental state and corruption. Indeed, the Albanian case shows that where the state is weak, more privatization can have a devastating impact on workers, communities and the environment and can further undermine the possibility of building a developmental state.

Agents for social change who can push for a more developmental state are still at an incipient phase. Recent student protests opposing further commercialization of public higher education and environmental degradation, and demanding a say in policy decisions regarding public spaces, may indicate the emergence of a new discourse which challenges some of the elements of the existing model of development. A comprehensive discourse on a progressive developmental model, however, requires a critical contribution from academia, which has been disturbingly silent on these issues. At the same time, the transformation of these protests into a movement for social change requires workers' voice and structural power. Relegated to the fringes of the public discourse on the most pressing problems facing the country, the existing trade unions have been reluctant to articulate their support for issues raised by students. Students' protests, however, may provide trade unions with a golden opportunity to shake off the apathy of the past decades and find their relevance. Thus, the unions' support and involvement is of critical importance not only for the future of students' movements, but first and foremost for the future of unions themselves. Also, students' protests may provide an emancipatory space for genuine trade unions to emerge, especially if the agenda of the protests is broadened to include workers' issues. A wide coalition of students, workers and academia can provide the space for consolidating the organizational and discursive power of these agents for social change, thus enabling them to push for a key role of the state in shaping a sustainable model of

---

[20] According to the U.S Department of State (2015): "The privatization process in Albania is nearing a conclusion, with only a few major privatizations remaining. These few opportunities include electricity distribution company, the state owned insurance company INSIG, 16 percent of the fixed line telephone company Albtelekom, the state owned oil company Albpetrol, and, 25 percent of oil refiner ARMO.... In order to promote investment in priority sectors, the government has announced that it may offer concessions to local or international investors for the symbolic price of one euro, but has not yet detailed specific concessions that will receive this treatment."

development anchored on the premise that decent work is essential to freedom from poverty and economic and social progress.

References

Abrahams, F. (2015): *Modern Albania: From dictatorship to democracy in Europe*, New York: Nuy Press.

Albanian Helsinki Committee (2015): Raport mbi situaten e respektimit te te drejtave te njeriut ne Shqiperi per vitin 2015. Accessible at: http://www.ahc.org.al/web/images/publikime/al/Raporti_per_te_Drejtat_Njeriut.pdf

Balkan Analysis (2012): Albanian oil industry enjoys revival, but investor-government relations remain a question. Accessible at: http://www.balkanalysis.com/albania/2012/02/05/albania-oil-industry-enjoys-revival-but-investor-government-relations-remain-a-question/

Bank of Albania (2015): Pozicioni i investimeve nderkombetare ne 31 Dhjetor 2014. Accessible at: https://www.bankofalbania.org/web/pub/pin_2014_analiza_30_09_2015_7629_1.pdf

Croucher, R., Stumbitz, B., Quinlan, M., Vickers, I. (2013): *Can better working conditions improve the performance of SMEs?: An international literature review*, Geneva: International Labour Organization.

Demeti, A., Rebi, E. (2014): Foreign direct investments (FDI) and Productivity in Albania. Accessible at: http://www.uamd.edu.al/new/wp-content/uploads/2015/01/Arber-DEMETI-21.pdf

E & Y (2014): Doing Business in Albania. Accessible at: http://www.ey.com/Publication/vwLUAssets/Doing_business_in_Albania_2014/$FILE/EY-doing-business-in-albania-2014.pdf

EITI – Extractive Industry Transparency Initiative (2014): Sektori hidrokarbur, nafta e gazi natyror. Accessible at: http://www.albeiti.org/industria-nxjerrese/sektori-hidrokarbur-nafta-e-gazi-natyror/

Ekolevizja (2015): Shperthimet e puseve me te shpeshta me teknologjine e re te perdorur nga Bankers. Accessible at: https://ekolevizja.wordpress.com/2015/04/02/shperthimet-e-puseve-me-te-shpeshta-me-teknologjine-e-re-te-perdorur-nga-bankers/

Eurofound (2012): *Work organisation and innovation*, Dublin: Eurofound.

Eurofound (2014): *Social dialogue in micro and small enterprises*, Dublin: Eurofound.

Felipe, J. (2012): Tracking the middle-income trap: What is it, Who is in it, and Why?, Asian Development Bank Economics Working Paper Series, No. 306. Accessible at: http://adb.org/sites/default/files/pub/2012/economics-wp-306.pdf

Fenwick, C., Howe, J., Trabsky, M., Summerbell, S. (2006): *Labour law and labour related laws in Micro- and Small Enterprises: Innovative regulatory approaches*, Melbourne: University of Melbourne.

Herr, H., Kazandziska, M., Mahnkopf-Praprotnik, S. (2009): The theoretical debate about minimum wages, GLU Working Paper, No. 6. Accessible at: http://www.global-labour-university.org/fileadmin/GLU_Working_Papers/GLU_WP_No.6.pdf

Herr, H., Schweisshelm, E., Vu, T. (Forthcoming): The integration of Vietnam in the global economy and its effects for Vietnamese economic development.

Hoxha, B. (2015): Rikthimi ne treg in naftes "Made in Albania". Monitor Journal. Accessible at: http://www.monitor.al/rikthimi-ne-treg-i-naftes-made-in-albania/

INSTAT (2011): Regjistri i ndermarrjeve 2011. Accessible at: http://www.instat.gov.al/media/157009/regjistri_ndermarrjeve_2011.pdf

INSTAT (2015a): Shkalla e papunesise 2007-2014. Accessible at: http://www.instat.gov.al/al/themes/tregu-i-pun%C3%ABs.aspx

INSTAT (2015b): Tregu i punes, Labour market 2014. Accessible at: http://www.instat.gov.al/media/291851/tregu_punes_2014____.pdf

INSTAT (2015c): Anketa e kostove te punes, Labour cost survey. Accessible at: http://www.instat.gov.al/media/291930/anketa_e_kostove_te_punes_2013.pdf

INSTAT (2015d): External trade in goods by enterprises characteristics. Accessible at: http://www.instat.gov.al/media/303319/tregtia_e_jashtme_sipas_karakteristikave_te_ndermarrjeve_2011-2014.pdf

INSTAT (2015e): Business register 2014. Accessible at: http://www.instat.gov.al/media/298854/regjistri_ndermarrjeve_2014.pdf

INSTAT (2016): Tregtia e Jashtme: Eksportet sipas grupmallrave dhe partnereve kryesore. Accessible at: http://www.instat.gov.al/al/themes/tregtia-e-jashtme.aspx

IOM (Undated): Migration and Albania. Accessible at: http://www.albania.iom.int/index.php/en/albania

Liperi, O. (2015): 100 Punedhenesit me te medhenj ne vend. Monitor Journal. Accessible at: http://www.monitor.al/100-punedhenesit-me-te-medhenj-ne-vend-2/

Liperi, O. (2016): Profili i ri i Shqiperise. Monitor Journal. Accessible at: http://www.monitor.al/profili-ri-shqiperise/

MAPO (2015): Mallkimi i naftes: Jeta midis ndotjes dhe vdekjes ne Patos-Marinze. Accessible at: http://www.reporter.al/mallkimi-i-naftes-jeta-midis-ndotjes-dhe-vdekjes-ne-patos-marinze/

Ministry of Energy and Industry (2016): Industria nxjerrese: Raportet e transparences per vitet 2013-2014. Accessible at: http://www.energjia.gov.al/al/njoftime/lajme/industria-nxjerrese-raportet-e-transparences-per-vitet-2013-2014

Monitor Journal (2014): Fasoni: Qeveria do te ngrije pagat per kater vjet. Accessible at: http://www.monitor.al/fasoni-qeveria-do-te-ngrije-pagat-per-kater-vjet/

Monitor Journal (2016): "Shqipëria, me pagën minimale më të ulët në Europë, për nga fuqia blerëse". Accessible at: http://www.monitor.al/shqiperia-pagen-mini male-te-ulet-ne-europe-per-nga-fuqia-blerese/

OECD (2012): Average annual hours actually worked per workers. Accessible at: https://stats.oecd.org/Index.aspx?DataSetCode=ANHRS

Open Data Albania (Undated): open.data.al/uploadserise/skedaret/ihd.xls

Panorama (2015) Shperthimet ne puset e naftes ne Marinze, prokuroria merr ne pyetje administratorin e "Bankers". Accessible at: http://www.panorama.com.al/shper thimet-ne-puset-e-naftes-ne-marinze-prokuroria-merr-ne-pyetje-administratorin-e-bankers/

Ristic, M. (2016): Albania, Kosovo top German 2015 asylum list. The Balkan Investigative Reporting Network. Accessible at: http://www.balkaninsight.com/en/article/albania-kosovo-top-german-2015-asylum-seekers-list-01-07-2016

Rusta, A. (2014): Aksidentet në miniera, kromi merr jetë njerëzish, në 2 vite 11 viktima. Newpaper "Shqiptarja". Accessible at: http://shqiptarja.com/m/aktualitet/aksi dentet-ne-miniera-kromi-merr-jete-njerezish-ne-2-vite-11-viktima-233981.html

Stiglitz, J.E. (1999): Whither Reform? – Ten years of the transition, Paper prepared for the Annual Bank Conference on Development Economics, Washington, D.C., April 28-30, 1999.

U.S Department of State (2015): Albania investment climate statement 2015. Accessible at: http://www.state.gov/documents/organization/241665.pdf

UNCTAD (2014): World investment report 2014 – Investing in SDGs: An action plan. Accessible at: http://unctad.org/en/PublicationsLibrary/wir2014_en.pdf

UNDP (2015): Human Development Report 2015: Work for human development. Accessible at: http://hdr.undp.org/sites/default/files/2015_human_development _report.pdf

UNDP, UNCTAD (2012): Foreign Direct Investment Report: Albania 2011. Accessible at: http://www.al.undp.org/content/dam/albania/docs/Foreign%20Direct %20Investment%20Report%20-%20Albania%202011.pdf

World Bank (2000): Albania Country Assistance Evaluation. Accessible at: http:// www-wds.worldbank.org/servlet/WDSContentServer/IW3P/IB/2001/03/01/00 0094946_01020805373780/Rendered/PDF/multi_page.pdf

World Bank (2001): Evaluating Public Sector Reform Guidelines for Assessing Country-Level impact of Structural Reform and Capacity Building in the Public Sector. Accessible at: http://unpan1.un.org/intradoc/groups/public/documents/ APCITY/UNPAN002283.pdf

World Bank (2009): Building competitiviness in Albania. Accessible at: http://www -wds.worldbank.org/external/default/WDSContentServer/WDSP/IB/2010/03/31/ 000333038_20100331010114/Rendered/PDF/478660ESW0v10A1C0disclosed0 31291301.pdf

World Bank (2015a): Country partnership framework for Albania for the period 2015-2019. Accessible at: http://www.worldbank.org/content/dam/Worldbank/document/eca/Albania/al-cpf-2015-eng.pdf

World Bank (2015b): Shqiperia, Gjenerata e ardhshme. Accessible at: http://pubdocs.worldbank.org/pubdocs/publicdoc/2016/1/948311453293073611/SCD-Executive-Summary-Albanian.pdf

World Bank (2015c): Albania World Bank Group Partnership Program Snapshot April 2015. Accessible at: https://www.worldbank.org/content/dam/Worldbank/document/eca/Albania-Snapshot.pdf

Xhafa, E. (2005): Shendeti dhe siguria ne pune ne industrine e tekstileve ne Shkoder. Unpublished report commissioned by Friedrich Ebert Stiftung, Tirana, Albania.

Xhafa, E. (2008): Micro and Small Enterprises in Albania – Closing the Representational Gap. Unpublished national report for the global research "Closing the representation gap in Micro and Small Enterprises".

Nicaragua 37 years after the Sandinista Revolution*

Trevor Evans

1. Introduction

Hansjörg Herr is renowned among friends and colleagues for his warmth and generosity and for the wide range of his interests in economics. In the summer of 1990, without even having met me, he very kindly arranged an office where I could work at the Berlin Social Science Centre for a few months. Then, in 1996 when I moved to Berlin from Latin America I joined a discussion group with Hansjörg and others, first discussing the drafts of the highly successful multi-paradigmatic textbook he was writing at the time with Michael Heine, and going on to discuss the work of various authors ranging from Hayek to Kalecki and recent post-Keynesian writers. Hansjörg – who at the time was in the process of developing his English – had a rare capacity to grasp the key points of an argument and to then improvise what he thought must be the intermediate steps in the argument, usually with remarkable perspicacity.

In 2006 I joined Hansjörg at the Berlin School of Economics, settling into an office next but one to his. Hansjörg showed himself to be an exceptionally gifted teacher, possessing a rare ability to explain complex issues in an accessible – and often amusing – way to students at the university. He was also always in great demand to speak to trade union and other non-academic audiences – occasionally even addressing meetings of conservatives who were also invariably bowled over by his ability to explain complex issues in a way that was accessible to non-economists.

---

* I am grateful to Nestor Avendaño, Eduardo Baumeister and Arturo Grigsby for helpful discussions about recent developments.

In the time that I worked with Hansjörg I was frequently amazed by his extraordinarily prolific output of publications. These ranged from wide-ranging theoretical texts to an extraordinarily extensive number of articles and books about contemporary economies, including Germany, Europe and, since the 1990s, developing economies – in particular China and other South-East Asian countries. Some of the issues which he confronted in these studies were ones which I had also had some contact with, although on a much smaller scale, while working in the Central American state of Nicaragua.

In 1979, a popular uprising led by the Sandinista National Liberation Front had overthrown the US-backed dictatorship which had ruled Nicaragua since the 1930s. Mass literacy and vaccination campaigns attracted widespread international praise but the process of social and economic transformation inaugurated by the new government was soon challenged by armed counter-revolutionary forces, organized and financed by the United States, and which – as intended – began to undermine the initial gains of the revolution.

2. From colonialism to dictatorship

Nicaragua was colonized by the Spanish in 1529 and the early settlers established unions with indigenous women to form the predominantly *mestizo* population. A white elite established large-scale haciendas on which cattle were reared, producing beef which was driven periodically to Guatemala and other Spanish possessions to the north. This dominant landed class formed the basis for the Conservative elite based in the city of Granada. By contrast, a Liberal, more market oriented elite involved in commerce and international trade began to develop with a base in the country's other main city, Leon.

Following the collapse of the Spanish empire in 1821, there was a short-lived attempt to establish a Central American Federation based on the former colonial provinces in the region, but this proved unstable. Nicaragua, like other countries in the region, was marked by conflict between Conservative and Liberal forces, and for several decades the country experienced what are known as the 'years of anarchy' with no effective central government. In 1857, a compromise was agreed between Conservatives and Liberals and the city of Managua – located roughly halfway between their respective seats of power – was established as the country's capital, initially under Conservative presidents.

The development of Nicaragua was transformed from the 1860s by the introduction of coffee production which, unlike the semi-feudal cattle haciendas, was based on waged labour and capitalist relations of production. The expansion of coffee production resulted in the rapid growth of the commercial bourgeoisie and this was reflected in the election in 1893 of a Liberal president, José Santos Zelaya. Zelaya pursued a project of national capitalist development, introducing public education and developing the telegraph and the country's system of railways and steam ships, but also using the state to oblige peasants to provide labour for the coffee plantations. Under Zelaya the region facing the Atlantic coast was also incorporated into the country. This had been under British control and was populated sparsely by former African slaves from the Caribbean and several small Indian communities.

Zelaya planned to raise foreign capital to build an inter-oceanic canal through Nicaragua, but this was strongly opposed by the United States, which had just invested huge amounts of capital in constructing the Panama Canal. In 1909 Zelaya was forced out of office after the US landed marines in Bluefields on Nicaragua's Atlantic coast in support of Zelaya's Conservative opponents. The marines withdrew after Conservative rule had been reestablished, but the new government quickly ran up debts with New York banks, and the marines returned in 1912 and ruled the country through a US appointed troika, forcing Nicaragua to cede the national bank and the country's railway and steam ships to the country's US creditors.

The US occupation was resisted by several small armies, but the US and its appointed government succeeded in negotiating some sort of deal with the leaders of most of these groups until only one remained: the guerilla army of workers and peasants led by Augusto César Sandino. Unable to secure a victory over Sandino, the US withdrew in 1933, having first set up a local military force, the National Guard, under the command of the English-speaking Anastasio Somoza. Sandino was murdered on Somoza's orders in 1934 while attending negotiations in Managua and Somoza became president shortly after, establishing a corrupt and repressive dictatorship that was continued by his two sons, and which lasted until 1979 supported, virtually to the end, by the US government.

Somoza took advantage of the income from gold mining during the Second World War to renationalize the national bank, the railway and the steamships. After the war the state then played a major role in promoting the expansion of agricultural exports, in particular cotton and sugar, as well as the more traditional exports of coffee and beef. In the 1960s, the government also began to promote a programme of import substituting industrialization based on a division of labour organized with neighbouring countries through the newly created Central American Common Market. However, the benefits of protracted economic growth were very narrowly distributed and peasant organisations and trade unions, together with political opponents, were subject to severe repression. Following the destruction of Managua by an earthquake in 1972, Somoza also lost the support of much of the middle class, who were disgusted at the way he appropriated much of the international aid that flowed into the country.

The most important opposition to the dictatorship emerged from the Sandinista National Liberation Front. This had its origins in a group, influenced by the Cuban revolution, which attempted to build a guerilla presence among peasants in the northern mountains of Nicaragua in the 1960s, drawing legitimacy from the support of some of Sandino's surviving combatants. A second group emerged in the 1970s, arguing that economic development meant that successful opposition should be based, not on rural peasants, but on the urban working class in the country's cities. Finally, as popular opposition to Somoza's rule became more widespread, a third group argued that, rather than a long-term struggle based on either the rural peasantry or the urban proletariat, discontent was so widespread that an immediate armed insurrection could topple the dictatorship, and advocated a multi-class alliance which included the middle class and even sectors of the bourgeoisie.

The first attempt at an insurrectionary rising in 1977 was put down by Somoza's forces but, in the aftermath, the three tendencies united and in 1979 popular uprisings led by the Sandinistas succeeded in overthrowing the dictatorship which had ruled the country for over 40 years.

3. The Sandinista Revolution

The new revolutionary government had enormous popular support and in 1984 the Sandinistas and their presidential candidate, Daniel Ortega, decisively won elections which, although condemned by the US, were widely praised by other international observers. Economic output, which had fallen during the uprisings against Somoza, began to recuperate at the start of the 1980s and the new government launched a major expansion of public education and health services, most notably in previously isolated rural areas. However, economic development soon faced a series of major problems. Under the impact of the deep international recession in the early 1980s, the prices of the country's agricultural exports fell sharply. In addition, counter-revolutionaries or *contras,* initially based on former members of Somoza's National Guard who had fled to Honduras, began to launch attacks on health centres and key economic infrastructure, armed and supported by the US government. Furthermore, the Sandinista's limited governmental experience and, in some cases, high handedness led to a growth in support for the contras in parts of the rural interior.

The economic model which the Sandinistas adopted was based on what they termed a mixed economy and involved three main sectors. The extensive farms and businesses of Somoza and his close supporters were expropriated, and formed the basis of a state sector known as the Area of People's Property. Small producers in the countryside and towns constituted a second sector. Finally, those capitalists who remained in the country and continued to be economically active (the so-called 'patriotic bourgeoisie') formed a third sector.

In the early 1980s, the state sector was seen as the basis for future economic development, and a number of major investment projects were launched with the aim of providing stable, well-paid jobs which could leap-frog the country out of underdevelopment. However, the elections in October 1984 alerted the Sandinistas to their weak support in some parts the rural interior, and in 1985 the government introduced a major shift in the focus of economic policy, giving priority to the peasant sector. The prices paid for basic agricultural products were raised – at the expense of urban consumers – and, in the face of rising shortages, rural stores were given priority in the allocation of scarce items. At the same time, land from some state farms was distributed to peasants, either as collective or individual property – something which had a beneficial effect on output, but did little to win back the support of estranged communities. Finally, with no apparent end to the US support for the contra and with new elections looming, in 1988 the Sandinista government introduced another major shift in policy, launching a market-based set of reforms which provided incentives to the capitalist sector in an attempt to arrest the declining level of output and to gain political support abroad, but which involved a further sharp decline in living standards for many of the urban and rural poor.

This last shift in economic policy was accompanied by the opening of negotiations with the contra, which secured a measure of peace in the countryside. As the election in 1990 approached, the US put massive pressure on the opposition parties to unite and managed to get all the parties to support the relatively moderate candidacy of Violetta de Chamorro, the widow of a distinguished Conservative newspaper editor who had been murdered by Somoza's National Guard in 1978. Chamorro's campaigned was skillfully managed by her son-in-law, Antonio Lacayo and, on the basis of a programme of national reconciliation, the coalition secured a majority of votes from the war-weary population.

4. Capitalist reconstruction

The Chamorro government ruled Nicaragua from 1990 to 1996, with Lacayo effectively acting as prime minister. The contra was – despite some hiccups – demobilized and, following agreements with the US Agency for International Development and the IMF, external financing was obtained, but with strict conditions. These involved highly restrictive macroeconomic policies with cuts in public spending, including the country's health and education programmes, and the privatization of virtually all the publicly owned enterprises and farms. This led a stagnation of output and a decline in employment and wages in the early 1990s and, while reestablishing the basis for a functioning capitalist economy, undermined any chance that Lacayo had of succeeding Chamorro.

At the elections in 1996, the main right-wing parties fielded joint candidates in order to prevent a Sandinista victory, and this resulted in the election of Arnoldo Aleman, a right-wing populist who had successfully united various warring Liberal parties, and who was president from 1997 to 2002. Under Aleman's government, investment and growth finally resumed, and real wages began to recuperate. Aleman was virulently anti-Sandinista but also highly corrupt and, after leaving office, he was condemned to 20 years in prison. In one of the country's great ironies, the Sandinista's veteran leader Daniel Ortega then negotiated a pact with Aleman which enabled him to serve his sentence in the comfort of his luxury farm – so long as he ensured that his party's deputies in the National Congress voted with the Sandinistas when called upon to do so! The deal was possible because many of the countries' judges had been appointed under the previous Sandinista government and remained loyal to Ortega.

At the following elections in 2001, the Liberals again fielded a single presidential candidate and won. Their candidate, Enrique Bolaños, had been the leader of the strongly anti-Sandinista private business confederation, COSEP, in the 1980s, and served as Vice-President under Aleman. Bolaños was president from 2002 to 2007 and pursued strongly pro-business policies which succeeded in attracting foreign investment to the country. The economy continued to expand and, although social policies were limited, real wages continued to recover, if more slowly. Nevertheless, Bolaños' ability to govern was limited by the fact that Ortega could now call on Aleman to mobilize Deputies from his party to vote for Sandinista positions in the National Assembly.

The Liberal parties were unable to agree on a joint candidate at the following elections in 2006 and, on his fourth attempt since 1990, the Sandinista candidate Daniel Ortega was able to win the presidency with 38 per cent of the vote. Although the constitution prohibits consecutive terms, Ortega stood for the presidency again in 2011 and, since the Supreme Electoral Council (staffed by Sandinistas and obedient Liberals) did not object, he was able to win a further term to 2016 with 62 per cent of the vote. Since returning to office in 2007 Ortega has pursued strongly pro-business policies but he has also introduced a series of programmes which have succeeded in reducing the most serious poverty and led to a growth of support for him amongst the urban and rural poor.

5. Economic developments

Although Nicaragua is geographically the largest of the Central American countries, it has a population of only just over 6 million people. Since the mid-1990s, the economy has generally expanded at some 4 per cent or more a year, but incomes remain very low. In 2015, the country's GDP was $12.1 billion, or about $2,000 per capita, although income is distributed very unequally. There are a small number of rich families who accumulated their wealth mainly in large-scale agriculture, commerce and finance, and this group has recently expanded to include new members, including some associated with the Sandinista leadership. There is also a large, prosperous sector of the middle class, which has profited from the growth of commerce.

Nicaragua: Economic growth, 1990-2015 (%)

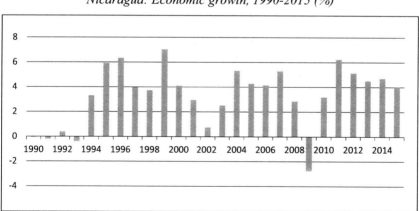

Source: Banco Central de Nicaragua, *Anuario Estadístico*, www.bcn.gob.ni

Nicaragua's economy is strongly dependent on exports of primary commodities and, like other Latin American countries, it has benefited from the boom in commodity prices which began in 2003 but which ended in 2012. Exports increased from $643 million in 2000 to reach $2,633 million in 2014. The main exports in 2014 were beef ($448 million, which includes large contracts with Venezuela), coffee ($394 million), gold ($385 million, recently revived due to significant foreign investment), sugar ($207 million) and dairy products ($196 million). Other exports include peanuts, beans, prawns and lobster. As the growth of exports has slowed, consumption expenditure – notably durable goods sold on credit – has accounted for a significant part of the growth. The economy has also been driven by strong investment, much of it by foreign firms which have been attracted by a combination of low wages and the relatively peaceful environment compared with some of the other countries in the region.[1] In particular, there has been a strong expansion of *maquila,* or free trade zones, where foreign companies are exempt from tax on re-exported products. Initiated in the early 1990s, by 2015 this involved 161 companies employing some 110,000, predominantly female, workers.

After the Ortega government took office in 2007, fees for public education and health services, which had been introduced under the previous governments, were abolished, although spending, particularly on education, remains low. In 2015, total public spending was equal to 31.5 per cent of GDP, and included a strong programme of public investment, notably on roads and other infrastructure. By contrast, central government income was equal to 27.6 per cent of GDP. The deficit after grants ran to 2.7 per cent of GDP. Taxes, however, are largely indirect, and there are many sectors that are exempt. A significant reform which would have extended the tax base, including to imported machinery and agricultural inputs, was inexplicably postponed in 2014.

Although Nicaragua's exports have increased strongly in recent years, imports have increased even more and the country has continually registered large current account deficits. The deficit has declined in recent years, aided by the provision of oil on very favourable terms by Venezuela, but in 2015 the deficit was still equal to 8.0 per cent of GDP. This is despite the country receiving large family remittances from Nicaraguans who have sought work abroad, notably in the United States, Costa Rica, and more recently Spain, which generated $1.2 billion in 2015 – almost half the value of the country's

---

[1] The Global Peace Index places Nicaragua after Costa Rica, Uruguay, Argentina and Panama as the safest countries in Latin America, considerably ahead of its northern neighbours Honduras, Guatemala and El Salvador (Institute for Economics and Peace 2015).

agricultural exports. The major source of external financing has been foreign direct investment, which was equal to some 6 per cent of GDP in 2015. The country has also benefited from relatively generous development assistance, although this has begun to decline, partly due to tensions between the government and some foreign donors. The government's external debt which stood at an extraordinary 700 per cent of GDP in the early 1990s has since been written down as a result of various bilateral and multilateral initiatives, and by 2015 was equal to 42.6 per cent of GDP, with foreign debt service amounting to only a little over 2 per cent of GDP.

6. Employment & wages

Nicaragua's population is increasing quite rapidly, and official figures show a steady rise in the economically active population, from 2.2 million in 2007 when the Ortega government took office to 3.2 million in 2014.[2] The largest sources of employment in 2011 (the last year for which figures were published) were agriculture (811,000), commerce (700,700), services (530,000), industry (326,300), construction (169,000), transport (104,000) and finance (95,000). The official rate of unemployment in 2011 was 5.9 per cent (180,200), and this increased in 2014 to 6.8 per cent (216,500), but these figures are sure to be underestimates as, in the absence of a proper job, people are forced to turn to some sort of work in agriculture or informal commerce to survive – or to work abroad.

The government has sought to promote enrolment in the country's social security system which provides preventative health care and a pension. The number of people insured has risen quite strongly, from 459,000 in 2007 to 710,000 in 2014, of whom 42 per cent were female.[3] But this still represents less than 20 per cent of the workforce. Although around half the workers employed in finance and in manufacturing industry have social insurance, the figure for construction is around 10 per cent and that for agriculture just over 5 per cent. There are, furthermore, reports in the press that some employers are attempting to shift workers back to uninsured, casual employment.

The government sets a minimum wage for 10 different branches of the economy, and this is revised once or twice a year following negotiations between the government, the employers and the unions, although in the event

---

[2] Banco Central de Nicaragua, *Anuario Estadistico 2014*.
[3] Institute Nicaragüense de Seguridad Social, *Anuario Estadístico 2014*, Table 1.1.

of disagreement (as occurred in 2015), a rate is imposed by the government. According to official figures, minimum wages have been raised significantly since Ortega returned to office in 2007, although they remain very low. A simple average of the different minimum wages increased from $88 a month in 1996, to $96 in 2006, and to $184 in 2014.[4] The lowest minimum wage, for agricultural workers, increased from $44 in 1996 to $57 in 2006 and to $112 in 2015; the highest minimum wages, for workers in construction and finance, increased from $98 in 1996 to $114 in 2006 and to $245 in 2015.

The average wage in each branch has also risen but, according to official figures, not as strongly as the minimum wage since the Ortega government took office in 2007. The average monthly wage for all workers increased from $169 in 1996 to $233 in 2006 and to $316 in 2015.[5] At the bottom of the scale, average wages for agricultural workers increased from $119 in 2006 to $154 in 2006 and $192 in 2015; the highest average pay was for workers in the mining sector, which increased from $227 in 1996, to $417 in 2006 and $598 in 2015, with workers employed in the provision of electricity and water closely behind, and those in transport and in finance averaging around $410 a month in 2015.

While average wages for all workers increased by 38 per cent in dollar terms between 1996 and 2006, and by 35 per cent between 2006 and 2015, minimum wages, which increased by a mere 10 per cent in dollar terms between 1996 and 2006, rose by 92 per cent under the two periods of the Ortega government. It should be noted that these figures are not adjusted for inflation and that not all workers actually receive the minimum wage, either because employers pay less, or due to short-time working. Nevertheless, the figures do appear to indicate a significant rise in wages for the very lowest paid.

The poorest sectors of Nicaraguan society have also benefited from anti-poverty programmes, notably in the countryside. According to figures published by the World Bank, the proportion of the population in Nicaragua living below the poverty line fell from 48.3 per cent in 2005 to 29.6 per cent in 2014.[6] However, this masks a significant difference between rural areas, where the count fell from 63.3 per cent to 50.1 per cent, and urban areas, where it fell from 30.9 per cent to 14.8 per cent. A recent independent study con-

---

[4] Banco Central de Nicaragua, *Anuario Estadístico*, Table III.8, converted at December exchange rates.

[5] Banco Central de Nicaragua, *Anuario Estadístico*, Table III.4, converted at December exchange rates.

[6] World Bank, *World Development Indicators*, 17 February 2016.

cluded that there had been a marked reduction in poverty, in particular acute rural poverty, between 2007 and 2011, but that the situation subsequently deteriorated again up to 2013, largely due to the weakening of primary commodity prices.[7] The study also noted that some 28.7 per cent of Nicaraguan households received remittances from abroad in 2013, and that this had been a significant factor in reducing poverty.

7. Towards elections

Since the Ortega government took office in 2007, the Nicaraguan economy has registered steady growth. However, there has been no radical programme to transform the economy, and the government has prioritised economic stability under the tutelage of the IMF, while seeking to attract private investment, in particular, from abroad. Government policies appear to have had an impact in reducing poverty but, while average wages have also risen, consumption spending by many households is dependent on receiving remittances from family members who have sought work abroad.

In the early 1990s, many members of the Sandinistas left the party in disagreement with the policies and centralised control exercised by Daniel Ortega and his allies. This included many feminists, who went on to establish an independent women's movement. Some of those that left the party were involved in the formation of a breakaway group, the Movement for Sandinista Renovation, but its support is small, and concentrated primarily in the urban middle class. The Sandinista leader, Daniel Ortega, himself was faced with a major scandal in 1998, when his step-daughter, Zoilamérica Narváez, alleged that from the age of eleven she had been repeatedly sexually abused by Ortega. Since Ortega was challenged about the truth of the allegations whenever he appeared in public, he subsequently left many public appearances to his partner, Rosario Murillo, who has denied the truth of her daughter's allegations. Since Ortega returned to the presidency, Murillo has conducted daily government press conference, and played a key role in coordinating policy between government Ministries. She has built up considerable support in the Sandinista's enthusiastic youth organisation, but she is less popular with many of the party's long-standing militants.

Nicaragua's main opposition parties are fragmented, and – in marked contrast to the 1980s – Ortega and the government enjoy excellent relations with

---

[7] FIDEG, *Dinámica de la pobreza en Nicaragua, 2009-2013*, 2014.

the country's main business confederation, COSEP. The leading families, as with the business sector as a whole, have boomed under the Ortega government, and show no sign of wishing to disrupt this highly profitable arrangement. The few open signs of discord have, in fact, emerged from key groups within the Sandinista's own base. One of the most controversial issues is that in 2013 a private Chinese investor was awarded a 100-year license to build an inter-oceanic canal through Nicaragua. The proposed canal, with an estimated cost of $50 billion, would be wider than the Panama Canal and divide Nicaragua in two. There are serious doubts about whether the canal itself will ever be built (the commercial infrastructure at the two mouths looks more likely), but it has provoked large demonstrations by peasant farmers due to lose their land. These involved traditional Sandinista supporters, but the riot police were deployed to break up the demonstrations and numerous demonstrators were injured or arrested. In another incident in 2015, traditionally pro-Sandinista miners at the Canadian-owned El Limon gold mine went on strike for higher pay. Again, riot police were deployed and numerous workers were arrested although – in a move of questionable legality – they were freed by command of Ortega himself for Christmas.

Nicaragua is due to hold elections before the end of 2016. It is widely expected that, health permitting, Daniel Ortega will stand again for the presidency, and there are suggestions that his wife, Rosario Morillo, might stand for the vice-presidency. The various Liberal and Conservative Liberal parties are in the process of selecting their candidates, but it looks unlikely that they will be able to agree on a joint campaign. At the most recent local elections in 2012, the Sandinistas secured the great majority of town halls, although there were allegations of widespread irregularities in some constituencies. Under Ortega, the Sandinistas have established strong popular support and early surveys indicate that they could obtain 65 per cent of the vote in the forthcoming presidential election.[8] But surveys also show that some 20 per cent were not decided, and tensions with some sections of the Sandinistas' traditional base could yet have an impact on the outcome.

---

[8] M & R Consultores, March 2015, http://www.myrconsultores.com/

Lebenslauf
Hansjörg Herr

1951	Geboren in Freiburg im Breisgau
1967-1969	Ausbildung zum Koch, u.a. im Hotel Berlin in Berlin
1970	Tätigkeit als Schiffskoch auf vier Handelsschiffen. Rettung nach Havarie als Schiffbrüchiger
1971-1973	Ausbildung zum staatlich geprüften Betriebswirt und Erwerb der mittleren Reife auf der Fachschule des Hotel- und Gaststättengewerbes Erwerb der Fachhochschulreife an der Porsche Oberschule Berlin
1973-1975	Studium der Betriebswirtschaftslehre an der Fachhochschule für Wirtschaft (heutige Hochschule für Wirtschaft und Recht Berlin)
1975-1981	Studium der Volkswirtschaftslehre und Wirtschaftspädagogik an der Freien Universität Berlin
1981-1986	Wissenschaftlicher Mitarbeiter am Institut für Wirtschaftspolitik der Freien Universität Berlin
1986	Promotion zum Dr. rer. pol. an der Freien Universität Berlin
1986-1993	Wissenschaftlicher Mitarbeiter/Projektleiter am Wissenschaftszentrum Berlin für Sozialforschung (WZB)
1991	Habilitation an der Freien Universität Berlin für das Fach Volkswirtschaftslehre
1994-2016	Professor für Supranationale Wirtschaftsintegration an der Hochschule für Wirtschaft und Recht Berlin

Curriculum Vitae
Hansjörg Herr

1951	Born in Freiburg im Breisgau
1967-1969	Apprenticeship as cook, one station being the Hotel Berlin in Berlin
1970	Work as ship's cook on four merchant ships. Saved after being shipwrecked
1971-1973	Apprenticeship as certified business economist and acquisition of advanced technical college entrance qualification at Porsche secondary school in Berlin
1973-1975	Studies of business administration at the Berlin School of Economics, later becoming the Berlin School of Economics and Law
1975-1981	Studies of Economics and Economic Pedagogy at the Free University Berlin
1981-1986	Junior Lecturer (Wissenschaftlicher Mitarbeiter) at the Institute of Economic Policy at Free University Berlin
1986	Promotion to Dr. rer. pol. at Free University Berlin
1986-1993	Academic researcher / project leader at the WZB Berlin Social Science Center
1991	Habilitation (venia legendi) in economics at Free University Berlin
1994-2016	Professor of Supranational Economic Integration at the Berlin School of Economics and Law

Publikationen von | Publications by
Hansjörg Herr

Monographien | Monographs

1. Geld, Kredit und ökonomische Dynamik in marktvermittelten Ökonomien – die Vision einer Geldwirtschaft, München (1986).

2. mit Spahn, H.-P.: Staatsverschuldung, Zahlungsbilanz und Wechselkurs. Außenwirtschaftliche Spielräume und Grenzen der Fiskalpolitik. Studien zur monetären Ökonomie, Bd. 5, Regensburg (1989).

3. mit Voy, K.: Währungskonkurrenz und Deregulierung der Weltwirtschaft. Entwicklung und Alternativen der Währungspolitik der Bundesrepublik und der Europäischen Gemeinschaften, Marburg (1989).

4. Geld, Währungswettbewerb und Währungssysteme. Theoretische und historische Analyse einer internationalen Geldwirtschaft, Frankfurt a.M., New York (1992) [japanische Übersetzung 1995].

5. mit Heine, M.: Volkswirtschaftslehre. Paradigmenorientierte Einführung in die Mikro- und Makroökonomie, München (1999).

6. mit Heine, M.: Volkswirtschaftslehre. Paradigmenorientierte Einführung in die Mikro- und Makroökonomie, 2., ergänzte Auflage, München (2000).

7. mit Heine, M.: Volkswirtschaftslehre. Paradigmenorientierte Einführung in die Mikro- und Makroökonomie, 3., grundlegend überarbeitete Auflage, München (2003).

8. mit Heine, M.: Die Europäische Zentralbank. Eine kritische Einführung in die Strategie und Politik der EZB, Marburg (2004) [2. Auflage 2006].

9. with Haiduk, K., Lintovskaya, T., Parchevskaya, S., Priewe, J., Tsiku, R.: The Belarusian Economy at a Crossroads, Moscow (2004).

10. with Priewe, J.: The Macroeconomics of Development and Poverty Reduction: Strategies beyond the Washington Consensus, Baden-Baden (2005) [das Buch erschien im Jahre 2006 in chinesischer Sprache im Publishing House der Southwestern University of Finance and Economics in Chengdu/ VR China].

11. mit Hübner, K.: Währung und Unsicherheit in der globalen Ökonomie. Eine geldwirtschaftliche Theorie der Globalisierung, Berlin (2005).

12. mit Heine, M. und Kaiser, C.: Wirtschaftspolitische Regime westlicher Industrienationen – theoretische Analyse und Fallstudien über Japan, Großbritannien, die USA und Deutschland, Baden-Baden (2006).

13. mit Heine, M.: Die Europäische Zentralbank. Eine kritische Einführung in die Strategie und Politik der EZB, Marburg, 3., grundlegend überarbeitete Auflage (2008).

14. mit Dullien, S. und Kellermann, C.: Der gute Kapitalismus – und was sich dafür nach der Krise ändern müsste, Bielefeld (2009).

15. mit Stachuletz, R.: Vietnam am Scheideweg. Analysen einer Ökonomie auf dem Drahtseil (= Perspektive), Berlin (2010).

16. with Dullien, S.: EU Financial Market Reform. Status and Prospects, Berlin, Bonn (2010).

17. mit Dullien, S.: Die EU Finanzmarktreform. Stand und Perspektiven im Frühjahr 2010. (= Internationale Politikanalyse). Berlin: Friedrich-Ebert-Stiftung (2010) [englische Übersetzung verfügbar].

18. with Kazandziska, M.: Macroeconomic Policy Regimes in Western Industrial Countries (= Routledge Frontiers of Political Economy), London (2011).

19. with Dullien, S. and Kellermann, C.: Decent Capitalism. A Blueprint for Reforming Our Economies. London: PlutoPress (2011) [also available in Chinese, Korean, Persian and Indonesian].

20. Europa vor einem verlorenen Jahrzehnt. Wege aus der Stagnation (= Perspektive), Berlin: Friedrich-Ebert-Stiftung (2012).

Herausgegebene Bücher | edited books

21. mit Heine, M., Westphal, A., Busch, U., Mondelaers, R. (Hg.): Die Zukunft der DDR-Wirtschaft, Reinbek (1990).

22. mit Westphal, A., Heine, M., Busch, U. (Hg.): Wirtschaftspolitische Konsequenzen der deutschen Vereinigung, Frankfurt a.M., New York (1991).

23. mit Westphal, A. (Hg.): Transformation in Mittel- und Osteuropa. Makroökonomische Konzepte und Fallstudien, Frankfurt a.M., New York (1993).

24. with Tober, S., Westphal, A. (eds.): Macroeconomic Problems of Transformation. Stabilization Policies and Economic Restructuring, Aldershot (1994).

25. mit Hübner, K. (Hg.): Der „lange Marsch" in die Marktwirtschaft. Entwicklungen und Erfahrungen in der VR China und Osteuropa, Berlin (1999).

26. mit Betz, K., Fritsche, U., Heine, M., Joebges, H., Roy, T., Schramm, J. (Hg.): Hajo Riese, Grundlegungen eines monetären Keynesianismus – ausgewählte Schriften 1964-1999, Band 1: Das Projekt eines monetären Keynesianismus, Band 2: Angewandte Theorie der Geldwirtschaft, Marburg (2001).

27. mit Sommer, A. und He Zerong: Nachholende Entwicklung in China. Geldpolitik und Restrukturierung, Berlin (2002) [Eine chinesische Übersetzung des Bandes erschien im Jahre 2003 beim Publishing House der Southwestern University of Finance and Economics in Chengdu, VR China].

28. with Priewe, J.: Current Issues of China's Economic Policies and Related International Experiences – The Wuhan Conference 2002. Part I: The Wuhan Conference 2002, Working Papers of the Business Institute Berlin at the Berlin School of Economics (FHW-Berlin), No. 16/I, Berlin (2003).

29. with Priewe, J.: Current Issues of China's Economic Policies and Related International Experiences – The Wuhan Conference 2002. Part II: Further monetary issues, Working Papers of the Business Institute Berlin at the Berlin School of Economics (FHW-Berlin), No. 16/II, Berlin (2003).

30. with Truger, A., Niechoj, T., Thomasberger, C., van Treek, T. (eds.): From Crisis to Growth? The challenge of debt and imbalances, Schriftenreihe des Forschungsnetzwerk Makroökonomie und Makropolitik (FMM), Marburg (2012).

31. with Gallas, A., Hoffer, F., Scherrer, C. (eds.): Combating Inequality. The Global North and South, London (2016).

Aufsätze in Büchern und Zeitschriften | Papers in books and journals

1999-2007 Mitglied der Redaktion der Zeitschrift Prokla, Zeitschrift für kritische Sozialwissenschaft.

32. Kapitalistische Weltwirtschaft und alternative Währungspolitik. In: Ernst-Pörksen, M. (Hg.), Alternativen der Ökonomie. Ökonomie der Alternativen, Argument-Sonderband 104, Berlin (1984).

33. Geld – Störfaktor oder Systemmerkmal. In: Prokla, Zeitschrift für Kritische Sozialwissenschaft, Heft 63, 16(2), 108-132 (1986).

34. Zentralbank und Spielräume alternativer Geldpolitik. In: Projektgruppe Grüner Morgentau (Hg.), Perspektiven ökologischer Wirtschaftspolitik: Ansätze zur Kultivierung von ökonomischem Neuland, Frankfurt a.M., 462ff. (1986).

35. Ansätze monetärer Währungstheorie – eine keynesianische Kritik der orthodoxen Theorie. In: Konjunkturpolitik, 33(1), 1-23 (1987).

36. Einige kritische Thesen zu Silvio Gesells Freiwirtschaftslehre aus Keynes'scher Sicht. In: Zeitschrift für Sozialökonomie, 73. Folge, 24. Jg., 10-14 (1987).

37. Die Sozialdemokraten und das Schuldenmachen. In: Neue Gesellschaft, Frankfurter Hefte, 34(12), 1128-1133 (1987).

38. Der Goldstandard und die währungstheoretische Diskussion der Klassik. In: Konjunkturpolitik, 34(1), 36-55 (1988).

39. Wege zur Theorie einer monetären Produktionswirtschaft – der keynesianische Fundamentalismus. In: Glombowski, J., Kalmbach, P. (Hg.), Ökonomie und Gesellschaft 6, Die Aktualität keynesianischer Analysen, Frankfurt a.M., New York, 66-98 (1988).

40. mit Westphal, A.: Europäisches Währungssystem: DM-Club oder demokratisches Westeuropa? In: WSI Mitteilungen, 41(7), 427-436 (1988).

41. On Post-Keynesian Crisis Theory: The Meaning of Financial Instability. In: Väth, W. (ed.), Political Regulation in the "Great Crisis", Berlin (1989).

42. Weltgeld und die Instabilitäten der 70er und 80er Jahre. In: Riese, H., Spahn, H.-P. (Hg.), Internationale Geldwirtschaft. Studien zur monetären Ökonomie, Bd. 2, Regensburg (1989).

43. mit Westphal, A.: Zum Verhältnis realwirtschaftlicher und monetärer Integration Westeuropas. In: Prokla, Zeitschrift für Kritische Sozialwissenschaft, Heft 75, 19(2), 72-96 (1989).

44. Die Instabilität der Weltwirtschaft in den 70er und 80er Jahren. Oder: Kann sich die Welt die Bundesrepublik Deutschland leisten? In: Riese, H., Spahn, H.-P. (Hg.), Geldpolitik und ökonomische Entwicklung – Ein Symposion, Studien zur monetären Ökonomie, Bd. 4, Regensburg, 95-109 (1990).

45. Der bundesdeutsche und japanische Merkantilismus. In: Spahn, H.-P. (Hg.), Wirtschaftspolitische Strategien – Probleme ökonomischer Stabilität und Entwicklung in Industrieländern und der Europäischen Gemeinschaft, Regensburg, 113ff. (1990).

46. Makroökonomische Chancen und Risiken der deutschen Vereinigung. In: Wirtschaftsdienst, 70(11), 569-575 (1990).

47. mit Westphal, A.: Außenwirtschaftliche Strategien der kleinen Länder Osteuropas und der europäische Integrationsprozeß. In: WSI Mitteilungen, 43(7), 442-451 (1990).

48. mit Westphal, A.: Konsequenzen ökonomischer Integration. Entwicklungsperspektiven der DDR als Region und als eigenständiger Staat. In: Heine, M., Herr, H. u.a. (Hg.), Die Zukunft der DDR-Wirtschaft, Reinbek, 151-170 (1990).

49. External Constraints on Fiscal Policy: An International Comparison. In: Matzner, E., Streeck, W. (eds.), Beyond Keynesianism. The Socio-Economics of Production and Full Employment, Aldershot, 161-182 (1991).

50. Zahlungsbilanz, Leitwährungsfunktion und die Zukunft des Dollars. In: Kredit und Kapital, 24(4), 443-467 (1991).

51. mit Westphal, A.: Economic Coherence and the Transformation of Planned Economies into Monetary Economies. In: Journal of Post Keynesian Economics, 13(3), 307-327 (1991).

52. mit Westphal, A.: Die Inkohärenzen der Planwirtschaft und der Transformationsprozeß zur Geldwirtschaft. In: Backhaus, J. (Hg.), Systemwandel und Wirtschaftsreform in östlichen Wirtschaften, Marburg, 139-168 (1991).

53. mit Westphal, A.: Polens Weg in die Geldwirtschaft. Wirkungen des Balcerowicz-Plans und Konfliktfelder in der Transformationsdebatte. In: Konjunkturpolitik, Vol. 37, 1991.

54. mit Westphal, A.: Probleme der monetären Integration Europas. Die Europäischen Währungsunion und die deutsche Vereinigung. In: Westphal, A., Herr, H., Heine, M., Busch, U. (Hg.), Wirtschaftspolitische Konsequenzen der deutschen Vereinigung, Frankfurt a.M., New York, 75-114 (1991).

55. mit Tober, S., Westphal, A.: A Strategy for Economic Transformation and Development in Eastern Europe. In: De Pecunia, 3(3), 95,135 (1991).

56. Die neuen Bundesländer nach dem Vereinigungsschock. Beschäftigungsobservatorium Ostdeutschland, Nr. 1, Kommission der Europäischen Gemeinschaften, Generaldirektion Beschäftigung, Arbeitsbeziehungen und Soziale Angelegenheiten (1992).

57. Der Transformationsprozeß in Polen, Ungarn und der CSFR. Beschäftigungsobservatorium Ostdeutschland, Nr. 3, Kommission der Europäischen Gemeinschaften, Generaldirektion Beschäftigung, Arbeitsbeziehungen und Soziale Angelegenheiten (1992).

58. Ökonomische Probleme einer europäischen Währung. In: Beirat für wirtschafts-, gesellschafts- und umweltpolitische Alternativen (Hg.), Vom „obsoleten" zum „adäquaten" marktwirtschaftlichen Denken, Marburg, 253ff. (1992).

59. mit Heine, M.: Der esoterische und exoterische Charakter der Marxschen Geldtheorie – eine Kritik. In: Schikora, A., Fiedler, A., Hein, E. (Hg.), Politische Ökonomie im Wandel. Festschrift für Klaus Kisker, Marburg, 195-209 (1992).

60. mit Heine, M.: Makroökonomische Koordinationsprobleme nach der deutschen Vereinigung. In: Burchardt, M., Falck, M., Heine, M., Herr, H., Maier, F., Preuss, S., Stadermann, H.-J., Politische Ökonomie des Teilens: wirtschaftliche und soziale Probleme und Konzepte in der deutsch-deutschen Vereinigung (= fhw-forschung 22), Berlin, 9-22 (1993).

61. Makroökonomische Budgetbeschränkung und Kreditmarkt. In: Steiger, O., Stadermann, H.-J. (Hg.), Der Stand und die nächste Zukunft der Geldforschung. Festschrift für Hajo Riese zum 60. Geburtstag, Berlin, 257-268 (1993).

62. Stabilisierung und Akkumulation in Transformationsökonomien. In: Herr, H., Westphal, A. (Hg.), Transformation in Mittel- und Osteuropa. Makroökonomische Konzepte und Fallstudien, Frankfurt a.M., New York, 19-47 (1993).

63. Budgetkrise und Entwicklungsperspektiven der Transformationsländer. In: Konjunkturpolitik, 40(1), 43-66 (1994).

64. mit Heine, M.: Binnen- und außenwirtschaftliche Koordinationsprobleme nach der deutschen Vereinigung. In: WSI Mitteilungen, 47(1), 30-36 (1994).

65. mit Heine, M.: Theoretische und wirtschaftspolitische Aspekte einer Regionalpolitik für die neuen Bundesländer. In: WSI Mitteilungen, 47(8), 488-498 (1994).

66. with Tober, S., Westphal, A.: Output Collaps and Economic Recovery in Central and Eastern Europe. In: Herr, H., Tober, S., Westphal, A. (eds.), Macroeconomic Problems of Transformation. Stabilization Policies and Economic Restructuring, Aldershot, 1-44 (1994).

67. Two Views on How a Deformed Monetary Economy Can Be Developed. In: Perczynsky, M., Kregel, J., Matzner, E. (eds.), After the Market Shock. Central and East-European Economies in Transition, Aldershot, 161-174 (1994) [published also in: Zhongliang Shi, Jiajun Wu (eds.), China's Industrial Development and Enterprise Reform, Economic Management Publishing House, Jiangxi University of Finanance and Economics, Nanchang, PR China, 2001].

68. with Tober, S., Westphal, A.: A Strategy for Economic Transformation and Development. In: Perczynski, M., Kregel, J., Matzner, E. (eds.), After the Market Shock. Central and Eastern Economies in Transition, Aldershot, 29-60 (1994).

69. Marktkonstellationen, Wirtschaftspolitik und Entwicklung – das Beispiel der Transformationsökonomien. In: Betz, K., Riese, H. (Hg.), Wirtschaftspolitik in einer Geldwirtschaft, Marburg, 143-174 (1995).

70. Die europäische Währungsunion zwischen politischer Wünschbarkeit und ökonomischen Zwängen. In: Thomasberger, C. (Hg.), Europäische Geldpolitik zwischen Marktzwängen und neuen institutionellen Regelungen. Zur politischen Ökonomie der europäischen Währungsintegration, Marburg, 199ff. (1995).

71. mit Priewe, J.: Entwicklungsstrategien für Transformationsökonomien am Beispiel der Republik Kirgistan – ein Diskussionsbeitrag. In: Osteuropa-Wirtschaft, 40(1), 51-71 (1995) [der Beitrag erschien 1995 auch in russischer Sprache in der Vierteljahreszeitschrift der Universität St. Petersburg].

72. Eine Außenwirtschaftsstrategie für Usbekistan. In: Dieter, H. (Hg.), Regionale Integration in Zentralasien, Marburg, 305-329 (1995) [der Sammelband erschien im gleichen Jahr auch in russischer Sprache].

73. Währungskooperation in Zentralasien – Vorteile, Modelle und Voraussetzungen. In: Dieter, H. (Hg.), Regionale Integration in Zentralasien, Marburg, 147ff. (1995) [der Sammelband erschien im gleichen Jahr auch in russischer Sprache].

74. Der Merkantilismus der Bundesrepublik Deutschland und Szenarien zukünftiger Entwicklung. In: Hengsbach, F., Emunds, B. (Hg.), Verfügungsrechte auf Finanzmärkte, Frankfurter Arbeitspapiere zur gesellschaftsethischen und sozialwissenschaftlichen Forschung 13, Oswald von Nell-Breuning-Institut für Wirtschafts- und Gesellschaftsethik, Frankfurt a.M., 20-31 (1995).

75. Außenwirtschaftliche Entwicklungsoptionen der Visegrád-Länder und der Europäischen Union. In: Miegel, M. (Hg.), Die Wirtschaftsbeziehungen der Visegrád-Länder mit den Ländern der Europäischen Union (Transformation. Leipziger Beiträge zu Wirtschaft und Gesellschaft; Schriftenreihe des Zentrums für Internationale Wirtschaftsbeziehungen der Universität Leipzig, Nr. 2), Leipzig, 102-120 (1995) [erschien auch in Roggemann, H., Sundhaussen, H. (Hg.), Ost- und Südosteuropa zwischen Tradition und Aufbruch, Berlin, 265-280 (1996)].

76. Globalisierung der Ökonomie: Entkopplung der Geldsphäre und Ende nationaler Autonomie? In: Eicker-Wolf, K. et al. (Hg.), Wirtschaftspolitik im theoretischen Vakuum? Zur Pathologie der politischen Ökonomie, Marburg, 251-272 (1996).

77. mit Heine, M.: Money Makes the World Go Round – Über die Verselbständigung der Geldsphäre und andere Mißverständnisse. In: Prokla, Zeitschrift für Kritische Sozialwissenschaft, Heft 103, 26(2), 197-225 (1996).

78. Probleme der Europäischen Währungsunion. In: SOWI, Sozialwissenschaftliche Information, 26(2), 108-119 (1997).

79. The International Monetary System and Domestic Economic Policy. In: Forsyth, D.J., Notermans, T. (eds.), Regime Changes. Macroeconomic Policy and Financial Regulation in Europe from the 1930s to the 1990s, Providence (RI), 124-168 (1997).

80. Keynesianische Wirtschaftspolitik in Transformationsländern. In: Stratmann, G., Kunze, C. (Hg.), Der Übergang zur Marktwirtschaft in Mittel- und Osteuropa als variables Ziel: Interessen, Strategien, Probleme (Transformation. Leipziger Beiträge zu Wirtschaft und Gesellschaft; Schriftenreihe des Zentrums für Internationale Wirtschaftsbeziehungen der Universität Leipzig, Nr. 5), Leipzig, 49-70 (1997).

81. Von der Stabilisierung zu wirtschaftlichem Wachstum: Herausforderungen für die Wirtschaftspolitik in Zentralasien, in: Dieter, H., Primbetow, S. (Hg.), Regionale Integration in Mittelasien. Chance und Risiko der ökonomischen Zusammenarbeit (1997) [der Band liegt nur in russischer Sprache vor].

82. Probleme der Stabilisierungspolitik in GUS-Ländern, dargestellt am Beispiel Kirgistan. In: Osteuropa-Wirtschaft, 42(4), 368-387 (1997).

83. mit Heine, M.: Keynesianische Wirtschaftspolitik – Mißverständnisse und Ansatzpunkte. In: Heise, A. (Hg.), Renaissance der Makrokönomik, Marburg (1998).

Aufsätze in Büchern und Zeitschriften | Papers in books and journals 449

84. mit Pan Deping: Über einige Probleme bei der Reform von Staatsbetrieben. In: Contemporary Finance and Economics, December, Nanchang, VR China [in chinesischer Sprache] (1998).

85. mit Tober, S.: Analyse der Differenzen volkswirtschaftlicher Transformationsprozesse. In: Economist, 1/1999, Southwestern University of Finance and Economics 1996-1998, Chengdu, VR China, 108-116 (1999) [in chinesischer Sprache; erneut abgedruckt in chinesischer Sprache in: Finance and Insurance, Heft 2, 2000].

86. mit Tober, S.: Unterschiedliche Marktkonstellationen. Was unterscheidet die Entwicklung in der VR China von den Ländern der ehemaligen Sowjetunion und den Visegrádstaaten? In: Herr, H., Hübner, K. (Hg.), Der „lange Marsch" in die Marktwirtschaft. Entwicklungen und Erfahrungen in der VR China und Osteuropa, Berlin, 77-118 (1999).

87. mit Hübner, K.: Einleitung: Wachstumsregime und ökonomische Transformation. Makroökonomische Entwicklungen und mikroökonomische Erfahrungen in vergleichender Perspektive. In: Herr, H., Hübner, K. (Hg.), Der „lange Marsch" in die Marktwirtschaft. Entwicklungen und Erfahrungen in der VR China und Osteuropa, Berlin (1999).

88. mit Heine, M.: Verdrängte Risiken der Euro-Einführung. In: WSI Mitteilungen, 52(8), 539-547 (1999) [erneut publiziert in polnischer und deutscher Sprache in: Wykłady Otwarte, Wyższej Szoły Bankowej w Poznaniu, 8/2000].

89. mit Heine, M.: Die beschäftigungspolitischen Konsequenzen von „Rot-Grün". In: Prokla, Zeitschrift für Kritische Sozialwissenschaft, Heft 116, 29(3), 377-394 (1999).

90. Finanzströme und Verschuldung. In: Hauchler, I., Messner, D., Nuscheler, F. (Hg.), Globale Trends 2000, Frankfurt a.M., 219-243 (1999).

91. with Priewe, J.: High Growth in China – Transition without a Transition Crisis? In: Intereconomics, 34(6), 303-316 (1999) [erneut in chinesischer Sprache publiziert in: Zhongnan Caijing Daxue Xuebao, Journal of Zhongnan University of Economics and Law, No. 1/2000, Wuhan, VR China und in Contemporary Finance and Economics, Jiangxi University of Finance and Economics, No. 5, 2001, Jiangxi, VR China].

92. Die Rolle des Eigentums im Transformationsprozeß von der Plan- zur Geldwirtschaft. In: Betz, K., Roy, T. (Hg.), Privateigentum und Geld. Kontroversen um den Ansatz von Heinsohn und Steiger, Marburg, 177-199 (1999).

93. Produktivität, Löhne und Beschäftigung. In: Hoß, D., Schrick, G. (Hg.), Beschäftigung und Produktivität oder: Die hohe Kunst des Bereicherns, Münster, 39-44 (2000).

94. Internationale Finanzströme und Entwicklung. In: Hengsbach, F., Emunds, B. (Hg.), Finanzströme in Entwicklungsländer – in welcher Form zu wessen Vorteil?, Frankfurter Arbeitspapiere zur gesellschaftsethischen und sozialwissenschaftlichen Forschung 24, Oswald von Nell-Breuning Institut für Wirtschafts- und Gesellschaftsethik, Frankfurt a.M., 13-23 (2000).

95. Das chinesische Akkumulationsmodell und die Hilflosigkeit der traditionellen Entwicklungstheorien. In: Prokla, Zeitschrift für Kritische Sozialwissenschaft, Heft 119, 30(2), 181-209 (2000).

96. Transformation und deformierte Finanzmärkte – Die VR China im Vergleich mit mittel- und osteuropäischen Transformationsländern. In: Osteuropa-Wirtschaft, 45(2), 140-164 (2000) [eine modifizierte Fassung in chinesischer Sprache erschien in: Contemporary Finance and Economics, 1999, Jiangxi University of Finance and Economics].

97. Die Finanzkrise in Russland im Gefolge der Asienkrise. In: APuZ – Aus Politik und Zeitgeschichte, 50(37/38), 29-38 (2000).

98. Finanzkrisen und die Architektur des internationalen Währungs- und Finanzsystems. In: Boris, D., Diaz, A.B., Eicker-Wolf, K., Käpernick, R., Limbers, J. (Hg.), Finanzkrisen im Übergang zum 21. Jahrhundert. Probleme der Peripherie oder globale Gefahr, Marburg, 319-361 (2000).

99. Keynes und seine Interpreten. In: Prokla, Zeitschrift für Kritische Sozialwissenschaft, Heft 123, 30(2), 203-225 (2001).

100. mit Heine, M.: Geld, Finanzierung und Einkommensbildung: Eckpunkte einer monetären Theorie der Produktion. In: Reich, U.P., Stahmer, C.,Voy, K. (Hg.), Kategorien der Volkswirtschaftlichen Gesamtrechnungen, Band 3: Geld und Physis, Marburg, 99-128 (2001).

101. Weltwährungssysteme im Rückblick – Lehren für die Zukunft. In: Heise, A. (Hg.), Neue Weltwährungsarchitektur, Marburg, 161-200 (2001).

102. mit Heine, M.: Das Eurosystem: Eine paradigmenorientierte Darstellung und kritische Würdigung der europäischen Geldpolitik (Auftragsstudie der GUE/NGL-Fraktion des Europäischen Parlaments), Rosa-Luxemburg-Stiftung, Manuskripte, Berlin, Februar (2001).

103. Theorien und Erfahrungen ökonomischer Transformation von Planwirtschaften in Geldwirtschaften. In: Hopfmann, A., Wolf, M. (Hg.), Transformationstheorie – Stand, Defizite, Perspektiven, Münster u.a. (2001).

104. Finanzströme und Verschuldung. In: Hauchler, I., Messner, D., Nuscheler, F. (Hg.), Globale Trends 2002, Frankfurt a.M., 267-287 (2001).

105. mit Evans, T. und Heine, M.: Weiche Kurse – Harter Fall? Die außenwirtschaftlichen Perspektiven der US-Ökonomie. In: Heise, A. (Hg.), USA – Modellfall der New Economy?, Marburg, 41-68 (2001).

106. Das Kaninchen vor der Schlange. Europäische Wirtschaftspolitik nach dem Anschlag vom 11. September. In: Prokla, Zeitschrift für Kritische Sozialwissenschaft, Heft 125, 31(4), 637-648 (2001).

107. Das Finanzsystem in der VR China – Funktionsweise und Reformdruck. In: Herr, H., Sommer, A., He Zerong (Hg.), Nachholende Entwicklung in China. Geldpolitik und Restrukturierung, Berlin, 21-51 (2002).

108. Tastendes Suchen. Chinas erfolgreicher Reformprozess. In: Internationale Politik und Gesellschaft, 3/2002, 26-48 (2002).

109. mit Heine, M.: Geldpolitik in Europa vor dem Hintergrund der Euro-Schwäche. In: WSI Mitteilungen, 55(5), 267-272 (2002).

110. mit Heine, M.: Zwickmühlen der europäischen Geldpolitik: Muddling Through mit John Maynard Friedman? In: Heise, A. (Hg.), Neues Geld – alte Geldpolitik? Die EZB im makroökonomischen Interaktionsraum, Marburg, 91-123 (2002).

111. Der Internationale Währungsfonds als internationaler Lender of Last Resort? In: Friedhelm Hengsbach, F., Behnen, J., Emunds, B (Hg.), Der IWF – Entwicklungshelfer oder Löschzugführer?, Frankfurter Arbeitspapiere zur gesellschaftsethischen und sozialwissenschaftlichen Forschung 36, Oswald von Nell-Breuning Institut für Wirtschafts- und Gesellschaftsthik, Frankfurt a.M., 88-103 (2002).

112. ECB Monetary Policy during the "Weak Euro" Period of 1999/2001. Theoretical Approach and Reality. In: Intereconomics, 37(6), 321-327 (2002).

113. Wages, Employment and Prices. In: Paying attention to wages. Labour Education 2002/3, No. 128, International Labour Office Geneva, 74-79 (2002).

114. Arbeitsmarktreformen und Beschäftigung. Über die ökonomietheoretischen Grundlagen der Vorschläge der Harz-Kommission. In: Prokla, Zeitschrift für Kritische Sozialwissenschaft, Heft 129, 32(4), 515-536 (2002).

115. The Monetary Policy of the European Central Bank during the "Weak Euro" Period of a 1999/2001 – Theoretical Approach and Reality. In: Herr, H., Priewe, J. (eds.), Current Issues of China's Economic Policies and Related International Experiences – The Wuhan Conference 2002. Part I: The Wuhan Conference 2002, Working Papers of the Business Institute Berlin at the Berlin School of Economics (FHW-Berlin), No. 16/I, Berlin, 38-48 (2003).

116. with Priewe, J.: Why China Should Not Liberalise the Capital Account. In: Herr, H., Priewe, J. (eds.), Current Issues of China's Economic Policies and Related International Experiences – The Wuhan Conference 2002. Part II: Further monetary issues, Working Papers of the Business Institute Berlin at the Berlin School of Economics (FHW-Berlin), No. 16/II, Berlin, 106-110 (2003) [chinesische Übersetzung in: Journal of ABC Wuhan Training College, Nr. 3, 2003, Serial No. 99].

117. Weltmarkt und Unterentwicklung. In: Mahnkopf, B. (Hg.), Management der Globalisierung. Akteure, Strukturen und Perspektiven, Berlin, 55-81 (2003).

118. mit Heine, M.: Der Neu-Keynesianismus als neues makroökonomisches Konsensmodell: Eine kritische Würdigung. In: Hein, E., Heise, A., Truger, A. (Hg.), Neu-Keynesianismus. Der neue wirtschaftspolitische Mainstream?, Marburg, 21-53 (2003).

119. Deregulierung, Globalisierung und Deflation. In: Prokla, Zeitschrift für Kritische Sozialwissenschaft, Heft 134, 34(1), 15-40 (2004).

120. Der Arbeitsmarkt in Deutschland im Jahre 2003 – Lage, theoretische Debatte und Reformvorstellungen. In: Zwengel, R. (Hg.), Gesellschaftliche Perspektiven. Arbeitsmarkt, Ökologie und Reformpolitik, EU-Erweiterung. Jahrbuch der Hessischen Gesellschaft für Demokratie und Ökologie, 29-54 (2004).

121. with Priewe, J.: Macroeconomic Aspects of Pro-Poor Growth. In: Krakowski, M. (ed.), Attacking Poverty: What Makes Growth Pro-Poor?, Baden-Baden, 61-88 (2004).

122. mit Fritsche, U., Heine, M., Horn, G., Kaiser, C.: Makroökonomische Regime und ökonomische Entwicklung: das Beispiel der USA. In: Hein, E., Niechoj, T., Schulten, T., Truger, A. (Hg.), Europas Wirtschaft gestalten. Makroökonomische Koordinierung und die Rolle der Gewerkschaften, Hamburg, 51-79 (2004).

123. China: Mit regulierter Marktwirtschaft auf Erfolgskurs. In: Orientierungen zur Wirtschafts- und Gesellschaftspolitik 101 (September), Ludwig-Erhard-Stiftung Bonn, 57-61 (2004).

124. with Fritsche, U., Heine, M., Horn, G., Kaiser, C.: Macroeconomic Regime and Development: The Case of the USA. In: Hein, E., Niechoj, T., Schulten, T., Truger, A. (eds.), Macroeconomic Policy Coordination in Europe and the Role of Trade Unions, Brussels, 69-110 (2005).

125. Deregulation, Currency Competition and Deflation in the Global Economy. In: Dauderstädt, M. (ed.), Towards a Prosperous Wider Europe. Macroeconomic Policies for a Growing Neighbourhood, Bonn, 59-69 (2005).

126. with Priewe, J.: Beyond the "Washington Consensus". Macroeconomics Policies for Development. In: Internationale Politik und Gesellschaft, 2/2005, 72-97 (2005).

127. mit Stachuletz, R.: Marktendogene Faktoren der Entstehung von Problemkrediten und Stabilisierungsstrategien. In: Clemens, J., Stachuletz, R. (Hg.), Workout. Management und Handel von Problemkrediten, Frankfurt a.M., 41-95 (2005).

128. mit Heine, M. und Kaiser, C.: Überforderte Lohnpolitik – Löhne im Spannungsfeld von Verteilung, Preisen und Beschäftigung. In: Hein, E., Heise, A., Truger, A. (Hg.), Löhne, Beschäftigung, Verteilung und Wachstum, Marburg, 93-118 (2005).

129. mit Heine, M.: Die Europäische Währungsunion im Treibsand. In: Prokla, Zeitschrift für Kritische Sozialwissenschaft, Heft 144, 36(3), 361-379 (2006).

130. with Priewe, J.: The Washington Consensus and (Non-)Development. In: Wray, L.R., Forstater, M. (eds.), Money, Financial Instability and Stabilization Policy, Cheltenham, UK, Northampton MA, USA, 171-191 (2006).

131. Das internationale Finanzsystem im Zeitalter der Globalisierung. Online Akademie der Friedrich-Ebert Stiftung (2006).

132. Geld und Währungen in der Weltwirtschaft. In: Steffens, G. (Hg.), Politische und ökonomische Bildung in Zeiten der Globalisierung, Münster, 35-53 (2007).

133. mit Evans, T., Heise, A., Kromphardt, J., Priewe, J., Thomasberger, C.: Tarifpolitische Chancen nutzen – Rückkehr zur produktivitätsorientierten Lohnpolitik geboten. In: WSI Mitteilungen, 60(3), 158-160 (2007).

134. with Heine, M. and Evans, T.: Elements of a Monetary Theory of Production. In: Hein, E., Truger, A. (eds.), Money, Distribution and Economic Policy. Alternatives to Orthodox Macroeconomics, Cheltenham, 47-65 (2007).

135. Die Rechnung zahlen die Armen – Internationale Finanzmärkte und Entwicklung. In: eins Entwicklungspolitik, 8/9, 36-39 (2007).

136. with Kazandziska, M.: Wages and Regional Coherence in the European Monetary Union. In: Hein, E., Priewe, J., Truger, A. (eds.), European Integration in Crisis, Marburg, 131-162 (2007) [erschien ebenfalls in: Lim, W. (ed.), Diversity and Dynamics of Globalisation: Socio-Economic Models in Global Capitalism, Seoul, 2007].

137. Ungelöste Probleme des Euro. In: Wagenknecht, S. (Hg.), Armut und Reichtum heute. Eine Gegenwartsanalyse, Berlin, 125ff. (2007).

138. mit Stachuletz, R.: „New Fashion in Finance" und Finanzmarktstabilität. In: WSI Mitteilungen, 60(12), 650-656 (2007).

139. Capital Controls and Economic Development in China. In: Arestis, P., de Paula, L.F. (eds.), Financial Liberalisation and Economic Performance in Emerging Countries, Basingstoke, New York, 142-172 (2008).

140. Das chinesische Wechselkurssystem. In: APuZ – Aus Politik und Zeitgeschichte, 58(7), 27-32 (2008).

141. mit Stachuletz, R.: Deregulierung, Finanzmarktdesaster und Reformoptionen: Die Hoffnung stirbt zuletzt. In: Internationale Politik und Gesellschaft, 3/2008, 11-27 (2008).

142. El proceso de crédito-inversión en China. In: Economía Informa, 355, 41-59 (2008).

143. Finanical Systems in Developing Countries and Economic Development. In: Hein, E., Niechoj, T., Spahn, P., Truger, A. (eds.), Finance-led Capitalism? Macroeconomic Effects of Changes in the Financial Sector, Marburg, 123-150 (2008).

144. Von der Finanzkrise zu Depression und Deflation. In: WSI Mitteilungen, Vol. 61(11+12), 638-640 (2008).

145. Global Imbalances and the Chinese Balance of Payments. In: Intervention. European Journal of Economics and Economic Policy, 6(1), 44-53 (2009).

146. Vom regulierten Kapitalismus zur Instabilität. In: WSI Mitteilungen, 62(12), 635-642 (2009).

147. The Labour Market in a Keynesian Economic Regime: Theoretical Debate and Empirical Findings. In: Cambridge Journal of Economics, 33(5), 949-965 (2009).

148. Fehlende Instrumente der Geldpolitik – die Zentralbank als Getriebene instabiler Finanzmärkte. In: Wirtschaftsdienst: Zeitschrift für Wirtschaftspolitik, 90(8), 511-515 (2010).

149. Credit expansion and development – A Schumpeterian and Keynesian view of the Chinese miracle. In: European Journal of Economics and Economic Policies: Intervention, 7(1), 71-89 (2010).

150. mit Stachuletz, R.: Die Immobilien-Bubble – Makro- und mikroökonomische Entstehungsmuster nachhaltiger Instabilitäten und Wege aus der Krise. In: Kühnberger, M., Wilke, H. (Hg.), Immobilienbewertung. Methoden und Probleme in Rechnungswesen, Besteuerung und Finanzwirtschaft, Stuttgart, 365-394 (2010).

151. with Kazandziska, M.: The Labour market and deflation in Japan. In: International Journal of Labour Research – Financial crisis, deflation and trade union responses: What are the lessons?, 28(1), 79-98 (2010).

152. mit Rogall, H.: Von der Traditionellen zur Nachhaltigen Ökonomie. In: Rogall, H., Binswanger, H., Ekardt, F., Grothe, A., Hasenclever, W., Hauchler, I., Jänicke, M., Kollmann, K., Michaelis, N., Nutzinger, H., Scherhorn, G. (Hg.), Jahrbuch Nachhaltige Ökonomie 2011/12. ...im Brennpunkt: „Wachstum", Marburg, 81-108 (2010).

153. Perspectives on High Growth and Rising Inequality. In: Scherrer, C. (Hg.), Chinas Labour Question, München, 7-27 (2011).

154. New Approaches to Monetary Theory. Interdisciplinary Perspectives, Expectations, Physics and Financial Markets. Paradigmatic Alternatives in Economic Thinking. In: Ganssmann, H. (Hg.), New Approaches to Monetary Theory. Interdisciplinary Perspectives, London, 212-236 (2011).

155. Making an unstable financial system work: Reform options. In: International Journal of Labour Research – Crisis: Causes, prospects and alternatives, 3(1), 133-155 (2011).

156. mit Priewe, J.: Macroeconomic Regimes for Growth and Stagnation in Developing Countries. In: Heise, A. (Hg.), Market Constellation Research. A Modern Governance Approach to Macroeconomic Policy, Frankfurt a.M., 63-89 (2011).

157. International Monetary and Financial Architecture. In: Hein, E., Stockhammer, E. (Hg.), A Modern Guide to Keynesian Macroeconomics and Economic Policies, Cheltenham, 267-293 (2011).

158. Das Finanzsystem als Rückgrat der chinesischen Entwicklungsdynamik. In: Journal für Entwicklungspolitik, 27(2), 47-66 (2011).

159. Cómo lograr que un sistema financiero inestable funcione? Análisis del sistema financiero apartir de las opciones fundamentales de reforma y globalización del mercado. In: Boletín international de investigación sindical – crisis: causas, perspectivas y alternativas, 3(1), 145-170 (2011).

160. mit Dullien, S. und Kellermann, C.: A Decent Capitalism for a good Society. In: Meyer, H., Rutherford, J. (Hg.), The Future of European Social Democracy. Building The Good Society. Hampshire, UK, 57-73 (2011).

161. Keynesianismus. In: Wullweber, J., Graf, A., Behrens, M. (Hg.), Theorien der Internationalen Politischen Ökonomie (= Globale Politische Ökonomie),. Wiesbaden, 49-66 (2013).

162. Financial Liberalisation, Deregulated Labour Markets and New Asset Market-Driven Capitalism. In: Bhowmik, S. (Hg.), The State of Labour. The Global Financial Crisis and Its Impact. New Delhi, 55-82 (2013).

163. with Ruoff, B.: Wage Dispersion as Key Factor for Changing Personal Income Distribution. In: Journal of Self-Governance and Management Economics, 2(3), 28-71 (2014).

164. with Sonat, Z.: The Fragile Growth Regime of Turkey in the post-2001 Period. In: New Perspectives on Turkey, 51, 35-68 (2014).

165. The European Central Bank and the US Federal Reserve as Lender of Last Resort. In: Panoeconomicus. Special Issue, 61(1), 59-78 (2014).

166. with Ruoff, B. and Salas, C.: Labour Markets, Wage Dispersion and Union Policies. In: International Journal of Labour Research, 6(1), 57-74 (2014).

167. Die Geld- und Schuldenwirtschaft in verschiedenen ökonomischen Paradigmen. In: Heimbucher, M., Krabbe, A., Quilisch, A. (Hg.), Wie auch wir vergeben unseren Schuldnern ... Geld – Glaube – Zukunft (= Erkenntnis und Glaube. Schriften der Evangelischen Forschungsakademie No. 45), Leipzig, 13-48 (2014).

168. Der Wechselkurs in ökonomischen Paradigmen. In: Dullien, S., Hein, E., Truger, A. (Hg.), Makroökonomik, Entwicklung und Wirtschaftspolitik / Macroeconomics, Development and Economic Policies. Festschrift für/for Jan Priewe (= Schriftenreihe des Forschungsnetzwerk Makroökonomie und Makropolitik (FMM) Band 16), Marburg, 43-70 (2014).

169. An Analytical Framework for the Post-Keynesian Macroeconomic Paradigm. In: Izmir Review of Social Sciences, 1(2), 73-105 (2014).

170. Дисперсия заработной платы и занятость – экономическое развитие и объяснение. In: Buzgalin, A., Traub-Merz, R., Voeikov, M. (Hg.), Неравенство доходов и экономический рост [= Einkommensungleichheit und Wirtschaftswachstum: Exit-Strategien aus der Krise], Moskau <russisch>, 78-94 (2014).

171. with Azarhoushang, B., Bramucci, A., Ruoff, B.: Value Chains, Under-Development and Union Strategy. In: International Journal of Labour Research, 7(1-2), 153-175 (2015).

172. with Detzer, D.: Theories of Financial Crises as Cumulative Processes – An overview. In: Hein, E., Detzer, D., Dodig, N. (Hg.), The Demise of Finance-dominated Capitalism. Explaining the Financial and Economic Crises, Cheltenham, UK, Northampton, US, 115-162 (2015).

173. with Chang, R.: The Main Challenges for Chinese Economy in the New Normal Time. In: People's Tribune, 499, 1-2 (2015).

174. Geld, Währungskonkurrenz und die Instabilität des marktfundamentalen Globalisierungsprojektes. In: Prokla, Zeitschrift für kritische Sozialwissenschaft. Heft 179, 45(2), 237-256 (2015).

175. with Dodig, D.: Financial Crises Leading to Stagnation – Selected Historical Case Studies. In: Hein, E., Detzer, D., Dodig, N. (Hg.), The Demise of Finance-dominated Capitalism. Explaining the Financial and Economic Crises, Cheltenham, UK, Northampton, US, 162-218 (2015).

176. Europe's Lost Decade: Path out of Stagnation. In: Pons-Vignon, N., Nkosi, M. (Hg.), Struggle in a Time of Crisis, London, 42-46 (2015).

177. Der Aufstieg Chinas zu einer ökonomischen Großmacht – Erfolge und Herausforderungen. In: Linke, M., Sablowski, T., Steinitz, K. (Hg.) China: Gesellschaftliche Entwicklung und Globale Auswirkungen (= Manuskripte Neue Folge Rosa Luxemburg Stiftung, No. 16), Berlin, 84-113 (2015).

178. with Dodig, N.: Current Account Imbalances in the EMU: An Assessment of Official Policy Responses. In: Panoeconomicus, 62(2), 193-216 (2015).

179. Market regulation, inequality and economic development. In: Gallas, A., Herr, H., Hoffer, F., Scherrer, C. (eds.), Combating Inequality. The Global North and South, London, 229-242 (2016).

180. After the Financial Crisis: Reforms and Reform Options for Finance, Regulation and Institutional Structure . In: JEB – Journal of Economics Bibliography, 3(2), 172-202 (2016).

181. with Detzer, D.: Financial Regulation in Germany. In: Kattel, R., Kregel, J., Tonveronachi, M. (eds.), Financial Regulation in the European Union, London, 41-77 (2016).

182. with Ruoff, B.: Labour and financial markets as drivers of inequality. In: Gallas, A., Herr, H., Hoffer, F., Scherrer, C. (eds.), Combating Inequality. The Global North and South, London, 61-79 (2016).

Sonstige Beiträge | other contributions

183. mit Fischer, J., Voy, K.: Der Weg der Dollarmacht. Zur Entwicklung des Weltwährungssystems nach dem II. Weltkrieg. In: Kommune, 1(9), 38ff. (1983).

184. Die Schwindsucht der nationalen Autonomie. Labilität des Währungssystems seit den 70er Jahren. In: Kommune, 3(10), (1985).

185. mit Voy, K.: Übereinstimmung im einzelnen, Differenz im ganzen. Eine Auseinandersetzung mit sozialdemokratischer Wirtschaftsprogrammatik. In: Kommune, 3(12), (1985).

186. Mit Keynes gegen den Nachfragekeynesianismus. Oder: Was hat Keynes in der heutigen sozialdemokratischen wirtschaftspolitischen Diskussion noch zu sagen? In: spw-28 (1985).

187. mit Westphal, A.: Wirtschaftsweltmacht EG? Die Weiterentwicklung des Europäischen Währungssystems.In: Die Neue Gesellschaft / Frankfurter Hefte, 35(10), 908-914 (1988).

188. mit Pan Deping: Der Unternehmenssektor als Wachstumsmotor und Schwachstelle des Transformationsprozesses in der VR China. In: Kunze, J. (Hg.), Aspekte des chinesischen Transformationsprozesses (= Internationale Entwicklungen und Perspektiven, No. 3, Fachhochschule für Wirtschaft Berlin), Berlin (1997).

189. Auf der unsicheren Seite der Weltwirtschaft. Droht den Transformationsländern Mittel- und Osteuropas eine ähnliche Krisenentwicklung wie den asiatischen Tigerstaaten? In: der Freitag 11 vom 6. März 1998 (1998).

190. In der Währungs-Falle – IWF. Warum universell liberalisierte Kapitalmärkte nicht zu stabilisieren sind. In: der Freitag 17 vom 17. April 1998 (1998).

191. Teure Notgroschen – IWF, Stabilisierungsfaktor der Weltwirtschaft oder Selbstbedienungsladen für Spekulanten. In: der Freitag 31 vom 24. Juli 1998 (1998).

192. mit Heine, M.: Modell aus der Gusseisen-Zeit? Schwächelnder Euro – kraftstrotzender Dollar. In: der Freitag 7 vom 11. Februar 2000 (2000).

193. Gradualismus und Transformationskrise in China. In: Kunze, J. (Hg.), China an der Schwelle zum neuen Jahrtausend (= Internationale Entwicklungen und Perspektiven, No. 4, Fachhochschule für Wirtschaft Berlin), Berlin (2000).

194. mit Kunze, J.: Wirtschaftsmacht des nächsten Jahrhunderts. In: Kunze, J. (Hg.), China an der Schwelle zum neuen Jahrtausend (= Internationale Entwicklungen und Perspektiven, No. 4, Fachhochschule für Wirtschaft Berlin), Berlin (2000).

195. mit Heine, M.: Die Schwäche des Euro. In: FHTW-Magazin, Fachhochschule für Technik und Wirtschaft Berlin (2000).

196. Die zunehmende Rolle der Aktien in der Weltwirtschaft. In: Evangelische Kommentare, 33(8), 6-8 (2000).

197. Neues aus der Wissenschaft. Stellungnahme zu K.S. Rogoff: Why are G3 Exchange Rates so Fickle? In: Entwicklung und Zusammenarbeit, Vol. 43, November (2002).

198. Stichwörter. In: Behnen, M. (Hg.), Lexikon der Deutschen Geschichte, 1945-1990, Stuttgart (2002).

199. Die Wirtschaftliche Situation in China. In: Broschüre über die Bundesbranchenkonferenz Aluminiumindustrie 2006 am 11. und 12. Oktober in Berlin „Total global – und wo bleiben wir"?, IG-Metall Vorstand (2007).

200. Counting Surpluses. China's Export and its Exchange Rate Regime. Business Forum China, Issue 4, July-August (2008).

201. Es sind die Löhne. Le Monde Diplomatique, deutsche Ausgabe, Februar 2009.

202. mit Dullien, S. und Kellermann, C.: Der gute Kapitalismus – und was sich dafür nach der Krise ändern müsste. In: Internationale Politikanalyse, Oktober 2009.

203. with Dullien, S. und Kellermann, C.: Good Capitalism – And What Would Have to Change for That. In: Social Europe Journal, 4(4), 26-34 (2009).

204. mit Dullien, S.: Länder Fact-Sheet – Deutschland. In: Pohlmann, C., Reichert, S.; Schillinger, H. (Hg.), Die G-20: auf dem Weg zu einer Weltwirtschaftsregierung?, Berlin, 27-29 (2010).

205. Guter Kapitalismus. In: Le Monde Diplomatique (Slowenische Ausgabe) vom 01.01.2011, S. 1 (2011).

206. Europe's Lost Decade – Path out of Stagnation. In: Global Labour Column. Bd. Blog Archiv. H. 06/2012, S. 1-2 [http://www.global-labour-university.org/fileadmin/GLU_Column/papers/no_101_Herr.pdf] (2012).

207. mit Horn, G.: Lohnpolitik heute. (= IMK Policy Brief Mai 2012). Düsseldorf: Hans-Böckler-Stiftung (2012).

208. Japan. In: van Klaveren, M., Gregory, D., Schulten, T. (Hg.), Minimum Wages, Collective Bargaining and Economic Development in Asia and Europe, Basingstoke, 78-100 (2015).

Arbeitspapiere | Working Papers

mit Bruche, G. und Rieger, F.: Herausgeber der Working Papers des Business Institute Berlin an der FHW Berlin, ab 1998.

Mitglied der Redaktion | member of the group of editors: Global Labour University Working Papers, Global Labour University, ab | since 2008.

209. Weltgeld und Währungssystem. Discussion Paper IIM/LMP 86-25, Wissenschaftszentrum Berlin für Sozialforschung (1986).

210. Der Euro-DM-Markt: Theoretische Erfassung, empirische Entwicklung und Einfluß auf die nationale Geldpolitik. Discussion Paper IIM/LMP 87-7, Wissenschaftszentrum Berlin für Sozialforschung (1987).

211. Kredit und Akkumulation in einer Geldwirtschaft. Diskussionsbeitrag zur gesamtwirtschaftlichen Theorie und Politik, Forschungsgruppe „Postkeynesianische Ökonomie", Bremen: Fachbereich Wirtschaftswissenschaften (1987).

212. Zur Stabilisierung ökonomischer Prozesse durch institutionelle Regulierungen. Discussion Paper IIM/LMP 87-13, Wissenschaftszentrum Berlin für Sozialforschung (1987).

213. World Money, the Monetary System, and the Instability of Economic Development in the 1970s and 1980s, Discussion Paper FS I 88-4, Wissenschaftszentrum Berlin für Sozialforschung (1988).

214. mit Voy, K.: Neuorientierung der bundesdeutschen Währungs- und Finanzpolitik im internationalen Rahmen. Gutachten im Auftrag der „Arbeitsgemeinschaft Weltwirtschaft und Entwicklung – verantwortbares Produzieren und Konsumieren in einer Welt" der Fraktion DIE GRÜNEN im Bundestag (= Schriftenreihe des IÖW 22/88), Berlin (1988).

215. Mercantilistic Strategies, Cooperation and the Option of the European Monetary System. Discussion Paper FS I 89-2, Wissenschaftszentrum Berlin für Sozialforschung (1989).

216. mit Westphal, A.: Die Transformation von Planwirtschaften in Geldwirtschaften. Ökonomische Kohärenz, Mindestschwelle und Sequencing der Transformation, außenwirtschaftliche Strategien. Discussion Paper FS I 90-9, Wissenschaftszentrum Berlin für Sozialforschung (1990).

217. with Tober, S.: Monetary stability and economic development, Diskussionspapiere / Institut für Wirtschaftsforschung Halle, 35 (1995).

218. mit Pan Deping: Untersuchungen zu finanzwirtschaftlichen Problemen bei der Restrukturierung chinesischer Staatsbetriebe, Working-Papers der Southwestern University of Finance and Economics 1996-1998, Chengdu, VR China [in chinesischer Sprache] (1998).

219. mit Tober, S.: Explaining the Difference in the Economic Development of Countries in Transition. Working Paper 85, Cseka Narodni Banka, Institut Ekonomie (1998).

220. with Tober, S.: Pathways to Capitalism − Explaining the Differences in the Economic Development of the Visegrád States, the States of the Former Soviet Union, and China. Working Papers No 5 des Business Institute Berlin an der Fachhochschule für Wirtschaft Berlin (1999).

221. Wages, Employment and Prices. An Analysis of the Relationship Between Wage Level, Wage Structure, Minimum Wages and Employment and Prices, Working Papers of the Business Institute Berlin at the Berlin School of Economics No. 15, Berlin (2002).

222. mit Priewe, J.: The Macroeconomic Framework of Poverty Reduction − An Assessment of the IMF/World Bank Strategy − A Critical Review of the PRSP Sourcebook Chapter 6 from September 21, 2000. Working Papers of the Business Institute Berlin at the Berlin School of Economics (FHW-Berlin), No. 17 (2003).

223. Time, Expectations and Financial Markets. Working Paper No. 03/2009, Institute for International Political Economy Berlin (2009).

224. From Financial Crisis to Depression and Deflation, GURN Policy Brief No.1, January, Geneva (2009).

225. with Kazandziska, M., Mahnkopf-Praprotnik, S.: The Theoretical Debate About Minimum Wages. Global Labour University Working Papers, no. 6, February, Berlin (2009).

226. with Kazandziska, M.: Principles of Minimum Wage Policy – Economics, Institutions and Recommendations, Genf: Global Labour University Working Papers 11 (2011).

227. with Horn, G.: Wage Policy Today. Genf: International Labour Office Working Paper 16 (2012).

228. with Detzer, D., Dodig, N., Evans, T., Hein, E.: The German Financial System. Financialisation, Economy, Society & Sustainable development, FESSUD Studies in Financial Systems 3), Leeds: University of Leeds (2013).

229. with. Sonat, Z.: Neoliberal unshared growth regime of Turkey in the post-2001 period, Global Labour University Working Paper 19, Geneva: International Labour Organization (2013).

230. with Ruoff, B.: Wage dispersion: empirical developments, explanations and reform options, Global Labour University Working Paper No. 24, Geneva: International Labour Organization (2014).

231. with Dodig, N.: Previous financial crises leading to stagnation – selected case studies, FESSUD Working Paper Series No. 24, Leeds: University of Leeds (2014).

232. with Detzer, D.: Theories of Financial Crises, FESSUD Working Paper Series No. 25, Leeds: University of Leeds (2014).

233. with Detzer, D.: Financial Regulation in Germany, FESSUD Working Paper Series No. 55, Leeds: University of Leeds (2014).

234. with Horn, G.A.: Wage Policy Today, Global Labour University Working Paper No. 16, Geneva: International Labour Organization (2014).

235. with Detzer, D.: Theories of Finance and Financial Crisis – Lessons for the Great Recession, Working Paper – IPE Institute for International Political Economy 48/2015, Berlin: Hochschule für Wirtschaft und Recht Berlin (2015).

236. with Evans, T.: Synthesis of the sectoral studies of the currency, energy and residential property market, FESSUD Working Paper Series No. 113, Leeds: University of Leeds (2015).

237. with Dodig, N.: EU Policies Addressing Current Account Imbalances: An Assessment, Working Paper – IPE Institute for International Political Economy 46/2015, Berlin: Hochschule für Wirtschaft und Recht Berlin (2015).

238. After the financial crisis: Reforms and reform options for finance, regulation and institutional structure, Working Paper, Institute for International Political Economy Berlin, No. 63/2016, Berlin (2016).

239. with Evans, T.: Financialisation in currency, energy and residential property markets, Working Paper, Institute for International Political Economy Berlin, No. 62/2016, Berlin (2016).

240. with Rüdiger, S., Pédussel Wu, J.: The Federal Reserve as lender of last resort during the subprime crisis: Successful stabilisation without structural changes, Working Paper, Institute for International Political Economy Berlin, No. 65/2016, Berlin (2016).

Autor_innen und Herausgeber_innen
Authors and Editors

Patrick Belser is Senior Economist at the International Labour Office (ILO) in Geneva, and is the principal editor of the ILO Global Wage Report, an ILO flagship report published every two years since 2008. He has a D.Phil. in Economics from the Institute of Development Studies (IDS) at the University of Sussex, and has previously worked on the economic dimensions of forced labour and human trafficking.

Sharit K. Bhowmik is a Sociologist who specialises in labour studies. He was Professor of Labour Studies at Tata Institute of Social Sciences and was earlier the coordinator (India) of the Global Labour University. He is National Fellow (Sociology), Indian Council of Sociel Sciences Research.

Kajsa Borgnäs, doctoral student at Potsdam University and former President of the Swedish Social Democratic Student Association.

Daniel Detzer, M.A. International Economics, is a Research Fellow in the project Financialisation, Economy, Society and Sustainable Development (FESSUD) at the Berlin School of Economics and Law and a PhD student at Carl von Ossietzky University Oldenburg.

Sebastian Dullien ist Professor für VWL, insbesondere International Economics, an der Hochschule für Technik und Wirtschaft (HTW) Berlin und Senior Policy Fellow beim European Council on Foreign Relations. Seine Forschungsinteressen sind internationale Makroökonomie und internationaler Handel, Europäische Integration und Wirtschaftspolitik.

Trevor Evans war bis 2015 Professor für Geldtheorie, Geldpolitik und internationale Währungsbeziehungen an der Hochschule für Wirtschaft und Recht Berlin. Zuvor war er langjähriger Wissenschaftlicher Mitarbeiter am ‚Coordinadora Regional de Investigaciones Económicos y Sociales' (CRIES) in Managua, Nicaragua. Er ist Mitglied der Koordinations-Gruppe der ‚European

Economists for an Alternative Economic Policy in Europe' und hat zahlreiche Veröffentlichungen zur Marxschen und Post-Keynesianischen Geld- und Finanztheorie sowie zur Politischen Ökonomie der Vereinigten Staaten von Amerika, der Eurozone und Zentralamerikas verfasst.

Khayaat Fakier is a Senior Lecturer at the University of Stellenbosch, where she teaches and supervises students in the sociology of work and the sociology of migration. Her work has been published in journals such as Antipode and the International Feminist Journal of Politics. She has recently co-edited a volume titled, *Socio-Economic Insecurity in Emerging Economies: Building New Spaces,* published by Routledge with Ellen Ehmke.

Barbara Fritz, Professor for Economics at the Institute for Latin American Studies and the Economics Department at the Free University Berlin. Her research focuses on monetary macroeconomics of emerging market countries.

Alexander Gallas is an Assistant Professor at the Department of Politics at the University of Kassel, Germany. His research interests include strikes and industrial action, labour relations in Europe, class theory and state theory. He is Editor of the *Global Labour Journal* and has written a monograph entitled *The Thatcherite Offensive: A Neo-Poulantzasian Analysis.*

Eckhard Hein, Professor of Economics at the Berlin School of Economics and Law, Co-Director of the Institute for International Political Economy Berlin (IPE), and managing Co-Editor of the *European Journal of Economics and Economic Policies: Intervention.*

Michael Heine war bis 2015 Professor für Volkswirtschaftslehre an der Hochschule für Technik und Wirtschaft in Berlin. Seine Lehr- und Forschungsschwerpunkte sind Geldpolitik, Postkeynesianismus und Regionalökonomie. Von 2006 bis 2014 war er Präsident der Hochschule für Technik und Wirtschaft Berlin.

Alexander Herzog-Stein ist Referatsleiter für Arbeitsmarktökonomik am Institut für Makroökonomie und Konjunkturforschung (IMK) der Hans-Böckler-Stiftung und seit 2012 zudem Lehrbeauftragter an der Universität Koblenz-Landau (Abteilung Wirtschaftswissenschaft). Seine Forschungsinteressen sind vor allem Fragestellungen zu den Themen Arbeitszeit, Beschäftigung, Arbeitsmarktinstitutionen sowie der deutsche Arbeitsmarkt in der Großen Rezession.

Frank Hoffer is Senior Research Officer at the Bureau for Workers' Activities of the ILO. He is an economist and holds a PhD from the University of Bremen. Before joining the ILO he worked at the Center for Social Policy at the University of Bremen, the German Embassy in Moscow and the German Trade Union Federation (DGB) Moscow. He is also the international coordinator of the Global Labour University.

Gustav Horn ist seit 2005 Wissenschaftlicher Direktor des Instituts für Makroökonomie und Konjunkturforschung (IMK). Zudem ist er apl. Professor für VWL an der Universität Duisburg-Essen sowie Research Fellow der Generaldirektion Wirtschaft und Finanzen der EU-Kommission. Von 2011 bis 2015 war er Vorsitzender der Kammer für Soziale Ordnung der Evangelischen Kirche Deutschlands (EKD).

Praveen Jha is Professor of Economics with the School of Social Sciences Jawaharlal Nehru University. Currently he is also a Visiting Professor at Rhodes University, South Africa and Sam Moyo African Institute of Agrarian Studies, Zimbabwe. His main area of work is political economy of development with special focus on labour and agriculture.

Heike Joebges ist seit 2010 Professorin für Volkswirtschaftslehre, insbesondere International Economics, an der Hochschule für Technik und Wirtschaft (HTW) Berlin. Ihre Forschungsinteressen sind Finanz- und Währungskrisen, mit einem besonderen Fokus auf der Eurokrise, Handelsungleichgewichten und der Exportorientierung Deutschlands. Vorher war sie Referatsleiterin für Internationale Konjunkturanalysen und Prognosen am Institut für Makroökonomie und Konjunkturforschung (IMK) in der Hans-Böckler-Stiftung.

Christian Kellermann, Dr., co-author of "Decent Capitalism: A Blueprint for Reforming our Economies" and Head of Unit Sustainable Economy, Social Democratic Party of Germany Executive Board.

Martin Kronauer, Dr. phil., habil., Professor i. R. für Gesellschaftswissenschaft an der Hochschule für Wirtschaft und Recht Berlin.

Camille Logeay ist seit 2010 Professorin für Volkswirtschaftslehre an der Hochschule für Technik und Wirtschaft in Berlin (HTW). Von 2000 bis 2005 war sie wissenschaftliche Mitarbeiterin im Deutschen Institut für Wirtschaftsforschung (DIW Berlin) und von 2005 bis 2010 Referatsleiterin für Arbeitsmarktfragen am Institut für Makroökonomie und Konjunkturforschung (IMK) in der Hans-Böckler-Stiftung. Ihre Lehr- und Forschungsschwerpunkte betreffen Arbeitsmarktökonomie, Makroökonomie und Ökonometrie.

Zeynep M. Nettekoven, M.A., PhD Free University Berlin, Associate member of the Institute for International Political Economy Berlin (IPE), Berlin School of Economics and Law.

Torsten Niechoj is Professor of Economics and Political Science at Rhine-Waal University of Applied Sciences (Kamp-Lintfort, Germany), co-editor of the *European Journal of Economics and Economic Policies: Intervention* (EJEEP), and member of the coordination committee of the Research Network Macroeconomics and Macroeconomic Policies (FMM).

Siegbert Preuß, Diplom-Volkswirt, wiss. Mitarbeiter, Promotion zum Dr. rer. pol. an der FU Berlin. Selbständige Lehrtätigkeit zur Makroökonomie und Theorie der Wirtschaftspolitik. Langjähriger Lehrbeauftragter u.a. an der HWR Berlin, EHB, Studienkolleg der Universität Potsdam. Interessensgebiet: Stabilisierung von Marktwirtschaften, entscheidungstheoretische Modellierungen.

Jan Priewe war Professor für Volkswirtschaftslehre an der Hochschule für Technik und Wirtschaft bis 2014. Seit 2015 ist er Senior Research Fellow am IMK in der Hans-Böckler-Stiftung. Zusammen mit Hansjörg Herr leitete er von 2000-2009 die Macroeconomic Policy Studies (MPS), ein Kooperationsprojekt mit der People's Bank of China zur Weiterbildung von Mitarbeitern der chinesischen Zentralbank, gefördert von der Bundesregierung. Er befasst sich vorwiegend mit Makroökonomie, Entwicklungsökonomie und Wirtschaftspolitik.

Hajo Riese, Diplomvolkswirt, Promotion an der Universität Kiel, Habilitation an der Universität Basel, war von 1970 bis 2001 Professor für Volkswirtschaftslehre am Institut für Wirtschaftspolitik und Wissenschaftsgeschichte. Sein wissenschaftlicher Schwerpunkt liegt in der Ausarbeitung einer monetär-keynesianisch fundierten Theorie der Wirtschaftspolitik. Autor zahlreicher Bücher und Aufsätze.

Bea Ruoff, M.A. International Economics, ist wissenschaftliche Mitarbeiterin an der Hochschule für Wirtschaft und Recht Berlin und Mitglied des Institute for International Political Economy Berlin (IPE).

Carlos Salas is a Professor at Instituto de Economia Unicamp, Brazil and researcher at CESIT (Center for the study of unions and labor economics) at Unicamp. He has written extensively on labor economics, in particular on Latin American countries. Currently, he is working on occupation segmentation by regions and gender in Mexico and Brazil.

Christoph Scherrer, economist and political scientist, he is Professor of globalization and politics and Executive Director of the International Center for Development and Decent Work at the University of Kassel and a member of Steering Committee of the Global Labour University. He has received the Excellency in Teaching Award of the State of Hessia and the Excellence in Development Cooperation Award from the DAAD. Recent English language publications include: *"Combating Inequality: The Global North and South"*, London: Routledge (2015, co-ed. with A. Gallas, H. Herr, and F. Hoffer), *"The Transatlantic Trade and Investment Partnership: Implications for Labor"*, Hampp Verlag (2014, ed.)

Claus Thomasberger, Diplomsoziologe und -volkswirt, Promotion an der Universität Bremen, Habilitation an der FU Berlin, ist Professor für Volkswirtschaftslehre und Außenwirtschaftspolitik an der Hochschule für Technik und Wirtschaft Berlin. Er lehrte als Gast- und Vertretungsprofessor an der Knoxville University, der Universität Osnabrück und der Wirtschaftsuniversität Wien. Autor und Mitherausgeber zahlreicher Bücher, darunter: *Der neoliberale Marktdiskurs* (2009) *From Crisis to Growth* (2012) und *Das neoliberale Credo* (2012). Forschungsschwerpunkte: Internationale Währungsbeziehungen, europäische Integration, politische Philosophie.

Achim Truger is Professor of Economics, in particular Macroeconomics and Economic Policy at the Berlin School of Economics and Law where he is also the Vice Dean of the Faculty of Economics and Business Administration. He is a Senior Research Fellow at the Macroeconomic Policy Institute (IMK) at Hans Boeckler Foundation in Düsseldorf, Germany. He is a member of the coordination committee of the Research Network Macroeconomics and Macroeconomic Policies (FMM), and managing co-editor of the *European Journal of Economics and Economic Policies: Intervention*.

Klaus Voy, Dr. rer. pol., war von 1978 bis 2013 im Statistischen Landesamt Berlin und im Amt für Statistik Berlin-Brandenburg in verschiedenen Bereichen und Funktionen tätig, u.a. Wirtschafts- und Bevölkerungsstatistiken und

Volkwirtschaftliche Gesamtrechnungen. Arbeitsschwerpunkte: Theorie, Konzepte und Geschichte der Volkswirtschaftlichen Gesamtrechnungen, Geschichte der Geldwirtschaft und Buchführung, Geschichte der Wirtschaft und Wirtschaftspolitik.

Edward Webster is a Research Professor in the Society, Work and Development Institute (SWOP) at the University of the Witwatersrand (Wits). He is the author of seven books and over one hundred academic articles. He was a Senior Fulbright Scholar at the University of Wisconsin (Madison) in 1995/1996 and the first Ela Bhatt Visiting Professor at the Centre for Development and Decent Work (ICDD) at Kassel University in 2009/2010.

Michael Wendl, Soziologe, hat von 1980 bis 2016 für die Gewerkschaften ÖTV und ver.di gearbeitet und für diese Tarifverhandlungen geführt. Seine Arbeitsschwerpunkte sind Tarifpolitik und Geldpolitik. Er ist Mitherausgeber der Zeitschrift ‚Sozialismus'.

Edlira Xhafa has a Masters in Labour Policies and Globalisation from the Global Labour University-Germany (2005/2006) and has obtained her PhD in Labour Studies from the University of Milan, Italy (2012). She started working with Albanian trade unions in 2000 and has since worked with a number of national and international labour organisations. Edlira has (co)authored a number of peer-reviewed book chapters and articles published in internationally-recognised journals and other academic publications.

Yang Laike is full-time Professor at East China Normal University in Shanghai and currently the Dean of the department of international trade. He holds a Ph.D. in economics from Xiamen University and did his post-doctoral fellow at the Chinese Academy of Social Science (CASS). His research interests include trade and environment, Asian economic integration, Sino-US trade relationships.

Zhen Guojiao is a Ph.D candidate in East China Normal University in Shanghai.